# PRACTICES OF WEALTH DEPOSITING

## in the 1st–9th century AD Eastern Baltic

Sidestone Press

# PRACTICES OF WEALTH DEPOSITING in the 1st–9th century AD Eastern Baltic

ESTER ORAS

Published by Sidestone Press, Leiden
www.sidestone.com

This dissertation was submitted for the degree of Doctor of Philosophy
Division of Archaeology, University of Cambridge

ISBN 978-90-8890-307-6

Photograph cover: A disc brooch from Vagula wealth deposit (from the collections of the Institute of History, Tallinn University, AI 2616)
Back cover: A neck-ring from Metsküla wealth deposit (from the collections of the Institute of History, Tallinn University, AI 2513:88)

Lay-out & cover design: Sidestone Press

*Also available as:*
e-book (PDF): ISBN 978-90-8890-308-3

This research was supported by the Foundation Archimedes Kristjan Jaak Scholarship Programme for Doctoral Study Abroad, Estonian Ministry of Education and Research institutional research funding IUT20-7 "Estonia in Circum-Baltic space: archaeology of economic, social, and cultural processes", and the European Union through the European Regional Development Fund (Centre of Excellence CECT).

Investing in your future

European Union
Regional Development Fund

*Pühendusega emale*
To my mother

*Contents*

# Preface

This dissertation is the result of my own work and includes nothing which is the outcome of work done in collaboration except where specifically indicated in the text.

This dissertation does not exceed the word limit set by the Archaeology and Anthropology Degree Committee. The application to extend the thesis word length to 85,000 words has been approved by the Archaeology and Anthropology Degree Committee and the Board of Graduate Studies at the University of Cambridge.

Ester Oras

Wolfson College, Cambridge
July 2014

# Abstract


## Practices of Wealth Depositing in the 1st–9th Century AD Eastern Baltic

by Ester Oras

This PhD thesis discusses the practices of wealth depositing based on the 1st-9th century AD eastern Baltic (Estonia, Latvia, Lithuania) material. Wealth deposits are one or more valued object/s that is/are hidden deliberately as an intended separate deposition of selected object(s) into a selected place in a specific, distinguishable manner. Wealth depositing is regarded as an important cultural practice which relates to and derives from various past social phenomena and changes respectively in spatial and temporal terms. It is emphasised that wealth deposits should be analysed as a cohesive corpus of material, regardless of specific artefact types, functional groups, production material, environment of concealment, and most importantly without any predetermined interpretational categorisations. The thesis presents different patterned practices of wealth depositing in the 1st-9th century AD eastern Baltic through detailed contextual analysis of their main material characteristics: artefacts, their assemblages and appearance, the environment of concealment, chronology and the location of the deposit in the cultural landscape. The study demonstrates how depositional practices change in time and space, and analyses relations between specific depositional practices and developments on a wider social scale. A comparative analysis of wealth deposits and important social changes in the contemporary society as expressed by data from other archaeological sites and overall material culture is presented. The key regional and cross-regional practices of wealth depositing in the 1st-9th century AD eastern Baltic are identified. Additionally, further comparisons are drawn between the wealth depositional practices in the eastern Baltic and other parts of the Baltic Sea region, especially Scandinavia. The thesis contributes to the discussion of the concepts of value and depositional practices in a long-term and cross-regional perspective. The further aim is to look beyond the problematic 'why?'-questions posed in the studies of wealth deposits and move instead to the more comprehensible questions of 'how?': how do depositional practices change in time and space, and how are these processes related to the developments in a broader social context?

# Acknowledgments

My sincerest gratitude belongs to my supervisor Catherine Hills for her tremendous help and support throughout my PhD studies. Her trust, encouragement, and supervision made my time in Cambridge most rewarding and I am very grateful for this wonderful opportunity to work with her. I also wish to thank my advisor Marie Louise Stig Sørensen for her advice and assistance. My external advisor Valter Lang (University of Tartu) has supported my academic endeavours since my undergraduate studies and I thank him for his sympathy, kind words, and guidance for evermore.

There are numerous people who made this thesis possible by allowing me to study their collections and providing help with data gathering. I wish to thank Ülle Tamla, Priit Lätti, Mirja Ots (Institute of History, Tallinn University), and Krista Sarv (Estonian History Museum) from Estonia; Jānis Ciglis and Zane Buža (Latvian National Historical Museum), Antonija Vilcāne (Institute of Latvian History) and Aldis Barševskis (Jelgava Museum) in Latvia; Audronė Bliujienė and Vykintas Vaitkevičius (Klaipėda University), Eglė Griciuvienė and Gediminas Petrauskas (Lithuanian National Museum), Kęstutis Šeškevičius (Vytautas the Great War Museum), Edita Lansbergienė and Tatjana Niedvarienė (Sėla Museum), Ernestas Vasiliauskas (Aušra Museum), Dalia Karaliene (Alka Samogitian Museum), Vaidotas Suncovas (Vilnius University) in Lithuania; and Tatjana Borisovna Sinechenkova (The State Hermitage Museum) in Russia. I also wish to thank the Section for Prehistoric Archaeology at Århus University, Society of the Lithuanian Archaeology, Kretinga Museum and the archaeology collections at the University of Tartu. Special thanks are dedicated to my good friend Agnė Žilinskaitė who always made my visits to Lithuania most pleasant. This thesis would have been impossible without these people and institutions.

Many friends and colleagues have read and commented parts of this thesis. I would like to thank John Robb, Tõnno Jonuks, Mari Tõrv, Mette Løvschal, Barbara Hausmair for their help, comments, and feedback that made me write a better thesis. I am grateful to Anna Bitner-Wróblewska, Andres Tvauri, Sonja Hukantaival and Timo Muhonen for their literature recommendations. My sincere gratitude belongs to David Redhouse for providing necessary data for the maps in this thesis. I also wish to thank Thomas Higham and Oxford Radiocarbon Accelerator Unit for the help with dating analysis. My special thanks go to Tamsin O'Connell for inspiring my interest in archaeological science as well as for the encouragement and support to continue in this field.

This research would not have been possible without the support of several funding bodies. First I would like to thank Foundation Archimedes Kristjan Jaak Scholarship Program for PhD Studies abroad who provided me with the scholarship for my studies in Cambridge. My fieldwork was supported by the Worts Travelling Scholars Fund, Ridgeway-Venn Travel Studentship, University of Cambridge Scandinavian Studies Fund, Dorothy Garrod Memorial Trust, Wolfson College Travel Fund, and the Lane Cox Fund at the University of Cambridge. My studies and research were also supported by the Cultural Endowment of Estonia, Estonian

Students' Fund in the USA, Estonian Educational Trust, the research projects "Social, Economic and Cultural Processes in Estonia in Prehistoric, Medieval and Modern Times", Centre of Excellence in Cultural Theory at the University of Tartu, and a research grant "The Materiality of Religion – Religious Artifacts in Estonian archaeological Collections" at the Estonian Literary Museum.

This work would have been impossible without my supportive family who cheered me up and kept me down-to-earth whenever I needed that. Thank you, my beloved mother Anne, my sister Jana and brother Janek and their families.

And finally, I take the liberty of expressing my sincerest gratitude to my dearest and best friend in my mother tongue, Estonian: *Aitäh Sulle, Martti!*

# List of tables

# List of figures

Fig. 9.2.1. Distribution map of major materials of eastern Baltic wealth deposits and their chronology. Number on the symbol indicates the dating of the deposit.

Fig. 9.2.2. Distribution map of major artefact groups of eastern Baltic wealth deposits and their chronology. Number on the symbol indicates the dating (century AD) of the deposit.

Fig. 9.2.3. Distribution map of major material, environment of concealment and chronology of eastern Baltic wealth deposits. Number on the symbol indicates the dating (century AD) of the deposit.

Fig. 9.2.4. Distribution map of major artefact group, environment of concealment and chronology of eastern Baltic wealth deposits. Number on the symbol indicates the dating (century AD) of the deposit.

*Chapter 1*

# Introduction

Wealth deposits as intentional separate artefact deposits are one of the most controversial archaeological find groups. One the one hand, these precious objects often become local objects of pride. The discoveries of those intriguing artefacts live on in the memories of local people, they are proudly displayed in national museums and admired by foreign visitors. Finds of prehistoric gold and silver might even become regional symbols, such as the Gallehus golden horn from Denmark or the Snettisham torcs from England. The discoveries of wealth deposits could be considered as one of the main instances where the interests of archaeologists and the general public intersect: discovered accidentally by local farmers or land-owners they bring history closer and make it tangible for ordinary people.

Wealth deposits may also cause disputes between scholarly and public interest groups. One of these is the question of looting and threat to the local heritage by illegal trade. These issues have been discussed in western Europe for over a decade (Brodie *et al.* (eds) 2001; Brodie & Tubb (eds) 2002; Gaimster 2004; Robson *et al.* 2006) and they have also received the attention of Baltic archaeologists (Kangert 2009; Ulst 2010). Different countries have different legislative means to deal with this issue. As the experience of the Portable Antiquities Scheme[1] and several case studies in England, Wales and elsewhere indicate (Thomas & Stone (eds) 2009; Campbell & Thomas (eds) 2013; Dobat 2013) there is a possibility for fruitful cooperation between archaeologists and metal detectorists. However, conflicts between different parties are inevitable if personal, in most cases economic, interests outweigh wider public or national objectives. This can easily result in a situation where new finds are not reported and they end up in international, often illegal, trading networks. As the past situation in the eastern Baltic shows, the response by archaeologists has sometimes been to attempt to keep information secret. The details about the finds and relevant fieldwork are kept within a small circle of people and the public might easily feel left out from the creation of history and local identity. This situation has started to change in some parts of the eastern Baltic where new legislation about metal detecting has come into force (Kraut 2012; Ulst 2012).

On the other hand, the scientific and heritage-related attention paid to such archaeological discoveries can be quite uneven in the eastern Baltic. Find-spots of wealth deposits rarely become nationally protected designated archaeological monuments. In most cases the sites that once provided literally the richest evidence of the past after a couple of decades become vague village names in the head of the researcher. Some scholars may have visited the site of discovery, although often years later. It also depends on who makes the discovery and what

1 http://finds.org.uk/.

actions are followed after that. Several good examples of how detector finds can contribute to archaeological research can be found in the Portable Antiquities Scheme research projects, but similar examples in the eastern Baltic are still rare. The situation has changed considerably in the last decades and more find-spots are studied after new shiny (or not so shiny) objects have been unearthed. With the development of new landscape survey techniques the areas can be mapped more precisely and checked with metal detectors. Sometimes these attempts result in successful new additions to the initial assemblage. However, considering the sheer number of wealth deposits, proportionally only a very small part of those sites has received a significant amount of scientific input. In contrast, the objects that reach the archaeological collections are more often elaborately studied and analysed. This is especially related to the development of scientific methods and application of different chemical and physical analysis such as microscopes, new dating methods, XRF, SEM etc. Therefore, unlike many other archaeological sites such as settlements, hill-forts or burials, wealth deposits often tend to gain object-based not site-related scientific investment.

This affects the ways in which wealth deposits have been studied and included in the general interpretations of past societies. Most of the analyses are concentrated on artefacts. Often seen as closed find complexes, wealth deposits are good study material for artefact chronology and typology. With the help of new scientific methods questions of production, material provenance and artefact use can be considered. Much less systematic attention has been paid to the landscape situations, historical changes in the environments of concealment and relations to other archaeological sites. The reason is simple – it takes an extra effort to gain these aspects of information about the deposits due to the inherent nature of their discovery.

As a result, for a long time wealth deposits remained an autonomous and self-contained archaeological find group. For example, most of the eastern Baltic studies from the first half of the 20th century concentrate on the specific find-group of wealth deposits only. The material is analysed on the basis of artefacts and resulting typo-chronological or provenance questions (e.g. Schmiedehelm 1934; Moora 1935). The second largest strand of traditional scholarly work includes the question of the environment of concealment of deposits. This often resulted in limiting the data according to a single environment of concealment: bogs, rivers, temple contexts (Torbrügge 1972; Tamla 1977; 1985; Bradley 1990; Stjernquist 1997; Bliujienė 2010). The third largest approach is to study only specific functional groups or types of objects (weapon deposits, vessels, silver) (Becker 1971; Harck 1984; Fabech 1991a; Randsborg 1995; Hårdh 1996; Jørgensen *et al.* (eds) 2003). Both of the latter approaches often result in interpretational categorisation of the material, mainly into oppositional groups of religious-related or economic deposits. There are very few comparative and holistic studies of the overall assemblages of wealth deposits and those that exist, mostly cover small geographical regions (e.g. Kiudsoo 2005; Henriksen 2010).

There is therefore often an impression that all wealth deposits, whether defined by artefact groups or environments of concealment, are the remains of a single unique and self-sufficient act: their relations to each other and developments in time are less considered. It seems that wealth deposits as a find category do not form a broader concept of widely followed, socially and materially constituent patterns of practices that can be expected in the other past activities such as the traditions of burials, iron production, religious devotion, diet or house constructions. More importantly, little discussion has been provided about the wealth depositing practices and their relation to other cultural activities and broader social contexts.

This situation has started to change. Recently discussions about the problems of deposit categorisation and their relation to the bigger picture of past society have been represented in the studies by and discussion between Fabech (1991a-b, 1994a-b, 1999a-b; 2001) and Hedeager (1992; 1999; 2003). Landscape studies, both physical and cultural landscape, including the surroundings of stray finds and separate deposits have become more elaborate (e.g. Hansen 2006; Henriksen 2010). However, these often result in interpretational consideration about the meanings of deposits in the past and concentrate on the why-questions: why deposits were concealed? why some artefacts end up in burials and others in wealth deposits? why specifically those areas were chosen for hiding valuables? etc. (Levy 1982; Hedeager 1992; Fontijn 2002; Jørgensen *et al.* (eds) 2003; Haselgrove & Wigg-Wolf (eds) 2005).

These main traditional approaches to the material of wealth deposits – particular artefact or environment-based selection of data, lack of discussion about more widely followed practices, interpretationally determined research questions, and isolation of wealth deposits from broader social contexts – were the main reasons for starting the current research project. In this study I want to break away from these traditional ways of approaching wealth deposits and pose some new questions to this particular archaeological find group. Firstly, I would like to question whether wealth depositing should be seen as a self-sufficient cultural action that does not follow any wider social rules and conditions. Secondly, I want to emphasise the advantages of analysing the material of wealth deposits as a whole, in an all-inclusive way and long-term perspective. Finally, I aim to demonstrate the importance of studying wealth deposits in the context of the developments taking place on a larger social scale. The latter is derived from the materialities and practices taking place in various other archaeological sites and information about environmental conditions. A further aim is to provide both theoretical and methodological approaches for carrying out such a long-term, all-inclusive and socially determined analysis of wealth deposits.

The hypothesis of the current study is that, like any other past activity, wealth depositing is an important cultural practice which relates to and derives from various past cultural phenomena. More specific research questions that should help to verify or falsify this hypothesis are as follows: what, if any, depositional practices can be traced in the eastern Baltic 1st-9th century material?; how do these depositional practices change in time and space?; if and how depositional practices relate to the developments taking place on a wider social scale?; is it possible to trace the reasons for the choice of artefact(s) and locations of deposition?

The first step is to analyse which practices of wealth depositing can be traced in the archaeological record. This starts from a detailed description of different contextual and content-based information: artefacts, their functional groups and types, materials, appearance, environment of concealment etc. From these one can distinguish deposits with similar characteristics. If they also relate in spatial and temporal terms it can be argued that one has identified more widespread depositional practices. This also highlights unique depositional cases that do not fit into the pattern of more widely followed practice. Adding chronological and geographical scale to this information helps to show how depositional practices change in time and space.

There is one important premiss when asking questions about different practices of wealth depositing and their developments in time: it is necessary to include all the materials, artefact groups and environments of concealment. The selection of material must be all-inclusive as long as intentional and acknowledged artefact depositions can be discerned. The data selection should not be limited to specific materials, artefact functional groups or types and environments of concealment.

The second question relates to the broader social context and interdependency of content and context of wealth deposits and social developments. Comparison of wealth depositing with other past practices provides a broader social context. This information can be derived from analysing contemporary archaeological sites, especially the processes of change. The whole range of different sites (hill-forts, settlements, burials, field systems, production sites, etc.), the broader social circumstances indicated by them (assumptions about economy, religion, social hierarchy, foreign contacts etc.), and environmental data should be considered. This enables one to create a picture of the social context in which any particular wealth depositing practice takes place. Although this information is biased towards the current state of research, available material and specific research questions, it still is the best way to reconstruct the developments and topical issues in a particular past society. Adding chronological analysis makes it possible to see how the changing materialities in other archaeological sites and environmental data correlate with developments in the practices of wealth depositing.

In this PhD thesis the material from the three Baltic countries – Estonia, Latvia and Lithuania – is considered. The region is named as the eastern Baltic throughout the thesis, although the detailed analysis does not include data from Poland, Finland or north-western Russia. The chronological period for the study is the 1st-9th century AD. There are several reasons for those geographical and chronological frames. First, it builds on and develops further previous research by the author, especially in Estonia. Secondly, due to the history of those countries and their scholarly tradition, including publication policy and languages, very little is known about the wealth deposits in this region in western archaeological scholarship. Most of the material is published in local languages or in Russian, often decades ago. Thirdly, although regionally very close and sharing very similar recent and distant past (including the main archaeological sites and features), there are very few studies which compare all of the eastern Baltic wealth deposits. As the current study shows, this larger scale comparison helps to reveal some regional divisions and correlations within the eastern Baltic which would not be apparent if the focus was only on a single country. Additionally, broader regional conclusions about the practices of wealth depositing make it possible to create a cohesive and comparative discussion about the practices of wealth depositing around the Baltic Sea. Scandinavian Iron Age depositional material is well known and widely published. Adding eastern Baltic material enables a juxtaposition of the two coasts in order to create a bigger picture of Iron Age wealth depositional practices in the Baltic Sea area.

The chronological limits are dictated by the material itself. In contrast to Scandinavia and the southern coast of the eastern Baltic, there are very few examples of wealth deposits preceding the turn of our era. The numbers of Stone and Bronze Age deposits can be counted in tens and their chronological distribution covers thousands of years. There are slightly more examples from the Pre-Roman Iron Age, but even these are very scarce. As the spatial and temporal gaps are very large for the centuries BC, the comparisons, associations and distinctions within the material would be very speculative. Therefore it was decided to set the start of the period of study at the beginning of the Roman Iron Age (1st century AD) because this is a period when a considerable number of wealth deposits start to emerge in the eastern Baltic. The end of the period is dictated by the beginning of the Viking Era. Several developments and changes in the archaeological material take place between 800-1050 AD, but for the studies of wealth deposits the most important are coin finds. Large numbers of coins and other silver objects are found in the eastern Baltic, because this region played an important role in the eastern road of the Viking trade networks. If this period were included it would have involved the inclusion of a far larger body of material. Besides, Viking Age and later periods would require an advanced knowledge of numismatics and experience in analysing coin finds. Acquiring such skills would exceed the limits of time and effort available for the current PhD thesis. Therefore it was decided, that as the Viking Age involved a whole new system of valuables and their movement, significant changes and developments in the economy and social structure, this period should be excluded from the current study.

The detailed contextual analysis also excludes Roman coin hoards, because this would also require specialist numismatic expertise. In addition, the history of numismatic research in the eastern Baltic means that although the descriptive and chronological aspects of the coin finds are often recorded in great detail, there is less interest in the detailed contextualisation and further interpretation of these finds. For these reasons the deposits consisting of coins alone have been omitted from the detailed analysis of the artefacts. However, a general overview of the coin hoards is provided and the main numismatic publications are introduced. I also include coin finds as a comparison when analysing practices of wealth depositing and their long-term changes in the final chapters. Additionally, assemblages where coins are found with other artefacts are included.

Even when considering the most abundant period of wealth deposits in pre-coinage period eastern Baltic – the 1st-9th century AD –, the material does not stand out for its abundance. The total number of wealth deposits in these 800-years remains just over one hundred, from which only 69 can be included in the detailed analysis of this thesis, because the Roman coin finds are excluded from the detailed analysis for the reasons given above. Several deposits, including numerous coin hoards, lack a sufficient level of information about the content and context of the find. As a result of these exclusions the material is quite limited. However, it is therefore even more noteworthy that the analysis of widely followed depositional practices proved largely successful (see Chapters 6-9). The exact methods for selecting, systematising and analysing data are explained in Chapter 4 and thus there is no need to introduce them here in more detail.

Before going to the detailed analysis of eastern Baltic wealth deposits it is necessary to provide an outline of eastern Baltic Iron Age archaeology. The periodization of prehistory in the eastern Baltic is broadly similar to the Scandinavian tradition. The Pre-Roman Iron Age starts around 500 BC. It is followed by the Roman Iron Age after which comes the Middle Iron Age, including the Migration Period (400/450-550 AD) and Pre-Viking Age (550-800 AD), and then the Viking Age starts (800 AD) (see Fig. 1.1.). The major difference from

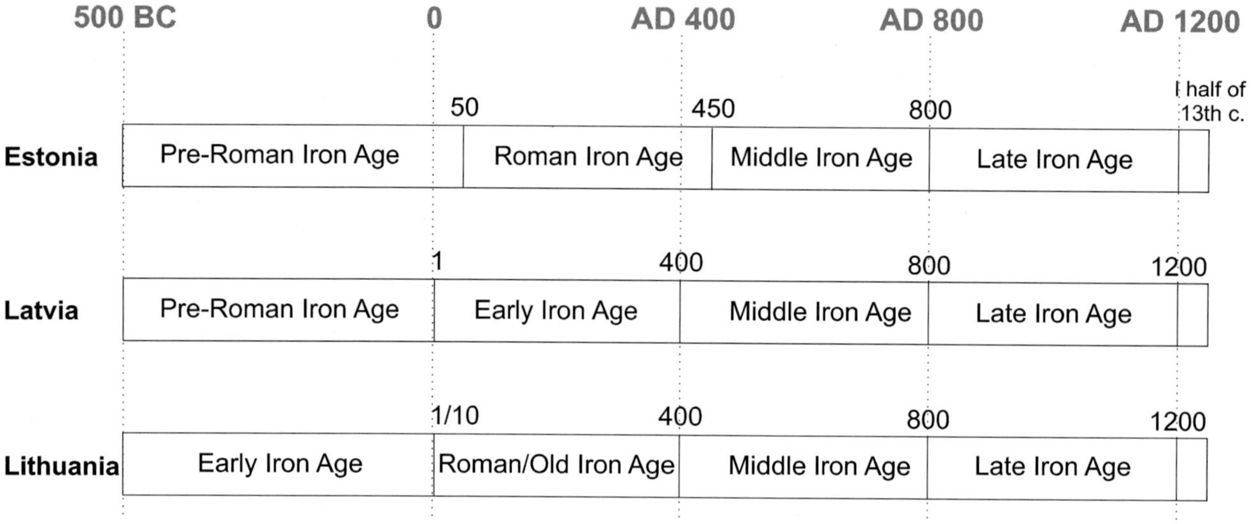


*Fig. 1.1. Iron Age chronology in the three Baltic countries (from Oras 2012a).*

Scandinavia and most of Europe is the fact that the Iron Age lasts up to the early 13th century AD in the eastern Baltic. The Viking Age is followed by the Final Iron Age and these two periods together create the Late Iron Age. The Middle Ages start in the region only with the northern Crusades at the end of the 12th – beginning of the 13th century.

The archaeological material in the eastern Baltic is similar in terms of the main archaeological sites and their state of research. The main overview of Iron Age material can be found in the general publications on the prehistory of each country (Apals *et al.* 1974; Jaanits *et al.* 1982; Apals *et al.* 2001; Banytė-Rowell *et al.* 2007). The list of primary publications also includes period specific and older native language publications with German or English summaries (Michelbertas 1986; Tautavičius 1996), but more recent publications can be found in English (Lang 2007b; Tvauri 2012).

As in many other countries burial grounds are the most abundant and thoroughly studied archaeological monuments. They vary regionally. Some burial traditions spread across current political borders, while others are very small-scale and local phenomena. The eastern Baltic Iron Age material includes examples of cremations and inhumations, stone constructions, flat underground burials, barrows and pits. Burial goods, both in quantity and content, are also very variable depending on the specific burial tradition. The history of studying those sites goes back to the pre-academic period with the first excavations carried out by local antiquarians already in the 18th and 19th centuries.

Hill-forts are the second largest group of Iron Age monuments. These easily recognisable earth-built fortifications have been studied from the beginning of the academic discipline in the region. Their numbers, distribution density, form and dates vary country by country. As many of the hill-forts date from the Iron Age, these sites are one of the characteristic sites of the period. They have a long-term excavation tradition from the early 20th century onwards.

One of the least studied archaeological sites are settlements. Although a considerable number of settlements are known, these are the least excavated and analysed archaeological monuments in the eastern Baltic. They are usually found during landscape surveys, but not studied thoroughly. Thus, there is a gap in the information on the day-to-day life of Iron Age people in the eastern Baltic. This means there are limitations to discussion of the social context of those societies. The only settlement sites that are more thoroughly studied, mainly in relation to excavations at the hill-forts, are settlements at the foot of hill-forts.

Some other types of archaeological sites are found in all three Baltic countries. One is ancient field systems, the so-called fossil fields, Celtic fields, clearance cairns, etc. These monuments have been mostly studied in Estonia, to lesser extent also Lithuania. The other common archaeological site group which has resulted in some specialist publications are iron production sites. For both of those economy-related sites the scholarship goes back to the mid-20th century. The final larger group of monuments is sites related to religion. These are usually remarkable natural sites that can be used in later historical periods, mentioned in written sources or folklore. Some of them contain remains of prehistoric human activity, but the exact interpretation of human activities during Iron Age and earlier periods remains a matter for discussion. A more detailed account of some of the examples of burial grounds and goods, information about hill-forts, settlements and other sites is discussed under the specific case-studies in the core chapters of the thesis.

One additional phenomenon to be discussed in relation to eastern Baltic Iron Age scholarship is the question of ethnozones which partly relates to the concept of migrations. There is a long-term tradition of dividing archaeological material between smaller regions that are assigned to specific ethnic groups such as Curonians, Livs, Semigallians, Selonians etc. with their distinct material culture. On the basis of the latter also prehistoric migrations have been followed. In Estonia the question of smaller ethnic divisions within a country features less in current research, but for understanding Latvian and Lithuanian publications the knowledge of smaller local cultures and regions is essential in order to follow the discussion of eastern Baltic Iron Age site distribution and social developments. This approach has several interpretative problems: it relies on references to ethnozones in the early written sources and equals the emergence of specific artefact types with certain ethnic groups. Those ideas go back to the 19th century historical scholarship and are rooted in the early 20th century culture-historical framework as well as Soviet period archaeological tradition (see Oras 2012a). They are largely defined on the basis of material from Iron Age burial grounds, especially from the Roman Iron Age onwards. Some of those regions are mentioned later in relation to the distribution of wealth deposits and their contemporary social context, but keeping in mind the highly-problematic nature of tracing distinct ethnozones in prehistory these small scale divisions are preferably avoided in further discussions. The traditionally identified smaller ethnic regions within the eastern Baltic are represented in Fig 1.2.

Estonian Iron Age wealth deposits (Estonian *aarded* (hoards), *peitleiud*, *peitvarad* (*peit* meaning 'hidden', *-leiud* 'finds', *-varad* 'valuables/wealth')) are covered by different publications quite well. The deposits of artefacts are mentioned on the pages of general overviews of Estonian prehistory. In some cases it is possible to find separate (sub-)chapters about the topic (Jaanits *et al.* 1982; Lang 2007a-b; Tvauri 2012). In many books the information is scattered across various pages (Tallgren 1925; Moora *et al.* 1936; Tvauri 2006). From the more recent publications, there is an exhibition catalogue of the Institute of History of Tallinn University by Tamla and Kiudsoo (2005) which introduces Estonian wealth deposits from prehistory to the historic periods (published also in English in 2009). The other relevant publication is the research on Estonian prehistoric

*Fig. 1.2. Ethnic groups in the Iron Age eastern Baltic (from Oras 2012a).*

religion by Jonuks (2009) where different characteristics and interpretations of wealth deposits are discussed. The newest and most exhaustive overview of Middle Iron Age deposits is by Tvauri (2012). Some relevant literature is found in specific area studies (Aun 1992; Lang 1996; Tamla 1996; Laul 2001; Mandel 2003).

The most important publication group for current research is specialist papers. Most of these concentrate on single finds and are often published soon after the discovery (Hausman 1905; 1914; Schmiedehelm 1924; Tallgren 1924; Moora 1925; Schmiedehelm 1934; Moora 1935; 1962; Mandel & Tamla 1977). There are also some studies which focus on specific environments of concealment such as springs and bog finds throughout prehistory (Tamla 1977; 1985; 1995). A couple of articles look at the whole material of wealth deposits either within a smaller area, including the material from historic and prehistoric periods (Kiudsoo 2005), or consider slightly later periods than the one under discussion in the current study (Tõnisson 1962). Before the MA thesis of the present author there was no special study of the Middle Iron Age wealth deposits in Estonia (Oras 2009; 2010). In addition to that, Estonian Roman Period finds are incorporated into current thesis.

Latvian Roman and Middle Iron Age wealth deposits (Latvian *depozīti)* were studied most thoroughly in the 1960s and 1970s by Vladislav Urtāns, who also worked at the National History Museum of Latvia where most of the finds are stored. He has published a detailed monograph about Latvian wealth deposits up to the year 1200 AD (Urtāns 1977). Another paper focuses on the finds from the 5th-9th century AD (Urtāns 1964). These publications include a catalogue section with information about the artefacts and their finding circumstances based on the archive materials at the museums. Another important publication is a book about Roman Iron Age Latvia, written by Moora (1929; 1938). At least some of the Latvian deposits, from the Roman Iron Age and the following period, are introduced on the pages of those publications. These two books also point out some interesting parallels to Latvian finds in the Estonian and Lithuanian material.

There are general overviews of Latvian prehistory which include some information about the wealth deposits. Starting chronologically, the first one is the catalogue of the 10th archaeological congress in Riga in 1896. The next is a catalogue of the Baltic archaeologists' congress in Riga in 1930. There are also books on Latvian prehistory from the first period of independence i.e. 1920s and 1930s where the material of wealth deposits is briefly introduced (Tallgrens *et al.* 1926; Balodis & Tentelis (eds) 1938). To this list the previously mentioned general overviews of Latvian prehistory can be added (Apals *et al.* 1974; Apals *et al.* 2001). Some exhibition catalogues provide information about Latvian deposits, for example a publication by Carnap-Bornheim *et al.* (2008) and an edited volume by Bitner-Wróblewska (2007). Besides those general overviews some special articles can be found (Riekstiņš 1931; Urtāns 1962; Graudonis 1964; Žeiere 2008; Brīvkalne 2009).

Publications relating to coin finds from Latvia are quite numerous. Besides the works by Urtāns there is a general overview of Roman coins found in the area of contemporary Latvia by Riekstiņš (1936). Kropotkin (1961) writes solely about the Roman coin finds in the territory of the former Soviet Union, including Latvia. The most recent is a publication about the 1st-20th century AD coin hoards in Latvia (Ducmane & Ozolina 2009) which includes a detailed catalogue.

Some publications cover the finds of wealth deposits from both Latvia and Lithuania. Most recent are the catalogues published by the Lithuanian National Museum (Griciuvienė 2005; 2007; 2009). These books are based on the traditional studies of historic and prehistoric ethnic groups in Lithuania and Latvia and focus therefore on the small ethnic regions of Semigallians, Selonians and Curonians. Another useful article which covers both countries was published by Bliujienė (2010). Her research discusses Baltic bog deposits in the area between two major rivers, Nemunas (in Lithuania) and Daugava (in Latvia). It includes a useful catalogue and covers all the Iron Age periods in these regions focussing on sacrificial interpretations of the finds.

Compared to Estonia and Latvia the studies of Lithuanian Iron Age hoards and other deposits of artefacts (Lithuanian *lobis*) are not very exhaustive. The most helpful starting point that gives an overview of the finds is an atlas-catalogue from 1977 compiled by Tautavičius which lists all the hoards from the 2nd to 13th centuries (1977, 130-133, map 5). Another relevant publication is a book by Michelbertas (2001) about the Roman finds in Lithuania, which also lists 18 Roman coin hoards. More general is the short overview of coin hoards in Lithuania by Sajauskas (2007).

There are a number of publications where wealth deposits and hoard finds have been discussed as one (usually rather brief) part of more general overviews. Some of the finds are discussed in relation to prehistoric metal finds (Volkaitė-Kulikauskienė 1943; Nakaitė 1959; Merkevičius 1973; Vaitkunskienė 1981), the others in relation to particular study areas (Hollack 1908; Engel 1931; Žulkus 2004) or period- or phenomenon-specific topics (Michelbertas 1972; Vaitkevičius 2004; Kazakevičius & Malonaitis 2006; Bliujienė 2008). There are also a couple of very broad overviews with some references to the hoards from Lithuania (Volkaitė-Kulikauskienė 1958, 112 ff; Kulikauskas *et al.* 1961; Michelbertas 2007). Special articles introducing a single find from this specific period are unfortunately very rare (e.g. Valatka 1966).

To complete the list of relevant publications, the deposits have been also mentioned on the pages of different Balto-German societies' publications, i.e. different periodicals of the so-called *Sitzungsberichtes*. Important information on finding circumstances such as environment, artefact placement and exact location was also obtained from different archive materials, mainly museum catalogues.

A common denominator for most of the publications, especially the older ones, is that they tend to put stress on the chronology and description of artefacts and focus less on contextual aspects. Although some information about environment of concealment and exact circumstances of discovery is available in the catalogues, there is usually very little systematic and comparative analysis of detailed artefactual data, aspects of environment of concealment, cultural landscape and artefact placement. The second characteristic is the limited selection of material either on the basis of a specific environment of concealment (e.g. bog finds, watery conditions) or geographical areas and periods. There are only a few studies that look beyond the borders of contemporary political territories or approach the material in a long-term perspective (Tamla 1985; Kazakevičius & Malonaitis 2006; Bliujienė 2010).

In terms of interpretative frameworks, the older publications seem to avoid interpretative discussion of the reasons for concealment, but such analyses are more characteristic of recent publications. The prevailing concepts applied to the eastern Baltic wealth deposits still relate to dividing deposits between utilitarian (profane) and religious (sacred). This division is clearly followed in most of the recent publications (Tamla & Kiudsoo 2005; Lang 2007b; Bliujienė 2010; Tvauri 2012; Sperling 2013). Comparative analysis stressing depositional practices and their relation to broader social developments are so far in the minority, or non-existent, in the eastern Baltic archaeology. This is the reason for choosing the questions and problems posed in the current thesis.

In outline this thesis is divided into eight main chapters. The first three chapters concentrate on the theoretical and methodological issues of the thesis. Chapter 2 focuses on terminology and its significance. It analyses different terms and concepts applied in the studies of intentional artefact concealment. In its second part the new term 'wealth deposit' is introduced and discussed in detail, explaining why this term is preferred to all the other traditional terms used in the studies of intentional artefact concealment. The third chapter discusses the theoretical questions of the thesis. It defines and analyses the main ideas applied to the study of practices of wealth depositing in a long-term perspective including events and practices, micro and macro scale, relationships between them and the role of long-term approach. The last chapter before the core part of the thesis is dedicated to methodological questions. It describes how the data for the current study was collected and systematised. This is followed by the methodological discussion about which aspects of this data are the most meaningful in order to answer the questions and control the hypothesis of the current thesis. In the final part of this chapter the specific methods employed in data analysis are discussed.

Chapter 5 gives a general overview of the main characteristics of and the topical questions relating to the material of Iron Age wealth deposits in the Baltic Sea area. The majority of this chapter concentrates on the Scandinavian examples because this material is particularly abundant and thoroughly studied. In the final subchapters the main characteristics of Polish and Finnish Iron Age wealth deposits are introduced. The aim is to provide a background in terms of comparisons and main interpretative frameworks for the Estonian, Latvian and Lithuanian material.

Chapters 6-8 form the core chapters of the thesis. The material of the eastern Baltic wealth deposits in the 1st-9th century AD is introduced country by country. I discuss the general characteristics of the find material, but also the main problems that occurred during data collection and the exclusions of material. Thereafter comes the presentation of artefact groups and environments of concealment represented in each country followed by the analysis of different combinations of artefacts and environments of concealment. Putting the latter results in a chronological and geographical context provides the conclusions about the particular practices of wealth depositing for each country. This also identifies the unique outliers which do not form parts of broader wealth depositional practices.

The final chapter is the principal part of the thesis. It combines the contextual characteristics of wealth deposits from all the three Baltic countries. As a result some very significant depositional traditions are identified, some of which spread across all the three countries, while others are very local and small-scale. These are discussed in relation to their broader social context. The aim is to analyse regional and cross-regional depositional practices in order to discuss the question of cultural borders and the influence of social context on the practices of wealth depositing. It brings together the case studies that best exemplify the importance of the analysis of wealth deposits on a larger scale, illustrating why and how the practices of wealth depositing make a significant contribution to the study of past people and social developments. This chapter is considerably longer, because it combines data from all the three countries and provides detailed information on social contexts for each case study. It identifies spatial and temporal developments of depositional practices, forming a cohesive comparative picture of the eastern Baltic depositional practices. Therefore it was decided to present this material within a single key chapter. The final part of this chapter draws some general conclusions about the similarities and differences of wealth depositional practices around the Baltic Sea. It concentrates on comparing eastern Baltic material with the Scandinavian and southern Baltic counterparts. As a result, for the first time, a picture of general and regional distribution areas of the practices and traditions of wealth depositing across the Baltic Sea region is provided.

The broader aim of the current thesis is to move beyond the traditional interpretational "why"-questions posed to wealth deposits and move instead to the questions of "how". I argue that on an interpretational basis, archaeologists can never get to the initial meaning of a wealth deposit. The functions, uses and meanings of different artefacts, environments and actions in the past are so variable and so much context- and person-dependant that the gap between current researchers and past people makes it very difficult to provide any firm conclusions to such questions. I do not want to dismiss those questions entirely and agree that they are important and interesting. But I believe that they can be answered only in exceptional cases when the fragmentation of the material is minimal and the record is reliable and detailed. For most of the data on wealth deposits these conditions do not apply. What one can study in these cases is how different materialities develop and change in time and space and how they relate to each other. These questions are less loaded with interpretative problems and help to get closer to past human actions and the relations between material selections and social conditions than problem settings that ask for a specific meaning and a reason of concealing wealth deposits.

*Chapter 2*

# Defining the wealth deposit

Terms and definitions are important components of all research. Use of specific terms without definitions may result in serious misunderstandings. In the following chapter I give an overview of the terms used by other scholars so far in studying different deposits of artefacts. I will analyse different terms and definitions in relation to my current research, pointing out their limitations and strengths. I then define the term 'wealth deposit' and explain why it is most appropriate for the current study. I have briefly discussed some of these questions in my previous publications (Oras 2008; 2009, 3-7; 2010; 2012b), but will examine them more closely on the following pages.

## 2.1. Problems with terms and definitions

The main problem in studying different types of artefact assemblages lies in predetermined interpretations of these sets of objects. Most of the terms – hoards, treasures, votive or ritual deposits, etc. – are loaded with preconceived ideas as to why artefacts were deposited. Additionally they relate to both everyday and academic traditional employment of these words. There is an obvious question whether our interpretation of the find necessarily correlates with its meaning, function and usage in the past or if there can be a single interpretation at all. The lines between archaeological finds and their past functions and meanings are drawn by current researchers centuries after the original deposit. Often the possibility of fluidity and the changing nature of an artefact's function and meaning is forgotten. It has to be acknowledged that no matter how hard we try we will never be able to get into the mind of past people and provide definite statements about their original intention when making a wealth deposit.

### 2.1.1. Interpretational terms

Amongst the oldest interpretational terms used are the terms 'hoard' and 'treasure'. According to the Oxford English Dictionary[2] a hoard is "an accumulation or collection of anything valuable hidden away or laid by for preservation or future use; a stock, store, esp. of money; a treasure". According to the same source a treasure is "wealth or riches stored or accumulated, esp. in the form of precious metals; gold or silver coin; hence in general, money, riches, wealth". There are two main aspects here that need to be stressed: first, that the words both denote an assemblage of objects; second, that in the case of a hoard it is deliberately hidden for storage or further use i.e. meant to be retrieved; and third, that treasure is usually related to precious metal and/or precious stones. Treasures and hoards may not be identical, but they do overlap, and thus here I use the term 'hoard' for both

2 http://www.oed.com/.

of them. It is interesting that the word 'treasure' is used less frequently in academic texts (Johns 1994; 1996). Millett has pointed out that the reason for this might be its connection to common and somehow vulgar usage of words, often associated with treasure hunters (1994, 101).

The idea of retrievable precious (metal) artefact assemblages is related to the need for safe storage and protection of something to be recovered when needed. In the context of the United Kingdom at least these terms and definitions are influenced by the 12th century law of Treasure Trove which was supposed to ensure that the Crown acquired newly discovered valuables that were without legal ownership (Millett 1994, 102; for legal discussions of Treasure Trove see Hammond 1982; Sparrow 1982; Cookson 1992). As this law stated, hoards consist of valuables of precious metal meant to be retrieved, but never recovered for some reason by the owner, who can no longer be traced. This certainly influences the current and traditional definitions of the term and might easily lead to the conclusion that a hoard or a treasure must be an assemblage of precious metal artefacts related to safe keeping of valuables for economic reasons. However, working out the aims of the past depositor e.g. whether the objects were meant to remain in the ground or not, is very speculative. Therefore the new Treasure Act which took effect in 1997[3] and was amended in 2002 as The Treasure (Designation) Order[4] covers also the assemblages of other metal objects of prehistoric origin. More importantly, the idea of distinguishing retrievable and non-retrievable finds has been abandoned and attempts to determine the intentions of the depositor have been given up.

In the academic sphere, archaeologists have provided various definitions of the term 'hoard', where the mixture of characteristics causes further definitional problems. There seems to be continuous disagreement about the material of artefacts, quantity of objects, acceptable environment of concealment, and interpretations of the reasons for hiding the object(s).

First, there is discussion about the characteristics of artefacts forming a hoard: does this include any kind of valuables or only specific categories? The dependency of value on artefact material is an ambiguous concept if we think about different prehistoric periods. For example in the Stone Age we often lack silver, bronze or gold and artefact assemblages may consist of stone and organic material alone (Bradley 1988, 250). Similar ideas have been expressed when discussing Roman Period hoards which traditionally consist of silver and gold, whereas the preceding and following periods provide examples of non-precious metal artefact assemblages which might also be regarded as valuables and thus seen as hoards (Millett 1994, 104; Johns 1996, 1; Verlaeckt 2000, 194). The latter problem is touched on by Hingley in his study of iron objects in Iron Age and Roman Period Britain, where he refers to the assemblages of iron objects as 'hoards' (*sic!* in quotation marks) (2006, 214-215).

Second, there is the question of counting artefacts. There are two controversial opinions as to how many artefacts constitute a hoard. The first one says that a hoard must be a collection, an assemblage of artefacts (Johns 1996, 1; Chapman 2000, 112; Verlaeckt 2000, 194). This approach tries to minimize the possibility of confusing a hoard with accidental loss of artefacts. The others refer to the value of an object and stress that the quantity should not be the main characteristic

3 http://www.legislation.gov.uk/ukpga/1996/24/contents.
4 http://www.legislation.gov.uk/uksi/2002/2666/contents/made.

(e.g. one golden bracelet compared to a couple of coins). Authors sometimes contradict themselves (compare for example Chapman 2000, 46, 112) leading to the conclusion that the conception of a hoard as a multi-object find might be too strict (Geißlinger 1984, 321; Aitchison 1988, 271; Hingley 2006, 215-216). For instance, it has been shown that finds of Neolithic stone axes in the Netherlands often consist of one object alone (Wentink & van Gijn 2008, 35). The same goes for some Bronze Age deposits in the same area (Fontijn 2008, 13). Thus, as Hingley (2006, 220) also points out, if distinguishable from possible accidental loss as acknowledged and deliberate deposition, single objects should not be dismissed from the overall analysis of deposits.

One solution proposed in this debate on counting artefacts is that in the case of just one object, it would be possible to use the word 'cache' (Johns 1996, 2). But a cache means something hidden or just a hiding place according to the Oxford English Dictionary[5]. It might just as well refer to many objects and is often used in discussing artefact deposits in the New World (compare Johns 1996, 2, 11, 15; see also Walker 1995, 76-77; Mills 2004, 243; Pauketat & Alt 2004, 779). So, this term again includes different interpretations with different implications.

Another point relating to counting objects is the formation process of a hoard. Shall we consider a hoard to be a single depositional act or perhaps include the possibility of adding and removing artefacts over time (Aitchison 1988, 271; Johns 1996, 7, 9-11; Hingley 2006, 215)? It is highly likely that once a safe spot was found for valuables objects might have been added and removed according to the owner's needs. The same is also discussed in relation to votive or ritual depositing in Roman Period temples (Johns 1994, 111-114; 1996, 9-11). Thus counting objects might not actually give a direct answer as to how the assemblage of objects or a find of one object was formed.

Third, discussing hoards and the reasons for their concealment often becomes a matter of debate about contexts, which is closely related to interpretation of find assemblages. For instance, it has been seen problematic not to include finds from rivers, lakes, bogs and other watery conditions in the analysis of Western-Europe 1st millennium BC hoards (Bradley 1988, 249), because finds from watery conditions seem to be distinguished from economic hoards. In recent decades this debate has subsided (Levy 1982; Pauli 1985; Needham 1988; Bradley 1990; Fontijn 2002; Rossenberg 2003; Hamon & Quilliec 2008, 1; Yates & Bradley 2010; Joy 2011), and although grouped separately, deposits of artefacts from different environments are analysed together. In this context, also the question of deposits in specific archaeological sites (shrines, temples, settlements, hill-forts) and their relation to the interpretation of hoards has come into question (Hingley 2006, 215). This is related to the categorization of archaeological sites as if they and the artefacts from them had a single function.

And last but not least there is the problem of opposed terms and definitions, which is the most difficult scholarly tradition to overcome. The most widely debated issue in this context is the relationship and distinction between ritual and/or religious related hoards (aka offerings, sacrifices, dedicated or votive deposits/hoards) and economic safe-keeping or storage hoards. Often these two categories are opposed to each other as pragmatic, utilitarian, profane, secular, and symbolic, special, ritual, religious, sacred (Levy 1982; Geißlinger 1984, 322; Reece 1988,

---

5 http://www.oed.com/.

264; Bradley 1990; Hedeager 1992, 33-36; Hårdh 1996, 131-132). At times it seems as if there is even a bias in favour of one or another interpretation within different groups of scholars, who separate these two depositional aspects and speak in favour of one and against the other. Sometimes the interpretational terms are also closely related to the period or area under discussion. For instance, prehistoric, especially in the case of non-monetary societies, deposits seem to be more often related to ritual or religious hoards whereas later periods that are characterized at least to some extent by circulation of coins tend to be seen as economy related (Randsborg 2002, 415). Similar tendencies for generally approved and acceptable interpretations also vary geographically (see Bradley 1982, 111; 1990, 15-17, 28-29).

An example of these opposing interpretational terms and definitions is Osborne's (2004) article about dedicated objects, which according to him might include different artefact sets like votives and dedications, ritual deposits or hoards, offerings. His main aim is to highlight the concept of hiding artefacts for religious and symbolic reasons, claiming that there are assemblages of artefacts dedicated to the supernatural, often characterized by special depositional locations or special choice of artefacts. Although he sets out some characteristics for distinguishing dedicated objects, it is still problematic as a basis for definition. The special character of objects does not necessarily relate to visible unusual features of the artefact, but might be created through the dedication act itself (Johns 1996, 9; Bradley 2003, 11; Osborne 2004, 2). Thus a most ordinary and undistinguished daily object might become dedicated. On the other hand, what might look like a special location to a modern researcher does not necessarily relate to religious activities in the past. There are examples of hiding valuables in the water to keep them safe (Geißlinger 1984, 322-323; Johns 1994, 114; Randsborg 2002). Artefacts in temples or other religious sites are often seen as votives, but some of them were meant for further use at the same time (Johns 1994, 111-114; 1996, 9-10) or are the examples of so-called ritual rubbish as discarded ritual attributes or ceremonial trash (Garfinkel 1994; Clayton *et al.* 2005; Stanton *et al.* 2008). It is also debatable how far it is possible to make a clear division between directly supernatural-related (religious) and other social ceremonial (ritual) activities (Brück 1999; Bradley 2005). So, distinguishing special, dedicated and religion-related deposits by material means might be a very complicated task.

Of course there are cases where it can be argued that some artefacts were deposited in relation to ritual and perhaps even religious activities and the others for safekeeping to be retrieved after the threat has passed. But the archaeological material is not always clearly attributable to either. It is grey-scale and provides researchers with very different objects from various environments and landscape features that are difficult to understand and explain. Additionally, even with an idea of how religious or supernatural aspects might have been expressed (special artefacts and hiding contexts) it is, first, not to be seen as universal and supra-cultural; and second, not to be related to religious activities alone.

Several other scholars have argued recently that there should not be a distinction between pragmatic and more symbolic acts of depositing artefacts, or at least that different interpretational groups should be analysed together (Bradley 1987; 1988, 249-250, 258; Brück 1999; Verlaeckt 2000, 194; Bradley 2003; Insoll 2004; Bradley 2005; Mills & Walker 2008; Joyce & Pollard 2010; Berggren & Stutz 2010). These arguments try to combine different interpretational conceptions which often seem separated, and stress the variability of different practices of artefact depositing. This brings us to the following discussion of more neutral and less-interpretation based terms and definitions which should include different interpretational groups.

## 2.1.2. Neutral terms

One way to avoid the interpretational terms is the usage of more neutral ones – either based on purely physical characteristics or on more abstract concepts relating to practices of creating deposits of artefacts. Describing and grouping artefact finds according to single physical characteristics stresses just one aspect of the find assemblage and enables one to concentrate on just a fraction of the whole deposits' material. Examples of such terms might be as follows: metal deposits, ornament deposits, weapon deposits, iron deposits, bog finds, etc. These terms seem more neutral, but on the other hand are very dull, because they do not actually say anything about the intrinsic nature of depositing practices. If we are to accept the importance of broad analysis of different deposits of artefacts, this might turn out to be problematic. For instance, we know different long-term traditions of Scandinavian bog finds from human sacrifices to weapon offerings (see Chapter 5), which vary considerably in their characteristics and probably also meanings. Is the most important denominator really just a bog or are we actually talking about completely different depositional traditions...?

The other solution to the question of interpretationally loaded terms without falling into a purely descriptive approach is to consider more practice related and intention-focussed use of terms and definitions. In these cases the term 'deposit' or 'depositions' is often used (see also Joyce & Pollard 2010, 294 and the literature cited), which again suggests more general and neutral use of words. They are based on ideas of socially constructed and acknowledged depositional practices which result in repeated and patterned material characteristics.

A ground-breaking study in this field followed by numerous scholars for decades was Richards and Thomas' article about Neolithic Wessex (1984), where they introduced the term 'structured deposits' as special features in the material record (see Garrow 2012). Although more neutral at first sight, their concept is still closely related to the study of ritual in the archaeological record. They see a specific structuration in the deposits as means to decode past ritual activities, because ritual is regarded as something highly formalized and repetitive (Richards & Thomas 1984, 191-192).

The other term which emphasises the historical and social background of deposit creation is 'selective deposits', which was first used by Needham in his study of Early Bronze Age metal finds in Britain (1988). He illustrated the concept by showing that different find assemblages (burials and metal deposits) have different contents and hiding contexts. Therefore it is evident that there must have been an acknowledged selection of artefacts and their placement according to the goals and aims of those making the deposit. Similar ideas have been reflected later in the Netherlands' scholarship (Fontijn 2002; 2008; Wentink & van Gijn 2008). These are based on the ideas of selection of deposited artefacts according to their context of concealment, especially burials *versus* hoards, but they also put emphasis on the characteristics of ritual and religious deposits.

The third term, also closely related to studies of past ritual, is 'special deposits'. These have been defined as specially or carefully treated deposits – either in artefact handling and/or their placement. The latter is believed to be caused by the ideas of the appropriate and right way of depositing artefacts according to the aims and intentions of the participants (Pollard 2008, 45). Examples of such studies of special deposits include discussions of Iron Age or Anglo-Saxon Period osteological material (both human and animal) in settlement contexts (mainly sunken-featured houses and pits) (Hill 1995; Hamerow 2006). But the same term has been also used about British Roman and Iron Age deposits (Cunliffe 1992; Clarke 1997; Hamerow 2006, 19-20), metal finds (Hingley 2006, 213) and Neolithic material (Pollard 2008).

There are many other similar and at first sight more neutral or abstract terms e.g. intentional, odd, deliberate, placed etc. deposits. But all these are problematic solutions because they often result in ritual related interpretations and their identification in archaeological material is complicated. In fact, most of these concepts have been regarded as derivations of a general umbrella concept of 'structured deposits' (Garrow 2012, 93).

The problems with these neutral terms are multifaceted. First, we must ask whether we are able to make the kind of distinction in the archaeological record that these terms – structured, intentional, selective, and special – refer to. It has been pointed out that the concept of structured deposits includes the possibility that there must have been unstructured ones as well (Pollard 2008, 9). However, all the deposits from rubbish to valuable artefacts are the results of specific activities and all the activities are in essence structured (Moore 1982; Hill 1995, 96; Pollard 2001, 316) and thus selective. In addition, every acknowledged act probably has intentions and aims. Therefore, almost all acts are to some extent rule based, repeated, selective and intended. Even routine cleaning and rubbish discarding or artefacts left behind because of seasonal movements must have been acknowledged, intentional, selective and even rule bound. Thus the distinctions between structured, intentional or selective deposits or ordinary archaeological material remain unclear.

The other aspect of critique includes the discussion that the concept of structured deposits threatens to exclude deposits where structure and repeated selection is not evident, labelling such deposits as non-functional and difficult to explain (Pollard 2008, 43). The concept of extraordinary as out of pattern may result in very unusual deposits being impossible to study because they have no characteristics which would allow comparison with and relation to others. They remain unique and special.

However, even the special is difficult to distinguish, because we are talking about past cultures, experiences and perceptions. An example of this is Hill's (1995) study of Iron Age pits in Wessex: although accepting himself that he is talking about probable ritual special deposits, he still prefers to use 'articulated or associated animal bone groups' (1995, 16). It should be remembered that the structure or speciality of deposits is created, described and thereafter looked for by contemporary researchers (Brudenell & Cooper 2008, 24; Mills & Walker 2008, 21) and thus in essence this approach is to some extent biased.

My own critique of these abstract terms is that they seem to distance us from the previously introduced concepts of hoarding and economy-related reasons for hiding valuables. As mentioned, all these neutral terms are either derived from or tend to result in studies of past ritual. Therefore they can be seen as interpretational definitions disguised behind more neutral terms. In them lies a threat of exclusion of some artefact assemblages at the beginning of the study just because they do not seem selective, special or structured enough.

However, those neutral concepts and terms have been developed further into studies which emphasise the act of deposition and its broader cultural context. Although some of them even use the same adjectives, like structured, they stress the intentionality behind depositional practices, practices and processes of deposition formation, phenomenology and perceptions of past practices (Pollard 1995, 137; Chapman 2000, 130; Joyce 2008, 27-28; Mills & Walker 2008, 17; Joyce & Pollard 2010). To some extent they try to leave the concepts of ritual behind.

If we are to stress the importance of depositional practice as our primary goal instead of distinguishing oppositional groups, the elimination of some material sources must be avoided. If we want to get closer to past peoples' understanding of valuables, their variable use, function and ways of deposition, the source material should be inclusive not exclusive. From all of those more neutral terms discussed above, the idea of selective deposits is probably the closest one to this aim. However, it clearly emphasises the need for detailed comparative analysis of all the possible contemporary archaeological sites and the material culture therein. The latter is beyond the limits of the current thesis in the case of 1st-9th century AD eastern Baltic deposits. Due to the scale of the study as well as limited excavations at some specific sites there is a lack of detailed analyses, in-depth and reliable chronology for some archaeological monuments (see Chapter 9.2).

Summing up, even though interpretational terms are problematic, more neutral and abstract terms – based on either pure physical characteristics or practice and its aim related concepts – have also limitations. But perhaps there is a third way: a possibility to say more about different practices of depositing artefacts in the past without grouping artefact assemblages according to current researcher interpretation or mere physical characteristics. At this point I would like to introduce and discuss the term 'wealth deposit'.

## 2.2. Wealth deposit

Having discussed different terms for the deposits of artefacts and pointed out the pros and cons of their usage, I am left in the situation where none of them is quite suitable for my current research. Some of them define the data according to material. Concentrating on a single type of find-spot context (environment) would allow me to look at just one part of the phenomenon. Interpretational terms would make me separate the material into either-or categories (sacred/profane, ritual/functional, etc.). Ideas of structured, selective and special deposits might raise questions about distinguishing some artefact assemblages from the overall archaeological record. Besides, traditionally these terms are used with ritual-related interpretations. My source material covers different metal artefacts, sometimes with some organic or even mineral objects included, and various hiding environments from natural places to archaeological sites. I am interested in the spatial and temporal changes in the practices of artefact depositing as well as their relation to broader social context and cultural development. Thus, I need to look at and analyse my source material as a whole, not divide it into different categories from the start. Therefore, none of the previously discussed terms suits my research material and questions.

The concept that I have decided to use is the term 'wealth deposit'. This term is wide enough to cover all the different characteristics of artefact assemblages and contexts in my research area and period, and limited enough to be understood as a separate archaeological find group. By the term 'wealth deposit' I refer to one or more valued object/s that is/are hidden deliberately as an intended separate deposition of selected object(s) into a selected place in a specific, distinguishable manner (see also Oras 2010; 2012b and below). That term covers all the possible artefact groups from various find-spots without preconditioned interpretation. It combines two important words in the scholarship of artefact concealments: 'wealth' or 'value' and 'deposit'. The more widely used term 'deposit' has a connotation of distinguishing specific and intentional artefact concealments from the artefacts left behind by other human activities on different archaeological monuments (burials, settlements, forts, field-systems, etc.). It has even been argued that unlike a hoard, a deposit might consist of a single object or can be created over time (Aitchison 1988, 271) making the inclusion criteria correspondingly wider. 'Deposit' and 'depositing' stresses the importance of the act (or practice) of making a deposit in a widest sense and leaves space for very different interpretations. Therefore the word 'deposit' as part of the specific term is more appropriate for my source material and research questions. The term 'wealth' is more complicated and requires a more detailed discussion.

### 2.2.1. Wealth and value

In the context of providing preliminary definitions, the use of the term 'wealth' needs further explanation. It has been used as 'wealth deposition' in Parker Pearson's study where he is referring to any kind of deposition of wealth either in burial contexts or as separate deposits of artefacts (1999, 87) or in relation to economic coin hoards in the context of Iron Age England (Holman 2005). The term 'wealth' is closely related to the concepts of value and valuables: being wealthy means owning something valuable.

The concept of value is multifaceted, because it includes measurable and universal ideas of valued objects, but also the creation of artefact value through symbolic and contextually created meanings. Value is both an *emic* and an *etic* (cf. Harris 1976) concept, which therefore derives from cultural and cross-cultural concepts of valuables, as pointed out by Renfrew (1986, 146). Anthropology and history abound with such culture-dependant examples of contextually created and maintained valuables: cloth, pigs and shells in the Pacific (Munn 1986; Thomas 1991; Mauss 2002), evaluation of glass beads and iron by natives in the New World (Pugh 2009), etc.

There are some objects which can be accepted as representing general and universal wealth and value. One such category is precious metal objects. These can be described as rare, durable and attractive, often used as prestige and symbolic items (Haselgrove 1982; Renfrew 1986, 148-149; Lesure 1999, 33; Parker Pearson 1999, 79). The other way of decoding valuables is through production effort: the more labour it takes to produce the raw material and to make the artefact from it, the more valuable an object probably is. This becomes more debatable if one tries to distinguish the rate of value among specific artefact groups and types (see e.g. Arnold 1980, table 4.5.). But it still can be assumed that bigger and elaborately decorated items were of higher value. Evaluation of an artefact might be related to its scarcity, but also to the ways it was acquired or derived from its belonging to artefact sets forming an ensemble (Randsborg 1973, 565; Lesure 1999, 31; Hamon & Quilliec 2008, 2).

But value is not constituted by economic and material, measurable and visible characteristics alone. Very often it has been pointed out that contemporary archaeologists should not take their own concepts of value and its usage as universal and cross-cultural (see discussion between Millett 1994, 101 and Johns 1994, 109; also Moore 1982, 75-76; Lucero 2008, 190). It is important to see not only the intrinsic value of an artefact in measurable terms (weight, material), but its value in its overall social context (Lucero 2008, 190).

There is a concept of symbolic value which relates to the use and circulation of specific artefacts in their historical and social contexts (Appadurai 1986, 23). The evaluation of objects relates to numerous cultural concepts: objects of prestige and status (Haselgrove 1982, 82); objects that have sentimental and individual-related value (Renfrew 1986, 158-159; Lillios 1999); inalienable or singularized symbolic objects as symbols of group or individual personification, identity and socialisation (Davenport 1986; Kopytoff 1986, 73-74; Thomas 1991; Weiner 1992; Miller 2001, 108; Myers 2001, 9, 58). These objects do not necessarily have to be made of rare materials with high labour effort and they might not be usable in the practical utilitarian sense. In these cases artefact values are assigned by the society: they are created, maintained and changed in its own social contexts. One such example is iron, the production and value of which is highly symbolic in many societies, often ritual and religion related (Rowlands 1971; Budd & Taylor 1995; Walker 1995, 77; Peets 2003; Gansum 2004; Haselgrove & Wigg-Wolf 2005, 11-12; Hingley 2006, 217). It has been argued that objects with their specific culturally created and accepted values are active agents in cultural practices: they may dictate human action and make people act (make people to deposit them) in specific ways (Robb 2004, 133; Miller 2005; Pollard 2008, 48-49). Therefore it can be argued that the process of evaluation is not only a matter of materials and production. The socially created evaluation and symbolic value of objects might be based on practices, institutions and histories with which these objects are associated and thus the value is not just a static characteristic, but may change over time (Keane 2001, 70; Myers 2001). These fluid concepts lead to the idea of 'social and mental valuables'.

How do we then recognise those 'mental' valuables and wealth deposits in archaeological material? The answer lies in the way these valuables have been treated expressing this evaluation – through their depositional contexts and in the broader background of their social contexts. These evaluative characteristics might be special sites or features related to communal activities and collective possessions. Examples might be archaeological sites which were presumably used collectively (temples, burials areas, etc.) or artefact assemblages which probably cannot have been the possession of a single owner e.g. one specific artefact group represented in unusually large numbers. There is also an idea that valuables were not used always and everywhere, but in specific cases and specific locales (Lesure 1999, 33). Therefore they are probably not widespread in different archaeological sites. Rare(r) and/or unparalleled objects which might be related to prestige and personal status attributes were probably evaluated regardless of their material or decorative appearance (Mills 2004, 247).

There are two main ideas to be applied to the eastern Baltic material. First the concept of universal value that mainly relates to the scarcity of material and labour-effort invested into production. In the context of Iron Age eastern Baltic all metal artefacts were valuables and regarded as wealth (see Chapter 9.2.), because no precious metal is available in these areas and it takes quite an effort to produce iron from bog ore. The production of these objects must have been quite labour-intensive and some of them are imported artefacts or materials being therefore rare rather than ordinary. The second idea is about tracing socially constituted valuables. This helps to broaden the concept of wealth and distinguish wider categories of valuables in the eastern Baltic Iron Age. The latter might include unparalleled artefacts (e.g. lacking from settlements and burials) and also specific numbers or combinations of them. Regarding the hiding locations, special natural objects or collectively used archaeological sites might serve the purpose of being a suitable depositional context for 'mental' valuables. Often these evaluative special treatments can be recognisable through repeated contextual characteristics, overlapping depositional patterns (Walker 1995, 72-73, 79; Pollard 2001) occurring in the contexts of these deposits in different cases. This might also help to distinguish valued objects. There must be similarities and parallels in these depositional practices in order to argue for culturally created and accepted object evaluations through their depositional practices.

What I wish to emphasise in the previous discussion is the importance of keeping in mind that besides universally accepted concepts of valuables based on their exchange and market value, objects' value is also expressed in how, where and with what artefacts were deposited. Even quite ordinary and everyday materials and objects might become special and valued. How far this can actually be distinguished in archaeological material depends on the availability and characteristics of the source material and its previous documentation as well as collection history and strategies. For example, in the eastern Baltic Iron Age material there are very few wealth deposits which contain other material than metal. However, these field-specific problems should not make us deny the variability and context-dependency of the concept of value.

### 2.2.2. Importance of the concept of wealth deposit in the current study

Based on the available data of intentionally concealed and separate artefact deposits from the 1st-9th century AD eastern Baltic material and the multifaceted concepts of value I find it useful to start using a new term – wealth deposit – as defined above: one or more valued object/s that is/are hidden deliberately as an intended separate deposition of selected object(s) into a selected place in a distinguishable manner (see also Oras 2010; 2012b). This definition infers that the act of depositing has been intentional and acknowledged by the participant(s) and not an accidental loss. It is also separated from the other depositional practices of which the primary essential and functional background is different (e.g. burials, rubbish pits, etc., see below).

I prefer the term "wealth deposit' to any current terms for the following reasons. First, the term leaves the discussion open in the sense of physical and material as well as interpretational characteristics. It does not restrict the choice of primary data through the number of artefacts and includes deposits formed over longer time periods as well as those created at one time. I agree that methodologically it is not always possible to distinguish between deliberate deposits and accidental loss, especially in the case of single finds. But single objects were valuable, some of them perhaps even more than sets of artefacts so less likely to be lost. This brings us to the matter of depositional contexts. Although I will use the term 'context' in a broader sense later on (see Chapter 4), here I use it in the traditional sense of the environment of concealment and artefact location in relation to other archaeological sites and features. It is important to understand the past environment where the deposits were discovered in order to interpret them, perhaps even recognize them at all. Firstly, because the environment of concealment at the time of depositing is one crucial characteristic of every find. But secondly, patterns of contextual characteristics in combination with specific artefacts might help in recognition of the evaluation process of deposited artefacts (Barrett 2001; Pollard 2001; Lucero 2008, 189; Mills & Walker 2008, 16; Berggren & Stutz 2010). Often, it is only through hiding contexts, which have similar characteristics to known deposits, that acts of deliberate and patterned depositional practices become evident (Verlaeckt 2000, 194-195; Hamon & Quilliec 2008, 1). Some past cultural practices with specific artefacts are related to specific locations and thus through similar characteristics make us see deliberate depositional practices i.e. there is a dynamic between some artefacts and sites (Needham 1988; Bradley 1998, 27-28; Pollard 2001, 315-316). Similar ideas can be also followed in the contexts of artefact placement – sometimes it is evident that the deposit could not have been accidental, but planned and intentional.

However, even though appropriate in many aspects, the term 'wealth deposit' carries its own flaws. As it has been pointed out by different audiences to which I have presented my research in various conferences and presentations, to many the word 'wealth' still relates to the economic sphere of life. Therefore its use might carry biased connotations which I am trying to avoid. The solution here is to keep in mind the emphasis of the concept of value as discussed above. Seeing value as something culturally but also personally created and maintained should be reflected in more abstract and wider use of the term 'wealth'. Hereby I prefer to use the term 'wealth' in the ways in which various anthropological studies have elaborated on this concept through the ideas of entanglement, inalienability, singularisation and decommoditization (Mauss 2002; Weiner 1985; Thomas 1991; Weiner 1992; 1994). Wealth can be economic, but also individual, social and cultural, why not even emotional and educational concept. Having played with different pairs of words in my mind, I have not managed to come up with any more abstract or less meaning-laden term than 'wealth deposit'. For example, 'deposits of value' or 'value deposits' do not sound semantically correct; 'artefact deposit' is too broad and may apply to all archaeological finds; the use of traditional terms was discussed above already.

The problem remains that the idea of culturally created value still includes a degree of interpretation. However, if valuable artefacts were distinguished by special treatment, it is not such an impossible task to recognize these deposits in comparison with other archaeological sites and features. The overall contextual record and wider spatial and temporal comparisons indicate the evaluation of objects. The specifics of artefact choice, hiding place and manner in which they are deposited enables the distinction from other past practices.

It is necessary to keep in mind how much the archaeological material and the research questions influence the choice as well as the creation of research terminology. First, deriving from the current research question – what dictates the choice of where, what and how artefacts are deposited and what are the relations between artefact deposits and their broader social context in a long-term perspective – it is essential to include all the finds that can be distinguished as separate artefact concealments. This means that the data must include all the variety of material regardless of their artefact numbers, material and assemblage, environment of concealment or location in relation to other archaeological sites. As long as we can be sure that we are dealing with intentionally and separately concealed objects everything must be included in the analysis. The set of data is therefore very broad in terms of material characteristics. This results in the situation where there is a need for a general umbrella term which at the same time would grasp and describe a kind of common-denominator for the whole material.

It should be added that the concept of wealth deposit does not necessarily have to be used in neutral and abstract ways alone. It is possible to add adjectives based on overall analysis e.g. ritual, hoarded, selective, etc. without raising the problem of controversy in traditional terms (like votive hoards or treasures, economic special deposits). These adjectives can be the results of a final interpretation, not predetermined interpretations: the interpretational categorisation can follow only after a thorough analysis and well-argued discussion.

I have argued for the use of this combination – wealth + deposit, in the framework of the current research topic. It is less interpretationally and traditionally preconditioned and avoids the oppositional categorisation of material. By virtue of including very different contents and contexts and focussing on patterns of material characteristics in depositional practices it becomes possible to look for differently aimed past practices not dichotomised interpretational groups. I am not arguing that one should dismiss all the previously discussed terms. There are research questions, study areas and periods to which they are appropriate, but this is not the case in the frame of the current study.

## 2.3. Wealth deposits and other archaeological structures

All studies of intentional artefact deposits include the problem of distinguishing whether a specific object(s) really was (were) deliberately hidden and not an accidental loss or a result of any other past practice or feature with a quite different functional background, like the ordinary use of settlements, hill-forts, burial grounds (Urtāns 1964, 39; Fitzpatrick 1984, 178; Geißlinger 1984, 320-321; Verlaeckt 2000, 194). However, one cannot deny the possibility of having intentional and separate deposits within other archaeological sites. Being able to distinguish objects of study and primary sources must be a starting point for all research. In the case of wealth deposits, especially with a broader definition based on the value of objects and ideas of deliberate hiding, the process of making the distinction is complicated. Thus there is a need to explain the premises used in identifying my primary sources. Most of the illustrative examples below are deliberately chosen from the study area and/or period of the current thesis.

One of the main difficulties is distinguishing separate deposits of artefacts from burials. Often these two archaeological find groups are seen together as consumptions of wealth (Needham 1988; Parker Pearson 1999, 87). Although in some instances it might be just a question of whether we have the evidence of human remains, there are also more complicated issues. One example is cenotaphs where artefacts have been buried in order to commemorate a missing person without the body itself. In that case we are dealing with an artefact assemblage without osteological evidence. Chapman (2000, 122) argues for the examples from the Balkan Copper Age, that if the artefact collection resembles personal sets with specific age and gender related objects, especially when it is found in the vicinity of a burial area or related to some other osteologically proved burial, it should be related to burial traditions. The same explanation based on the distinction of sets of personal artefacts has been used by others (Bradley 1980, 174-175; Fabech 1991a, 94-95; Hines 1989, 198-199; Mills 2008, 100, 106; in Estonian Stone Age material by Tamla & Kiudsoo 2005, 6; Ots 2006, 79, 83-86 and Mari Lõhmus (University of Tartu) pers. comm.; see also Mägi 2000; Mandel 2003, 137).

On the other hand, there seems to be a tradition where large artefact assemblages were buried close to burial areas without any hint of human remains (Grinsell 1967; Aitchison 1988, 275-277). Such examples occur in the Iron Age eastern Baltic (e.g. Paali I and II, Villevere, Kardla, Kriimani in Estonia; Priedkalni, Cibēni, Rūsiši in Latvia). They can be located at a short distance from the central burial area and can date from later periods than the usage of burial ground itself e.g. Kriimani. An obviously detached location and later date compared to the burial ground would be an argument for separate deposition of artefacts.

To make things more complicated, if we consider the definition of wealth deposit as relating to objects of value, bone deposits might be also included in the analysis. These might include animal bones (Hamerow 2006; McNiven 2012), but there are plenty of examples of human bone deposits (Grant 1984; Scott 1991; Hill 1995; Bradley 2003; Brudenell & Cooper 2008, 25-30; Chadwick 2012; see also Scandinavian examples in Chapter 5). It is very difficult to make a distinction between possible human burial (with the find context as a final resting place) and possible other ritual-ceremonial activities. In this context we can also think about medieval Christian relics and remains of saints (see e.g. Geary 1986). One possibility would be to consider the skeleton fragments: it is likely that burial practices would consist of more than just a couple of bones (skulls, long bones). Still, this explanation is not reliable if we take into account cremation burials and manipulation of bones as part of ancestral cult after the burial. The other approach would be to consider the overall function of the find-spot and its close vicinity: burial areas should probably contain more human remains, often with similar characteristics of depositional practices (burial goods, placement of the deceased, relation between the bodies and their placement in the ground). Single and specific (also in some ways specially treated) skeletal remains in non-burial contexts might be related to other ritual activities – especially, if there is a wider tradition of such deposits known in this specific cultural context (cf. Grant 1984; Hill 1995). However, there still remains a problem where and when does the burial and its remains turn into other ritual(?) activity, including intentional wealth depositions.

The other site group to consider in relation to wealth deposits is settlements and forts (hill-forts, enclosures, fortified settlements). Valuables can be concealed in the daily activity areas and fortifications. It might be just a matter of another selection of where to put your valuables according to the aims and reasons for their hiding. The distinction from ordinary dwelling deposits is clear-cut due to the selection of artefacts, especially in the case of metal objects, and their placement, perhaps also the selection of depositional location e.g. markers such as relation to rampart, hearth, etc. There are examples where artefacts have been buried at settlement sites (e.g. Latvian Ķente, Ķišukalns, Mūrnieki) or hill-forts (e.g. Lithuanian Velžiai; Latvian Ķente, Vecmokas, Mežotne and Mūkukalns deposits). The reasons for such deposition might vary: from hiding valuables in times of trouble, to a concern about accessibility to retrieve artefacts later, communal ceremonies, etc.

But in the case of organic material and other daily objects (tools, ceramics) there is a problem related to distinguishing cases when we are dealing with ordinary daily activities (rubbish pits, household remains) or intentional deposits of artefacts. As with burial areas, it is a question of complex contextual analysis as convincingly presented for example by Walker (1995), Hill (1995), Pollard (2001), Bradley (2003; 2005) and McNiven (2012). This means that detailed contextual analysis – for instance, which parts of skeleton or other artefacts, where and how were deposited – should enable us to distinguish the practices that were intentional and acknowledged artefact deposition from ordinary daily depositional processes. This might be based on an assumption that deliberate deposits were preceded by acknowledged selections based on traditional concepts of the proper way of making a deposit. Such indications of deliberate and perhaps also non-daily practices might be the patterned deposits of similar artefacts and their specific combinations, similar depositional features and locales, unusual artefact placement etc.

However, sometimes similar objects in terms of materialities, but quite different in terms of aims, function and meaning, might end up in the same contexts e.g. foundation deposits, ritual offerings to grain storage pits, in comparison with daily rubbish or simple household pits etc. (Grant 1984; Hill 1995; Bradley 2003; 2005). Additionally, as Brudenell and Cooper have demonstrated (2008) not all the human bone deposits from settlement sites necessarily need to be acknowledged, intentional and special even though in general human bones as deposit might be regarded as remarkable finds. They give examples of possible accidental incorporation of human bones into settlement deposits but also discuss the possibility of quite different burial and commemorative practices unexpected in terms of current archaeologists' ideas about the treatment of human remains (Brudenell & Cooper 2008, 29-30; Herschend 2009, 48-55). Thus, it becomes a matter of comparison between different contextual characteristics in the sense of materialities and broader cultural background that enables a researcher to distinguish different depositional practices. So far my sources do not include any organic material collections from ordinary settlements or cemeteries. This might be partly because the settlements of that period have unfortunately not been thoroughly studied in the eastern Baltic, or because that kind of special depositional practice has not yet caught the attention of the researchers in that area.

Lastly, there is a question of making distinctions between wealth deposits and lost artefacts. In some cases it has been suggested that we should not include single objects in the study of deliberate deposits because of the danger of misinterpretation. This, however, would mean discounting a large amount of important source material. So, how do we know that a single object was deposited intentionally and not lost by accident? Again, there is no single answer and, again, all the possible contextual features should be considered: how likely it was that the 'lost' artefact became irretrievable even if wanted by the loser in the specific depositional environment (watery conditions and dry land); is the 'losing' of objects frequent in the area (other similar 'losses' of artefact); are there any distinct patterns and similarities in depositional practice (artefact placement or treatment) in these stray finds in the relevant study area (is it a widespread phenomenon?). There are examples of single silver neck-rings or single vessels in Estonia, where the environment does not necessarily exclude the possibility of retrieving large artefacts (e.g. Navesti, Kriimani, Varnja). So we can say that there clearly is a depositional practice involving single artefacts. Certainly, some of the single object finds and especially everyday artefacts will remain invisible even though they might have been deposited as deliberate, unusual and somehow special valuables. And on the other hand we will probably include some lost artefacts in the discussion of deliberate deposits. But that is a risk we simply have to acknowledge.

In conclusion the context of the artefacts is most important. This does not only mean the environment and find-spot, but a wider set of deposition-related characteristics: artefacts, their handling, their placement, location in the cultural landscape and in relation to geographical features, cultural background and depositional patterns in the study area, etc. (for further discussion of the importance of context see Chapter 3 and 4). There is no single criterion or check-list for identifying wealth deposits in the archaeological record. It is a complex combination of different characteristics, which may sometimes be clear and convincing, sometimes a matter of debate. I will discuss the problems I faced in my source material in detail in Chapters 6-8.

*Chapter 3*

# Theoretical standpoints

This chapter outlines the theoretical framework for analysing practices of wealth depositing. The basic concepts of practice and agency theory as discussed by Anthony Giddens and William H. Sewell are introduced. This is followed by a discussion of different elements of social practices and how they can be traced in the archaeological record, especially in wealth deposits. The elements analysed include the concepts of events, socially followed practices, micro and macro scales, and long-term perspective. Along with a detailed overview and definitions I discuss their interrelations and applicability for analysing practices of wealth depositing.

In a wider perspective I would like to propose an alternative theoretical framework for studying wealth deposits. I argue that instead of asking interpretational 'why' questions – *sensu* applying the opposed concepts of sacred and profane to wealth deposits –, it should be aimed at analysing how depositional practices vary in time and space and how they relate to the events and processes taking place in a particular society and period. I do not wish to fall into positivist and purely descriptive approach. Instead my aim is to change the perspective of the questions posed to this source material in order to understand wealth deposits in their wider social context and discuss the relations between the two (see below).

## 3.1. Agency and practice theory

Different archaeologists provide quite different meanings and definitions of agency and practice theory (Robb 1999; Dobres & Robb 2000; Dornan 2002; Knapp & van Dommelen 2008; Robb 2010). Although mostly based on the classic works of Pierre Bourdieu (1977; 1990), Anthony Giddens (1979; 1999 [1984]) (see also Ortner (1984)) and more recently on Bruno Latour (2005), approaches to archaeological material through the concepts of agency, actors, materiality, networks and practice vary considerably.

Three main strands can be distinguished. The first attempts to put people back in the big picture of the past, emphasising individual agency and relating this to the studies of power, hierarchy and gender (Wolf 1990; Conkey & Gero (eds) 1991; Flannery 1999; Knapp & van Dommelen 2008; Robb 2010, 496-497). The second is mostly inspired by the works of Alfred Gell (1998), Latour (2005) and Arjun Appadurai's edited book *The Social Life of Things* (1986) addressing the concepts of materiality from different perspectives. They mainly stress the importance of material agency and human-material relations in social contexts (DeMarrais *et al.* 1996; DeMarrais *et al.* (eds) 2004; Miller 2005;Tilley *et al.* (eds) 2006; Hicks & Beaudry (eds) 2010; Robb 2010, 501-504). The concept of materiality is seen through actively engaged and engaging material culture. I agree with the notion that different materialities interact with humans in various ways having variable and changing meanings and functions. However, I regard those engagements not as agency of material objects by themselves, but varying in human-initiated social context and primarily relating to what people (*sic!*) did to/with them (Gosden & Marshall 1999, 170; McCall 1999, 18; Martin 2005, 283-284).

The third approach sees agency as related to practices in the past that are part of broader historical processes and cultural developments (Barrett 1988; Shennan 1993; Barrett 1994; Thomas 1996, 66-68; Barrett 2000; 2001; Pauketat 2001a-b; Dornan 2002; Gardner 2002; (ed.) 2004; Joyce & Lopiparo 2005; Robb 2010, 497-501) partly relating to the concept of communities or fields of practice as discussed in social sciences (Bourdieu 1977; 1990; Wenger 1998). This is considered as appropriate for the current study and discussed in detail below. Following Dobres and Robb (2005) this chapter will not only be a discussion of theoretical concepts but aims to build a methodology which intertwines data, method and theory for studying the practices of wealth depositing in a long-term perspective.

### 3.1.1. Practice theory and the study of wealth deposits

My premiss is that wealth deposits are evidence of past practices that change and develop in time and reflect their social contexts. Very often the concepts of practice and agency are used in parallel and they are closely related to each other. I prefer to use the concept 'practice' in my theoretical discussion, because 'agency' has such a wide field of meanings, often relating to individual or material agency (Knappett 2005; Hoskins 2006; Knappett & Malafouris (eds) 2008). I regard practice as a socially accepted and more widely followed field of actions where cultural and material structures intersect with intentionally created single events.

My theoretical approach is based on the works of Giddens (1979; 1999 [1984]) and Sewell (1992). Giddens emphasises the dual relationship between agency as individual acts and structure as a social context. The foundation of Giddens's social theory is that every aspect of agency has its background in the broader social and material framework, in rules and resources – its structure. However, agency plays an active part in creating, sustaining and developing this structure. Therefore practices as the results of agency may change according to changing structure, but they may also change this structure itself. Sewell (1992) develops Giddens's concept further and explains structure as a collection of schemas (rules or procedures) and resources (materialities and people) that, on the one hand, are put into practice in various single events, and on the other hand, pattern those social practices themselves. Schemas are the virtual basis of structure, whereas resources are actual (Sewell 1992, 13) and it is through these schemas and resources that structures can change. He prefers to use the term 'structures', in plural, explaining that there are different structures at different social levels (Sewell 1992, 16-17). Structures are reflected in social practices, but through the use of schemas and resources in those practices, structures can also be transformed or transmitted. Changes in social structures are possible due to a) a variability of structures on different social levels and historical contexts from which social actors choose which to follow and also choose the resources – both human and material – to use in their actions; b) schemas as generalised procedures of social life that make up structures are still transformable and can be used in very different contexts; c) the accumulation of resources is unpredictable and they influence the structures or schemas; d) resources have multiple meanings and they are open to reinterpretation and mobilisation by agents; e) structures with their different resources and schemas can overlap or intersect, they can be combined in different ways in different situations (Sewell 1992, 15-19). In general, Sewells's idea of multiple structures, their variable inclusion of schemas and resources as well as active human agents choosing those schemas and resources enable the concept of structure to develop and change. These changes ought to be seen in social practices, but in the case of archaeology, in the changes of resources – material culture – that are evidences of those social practices.

This outline of practice theory gives a crucial theoretical framework for analysing practices of wealth depositing and their relation to contemporary social context. They combine different levels of human action that can be recognised in archaeological material. Concepts of agency and its resources can be equated with distinguishable single intentional acts or events in the material record – in the current context with a single wealth deposit. Patterned and repeated events of depositing show that they are followed by the broader audience and, thus, play an active part in this social structure. We can describe such sets of acts as socially accepted practices. Therefore, practices are related to and expressed in single events and can be analysed through the material remains of these single events. No single deposit exists in a vacuum, separated from its social context, because this social context provides both mental and material resources and schemas as rules for it. Thus, practices of wealth depositing reflect their underlying social structure – actualities, values, rules and available resources in the society in general. But deriving from Giddens and Sewell, practices do not only reflect the social structure. They also play an active role in either sustaining or changing this structure. Material remains of events allow us to see the changes and continuations of specific practices, but also of structures themselves. Alterations in the materialities of single acts and events may result in changes of practices. These alterations in practices and social structures, also their relationships in archaeology, can be best studied through long-term analysis. This means that it is necessary to create a timeline with detailed material characteristics of synchronic single events (micro scale), in order to see if these events form patterns as social practices, and analyse how these practices relate to and play out in the social structures (macro scale) on a diachronic long-term perspective.

The detailed study of wealth deposits by using the micro and macro scale comparisons in time and space enables an analysis of long-term developments of wealth depositional practices and their relations to social structure (Fig. 3.1.1.1.). The act of making a single wealth deposit is created by past human agents. In this they rely on social structure which contains schemas (rules and procedures) and resources (material and human). Through several single events more widely followed practices are created. These are seen in patterned and repeated materialities of wealth deposits. Agents with their single events and resulting widely followed social practices are actively involved in sustaining or changing this social structure. This altogether dictates the selection of schemas and resources for the next events.

Before considering the relations of social practices and structure it is necessary to explain what these events, practices and social structures are for archaeology: where do they come from and how do we actually get to them? After that it is possible to ask what the relationship between the micro and macro scales are and how can we see those relationships? (see also Murray 2006). In order to

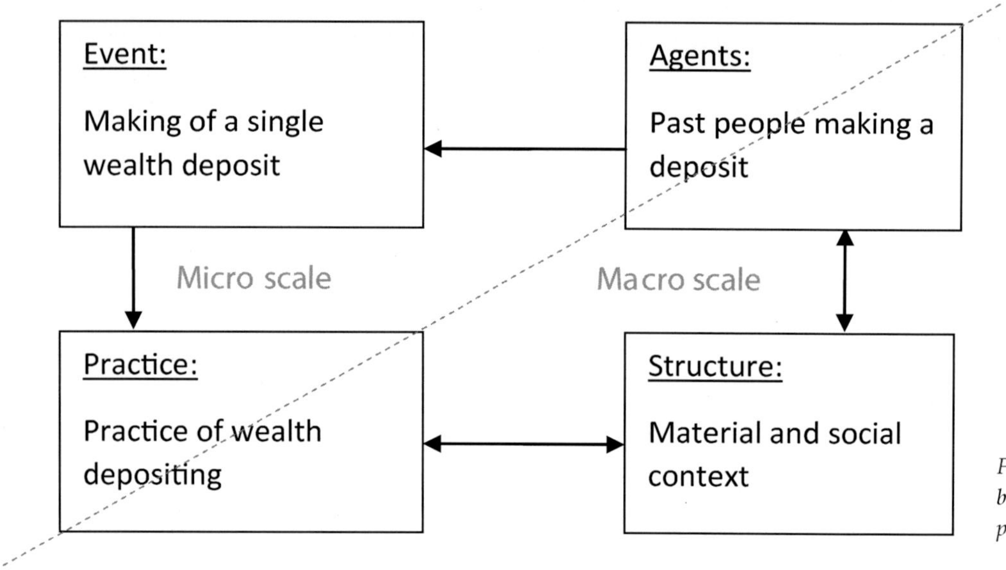


*Fig. 3.1.1.1. Relationship between agents, events, practices and structure.*

answer these questions I start with definitions. I also have to reemphasise that the following theoretical concepts have emerged from the specific study material and questions (cf. Harding 2005, 89). Therefore, the following definitions and solutions do not stand for universalities, but are rather tools that help to work with my data.

### 3.1.2. From events to practices: micro scale analysis

Prehistoric archaeology relies on the material record of the past. These different materialities are also the primary source for the analysis of the practices of wealth depositing. Artefacts reflect past events, because they are the results of what people did with and to them according to their social knowledge. To start analysing practices it is first necessary to define and describe events and their material contexts as the resources and building blocks of the broader fields of practices (Cornell & Fahlander 2002, 29-30; Fahlander 2003; Fletcher 2004; Harding 2005, 97-98; Pauketat & Alt 2005; Beck *et al.* 2007). This approach has its wider background in contextual archaeology, which emphasises the importance of searching for and decoding the materialities of the single events in the past through various material and social contexts (Hodder 1986; 1999; Johnsen & Olsen 2000; Thomas 2000).

As Lucas (2008, 62) proposed it is necessary to define the event deriving from objects at hand, because in reality archaeologists do not discover events, but objects and contexts as residues of those events. The concept of residue is used particularly because we are never able to uncover all the variety of materialities and social contexts behind one act (e.g. workshops where objects were made, house the depositor came from etc.). Although acknowledging that there is a whole conglomeration of preceding and proceeding events, practices (Bailey 2007, 209) behind making a single wealth deposit, I would argue that in the current research project it is necessary to regard the act of making a wealth deposit as one single event without going into exact details of other contexts and materialities contributing to its creation. That kind of premise allows us to frame the source material and start moving towards the practices of wealth depositing and their development in time.

The single event of wealth depositing is reflected in different material residues that derive from the material contexts of the deposit (see Fig. 3.1.2.1.) and provide us with a 'frozen' past moment. Wealth deposits are in this sense a much appreciated research material, because unlike constantly reused occupation sites or disturbed burials they have often remained in their environments of concealment. In a few cases they can be even found very much as they were deposited. Of course, it is still crucial to keep in mind that not everything unearthed reflects the exact elements of past events. It is necessary to acknowledge possible post-depositional events and processes, be it natural or anthropogenic, and take them into consideration when making further conclusions about the deposit. Unfortunately, very often these finds have been discovered by non-specialists and reached the collections after they have been removed from their initial context. Therefore, these considerations are not always available for the analysis. In addition there is always a possibility that the same site might have been disturbed or used on more than one occasion already in prehistory. In that case the chronology or detailed environmental analysis should provide relevant evidence. If we can trace the chronological differences or disturbances either in artefact dating or in stratigraphy, we can suspect multiple events of wealth depositing or later manipulations of the deposits. Lacking those clues one can assume that there was a single depositional event.

In the current study I refer to an event as a single action of making a wealth deposit by hiding materialities in a specific environment. This is the micro scale, the first building block for studying practices of wealth depositing. It can be traced and described through different material contexts of a single deposit (Fig. 3.1.2.1.). These ought to consider as detailed material contexts of one deposit as possible, starting from artefactual content and combinations, physical environment of concealment and its situation in cultural landscape.

A detailed study of a single event forms a basis for distinguishing broader practices. Thus, although starting an analysis from the materialities of a single event, it is not a study of one individual and separate action. The aim is a study of how numerous single events formed socially accepted and followed practices. Therefore it is essential to move from the detailed descriptions of single events towards socially accepted and widely followed practices, which are indicating

*Fig. 3.1.2.1. Materialities of an event of making a wealth deposit (micro scale of practice) in the presumed order of elements of making a wealth deposit.*

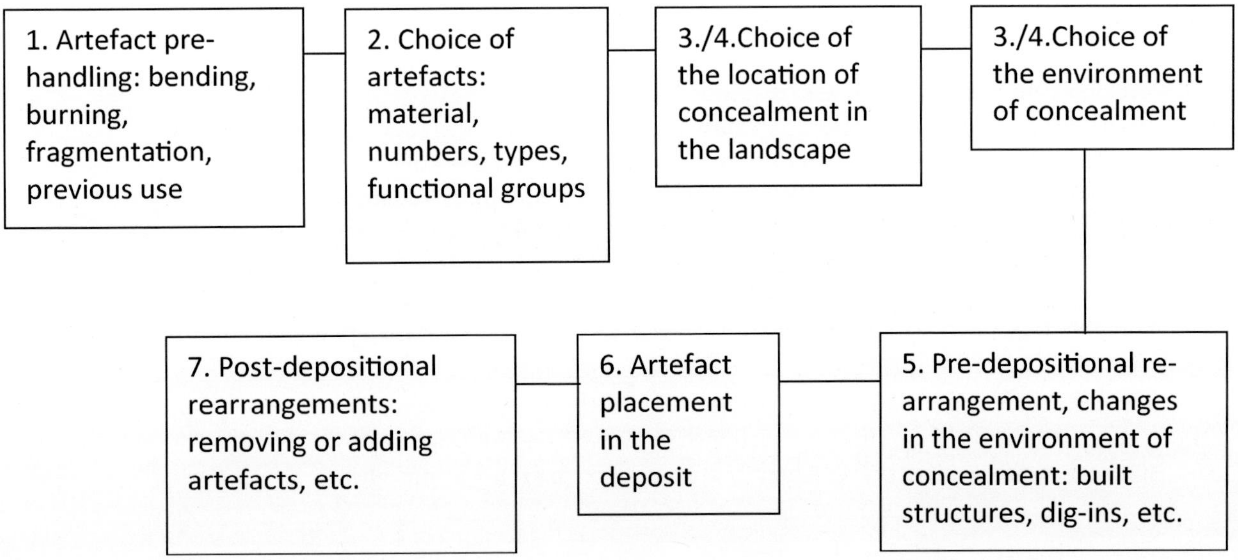

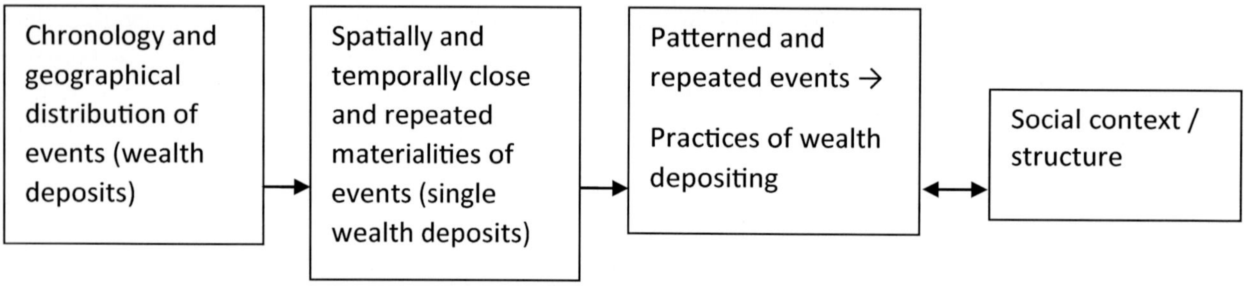


*Fig. 3.1.2.2. Creation and recognition process of practices of wealth depositing and their relation to the social structure.*

repeated and patterned materialities of events in close spatial and temporal contexts (Fig. 3.1.2.2.). Such a micro scale synchronic analysis of single events helps to uncover broader social practices formed by them.

These concepts rely on and support the ideas of Barrett (1988; 1994; 2000; 2001) that emphasise the importance of a single event and stress that every single action is based on its material preconditions, and the previous experience and knowledge of agents as created in their social contexts. Practices belong to their broader social context and cannot be understood without it. Alterations of events and practices (micro scale) might have influenced the changes of social structures (macro scale) but they also might have been the results of changes in the social structure. It is necessary to decode patterned and repeated events that form more widely followed practices in order to see how these practices created, secured or transformed broader social processes in time and space. This is where the importance as well as problems of decoding the macro scale, the social structure, has to be acknowledged.

### 3.1.3. Structure and practices: macro scale analysis

Having defined the concepts of event and practice, it is necessary to tackle the problem of the macro scale. Numerous scholars have discussed how to get from the materialities of a single event to social processes through the archaeological record (McGlade & Leeuw 1997; Harding 2005 and the comments in 2006). It has been argued that the aim of archaeologists should be to distinguish different social practices that were conducted by past people as their social negotiations (Pauketat 2000, 117; Robb 2004, 107; 2010, 503). Archaeological data should be studied in spatial and temporal terms because practices are historically conditioned. At the same time it needs to be kept in mind that social context is never a static entity, but a developing and changing process.

As discussed above, macro scale is usually regarded as a broader cultural context or social structure. It is an overall sum or a network of the ways in which materialities and mentalities of the society are combined and entwined, sustained and transformed by its different members. It is like an underlying, usually even unconscious influencing factor always playing an active role in human action as well as being played out by human actions. No action is in a vacuum from others, from the underlying material and mental structures of contemporary society, because people's choices of their actions must derive from somewhere, are based on something and lead to somewhere. The concept of the macro scale is very difficult to unravel and characterise, especially when only relying on fragmentary material traces of past societies. The whole is always more than just a sum of its elements and archaeologists are often lacking some very relevant elements. But it would be another extreme to deny and give up looking for the social structure.

To deal with this complex, but important concept, I have decided to apply a practical and empirical solution. I describe and define past macro scale through the empirically retrievable material remains of different archaeological features with an emphasis on the changes and stabilities of those features in spatial and temporal terms. In archaeology these macro scales are largely generalisations and interpretations about past social trends and tendencies that are based on different archaeological source materials: sites, artefacts and environments. It is important to notice changes created by social agents and their actions (Shennan 2004, 12; Pauketat 2001b, 80; Beck *et al.* 2007, 845), because changes or stabilities in sites and objects reflect what was seen as suitable, necessary, important, negotiable and also available in a society. Thus, I would argue that the sources telling us about past macro scales, their stabilities and transformations are the different materialities of possible find groups: hill-forts, settlements, burials, field systems, wealth deposits; but also environmental data such as population growth indicators, climate changes, etc. Archaeologists translate these different materialities into macro scale generalisations and abstractions when we talk about past economy, social relations, settlement patterns, religion, ideology, foreign contacts.

The important point is that it is probably never possible to give an exhaustive description of all these macro scale structures and their components at the specific moment of time. This is due to the fragmentary or residual (*sensu* Lucas 2008) nature of our source material, and second, large scale of the concept itself as well as our interpretational limitations (see also Harding 2006). But it is still possible to generate and pick out meaningful or relevant signposts according to what is regarded as most significant for specific research.

The macro scale that I provide for the current study is biased in terms of available data and its previous interpretations, but it can never be complete either. When looking at the material of wealth deposits and what happens to their materialities in time I relate these changing aspects to some macro scale processes that I believe to have relevance to the depositional practices. It is as if creating long lines of different event-based practices and looking for the temporal and spatial nodal points or continuity lines that stand for changes or stabilities in these practices. This forms a basis from which I can continue analysing whether these nodal points and continuity lines actually overlap or might be related to other archaeological features like wealth deposits in a specific time span (Fig. 3.1.3.1.). In addition, I would argue that it makes such an analysis easier if one has a prime phenomenon, a main study material, with which the other aspects of macro scale social contexts are compared, because it is very complicated to consider all the past practices on the same scale of details. In my case this main phenomenon is the material of wealth deposits.

Of course this kind of approach is very selective and dependant on a variety of factors from the state of research to preservation. However, its strength is that this approach helps to avoid seeing one phenomenon separated from its broader background, as if it existed in itself, apart from and unrelated to other past materialities and phenomena. It is just a way to look for the explanations of one phenomenon with the help of the others as well as to relate those phenomena to each other in order to get a more complete picture of the past.

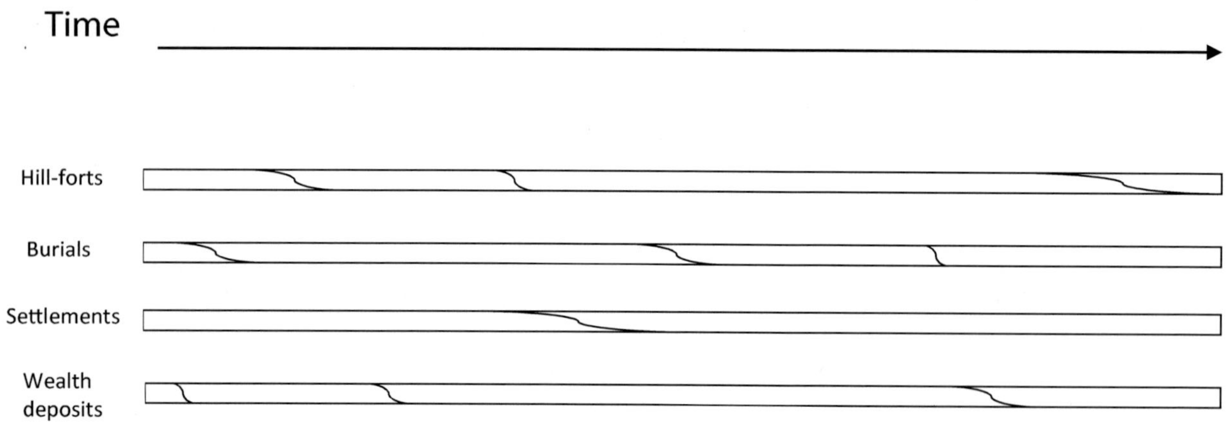


— Changes in the materialities represented in particular archaeological sites by single traceble events and following broader practices. The lenght of the line indicates possible time-span for a change.

*Fig. 3.1.3.1. Macro scale as created through stabilities, gradual developments and sudden changes in the social practices and seen by the particular material remains of different archaeological sites.*

When talking about the macro scale it is necessary to emphasize the importance of the long-term perspective. Due to the fragmented nature of our primary data it can be quite complicated to note changes and make comparisons between different past practices without a wider time span. The macro scale as defined above becomes visible in a long-term perspective, because different archaeological phenomena i.e. changes and stabilities in various past practices, can be seen only on larger scale. This approach can be regarded as either a burden or a blessing of archaeological research, but most certainly it is an inevitable approach when asking questions posed in the current thesis: how do depositional practices change in time and space, and how they relate to the developments in social structure?

### 3.1.4. Relating micro and macro scales: Importance of the long-term

To analyse the relationship between events and practices (micro scale) and their social context (macro scale) is not an easy task, a simple cause-effect relationship. The division of human actions into single events and broader social processes, like micro and macro scales in the current thesis, has been used quite often in archaeology (Ames 1991; Bradley 1991; Bintliff (ed.) 1991; Knapp (ed.) 1992; Bintliff 2004; Harding 2005; Bailey 2007, 213 and the literature cited). But this approach has also raised several debates about the usefulness of such a division of time, actions and processes (Bulliet 1992; Moreland 1992; Sherratt 1992; Leeuw & McGlade (eds) 1997; Harding 2005; Thomas *et al.* 2006; Bailey 2007; Lucas 2008; Robb & Pauketat (eds) 2013). First, there is a threat of anachronism in applying the analytical tools and categorisations of the contemporary researcher to past historical contexts, and second, there are difficulties in establishing what defines a reasonable scale for the analysis (see Harding 2005 and the comments by Thomas *et al.* 2006; Lucas 2008). The abstract concepts such as event, practice and social structure as discussed on the previous pages most definitely belong to such problematic tools, categories and scales. The wider problem is a circular connection between all those scales – no event is defined or limited by itself, but has a conglomeration of other previously or simultaneously concurrent events (Lucas 2008, 61-62). For instance, concealment of a wealth deposit must be preceded by manufacturing the artefacts to be deposited, choosing and perhaps arranging the environment for the deposit, act of taking the objects from one place to another etc., etc. All these small parts of an event are dependent on numerous other events, practices as well as social structure. Thus, the questions are – what constitutes events, practices and structures if they are always to some extent circular; and how can archaeologists at a large cultural and temporal distance from the past relate them to each other?

Bailey among others has made important contributions to answering those questions and I find his reasoning very useful for the current study. According to him there are different time perspectives that can be applied to archaeological research and it depends on those time perspectives what we as archaeologists notice. Different time scales are expressed by different resolutions and reveal different phenomena (Bailey 2005; 2007). As Bailey (2007) explains, micro scale phenomena are restricted in time and space, and relate to single events or short-term processes. Macro scale phenomena or processes, however, reveal themselves in a long-term perspective and larger areas. Which scale to use, depends on the research questions.

I acknowledge that those scales – events, practices and structures – are analytical tools anyway (Harding 2005; Lucas 2008, 59). Therefore, as being in some ways artificial it is necessary to explain which concepts are used, how and why they are limited, what is meant by them and why as well as how are these groups or levels of human action related to each other in the context of specific study. Although they can be artificial, they do help to categorize and make sense, but also relate and compare different archaeological data.

In my case this explanation is as follows. Micro scale is a high-resolution synchronic analysis of single short-term phenomena – events of making a wealth deposit – that are traced in detailed material characteristics of this single event. If these different events share their material characteristics and are close in spatial and temporal terms it provides an argument for more widely followed social practices. These practices, because of being widely followed, play a potentially active part in the creation, sustaining and changing of social structure. Macro scale refers to a diachronic low-resolution analysis of social practices as expressed by different archaeological phenomena. These two scales intersect and can be compared through a long-term perspective – long-term perspective is the link between them. The reason for comparing and analysing material in the micro and macro scale is to trace changes and continuities in different social practices and compare them with the changes and stabilities in wealth depositional practices. Such an analysis enables us to provide the answers to the questions such as how do depositional practices change in time and place; how do these practices relate to the processes taking place in a society on a larger scale; and what dictates the choice of which objects, where and how they are deposited? As the scale of my question is wide in spatial and temporal terms then my analysis starts from the event of making a wealth deposit. Most of the pre-depositional processes (artefact production, creation of the environment of concealment etc., origin and life-paths of depositors) are considered only indirectly and in much less details. The latter would be quite different if I were to work on a single wealth deposit and apply, for instance, a biographical approach to it. This altogether exemplifies once again the importance of the considerations of scales: the choice and definitions of scales and data analysed in a specific study depends on the questions asked.

### 3.1.4.1. Long-term perspective

To answer the questions posed in current study, as well as combine and compare micro and macro scale the use of the long-term perspective is unavoidable.[6] The concept of long-term perspective in archaeological studies is closely related to the *longue durée*. The *longue durée* itself is a concept of history based on the works of Fernand Braudel (1992) and the Annales school. Braudel divided history into geographical, social and individual time in which the first was a basis for the other two, an everlasting *longue durée*, which formed a long-term background for the others. It has been pointed out that this time division or structuring was not the primary goal of Braudel's work (Olivier 2006). However, it has been the main idea picked up by archaeologists (Bintliff 1991; Knapp 1992a; Gosden 1994, chapter 6). Archaeology as a discipline has an ability to take a retrospective view in long terms and broad areas which enables the analysis of long-term and wider trends of human activities.

So what is the usefulness of a long-term perspective in current study? First, the long-term perspective helps in understanding the background of a single event or set of practices on the deeper level. It sets an event or a practice into a perspective of what was there before and what followed. Long-term analysis that is based on the comparisons of unique micro processes and macro scale social structures helps to reveal broader social developments, the general mentality in the society (Bailey 1983, 184-185; Knapp 1992b; Pauketat 2001a; Lightfoot 2001, 241-242). It helps to say something more substantial about the past society and the practices therein.

Long-term perspective gives a methodological possibility to compare the variability of wealth deposits against other archaeological data and their changes in time. Interest in long-term social processes means interest in change. As noted, events and practices do not only sustain their contemporary structure, but can also alter it. Therefore it is important to start looking at single event and practices in the long-term scale to notice the changes in the first place. It also creates a link and enables temporal comparisons between different depositional practices.

Finally, the long-term approach that is based on the historical study of practices as constructed by single events, and the idea of changeable structure, helps to draw away from the problematic analysis of meanings and 'why?-questions' and propose a more comprehensible question of 'how?' (Pauketat 2001b; Robb 2004, 107, 133). Through the long-term perspective it becomes possible to ask how events and practices on the micro scale changed in time and space and influenced or were influenced by their macro scale. The questions to be asked might be thus the following: how were practices conducted? how changes occurred? how structures were reflected or changed in practices? etc.

The theoretical framework outlined above has been called a 'historical-processual' approach to archaeological material (Pauketat 2001b). Whatever the label, I hope that these pages have defined and explained the background for the concepts that are employed in current study. The scales of analysis and

---

6 I want to stress, that I am consciously avoiding further discussions of what kind of time scales existed in the past society itself and whether or how the time scales of archaeologists relate to that (see e.g. Bailey 1983; Gosden & Lock 1998; Bradley 2002; Bailey 2005, 271).

choice of data is always problematic and has to be elaborated on, but it is also directly related to the research questions. My concepts of events, practices, social structure, the way they are set in micro and macro scale comparisons and seen in long-term perspective derive directly from the problem setting of this particular research. I would argue that these concepts enable one to combine and compare different human actions and their social conditions, notice changes and the possible correlations of changes in depositional practices and other contemporary social practices.

The theoretical approach proposed in the current thesis aims at changing the sets of questions posed to the material of wealth deposits. The emphasis is put to the questions of 'how' – how depositional practices change and vary in time and space and how they relate to contemporary social developments. This is an indirect objection to the more traditional questions of 'why' posed to this data: asking about the functions and meanings of wealth deposits, especially their more specific interpretations as economy- or ritual related activities. Nevertheless, the 'how' questions are not intended to turn the study of wealth deposits into purely descriptive empirical endeavour dismissing more profound and socially-derived explanations. The idea is rather to tackle these subjects from detailed data substantiation and change the angle of 'why' questions – from seeing wealth deposits as self-contained and single meaning laden materialized entities to socially embedded practices. Thus, the material represented in the core chapters of the thesis indeed follows the lines of 'how', but in doing so answers the 'why-s' by an all-encompassing comparative analysis of depositional practices and their contemporary social context. In my opinion these questions and relations are far more available to current researcher and closer to the considerations of past people than any oppositional categorisation and division of wealth deposits, or quest for the exact single meaning of a particular deposit.

*Chapter 4*

# Methodology

In this chapter the methods used for studying the practices of wealth depositing in the 1st-9th century AD eastern Baltic are introduced. First, some theory related methodological principles are discussed. Thereafter an overview is given of the data collection, systematisation and categorisation. The latter includes also problems encountered during data collection and the possible impact this might have on final results. Finally, the contextual criteria taken into account for analysing practices of wealth depositing are discussed. The form of information used, and the way material is represented in the appendices of the thesis is also explained. Additionally a brief overview of statistical methods is provided.

## 4.1. Contextual approach for studying practices of wealth depositing

In order to start analysing practices of wealth depositing, it is necessary to create a detailed record of the material contexts of every deposit. This information, its details and recording principles, must have a similar basis for each deposit. Otherwise the data is not comparable at the same level and detectable patterns lose their potential for arguing for or against specific depositional practices. For example, without information about the environment of concealment, such deposits cannot be used for further analysis about the practices of wealth depositing, because the choice of the environments of concealment is one important element in that practice. Depending on the circumstances of discovery, the information about the contextual criteria and its exact details vary. It is then necessary to decide what is a sufficient level of information that allows one to analyse the patterns of the deposits' material contexts. For instance, is the artefact placement in the deposit the key piece of data, or is the broader environment of concealment sufficient level of information.

Based on these principles a decision was made that my primary data collection must include the following criteria:

- artefacts and their assemblages: artefact functional groups (e.g. ornaments, weaponry, tools, etc.); artefact groups (e.g. axes, neck-rings, knives etc.); artefact types (socketed axes, cross-bow brooches etc.) and appearance (e.g. intact or damaged; signs of wear);
- environment of concealment: water-related conditions, dry land (also referred to as solid ground), archaeological sites, if possible also different markers in the landscape; depth of the deposit; if possible also artefact placement in the deposit;

- location in the cultural landscape: adjacent sites from the same or close archaeological periods (e.g. relation to contemporaneous burial grounds, settlements, etc); relation to geographical features (hills, river-beds, coasts etc.);
- chronology and geographical distribution.

The exact details of discovering or reconstructing these contexts as well as disadvantages or problematic issues in doing so are discussed below.

However, when talking about the contexts of the find, one should also not forget the social context. As discussed in the previous chapter, social and cultural context is the basis on which single events, such as depositional acts, are built, and they are also formed by these events. To create the social context for particular depositional practices I drew a 'timeline' of the main and major changes, developments and stabilities in an archaeological record of the eastern Baltic 1st-9th century AD material (see case studies in Chapter 9.2.). This is divided into smaller regions and time periods in which particular depositional practices emerge. In the descriptions of the contemporary social context I consider the main characteristics and changes of very different archaeological features in those particular regions and periods: hill-forts, settlements, burial grounds, production sites, environmental conditions, artefact comparisons in wealth deposits and other archaeological sites. This all is largely based on previous scholarly work and is thus somewhat biased towards topical questions and material which has been studied. However, it aims at providing a more tangible and explicit account of a very broad cultural background on which to place the material of wealth deposits.

## 4.2. Data collection

The list of wealth deposits included in this thesis is not exhaustive. The database is largely based on previous publications and it is likely that the most recent or unpublished finds have been left out. The preferences and decisions made by local scholars have sometimes determined which finds have been regarded as separate and intentional artefact deposits and which have been seen as results of other past practices (burial rituals, settlement activities, etc.). For instance, there are cases in the literature where some finds from burial areas or even stray finds could be in fact regarded as wealth deposits according to the definition of the term in this thesis. However, without the detailed background and reasoning behind distinguishing different find categories I have decided to rely on judgements made by local specialists. Thus, the following is to some extent biased and relies on the traditions of the local archaeological scholarship of specific archaeological sites and find material.

The first step in research is to acquaint oneself with the data, collect it and systemise it in a way that enables analysis according to the research questions. For that purpose I created a simple MS Access database of the eastern Baltic 1st-9th century AD wealth deposits consisting of seven main tables (with several data-feed tables) that were merged into five forms:

- Core data: main information about the circumstances of discovery, coordinates, chronology, archaeological collections and publications.
- Main artefact characteristics: the basic description of the composition of the deposit (including material and functional groups).

- Artefact description: detailed description of artefacts, their typological characteristics, appearances, further descriptions, collection numbers.
- Find-spot: detailed overview of the environment of concealment and nearby archaeological sites.
- Cultural landscape: information about the nearby archaeological sites (dating, location, number of registration as given by the local Heritage Boards).

This database allows different queries about the main characteristics of the finds in a temporal-spatial scale and also mapping the data in the micro scale cultural landscape or in more general geographical distribution maps. The database also forms the basis of primary data for further statistics and simple qualitative analysis when looking for the patterns in the contextual characteristics of the deposits in time and space. This database covers information about all the eastern Baltic wealth deposits that can be dated to 1st-9th century AD, including coin hoards and the ones that lack sufficient data about the environment of concealment or exact artefact assemblage and thus cannot be included in the further analysis (see Appendices).

The information about the Estonian material is largely based on my previous research: MA thesis on Estonian Middle Iron Age wealth deposits and one year of PhD studies in Estonia (University of Tartu), during which information about the Estonian Roman Iron Age deposits was gathered. However, these datasets have been amended to incorporate new and more detailed information. The information about Latvia and Lithuania has been collected between 2010 and 2012.

### 4.2.1. Data on artefacts

The first level data on artefacts in the deposits is based on previous publications. These vary considerably from general overviews to special articles. They also include 19th century published overviews from local antiquarian collections including so-called Learned Societies and larger museums.

After gathering preliminary information all the relevant archaeological collections were visited. Altogether there were eleven different archaeological collections or museums: four in Estonia (Archaeology collections of the University of Tartu, Institute of History at Tallinn University, Estonian History Museum and Valga County Museum), two in Latvia (The National History Museum of Latvia, Ģ. Eliass Jelgava History and Art Museum – Academia Petrina), five in Lithuania (Vytautas the Great War Museum in Kaunas, National Museum of Lithuania, Telšiai Museum "Alka", Šiauliai Museum "Aušros", Biržai Museum "Sėla") and the State Hermitage Museum in St Petersburg in Russia. The aim of these visits was to document and describe the artefacts in detail, photograph the finds and read relevant archive materials, including catalogues, in order to establish more detailed information about the circumstances of discovery. Not all the artefacts could be described or photographed during these visits. Some of them had been lost in the past (especially during the World Wars), the others were on display or unidentifiable among other artefacts of the collections. Relevant comments can be found in the catalogue part of the thesis. Besides the institutes visited, several other collections were contacted to create as detailed and complete database about the eastern Baltic wealth deposits as possible.

The first prerequisite of the deposit for inclusion in the further analysis is the presence of artefacts or at least a detailed description and documentation of objects. Simple as this seems, the situation can turn out to be complicated. Some artefacts have been lost over time, especially during the wars, evacuations and moving, or even immediately after the discovery through selling or dividing the objects among the finders. Thus, sometimes there is only an archive record that describes the number of originally found items. Although these finds cannot now be identified and documented, a decision was made that when they have been documented in previous decades at an acceptable level of detail and can be dated, they will be included in the analysis. Otherwise the picture would be biased towards the state of current archaeological collections and its history and would not describe the past context. Of course, if the chronology of the items cannot be estimated, the deposit cannot be used in further analysis. As a middle-ground solution, whenever possible at least the previous pictures or drawings of the finds, if the artefacts themselves are no longer available, are included in the catalogue.

The other major problem was with the numbers of artefacts. Usually it is straightforward, but depending on the characteristics of the find or its destiny after the discovery very vague numbers can be given. These include amounts such as 'tens of', 'some', 'more than', 'numerous' etc. Such examples are particularly common when the deposit, or actually a small part of it, has reached the collections years after the discovery and most of the objects have been either lost or redistributed. The other problem is when different scholars have identified objects in different ways. The latter is especially evident with some corroded iron artefacts where it has been, and sometimes still is, difficult to identify its function e.g. spearhead, pointy iron object, iron rod etc. In these cases it is difficult to estimate what should be the number of object types recorded in the database. Again, in order to get as close as possible to the past event, I have relied on the given description, however, stating the minimum possible number. For example, if 'tens' were mentioned, the number given is 10; if 'some' then 1 was counted; 'more than' followed by number was equated with the given number. The most important thing to ascertain, was to be able to give the functional group and the material of artefacts. When difficulties in defining the functional group of the artefact occurred, it was put under a broader category of iron object not arrow head etc. Exact explanations and details are provided in the catalogue.

Some problems emerged with categorisation of artefacts into functional groups. Although in most cases it is fairly evident whether one deals with tools, weapons or ornaments, sometimes this grouping might turn out to be more complicated with some items, for example knives, axes (both weapons or tools?), arrowheads (weapon or hunting tool), horse gear, belt parts (weaponry or ornaments?), different rings. It seems that very often there is no single right answer to such questions. An axe might serve as a weapon as well as a tool (see e.g. Christensen 2005a, 60-62); belt parts are both related to warriors and also ordinary people. However, the decision must be made when trying to define numbers for the further analysis of the material on similar bases. Regarding the axes, the examples with narrow blades or some distinctive decorative features are usually considered as weapons (Simniškytė 2006b, 66; Lang 2007b, 141, 187; Tvauri 2012, 123-124), and quite often the axes from wealth deposits are of that kind. As distinguishing between battle axes and tool axes can be very complicated and speculative, then for the sake of clarity all the axes in the following analysis are grouped under weapons (Moora

| Functional group | Artefact types |
|---|---|
| Weapons | Arrowhead, Axe, Battle knife, Horse gear (bit, bridle, horse shoe, spur, stirrup), Other weapon (Scabbard mounting, shield, shield boss), Spearhead, Sword |
| Tools | Knife, Other tool (anvil, awl, hammer, harpoon, hoe, mattock/pick, nail, shear, spindle whorl, strike-a-light stone, strike-a-light, trowel, whetstone), Sickle/Scythe |
| Ornaments | Bead, Belt part (buckle, belt mounting), Bracelet, Brooch, Dress pin, Ring, Neck-ring, Other ornament (bronze spiral and cylinder, chain, pendant), Finger-ring |
| Coins | Coin |
| Raw material | Raw material (e.g. rod/bar, unfinished items) |
| Other | Other (miscellaneous items including comb, lamp, slag, organic material items e.g. bag, band, toggle, stick, textile, worked timber and bone fragments), Other iron object (unidentified objects), Vessel (drinking horn, metal vessels) |

*Table 4.2.1.1. List of artefact groups and types in the database.*

1938, 508; Jaanits *et al.* 1982, 292; Simniškytė 2006b, 66). The same goes for different items of horse gear that have been mainly related to warriors, and thus might relate to weapons (as in Tautavičius 1978, 150; Tvauri 2012, Chapter 4.4., 180). Arrowheads were considered as weapons. Although different belt parts and rings might in principle belong to horse gear equipment, in the analysis they are grouped under the section of ornaments. Knives are regarded as tools, the same goes for whetstones and strike-a-light stones. The categories of artefacts are listed in Table 4.2.1.1.

Some deposits include more than one material. All the different artefact materials were recorded, but ordered according to the largest one. Material 1 is thus the main one in the deposit, followed by Material 2, sometimes also Material 3. This division is necessary in order to compare the combinations of artefact materials in different environments. It is important to notice here, that in most cases there was no difficulty in defining the main material as in nearly all some artefact groups and materials were clearly in the majority in comparison with others. The materials occurring in the database are Bone, Bronze, Gold, Iron, Organic (including horn, leather, wood, wool), Other, Silver, and Stone. The need for making subdivisions within the specific material (organic, metal, mineral) into autonomous categories (wood, leather, bone; iron, silver, gold; stone, clay, glass) was decided on the basis of the quantity of specific material in the dataset.

Finally the way in which the chronology of the deposits is estimated needs to be explained in detail. First, within the constraints of the thesis I have not attempted to create new chronological and typological analyses of all the artefacts from the deposits in the three Baltic countries. Therefore, in dating the artefacts and deposits I rely largely on my predecessors and their estimations. Only when the previous scholars have estimated too wide a time span, have I tried to narrow it. Again, the relevant remarks are in the catalogue. In general I have estimated the chronology of the wealth deposits with the most likely century of concealment, based on its artefact chronology. This reasoning for relying on such a wide time span is based on the decisions made by previous scholars who have studied similar artefact deposits. For instance while Hårdh (1996) in her study of Viking Age silver has limited her chronological divisions to half a century phases or more precisely if coins are available, then Levy (1982) in her study of Bronze Age deposits relies on the six Bronze Age periods which cover several centuries each. Lacking the numismatic material but having fairly detailed and reliable typological chronology of artefacts I reckon the estimation within a century is a satisfactory result for general analysis. If more detailed chronology can be established it is provided in the appendices and catalogue.

The chronological estimations of previous scholars were translated into numeric values. For instance the first half of the 5th century is marked as AD 400-450, around 800 as 775-825. One issue is the determination of the dating of the deposit as based on the chronology of its components. The first general rule that was followed is the one from the numismatist concept of *tpq* i.e. the dating of the deposit has to be later than the earliest date of the latest object. If this estimation covers several consecutive centuries, then usually the later one was taken as the date of the deposit. Additionally, I tried to find the closest dating of different artefacts by considering the possible chronological distribution of all the objects and finding the most likely latest overlapping area for all of them. If the time span is even wider (sometimes up to 400 years) the most likely estimation of chronology is based on similar finds from other wealth deposits or archaeological contexts. Such comparisons and controls with overall archaeological material in the region are also taken into consideration when more precise chronology is available. Thus, the chronology of the deposits is derived from combinations and comparisons of objects' *tpq* and parallels from other archaeological contexts. The chronology of the deposits is one of the most problematic issues and some of the estimations might be less reliable than others. At the same time, it is necessary to make a best judgement or indeed a guess of deposits' chronology in order to carry out any analysis and long-term comparisons. But sometimes it is even more complicated because there is a possibility that one and the same area has been used for depositional practices over the centuries. The decision in such cases is made deposit by deposit according the characteristics of the specific assemblage: its overall chronology of artefacts, artefact placement in the deposit, and proportions of different chronological sequences. If this situation can be presumed on the basis of various contextual criteria of the find, relevant specifications of wider time spans for the chronology of the deposit are provided.

In the case of very broad dating usually the latest possible century is taken into account, although it cannot be excluded that some of the deposits might belong to the earlier periods. For these reasons also the deposits with dates which reach the Viking Age (e.g. broad dating of 8th-9th century, up to 899 AD) are included in the analysis despite the fact that this period is already beyond the limits of the current study. Although the latest possible dating of such later finds extends to the Viking Age, the earlier chronology situates the finds to the end of the 8th century. Thus they cannot be entirely excluded from the Middle Iron Age material. The more exact and/or wider chronological spans of artefact assemblages themselves are provided in the catalogue.

### 4.2.2. Data on the environment of concealment

Data on the environmental context and character of deposition is more fragmentary, because it depends on the circumstances and the level of documentation of the discovery. Unusual finding contexts (such as watery conditions and clear markers above the ground) have been noted in the publications and archive materials, but the records of artefact placement, possible vessels and exact depth are scarcer. Numerous deposits have been discovered during field ploughing so their depth has been assumed as ca. 20-40 cm. From time to time remarkable geographical landscape features (e.g. limestone cliffs, hills, river valleys etc.) have been noticed only after visiting the sites during the landscape surveys, but they are not characteristic to all the find-spots.

The initial data on the find-spot, including the environment of concealment, artefact placement, depth of the deposit and markers in the landscape, is based on previous publications. Some important additional data was gathered from the archives of the archaeological collections, which sometimes include remarks about the circumstances of discovery. These sources include museum catalogues, also fieldwork reports or additional documentation about the find, compiled by the museum workers when the items were handed over. For the Estonian material it was also possible to use one specific archive material group – descriptions of archaeological sites of Estonian historic parishes compiled mainly in the 1920s and 1930s by the archaeology students at the University of Tartu. These descriptions of parishes (Est. *kihelkonnakirjeldus, kihelkonnakirjeldused* in plural) were gathered by students while visiting the areas and questioning the people, recording known, destroyed or new archaeological sites. Very often the pages of parish descriptions include memories of local people and even small details about the finding circumstances of deposits. Due to the topographic and toponymic data mentioned in these descriptions, the localisation of the find-spots in the landscape is more precise. In addition to hard-copy archive materials, much help was gained from an electronic database of Estonian archaeological and folklore sites created by the *Kabinet* of archaeology at the University of Tartu.

In the eastern Baltic, wealth deposits are usually not registered, listed or mapped on the same basis as other archaeological sites. Thus, the first aim in working with the find-spot of the deposits was to situate the sites in the contemporary landscape. This was necessary in order to create general distribution maps as well as for analysing the location of the depositions in relation to other contemporary archaeological sites (see below). As with artefactual material a minimum set of information was defined: a find-spot of the wealth deposit must be identifiable at the level of village name (farm name if possible) and localised to an area of ca. 1 km$^2$. If there was not enough information to answer those questions, deposits were not included for the further analysis. Such wealth deposits are listed in Appendix 1.1.

In most cases the village name was documented in the publications, and archive materials often had additional description relating to farm or its owner's name. Sometimes remarks describing the landscape features such as boggy areas, rivers, hills etc. helped to localise the find-spot in the landscape with the use of contemporary electronic map resources. In the case of Estonia the Estonian Land Board Geoportal was used.[7] Mapping of Lithuanian sites was done with the help of the electronic mapping devices of the Department of Cultural Heritage.[8] Latvian find-spots were localised by combining the electronic maps of the Latvian Geospatial Information Agency[9] and electronic maps of KurTuEsi.[10] Most of the find-spots were identifiable and given geographic coordinates with the help of those mentioned electronic map services.

7 http://geoportaal.maaamet.ee/est/Kaardiserver-p2.html.
8 http://www.heritage.lt/km/.
9 http://kartes.lgia.gov.lv/kartes.html.
10 http://www.kurtuesi.lv/maps#.

However, as some of the farms, sometimes even manors, have been renamed or even disappeared over time, the use of available historical maps became extremely helpful. The previously mentioned Estonian Land Board GIS server includes various layers of historical maps from the 19th and the first half of the 20th century. In addition very useful information was obtained from the Register of the maps in the National Archives of Estonia.[11] In Lithuania the map server of cultural heritage also has some references to historical maps that turned out to be useful when localising older discoveries. In Latvia, some help was provided by the archive materials at the National History Museum of Latvia and from Soviet period military maps available at the KurTuEsi map-server. So, combining the data from archaeological publications and archives with contemporary electronic map devices, including historical map layers, and if necessary consulting with the old and undigitised historical maps, it was possible to determine the location of the wealth deposits. When the location remained debatable, the relevant comments are included in the catalogue.

Determination of the environment of concealment is again based on the description of the discovery circumstances. Archive materials are often more detailed in these questions. However, the thoroughness of information varied considerably depending on whether the deposit was found by a specialist or layman, and in case of the latter, whether archaeologists were invited to inspect the site or not, or how much attention was paid to the environment of the deposit while digging up the finds. For these reasons, records of the exact placement of artefacts in the deposits are infrequent. Possible vessels in which the artefacts might have been hidden are mentioned only if they were really evident and well preserved. Therefore hints of organic material are very rare. The same goes for the traces of possible markers in the landscape: in some instances stones have been mentioned, but less obvious markers, such as organic posts etc., were of course rarely noticed. The depth of the find is given sometimes or in some cases it can be at least presumed according to the descriptions. It is aimed to include as detailed information as possible about the environment and circumstances of concealment in the catalogue, although the amount of information varies to some extent from one deposit to another.

There remains one problem about the determination of the environment of concealment. The environments were divided into main categories: dry land/ solid ground (divided into archaeological site and ordinary dry land at the second level); watery condition (bog, lake, marsh, river, spring at the second level) and unknown. To compare different environments of concealment it is necessary to try to estimate and take the context of discovery back in time to its moment of concealment. Landscape features change in time which might alter the estimation of the initial environment of concealment. These deposits were made 1000-2000 years ago and landscape change is inevitable for such a long period (see similar discussion in Scandinavia e.g. Henriksen 2010, 406). However, when dealing with the main geographical features such as water bodies or geographical formations, the change should not be so dramatic. The problem is also less evident with the finds from dry land or archaeological sites. With the latter there is always a problem of overlapping, preceding or succeeding chronologies of different sites which can make a considerable difference. For instance the interpretation of the

11 http://www.ra.ee/kaardid/index.php/et.

deposit might differ according to the use of the environment of concealment. It makes a difference if the deposit was made into an actively used or abandoned settlement or burial area and these changes might happen within a generation. Since in archaeology very often the determination of the chronology of the site is somewhat approximate and broad, without detailed analysis it is likely that some crucial information is lost. At the same time, as long as there is a lack of very precise chronology for sites it is almost impossible to control the correlations between the time of concealment of wealth deposits and their surrounding features. One has to rely on the available data.

Perhaps the most problematic in the context of environment is the question of watery conditions e.g. bogs and marshy areas, springs, lakes, flooded areas. These formations are more changeable and their areas as well as special characteristics might easily alter over time. Seasonal changes, especially in watery conditions, might influence the interpretation of the environment considerably (flooded, drained or frozen lakes). As we unfortunately do not know at what time of the year the deposit was made then this cannot be taken into account. Estimation and construction of past environments and landscapes with their detailed features is a specialist discipline which requires special knowledge, experience and resources. Therefore it was not possible to carry out such in-depth studies in the framework of the current project. Instead it was necessary to find out the least elaborate and most cost-effective possibilities for estimating the landscape and environment of concealment for every wealth deposit.

Firstly, an attempt was made to consider the more permanent landscape features (valleys, waterlogged areas, hilltops etc.) that most probably influence the watery conditions. This is why it was very important to actually visit the sites during several fieldwork seasons to have at least a glimpse of the surrounding geography and geology. Besides that, historical maps became particularly useful, especially the ones predating Soviet period large-scale land improvement activities that changed the landscape in the Baltic countries considerably. As most of the deposits in the current database were discovered prior to the 1950s then the description of environments and landscapes surrounding the deposits were in these cases still unaffected by large scale and mechanised land improvement activities. The land improvement in the 19th century was at a smaller and local scale, in fact many deposits were discovered as a result of those earth works. Thus in most cases we are privileged to have a documentation of the environment of concealment which remains at the time of pre-land improvement works, although this neither has to overlap with the exact environment centuries earlier. Finds from the second half of the 20th century were mostly discovered during archaeological excavations or at least have been documented by archaeologists. Of course, there always remains some doubt as to whether artefacts were concealed in the bog surface, dug in it, whether the marshy area was actually waterlogged at the time of concealment, if the springs were part of the lake or separated etc., but in the absence of detailed geomorphological and ecological studies it is only possible to rely on the currently available data.

### 4.2.3. Cultural landscape

One of the important aspects for the interpretation of wealth deposits and identifying the past practices of wealth depositing is their location in the contemporaneous cultural landscape and relation to other archaeological sites. Such detailed information about the distribution of different archaeological sites around deposits might open several new discussions and lead to conclusions about the choice of location where items were concealed. For instance, they might indicate more or less densely settled regions, uninhabited and border areas between settlement clusters, possible connections with burial areas or hill-forts etc. Such micro scale maps would help to broaden the discussion of past landscape use and choice of places that were regarded suitable for depositing precious items. Indeed, the results of such analysis for the Estonian Middle Iron Age material provided several interesting results and further discussion about the selection of the location where artefacts were hidden (see e.g. Oras 2009; 2010).

Although acknowledging the usefulness and potential of this endeavour, the creation of such micro scale maps includes several problems. As the aim of such maps is to broaden ideas about the cultural landscape at the time of the concealment of the deposit, only the chronologically closest sites – contemporary or temporally close archaeological features – should be recorded. However, the question of the chronology of these sites is problematic. Most have not been excavated and their chronological estimation is often very general (first half of the 1st millennium AD). Dating is often based on parallels with previously excavated sites or are just estimations built on the general appearance of the object. It is only in rare cases that the surrounding sites of ca. 5 km radius have been studied more thoroughly. Thus their dating and relation to wealth deposits ends up being speculative.

The second problem is related to official records and information available about different archaeological sites. Not all the archaeological sites are recorded and listed in publicly available databases. For instance stray finds and officially unprotected or not yet listed sites are often recorded in different archives of local museums, institutions and archaeological collections and thus the data is dispersed. Therefore, collecting the necessary data is time consuming and not all the relevant information is publicly attainable. There are freely available databases about designated archaeological sites with related GIS solutions created and maintained by the local national heritage boards in Estonia and Lithuania. The Estonian Land Board has a long-term cooperation with the Estonian National Heritage Board and all protected historical and archaeological sites are mapped in their GIS server called X-GIS.[12] The sites on the map are linked with the heritage register so that the preliminary chronology and main characteristics of the specific sites can be easily found. In Lithuania, there exists a GIS based map of the protected historical and archaeological sites at the Register of Cultural Heritage.[13] From there one could in principle work out which objects remain at the close vicinity of the deposits and additional data about the chronology of those sites is soon to be publicly available.[14]

12 http://xgis.maaamet.ee/xGIS/XGis.

13 http://kvr.kpd.lt/heritage/.

14 I would like to thank Dr Vykintas Vaitkevičius (Klaipėda University), and members of Archeokrastovaizdis project, who were kindly willing to share their database information.

The recording of protected sites in Latvia is currently, however, far more complicated: there is no GIS based map of protected sites. There exists a state register or a list of cultural heritage[15], but it gives information on an administrative basis and is thus not much help when trying to work out which archaeological sites actually are in the close vicinity of the wealth deposits. The GIS map for heritage sites is still under construction and at the moment the sites are only recorded on the hardcopy maps at the archaeology archives and the State Inspection for Heritage Protection of Latvia. Another way to collect primary data about the archaeological sites in the vicinity of the deposits in Latvia would have been using the maps of local municipalities. As Latvia is in the process of planning a large scale municipality reformation, all the local administrative units have mapped their areas in various details, including protected archaeological sites. These maps are available to the public at the homepages of the municipalities. However, these are not yet linked with the geographical coordinates. Therefore, in the frameworks of the current project, it became too time-consuming and costly to map all the archaeological sites around 25 Latvian wealth deposits. It would have meant considerable manual labour with un-digitised and/or electronically unmapped data which additionally should have been georeferenced in order to make this data suitable for mapping with GIS programs as needed for the current thesis.

A third complication arose while carrying out landscape research in the three countries. Namely, after localising the find-spots of wealth deposits in the contemporary landscape and maps several landscape surveys were carried out in those areas. The aim was to gain better understanding about the geographical characteristics of the find-spot and photograph the landscape situation. The latter was also used for better description of the possible environment of the concealment for every deposit. In the case of Estonia an extra goal of these landscape surveys was to search for new archaeological sites, especially in the close vicinity of the deposits themselves. However, due to heritage related legal restrictions and the extra effort that occurs when finding tangible heritage or portable antiquities in a foreign country (cleaning and numbering, reports, suitable storage facilities and collections, etc.), this goal was not followed in Latvia and Lithuania. In the case of the latter two, sites were visited in summer, during the high vegetation seasons and no effort was put into looking for new archaeological features. This also results in somewhat biased information in favour of Estonian material, enabling more detailed cultural landscape mapping and final conclusions compared to Latvian and Lithuanian finds.

As a result, it was not possible to create cultural landscape maps for all the three Baltic countries based on the same mapping principles. The region under study covers three different countries and it would have been very time-consuming to bring the level of information recording about the cultural landscape and other archaeological sites on the same detailed basis for all these regions. It would have been worth the effort for some single case studies, but not with 69 examples. Thus, although acknowledging the potential usefulness of taking into account the broader cultural landscape around wealth deposits, this initial idea had to be abandoned in the context of the current project. Instead, it was decided to collect data only about the closest (sites right next to deposits) and clearly contemporary archaeological sites in the vicinity of the deposits. This information is recorded and presented in the relevant tables, database and catalogue, and used in the final analysis of the data.

---

15 http://www.mantojums.lv/?cat=742&lang=lv.

## 4.3. Methods of analysis

In order to start analysing the data it is first necessary to decide which contextual criteria are relevant and meaningful in terms of describing potential acknowledged choices behind the act of depositing artefacts. As evident from the above subchapter the amount of data collected is vast. However, partly due to the variability of documented details during the discovery, partly in relation to what has happened to the collections over time, it is not possible to take into account all the contextual characteristics in a similar way for all the deposits. Thus, it was necessary to bring down the choice of contextual criteria to the level that is on the one hand meaningful in terms of answering the questions of patterned depositional practices, but on the other hand also available for all the deposits analysed.

All the deposits are in principle intersections of three very simple criteria: objects, time and place (environment). If one has information about those large categories, it becomes possible to, first, define and distinguish wealth deposits as a find category (see Chapters 2-3 for details), and second, to characterise the specifics of each wealth deposit. Of course there is one more important criterion – the actor(s) who make the deposit and choose the items, place and time for creating it. Understandably this is the information that at least prehistoric archaeologists are often lacking a detailed account of. However, exactly this active human dimension is derived from the material remains of their actions in the past.

These three main data criteria – objects, dating/chronology and place – can be subdivided into several additional subcategories, some of which were more available for current analysis, the others less relevant or unavailable. For instance, the category of objects also includes different artefact functional groups e.g. weapons, tools, ornaments which can be divided again into subgroups such as neck-rings, bracelets, dress pins and brooches. Additionally, artefacts can be subdivided into even smaller categories and types such as cross-bow brooch, penannular brooch, star-shaped foot fibula etc. Besides all those, it is possible to take into account the production material of items, in rare cases also their handling such as intentional fragmentation, burning, bending, signs of use etc. The category of time is in most cases derived from specific artefacts typology and chronology. Only in rare cases do we have more precise and direct radiocarbon or other kind of dating of remains associated with the deposit. The third category – place – has also several sub-characteristics. It is first of all an environment of concealment which in the broadest sense can be divided into water related or dry land. These additionally include several more specific criteria. In the case of watery conditions we can talk about open water sources (spring, lake, river), marshes and bogs; in the dry land context the discovery from an archaeological site might be possible besides the ordinary dry land context. But besides those direct place-related characteristics there is also a possibility to analyse the location of each deposit in the context of other indirectly related aspects such as border regions between forests and arable land, river valleys, mountains; or contemporary cultural landscape including archaeological sites in the closer vicinity or further away from the deposit. The latter are most likely the occupation and main activity sites of the people who deposited the items or at least were to some extent related to the depositional act, and thus they too can provide additional information about the practices of wealth depositing. As part of the concept of place, artefact placement and markers in the landscape could be also considered.

However, for the reasons mentioned already above it is not possible to provide such a detailed record of information for every single deposit. If items were never stored in the archaeological collections or have been lost, it is difficult to give a detailed description of objects, sometimes even their exact quantity. Partly in relation to that, it is difficult to estimate the fragmentation and pre-depositional handling such as burning and use-wear of all the objects in the deposit. There are also several problems with establishing specific details of the environment of concealment. The depth of the find, exact placement of the objects and possible markers are in some cases clear and obvious, but in others very uncertain. The problems of mapping the detailed cultural landscape situation around the deposit include not only the estimation of the chronology of the nearby sites, but also the level at which other archaeological sites have been recorded in the specific region. Therefore it was decided to exclude all those questionable and uncertain characteristics, which might describe either post-depositional processes or be highly interpretative estimations or just rely on incomplete information. Instead, only the most detailed but universally available contextual criteria were employed.

The contextual criteria used in the further analysis of practices of wealth deposits were the following:

- object = its functional categories (weapons, tools, ornaments), object types (swords, knives, pins, etc.), and materials. Depending on the specific questions or methods used it was possible to include either exact numbers, or categories, their combinations, or only main groups or types of objects (see below);
- dating/chronology = estimation according to the period or century. This category also makes it possible to give a long-term perspective to practices of wealth depositing and to identify changes of those practices at the narrower timescale;
- place = direct environment of concealment and the relation to contemporaneous archaeological sites, also general geographical distribution.

The categories of dating and place can be expressed by a single criterion, because there is one date and one place of concealment for each depositional act. The object category, however, often consists of an assemblage of items, their different sub-categories e.g. object groups, types, and material(s). These all are meaningful in terms of indicating the choices and combinations of different contextual criteria for carrying out the depositional act. Therefore the analysed categories in the case of objects have to be expressed through several subdivisions into artefact groups, artefact types and artefact material (see the results in the following chapters).

Those three main contextual criteria – artefacts, chronology and place – indicate depositional practices when their combinations are analysed and they result in showing particular patterning, overlapping and shared contextual characteristics, especially on a spatial and temporal scale. To identify those patterns several combinations of contextual criteria were taken into account as described in Table 4.3.1.

This table explains which contextual criteria were taken into account. The significant characteristics and the ones of no significance in terms of selection are expressed with a tick and a cross respectively. It is logical that some criteria can be combined with each other while it is impossible or irrelevant for others. For

| | Dating | Objects (Functional groups & object types) | Material of objects | Place (Environment, geographical distribution) |
|---|---|---|---|---|
| Dating | × | √ | √ | √ |
| Objects (Functional groups & object types) | √ | √ | ? | √ |
| Material | √ | ? | √ | √ |
| Place (Environment) | √ | √ | √ | × |

√ - meaningful correlation for discovering practices of wealth depositing

× – not meaningful correlation for discovering practices of wealth depositing

? – questionable correlation for discovering practices of wealth depositing

*Table 4.3.1. The combinations of the main contextual criteria describing the selections behind the practices of wealth depositing.*

instance, there can be only one estimation for environment of concealment or chronology. However, combinations of chronology would be relevant if one were to suspect that the same place has been used for depositing for several different occasions. For analysing the selections and combinations of different artefacts within a deposit it is necessary to look which combinations of functional groups or types are represented. The importance of production material in relation to artefact groups or types is questionable in the current project, because it is obvious that the function of an object largely determines its material. In most cases in the Iron Age eastern Baltic weapons and tools are made of iron and ornaments of bronze or silver. However, that kind of analysis might provide very interesting results for other types of objects and material like vessels, beads, spindle whorls etc. When it comes to comparing the selection of objects and the relation between specific artefacts and environments both production material and artefact group have equal importance, although in most cases they overlap with each other. These specifics have even more weight when it comes to comparisons on a temporal scale and analysing the change of preferred materials for producing some items in long-term perspective e.g. bronzes for ornaments in earlier and silver in later centuries (see Chapters 6-9).

In addition to those paired combinations of main categories as expressed in the table above, the final results of practices of wealth depositing in temporal scales can be achieved by adding up all the four main categories: artefact types, material, environment of concealment and chronology. If there are coinciding contextual criteria and similarities within specific combinations of artefact (material) and environment, and they are close in temporal, even better in spatial terms, then it becomes possible to argue for socially accepted and widely followed depositional practices. The lack of parallels and thus unusual combinations indicate unique single acts that remain beyond the realm of socially accepted, perhaps even expected, depositional practices.

Although much of the data that has been collected is omitted from the statistical analysis, they are still to a large extent included in the catalogue part of the thesis. More significant correlations within depositional patterns and more specific criteria of objects or environments of concealment that are not included in general analysis (e.g. imported items, intentional fragmentation etc.) are provided in the more detailed discussions of specific depositional practices under relevant case studies (see Chapters 6-9).

### 4.3.1. Statistical methods, data input and graphical output

It has to be acknowledged that the dataset used in the current thesis is not large – altogether 69 deposits with over 2400 artefacts. In general terms there are very few elaborate statistical methods that would be suitable for such a small dataset and there are some statistical problems inherent in the results, especially in the analysis which include more detailed subcategorisations of the dataset. However, most of the results and especially their graphical outputs do provide identifiable patterns of different contextual criteria and therefore it was decided in favour of using them despite the complications deriving from the small dataset. Additionally, throughout the thesis, it has been attempted to combine both simple quantitative (Excel graphs) and more elaborate qualitative (crosstabulation, correspondence) analysis to back-up the final results and discussions at different levels of information.

Several books on statistical methods used in archaeology concentrate on analysing quantitative data: numerical and measured values, ordinal and ratio variables of artefacts or sites. The data used in this thesis are mostly qualitative: nominal and based on multivariate categories. This sets limits and prescriptions to the statistical methods that can be used in relation to particular questions of interest (combination of different nominal categorical values of the contexts of wealth deposits).

The majority of the statistical methods used in the current analysis are taken from specific handbooks (Drennan 1996; Shennan 1997; Baxter 2003). The most useful in terms of multivariate analysis is Baxter (1994) and edited volume by Madsen (1988). These are both dedicated to this particular data category and provide case studies which help to conduct qualitative multivariate analysis on the basis of the data that has been collected during this research project. Some additional help for artefact categorisation was gained from Read (2007).

The simplest quantitative analyses were carried out with Microsoft Excel which also has a very simple and flexible graphic output. These graphs give a general overview of the main characteristics of deposits, some combinations of artefacts and the chronological developments of the main contexts country by country. For more complex methods two different programmes were used. SPSS was employed for crosstabulation and (multiple) correspondence analyses. Freeware PAST (Hammer *et al.* 2001)[16] provided by the University of Oslo and initially created for analysing palaeontological material was used for correspondence, some multiple correspondence and testing seriation analysis. The preferences were made according to the suitability of graphic output of those programmes. These more specialised programmes were used for analysing different combinations between materials, artefact groups and their relations to specific environments of concealment, including on a chronological scale. They were also used for analysis of the development of depositional practices in a long-term perspective. The choice of artefact categories (functional groups or artefact groups) and the form of input (exact numbers or presence/absence) was determined according to specific questions and is explained in more detail in the relevant paragraphs and graphs in Chapters 6-9 below.

16 http://folk.uio.no/ohammer/past/.

The most complicated task was the choice of format for artefact categories, because there are different subsets included in this data category. First, the exact quantity of objects is not known in all the cases. Sometimes a rough estimate can be made and thus some uncertainty is included in the results of the quantitative analysis. However, in qualitative analysis it is attempted to minimise such drawbacks by focusing only on the major artefact groups as qualitative nominal categorical variables instead of an exact number of items. Due to the uncertainty over exact numbers of items, the estimate of artefact groups represented is expressed by presence and absence (respectively 1 and 0 in the dataset) of those particular object groups. The format of the dataset – whether the latter solution or only the main artefact group or material is taken into account – is indicated in the subtitles of the relevant graphs and in the paragraphs explaining the results of the analysis. There is only one exception – in the analysis of production material combinations of the exact numbers of each artefact according to its production material is given instead of just domination or presence-absence estimation. This helps to emphasise a dominance of one material within a deposit and make a clearer case for limited material combinations within eastern Baltic wealth deposits. In the analysis where the second most frequent artefact groups were considered, either for artefacts or materials, only those items that constituted at least 20% of the deposit were taken into account.

There were problems with data estimation and input for those qualitative and quantitative statistical methods that needed extra considerations and approximate decisions. In most cases the determination of major artefact group or material is straightforward and there is a clear dominance towards a single material or artefact functional group. In a couple of cases a rough estimation had to be made. Most of the problems with estimating major artefact group relate to iron deposits which include both weapons and tools, because sometimes the numbers exceed each other by only a few (e.g. Igavere and Paluküla in Estonia; Cibēni, Mūkukalns III in Latvia). In those cases the group with a largest number of items was taken into account, but the division is not always clear-cut. However, as the deposits of weapons and tools seem to form a rather uniform depositional practice in which the material of items seems to be more important than their exact function (see Chapters 6-9) the bias is not that substantial.

The same applies to the estimation of the main material. In most cases the dominance of one material is clear, but in a couple of cases the numbers of objects made of different materials are very close (e.g. Paluküla in Estonia). As a result of counting main artefact groups and materials represented there are also some instances that might appear contradictory. One of them is a deposit from Rūsiši which has 15 ornaments forming a majority of the deposit. However, the main material is listed as iron because seven weapons, nine tools, some of the ornaments and items from the group 'other' are made of iron. The second problematic deposit is the Tīras purvs find which contains the belongings of a male warrior: shield parts, tools, belt-parts, parts of drinking horn but also personal ornaments such as a brooch and a bracelet. When counting the items the largest amount of items is provided by different organic fragments such as textiles, wooden toggles and worked sticks, bone objects, leather items etc. Thus the general characterisation of this deposit is controversial: although the items clearly belong to a male warrior, the predominant artefact group is 'other' and material 'organic'. Most of those problematic examples fall within the category of unique and less widely followed depositional practices, emphasising their special character even more. The exact numbers of artefact functional groups and materials are provided in the catalogue and appendices of Chapters 6-8.

In terms of visual aids the colour selection for displaying data and statistical results in the graphs and maps is chosen with the aim of expressing relations between different artefact groups or environments of concealment. In the case of artefact types the logic is as follows: warm colours from pink-violet to red and yellow express ornaments (also materials of silver and bronze respectively); cold colours of various grey, purple and blue stand for weapons; and green colours indicate tools (iron or mineral objects respectively). Other more exceptional types of objects are given in a more unusual palette of colours. For detailed environments of concealments watery conditions are given in blue and purple, archaeological sites in red and dry land/solid ground in green. This enables visual grouping and merging of artefact groups or specific context in graphs or maps on the basis of their specific artefact type or environment similarities.

For data mapping the programme of ArcGIS was used. The base-maps were kindly provided by David Redhouse (University of Cambridge) using the following data-sets: Boundary data: Global Administrative Areas[17]; Elevation data: ASTER GDEM is a product of METI and NASA; Hydrographic data: CCM River and Catchment Database Copyright European Commission---JRC, 2007 (Vogt *et al.* 2007)[18]; Place name data: NGA GEOnet Names Server[19]; Soils data: European Soil Database (Panagos *et al.* 2012). In order to retain compatibility with ArcGIS some letters in site names had to be replaced by English characters, e.g. avoiding umlauts, or using sh or zh instead of š or ž respectively. Thus, for accurate site names please refer to main text or catalogue.

17 http://www.gadm.org/.
18 http://ccm.jrc.ec.europa.eu/.
19 http://earth-info.nga.mil/gns/html/.

*Chapter 5*

# Iron Age wealth deposits in the Baltic Sea area

This chapter provides an archaeological background for the eastern Baltic wealth deposits' material and forms a basis for further comparisons between the depositional practices in the east and west of the Baltic Sea presented in Chapter 9.4. It gives an overview of the major types of Iron Age deposits on the Baltic Sea region (excluding southern Poland and northern Germany) dating from the Iron Age up to the Viking Age (AD 800). Drawing on previous research, the subchapters are based on geographical areas and focus on the major subgroups of the depositional material.

Studies of intentional prehistoric artefact deposits in the Baltic Sea area are numerous. Looking at the geographical context they are more abundant and elaborately studied in Scandinavia than in the eastern part of the Baltic Sea region. The same applies to chronology: in the western Baltic countries the material of various deposits goes back to the Mesolithic and Neolithic (Stjernquist 1997; Koch 1999; Bennike 1999; Berggren 2010). Scandinavian Bronze Age metal deposits are particularly rich (Levy 1982; Larsson 1986; Johansen 1993; Verlaeckt 2000; Lund & Melheim 2011). In comparison there are quite a few Bronze Age deposits in the southern part of the eastern Baltic region, especially Poland, and coastal regions of Lithuania (Sidrys & Luchtanas 1999; Čivilytė 2009; Merkevičius 2011). However, only six Bronze Age deposits have been discovered in Latvia and most of those are from the coastal regions or related to larger water routes (Urtāns 1977, 129-132; Vasks & Vijups 2004). From Estonia only one Bronze Age deposit, Tehumardi at the coast of Saaremaa Island, is known (Sperling 2013). The majority of the wealth deposits in the eastern Baltic area are dated to the Iron Age (500 BC – ca. 1200 AD). In the Pre-Roman Iron Age (500 BC – 10/50 AD) the number of deposits is still very small and most of them are found in Lithuania. A considerable increase in wealth deposits emerges with the Roman Iron Age.

## 5.1. Iron Age wealth deposits in Scandinavia

The Scandinavian Iron Age provides abundant examples of intentional artefact concealments. They include very variable material from artefacts and natural objects to human remains and other organic material. In order to present this rich material more clearly I have divided the following subchapters according to the main find categories: finds from bogs and precious metal deposits. Most of the examples are found in southern Scandinavia: Denmark and Scania in Sweden. The number of Iron Age wealth deposits decreases considerably in the central and northern regions of Scandinavia.

### 5.1.1. Booty sacrifices and bog deposits in Scandinavia

The most famous deposits from the Scandinavian Iron Age are the so-called booty sacrifices (Danish *krigsbytteofringen*) – finds of military equipment, mainly weapons, from boggy areas. The majority of these are from Jutland and the Danish islands, but there are also some examples from Sweden (see Ørsnes & Ilkjær 1993; Ilkjær 2000, 15; 2003; Jensen 2006a, 507-584; 2006b, 88-93). They are mostly dated to the second half of the Roman Iron Age, although there are also some later and earlier examples (see below). Usually these finds are interpreted as war booty sacrifices marking victories over intruders whose equipment was demolished, sometimes also burnt, and cast into watery conditions such as lakes and bogs as a ritual act. The tradition of studying those deposits goes back to the 19th century. Several sites such as Thorsbjerg, Kragehul, Nydam, Vimose were studied already in the 19th century by Conrad Engelhardt (1863; 1866; 1867; 1869). Some of those discoveries had a strong politico-historical connotation resulting in dispute between Denmark and Germany about the ownership and interpretation of those deposits (Wiell 2003).

The earliest example of booty sacrifice in Scandinavia is the Pre-Roman Iron Age Hjortspring find from ca. 350 BC (Randsborg 1995; Crumlin-Pedersen & Trakadas (eds) 2003). It consists of the equipment of a small army containing weapons, including bone spearheads, and a few tools deposited with a boat. There are also evidences of earlier ritual activities on the site indicated by animal bones (Kaul 2003).

The most extensively studied booty deposit is from Illerup in Jutland, which consists of several thousands of objects and animal bones. It was first excavated in the 1950s by Harald Andersen in relation to drainage of the bog. From the mid-1970s onwards it was studied thoroughly by Jørgen Ilkjær (Ilkjær 1984; 2000 and web-site Illerup Ådal[20]). Research at this site has resulted in 15 volumes of detailed material analysis published in the series of the Jutland Archaeological Society Publications (Jysk Arkæologisk Selskabs Skrifter). The boggy area has been used for depositing different weaponry – some of Roman origin –, but also personal items and tools concealed on at least three different occasions from the 3rd to early 6th century AD. The total number of objects exceeds 15 000 including some which have been intentionally demolished, bent and even burnt prior to deposition.

Similar large-scale deposits of army equipment, often also accompanied by tools and personal items, are also known from other Danish sites. A discovery at Ejsbøl preceded the large-scale excavations in Illerup in the 1970s. This find comprises over 1000 objects, deposited on at least four or five different occasions during the Roman Iron Age, but the site also includes some Pre-Roman Iron Age potsherds and bone material (Ørsnes 1963; 1988). The Nydam find includes boats besides the weaponry and was created on four or five different occasions from the mid-3rd to late-5th century AD (Rieck & Jørgensen 1997; Bemmann & Bemmann 1998; Gebühr 2000; Rau 2010). There were also some traces of Pre-Roman and/or Roman Iron Age ritual activities in the area, indicated by the sherds of ceramic vessels (Rau 2010, 12-13). The Vimose find of weapons, tools and some ornaments dates from the 1st to 7th century AD, though mostly from the Roman Iron Age (Christensen 2005a; Pauli Jensen 2008; Dobat 2008). And again, the same pattern of Pre-Roman Iron Age ceramic vessels in the same bog was evident.

20 http://www.illerup.dk/.

The Thorsberg deposit from what is now northern Germany consists mainly of 3rd century weapons, some of which seem to have been deposited after intentionally sorting and grouping the artefacts (Lønstrup 1984; Raddatz 1987; Gebühr 2000). The Danish Porskjær find includes mainly weapons and ornaments and shows a continuous use of the same depositional area from the early 3rd to 6th century AD (Nørgård Jørgensen 2008a-b). The find from Kragehul has over 500 objects dating from the Pre-Roman Iron Age, although the majority of deposits (four out of five) are from the 4th and 5th century and consist mainly of weapons (Iversen 2008; 2010). An unusual example is the Tranbær find from 2nd-3rd century AD which mainly includes organic objects such as wheels, wooden weapon parts, ceramic vessels and does not include any iron artefacts (Schovsbo 2007).

There are also examples of relatively smaller numbers (up to 30 objects) of artefacts deposited in water-related conditions during the 3rd-7/8th century AD (Nørgård Jørgensen 2008a, fig. 61, 100, 104-120). Examples include Knarremose, Dallerup and Balsmyr. The latter contains items from the Bronze and Pre-Roman Iron Age (Nørgård Jørgensen 2008a, 104-113). A find from Illemose with its 40 metal and organic artefacts and bone material might be also added to this list of booty deposits (Stenbak 1994).

Compared with Denmark, the weapon deposits from other parts of Scandinavia during the Roman and Germanic Iron Age are somewhat smaller or studied in less detail (Burenhult 1991, 150-153; however, see Hagberg 1984). There are weapon and personal equipment finds sometimes accompanied by riding gear such as Vännebo, Jönköping and Nedersten in southern Sweden which all belong to the first half of the 1st millennium AD. The find from Skedemosse on Öland includes weapons, animal and human bones, and a remarkable amount of gold objects dating from the Pre-Roman Iron Age up to the 5/6th century AD (Hagberg 1964; 1967). The second largest and most recently studied find is in Finnestorp in southern Sweden. So far ca. 300 objects from the 3rd to 6th AD century have been found. They include bone material, numerous weapons, riding gear and personal dress accessories (Nordqvist 2006; 2007).

There are some indications of a widespread tradition of weapon deposits in other parts of Scandinavia. Several Swedish stray finds or deposits of weapons come from watery conditions and are dated to the Roman Iron Age (Nicklasson 1997, 159, 179-180). Although most of them have not been excavated the author quotes examples of Roman Iron Age weapon deposits from the Mälar area, for example Västmanland and Närke, that can be interpreted as markers of sacrifices in borderlands (Nicklasson 1997, 179). He also mentions that in Scania there are seven Pre-Roman Iron Age deposits of bone or horn arrowheads. Five of them are from boggy areas which gives a reason to draw a comparison with the Hjortspring find (Nicklasson 1997, 96-97, 178). There are elaborate studies on the weapon deposits in Sweden, Norway and Denmark by Lund (2004; 2005; 2006; 2008; 2009), but these – often single deposits in the same area over a long period – are mainly dated to the Viking Age or Early Medieval Period.

As the traditional term 'booty sacrifices' already implies, most of these weapon finds have been interpreted as signs of ritual activities relating to war victories, also mentioned in Roman sources. Often the discussion focuses on the origin of defeated troops and sacrificing communities. For instance in the case of the Illerup find the invaders have been located to various areas in eastern, western and southern Scandinavia and northern Germany (Ilkjær 2000, 68-73; Carnap-

Bornheim & Ilkjær 1996, 471, 483, however, see also Kaul 1997; Fuglevik 2007). The second, closely related interpretation, is that some of these deposits might have been Germanic 'copies' of Roman triumphs: victors brought the equipment of defeated armies back home and sacrificed them into local water bodies (Jørgensen 2001, 15-16 and the literature cited).

The abundant and violently handled weapon finds have attracted a lot of attention, but they have mainly been employed in the discussion of single or a series of similar remarkable events in a rather short-term perspective, especially since the discovery of Illerup find. The additional point of discussion is the origin of the owners of deposited material. In relation to the geographical origin of the invaders Nørgård Jørgensen (2008a, 117-119) has argued that Late Roman Iron Age and Germanic Iron Age deposits include weapons of such widespread geographical origin that it cannot be demonstrated where the owners came from. In this context, comparisons of different depositional activities over longer time period provide new perspectives. The bogs with large weapon deposits have often been used in preceding periods. In addition, they continue to be used in later times, although in these cases the quantity of artefacts is diminished to just a few instead of hundreds. Different depositional traditions in the same places throughout the 1st millennium AD might indicate that the reasons and backgrounds for depositing the objects have varied (Christensen 2005b; Nørgård Jørgensen 2008a, 119-120; Iversen 2010, 151-152). This long-term perspective and comparison of changes in depositional material as presented in more recent publications provides some interesting discussions of the development and changes in wealth depositing (see also Fabech 1994a-b; 1999b; Hedeager 1999). One example of variable depositional practices which help us to see the booty sacrifices from a slightly new point of view are weapons in non-watery conditions. A recent discovery at Uppåkra in Scania is a collection of weapons next to a possible temple interpreted as offerings related to warfare activities and warrior ideology (Helgesson 2004). There are also some instances of weapons deposited in settlement contexts, often relating to buildings that chronologically overlap with the booty sacrifices for example Østerhåbsalle near Horsens, Bejsebakken near Ålborg and from Sorte Muld (Lund Hansen & Vennersdorf 2009, 30-33; Iversen 2010, 143-144, 152).

The second point that opens up a bigger picture about bog deposits is that bogs were not only used for depositing army equipment (Hedeager 1992, 37-81; 1999; Fabech 1999b). Although mostly from the Pre-Roman Iron Age, the finds of metal cauldrons in Denmark have provided the examples of Gundestrup (Kaul 1991; Nielsen *et al.* 2005), Rynkeby, Mosbæk and Ringsebølle (Kaul 2009). The tradition of casting pottery, sometimes accompanied by natural objects (stones, stakes) and bone material into watery conditions goes back to the Neolithic Period. There are several examples of such finds in Danish and northern Germany Pre-Roman and Roman Iron Age material (Becker 1971; Harck 1984). Harck (1984, 115-116) also points out that these depositional practices have not been noted in Roman sources in the same way as the weapon deposits and therefore we must be looking at less dramatic ritual activities of ordinary people. The Danish find from Valmose might be interpreted in that way. Besides some artefacts and pots this mainly consisted of natural objects and animal as well as human bones that were deposited over a longer period in the Iron Age (Ferdinand & Ferdinand 1962). Similar to that is the Pre-Roman Iron Age find at Hedemark in Norway where three human skeletons with marks of violence had been deposited in a possible lake (Resi 2011). Bone, stone, organic material and pottery deposits were found in the Röekillorna deposit, which covers the time span from the Neolithic to the Middle Ages (Stjernquist 1997). Another example of depositing pots, wooden artefacts, and some bones in watery conditions in Sweden is the Käringsjön deposit (Burenhult 1991, 150; Carlie 1998). The most recent discovery which broadens our ideas about Scandinavian Iron Age bog deposits is from Alken Enge (Skandeborg Museum[21]; Holst 2013), not far from the Illerup deposit. There disarticulated bones of over 200 individuals, some of them with signs of violence, have been discovered. Accompanying artefacts include just few weapons-tools and sherds of pottery. The dating of this deposit is at the turn of our era, which precedes the earliest Illerup find by a couple of centuries. However, even at this site, the tradition of depositing animal bones and pottery has a long time span from the Pre-Roman Iron Age to the Middle Ages.

And finally, this list of various water-related deposits would not be complete without a brief mention of Pre-Roman and early Roman Iron Age bog bodies e.g. Grauballe Man, Tollund Man (for general overview see Glob 1969; Sanden 1996). Most often these are interpreted as evidence for various (agricultural and fertility) rituals – mainly sacrificial practices relating to religious communication with the gods and communal gatherings.

Thus the picture of bog deposits is very multifaceted and weapon deposits form only one part of them. The examples provided emphasize that bogs and other watery conditions show a considerable variety of depositional practices throughout prehistory.

### 5.1.2. Precious metal deposits in Scandinavia

The precious metal deposits of the Scandinavian Iron Age – from Roman coins to ornaments, special products and hacked objects – open a new field of research and interpretations, which only partly overlaps with the previously presented weapon and other bog finds. The precious metal finds have been traditionally seen as either hoards for safekeeping and hidden for economic reasons, or interpreted as materialities of different ritual activities (see also Hines 1989; Hedeager 1992, 70-82). In the case of the Scandinavian Iron Age, especially during the Migration Period, the second interpretation seems to dominate the literature.

The examples of ritualistic interpretations of precious metal finds relate mainly to Migration Period central places. Some sites stand out for their large quantities of gold finds: Sorte Muld in Bornholm (Adamsen *et al.* (eds) 2009), Lundeborg and Gudme in the Island of Funen in Denmark (Randsborg 1990; Nielsen *et al.* (eds) 1994; Henriksen 2010), Helgö (Lamm 2004) and Uppåkra in Sweden (Hårdh & Larsson (eds) 2002; Hårdh (ed.) 2003; Larsson (ed.) 2004). These sites include large amounts of precious metal objects from jewellery to coins. Among them are the gold foil figures (Danish *guldgubber*) – tiny gold foil plaques with human figures on them. They have been most often interpreted as a kind of temple money used in ritual activities in the religious areas at the central places (Lamm 2004; Watt 2004; Ratke & Simek 2006).

But gold foil figures are only one example of the types of gold artefacts deposited in Scandinavia. There are also numerous finds of gold bracteates. These are round golden pendants with different decorative depictions varying from a bust of a man,

21 http://www.skanderborgmuseum.dk/Alken_Enge-English_version-1070.aspx.

reminding Roman emperors on coins, to different and sometimes very abstract scenes picturing humans and animals (see e.g. Stenberger 1977, 322-328; Hines 1989; Hauck & Axboe 1985; Andrén 1991; Hedeager 1992, 56-60; Jensen 2006b, 110-111, 124-136; Behr 2010). They are discovered mainly as hoards in the core area, southern Scandinavia, but as burial goods in Norway, northern Germany and England (however, for the possibility of hoards in England see Behr 2010). In the latter cases they are most often found in female burials. In deposits the bracteates have often been concealed with beads and brooches similar to female dress accessories. Therefore, these finds have been related to women's attributes and interpreted in relation to the female life cycle, including surrogate burials of a woman (Hines 1989, 197-199; Arrhenius 1995; Gaimster 2001; Behr 2010). However, there are some examples of bracteates in male graves, and a set of female accessories is not evident in all the bracteate deposits. Therefore, their interpretation in terms of gender is ambiguous. It appears that regional variability in depositions reflects different meanings of those objects – such as items of status symbol, personal ornaments and sacrifices to gods – rather than a homogenous depositional practice throughout Scandinavia (Lindeberg 1997; Axboe 2001; Hedeager 2011).

Besides bracteates and gold foil figures there are abundant Danish finds of gold rings, including bracelets as well as neck-rings (Hedeager 1991; 1992, 60-64; Jørgensen & Petersen 1998; Magnus (ed.) 2001; Jensen 2006b). Finds of rings and bracteates are also numerous in southern and eastern Sweden and its islands (Stenberger 1977, 290-294; 314-322; Hagberg 1984; Andersson 2011). These gold items are found both in watery conditions and dry land. The watery context of concealment has been interpreted as border markers that provide magical protection for the settlement (Wiker 1999; Hedeager 1999). Also, some Danish and Swedish stray finds of elaborately ornamented brooches in bog areas have been interpreted as offerings to a female goddess who was supposed to dwell in the lakes (Magnus 1999, 80-81).

But collections of gold and silver rings and bars as well as hackgold are also known from dry land (Hedeager 1992, 65-66). The 5th century AD Timboholm deposit from southern Sweden, consisting of high quality gold rings and gold bars, over 7 kg in total, is the largest gold find from the country (Arne 1906; Stenberger 1977, 317-318; Burenhult 1991, 40, 44-47, fig. 21; Gullman 1995). A more recent discovery of gold items at Vittene, also from southern Sweden, was again found in a settlement context and is dated to the Pre-Roman and Roman Iron Age (Lamm 1997; Rasch 2004; Nordquist 2007, 223). Another example of precious metal in a settlement context is a Swedish Roman Iron Age deposit from Havor in Gotland that consisted of Roman vessels as well as a remarkable gold neck-ring (Nylén *et al.* 2005).

There are also examples of hacksilver hoards from the mid-1st millennium AD (Hedeager 1992, 50-53, 66; Jensen 2006b, 58-59, 111-113). Such finds are known in Denmark e.g. Simmersted, Høstentorp, Gudme-Stenhøjgård, Søtoftegård and Hardenberg (Voss 1954; Fabech 1990, 113-116; Vang Petersen 1994; Rau 2010, 454-456 and the literature cited). Similar examples in Sweden are Sjörup, Fulltofta and Sösdala, which contain also numerous fragments of riding related equipment (Hagberg 1984; Fabech 1990). A hacksilver hoard has been discovered at Gudme (Munksgaard 1987; Jørgensen 1994; Vang Petersen 1994). A recent find is the Mannerup hoard from the Roskilde area where a ceramic vessel filled with gold and silver objects from the 5th century AD was discovered (Roskilde

Museum[22]). Similar finds of hacksilver and -gold are Djurgårdsäng in Sweden (Stenberger 1977, 327-328) and Slipshavn in Funen (Jørgensen & Petersen 1998, 195; Henriksen 2010, 417, figs 30-31).

Final examples of the variability and abundance of Scandinavian deposits are several instances of iron bar deposits that most often have been discovered in dry land, also marked with larger stones, and interpreted as important collections of valuable raw material (e.g. Resi 1995). More recent studies have started to investigate various artefact deposits – vessels, weapons, ornaments, bone material – from settlement contexts and to interpret them as signs of domestic ritual or magic related practices (Hansen 2006; Webley 2008, chapter 7; Iversen 2010, 143-144, 152).

Therefore the whole range of Scandinavian Iron Age wealth deposits is very diverse with different forms, contexts and contents of depositional practices. The earliest are different deposits of ceramic vessels and organic or mineral material in bogs. One of the largest group of finds are weapon deposits in watery conditions. These are mainly dated to the Roman Iron Age, but there are also examples from preceding and following periods. From the Migration period onwards gold and silver deposits become more numerous. These are found in both watery conditions and dry land, including settlement contexts.

## 5.2. Eastern Baltic Iron Age wealth deposits

Similar studies of Iron Age artefact deposits up to the Viking Age (800 AD) on the opposite side of the Baltic Sea, especially in its northern part, are more limited. The reason on the one hand is the smaller amount of source material, on the other, the lack of interest by more recent scholars. This is especially evident in the case of general overviews looking beyond single examples or smaller regions. The material from the Baltic countries will be analysed in detail in the following pages of this thesis. In this sub-chapter a brief account of Finnish and Polish material is given.

### 5.2.1. Iron Age wealth deposits in Finland

Iron Age deposits from Finland are not very abundant. Although artefact deposits have been discovered from the Stone, Bronze and even Pre-Roman Iron Age, there is a gap in the 1st-9th centuries AD, followed again by richer material from the Viking Age onwards (Luoto 2010; Siljander & Poutianinen 2010). According to the general overview of the Finnish Iron Age by Kivikoski (1973), the total number of identifiable intentional artefact deposits remains below ten. Kivikoski divides the material on the basis of the content of the find into precious metal hoards (Germ. *Schatzfunde*), or iron and bronze deposits (*Depotfunde* or *Verwahrfunde*), but she also uses some distinctions according to the context of discovery, the content of the find or further interpretation of the data e.g. offerings (*Opferfunde*), bog deposits (*Moorfunde*), silver finds (*Silberfunde*) and weapon finds (*Waffenfunde*).

In Finland, there are only a few deposits that can be dated to the Pre-Roman Iron Age (500 BC-50 AD). One is a deposit of imported iron daggers discovered in the bog at Savukoski parish in northern Finland (Kivikoski 1973, 9, 14; Huurre 1995, 123). The second is the Pernaja-Malmsby deposit of weapons and iron tools, which was found in a watery environment and has been interpreted as either an offering or a collection of smith's belongings (Kivikoski 1961, 119, fig. 10;

---

22 http://www.roskildemuseum.dk/Default.aspx?ID=651.

Salo 1968, 83; Huurre 1995, 120; Luoto 2010, 23-24). There is also a find of three bronze neck-rings of so-called Bräcksta type imported from Scandinavia that were discovered in watery conditions in Panelia-Kiukainen (Meinander 1954, 52-53, table 15). An interesting find is a Roman Iron Age, namely a 3rd century single gold neck-ring from Nousiainen (Hackman 1905, 213-214). This is a Scandinavian torc-like ring with animal-head terminals. In fact, there were probably two rings concealed, but the details and whereabouts of the second has remained unknown to archaeologists (Kivikoski 1961, 133; Luoto 2010, 23).

During the following Migration and Merovingian Periods (400/450-550/600 and 550/600-800 AD respectively) wealth deposits decrease suddenly. One Migration Period find from Pylkönmäki-Multapekko consists of lance heads and has been interpreted as either an economic artefact deposit or an offering (Kivikoski 1973, 14, 79). There are also two unusual bog finds from Isokyrö-Levänluhta and Vöyri-Käldamäki. They consist mainly of human remains, but also include some artefacts and animal bones. For a long time they were interpreted as evidence of ritual and religion-related practices (Meinander 1950, 136-145; Seger 1982, 192; Niskanen 2006; Luoto 2010, 27), but the most recent scholarship seems instead to relate them to unusual burial practices (Wessman 2009).

There are only a few more artefact deposits which include artefacts from the last centuries of the Merovingian Period but are mostly dated to the first century of the Viking Age already. The Hämeenlinna-Hattemala and Kiika-Friedhof finds consisted of bronze ornaments and some personal items (Ailio 1928; Kivikoski 1973, 11-12, 67-68). In the first some of the artefacts are dated to the Viking Age and have been interpreted as collected by a bronze smith possibly looted from burials (Ailio 1928; Taavitsainen 1990, 45). The other examples preceding or partly overlapping with the Viking Age are ornaments from Nastola-Vehkosilta and Kuhmoinen-Papinsaari (Siljander & Poutiainen 2010, 83-87). A weapon find from Asikkala-Saukkola could be added to this list (Luoto 2010).

There is one more find-group that can be categorised under the concept of intentional artefact deposits in Finland. These are oval strike-a-light stones from the Roman Iron Age, Migration and Merovingian Period mostly found in the south-western Finland, but also inland regions and interpreted as possible ritual depositions by some scholars (Salo 1984, 237-239). However, as single stray finds without detailed analysis of the find contexts, the inclusion of those finds under wealth deposits is problematic.

It is apparent that the total number of 1st-9th century AD deposits from Finland is remarkably small, especially when excluding the problematic finds with a possible Early Viking Age date. Most deposits are from the western and central part of Finland. This cannot be explained as reflecting state of research in different areas or periods, because there are numerous hoards from the Viking and Late Iron Age throughout Finland (Talvio 2002). An interesting separate scholarship of artefact deposits in Finland is the discussion of Sámi sacrificial sites with metal deposits from the Late Iron Age and Medieval periods (Zachrisson 1984; Spangen 2009).

Therefore, the total number of recorded Pre-Viking Age deposits in Finland is genuinely small. Comparing the data with Scandinavian and eastern Baltic material (see Chapters 6-9) it is also noticeable that the number of weapon finds as well as precious metal ornaments is very limited. The finds seem to consist of organic material or bronze ornaments with only rare silver and gold objects. This suggests quite different depositional traditions that are expressed in different numbers as well as composition of deposits in the northern part of the eastern Baltic.

### 5.2.2. Iron Age wealth deposits in Poland

Poland, especially its northern and coastal regions, provides several examples and parallels to eastern Baltic and Scandinavian depositional traditions. There seems to exist a similar booty sacrifice tradition in the southern part of the eastern Baltic as in Scandinavia, although at a considerably smaller scale. In some instances even a similar ritual destruction of weapons is evident (see e.g. Makiewicz 1992). The finds are often related to the main water routes of the country and concentrate in its northern part. One such find is a deposit of Roman Iron Age weapons from Wolka-See in East Prussia (Raddatz 1993). It consisted of military objects, horse gear and personal items. The most recent discovery is from Czaszkowo, Lake Nidajno near Mrągowo, in Masuria district (Nowakiewicz & Rzeszotarska-Nowakiewicz 2012). This deposit was possibly cast into a lake and contains elaborately ornamented buckles and other precious-metal artefacts. There are also some remains of iron objects, including weapons, although the preservation of iron is very poor. It has been dated to the 3rd-6th century AD. Similarly to Wolka-See, this find has been interpreted in the context of Scandinavian booty sacrifices. There are also some instances of possible weapon sacrifices in a Roman Iron Age settlement context like the Żarnowiec and Inowrocław deposits of weapons and tools with riding equipment (Makiewicz 1988, 110-111). These are interesting comparative parallels to Scandinavian weapon deposits in the central places.

The Polish Iron Age depositional material is quite similar to Scandinavian data in other respects as well. Firstly, there seems to be a tradition of depositing organic as well as mineral material, for example wooden objects, stones, bones and pottery, and also some ornaments, coins and statuettes, into watery conditions and dry land throughout the Pre-Roman and Roman Iron Age (Makiewicz 1988; 1993; Cofta-Broniewska 1993; Kokowski 1993). Some of those deposits have been related to ritual sites either in the vicinity of settlements or burial areas, located on higher hills (Cofta-Broniewska 1993). This includes the Otalążka find which has a specially built stone and wooden structure surrounding the possible ritual site (Makiewicz 1988, 83-93).

Secondly, numerous Roman coins of mainly bronze, but also silver and gold have been discovered in Poland (Godłowski 1980, 74; Bursche 1992; Ciołek 2010; Zapolska 2012). There are tens of Roman coin hoards from the vicinity of the Baltic Sea coast. The total number of Roman coins finds in Poland is counted in thousands.

Thirdly, the gold and silver deposits in the northern part of the country also resemble the Scandinavian material both in terms of content and context (Godłowski 1980). The data from the Baltic Sea coast, Pomerania, gives abundant examples of Migration Period deposits of gold and silver. These deposits include coins and ornaments, sometimes reflecting separate selective depositional traditions, sometimes a mixture of all types of valuables. They include single gold neck-rings from Radosiew, Piotrowice, Stargard and Młoteczno deposited around 5th-6th centuries AD (Godłowski 1980, 74). There are also combinations of gold ornaments, sometimes concealed with coins, such as Wapno, Karlino and Friedrichstahl, while the latter included also sword parts similar to some of the Scandinavian rich finds (Godłowski 1980, 72-73). There is also a scrap metal hoard consisting of hacksilver pieces from Frombork (Frauenburg) (Bitner-Wróblewska 2010, 150-151).

The interpretations of all these Polish finds vary from possibly religion-related deposits to economic concealment and safe-keeping. More importantly, the general picture of Polish Iron Age wealth deposits is remarkably similar to the Scandinavian material. Although smaller in the numbers of deposits, the resemblance is evident in terms of content and context of the main depositional traditions.

# *Chapter 6*

# Practices of wealth depositing in Estonia

## 6.1. 1st-9th century AD wealth deposits in Estonia

There are altogether 33 wealth deposits known from the territory of Estonia from the 1st to the 9th century AD. As explained coin hoards will not be included in the detailed analysis of the material. Besides the two reliable coin hoards from Estonia – Juminda and Kastna – three other finds (Aesoo I and II, North-Estonian find) are excluded due to the lack of information about the artefacts or circumstances of discovery (see below). That leaves us with a total number of 28 wealth deposits from Estonia. The main characteristics and descriptions of those 28 finds are found in Tables 6.1.1.-6.1.3.

*Table 6.1.1. Chronology, artefact functional groups, and materials represented in Estonian wealth deposits.*

| Wealth Deposit | Dating of artefacts (AD) | Dating (century) | Weapons | Tools | Ornaments | Coins | Raw Material | Other | Material 1 | Material 2 | Material 3 |
|---|---|---|---|---|---|---|---|---|---|---|---|
| Metsküla | 1-200 | 2 | | | 2 | | | | Bronze | | |
| Kiiu | 200-300 | 3 | | | 5 | | | | Bronze | | |
| Liimala | 275-325 | 4 | | | 2 | | | | Bronze | | |
| Mustmätta | 275-325 | 4 | | | 16 | | | | Bronze | | |
| Kaali | 200-450 | 4 | | | 3 | | | | Silver | | |
| Kavastu | 1-200 | 5 | | | | | 4 | 1 | Bronze | | |
| Piilsi | 450-500 | 5 | | | 41 | | | | Bronze | Iron | |
| Reola | 450-500 | 5 | | | 11 | | | 1 | Bronze | Bone | |
| Vagula | 450-525 | 5 | | | 1 | | | | Bronze | | |
| Kardla | 500-550 | 6 | | | 24 | | | 1 | Silver | Gold | Bronze |
| Paali_I | 500-550 | 6 | | | 3 | | | | Silver | Bronze | |
| Paali_II | 500-550 | 6 | | | 15 | | | | Silver | Bronze | Iron |
| Uuri | 500-550 | 6 | | | 5 | | | | Silver | Bronze | |
| Viira | 450-550 | 6 | | | 11 | | | | Silver | | |
| Villevere | 450-550 | 6 | | | 12 | | | | Silver | Bronze | |
| Kriimani | 475-600 | 6 | | | | | | 1 | Silver | | |
| Varnja | 491-600 | 6 | | | | | | 1 | Silver | | |
| Rikassaare | 550-650 | 7 | 61 | | | | | | Iron | | |
| Igavere | 500-700 | 7 | 9 | 8 | | | | | Iron | | |
| Hummuli | 700-725 | 8 | | | 3 | | | | Silver | | |
| Navesti | 700-725 | 8 | | | 1 | | | | Silver | | |
| Kunda_II | 600-800 | 8 | | 1 | 3 | | | | Bronze | | |
| Kaabe | 400-800 | 8 | 2 | | | | | | Iron | | |
| Koorküla_Valgjärv | 700-900 | 9 | 4 | 1 | | 1? | | 1 | Iron | Bronze | |
| Loosi | 750-900 | 9 | | | 3 | | | | Silver | | |
| Paluküla | 750-900 | 9 | 35 | 1 | 32 | | | 3 | Iron | Bronze | |
| Kunda_I | 1-700 | 1-3; 6-7 | 15 | 2 | | | | 6 | Iron | | |
| Alulinn | 100-1200 | 2-3; 6-7; 12/13 | 67 | 28 | | | | 3 | Iron | | |
| **Total: 28** | | | **193** | **41** | **193** | **1?** | **4** | **18** | | | |

| Wealth Deposit | Dating (c.) | Swords | Axes | Battle Knives | Spearheads | Other Weapons | Knives | Horse Gear | Sickles/ Scythe | Other Tools | Other Iron Objects | Neck-rings | Bracelets | Brooches | Finger-rings | Rings | Belt Parts | Dress Pins | Other Ornaments | Vessels | Coins | Raw Material | Other | Comments on 'other' |
|---|---|---|---|---|---|---|---|---|---|---|---|---|---|---|---|---|---|---|---|---|---|---|---|---|
| Metsküla | 2 | | | | | | | | | | | 2 | | | | | | | | | | | | |
| Kiiu | 3 | | | | | | | | | | | 3 | | 1 | 1 | | | | | | | | | |
| Liimala | 4 | | | | | | | | | | | 2 | | | | | | | | | | | | |
| Mustmätta | 4 | | | | | | | | | | | 16 | | | | | | | | | | | | |
| Kaali | 4 | | | | | | | | | | | 1 | 2 | | | | | | | | | | | |
| Kavastu | 5 | | | | | | | | | | | | | | | | | | | | | 4 | 1 | Roman bronze lamp |
| Piilsi | 5 | | | | | | | | | | | 6 | 17 | 4 | | 11 | | | 3 | | | | | |
| Reola | 5 | | | | | | | | | | | | 8 | 3 | | | | | | | | | 1 | Bone artefact (lost) |
| Vagula | 5 | | | | | | | | | | | | | 1 | | | | | | | | | | |
| Kardla | 6 | | | | | | | | | | | 12 | 6 | 4 | | 2 | | | | | | | 1 | Ring-like iron rod with silver rings on |
| Paali_I | 6 | | | | | | | | | | | 2 | | 1 | | | | | | | | | | |
| Paali_II | 6 | | | | | | | | | | | 2 | 2 | 3 | 1 | | 3 | | 4 | | | | | |
| Uuri | 6 | | | | | | | | | | | 3 | 1 | 1 | | | | | | | | | | |
| Viira | 6 | | | | | | | | | | | 11 | | | | | | | | | | | | |
| Villevere | 6 | | | | | | | | | | | 8 | 1 | 1 | | 1 | | | 1 | | | | | |
| Kriimani | 6 | | | | | | | | | | | | | | | | | | | 1 | | | | |
| Varnja | 6 | | | | | | | | | | | | | | | | | | | 1 | | | | |
| Rikassaare | 7 | | | 7 | 54 | | | | | | | | | | | | | | | | | | | |
| Igavere | 7 | 1 | 5 | | 1 | 1 | | 1 | 1 | | 7 | | | | | | | | | | | | | |
| Hummuli | 8 | | | | | | | | | | | 3 | | | | | | | | | | | | |
| Navesti | 8 | | | | | | | | | | | 1 | | | | | | | | | | | | |
| Kunda_II | 8 | | | | | | | | | 1 | | | | | 1 | | | 2 | | | | | | |
| Kaabe | 8 | 1 | 1 | | | | | | | | | | | | | | | | | | | | | |
| Koorküla_V | 9 | | 1 | | 3 | | | | | 1 | 1 | | | | | | | | | | 1?? | | | |
| Loosi | 9 | | | | | | | | | | | 3 | | | | | | | | | | | | |
| Paluküla | 9 | 5 | | | 24 | | 5 | 1 | | 1 | 1 | 2 | 5 | 23 | | | | 2 | | | | | 2 | Timber fragments |
| Kunda_I | 1-3; 6-7 | 1 | 9 | | 5 | | | | | 2 | 6 | | | | | | | | | | | | | |
| Alulinn | 2-3; 6-7; 12/13 | 3 | 13 | | 51 | | | | 27 | 1 | 3 | | | | | | | | | | | | | |
| **Total: 28** | | **11** | **29** | **7** | **138** | **1** | **5** | **2** | **28** | **6** | **18** | **77** | **42** | **42** | **3** | **14** | **3** | **4** | **8** | **2** | **1?** | **4** | **5** | |

*Table 6.1.2. Artefact groups in Estonian wealth deposits.*

## 6.1.1. Roman import and coins

The number of Roman imports on Estonian territory is generally moderate: besides the coins there are some brooches, a bronze lamp from Kavastu, a bronze bell from Kambja (Nowakowski 1988, fig. 13; 1994, 136) and more than 100 glass or gold foil beads of provincial origin (Lang 2007b, 257; Štšogoleva 2009).

The total number of documented Roman coins, both silver and copper, found from Estonia is over 50, most found in uncertain contexts or as stray finds (Lang 2007a, 163; Lang 2007b, 257). This number is remarkably small compared to Latvia and Lithuania (see below). Around 20 find-spots of Roman coins are known (Kropotkin 1961, 103 for details), but there are only two Roman coin hoards known in Estonia. First is the Juminda find of four Roman copper sesterces minted during the reign of Marcus Aurelius (161-180) which was discovered in the Juminda peninsula (Molvõgin 1976; Tamla & Kiudsoo 2005, 14-15; Lang 1996, 328; Lang 2007b, 247, 257). Second is a very recent find of 17 copper coins from the 2nd century AD from Kastna at the western coast of Estonia (Kiudsoo 2013).

| Wealth Deposit | Dating (c.) | Environment | Environment Subtype | Depth (cm) | Markers | Archaeological Site |
|---|---|---|---|---|---|---|
| Metsküla | 2 | Watery condition | Marsh | 120 | | |
| Kiiu | 3 | Solid ground | | | Big stone | Burial area? |
| Liimala | 4 | Solid ground | | | Stones? | Burial area? |
| Mustmätta | 4 | Solid ground | | 20-30 | | |
| Kaali | 4 | Solid ground | Archaeological Site | | | Fortified settlement / enclosure / sacrificial site |
| Kavastu | 5 | Watery condition | Bog | 120 | | |
| Piilsi | 5 | Watery condition | River | 80-90 | Wooden platform? | |
| Reola | 5 | Watery condition | Bog | 100 | | |
| Vagula | 5 | Watery condition | Lake | | | |
| Kardla | 6 | Solid ground | Archaeological Site | 45 | Big stone | Burial area |
| Paali_I | 6 | Solid ground | Archaeological Site | 20-40 | Stone | *Tarand*-grave |
| Paali_II | 6 | Solid ground | Archaeological Site | 100 | | *Tarand*-grave |
| Uuri | 6 | Watery condition | Marsh | 30 | | |
| Viira | 6 | Solid ground | | 120 | | |
| Villevere | 6 | Solid ground | Archaeological Site | 30-40 | | Burial area |
| Kriimani | 6 | Solid ground | Archaeological Site | 10-30 | Heap of stones | Possible stone (*tarand*) grave |
| Varnja | 6 | Solid ground | | | Stone | Burial area? |
| Rikassaare | 7 | Watery condition | River | 20-40 | | |
| Igavere | 7 | Watery condition | Marsh | 15-20 | | |
| Hummuli | 8 | Watery condition | Marsh | 30-40 | | |
| Navesti | 8 | Watery condition | Marsh | 20 | | |
| Kunda_II | 8 | Watery condition | Bog | | | |
| Kaabe | 8 | Watery condition | River | 150 | | |
| Koorküla_Valgjärv | 9 | Watery condition | Spring | | | |
| Loosi | 9 | Watery condition | Marsh | | | |
| Paluküla | 9 | Watery condition | Marsh | 30-40 | Stone | |
| Kunda_I | 1-3; 6-7 | Watery condition | Bog | | | |
| Alulinn | 2-3; 6-7; 12/13 | Watery condition | Bog | 30-40 | | Hill-fort / enclosure |
| **Total: 28** | | | | | | |

*Table 6.1.3. Environments of concealment of Estonian wealth deposits.*

## 6.1.2. Problems and exclusions

Besides the Juminda and Kastna coin hoards three more deposits from Estonia are excluded from further analysis. First is a find of over 50 sickles/scythes, more than 20 spearheads, a couple of axes and some battle knives which lacks information about the finding place and environment (Tamla 1977, no. 51, 156; Tamla 1995, 103). The only available information so far is that all the artefacts were discovered together some time in the 19th century and the find used to belong to the collections of the Estonian Museum in Tallinn. In January 1928 it was handed over to the collections of the *Kabinet* of Archaeology at the University of Tartu from where it went to the collections of the Institute of History during the Soviet time (now affiliated with Tallinn University). Unfortunately the collection number from the first museum has been lost and it has become impossible to re-contextualise the find. According to the historical tradition the Estonian Museum in Tallinn used to collect archaeological finds from the northern part of the country and it has been assumed that the find was discovered in northern Estonia (pers. comm. Toomas Tamla). However, without certainty about the exact place of discovery and context, this deposit cannot be included in the current thesis.

Two other finds that cannot be included in the analysis are the finds from Aesoo, from the south-western part of Estonia. In the archive (Laid 1924, 138-139) it is mentioned that weapons and tools which according to the descriptions might belong to the Middle Iron Age were discovered at Aesoo village probably at the beginning of the 20th century. It is possible that two separate deposits were found, but they might also belong to a single deposit. As the finds have been lost it is not possible to specify the chronology of the artefacts and thus the deposit(s) cannot be considered in the current thesis.

There are two finds which are problematic in terms of estimating their date. Namely, in the case of the Metsküla and Kaali finds it has been argued that the artefacts themselves might actually belong to the Pre-Roman Iron Age (Schmiedehelm 1955, 163; Mägi 2003, 5; Lang 2007b, 247; Rzeszotarska-Nowakiewicz 2010). According to the finding context and other similar find assemblages in the region the deposits are still thought to belong to the Roman Iron Age (Jaanits *et al.* 1982, 221, 231; Lõugas 1996, 59-62; Tamla & Kiudsoo 2005, 16-17; Lang 2007a, 162; Lang 2007b, 76-77, 246-247). However, relying on the artefact chronology it is more likely that in the case of Metsküla we are looking at a deposit from the first centuries of the Roman Iron Age (Lang 2007b, 247; Rzeszotarska-Nowakiewicz 2010, 324, 329-330, plate IX: 14). Therefore this particular deposit has a possible time of concealment set for the 2nd century AD. In the case of the Kaali find we are dealing with an unique find and context of concealment. It is the earliest silver deposit in Estonia found in the enclosure site at the bank of Kaali meteor crater in Saaremaa Island. Although the find material from the enclosure has been mainly dated to the Late Bronze and Pre-Roman Iron Age, it also includes some finds from the Roman Iron Age (Lõugas 1996; Lang 2007b, 75-77). As no similar silver ornament deposits are thus far known from either Scandinavia or other Baltic countries and the first silver finds for instance in Lithuania are from the Roman Iron Age (Vaitkunskienė 1981), the Kaali deposit has been dated to the second half of the Roman Iron Age (3rd-5th century AD).

One of the Estonian finds, the Kavastu deposit, stands out for its content and dating. It is a deposit of a Roman bronze lamp and four bronze bars (two of them possibly fragments of a lamp-stand) that was found in the Kavastu bog during peat cutting. According to the artefact chronology the lamp belongs to the first centuries of the Roman Iron Age (ca 1-200 AD). It was made in the Mediterranean area of the Roman Empire. To control the correlation of artefact chronology and possible time of deposition an AMS dating of the lamp fuel residue was carried out at the Oxford Radiocarbon Laboratory. The results were remarkable – 1561±25 BP, 95.4% probability cal. 427-557 AD (OxA-27781). This indicates that the deposition of the artefact must have taken place some time after that date. As the calibration curve for this dating is very flat the time span is wide. It was decided to include the deposit in the group of Roman Iron Age finds of the first half of the 5th century on the basis of its general appearance, main production material, other Estonian Roman import finds and earliest possible dating. However, in principle it might also belong to the earliest decades of the Middle Iron Age.

### 6.1.3. General overview of analysed material

Most of the deposits represent only one material (for details see Table 6.1.1.). There are seven deposits where two materials (iron and bronze, or silver and bronze) are represented, and in two deposits three materials are evident. However, in most of these examples a clear domination of a single raw material of an artefact and the assemblage itself can be seen. The only exception is perhaps the find from Paluküla where the numbers of iron and bronze objects are nearly equal.

In terms of counting all the artefacts represented in wealth deposits the main material is iron, followed by bronze and silver (Fig. 6.1.3.1. (A)). The distribution alters when taking into account the predominant material within every single wealth deposit. Then silver clearly exceeds all the other materials (Fig. 6.1.3.1. (B)), followed by bronze and only then by iron. These are the only main materials represented in Estonian 1st-9th century AD wealth deposits.

The 28 Estonian wealth deposits contain 450 objects of various kinds. The most abundant artefact groups are weapons and ornaments which each form over 40% of the artefacts (Fig. 6.1.3.2. (A)). Tools as the third largest group form less than 10% of all items deposited. Raw materials are represented by four items all of which belong to the Kavastu find. The find group 'other' is quite numerous in Estonia. It is formed by a mixture of different artefacts that do not belong to the previously mentioned find groups. For instance, various vessels belong to this group: a Roman bronze lamp from Kavastu, Byzantine silver vessels from Varnja and Kriimani, as well as unidentifiable iron objects from Kunda I, Koorküla Valgjärv, Paluküla and Alulinn find (see the Catalogue for references and details). However, looking at the distribution according to the predominant artefact functional group within a deposit, the picture changes considerably (Fig. 6.1.3.2. (B)). Over half of the wealth deposits contain ornaments as the major artefact group, weapons are in majority in only quarter of the deposits and tools are never found as the main artefact group in the deposit.

The detailed overview of the artefact groups reveals that the most numerous type of artefact in Estonian 1st-9th century AD wealth deposits is the spearhead with 138 examples (Table 6.1.2.). Next are neck-rings with 77 items, and bracelets and brooches (both with 42 items). Only after those come axes with 29 and sickle/scythe with 28 objects. The other artefact groups are not often represented.

Turning towards the environment of concealment (see Fig. 6.1.3.3.) it is evident that water related contexts, open water, marshy areas and bogs, are most numerous. From 28 Estonian wealth deposits altogether 17 relate to watery context

*Fig. 6.1.3.1. Distribution of all artefact materials (A) and major materials (B) in Estonian wealth deposits.*

A

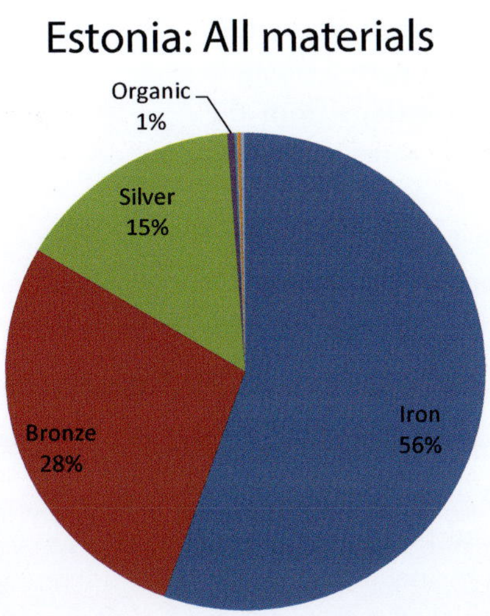


| | |
|---|---|
| Iron | 250 |
| Bronze | 126 |
| Silver | 69 |
| Organic | 2 |
| Bone | 1 |
| Gold | 1 |
| Stone | 1 |

B

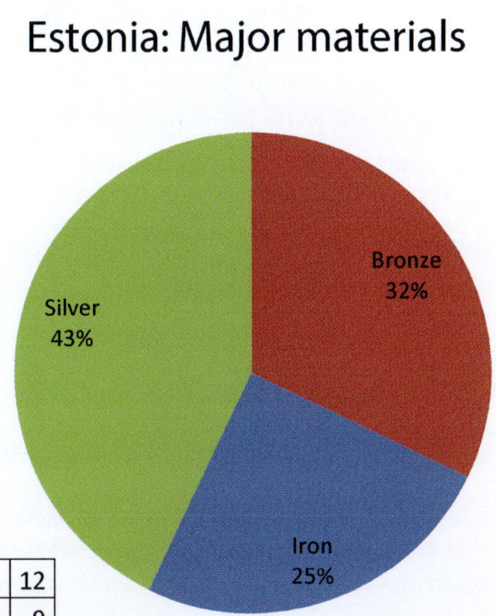


| | |
|---|---|
| Silver | 12 |
| Bronze | 9 |
| Iron | 7 |

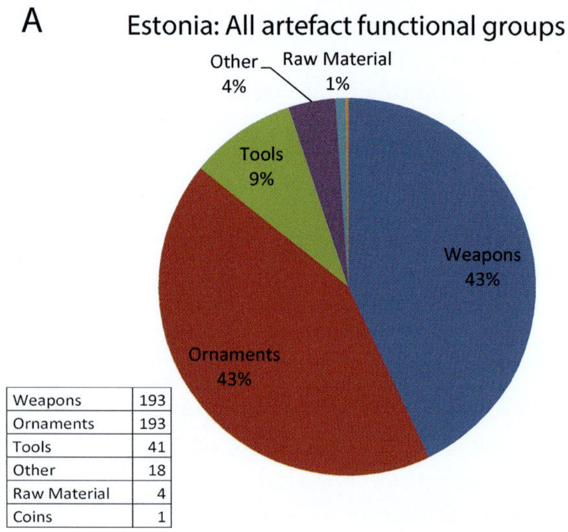


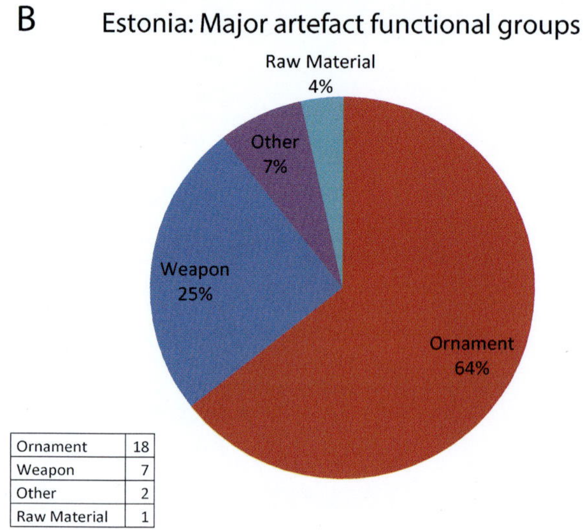


*Fig. 6.1.3.2. Distribution of all artefact functional groups (A) and major functional groups (B) in Estonian wealth deposits.*

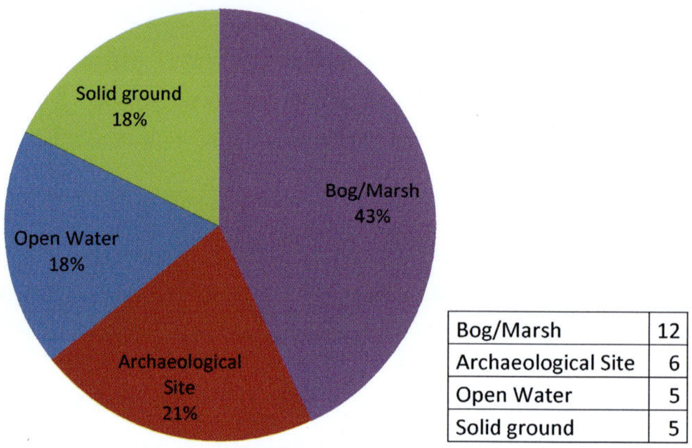


*Fig. 6.1.3.3. Environments of concealment of Estonian wealth deposits.*

(Table 6.1.3.), of which the most common are marshy areas and bogs (seven and five respectively). There are three finds relating to a river, one with a lake and one with a spring. Eleven deposits come from the dry land. However, six of these are actually not only from the dry land but related to a nearby archaeological site – mostly to a burial ground –, and two more if not three deposits have a possible connection with burial areas. Therefore the number of ordinary finds from the dry land without any relation to other archaeological sites is only three. However, the dominance over finds from dry land, including also archaeological sites, is not overwhelming. One important note is that in terms of non-watery conditions, there are more deposits from archaeological sites than from ordinary dry land.

A marker might be presumed in seven cases in all of which a stone or a cluster of stones have been mentioned. Of course, it is possible that organic markers were used. Such features will not be preserved and the slight traces of them might be unnoticed by non-archaeologists. There is a similar problem with the possible containers in which artefacts were hidden. In only two cases (Villevere and Paali II) has a possible container been mentioned (textile wrapping and birch bark vessel respectively). Remarks on artefact placement have seldom been included and are known in just four cases: in Rikassaare and Koorküla Valgjärv the spearheads were thrust into the ground (probably with a shaft), in Paluküla the artefacts were placed

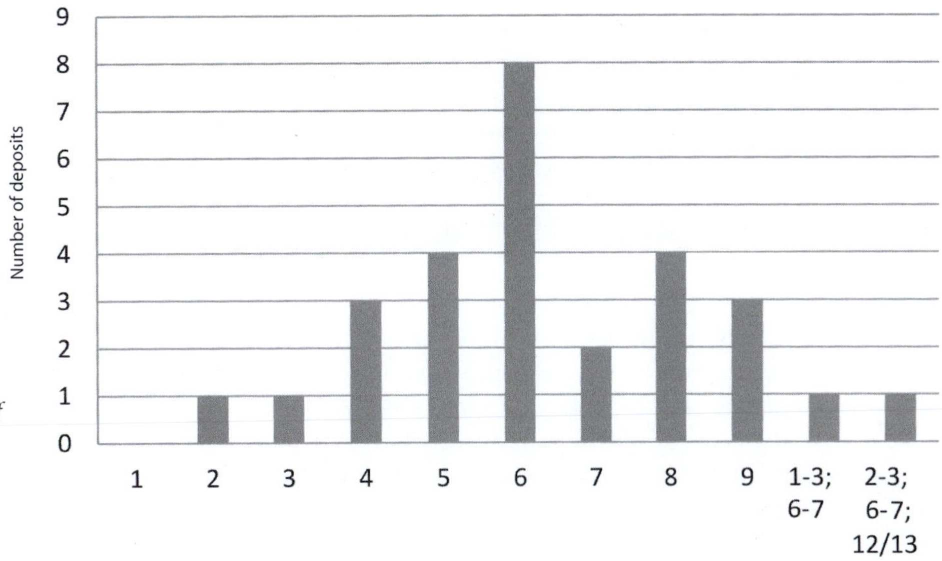


*Fig. 6.1.3.4. Chronological distribution (centuries AD) of Estonian wealth deposits.*

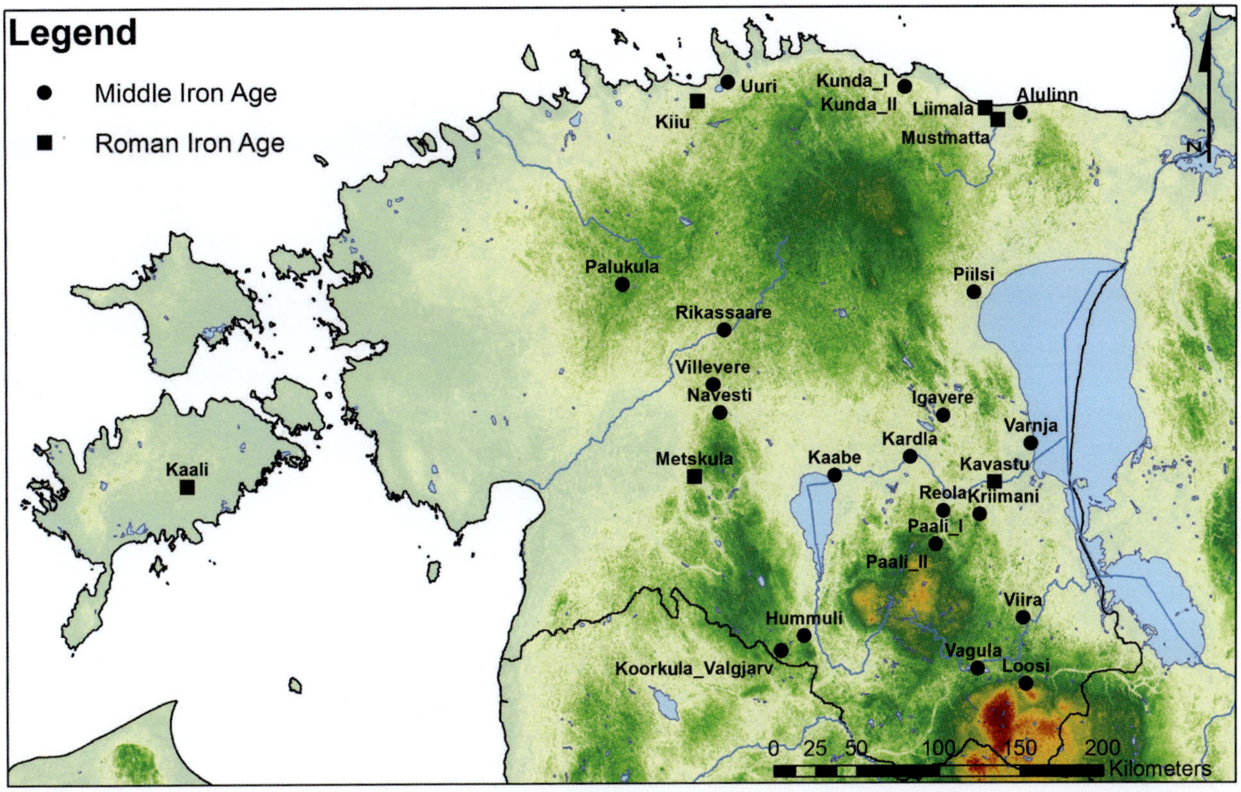


*Fig. 6.1.3.5. Map of Estonian wealth deposits.*

between three bent swords and in the Paali I deposit neck-rings were placed on top of each other, a brooch put in the middle of them. It remains unclear how much of such evidence has been noticed and recorded or has been just ignored by the finders.

Finally, the spatial and temporal distribution of Estonian 1st-9th century finds needs to be pointed out (Figs 6.1.3.4., 6.1.3.5.). There are no deposits from the first century of the Roman Iron Age and the first finds are from the 2nd century onwards. The Roman Iron Age (50-450 AD) is represented with altogether six deposits, the Middle Iron Age (450-800 AD) provides the major part of the overall material. A considerable peak can be seen in the 6th century, when altogether eight wealth deposits are concealed. The preceding and following centuries give examples of deposits in the range of two to four per century.

There are two quite interesting finds in terms of dating – Kunda I and Alulinn. The artefacts, in those finds cover a broad time span from the beginning of the Roman Iron Age. In the Kunda I deposit some finds have been dated to the first century of the 1st millennium AD, but the Alulinn deposit includes artefacts from the first centuries AD, from the middle of the millennium and also a spearhead that has been dated to the 12th/13th century AD. Traditionally both of these find assemblages have been discussed within an analysis of the Middle Iron Age material, because most of the artefacts belong to those centuries. According to descriptions of the discovery, the artefacts that form these deposits were found together at the same place or at least near to each other. Thus most likely in those two cases the same location has been used for depositional activities for a very long period.

The geographical distribution of Estonian wealth deposits (Fig. 6.1.3.5.) shows that the majority of the finds concentrate in the eastern part of the country. There are only a few deposits from the central part and almost none from the western half of the country, with the exception of Kaali in Saaremaa. As we will see later, the deposits in the western regions are also outliers in terms of their artefact composition. Most abundant are the finds from south-eastern part of the country and across the north-eastern and northern coastal areas. This indicates that there are concentration areas even within such a small region as Estonia and that the practice of wealth depositing is current in some parts of the country and not in others. The possible reasons for this will be discussed in the second half of this and in the final chapter.

### 6.1.4. Selection of artefacts

The first clear indication of deliberate choice of deposited objects is the simple choice of production material (Fig. 6.1.4.1.). The following is based on the predominant and second largest quantity of artefact production material. In most cases the predominant material remains the only material represented in a deposit (see blue bars and crosstabulation (crosstab) tables without column heading in Fig. 6.1.4.1.). The majority of Estonian wealth deposits are dominated by either bronze or silver artefacts. The combinations of materials are quite significant. Bronze objects are associated only with bone or iron artefacts (one example for a combination). If silver is the main material, no iron objects have been discovered as the second major artefact group. Silver is combined with either bronze or gold artefacts. Where iron is the main material, only bronze items can be associated with it.

Looking at the correspondence analysis (CA) graph which takes into account all the materials represented in every wealth deposit and the exact numbers of artefacts made of each material, some material based clusters are evident (Fig. 6.1.4.2.). With the Axis 1 and 2 representing 45.5% and 35.9% of the inertia we can see that there exists a clear separation between silver and gold objects from iron deposits. The third larger group is formed of deposits that mainly include bronze objects, but also occasionally some stone, bone or other organic artefacts. Two deposits (Paali II and Paluküla) stand out from the overall patterns, because they include either similar numbers of silver and bronze or iron and bronze objects. However, there is a consistent choice of materials that are deposited together which can be followed in the three main groups of deposits: precious metal, mainly bronze and mainly iron object deposits. Precious metal is

| | | Second Material | | | | | |
|---|---|---|---|---|---|---|---|
| | | None | Bone | Bronze | Gold | Iron | Total |
| Major Material | Bronze | 7 | 1 | 0 | 0 | 1 | 9 |
| | Iron | 5 | 0 | 2 | 0 | 0 | 7 |
| | Silver | 7 | 0 | 4 | 1 | 0 | 12 |
| | **Total** | **19** | **1** | **6** | **1** | **1** | **28** |

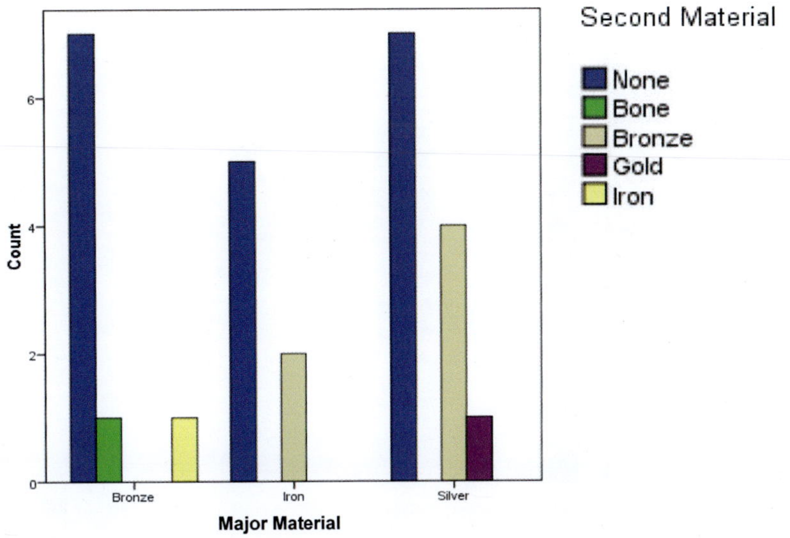


*Fig. 6.1.4.1. Crosstabulation and bar charts of combinations of main production materials represented in Estonian wealth deposits.*

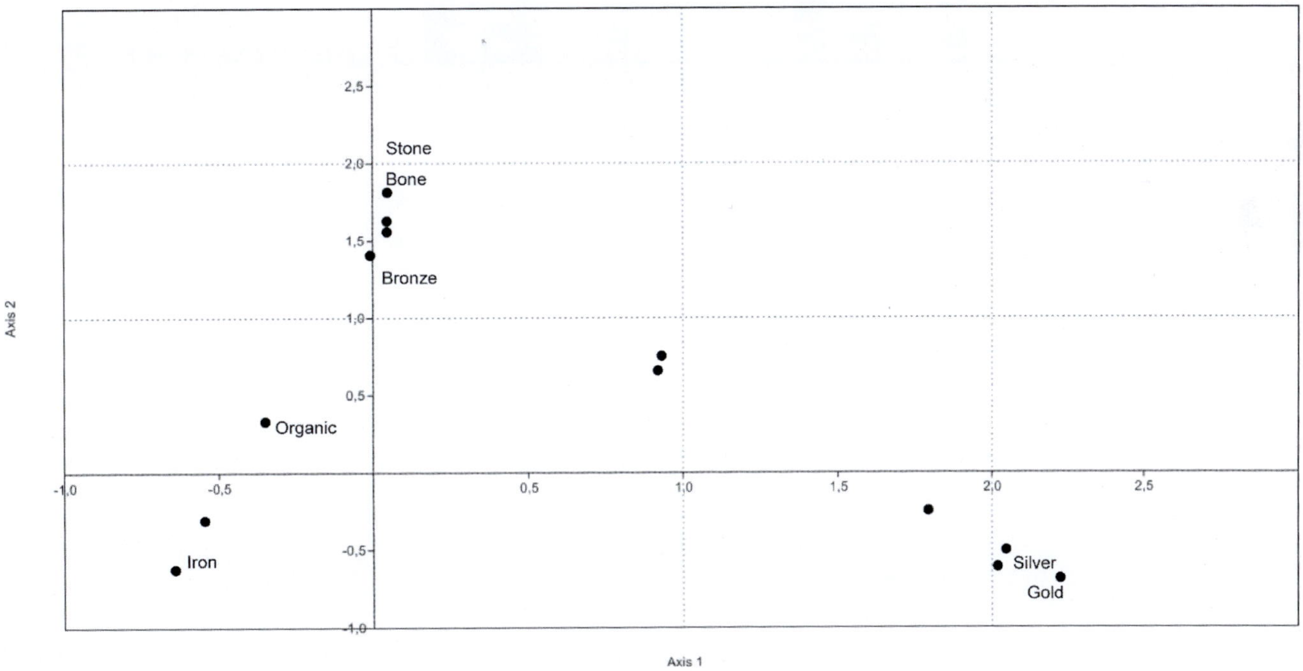


*Fig. 6.1.4.2. Correspondence analysis of combinations of all materials represented in Estonian wealth deposits according to the number of represented artefacts.*

never found with iron objects. When one material is in majority then the deposits contain very few other materials at all.

Analysing the functional groups of artefacts deliberate choices become even more evident (Fig. 6.1.4.3.). There are altogether 19 deposits which include only one artefact group. The most numerous are ornament deposits, which form over half of the total number of deposits. Only occasionally can we find that ornament

| | | Second Artefact Group | | | | |
|---|---|---|---|---|---|---|
| | | – | O | Oth | T | Total |
| Major Artefact Group | O | 15 | 0 | 2 | 1 | 18 |
| | Oth | 2 | 0 | 0 | 0 | 2 |
| | R | 0 | 0 | 1 | 0 | 1 |
| | W | 2 | 1 | 0 | 4 | 7 |
| | **Total** | **19** | **1** | **3** | **5** | **28** |

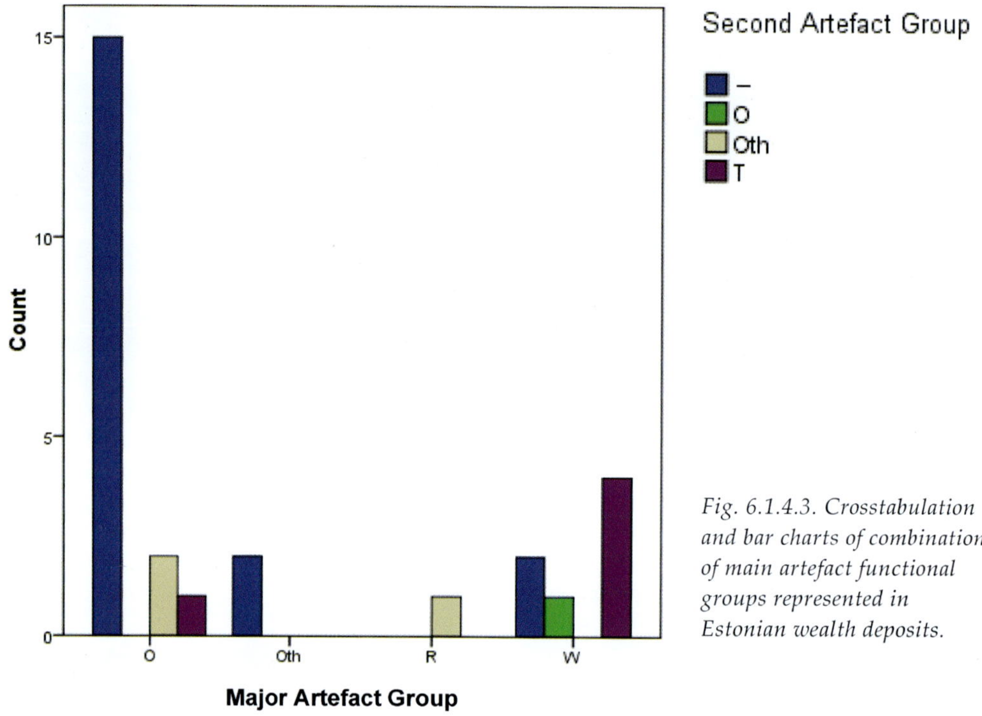


O – Ornaments, Oth – Other, R – Raw Material, W – Weapons, T – Tools.

*Fig. 6.1.4.3. Crosstabulation and bar charts of combinations of main artefact functional groups represented in Estonian wealth deposits.*

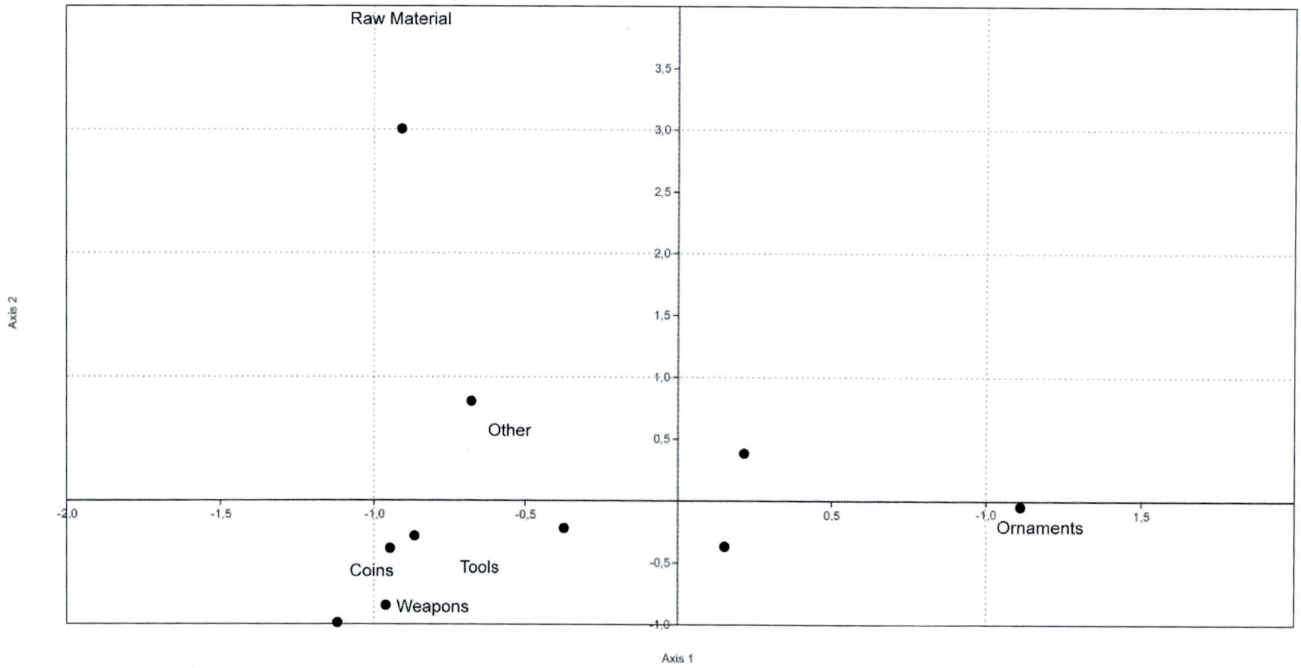


*Fig. 6.1.4.4. Correspondence analysis of combinations of all artefact functional groups represented in Estonian wealth deposits.*

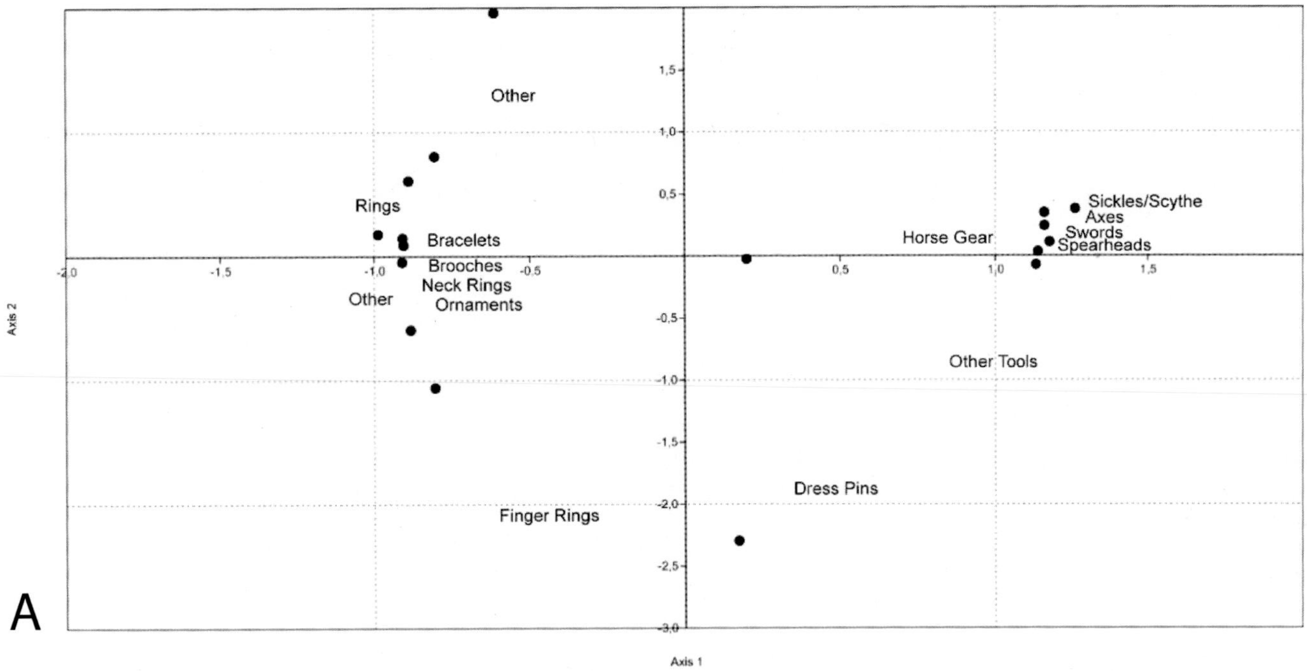


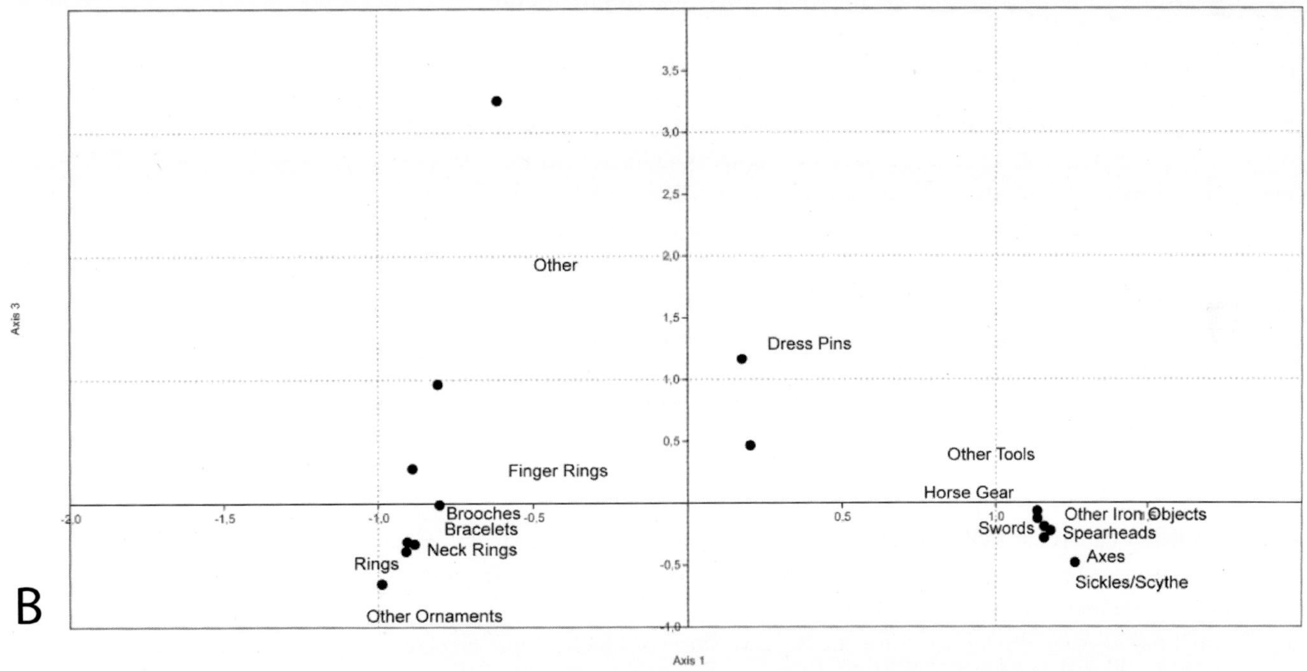


*Fig. 6.1.4.5. Correspondence analysis of combinations of artefact types represented in Estonian wealth deposits. A – Axes 1 and 2; B – Axes 1 and 3.*

deposits include either a single tool (Kunda II) or the functional group 'other'. The group of finds containing 'other' includes two silver vessel deposits (Kriimani and Varnja). There are only two deposits that contain solely weapons. In most cases weapons are discovered with tools and there is only one example where ornaments are found in the deposit where weapons are in majority. This is the unique Paluküla deposit.

Correspondence analysis (CA) based on the representation of artefact groups found in every deposit also indicates clear choice of which functional groups belong together and which not (Fig. 6.1.4.4.). With the Axis 1 and 2 representing 39.3% and 28.4% of the inertia respectively, it can be still seen that ornaments form their own group of deposits. Weapons are most often found with tools, but in a single case (Koorküla Valgjärv) also with coins. Distinct groups are deposits of 'other' and raw material: the first are again formed by single silver vessels mentioned above, the latter by a unique deposit of bronze bars and a Roman bronze lamp from Kavastu.

Finally specific artefact types within wealth deposits are analysed. This indicates which exact artefact types have been combined in single deposits. The CA based on the selections and criteria set by Shennan (1997, 327-341) that takes into account only those deposits that include more than one artefact type and only those artefact types that are represented in more than one deposit indicates more detailed selections of artefacts within a deposit. A graph with the Axis 1, 2 and 3 representing 32.9%, 16.3% and 14.6% of the inertia respectively still separates clearly deposits with various ornaments and clothing related objects and the ones relating to warrior equipment *e.g.* swords, spearheads, axes, accompanied by sickles and scythes as most numerous tool types and also unidentifiable iron objects (see Fig. 6.1.4.5.). It is, however, noticeable, that dress pins do not seem to belong together with other ornaments in either of the axis combinations.

## 6.1.5. Selection of environment

Around 60% of Estonian finds have been discovered in water related conditions such as bogs, marshy areas and open water sources. The remaining 40% of material is distributed evenly between either ordinary dry land or archaeological sites (see Fig. 6.1.3.3.). More specific selections within different environments of concealment become evident when combining them with the artefacts.

There are three groups of predominant materials. Their distribution between different environments is generally speaking quite equal (Fig. 6.1.5.1.). However, a closer look shows that silver objects are only found in either archaeological sites or dry land and iron artefacts are only discovered in watery conditions. Taking into account the second major material in the deposit, the distribution between environments remains by and large the same (Fig. 6.1.5.2.) and it seems that the main material dictates the environment of concealment. Looking at the multiple correspondence analysis (MCA) plot of distribution of main material and environment of concealment, some visible patterns in the choice of environment according to the material of objects emerge (Fig. 6.1.5.3.).

It can be seen that distinctions are made according to which major artefact groups are concealed: ornaments and find group 'other' (two silver vessels) are in a clear majority in the dry land, weapons and raw material deposits are found in watery conditions only, although ornament finds have also been discovered in the latter (Fig. 6.1.5.4.). The more detailed divisions between environments (Fig. 6.1.5.5.) seem to overlap with the broader categorisation of environment. However, it can be seen, that if ornaments are in watery conditions, they tend to be more often deposited in boggy and marshy areas than in open water. The same also applies to the deposit of raw materials in watery conditions, *e.g.* Kavastu. Finds of weapons as the major artefact group are quite evenly distributed among

| | | Major Material | | | |
|---|---|---|---|---|---|
| | | Bronze | Iron | Silver | Total |
| Environment Subcategory | Archaeological Site | 0 | 0 | 6 | 6 |
| | Bog/Marsh | 4 | 4 | 4 | 12 |
| | Open Water | 2 | 3 | 0 | 5 |
| | Solid Ground | 3 | 0 | 2 | 5 |
| **Total** | | **9** | **7** | **12** | **28** |

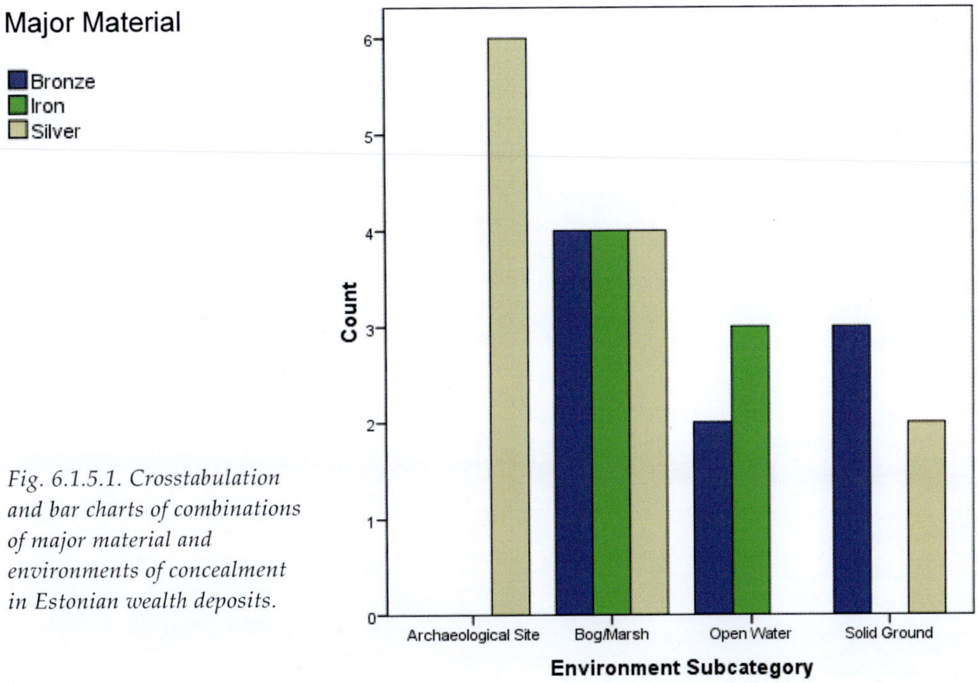


*Fig. 6.1.5.1. Crosstabulation and bar charts of combinations of major material and environments of concealment in Estonian wealth deposits.*

*Fig. 6.1.5.2. Crosstabulation of combinations of major and second material and environments of concealment in Estonian wealth deposits.*

open water and bog areas. Similar patterns remain the same when taking into account the second major find groups (Fig. 6.1.5.6.). The only addition is that weapons accompanied with tools are only found in bogs, whereas weapons-only deposits are in slight majority in open water environments.

| Major Material | | | Environment Subcategory | | | | Total |
|---|---|---|---|---|---|---|---|
| | | | Archaeological Site | Bog/Marsh | Open Water | Solid Ground | |
| Bronze | Second Material | | 0 | 3 | 1 | 3 | 7 |
| | | Bone | 0 | 1 | 0 | 0 | 1 |
| | | Iron | 0 | 0 | 1 | 0 | 1 |
| | Total | | 0 | 4 | 2 | 3 | 9 |
| Iron | Second Material | | 0 | 3 | 2 | 0 | 5 |
| | | Bronze | 0 | 1 | 1 | 0 | 2 |
| | Total | | 0 | 4 | 3 | 0 | 7 |
| Silver | Second Material | | 2 | 3 | 0 | 2 | 7 |
| | | Bronze | 3 | 1 | 0 | 0 | 4 |
| | | Gold | 1 | 0 | 0 | 0 | 1 |
| | Total | | 6 | 4 | 0 | 2 | 12 |

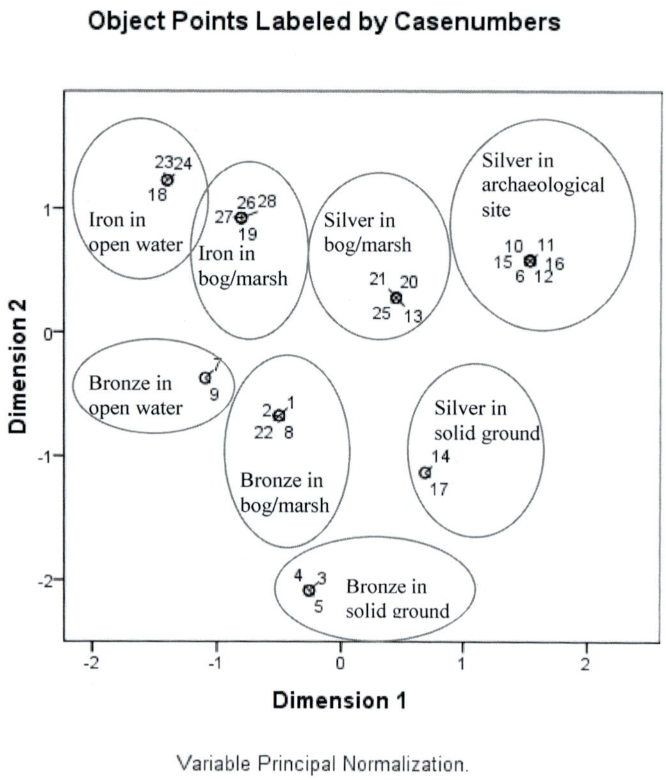


| |
|---|
| 1-Metsküla |
| 2-Kavastu |
| 3-Kiiu |
| 4-Liimala |
| 5-Mustmätta |
| 6-Kaali |
| 7-Piilsi |
| 8-Reola |
| 9-Vagula |
| 10-Kardla |
| 11-Paali_I |
| 12-Paali_II |
| 13-Uuri |
| 14-Viira |
| 15-Villevere |
| 16-Kriimani |
| 17-Varnja |
| 18-Rikassaare |
| 19-Igavere |
| 20-Hummuli |
| 21-Navesti |
| 22-Kunda_II |
| 23-Kaabe |
| 24-Koorküla_Valgjärv |
| 25-Loosi |
| 26-Paluküla |
| 27-Kunda_I |
| 28-Alulinn |

*Fig. 6.1.5.3. MCA plot of combinations of major material and detailed environments of concealment in Estonian wealth deposits.*

| | | Major Artefact Group | | | | |
|---|---|---|---|---|---|---|
| | | O | Oth | R | W | Total |
| Environment | Solid ground | 9 | 2 | 0 | 0 | 11 |
| | Watery condition | 9 | 0 | 1 | 7 | 17 |
| **Total** | | **18** | **2** | **1** | **7** | **28** |

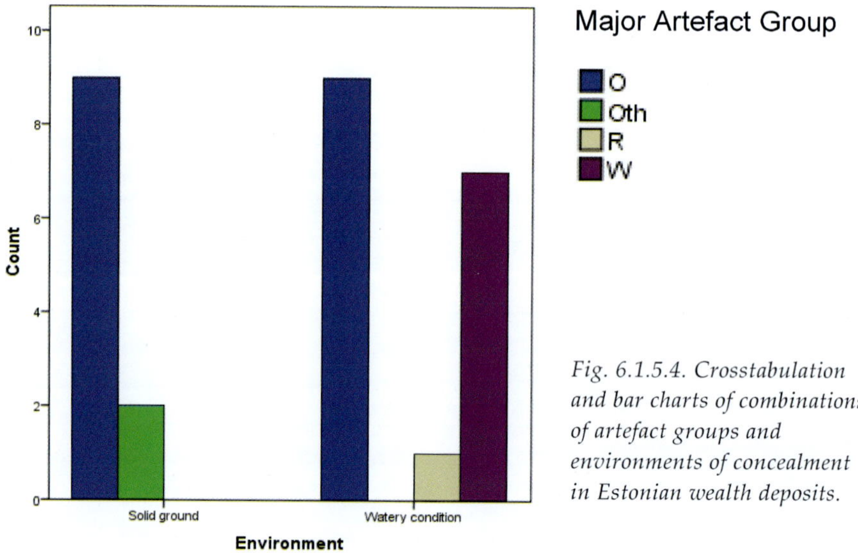


*Fig. 6.1.5.4. Crosstabulation and bar charts of combinations of artefact groups and environments of concealment in Estonian wealth deposits.*

O – Ornaments, Oth – Other, R – Raw Material, W – Weapons.

| | | Major Artefact Group | | | | Total |
|---|---|---|---|---|---|---|
| | | O | Oth | R | W | |
| Environment Subcategory | Archaeological Site | 5 | 1 | 0 | 0 | 6 |
| | Bog/Marsh | 7 | 0 | 1 | 4 | 12 |
| | Open Water | 2 | 0 | 0 | 3 | 5 |
| | Solid Ground | 4 | 1 | 0 | 0 | 5 |
| **Total** | | **18** | **2** | **1** | **7** | **28** |

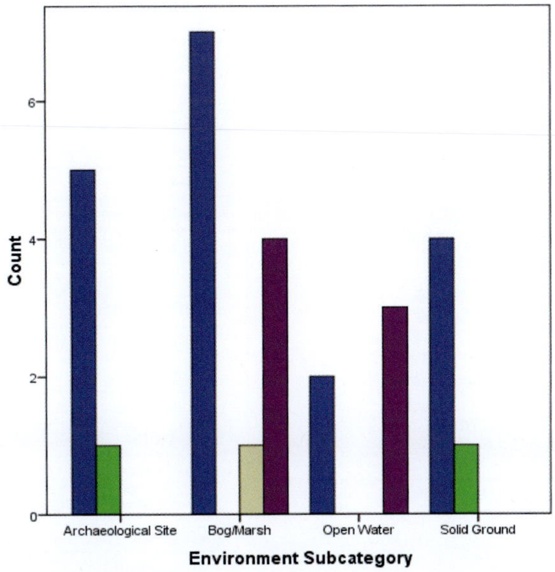


*Fig. 6.1.5.5. Crosstabulation and bar charts of combinations of artefact groups and detailed environments of concealment in Estonian wealth deposits.*

O – Ornaments, Oth – Other, R – Raw Material, W – Weapons.

| | | Major Artefact Groups | | | | | Total |
|---|---|---|---|---|---|---|---|
| | | O | Oth | R+Oth | W | W+T | |
| Environment Subcategory | Archaeological Site | 5 | 1 | 0 | 0 | 0 | 6 |
| | Bog/Marsh | 7 | 0 | 1 | 1 | 3 | 12 |
| | Open Water | 2 | 0 | 0 | 3 | 0 | 5 |
| | Solid Ground | 4 | 1 | 0 | 0 | 0 | 5 |
| **Total** | | **18** | **2** | **1** | **4** | **3** | **28** |

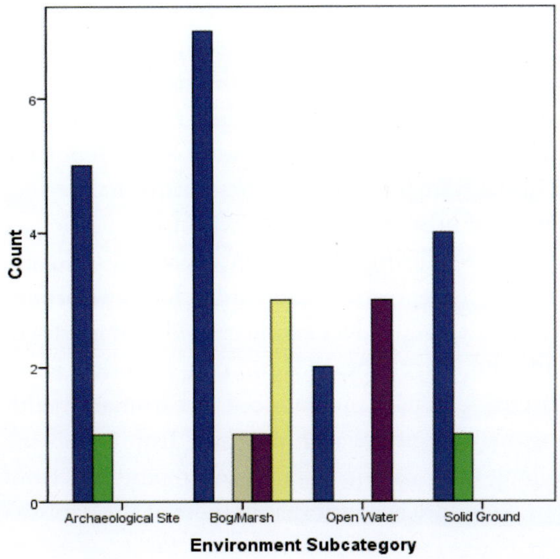


*Fig. 6.1.5.6. Crosstabulation and bar charts of combinations of major and second artefact group and detailed environments of concealment in Estonian wealth deposits.*

O – Ornaments, Oth – Other, R – Raw Material, W – Weapons, T – Tools.

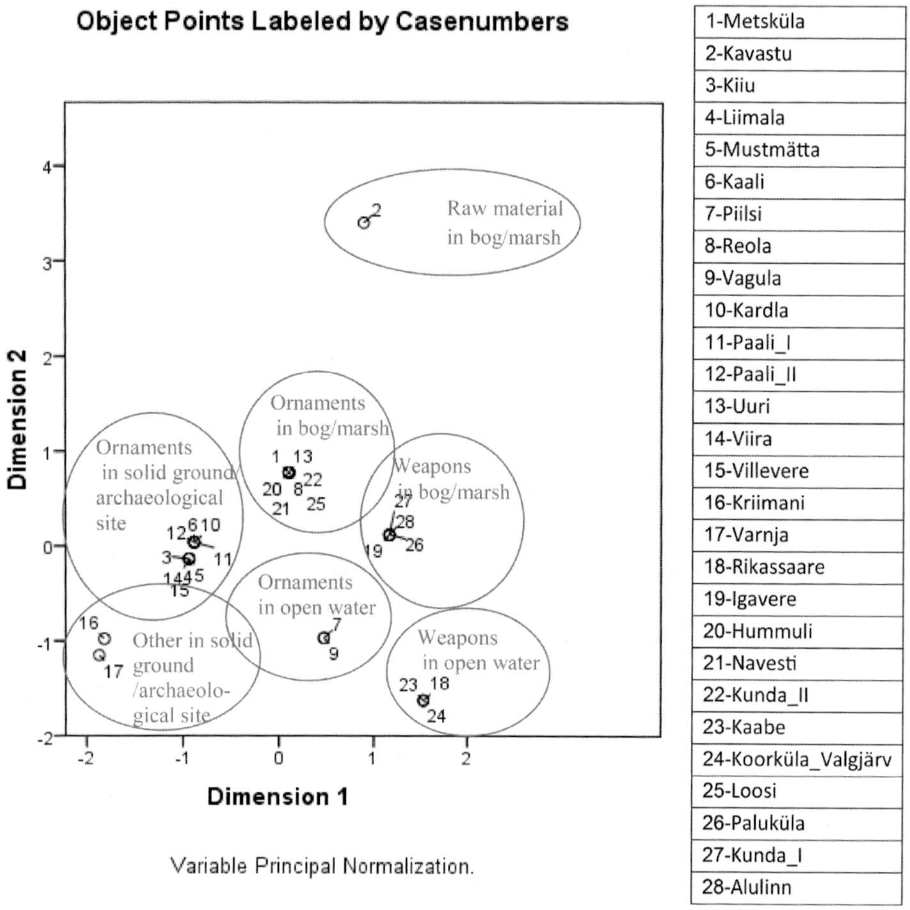


*Fig. 6.1.5.7. MCA plot of combinations of major artefact groups and detailed environments of concealment in Estonian wealth deposits.*

Some preliminary clusters and patterns emerge when putting the information on major artefact groups and subcategories of environments of concealment into a MCA plot (Fig. 6.1.5.7.). Although few in numbers, these show the patterns in the selection of artefact groups and environments of concealment.

## 6.1.6. Chronological distribution

Adding a time dimension some more patterns become evident. Looking at the deposited materials in terms of numbers of objects in a time scale (Fig. 6.1.6.1.) there is a clear difference between the deposited materials in the Roman Iron Age (50-450 AD) and Middle Iron Age (450-800 AD). During the first period, clear dominance is given to bronze objects, only in the unique case of Kaali deposit is silver the main material of deposit in the Roman Iron Age. The transitional period, the 5th century, shows a continuation of bronze dominance with only a few iron and bone objects added. A change happens during the 6th century when suddenly silver becomes the main material in wealth deposits, accompanied by some bronze and by just single iron and gold items. Although silver can be traced in deposits in some of the following centuries, it is no longer the predominant material. From the 7th century onwards a new material – iron – is introduced in Estonian wealth deposits. In the 7th century iron is the only material in deposits. Iron is also the single material represented in two long-term use sites which cover centuries from both Roman and Middle Iron Age. Taking into account that in most of the deposits a clear dominance of a single material exists and analysing the deposits according to most common materials, the temporal distributions overlap with the detailed graph (compare Fig. 6.1.6.1. A and B). However, the more general graph helps to show that although large in quantity, the 7th century iron deposits consist of just two separate deposits. The deposits in the 8th century on the contrary include fewer items, but the number of deposits is larger than during the previous century. The peak of silver deposits remains in the 6th century. From the 6th century onwards the deposits can be divided into two larger groups – iron deposits with larger amount of objects and silver deposits with small amount of items. There is only one artefact deposit which contains mainly bronze items from this period.

A

Estonia: Temporal distribution of all deposited materials

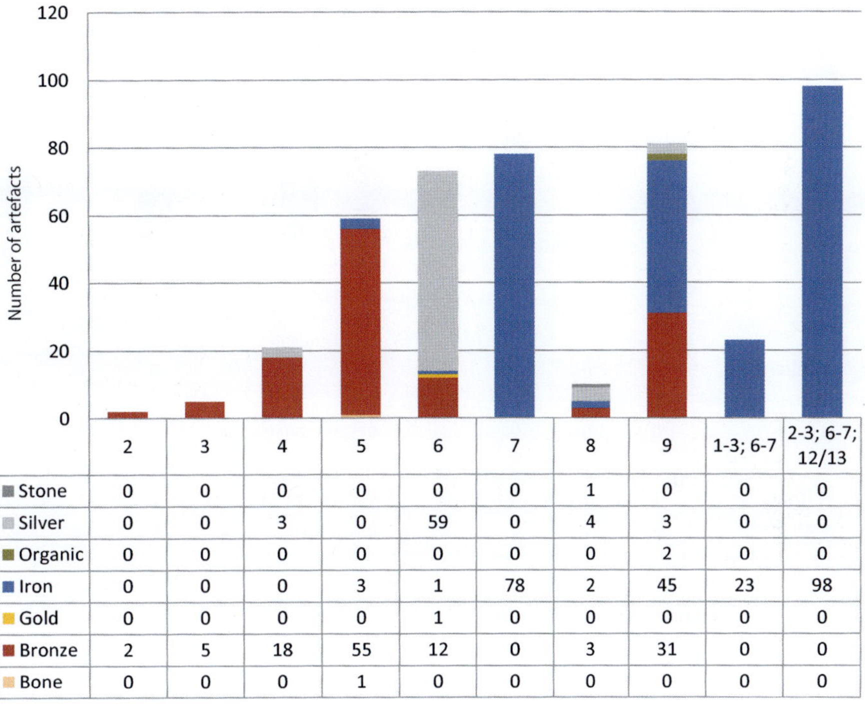


| | 2 | 3 | 4 | 5 | 6 | 7 | 8 | 9 | 1-3; 6-7 | 2-3; 6-7; 12/13 |
|---|---|---|---|---|---|---|---|---|---|---|
| Stone | 0 | 0 | 0 | 0 | 0 | 0 | 1 | 0 | 0 | 0 |
| Silver | 0 | 0 | 3 | 0 | 59 | 0 | 4 | 3 | 0 | 0 |
| Organic | 0 | 0 | 0 | 0 | 0 | 0 | 0 | 2 | 0 | 0 |
| Iron | 0 | 0 | 0 | 3 | 1 | 78 | 2 | 45 | 23 | 98 |
| Gold | 0 | 0 | 0 | 0 | 1 | 0 | 0 | 0 | 0 | 0 |
| Bronze | 2 | 5 | 18 | 55 | 12 | 0 | 3 | 31 | 0 | 0 |
| Bone | 0 | 0 | 0 | 1 | 0 | 0 | 0 | 0 | 0 | 0 |

B

Estonia: Temporal distribution of major deposited materials

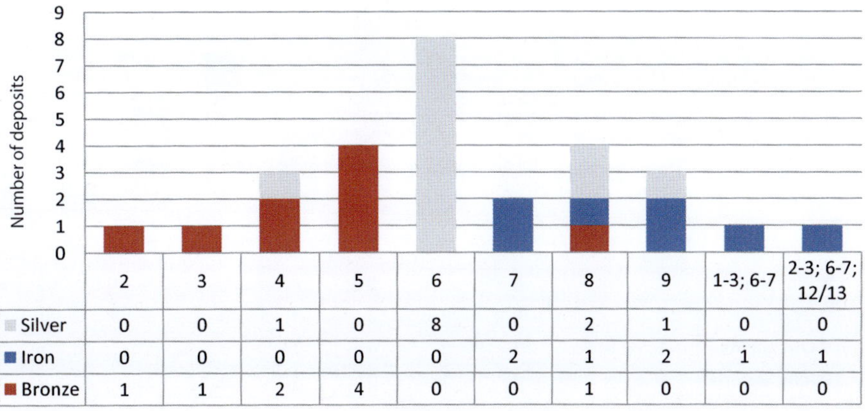


| | 2 | 3 | 4 | 5 | 6 | 7 | 8 | 9 | 1-3; 6-7 | 2-3; 6-7; 12/13 |
|---|---|---|---|---|---|---|---|---|---|---|
| Silver | 0 | 0 | 1 | 0 | 8 | 0 | 2 | 1 | 0 | 0 |
| Iron | 0 | 0 | 0 | 0 | 0 | 2 | 1 | 2 | 1 | 1 |
| Bronze | 1 | 1 | 2 | 4 | 0 | 0 | 1 | 0 | 0 | 0 |

*Fig. 6.1.6.1. Temporal distribution (centuries AD) of all artefact materials (A) and major materials (B) in Estonian wealth deposits.*

Turning towards objects' functional groups and their distribution throughout 1st-9th century AD (Fig. 6.1.6.2.) there is a considerable overlap with the material based distribution (compare Figs 6.1.6.1. and 6.1.6.2.). The distributions of artefact groups and detailed content according to deposits are represented in Figs 6.1.6.3. and 6.1.6.4. These graphs provide a good general overview for identifying patterns in artefact distributions on a temporal scale.

During the Roman Iron Age a majority of deposited artefacts are ornaments, with the exception of the Kavastu deposit which includes raw material and a find group of 'other' indicating a bronze lamp. The same tradition of ornament deposits continues up to the 7th century and includes also the previously mentioned sudden increase of deposited silver ornaments in the 6th century. This peak also contains two silver vessel deposits categorised under the group 'other'. As seen in the analysis of materials, obvious change happens in the 7th century,

A

Estonia: Temporal distribution of all artefact groups

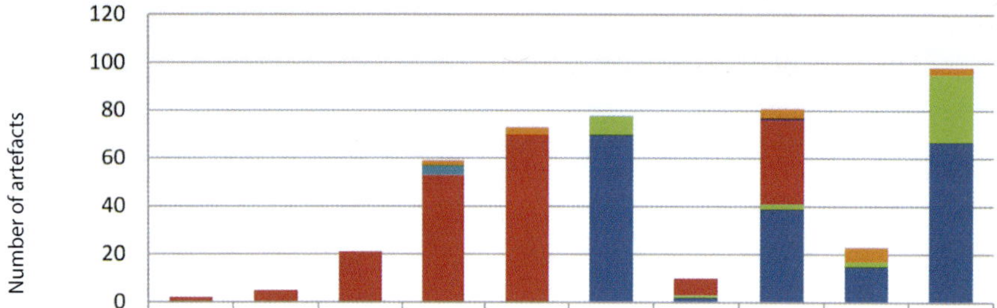


| | 2 | 3 | 4 | 5 | 6 | 7 | 8 | 9 | 1-3; 6-7 | 2-3; 6-7; 12/13 |
|---|---|---|---|---|---|---|---|---|---|---|
| Other | 0 | 0 | 0 | 2 | 3 | 0 | 0 | 4 | 6 | 3 |
| Raw_Material | 0 | 0 | 0 | 4 | 0 | 0 | 0 | 0 | 0 | 0 |
| Coins | 0 | 0 | 0 | 0 | 0 | 0 | 0 | 1 | 0 | 0 |
| Ornaments | 2 | 5 | 21 | 53 | 70 | 0 | 7 | 35 | 0 | 0 |
| Tools | 0 | 0 | 0 | 0 | 0 | 8 | 1 | 2 | 2 | 28 |
| Weapons | 0 | 0 | 0 | 0 | 0 | 70 | 2 | 39 | 15 | 67 |

B

Estonia: Temporal distribution of major artefact groups

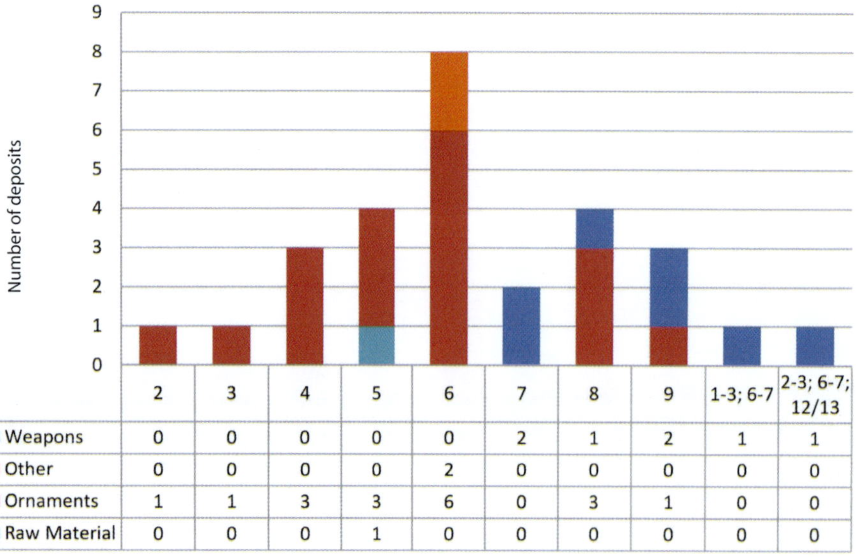


| | 2 | 3 | 4 | 5 | 6 | 7 | 8 | 9 | 1-3; 6-7 | 2-3; 6-7; 12/13 |
|---|---|---|---|---|---|---|---|---|---|---|
| Weapons | 0 | 0 | 0 | 0 | 0 | 2 | 1 | 2 | 1 | 1 |
| Other | 0 | 0 | 0 | 0 | 2 | 0 | 0 | 0 | 0 | 0 |
| Ornaments | 1 | 1 | 3 | 3 | 6 | 0 | 3 | 1 | 0 | 0 |
| Raw Material | 0 | 0 | 0 | 1 | 0 | 0 | 0 | 0 | 0 | 0 |

*Fig. 6.1.6.2. Temporal distribution (centuries AD) of all artefact groups (A) and major groups (B) in Estonian wealth deposits.*

when weapons become the most numerous items in the deposits. They continue to be represented until the end of the Middle Iron Age. The total number of weapon deposits per century remains around one or two and in most of the cases tools are the second major object category in those deposits. The 8th and also 9th century give examples of different artefact deposits, although the total number of deposited artefact in the 8th century remains very small. Sites with a long use period containing iron objects are mostly comprised of weapons and tools.

The main conclusion is that in the 7th century there is a clear shift from ornament dominance, be it bronze or silver, to weapon deposits which often include other iron items. The long-term deposits do not contain ornaments at all. In the centuries where weapons-tools combinations are evident, the quantity of ornaments deposited at the same time is very small. Looking at the detailed artefact descriptions they invariably consist of up to three silver neck-rings, in one case also a set of bronze ornaments including dress pins, a ring and a strike-a-light stone. Therefore the 7th century is an important divider between the two different traditions of ornament deposits: abundant and combined ornament assemblages before, and very few similar types of ornaments after this century.

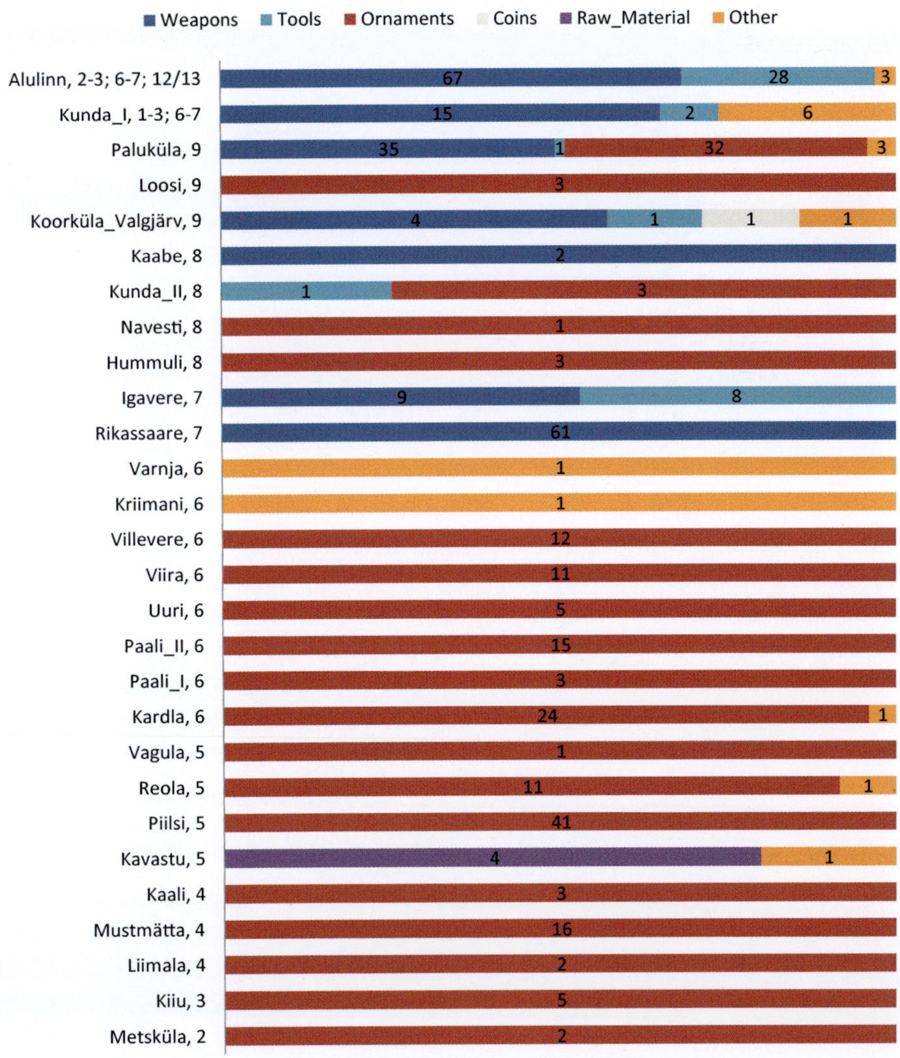


*Fig. 6.1.6.3. Temporal distribution (centuries AD) of artefact groups according to deposits in Estonian wealth deposits. The number in deposit name indicates century.*

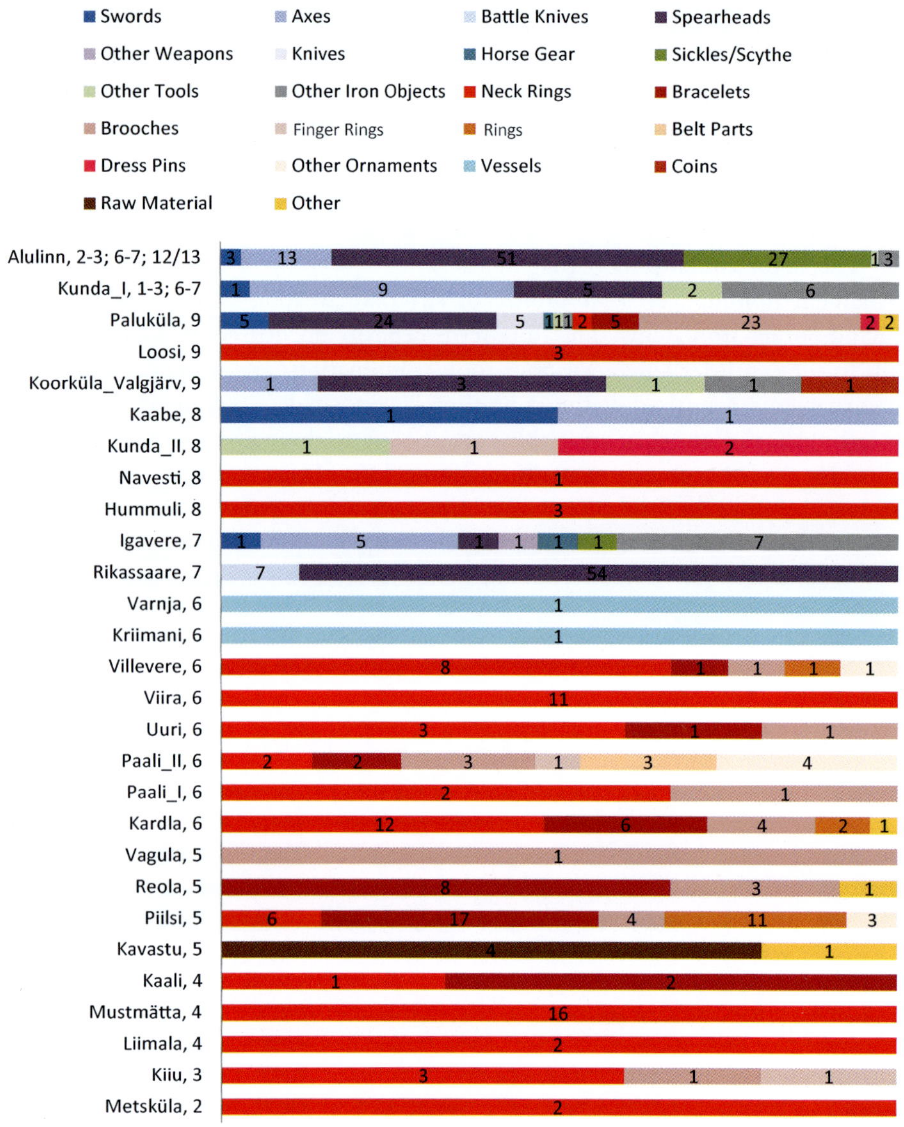


*Fig. 6.1.6.4. Temporal distribution (centuries AD) of artefact types according to deposits in Estonian wealth deposits. The number in deposit name indicates century.*

The chronological distribution of the environment of concealment adds to this (Fig. 6.1.6.5.). Although at first sight there seems to be no clear temporal distinction between the environments throughout the centuries, it can be concluded that dry land contexts are more prevalent in the Roman Iron Age. Watery conditions are popular in the 5th century, but they become more frequent from the 7th century onwards. The first two deposits in the Roman Iron Age come from watery conditions, but the deposits from the second half of the period are from dry land/archaeological site context. The peak century, the 6th century contains mainly deposits from dry land and archaeological sites, where the detailed overview indicates a relationship with contemporary or earlier burial areas. The long time period deposits are both discovered in bogs.

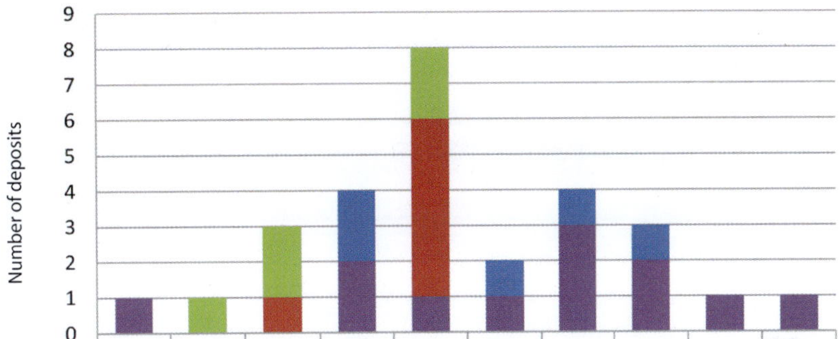


| | 2 | 3 | 4 | 5 | 6 | 7 | 8 | 9 | 1-3; 6-7 | 2-3; 6-7; 12/13 |
|---|---|---|---|---|---|---|---|---|---|---|
| Solid Ground | 0 | 1 | 2 | 0 | 2 | 0 | 0 | 0 | 0 | 0 |
| Open Water | 0 | 0 | 0 | 2 | 0 | 1 | 1 | 1 | 0 | 0 |
| Archaeological Site | 0 | 0 | 1 | 0 | 5 | 0 | 0 | 0 | 0 | 0 |
| Bog/Marsh | 1 | 0 | 0 | 2 | 1 | 1 | 3 | 2 | 1 | 1 |

*Fig. 6.1.6.5. Temporal distribution (centuries AD) of environments of concealment in Estonian wealth deposits.*

## 6.2. Practices of wealth depositing in Estonia: Long-term perspective and the question of change

The following discussion of practices of wealth depositing in Estonia in a long-term perspective is based on the previous charts, tables and paragraphs. For the sake of fluent discussion repetitive cross-references to them are omitted from the text, but references should be made to Figures 6.1. and relevant catalogue pages for supporting data.

Comparison of the combinations of major artefact groups, environment of concealment, and chronology according to century in the MCA analysis plot show the major patterns of practices of wealth depositing (see Fig. 6.2.1.). In most cases it is possible to add more precise chronology of the deposits. This plot also identifies some of the outliers and unique cases (e.g. nos 1-Metsküla, 22-Kunda II). However, as the criteria are set according to the main artefact group and material, environment as well as century based chronology, the plot has included some of the items in various clusters that according to the detailed analysis do not entirely fit there (e.g. nos 6-Kaali and 26-Paluküla). This provides an indication of possible problems inherent in statistical analysis and data categorisations. The exact details of such outlying finds will be discussed below, taking into account the results of statistical analysis as well as detailed contextual characteristics of each deposit. The mapping results of different contextual criteria of Estonian 1st-9th century wealth deposits are represented in Figs 6.2.2.-6.2.4.

There are altogether six deposits which are dated to the Roman Iron Age: **Metsküla, Kiiu, Liimala, Mustmätta, Kaali, Kavastu**. The first conclusion is that Roman Iron Age depositional practices are clearly clustered around ornament deposits. Most of the deposits contain only bronze items the majority of which are neck-rings, including some very massive examples. There seems to be a slight dominance of dry land environments, with the addition of one archaeological site, the Kaali silver ornament deposit. The latter also stands out from other contemporaneous finds because it is the earliest silver wealth deposit in the country.

There are two Roman Iron Age exceptions that stand out from the others. The first is a deposit of four bronze bars and a Roman bronze lamp from **Kavastu**. Although different in terms of environment of concealment and deposited items

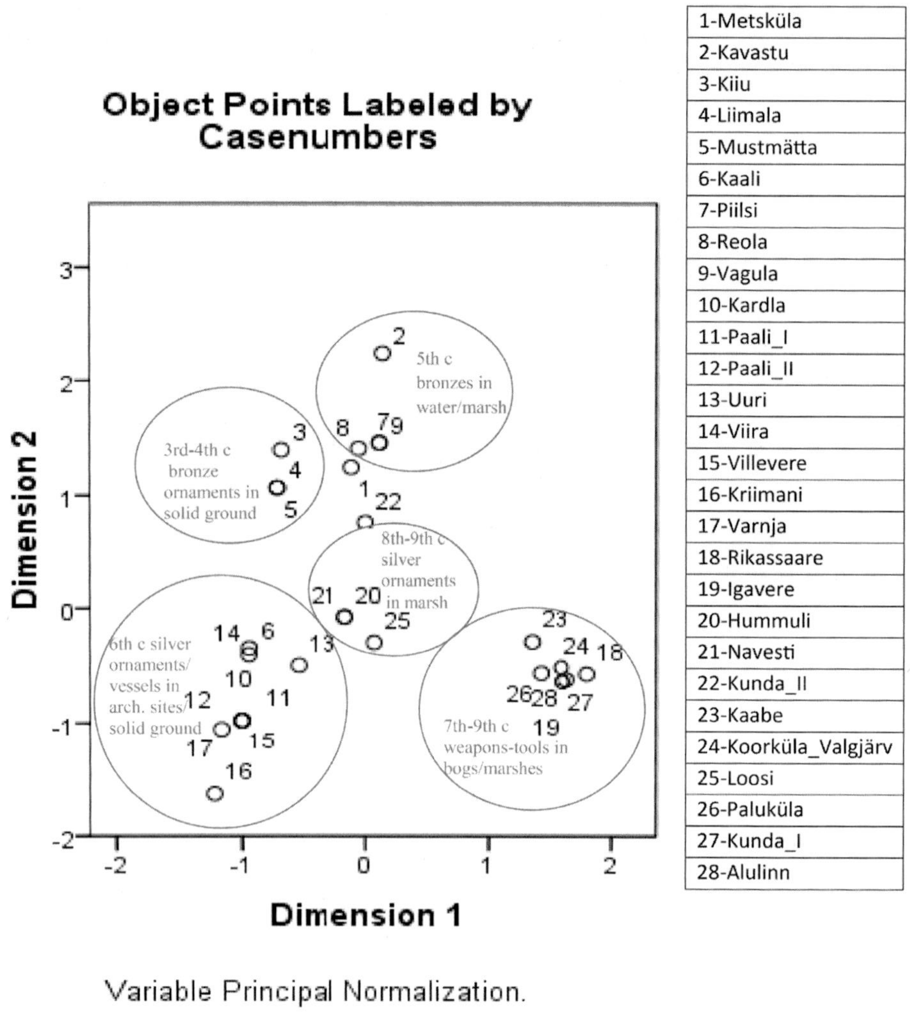


*Fig. 6.2.1. MCA plot of combinations of major artefact groups, materials, detailed environments of concealment and dating of Estonian wealth deposits.*

(bog as opposed to dry land in most Roman Iron Age deposits), in terms of material it still falls into the same category with other Roman Iron Age deposits. The second unique find is the earliest bronze neck-ring deposit from **Metsküla**. Unlike all the other bronze ornament deposits, this was possibly deposited in a watery environment.

Both the Kavastu and the Metsküla deposits include imported objects: a unique Roman bronze lamp and a massive crown-like neck-ring from the south, possibly Prussia in northern Poland, respectively. They stand out in terms of environment of concealment but for their bronze content they follow the same pattern in terms of deposited materials and/or artefact types. However, if Metsküla is the earliest example of a Roman Iron Age deposit in Estonia, then Kavastu belongs to one of the last deposits of the period according to the AMS dating of the lamp fuel residue which covers a time span of 427-557AD (OxA-27781). Thus the deposit might instead be dated to the first century of the Middle Iron Age. Metsküla might be related to possible previous depositional traditions in the Pre-Roman Iron Age and Bronze Age. However, this remains tentative, because as mentioned in Chapters 1 and 2 there is only one known wealth deposit from the preceding periods: a scrap bronze hoard from Tehumardi found at the coast of Saaremaa Island, dated to the first half of the 1st millennium BC. Kavastu, however, seems

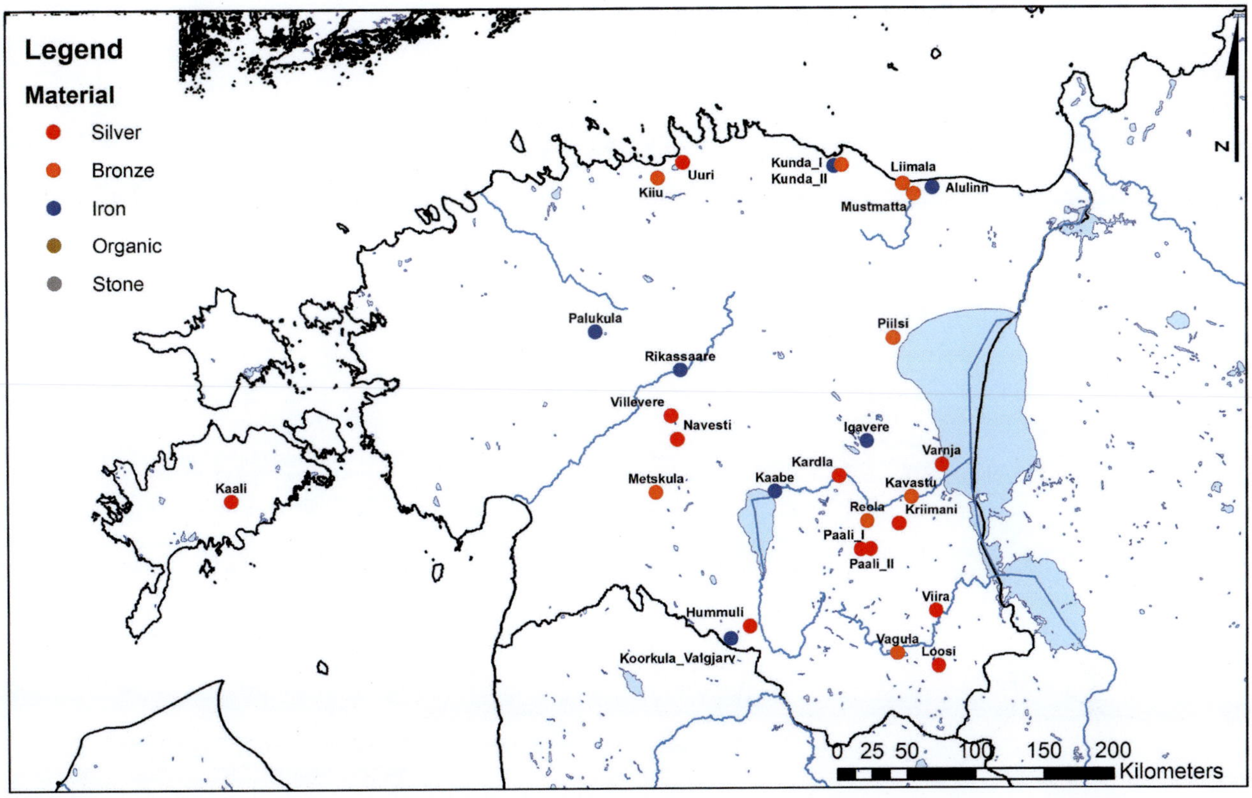


*Fig. 6.2.2. Map of major materials represented in Estonian wealth deposits.*

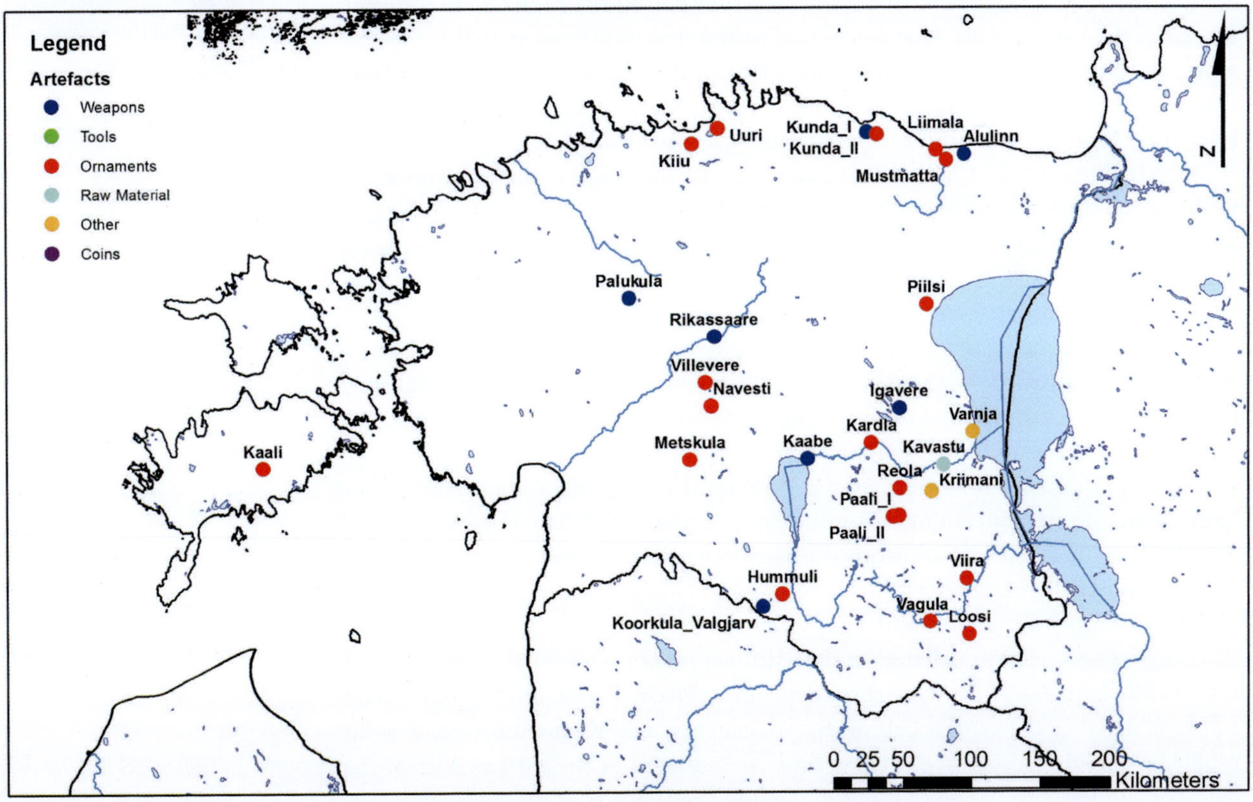


*Fig. 6.2.3. Map of major artefact groups represented in Estonian wealth deposits.*

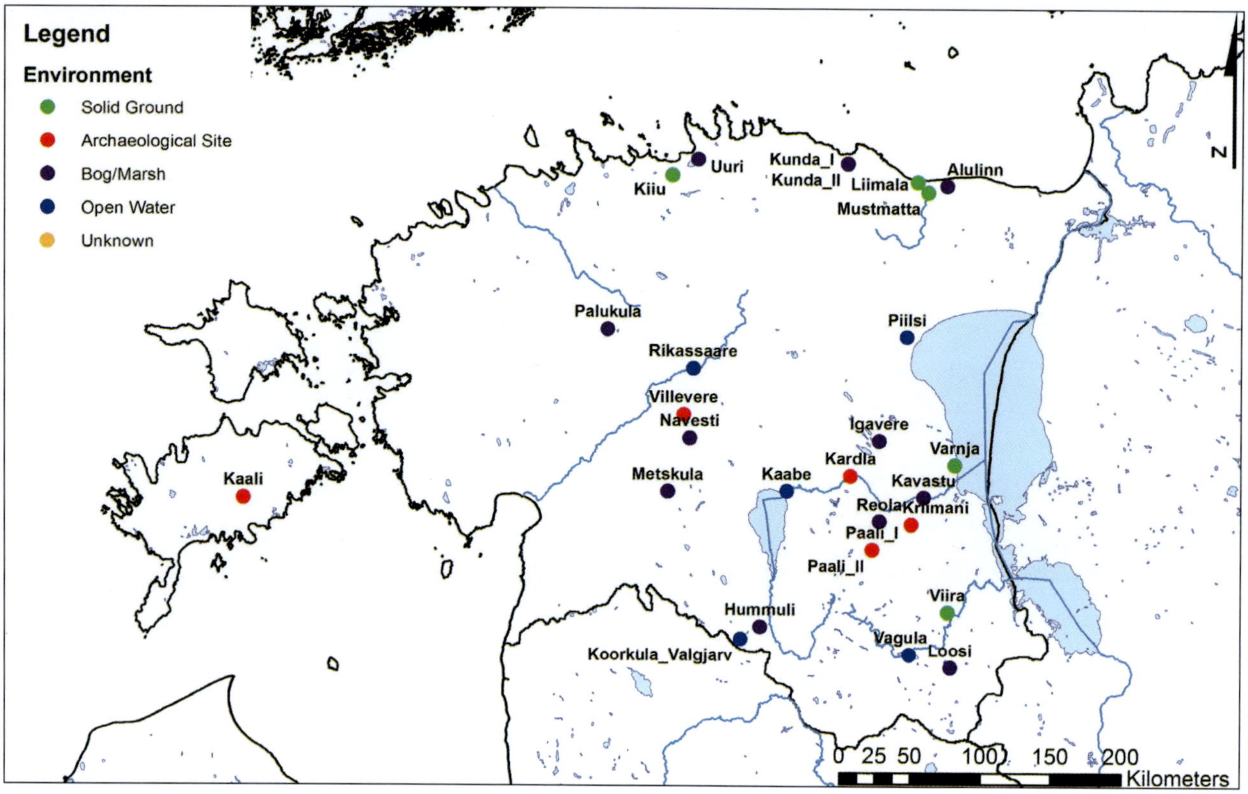


*Fig. 6.2.4. Map of environments of concealment of Estonian wealth deposits.*

to form a link between Roman Iron Age deposits of bronzes and the earliest Middle Iron Age bronze deposits: if in the earlier period the bronzes are found in dry land, then in the later they are related to watery conditions as is also the case with the Kavastu deposit. Therefore these two finds are regarded as outliers from the general Roman Iron Age depositional pattern. At the same time they are still important links with the earlier and later depositional traditions.

In this context it is also worth emphasising that although small in number, the tradition of bronze/ornament deposits in the Roman Iron Age shows consistent and traditional depositional practices. There are no clear peaks or significant changes within the 400-years period: bronzes, mainly ornaments, are the main artefacts within almost every deposit throughout the Roman Iron Age.

Partly related to this time period are the two coastal sites of **Kunda I** and **Alulinn**. The artefacts in these deposits, which have a long-term accumulation process, contain examples of both weapons and tools from the Roman Iron Age, although the majority of the weapons date from the following period.

In geographical terms most of the Roman Iron Age deposits relate to the larger water routes, including coastal areas (see Fig. 6.1.3.5.). The majority of Roman Iron Age deposits are from the northern coast of the country. Only the two previously discussed exceptional finds – Kavastu and Metsküla – are located in the southern part of the country.

There is no significant change in depositional practices in the first centuries of the Middle Iron Age. There are three deposits – **Piilsi, Reola** and **Vagula** – with artefacts dated to the second half of the 5th century. The **Kavastu** bronze deposit might be added to this list. All those finds are situated in the eastern part of the country. Similarly to the preceding time period they consist of bronze ornaments.

However, now the content of the finds is more variable: the rings of all kinds are most frequent, but neck-rings are now in a minority and the deposits include more bracelets and brooches, also bronze vessel rims. All these deposits come from watery conditions, either bogs or open water sources. Unfortunately due to the lack of detailed environmental knowledge about the exact find-spot, it remains an open question whether they were deposited in the open water or flooded area or marshy land, in the vicinity of the water source. Despite that these three earliest Middle Iron Age deposits form an important link with the previous Roman Iron Age depositional traditions in terms of content and material.

A considerable change happens in the 6th century. There is a remarkable increase in the number of deposits providing us with altogether eight finds – **Kardla, Paali I & II, Uuri, Viira, Villevere, Kriimani, Varnja**. This is almost the same number of deposits as the total from previous centuries. Now for the first time the main material of deposits is silver. Similarly to 5th century bronze deposits, the majority of artefacts are ornaments, although neck-rings are the most numerous items. An interesting addition to those ornament deposits are two silver vessel deposits from Kriimani and Varnja. Most of those eight deposits were hidden in a non-watery environment and in altogether five instances (Kardla, Paali I & II, Villevere, Kriimani) they are found either within or in the close vicinity of contemporary or earlier burial grounds. The only exception is Uuri at the northern coast of Estonia which most likely was hidden in a marshy area. The analysis of detailed characteristics of the finds shows that all the objects, whether ornaments or silver vessels, are imports: the ornaments are of southern origin i.e. Baltic-types, the vessels are made in Byzantine Empire. Seven out of eight finds are located in the central-southern part of Estonia related to larger water routes.

Another significant change takes place in the 7th century and this new concept of depositing continues until the end of the Middle Iron Age. First, the total number of deposits per century decreases considerably compared to the previous century. A new type of deposit assemblage – weapons and/or tools – emerge. In the 7th century all finds are of weapon deposits, namely **Igavere** and **Rikassaare**. Deposits of weapons occur also in the 8th and 9th century, **Kaabe**, **Koorküla Valgjärv** and **Paluküla** respectively. However, the latter two also contain some other artefact groups and are examples of more unusual assemblages within a single deposit (see below). In relation to weapon and tool deposits it is also necessary to point out the two long time period deposits of **Kunda I** and **Alulinn**. These both include tools and weapons from the Roman and Middle Iron Age, but the main chronology of the weapons is around the 6th-7th century AD. Considering the chronology of these deposits it seems highly likely that they belong to the 7th century and therefore are contemporary with the other 7th century weapons-only deposits. The homogeneity of a tradition of weapons-tools deposits is confirmed by their similar environment of concealment: all iron deposits have been discovered in watery conditions, either in or in the close vicinity of open water sources or in bogs/marshes. Two or three finds of iron items with insufficient data about the context of discovery and/or exact items concealed – Aesoo I and II, Põhja-Eesti (North-Estonia) (see Appendix 1.1. for details) – fit into the same pattern neatly.

In relation to weapon deposits the slightly unusual character of the **Koorküla Valgjärv** deposit needs to be explained. It contains mostly weapons, but also a coin, pair of shears and other iron objects were recorded. Unfortunately the latter are now lost and their exact relationship to the 9th century weapon deposit remains unclear. The spring was also used in ritual activities in the historic periods (Tvauri 2012, 249) and some of its non-weaponry content might be later. It is likely with regard to the Middle Iron Age objects that this find falls into the weapons-only category found in open water (in a spring) forming a homogeneous group with other weapon deposits in the 7th and 8th century.

The 7th-9th century weapons-tools deposits seem to be the only practice which is distributed across most of the area where deposits have been found (Fig. 6.2.3.). In the 7th-8th century weapons-tools finds are situated in either the north-eastern coastal or central part of Estonia. Only the Koorküla Valgjärv deposit from the 9th century comes from the southern part of the country.

There is one clear outlier in the 9th century material, the **Paluküla** find. The find was discovered in marshy area. Unlike all the deposits discussed above it includes a mixture of different artefact functional groups and materials. It contains a similar quantity of weapons and ornaments as well as bronze and iron objects. The Paluküla deposit also stands out for its geographical location: it is the westernmost deposit in mainland Estonia about 50 km away from the closest Middle Iron Age deposit. No silver items are known from this find and several items show signs of burning and fragmentation. These details may help to decode this unique find: it looks as if some items have gone through burial rituals, the objects have been collected, mixed and concealed for their material value. The area where objects were found is rich in iron fragments which might indicate a possible smithy site. Therefore it has been interpreted as a deposit of scrap metal, perhaps a grave robbery, meant to be raw material for new objects (Tvauri 2012, 223).

In the last half of the Middle Iron Age another interesting depositional practice emerges. There are four deposits from the 8th and 9th century that mainly include small numbers of ornaments: **Hummuli, Navesti, Loosi, Kunda II**. The first three include 1-3 silver neck-rings and are all located in the south-eastern part of the country. The Kunda II deposit is different because it contains bronze items, dress pins, a ring and a strike-a-light stone, and it is located in the coastal area of north-eastern Estonia, not far from the Kunda I weapons-tools deposit. The Kunda II find is also an outlier because all the items in this deposit are very rare in the overall depositional material. All these four ornament finds are from marshy areas relating to watery conditions that also prevail in the weapons-tools deposits in the same centuries. Therefore it might be likely that although different in terms of artefact groups, they follow the same pattern of preference for watery conditions as suitable environments for depositing in the last half of the Middle Iron Age. Although to some extent a link might be made with the 6th century silver deposits in burial areas, a difference in artefact types (neck-rings only vs. ornament assemblages) and numbers of ornaments (up to three vs. mostly around 10 or more) can be seen. Therefore it confirms the idea that there is a considerable change in the traditions of ornament deposits from the 7th century onwards.

In conclusion, it can be seen that there are several significant differences in the practices of wealth depositing in a long term perspective. The Roman Iron Age is dominated by bronze deposits with around 2-3 finds per century. The earliest deposit is a unique import item found in a water related environment in the southern part of the country. During the second half of the Roman Iron Age mainly bronze objects, dominated by neck-rings, are found in dry land and those finds concentrate around the northern coast of the country. In the 5th century we see the continuation of the tradition of previous period deposits. However, the variability of deposited objects increases and all of them are now hidden in water-related contexts in the eastern part of the country. The first large-scale, but also a very short-term change in depositional practices takes place in the 6th century when we see the sudden emergence of imported silver ornaments or vessels deposits in solid ground, the majority of them relating to burial areas. The number of such deposits is several times greater than the number of deposits in previous and following centuries. This new tradition vanishes with the 7th century, when suddenly weapons and tools occur as the major material of depositions and watery conditions become the only acceptable environment of concealment. This continues until the end of the Middle Iron Age, providing a couple of examples in each century. Most of those iron artefact deposits are found in the northern coastal area or central part of the country, but there is also a single and slightly later find of this kind from the southern border of Estonia. At the same time as the later weapon and tool deposits there is a new tradition of depositing up to three silver neck-rings in southern-central Estonia in the 8th-9th century. There are only two long-period deposits. These are weapons-tools deposits in bogs in the north-eastern coastal region containing objects from both Roman and Middle Iron Age. Although not large in numbers, their geographical proximity as well as chronological and artefactual similarities seem to indicate a specific regional depositional tradition which is not found in any other part of the country.

*Chapter 7*

# Practices of wealth depositing in Latvia

## 7.1. 1st-9th century AD wealth deposits in Latvia

There are altogether 40 wealth deposits from the 1st-9th century AD in Latvia. Twelve are Roman coin hoards of which eight are uncertain. There is also a find that includes Arabic coins from the end of the 8th century (Uņģeni), but which was probably hidden in the 9th-10th century. This leaves us with 27 wealth deposits from Latvia. Two of them lack information about the exact find-spot and thus the total number of analysable material from Latvia is 25. The main characteristics of Latvian wealth deposits are given in Tables 7.1.1.-7.1.3.

### 7.1.1. Roman and other coins

There are altogether approximately 500 Roman coins from the 1st-4th century AD from 42 find places in Latvia (Kropotkin 1961, 101-103; Apals *et al.* 2001, 213, fig. 156). Besides hoards, coins have also been found in burial places and settlements and the majority of them are from the 2nd-4th century AD (Apals *et al.* 2001, 213, fig. 156; Ducmane & Ozoliņa 2009, 40). Although the coins have been found all over Latvia, the most numerous finds are from the south-western and central part of the country and seem to relate to larger water routes (Apals *et al.* 2001, 214).

| Wealth Deposit | Dating of artefacts (AD) | Dating (century) | Weapons | Tools | Ornaments | Raw Material | Other | Material 1 | Material 2 | Material 3 |
|---|---|---|---|---|---|---|---|---|---|---|
| Alsungas | 300-425 | 4 | | | 1 | | | Bronze | | |
| Cibēni | 400-450 | 5 | 4 | 4 | 1 | | 1 | Iron | Stone | Bronze |
| Piltene | 400-500 | 5 | | | 1 | | | Silver | Gold | |
| Kokmuiža_I | 450-525 | 5 | 986 | 75 | 30 | 16 | 173 | Iron | Bronze | Stone |
| Kokmuiža_II | 450-525 | 5 | 42 | 33 | 36 | | 26 | Iron | Bronze | Bone |
| Ķente_I | 475-525 | 6 | | 4 | | | | Stone | Iron | |
| Mūkukalns_III | 475-525 | 6 | 7 | 7 | | | | Iron | | |
| Rūsiši | 475-525 | 6 | 7 | 9 | 15 | | 4 | Iron | Bronze | |
| Miškiņeva | 400-600 | 6 | | | 4 | | | Silver | | |
| Kalnamuiža | 400-600 | 6 | 74 | 4 | 9 | | | Iron | | |
| Lejaslepji | 400-600 | 6 | | | 7 | | | Silver | | |
| Vecmokas | 500-600 | 6 | 36 | 13 | 7 | | | Iron | Bronze | Stone |
| Lejasļūdi | 600-650 | 7 | | | 1 | | | Silver | | |
| Ķišukalns | 500-700 | 7 | | | 1 | | | Silver | | |
| Podži | 500-700 | 7 | | | 1 | | | Silver | | |
| Dumpji | 675-725 | 8 | | | 3 | | | Silver | | |
| Mūrnieki | 675-725 | 8 | | | 2 | | | Silver | | |
| Saulītes | 675-725 | 8 | | | 3 | | 1 | Silver | Organic | |
| Baltinava | 600-800 | 8 | | | 5 | | | Silver | | |
| Ķente_II | 700-800 | 8 | | | 2 | 3 | | Bronze | | |
| Mūkukalns_II | 775-825 | 9 | | | 1 | | | Bronze | | |
| Mežotne | 800-825 | 9 | | | 7 | | | Bronze | | |
| Tīras_purvs | 800-850 | 9 | 3 | 1 | 10 | | 85 | Organic | Iron | Bronze |
| Sauleskalns_I | 800-900 | 9 | | | 4 | | | Silver | Bronze | |
| Sauleskalns_II | 800-900 | 9 | 20 | | | | | Iron | | |
| **Total: 25** | | | **1179** | **150** | **151** | **19** | **290** | | | |

*Table 7.1.1. Chronology, artefact functional groups, and materials represented in Latvian wealth deposits.*

| Wealth Deposit | Dating (c.) | Swords | Axes | Battle Knives | Spear-heads | Arrow-heads | Other Weapons | Knives | Horse Gear | Sickles/ Scythe | Other Tools | Other Iron Objects | Neck -rings | Bracelets | Brooches | Finger-rings | Rings | Belt Parts | Dress Pins | Beads | Other Ornaments | Vessels | Raw Material | Other | Comments on 'other' |
|---|---|---|---|---|---|---|---|---|---|---|---|---|---|---|---|---|---|---|---|---|---|---|---|---|---|
| Alsungas | 4 | | | | | | | | | | | | 1 | | | | | | | | | | | | |
| Cibēni | 5 | | 1 | | 2 | | | 1 | 1 | 1 | 2 | | | | | | 1 | | | | | 1 | | | |
| Piltene | 5 | | | | | | | | | | | | 1 | | | | | | | | | | | | |
| Kokmuiža_I | 5 | 9 | 185 | | 792 | | | 3 | | 1 | 71 | 169 | 1 | 15 | 9 | 2 | 2 | | | | 1 | 4 | 16 | | |
| Kokmuiža_II | 5 | | 1 | | 41 | | | 9 | | | 24 | 6 | 1 | 1 | | | 2 | 28 | | 4 | | 1 | | 19 | Bone fragments & items |
| Ķente_I | 6 | | | | | | | | | 1 | 3 | | | | | | | | | | | | | | |
| Mūkukalns_III | 6 | | 2 | | 5 | | | 2 | | 5 | | | | | | | | | | | | | | | |
| Rūsiši | 6 | | | 1 | 1 | | | 4 | 5 | 2 | 3 | 1 | | 5 | 1 | | 2 | | 1 | | 6 | 2 | | 1 | Iron slag |
| Miškiņeva | 6 | | | | | | | | | | | | 4 | | | | | | | | | | | | |
| Kalnamuiža | 6 | 1 | | | 54 | 8 | 10 | 4 | 1 | | | | | | | | | 9 | | | | | | | |
| Lejaslepji | 6 | | | | | | | | | | | | 7 | | | | | | | | | | | | |
| Vecmokas | 6 | | 12 | | 24 | | | | | 11 | 2 | | 1 | | | | | | 6 | | | | | | |
| Lejasļūdi | 7 | | | | | | | | | | | | 1 | | | | | | | | | | | | |
| Ķišukalns | 7 | | | | | | | | | | | | 1 | | | | | | | | | | | | |
| Podži | 7 | | | | | | | | | | | | 1 | | | | | | | | | | | | |
| Dumpji | 8 | | | | | | | | | | | | 2 | | 1 | | | | | | | | | | |
| Mūrnieki | 8 | | | | | | | | | | | | 2 | | | | | | | | | | | | |
| Saulītes | 8 | | | | | | | | | | | | 3 | | | | | | | | | | | 1 | Leather belt |
| Baltinava | 8 | | | | | | | | | | | | 5 | | | | | | | | | | | | |
| Ķente_II | 8 | | | | | | | | | | | | | 2 | | | | | | | | | 3 | | |
| Mūkukalns_II | 9 | | | | | | | | | | | | 1 | | | | | | | | | | | | |
| Mežotne | 9 | | | | | | | | | | | | | 2 | 5 | | | | | | | | | | |
| Tīras_purvs | 9 | | | | | | 3 | | | | 1 | | | 1 | 1 | | 3 | 3 | | | 2 | 1 | | 84 | Wood & leather fragments & items |
| Sauleskalns_I | 9 | | | | | | | | | | | | 3 | | 1 | | | | | | | | | | |
| Sauleskalns_II | 9 | | | | | 20 | | | | | | | | | | | | | | | | | | | |
| **Total: 25** | | **10** | **201** | **1** | **919** | **28** | **13** | **23** | **7** | **21** | **103** | **176** | **35** | **26** | **18** | **2** | **10** | **40** | **7** | **4** | **9** | **9** | **19** | **108** | |

*Table 7.1.2. Artefact groups in Latvian wealth deposits.*

| Wealth Deposit | Dating (c.) | Environment | Environment Subtype | Depth (cm) | Markers | Archaeological Site |
|---|---|---|---|---|---|---|
| Alsungas | 4 | Watery condition | Bog | | | |
| Cibēni | 5 | Solid ground | Archaeological Site | 12-25 | Stones? | Burial area |
| Piltene | 5 | Watery condition | Marsh | 120 | | |
| Kokmuiža_I | 5 | Watery condition | Marsh | 45 | | Foot of hill-fort |
| Kokmuiža_II | 5 | Watery condition | Marsh | 45-60 | | Foot of hill-fort |
| Ķente_I | 6 | Solid ground | Archaeological Site | 38 | | Hill-fort |
| Mūkukalns_III | 6 | Solid ground | Archaeological Site | 52-70 | Stones | Hill-fort |
| Rūsiši | 6 | Solid ground | Archaeological Site | | Heap of burnt stones | Burial area |
| Miškiņeva | 6 | Solid ground | | | | |
| Kalnamuiža | 6 | Watery condition | River | 30-40 | Large granite stone | |
| Lejaslepji | 6 | Solid ground | | | | |
| Vecmokas | 6 | Solid ground | Archaeological Site | | | Foot of hill-fort |
| Lejasļūdi | 7 | Solid ground | | | | |
| Ķišukalns | 7 | Solid ground | Archaeological Site | | | Settlement, foot of hill-fort |
| Podži | 7 | Unknown | | | | |
| Dumpji | 8 | Solid ground | | | | |
| Mūrnieki | 8 | Solid ground | Archaeological Site | | | Settlement |
| Saulītes | 8 | Watery condition | Marsh | 45 | | |
| Baltinava | 8 | Solid ground | | | | |
| Ķente_II | 8 | Solid ground | Archaeological Site | 7-14 | | Settlement |
| Mūkukalns_II | 9 | Solid ground | Archaeological Site | 68 | Large stone slate | Hill-fort |
| Mežotne | 9 | Solid ground | Archaeological Site | | | Hill-fort |
| Tīras_purvs | 9 | Watery condition | Bog | 110-150 | Stakes? | |
| Sauleskalns_I | 9 | Solid ground | | 30 | Heap of stones | |
| Sauleskalns_II | 9 | Solid ground | | 30 | | |
| **Total: 25** | | | | | | |

*Table 7.1.3. Environments of concealment of Latvian wealth deposits.*

419 of the coins come from 12 hoards (Ducmane & Ozoliņa 2009, 40), but as mentioned eight of them have unreliable record (Urtāns 1977, 133-137; Ducmane & Ozoliņa 2009). From the four certain Roman coin hoards (Appendix 1.2.), the earliest one is Kazzemnieki, dated to the second half of the 2nd century AD. However, this dating is based on the two poorly preserved coins, whereas the number of artefacts found was larger than just two coins. There are three hoards from the 4th century AD: Daugavpils from the first half, Priedkalni and Jelgava from the second half of the century. The numbers of coins found are 34, 17 and

13 respectively. As Roman coin finds will not be included in the current study, these finds will not be discussed in more detail.

The find from Uņģeni consists of two silver spiral bracelets and two Arabic coins, one of which has been used as a coin pendant. It was recorded that six coins were discovered, but the others have now been lost. The coin pendant of the deposit is dated to the beginning of the 8th century. However, the dating of the latest coin is from the last decade of the 8th century. The bracelets are also characteristic of the type known from the Viking Age and most probably the hoard belongs to the end of the 9th – beginning of the 10th century AD (Urtāns 1977, 168; Ducmane & Ozoliņa 2009, 78, no. 13). Therefore it will not be included in the following analysis.

### 7.1.2. Problems and exclusions

There is one find that unfortunately cannot be included in further analysis, because information about the find-spot is lacking. This is a deposit about which it is only known that it was found somewhere in the Ikšķiles area. It consists of three silver neck-rings – one with profoundly faceted, the other two with saddle-shaped and loop terminals. They are stored in the collections of the State Hermitage Museum in St Petersburg. As no information about the detailed finding circumstances is available, this deposit has to be excluded.

The other problematic find is from Grobiņa. It consists of two crossbow brooches that have been dated to the end of the 7th century AD. One of them is a silver brooch with animal head-like terminals, the other is a gilded bronze brooch covered with animal ornament style, reminiscent of the animal-style finds from Scandinavia. In the Middle Iron Age and following periods the Grobiņa area had settlers of Scandinavian origin (Nerman 1958), so the find in itself is not surprising. However, the exact find-spot of the brooches is not absolutely definite and it might relate to either burial or a settlement site. It has been previously interpreted as a separate deposit find, but as it is lacking any further information about the exact find-spot it will not be included in the further analysis in the current study.

There are some other finds which are not absolutely definite separate and intentional artefact deposits. One of them is a silver neck-ring from Ķišukalns. In 1939 several artefacts were discovered and handed over to the National History Museum of Latvia in 1940. Among these is a silver neck-ring dating to the 6th-7th century AD which has been interpreted as a separate deposit discovered at the foot of the Ķišukalns hill-fort in the probable settlement area (Urtāns 1977, 153, fig. 59). In the archive materials of the Museum it is recorded that besides the neck-ring some other artefacts were bought including a bronze penannular brooch and fragments of a bronze bracelet, bronze cross pendants, spiral bracelets and an iron axe. Some bones were mentioned in relation to the artefacts handed over to the Museum, but they are most likely related to the settlement site, as no burial places are known in the vicinity of the Ķišukalns hill-fort. The exact find-spot is not entirely clear and we cannot be sure whether they were found together with or separately from the neck-ring. What is important here is that compared with the neck-ring, all the other mentioned artefacts belong to later periods (Viking Age and Late Iron Age in the 9th-11th century). Thus, the neck-ring will be included in the further analysis as a separate wealth deposit.

A

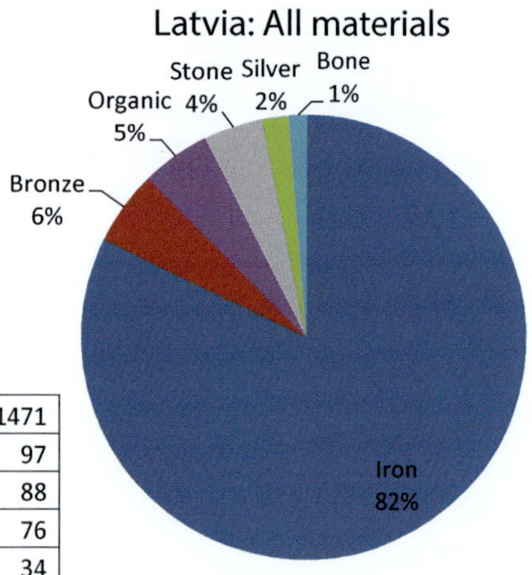


| | |
|---|---|
| Iron | 1471 |
| Bronze | 97 |
| Organic | 88 |
| Stone | 76 |
| Silver | 34 |
| Bone | 23 |

B

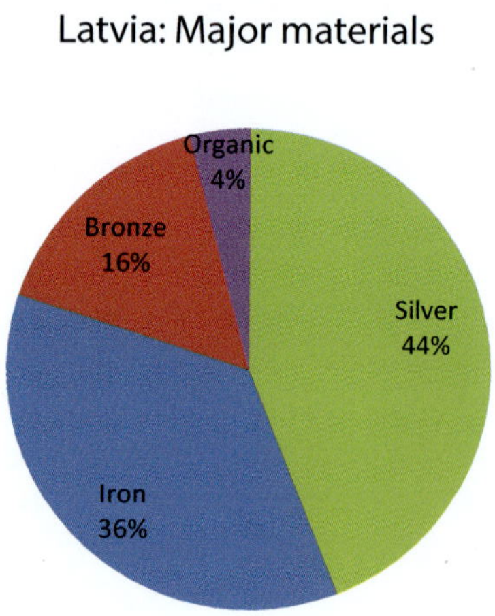


| | |
|---|---|
| Silver | 11 |
| Iron | 9 |
| Bronze | 4 |
| Organic | 1 |

*Fig. 7.1.3.1. Distribution of all artefact materials (A) and major materials (B) in Latvian wealth deposits.*

### 7.1.3. General overview of analysed material

More than half of the 25 Latvian deposits consist of solely one material (see Table 7.1.1.). Taking into account the numbers of single artefacts iron is clearly the main material. Only a small proportion of artefacts are bronze, organic, stone or silver (Fig. 7.1.3.1. (A)). In five cases two materials are represented and in five instances three different materials have been deposited. Especially in the case of ornaments sometimes an additional material is added due to gilding or decorative plates covering the original object. However, the graph of major material in every single deposit, shows very different result (Fig. 7.1.3.1. (B)). Now silver forms the predominant material in over 40% of the deposits, iron is second with 36% then bronze with 16% of deposits. Organic material is predominant in only one deposit.

The total number of deposited artefacts in Latvia is 1789. The biggest find group in terms of functional groups is clearly weapons with over 1179 representatives, followed by a vague find group of 'other' with nearly 300 objects (Fig. 7.1.3.2. (A)). Ornaments and tools are both represented with ca. 150 objects. Raw materials are evident in less than 20 finds. One deposit, Kokmuiža I, provides a total number of 1280 artefacts, including nearly 1000 weapons. Therefore a picture according to the major artefact group within a deposit provides a more balanced insight into the distribution of artefact groups in Latvian wealth deposits. As we can see from the pie chart created according to the predominant artefact group 60% of Latvian deposits consist of ornaments, only then follow deposits of weapons with 28% (Fig. 7.1.3.2. (B)). Tools and the find group of 'other' are predominant in single cases. However, it must be kept in mind that in the case of those Latvian deposits that include both weapons and tools, the dominance of one functional group over another is not always clear and the quantities are sometimes quite equal (see Chapter 4).

Artefacts represented in Latvian wealth deposits (Table 7.1.2.) are clearly dominated by spearheads with more than 900 objects, of which nearly 800 come from the Kokmuiža I find alone. The following groups are axes, and several unidentifiable or unusual iron objects and tools (201, 176, 103 objects). The find group 'other' is represented with over 108 finds formed by various organic objects and their fragments. Looking at ornaments, most numerous are belt parts

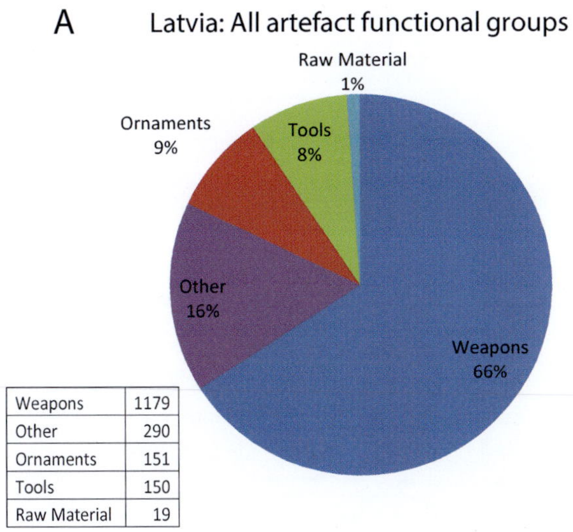


| | |
|---|---|
| Weapons | 1179 |
| Other | 290 |
| Ornaments | 151 |
| Tools | 150 |
| Raw Material | 19 |

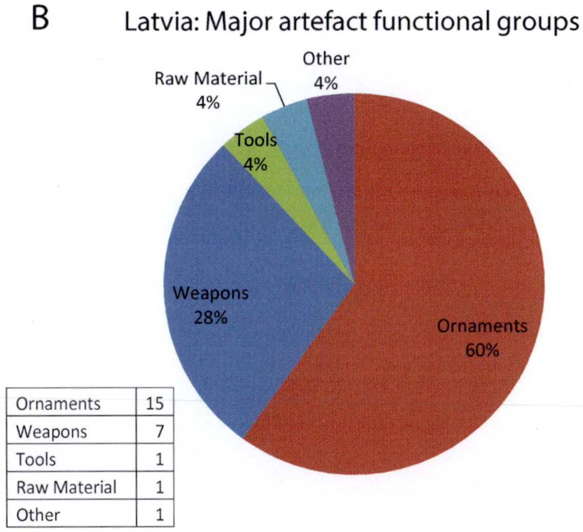


| | |
|---|---|
| Ornaments | 15 |
| Weapons | 7 |
| Tools | 1 |
| Raw Material | 1 |
| Other | 1 |

*Fig. 7.1.3.2. Distribution of all artefact functional groups (A) and major functional groups (B) in Latvian wealth deposits.*

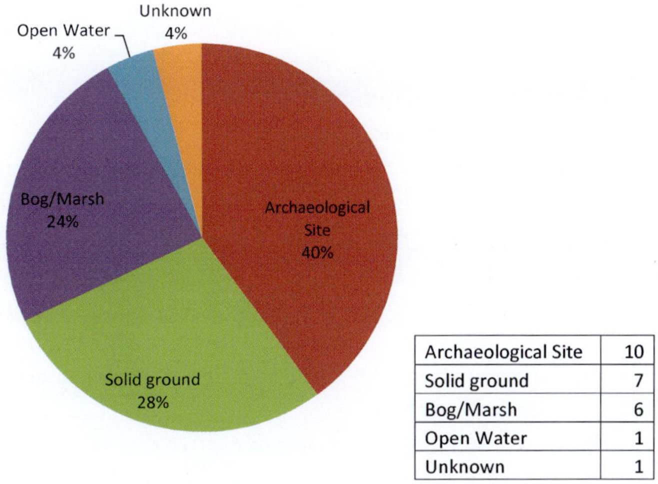


| | |
|---|---|
| Archaeological Site | 10 |
| Solid ground | 7 |
| Bog/Marsh | 6 |
| Open Water | 1 |
| Unknown | 1 |

*Fig. 7.1.3.3. Environments of concealment of Latvian wealth deposits.*

(40 objects), neck-rings (35) and bracelets (26). There are 28 arrowhead finds, most from the Sauleskalns II deposit. There are a few more than 20 knives and sickles/scythes represented in the overall material. The other artefact groups are represented with less than 20 objects.

When looking at the environment of concealment we see that archaeological sites are the most frequent context in which deposits have been discovered (Fig. 7.1.3.3.). Only after that come dry land and water related environments. Out of 17 dry land finds in ten cases the deposits have been found either in or in the close vicinity of contemporary archaeological sites. There are also some deposits from watery conditions that actually have been discovered close to an archaeological site. In most of these examples we are dealing with the finds relating to hill-forts (7 instances), though settlements and burial areas are also represented (3 and 2 instances respectively).

A possible marker of the hiding place has been documented in seven cases. Most of these are either stones or stone clusters, though in the bog find from Tīras purvs it is likely that some wooden stakes were left as visible markers in the bog. It

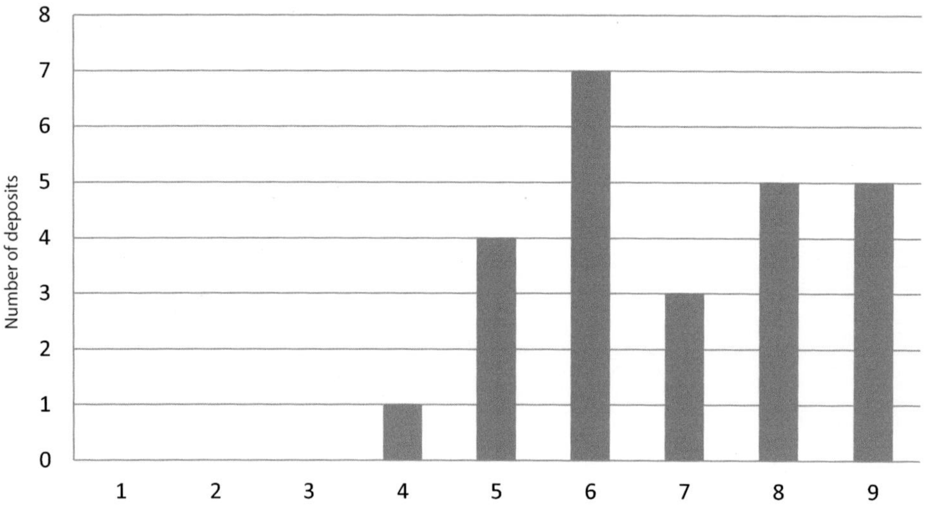


*Fig. 7.1.3.4. Chronological distribution (centuries AD) of Latvian wealth deposits.*

is also possible that they were used for attaching and keeping the artefacts below the water surface of the bog pool. A container is noticed in only three instances: in two of them a deposit or at least some of it has been wrapped in textile (Mežotne, Tīras purvs) and in one case a deposit was hidden in a wooden box (Ķente II). In two examples a ceramic vessel, or shards of it, have been mentioned in the vicinity of the deposit (Kokmuiža I, Mūkukalns III), but whether the deposit or part of it was hidden in the vessel or not remains unclear.

Regarding artefact placement there is some further information in seven examples. In the case of the Kokmuiža I and II finds it has been noticed that different artefact groups and materials were placed as if in layers. In the case of the Sauleskalns II and Mūkukalns III finds it has been recorded that the weapons were pointed in the same direction. In the Saulītes deposit neck-rings were on top of each other and in Ķente II small bracelets were placed inside each other. The find from Tīras purvs was surrounded by wooden pegs and a woollen cloth was placed on top of the deposit just after the concealment.

The chronological distribution (Fig. 7.1.3.4.) shows that after removing coin hoards from the analysis there is only one deposit from the Roman Iron Age, and no deposits from the first half of the Roman Iron Age at all. Out of 25 deposits the majority belong to the Middle Iron Age. A noticeable increase in the number of wealth deposits is in the 6th century AD when the total number of deposits reaches seven. During the preceding and following centuries the number of deposits remains between three and five. There is a sudden decrease in the number of deposits in the 7th century when the number is the smallest, so the number of deposits falls right after the 6th century peak.

The spatial distribution of Latvian deposits covers the whole country evenly without any clear concentration (Fig. 7.1.3.5.). Perhaps to some extent it can be concluded that there are no deposits in the northern part of the country and that a larger number of finds is known from the southern regions. The central and the south-western regions have several examples of deposits. Some deposits seem to cluster in the eastern region of Latvia. In this sense there is a kind of similarity with the spatial distribution of Estonian wealth deposits.

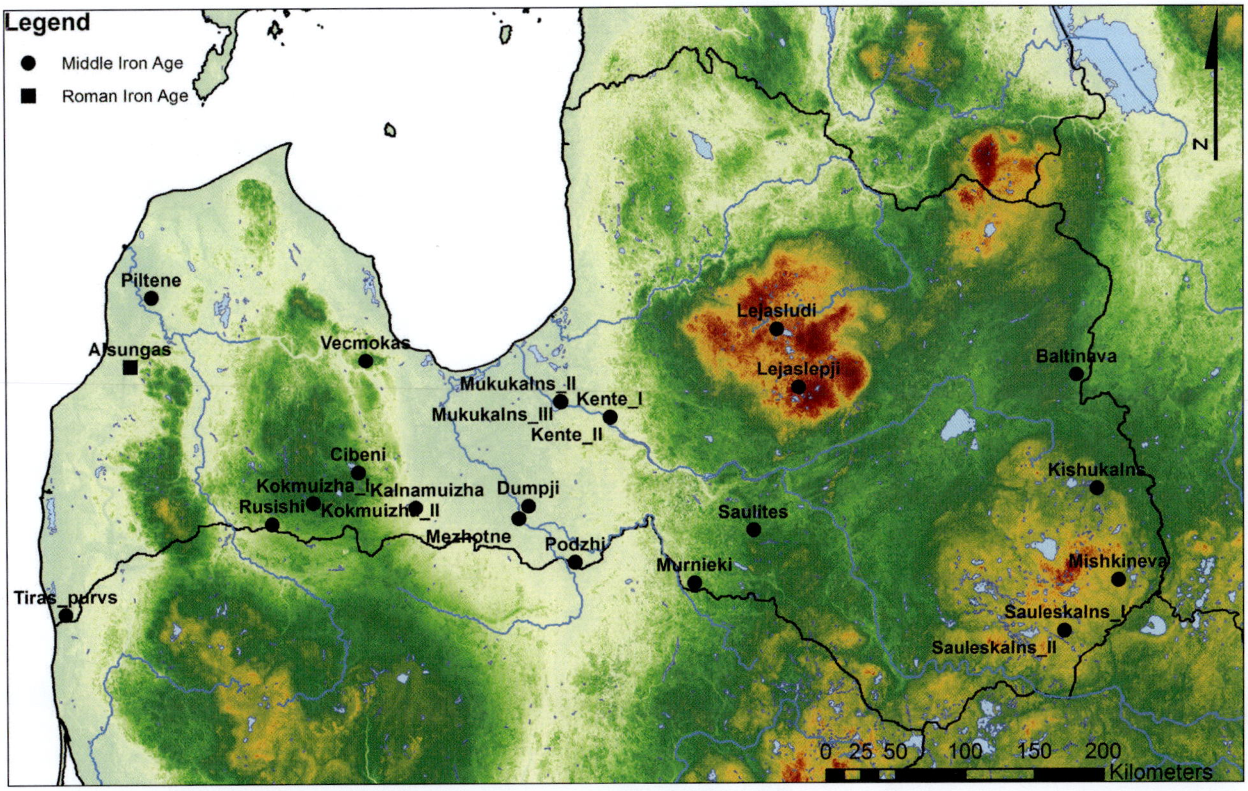


*Fig. 7.1.3.5. Map of Latvian wealth deposits.*

## 7.1.4. Selection of artefacts

There are several clearer selections in the combinations of artefacts in Latvian 1st-9th century AD wealth deposits. Starting from the production material we can recognise some patterns when comparing the main and second larger group of materials. As indicated in the crosstab cells without headings and blue bars in the chart (see Fig. 7.1.4.1.) when silver or bronze are in majority they are very rarely combined with any other material. On the other hand, iron is often found in combination with bronze. There are fewer solely iron deposits than iron in combination with bronze items. There are a couple of unique material deposits which contain either organic or stone as main material, but also iron objects are included in both of them.

Looking at the CA plot of material according to the exact numbers of objects and with the Axis 1 and 2 representing respectively 41.4% and 40.2% of the inertia we see two clear clusters of deposits (Fig. 7.1.4.2.). One clearer group is silver deposits, which forms a distinct whole in itself. The second are finds of iron in combination with stone items that are seen at the other end of the plot. Bronze objects stand out as a separate group, although they are more closely related to iron deposits. Two finds in the vicinity of the silver cluster are the Saulītes and Sauleskalns I deposits in which the majority of items are silver, but they also contain respectively a single organic or bronze object. A find from Tīras purvs is an interesting outlier because the largest quantity of objects in this find is provided by various organic objects.

| | | Second Material | | | | | | |
|---|---|---|---|---|---|---|---|---|
| | | None | Bronze | Gold | Iron | Organic | Stone | Total |
| Major Material | Bronze | 4 | 0 | 0 | 0 | 0 | 0 | 4 |
| | Iron | 3 | 4 | 0 | 0 | 0 | 1 | 8 |
| | Organic | 0 | 0 | 0 | 1 | 0 | 0 | 1 |
| | Silver | 8 | 1 | 1 | 0 | 1 | 0 | 11 |
| | Stone | 0 | 0 | 0 | 1 | 0 | 0 | 1 |
| **Total** | | **15** | **5** | **1** | **2** | **1** | **1** | **25** |

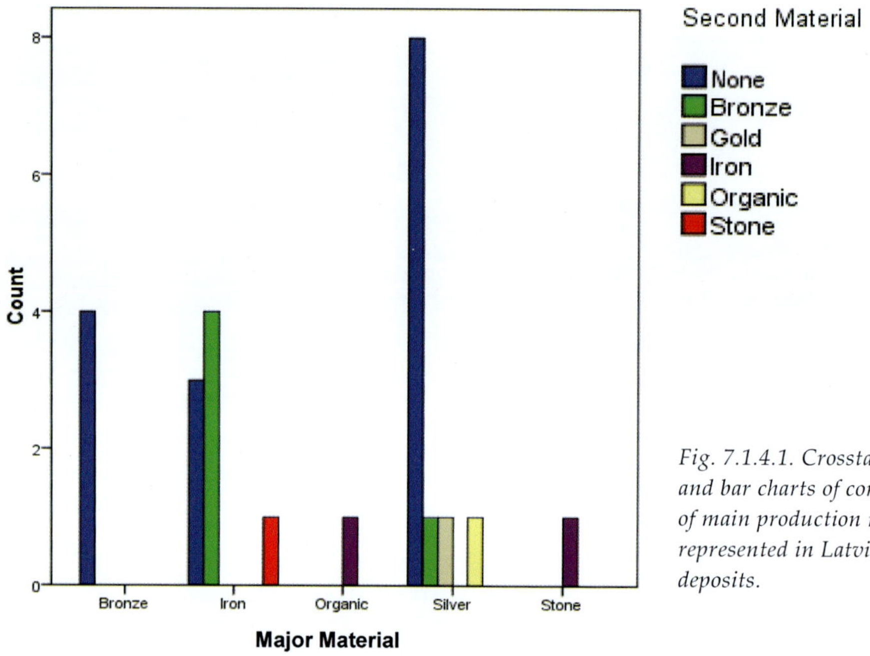


*Fig. 7.1.4.1. Crosstabulation and bar charts of combinations of main production materials represented in Latvian wealth deposits.*

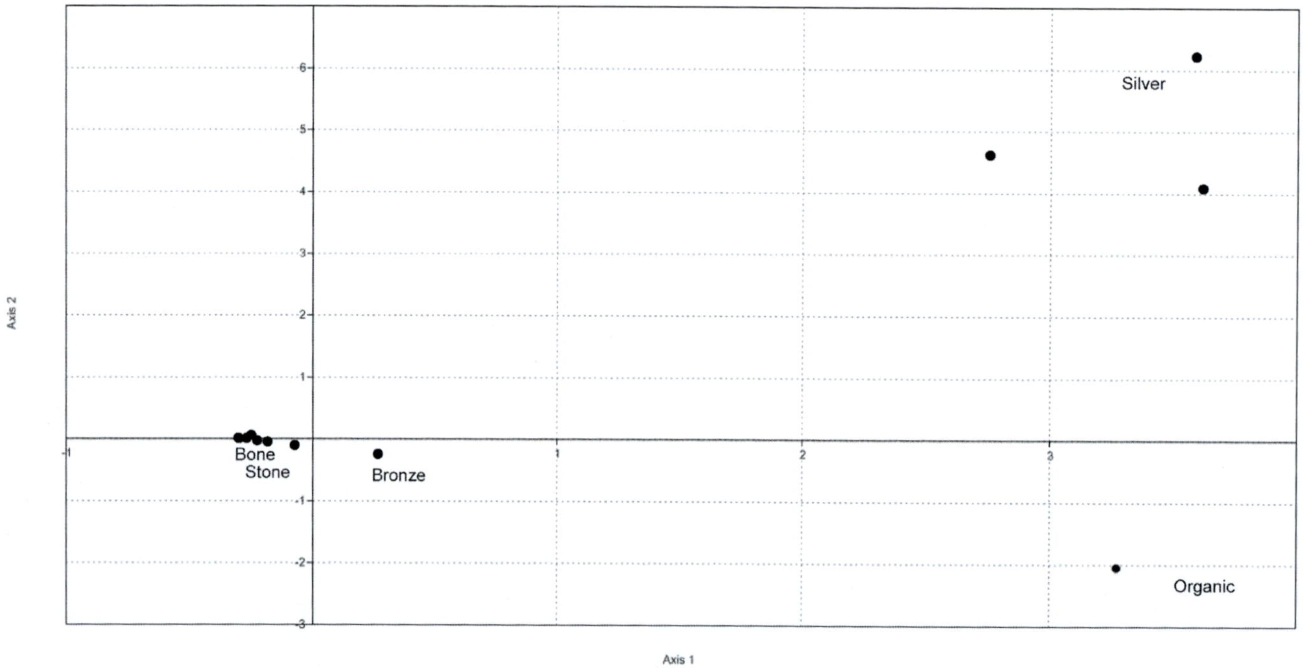


*Fig. 7.1.4.2. Correspondence analysis of combinations of all materials represented in Latvian wealth deposits according to the number of represented artefacts.*

| | | Second Artefact Group | | | | Total |
|---|---|---|---|---|---|---|
| | | – | O | Oth | T | |
| Major Artefact Group | O | 13 | 0 | 1 | 1 | 15 |
| | Oth | 0 | 1 | 0 | 0 | 1 |
| | R | 0 | 1 | 0 | 0 | 1 |
| | T | 1 | 0 | 0 | 0 | 1 |
| | W | 1 | 2 | 1 | 3 | 7 |
| **Total** | | **15** | **4** | **2** | **4** | **25** |

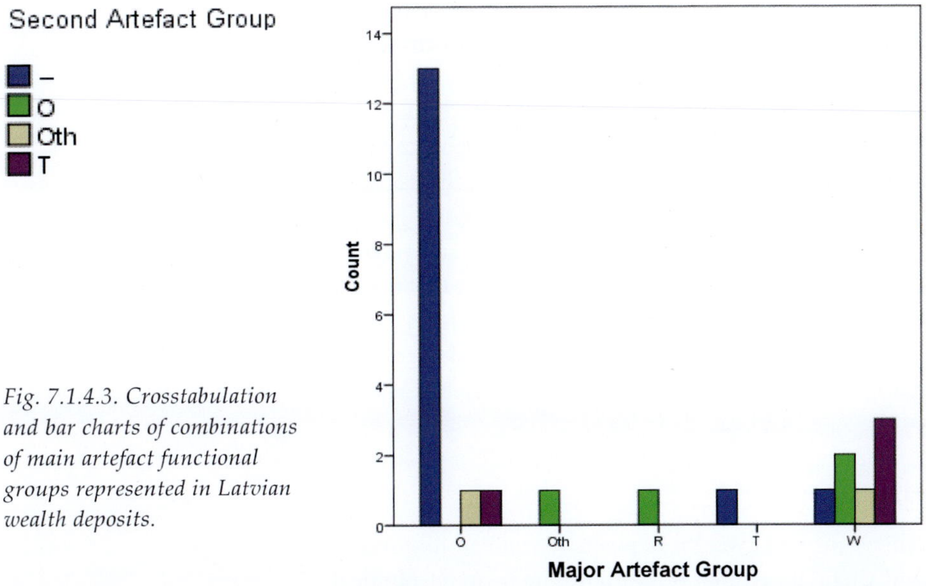


*Fig. 7.1.4.3. Crosstabulation and bar charts of combinations of main artefact functional groups represented in Latvian wealth deposits.*

O – Ornaments, Oth – Other, R – Raw Material, T – Tools, W – Weapons.

The distribution of artefact functional groups in deposits (Fig. 7.1.4.3.) shows a deliberate differentiation between different functional groups and combinations of artefacts. Where ornaments are deposited as the main artefact group, they are mostly found alone and only rarely with either tools or with the find group of 'other'. Additionally, when ornaments are the primary functional group no weapons are included in the same deposit. Looking at weapons as the main functional group we see that those deposits are more often combined with tools, ornaments or 'other' as the second functional group. At the same time there is only one weapon and one tool deposit which includes only those functional groups. There are only two examples where 'other' and raw materials are in majority and they are deposited in combination with ornaments.

CA according to the presence or absence of artefact groups in every deposit shows interesting results (Fig. 7.1.4.4.). Axis 1 and 2 represent the inertia respectively of 46.1% and 29.1%. As above, ornament deposits form a separate group, weapons and tools are mostly represented together and the find group 'other' is closer to the latter two than ornaments. An outlier or intermediate is the Kokmuiža I deposit which includes all the possible artefact groups. The second similar example is the Saulītes deposit which has mainly ornaments but also a find group of 'other' in it. However, as the latter is a leather belt the connection of which to ornaments is unclear, it is likely that this find fits into the general ornament cluster. Among the raw material is the unique Ķente I deposit which includes both ornaments but also raw material bars for the production of ornaments.

The CA plot takes into account only those deposits which include more than one type of object and only those object types that are found in more than one deposit. After removal of cells according to the described criteria 16 deposits remain to be analysed. Axis 1 and 2 give only 22.4% and 18.7% of the inertia. However, some selections and combinations of specific artefact types still emerge (Fig. 7.1.4.5.). On the one side of the scattergram we see a group of deposits that include ornament types, mostly neck-rings, but also bracelets and brooches are distributed on this side. On the other side is a cluster of all kinds of weapons (swords, axes, spearheads, also horse gear) but also tools (sickles/scythes, knives). In the latter there are also vessels, belt parts and rings. There one can find also some unusual ornament types called 'other ornaments' from three finds (Kokmuiža I, Rūsiši and Tīras purvs) which mostly include bronze spirals related to dress decorations. Indeed all those ornament types can be categorized as high status personal (clothing) objects or parts of horse riding or weapon carrying equipment which are most often related to elite male equipment. Additionally, as with Estonia, we see dress pins as liminal finds between the two separated groups. This last scatter indicates that there might be, if not gender, then at least status based distribution of artefact types in those 16 wealth deposits. Adding comparison with Axis 1 and 3 which provide the inertia of 22.4% and 15.5%, a subdivision in the weapon-tool cluster emerges: swords in combination with belt parts and horse gear becomes separated. All these items might indicate the possessions of high status male warriors.

## 7.1.5. Selection of environment

Nearly 70% of Latvian 1st-9th century AD wealth deposits have been discovered in dry land and the majority of them are related to contemporary archaeological sites (see Fig. 7.1.3.3.). One quarter of the finds is from boggy or marshy areas and there is only one example of a find from open water environment.

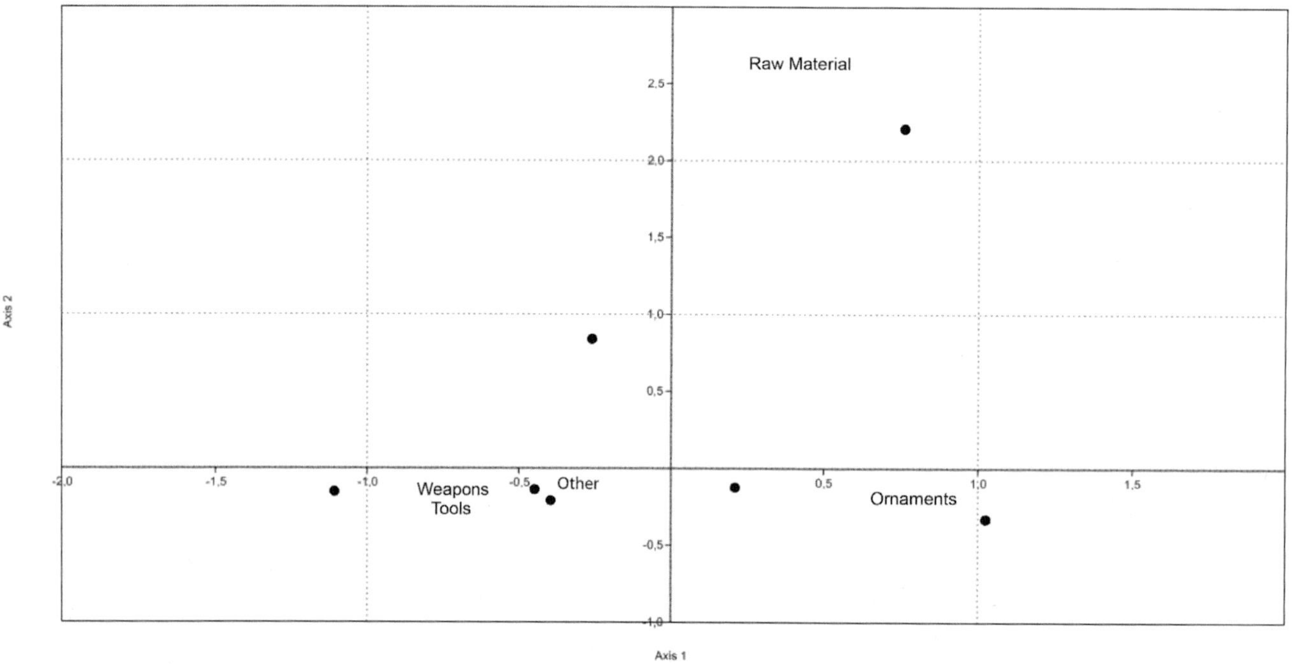


*Fig. 7.1.4.4. Correspondence analysis of combinations of all artefact functional groups represented in Latvian wealth deposits.*

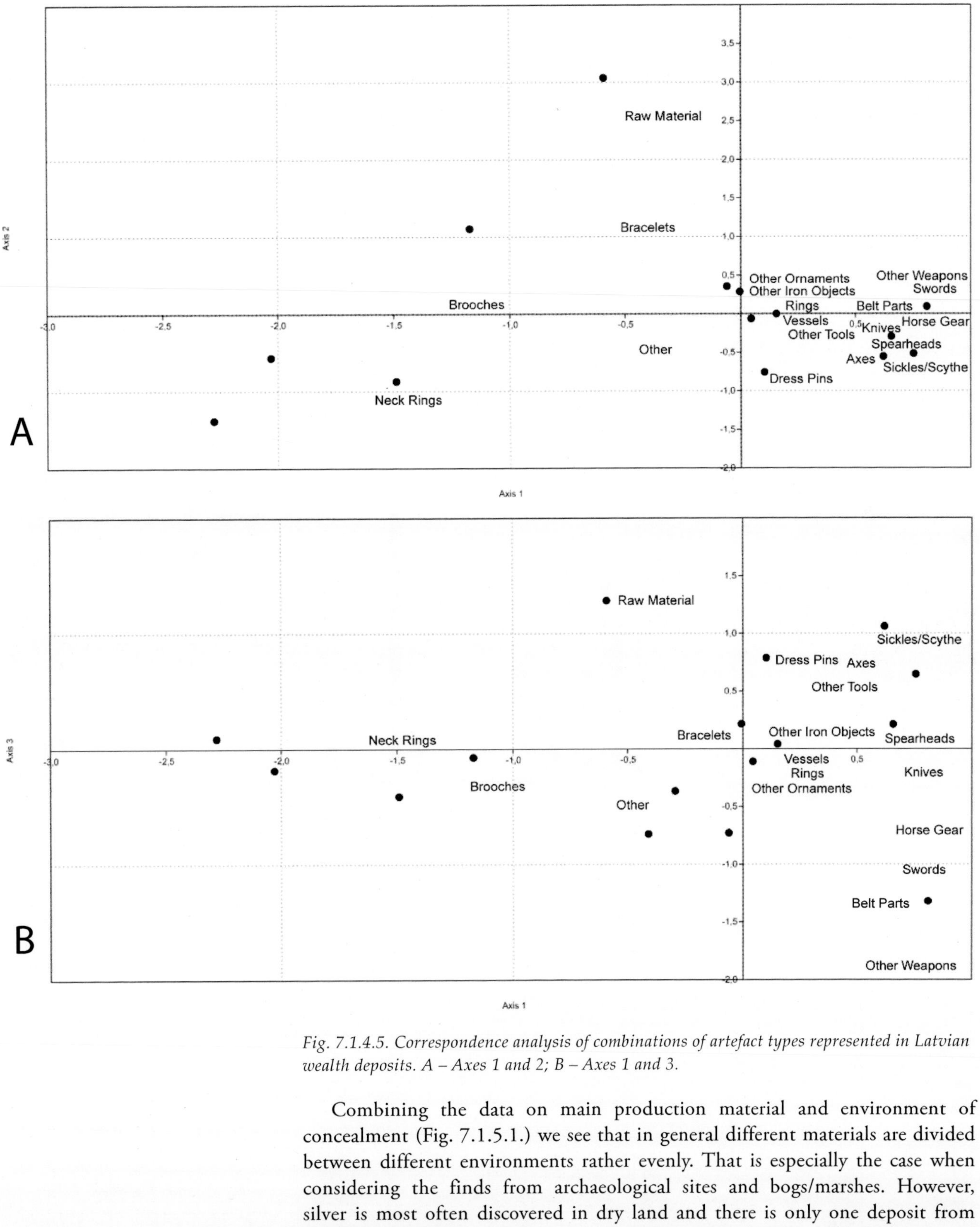


*Fig. 7.1.4.5. Correspondence analysis of combinations of artefact types represented in Latvian wealth deposits. A – Axes 1 and 2; B – Axes 1 and 3.*

Combining the data on main production material and environment of concealment (Fig. 7.1.5.1.) we see that in general different materials are divided between different environments rather evenly. That is especially the case when considering the finds from archaeological sites and bogs/marshes. However, silver is most often discovered in dry land and there is only one deposit from this environment in which iron is the main material. When adding the second main material within a deposit, the distributions by and large remain the same

(Fig. 7.1.5.2.). In addition, if bronze is the predominant material it is also the single material of the deposit, and the majority of such finds are deposited in archaeological sites. The MCA scattergram indicates some clusters (Fig. 7.1.5.3.) although there are more instances where some materials and environments seem to cluster and merge together (e.g. bronze and iron or bog/marsh and open water).

Looking at the artefact functional groups according to the environment of concealment the distinct selections of artefacts and environments become more evident. According to broader environment categories and main functional

| | | Major Material | | | | | |
|---|---|---|---|---|---|---|---|
| | | Bronze | Iron | Organic | Silver | Stone | Total |
| Environment Subcategory | Archaeological Site | 3 | 4 | 0 | 2 | 1 | 10 |
| | Bog/Marsh | 1 | 2 | 1 | 2 | 0 | 6 |
| | Open Water | 0 | 1 | 0 | 0 | 0 | 1 |
| | Solid Ground | 0 | 1 | 0 | 6 | 0 | 7 |
| | Unknown | 0 | 0 | 0 | 1 | 0 | 1 |
| **Total** | | **4** | **8** | **1** | **11** | **1** | **25** |

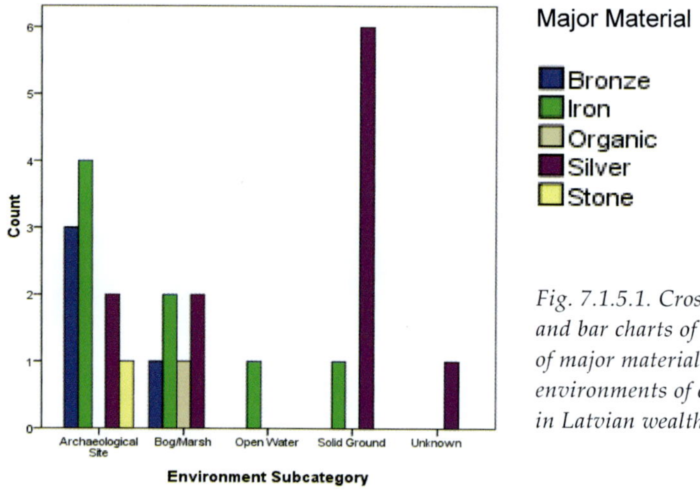


*Fig. 7.1.5.1. Crosstabulation and bar charts of combinations of major material and environments of concealment in Latvian wealth deposits.*

| Major Material | | | Environment Subcategory | | | | | |
|---|---|---|---|---|---|---|---|---|
| | | | Archaeological Site | Bog/Marsh | Open Water | Solid Ground | Unknown | Total |
| Bronze | Second Material | | 3 | 1 | 0 | 0 | 0 | 4 |
| | **Total** | | **3** | **1** | **0** | **0** | **0** | **4** |
| Iron | Second Material | | 1 | 0 | 1 | 1 | 0 | 3 |
| | | Bronze | 2 | 2 | 0 | 0 | 0 | 4 |
| | | Stone | 1 | 0 | 0 | 0 | 0 | 1 |
| | **Total** | | **4** | **2** | **1** | **1** | **0** | **8** |
| Organic | Second Material | Iron | 0 | 1 | 0 | 0 | 0 | 1 |
| | **Total** | | **0** | **1** | **0** | **0** | **0** | **1** |
| Silver | Second Material | | 2 | 0 | 0 | 5 | 1 | 8 |
| | | Bronze | 0 | 0 | 0 | 1 | 0 | 1 |
| | | Gold | 0 | 1 | 0 | 0 | 0 | 1 |
| | | Organic | 0 | 1 | 0 | 0 | 0 | 1 |
| | **Total** | | **2** | **2** | **0** | **6** | **1** | **11** |
| Stone | Second Material | Iron | 1 | 0 | 0 | 0 | 0 | 1 |
| | **Total** | | **1** | **0** | **0** | **0** | **0** | **1** |

*Fig. 7.1.5.2. Crosstabulation of combinations of major and second material and environments of concealment in Latvian wealth deposits.*

groups we see that dry land deposits contain mostly ornaments, but to a lesser extent also weapons. Watery conditions have a similar number of ornament and weapon finds and single instances of raw materials and tools are deposited in the dry land (Fig. 7.1.5.4.). More detailed categorisation of environmental contexts (Fig. 7.1.5.5.) indicates that ornaments are mostly found in dry land or archaeological sites (altogether 11 cases). Raw materials and tools come from archaeological sites only. Weapons have been deposited in all kinds of different environments with a slight domination in archaeological sites (3 cases) as opposed to bog/marsh and open water (2 and 1 case respectively). Taking into account all the major artefact groups in a deposit the pictures becomes more varied (Fig. 7.1.5.6.). Ornaments are most often found alone and mostly in archaeological sites or solid ground. Weapons are deposited most often with tools in archaeological sites, or with tools, ornaments and find group 'other' in bog/marsh. However, deposits containing weapons only are never discovered in archaeological sites, where weapons are always in combination with other functional groups.

There is a clear division in the selection of environments of concealment for ornament deposits in dry land or archaeological site, while weapons have been deposited in different contexts. The combinations of artefacts deposited together in archaeological sites and watery conditions are more variable. The latter is particularly evident when weapons are the most common objects in the deposit. There is only one deposit from open water environment in Latvia, most of the iron objects (be it tools or weapons) are from bog or marsh. However, the divisions

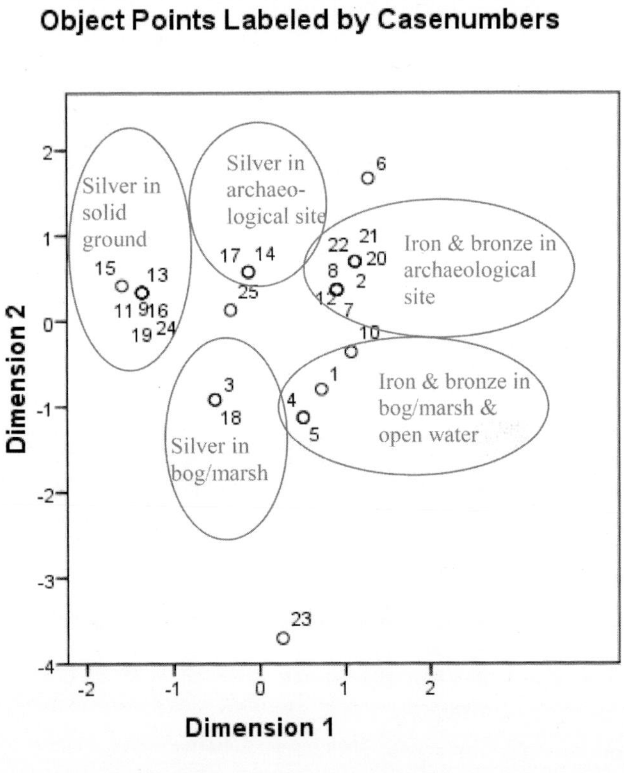


| |
|---|
| 1-Alsungas |
| 2-Cibēni |
| 3-Piltene |
| 4-Kokmuiža_I |
| 5-Kokmuiža_II |
| 6-Ķente_I |
| 7-Mūkukalns_III |
| 8-Rūsiši |
| 9-Miškiņeva |
| 10-Kalnamuiža |
| 11-Lejaslepji |
| 12-Vecmokas |
| 13-Lejasļūdi |
| 14-Ķišukalns |
| 15-Podži |
| 16-Dumpji |
| 17-Mūrnieki |
| 18-Saulītes |
| 19-Baltinava |
| 20-Ķente_II |
| 21-Mūkukalns_II |
| 22-Mežotne |
| 23-Tīras_purvs |
| 24-Sauleskalns_I |
| 25-Sauleskalns_II |

*Fig. 7.1.5.3. MCA plot of combinations of major material and detailed environments of concealment in Latvian wealth deposits.*

| | | Major Artefact Group | | | | | Total |
|---|---|---|---|---|---|---|---|
| | | O | Oth | R | T | W | |
| Environment | Solid ground | 11 | 0 | 1 | 1 | 4 | 17 |
| | Unknown | 1 | 0 | 0 | 0 | 0 | 1 |
| | Watery condition | 3 | 1 | 0 | 0 | 3 | 7 |
| **Total** | | **15** | **1** | **1** | **1** | **7** | **25** |

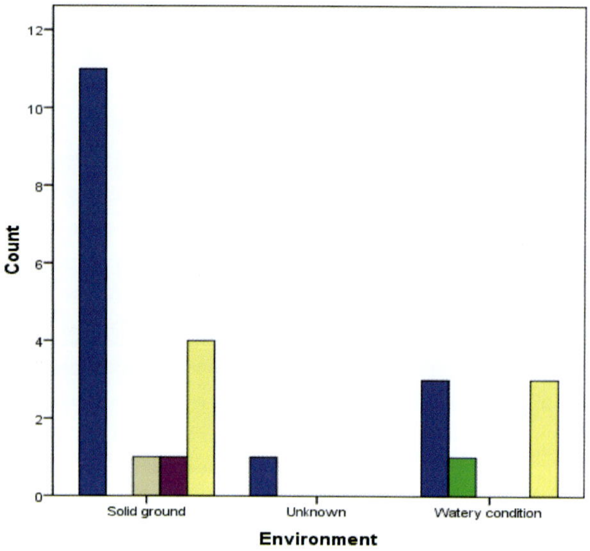

*Fig. 7.1.5.4. Crosstabulation and bar charts of combinations of artefact groups and environments of concealment in Latvian wealth deposits.*

O – Ornaments, Oth – Other, R – Raw Material, T – Tools, W – Weapons.

| | | Major Artefact Group | | | | Total | |
|---|---|---|---|---|---|---|---|
| | | O | Oth | R | T | W | |
| Environment Subcategory | Archaeological Site | 5 | 0 | 1 | 1 | 3 | 10 |
| | Bog/Marsh | 3 | 1 | 0 | 0 | 2 | 6 |
| | Open Water | 0 | 0 | 0 | 0 | 1 | 1 |
| | Solid Ground | 6 | 0 | 0 | 0 | 1 | 7 |
| | Unknown | 1 | 0 | 0 | 0 | 0 | 1 |
| **Total** | | **15** | **1** | **1** | **1** | **7** | **25** |

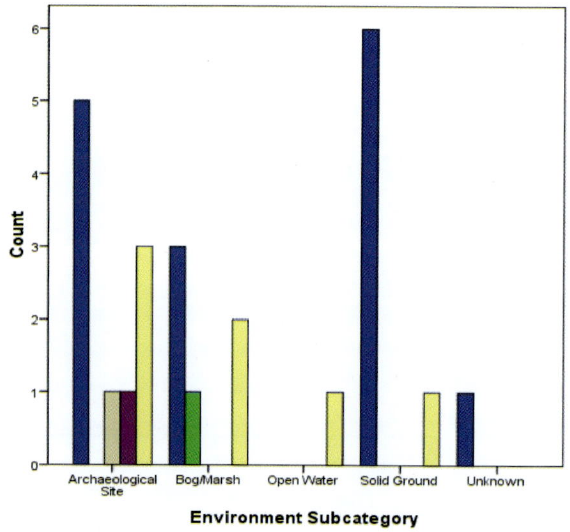

*Fig. 7.1.5.5. Crosstabulation and bar charts of combinations of artefact groups and detailed environments of concealment in Latvian wealth deposits.*

O – Ornaments, Oth – Other, R – Raw Material, T – Tools, W – Weapons.

| | | Major Artefact Groups | | | | | | | | |
|---|---|---|---|---|---|---|---|---|---|---|
| | | O | O+T+W | Oth | R+O | T | W | W+O+T+Ot | W+T | Total |
| Environment Subcategory | Archaeological Site | 4 | 1 | 0 | 1 | 1 | 0 | 0 | 3 | 10 |
| | Bog/Marsh | 2 | 0 | 1 | 0 | 0 | 1 | 2 | 0 | 6 |
| | Open Water | 0 | 0 | 0 | 0 | 0 | 1 | 0 | 0 | 1 |
| | Solid Ground | 6 | 0 | 0 | 0 | 0 | 1 | 0 | 0 | 7 |
| | Unknown | 1 | 0 | 0 | 0 | 0 | 0 | 0 | 0 | 1 |
| **Total** | | **13** | **1** | **1** | 1 | 1 | 3 | 2 | 3 | 25 |

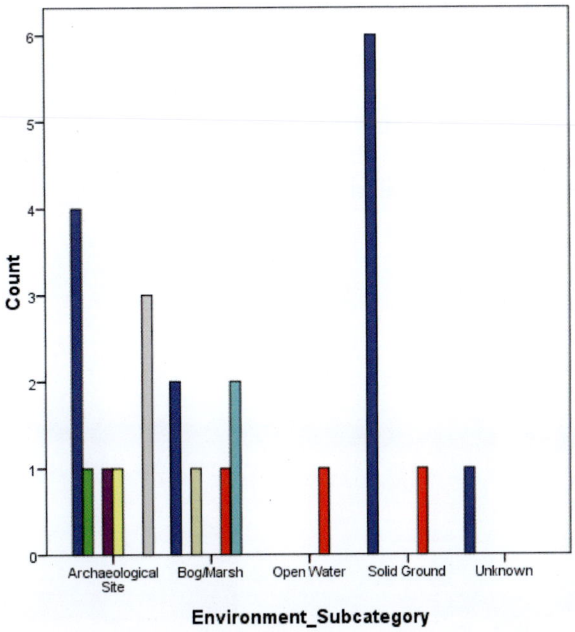


O – Ornaments, Oth – Other, R – Raw Material, T – Tools, W – Weapons.

*Fig. 7.1.5.6. Crosstabulation and bar charts of combinations of major and second artefact group and detailed environments of concealment in Latvian wealth deposits.*

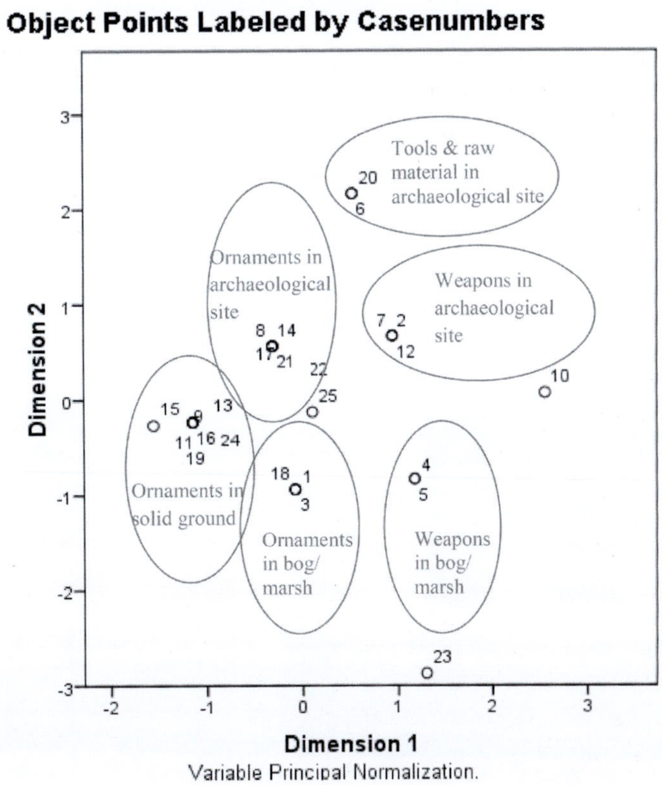


| |
|---|
| 1-Alsungas |
| 2-Cibēni |
| 3-Piltene |
| 4-Kokmuiža_I |
| 5-Kokmuiža_II |
| 6-Ķente_I |
| 7-Mūkukalns_III |
| 8-Rūsiši |
| 9-Miškiņeva |
| 10-Kalnamuiža |
| 11-Lejaslepji |
| 12-Vecmokas |
| 13-Lejasļūdi |
| 14-Ķišukalns |
| 15-Podži |
| 16-Dumpji |
| 17-Mūrnieki |
| 18-Saulītes |
| 19-Baltinava |
| 20-Ķente_II |
| 21-Mūkukalns_II |
| 22-Mežotne |
| 23-Tīras_purvs |
| 24-Sauleskalns_I |
| 25-Sauleskalns_II |

*Fig. 7.1.5.7. MCA plot of combinations of major artefact groups and detailed environments of concealment in Latvian wealth deposits.*

and correspondence between weapons-tools and ornament deposits in different environments are not as clear-cut as we saw in Estonian material.

Putting the data about main artefact groups and detailed environments of concealment into a scattergram plot quite similar patterns emerge (Fig. 7.1.5.7.). There are three clearer scatters of ornament deposits indicating that they are mostly found in dry land, then in archaeological sites, and then also in bog/ marsh. The other scatters have less examples. Weapons are most numerous in archaeological sites. The finds of raw material and tools in archaeological sites (nos 6 and 20) might be considered as outliers and both of them were hidden in one and the same hill-fort at Ķente. There are three other clearer outliers that remain without any comparative material: no. 10 is a single open water weapon deposit from Kalnamuiža; no. 23 is the unusual Tīras purvs bog deposit which

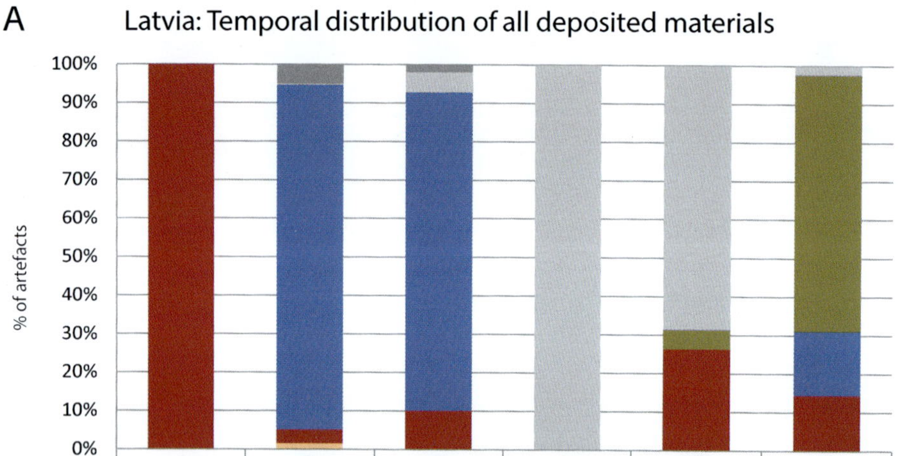


| | 4 | 5 | 6 | 7 | 8 | 9 |
|---|---|---|---|---|---|---|
| Stone | 0 | 72 | 4 | 0 | 0 | 0 |
| Silver | 0 | 4 | 11 | 3 | 13 | 3 |
| Organic | 0 | 0 | 0 | 0 | 1 | 87 |
| Iron | 0 | 1278 | 171 | 0 | 0 | 22 |
| Bronze | 1 | 51 | 21 | 0 | 5 | 19 |
| Bone | 0 | 23 | 0 | 0 | 0 | 0 |

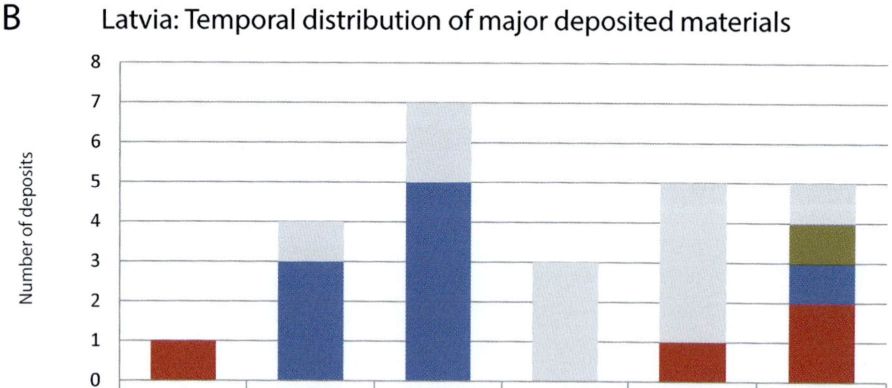


| | 4 | 5 | 6 | 7 | 8 | 9 |
|---|---|---|---|---|---|---|
| Silver | 0 | 1 | 2 | 3 | 4 | 1 |
| Organic | 0 | 0 | 0 | 0 | 0 | 1 |
| Iron | 0 | 3 | 5 | 0 | 0 | 1 |
| Bronze | 1 | 0 | 0 | 0 | 1 | 2 |

*Fig. 7.1.6.1. Temporal distribution (centuries AD) of all artefact materials (A) and major materials (B) in Latvian wealth deposits.*

included numerous organic, especially wooden and textile objects; and finally no. 25 is the Sauleskalns II find of 20 arrowheads found in dry land.

### 7.1.6. Chronological distribution

The chronological distribution shown in A parts of Figures 7.1.6.1. and 7.1.6.2. represent proportions of different material per century. This is because of the 5th century Kokmuiža I deposit which with its 1280 items provides nearly 90% of the material. As this distorts the numerical analysis the relevant proportions are given instead of exact numbers. The latter can be found in the table below the bars.

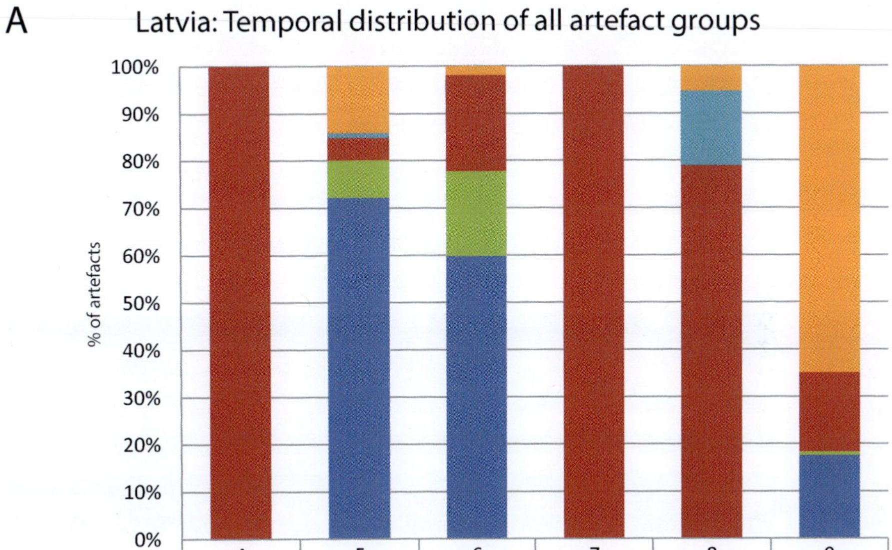


| | 4 | 5 | 6 | 7 | 8 | 9 |
|---|---|---|---|---|---|---|
| Other | 0 | 200 | 4 | 0 | 1 | 85 |
| Raw_Material | 0 | 16 | 0 | 0 | 3 | 0 |
| Ornaments | 1 | 68 | 42 | 3 | 15 | 22 |
| Tools | 0 | 112 | 37 | 0 | 0 | 1 |
| Weapons | 0 | 1032 | 124 | 0 | 0 | 23 |

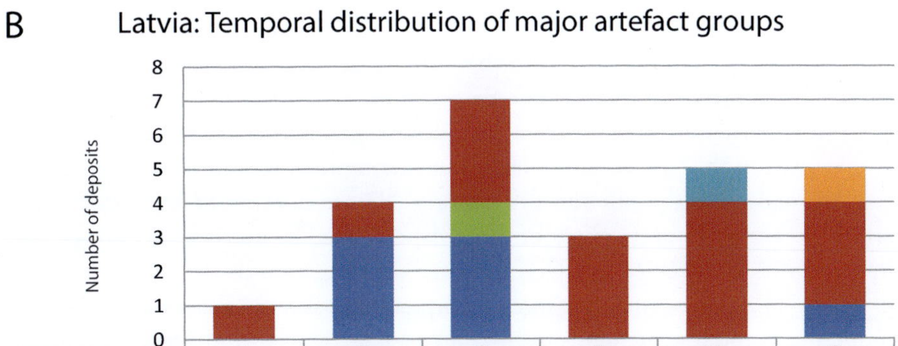


| | 4 | 5 | 6 | 7 | 8 | 9 |
|---|---|---|---|---|---|---|
| Other | 0 | 0 | 0 | 0 | 0 | 1 |
| Raw_Material | 0 | 0 | 0 | 0 | 1 | 0 |
| Ornaments | 1 | 1 | 3 | 3 | 4 | 3 |
| Tools | 0 | 0 | 1 | 0 | 0 | 0 |
| Weapons | 0 | 3 | 3 | 0 | 0 | 1 |

*Fig. 7.1.6.2. Temporal distribution (centuries AD) of all artefact groups (A) and major groups (B) in Latvian wealth deposits.*

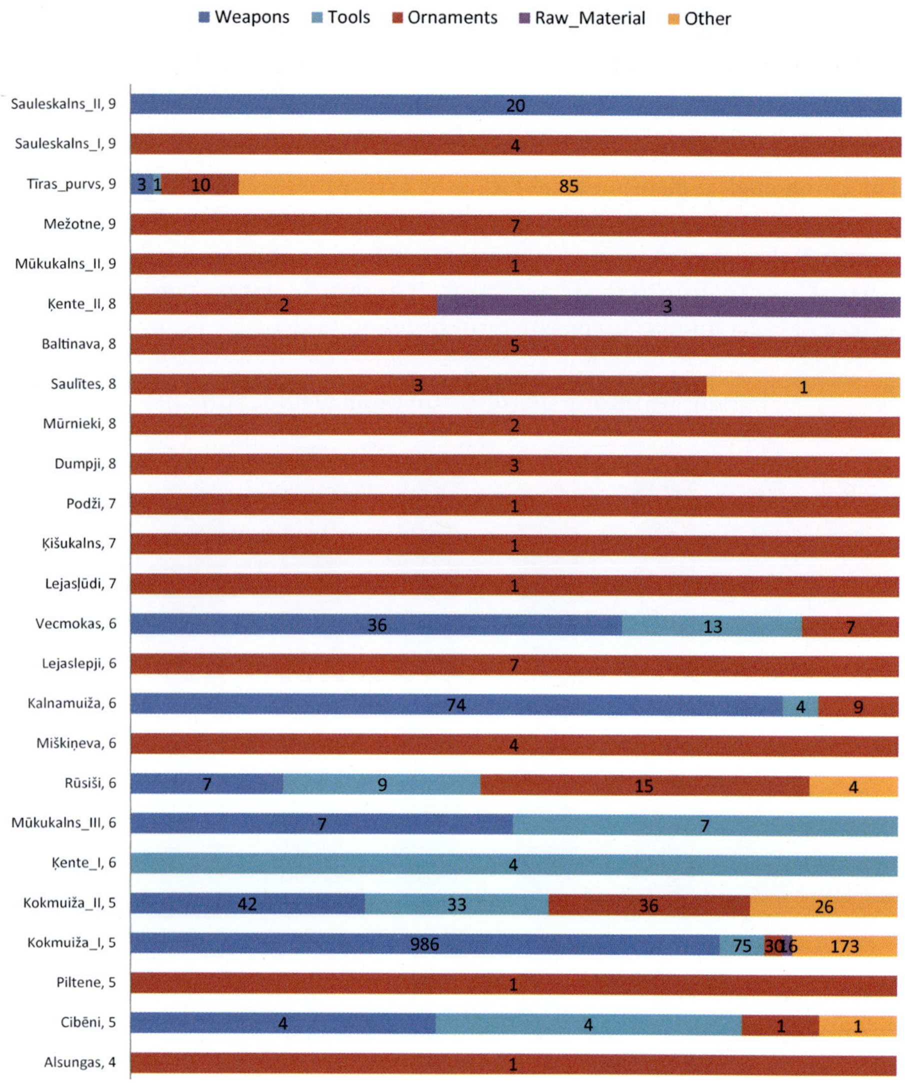


*Fig. 7.1.6.3. Temporal distribution (centuries AD) of artefact groups according to deposits in Latvian wealth deposits. The number in deposit name indicates century.*

The charts and tables representing the temporal distribution of different materials in Latvian wealth deposits (Fig. 7.1.6.1.) show that the first deposit dates only to the 4th century AD and contains bronze. In the 5th century a new material – iron – appears and the number of objects increases considerably. Most of the objects now are from only one find, Kokmuiža I. The same tendency towards dominance of iron and a relatively large number of deposited items is also evident in the 6th century. When considering the predominant material only (Fig. 7.1.6.1. (B)) the 5th and 6th century AD are dominated by iron but they also have examples of a couple of silver depositions. In the 7th and 8th century iron loses its dominance to silver, but there is a decrease in the total number of deposits. The 9th century provides examples of a variety of materials, the most numerous being organic items from again a single deposit, the Tīras purvs find.

Turning towards artefact groups it seems that the patterns overlap partly with the material distribution of wealth deposits. As above, the proportions of artefact groups are provided instead of exact numbers (Fig. 7.1.6.2.). Looking at the charts of numbers of objects of specific artefact groups and only the largest artefact group (Fig. 7.1.6.2. A and B), one sees that the earliest find is a single bronze ornament

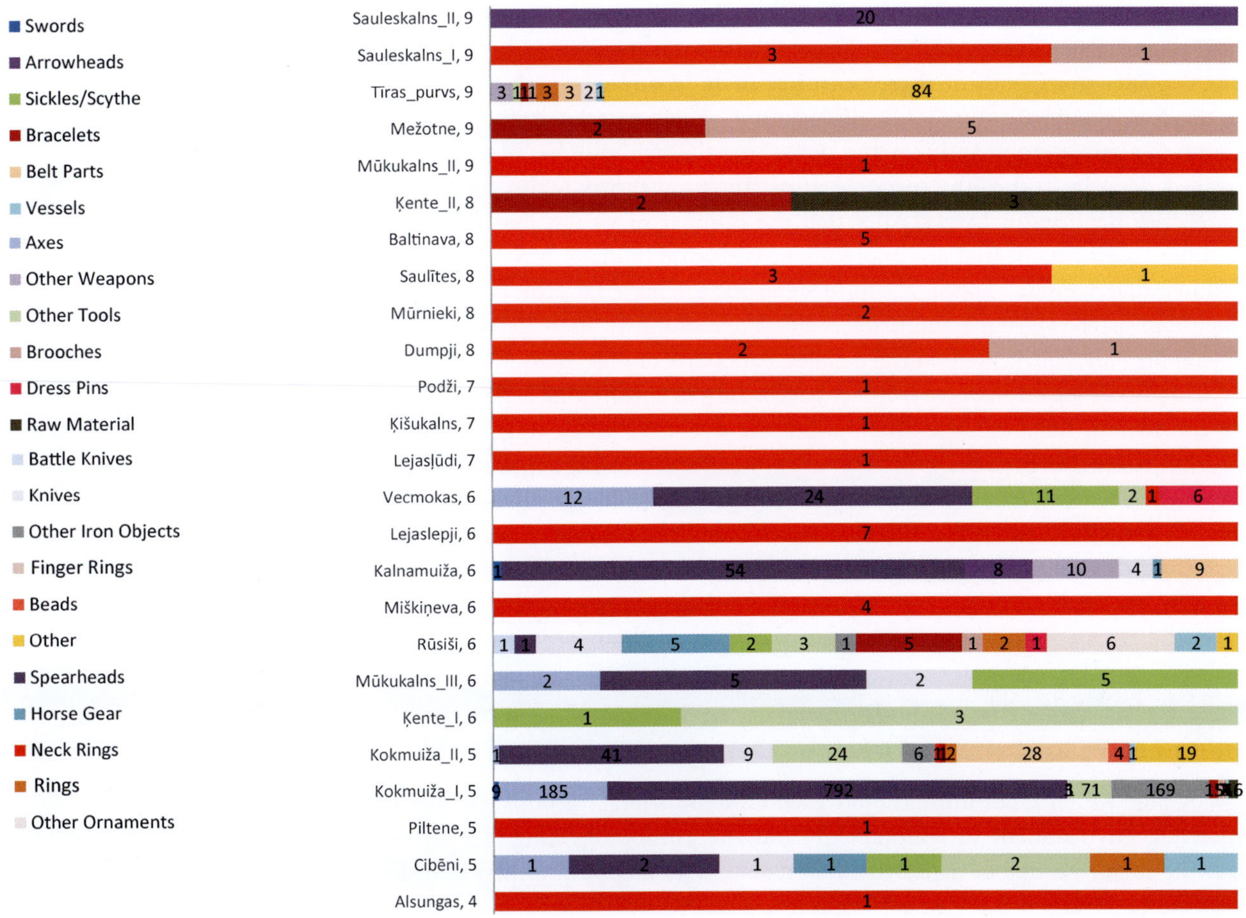


*Fig. 7.1.6.4. Temporal distribution (centuries AD) of artefact types according to deposits in Latvian wealth deposits. The number in deposit name indicates century.*

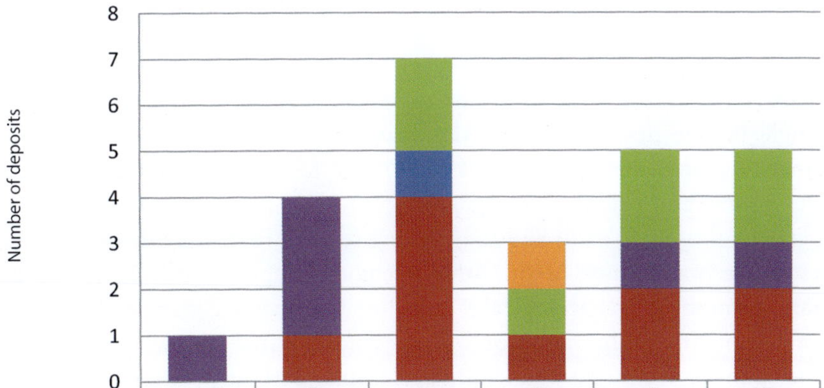


| | 4 | 5 | 6 | 7 | 8 | 9 |
|---|---|---|---|---|---|---|
| Unknown | 0 | 0 | 0 | 1 | 0 | 0 |
| Solid ground | 0 | 0 | 2 | 1 | 2 | 2 |
| Open Water | 0 | 0 | 1 | 0 | 0 | 0 |
| Bog/Marsh | 1 | 3 | 0 | 0 | 1 | 1 |
| Archaeological Site | 0 | 1 | 4 | 1 | 2 | 2 |

*Fig. 7.1.6.5. Temporal distribution (centuries AD) of environments of concealment in Latvian wealth deposits.*

deposit in the 4th century. This is followed by the clear domination of weapons in the 5th and 6th century AD. Weapons are the most numerous making up to 70% but deposits from both of these centuries include ornaments and tools as well as the find group of 'other'. The distribution of deposits according to the most common artefact group within a find shows that the total number of ornament and weapon deposits in the 6th century is equal. The 6th century is also a peak century for wealth deposits in Latvia. After that the number of wealth deposits decreases and the ornaments or find group of 'other' tends to dominate. It is only in the 9th century that weapons appear again in depositional material. The exact details of deposited artefact groups and artefact types according to each deposit and their chronology are represented on the detailed bar charts of Figs 7.1.6.3. and 7.1.6.4.

Finally the selection of environment according to chronology of deposits should be considered. Although the distributions are not too evident (Fig. 7.1.6.5.) it is possible to see that the earliest deposits are more often found in bog/marsh contexts. In the 6th century AD, when the total number of deposits peaks, archaeological sites and dry land are in the majority. In addition, the only open water deposit is also from this unusually rich century. From the 7th century AD onwards there is no clear preference in the environments of concealment: archaeological sites, dry land and after a couple of centuries' gap also bog/marsh are represented.

## 7.2. Practices of wealth depositing in Latvia: Long-term perspective and the question of change

MCA plot which takes into account predominant artefact groups, predominant material, environment of concealment and the chronology (Fig. 7.2.1.) points out the major groups of depositional practices. The mapping results of different contextual criteria of Latvian 1st-9th century AD wealth deposits are represented in Figs 7.2.2.-7.2.4.

Based on the previous analysis and the results of the MCA (Fig. 7.2.1.) some general patterns and unique outliers in the corpus of Latvian wealth deposits emerge. The clearest division is between weapon-tools in archaeological sites and watery conditions, and silver-bronze ornament deposits in dry land and watery conditions. However, looking at the more detailed characteristics of the finds and especially their chronology, some more specific patterns become evident. The earliest groups of deposits forming a particular depositional tradition are single neck-ring deposits from boggy-marshy areas. The earliest deposit is a 4th century single bronze neck-ring from **Alsungas** (375-425 AD). The **Piltene** find of a single gilded silver neck-ring has been dated to the transitional century between the Roman and Middle Iron Age (400-500 AD). There is a chronological overlap between those two finds and they belong to the ornament side of the MCA plot. However, while most of the other ornament deposits are discovered in either solid ground or archaeological sites, these finds were concealed in water-related environments. Additionally, both of the finds are from the western coastal area of the country. We might be looking at a similar early depositional tradition in the case of those two finds, although in the Alsungas example the material is more 'appropriate' for the Roman Iron Age, whereas the Piltene one forms a link with the silver deposits of the following period.

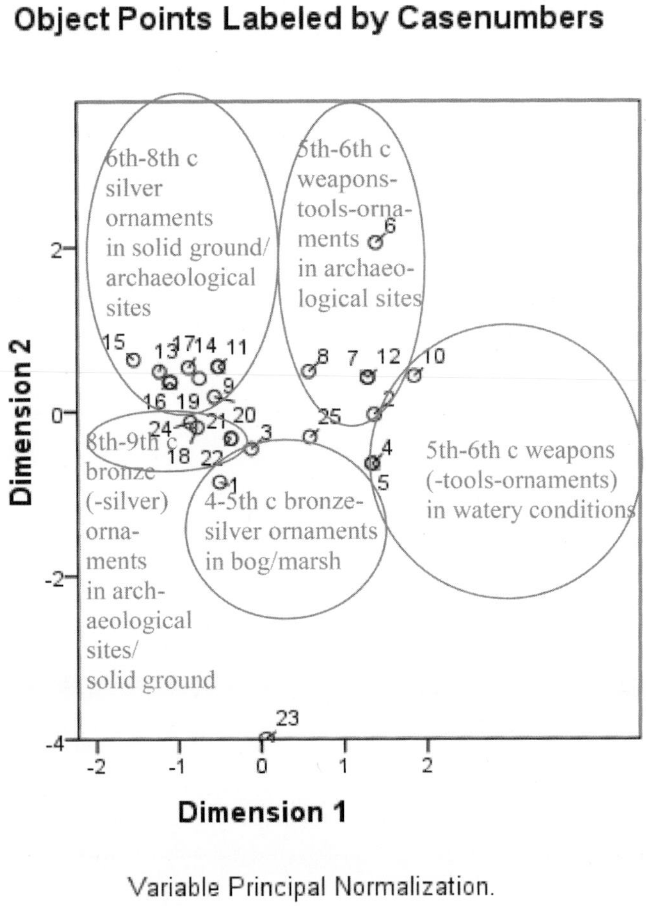


| |
|---|
| 1-Alsungas |
| 2-Cibēni |
| 3-Piltene |
| 4-Kokmuiža_I |
| 5-Kokmuiža_II |
| 6-Ķente_I |
| 7-Mūkukalns_III |
| 8-Rūsiši |
| 9-Miškiņeva |
| 10-Kalnamuiža |
| 11-Lejaslepji |
| 12-Vecmokas |
| 13-Lejasļūdi |
| 14-Ķišukalns |
| 15-Podži |
| 16-Dumpji |
| 17-Mūrnieki |
| 18-Saulītes |
| 19-Baltinava |
| 20-Ķente_II |
| 21-Mūkukalns_II |
| 22-Mežotne |
| 23-Tīras_purvs |
| 24-Sauleskalns_I |
| 25-Sauleskalns_II |

*Fig. 7.2.1. MCA plot of combinations of major artefact groups, materials, detailed environments of concealment and dating of Latvian wealth deposits.*

There are no other artefact finds in Latvia in the earliest part of the Roman Iron Age. This leaves the number of wealth deposits in Latvia in this period rather small, especially in comparison with the neighbouring countries. However, compared to Estonia there are considerably more Roman coin hoards from Latvia (Apals *et al.* 2001, 213, fig. 156; Ducmane & Ozoliņa 2009) although a large number of them are uncertain finds with insufficient data about the context of discovery. The majority are from the 3rd-4th century AD and they contain tens of bronze coins. If coin hoards are included the number of intentionally deposited artefact finds in Latvia during the Roman Iron Age rises to at least six.

A considerable change in deposited artefacts, quantity of objects and deposited materials takes place in the first century of the Middle Iron Age. There are two deposits – **Kokmuiža I** and **Kokmuiža II** – from the second half of the 5th century which both contain numerous weapons, but also some tools and ornaments in them. As emphasised above, those two finds, but especially the first one, provide the vast majority of artefacts in Latvian 1st-9th century AD wealth deposits. Both of them were hidden in the boggy area at the foot of the contemporary hill-fort close to the southern border of the country. To those finds the 6th century **Kalnamuiža** deposit can be added as a similar mixed deposit in which weapons are predominant. This was found at the Tērvete Rivulet bank, not far from the Tērvete hill-fort, under a granite stone. This find is also geographically closely situated to the previously mentioned Kokmuiža deposits. Thus we can see a specific depositional tradition in the southern region of the country in which a mixture

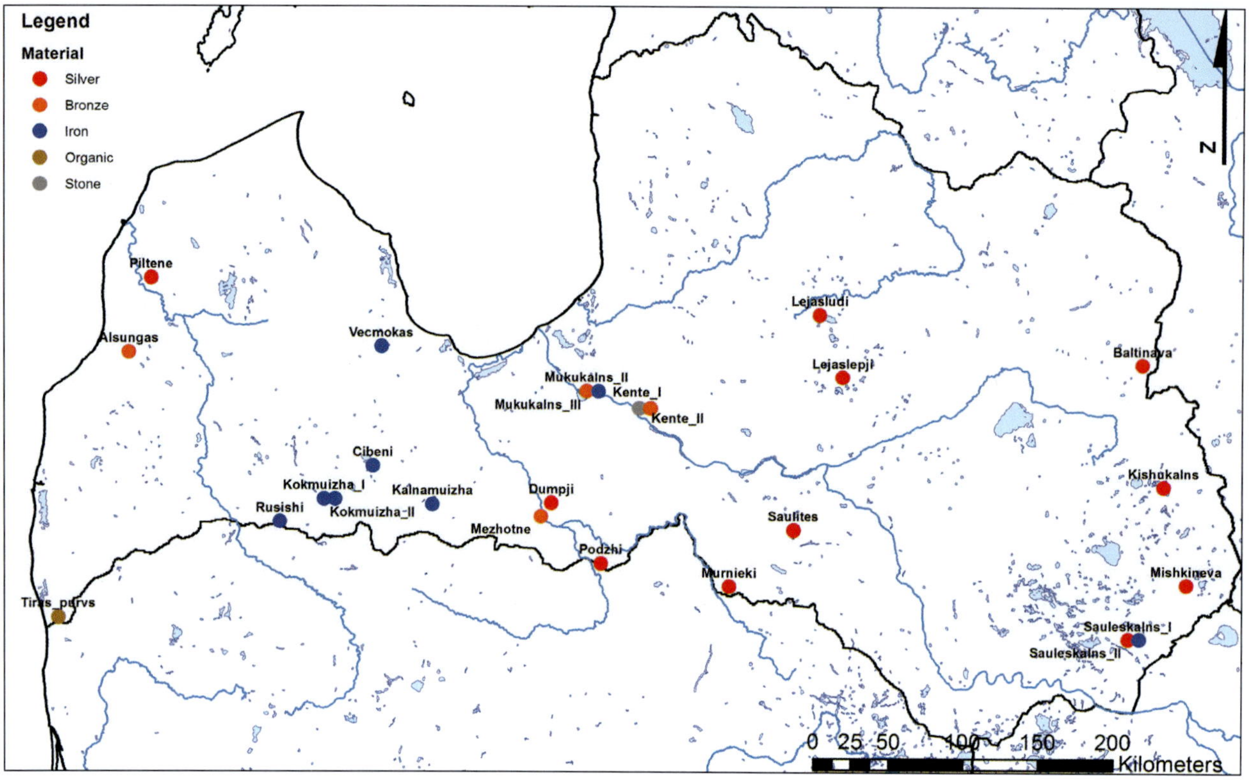


*Fig. 7.2.2. Map of major materials represented in Latvian wealth deposits.*

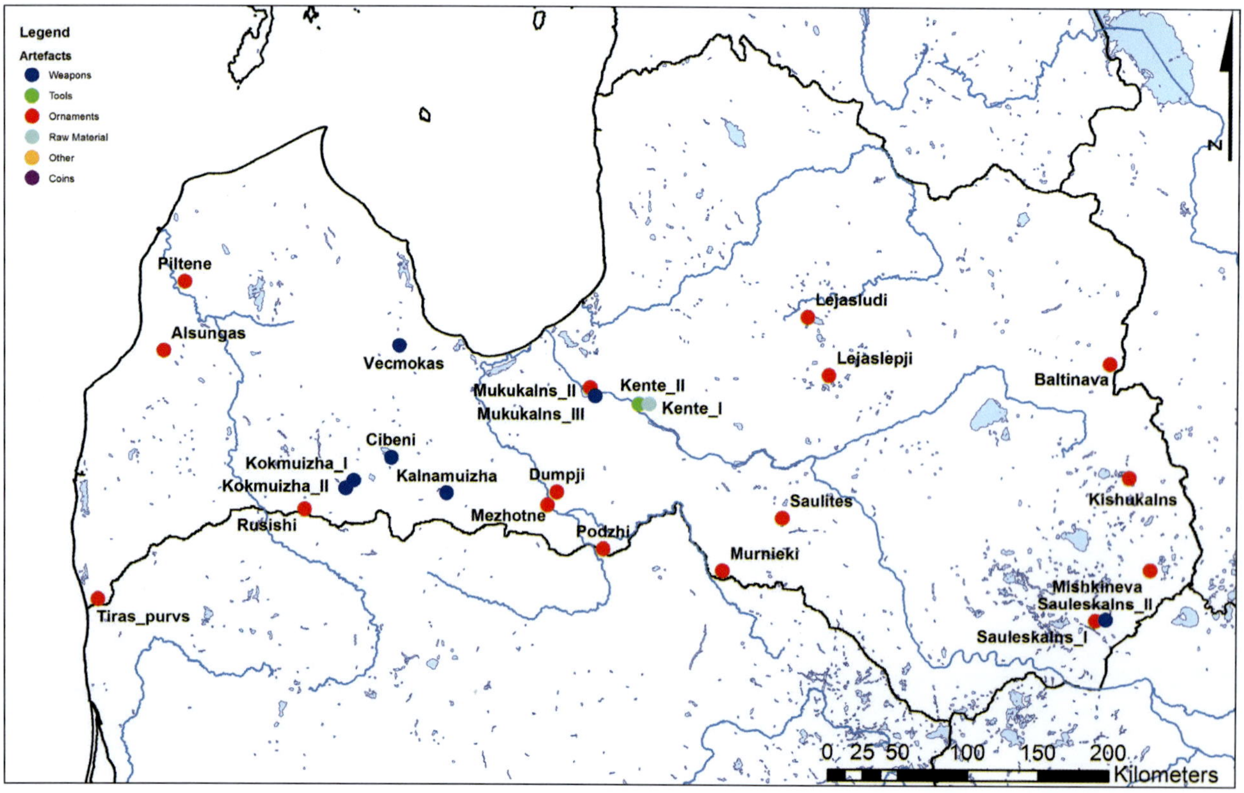


*Fig. 7.2.3. Map of major artefact groups represented in Latvian wealth deposits.*

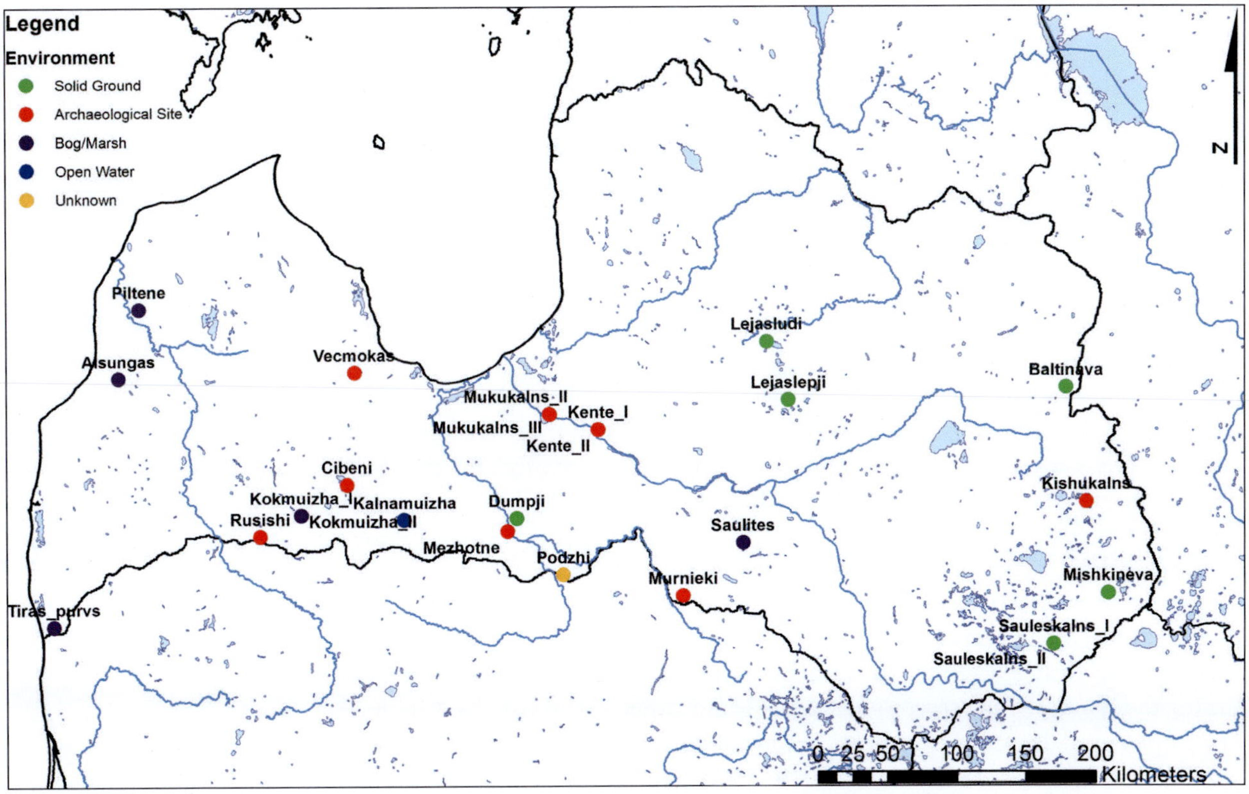


*Fig. 7.2.4. Map of environments of concealment of Latvian wealth deposits.*

of weapons, tools and ornaments (dominated by the first) are concealed in water related environments, in the vicinity of contemporary hill-forts, throughout the first centuries of the Middle Iron Age.

At the same time, the 5th-6th century AD, slightly different depositional traditions appear in the southern and central part of the country providing the examples of the **Cibēni, Ķente I**, **Mūkukalns III**, **Rūsiši** and **Vecmokas** deposits. What we see on a larger scale are the deposits of weapons, tools and ornaments, however, the first are not in such a clear majority as in the examples above, and the proportion of tools is larger. All those finds have been discovered either in archaeological sites or in dry land. The **Cibēni** and **Rūsiši** deposits are situated in the southern regions, not far from the previously mentioned weapon finds in watery environments. However, both of these deposits were discovered in the vicinity of a contemporary burial ground and consist of items that can be regarded as paraphernalia of an elite warrior, drinking horns and horse gear besides weapons and tools. This looks like another material manifestation of warrior-related ideology in this southernmost region in the 5th and 6th centuries AD, but in those two instances it is a different version, a possible cenotaph for a lost warrior. At the same time in the central region there are three 6th century finds: **Ķente I**, **Mūkukalns III** and **Vecmokas**. The first two were found in the rampart constructions of the hill-fort and they both contain large number of tools. Vecmokas deposit was discovered at the foot of the hill-fort and it contained some more weapons compared to the other finds. We do not have any detailed information about its discovery. However, the historic maps and the current landscape situation indicate boggy and marshy areas in the vicinity of the hill-fort. It seems likely that those items were concealed in water-related conditions, and indeed, that this find might go well with the examples from the previous paragraph i.e. large weapons-tools-ornaments in bogs/marshes like Kokmuiža I and II, and Kalnamuiža deposits.

At the same time as the weapon-dominated iron deposits another separate depositional tradition emerges. From the 6th century onwards up until the 8th century AD we see numerous silver ornament deposits: **Miškiņeva, Lejaslepji, Lejasļūdi, Ķišukalns, Podži, Dumpji, Mūrnieki, Saulītes, Baltinava**. Most of them contain nothing but neck-rings, found in either archaeological sites or dry land. However, there are some subdivisions within this large group of deposits. During the 6th century AD we see larger amounts of silver neck-rings deposited together. **Miškiņeva** and **Lejaslepji** deposits include four and seven silver neck-rings respectively. In the 7th century AD the number of deposited ornaments decreases considerably and now, as seen in the examples of **Lejasļūdi, Ķišukalns** and **Podži** only a single neck-ring is concealed. Although all the three latter finds are most likely found in dry land, the exact finding circumstances for the Podži deposit are not certain and the Ķišukalns find was most likely discovered in the settlement at the foot of Ķišukalns hill-fort. In the 8th century AD the number of deposited neck-rings increases again sometimes combined with other artefact types. However, as with the previous century, the choice of environment shows a mixture. **Dumpji** and **Baltinava** finds have been concealed in dry land, **Mūrnieki** is from a settlement site and **Saulītes** from a possible marshy area. The latter makes the Saulītes find exceptional, because no other ornament deposits have been discovered in water-related environments. The MCA plot sets it together with the later groups of ornament deposits in archaeological sites, but as we will see from more detailed analysis of those in the next paragraph, it seems to belong to the silver neck-ring deposits discussed here. All those finds are known from the eastern and central Latvia and no such silver neck-rings deposits are known from the western half of the country between the 6th and 9th century AD. The Ikšķile find of three 7th century silver neck-rings from central Latvia (Appendix 1.1.), but unfortunately without information about exact find-spot, fits well with this tradition of silver neck-ring deposits both chronologically and spatially. Thus there seems to be a continuous, long-term and widespread tradition of depositing silver neck-rings in the central and eastern regions of Latvia which are mostly related to dry land or archaeological sites, although there are also examples of water-related conditions. Additionally, if neck-rings are found in archaeological sites these are settlements or hill-forts not burial areas.

In the 8th and 9th century AD more diversity and a larger amount of unique depositional practices is seen, but there are also some more distinct clusters in the material. The tradition of depositing bronze ornaments in archaeological sites is represented in three examples: **Ķente II, Mūkukalns II, Mežotne**. All three were discovered in contemporary hill-forts. The common denominator for those finds is bronze ornaments and although Ķente II also contains raw material, these are raw materials for ornament production. Mūkukalns II contains a single bronze neck-ring. Mežotne find includes a large number of bracelets, but also brooches. All three finds are located in a small area in the central and southern part of Latvia. To this list we might perhaps also add the 9th century **Sauleskalns I** deposit of three silver neck-rings and a bronze brooch from the south-eastern corner of Latvia. This find was discovered in the dry land, but many scholars have connected the Sauleskalns area and finds therein with religious activities including a possible natural sacred site complex (Vaitkevičius 2004, 12; see also below).

An evident outlier is the **Tīras purvs** bog find from the coastal area of the south-western corner of Latvia. This is an atypical find which includes a large quantity of various well-preserved organic materials such as wooden and leather items and textile fragments. Besides those, the deposit also includes fragments of a shield, some tools, a bracelet and a brooch, some belt parts and fragments of a possible drinking horn. It looks like a combination of items related to male personal equipment. The remarkable preservation of organic material, the mixture of different artefact functional groups, but a small number of weapons and ornaments, and the later date (800 AD is the earliest possible dating for this find) sets it apart from all the other weapon or water condition related deposits in Latvia.

The **Sauleskalns II** find is a second outlier from the 9th century. This is a deposit of 20 arrowheads in dry land. As mentioned above the Sauleskalns area has been considered as a possible prehistoric sacred site. Arrowheads in general are very rare finds in the eastern Baltic wealth deposits, but here we have altogether 20 of them deposited at once. The description of the discovery indicates that arrows were placed in the same direction and as the wood fragments were still evident in the ground they were most probably deposited with shafts. What makes this deposit stand out besides the content is that most of the weapon-dominated deposits are in watery conditions, and the ones that include a considerable proportion of tools (also ornaments) are found in hill-fort or settlement contexts. Thus, the Sauleskalns II find as one of the latest examples of Latvian 1st-9th century AD wealth deposits remains unique both in terms of artefact content and environment of concealment. It might perhaps be related to the close by ornament deposit indicating indeed the significance of this area as possible sacred site in the 9th century AD.

In general terms, there are very few deposits in the first half of the Roman Iron Age and most of these consist of Roman coins. The number of deposits, including Roman coin hoards, increases in the second half of the Roman Iron Age, although non-monetary artefact deposits remain marginal. A sudden change happens at the beginning of the Middle Iron Age when we see if not a serious increase in the number of the deposits, then certainly an increase in the number of deposited artefacts. In the 5th-6th century AD for the first time the predominant material is iron and most of the finds are weapon deposits (in combination with smaller quantity of both tools and ornaments) in water related conditions or weapons-tools-ornaments deposits (without the clear dominance of weapons) in solid ground or archaeological sites. The latter include both hill-forts and burial sites. Those iron deposits are mostly found in the southern and central regions of the country. The peak of deposits in the 6th century AD is mainly provided by iron deposits, but there is also a large number of silver ornament deposits. This tradition of hiding silver neck-rings in dry land and archaeological sites continues up to the 9th century with the dominance of such deposits in the 7th and 8th centuries. Most of those silver neck-ring finds are located either in the eastern or central areas of Latvia. What we see here is a long-term, widely followed and clearly deliberate depositional tradition among the other quickly changing and variable depositional practices. There are no weapon deposits in the 7th and 8th century AD and the total number of deposits drops from seven to 3-5 in the following centuries. The 9th century AD brings a whole mixture of depositional ideas providing also two of the main outliers in terms of concealed objects and environments of concealment. At the same time the concept of depositing ornaments in the dry land and archaeological sites seems to continue although in this last century those ornament deposits show more variability of concealed objects which can be also made of bronze now. Thus the age of silver, especially silver neck-ring deposits seems to come to an end towards the transition to the Viking Age and weapon deposits never seem to re-establish their importance and dominance after their peak in the 5th and 6th century AD. The combinations of artefact and environments of concealment are more variable when dealing with iron and weapon-dominated finds. However, when it comes to ornament deposits it is possible to see some consistency throughout the centuries. It is only in the 9th century that we see the increased variability of different deposits within one century.

*Chapter 8*

# Practices of wealth depositing in Lithuania

## 8.1. 1st-9th century AD wealth deposits in Lithuania

There are 39 deposits of artefacts recorded from Lithuania dating to the 1st-9th century AD. Nineteen deposits are coin hoards (six of them uncertain), two hoards include coins and other artefacts. As the coin hoards will be excluded from the detailed contextual analysis and mixed assemblages will be included, this leaves us with 20 wealth deposits. However, due to problematic chronology and find-spots four more finds are excluded from the final analysis (see below), leaving 16 as the total number of wealth deposits in Lithuania. The main characteristics and descriptions of those 16 finds are found in Tables 8.1.1.-8.1.3.

### 8.1.1. Roman coins

The number of Antique coins (mainly Roman) discovered in the territory of contemporary Lithuania as hoards, single finds or in burials (Tautavičius 1977, 184) and other sites, is over 1000 (Kropotkin 1961, 98-101; Michelbertas 2001; Lang 2007a, 163). This number should be larger because quite often tens of coins have been mentioned in relation to the discovery, but unfortunately have been lost or the description of discovery does not give any further details.

Mostly deposits of coins include only numismatic material. However, there are two examples where coins were discovered with other artefacts (Dargiškė, Dirmeikiai). There are also two finds with just one coin recorded (Minija River valley, Pedievaitis). These might result from the accidental loss of a single small artefact such as a coin. However, the coin find from the Minija River valley is

*Table 8.1.1. Chronology, artefact functional groups, and materials represented in Lithuanian wealth deposits.*

| Wealth Deposit | Dating of artefacts (AD) | Dating (c.) | Weapons | Tools | Ornaments | Coins | Raw Material | Other | Material 1 | Material 2 |
|---|---|---|---|---|---|---|---|---|---|---|
| Miežaičiai | 1-200 | 2 | | | | | 8 | | Bronze | |
| Dirmeikiai | 161-250 | 3 | | | 1 | 2 | | | Bronze | |
| Dargiškė | 244-350 | 4 | | | 2 | 1 | | | Bronze | |
| Gudėniškės | 400-600 | 6 | 1 | | | | | | Iron | |
| Lėbartai | 500-600 | 6 | | | | | | 1 | Bronze | |
| Draustiniai | 500-700 | 7 | | | 5 | | | | Silver | Bronze |
| Migoniai_II | 500-700 | 7 | | | 3 | | | | Silver | |
| Migoniai_I | 600-700 | 7 | | | 3 | | 5 | | Bronze | |
| Velžiai | 600-700 | 7 | | | 1 | | | | Silver | |
| Baubliai | 600-800 | 8 | | | 3 | | | | Silver | |
| Negarba | 650-800 | 8 | | | 1 | | | | Bronze | |
| Šluostikiai | 500-900 | 8 | 3 | 1 | | | | | Iron | Stone |
| Palanga_I | 700-900 | 9 | | | 2 | | | | Bronze | |
| Vaineikiai | 700-1200 | 9 | | | 3 | | | | Silver | |
| Užpelkiai | 150-450 (150-300 & 350-450) | 2-3; 4-5 | | | 4 | | | | Bronze | Silver |
| Barstyčiai | 600-1100 | 7-8; 10-11 | 15 | | 3 | | | | Iron | Bronze |
| **Total: 16** | | | **19** | **1** | **31** | **3** | **13** | **1** | | |

| Wealth Deposit | Dating (c.) | Axes | Battle Knives | Spear-heads | Other Weapons | Other Tools | Neck-rings | Bracelets | Brooches | Belt Parts | Dress Pins | Other Ornaments | Coin | Raw Material | Other | Comments on 'other' |
|---|---|---|---|---|---|---|---|---|---|---|---|---|---|---|---|---|
| Miežaičiai | 2 | | | | | | | | | | | | | 8 | | |
| Dirmeikiai | 3 | | | | | | | | 1 | | | | 2 | | | |
| Dargiškė | 4 | | | | | | | 2 | | | | | 1 | | | |
| Gudėniškės | 6 | 1 | | | | | | | | | | | | | | |
| Lėbartai | 6 | | | | | | | | | | | | | | 1 | Bronze comb |
| Draustiniai | 7 | | | | | | 4 | 1 | | | | | | | | |
| Migoniai_II | 7 | | | | | | 3 | | | | | | | | | |
| Migoniai_I | 7 | | | | | | | 2 | 1 | | | | | 5 | | |
| Velžiai | 7 | | | | | | 1 | | | | | | | | | |
| Baubliai | 8 | | | | | | 3 | | | | | | | | | |
| Negarba | 8 | | | | | | | | | | | 1 | | | | |
| Šluostikiai | 8 | | | 3 | | 1 | | | | | | | | | | |
| Palanga_I | 9 | | | | | | 1 | | | | 1 | | | | | |
| Vaineikiai | 9 | | | | | | 3 | | | | | | | | | |
| Užpelkiai | 2-3; 4-5 | | | | | | 2 | | 2 | | | | | | | |
| Barstyčiai | 7-8; 10-11 | 2 | 1 | 11 | 1 | | | | 2 | 1 | | | | | | |
| **Total: 16** | | **3** | **1** | **14** | **1** | **1** | **17** | **5** | **6** | **1** | **1** | **1** | **3** | **13** | **1** | |

*Table 8.1.2. Artefact groups in Lithuanian wealth deposits.*

| Wealth Deposit | Dating (c.) | Environment | Environment Subtype | Depth (cm) | Markers | Archaeological Site |
|---|---|---|---|---|---|---|
| Miežaičiai | 2 | Unknown | | | | |
| Dirmeikiai | 3 | Solid ground | | | | |
| Dargiškė | 4 | Watery condition | Marsh | | | |
| Gudėniškės | 6 | Watery condition | Bog | | | |
| Lėbartai | 6 | Solid ground | | 40-50 | | |
| Draustiniai | 7 | Watery condition | Bog | | | |
| Migoniai_II | 7 | Solid ground | | | | |
| Migoniai_I | 7 | Solid ground | | 30-40 | | |
| Velžiai | 7 | Solid ground | Archaeological Site | | | Hill-fort |
| Baubliai | 8 | Watery condition | Marsh | 30-40 | | |
| Negarba | 8 | Watery condition | Bog | | | Hill-fort |
| Šluostikiai | 8 | Watery condition | River | | Flat boulder rock | |
| Palanga_I | 9 | Watery condition | Marsh | | | |
| Vaineikiai | 9 | Watery condition | Bog | | | |
| Užpelkiai | 2-3; 4-5 | Watery condition | Bog | 150 | | Hill-fort |
| Barstyčiai | 7-8; 10-11 | Watery condition | Bog | | | |
| **Total: 16** | | | | | | |

*Table 8.1.3. Environments of concealment of Lithuanian wealth deposits.*

worth considering because there are several Bronze Age finds from the nearby area: a bronze foundry axe mould, human figurine (Grigalavičienė 1980, no. 153, tab: IX: 3), and a bronze hoard (Čivilytė 2004, 227, figs 1, 2, 7; Bliujienė 2007, 51). Therefore, it has been proposed that this area might have been a Bronze Age offering site (Bliujienė 2010, 159) and the coin find might also be related to this offering tradition. In the case of the Pedievaitis find it has been stressed that numerous archaeological sites are known nearby (Bliujienė 2010, 159). This, however, does not eliminate but rather increases the possibility of accidental loss. Due to the high probability of accidental loss of single coin, these two finds are excluded from the overview table of Lithuanian coin deposits (see Appendix 1.3.).

Removing the six uncertain finds and two finds of just one coin leaves a total number of 194 coins discovered in 11 coin finds and two mixed deposits (Appendix 1.3.). These are mainly bronze coins. There is only one silver coin from Lileikėniai which unfortunately did not reach the museum collections. The largest documented hoard consists of 51, the smallest of just three coins. It is likely that coins circulated some time before they arrived in the modern Lithuania and were deposited. This is also evident in the cases where one hoard consists of coins from a wide time period (e.g. Raseiniai, Saulažoliai). The most numerous are the coins of Antoninus Pius (138-161) (23 coins), followed by Marcus Aurelius (161-180) (21 coins), then comes Trajanus (98-117) (12 coins). The earliest coin found in Lithuania is Augustus Octavianus (27 BC-14 AD), the latest is Constans I (337-350). The earliest hoards were concealed somewhere around the beginning of the second half of the 2nd century AD, the latest in the first quarter of the 5th century AD. The majority of the deposits of coins were probably hidden in the 2nd-3rd century AD.

Information about the finding circumstances of coin deposits remains often unknown and less attention has been paid to these aspects. There are cases where coins have been found in watery conditions, mainly river banks (Lileikėniai, Minija Valley), marsh (Dargiškė) or lake (Padievaitis). In most cases we are dealing with just one coin find or with a combination of coins with other artefacts. Only the find of Lileikėniai, of which only eight coins are certain, is an example of a small hoard found in watery conditions. In five examples (Dargiškė, Dirmeikiai, Kaunas, Noreišiai, Saulažoliai) the coins and sometimes other artefacts, were hidden in a clay vessel.

### 8.1.2. Problems and exclusions

Four finds, Sargėnai, Siraičiai, Rokiškis and Švėkšna, which are traditionally included in the list of 1st-9th century AD wealth deposits have been excluded from the current analysis. In the case of the Siraičiai the artefacts have been dated from the Roman Period until the 12th century AD. Most of the artefacts are from the later periods (after the 9th century AD). It was probably hidden somewhere in the Late Iron Age, after the 9th century AD. The only reason why this find has been mentioned in relation to the earlier periods of Iron Age is due to two small bronze beads/pendants that according to Bliujienė (2007, 162) belong to the Roman Iron Age. As the find-spot is close to the burial area it is questionable whether these beads belong to separate deposit or to the previous burials. The find has been interpreted as a Late Iron Age deposit of looted grave goods (Bliujienė 2008, 173).

Quite similar is the situation with the Sargėnai find. It includes objects from the 6th century AD, but it also has finds from later periods (Kazakevičius & Malonaitis 2006, 78, tab. 1; Bliujienė 2008, 173). It is thought to have been hidden somewhere in the 13th century AD and again interpreted as a deposit of plundered burial goods concealed after the period of interest in the current thesis.

The Rokiškis find of two silver neck-rings must be excluded, because the exact circumstances of discovery and thus the environment of concealment are unknown. It was found somewhere in the Rokiškis area, but this is unfortunately not enough to make any further conclusions about the context of the deposit.

For a long time the Švėkšna find of seven Egyptian origin bronze deity statuettes was regarded as an extraordinary deposit with no parallels from any other Lithuanian archaeological site. It was believed to be a wealth deposit that was discovered during the excavation of an Iron Age burial ground in the 19th century (LMAB F31-1440-96; Kraszewski 1860, 316-319; Tautavičius 1977, 133). Later critical enquiries revealed that the deposit was a fake archaeological 'discovery' fictionally related to a later period burial ground by young antiquarian Count Adam Plater who excavated the site at the time (Kolendo 1976; see also Čivilytė 2007). Therefore the find cannot be included in the current analysis either.

A problematic find is also the Gudėniškės deposit. Numerous different artefacts were found during the digging of quagmire in the 1970s, but only an axe was handed over to the museum. According to some scholars we might be looking at burial goods, because there is a burial mound very close to the find-spot (Bliujienė 2010, 158; Vaitkevičius 2006, 402). Unfortunately there is not enough data to decide for or against any of these interpretations and in the current study the find is regarded as a wealth deposit. However, it needs to be remembered that only an axe is counted in detailed analysis, because of the lack of information about any other artefacts.

A single complex pendant from Negarba is worth pointing out. Although it is a single find and in principle might be looked at as a simple loss of artefact, the size and finding circumstances suggest that it is an intentional deposit. It consists of several small attached pendants and long chains, which possibly belong to a set of breast decoration attached with a dress pin. It was discovered in what is now a boggy area at the foot of the Negarba hill-fort. The appearance of the item and context of discovery are evidences of an intentional deposit which is also supported by the local scholars (pers. comm. Audronė Bliujienė).

Some chronology-related issues have to be discussed in relation to the Palanga, Šluostikiai, Vaineikiai deposits. They include artefacts that can be dated to the later time periods i.e. Viking Age, but which according to some parallels have been considered as belonging to the latter part of the Middle Iron Age. As explained in the methodology chapter these finds are included in the current study due to their earliest chronology, because it cannot be excluded that those wealth deposits were concealed before the Viking Age.

### 8.1.3. General overview of analysed material

Looking at the production material, we can see that the variety of represented materials in Lithuanian wealth deposits is relatively smaller than in Estonia and Latvia. The majority of the deposits include single material (Table 8.1.1.). The most numerous are bronzes which form half of the material. They are followed by iron and silver with around a quarter of the items (Fig. 8.1.3.1. (A)). Considering only the major material the proportions remain the same (Fig. 8.1.3.1. (B)). However, the representation of silver now rises to one third leaving iron-dominated deposits in the third place.

*Fig. 8.1.3.1. Distribution of all artefact materials (A) and major materials (B) in Lithuanian wealth deposits.*

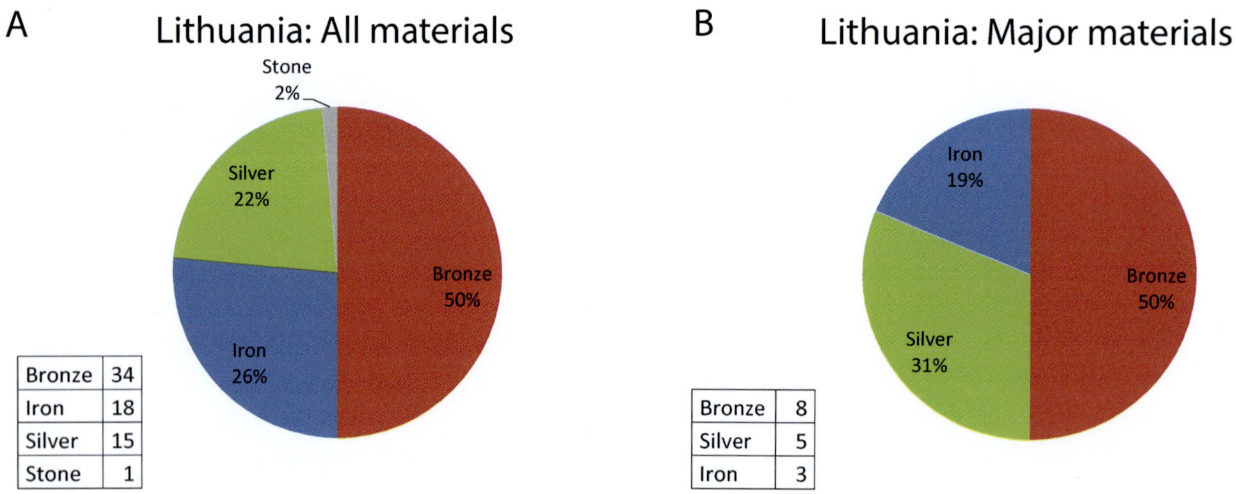


| | |
|---|---|
| Bronze | 34 |
| Iron | 18 |
| Silver | 15 |
| Stone | 1 |

| | |
|---|---|
| Bronze | 8 |
| Silver | 5 |
| Iron | 3 |

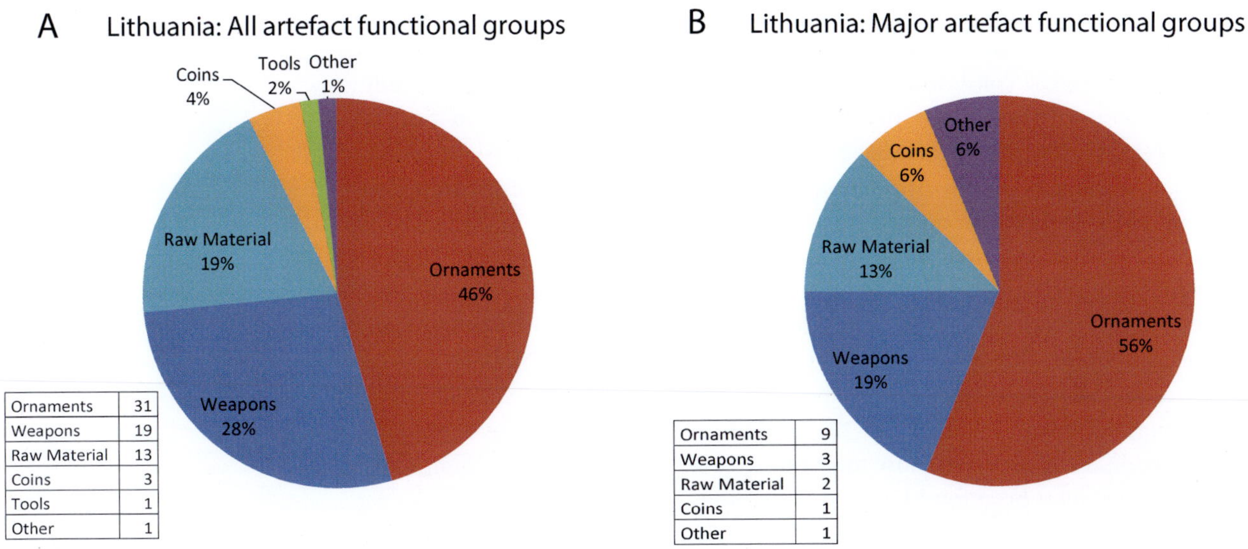


| | |
|---|---|
| Ornaments | 31 |
| Weapons | 19 |
| Raw Material | 13 |
| Coins | 3 |
| Tools | 1 |
| Other | 1 |

| | |
|---|---|
| Ornaments | 9 |
| Weapons | 3 |
| Raw Material | 2 |
| Coins | 1 |
| Other | 1 |

*Fig. 8.1.3.2. Distribution of all artefact functional groups (A) and major functional groups (B) in Lithuanian wealth deposits.*

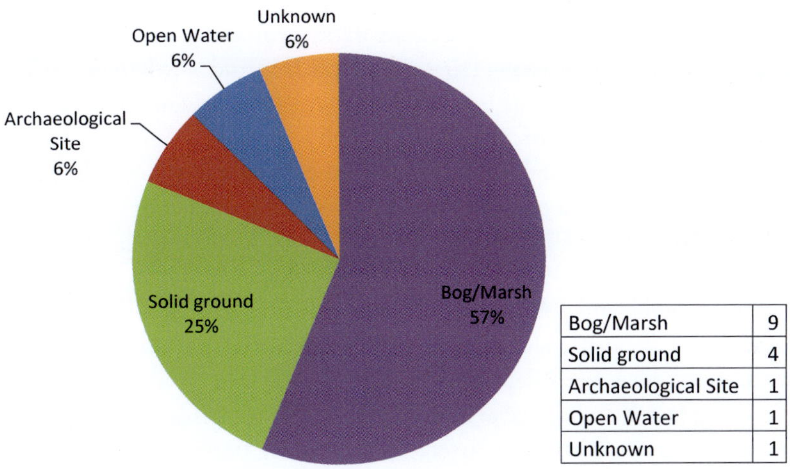


| | |
|---|---|
| Bog/Marsh | 9 |
| Solid ground | 4 |
| Archaeological Site | 1 |
| Open Water | 1 |
| Unknown | 1 |

*Fig. 8.1.3.3. Environments of concealment of Lithuanian wealth deposits.*

The most numerous artefacts in Lithuanian wealth deposits are ornaments (31 objects), followed by weapons (19) and raw material (13) (Fig. 8.1.3.2. (A)). Other artefact groups such as coins, tools and the find group of 'other' are less represented. Considering only the most common artefact group within every deposit these proportions change slightly (Fig. 8.1.3.2. (B)). Ornament deposits form half of the whole material and the proportion of weapon deposits is less than a fifth. There are two deposits where raw material is the largest artefact group. Coins and 'other' are in the majority in one case each. Tools are never in the majority in Lithuanian wealth deposits.

The most numerous artefact group among Lithuanian wealth deposits is clearly neck-rings (Table 8.1.2.). There are altogether 17 neck-rings from seven deposits. Most of them are made of silver, only two wealth deposits have bronze neck-rings. The next find group with 14 examples is spearheads, and they all come from two deposits (Barstyčiai and Šluostikiai). There are 13 items of bronze raw material from two deposits (Miežaičiai and Migoniai I).

In terms of environment of concealment we see quite a variety of contexts in which Lithuanian wealth deposits have been hidden. From 16 Lithuanian deposits ten relate to watery conditions, five have been found in the dry land (including one archaeological site) and the exact environment is unknown in one case (Table 8.1.3). Most often items have been placed into bogs and marshes, followed by dry land (Fig. 8.1.3.3.). Archaeological sites and open water environment are represented with one case each.

The depth of the deposits is often unknown. Compared to Estonian and Latvian finds where the depth can be sometimes derived from the description of the event of finding, e.g. during field ploughing, the situation with the Lithuanian material is quite different. At least in five instances (Gudėniškės, Draustiniai, Šluostikiai, Palanga, Vaineikiai) it is mentioned that the artefacts were discovered while digging drainage ditches in the marshy or boggy area. Thus it might be presumed that the depth of those might have been somewhat bigger compared to the finds that have been found during ploughing.

Information about possible markers or artefact placement in the deposits is very scarce. We know that Vaineikiai three neck-rings were attached with and placed on top of each other. The Šluostikiai find is the only example of having marker for the deposit: a flat granite boulder was placed on the spearheads and a spindle whorl which might have created an extra protection for the deposit. Containers are known in two cases – Dirmeikiai and Dargiškė – whereas both of these deposits contain Roman coins besides the ornaments in them.

The chronological distribution (Fig. 8.1.3.4.) shows some general tendencies of wealth depositing. During the Roman Iron Age there is a stable concealment of one non-monetary deposit in a century. The number of deposits starts to increase with the Middle Iron Age and peaks in the 7th century AD which is slightly later then we saw in the case of Estonia and Latvia. However, when this peak is compared with previous and following centuries it is not very significant. After that the numbers of deposits decline gradually. Sometimes it is also likely that some of the artefacts have been deposited in the same area in different occasions (Table 8.1.1.). For instance, Barstyčiai and Užpelkiai it is probable that we see the usage of the same area for depositing artefacts over a long period of time – up to Viking Age and Late Iron Age in Barstyčiai and throughout the Roman Iron Age in Užpelkiai.

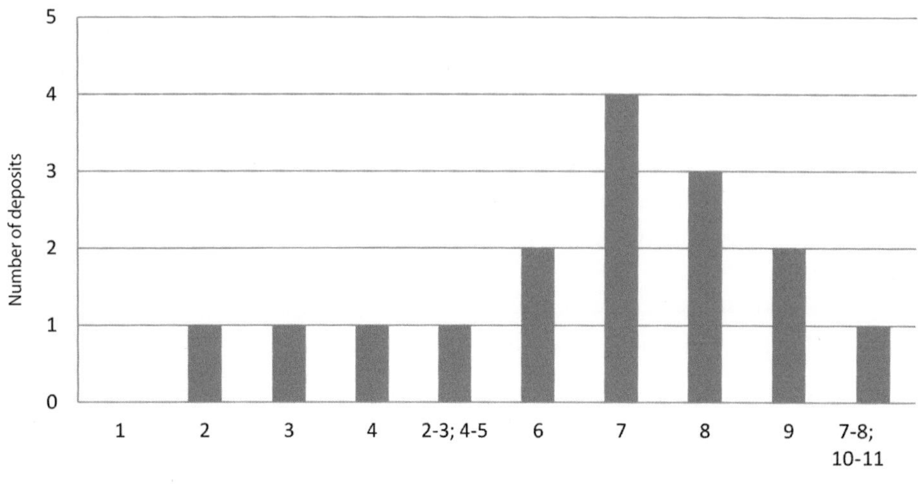


*Fig. 8.1.3.4. Chronological distribution (centuries AD) of Lithuanian wealth deposits.*

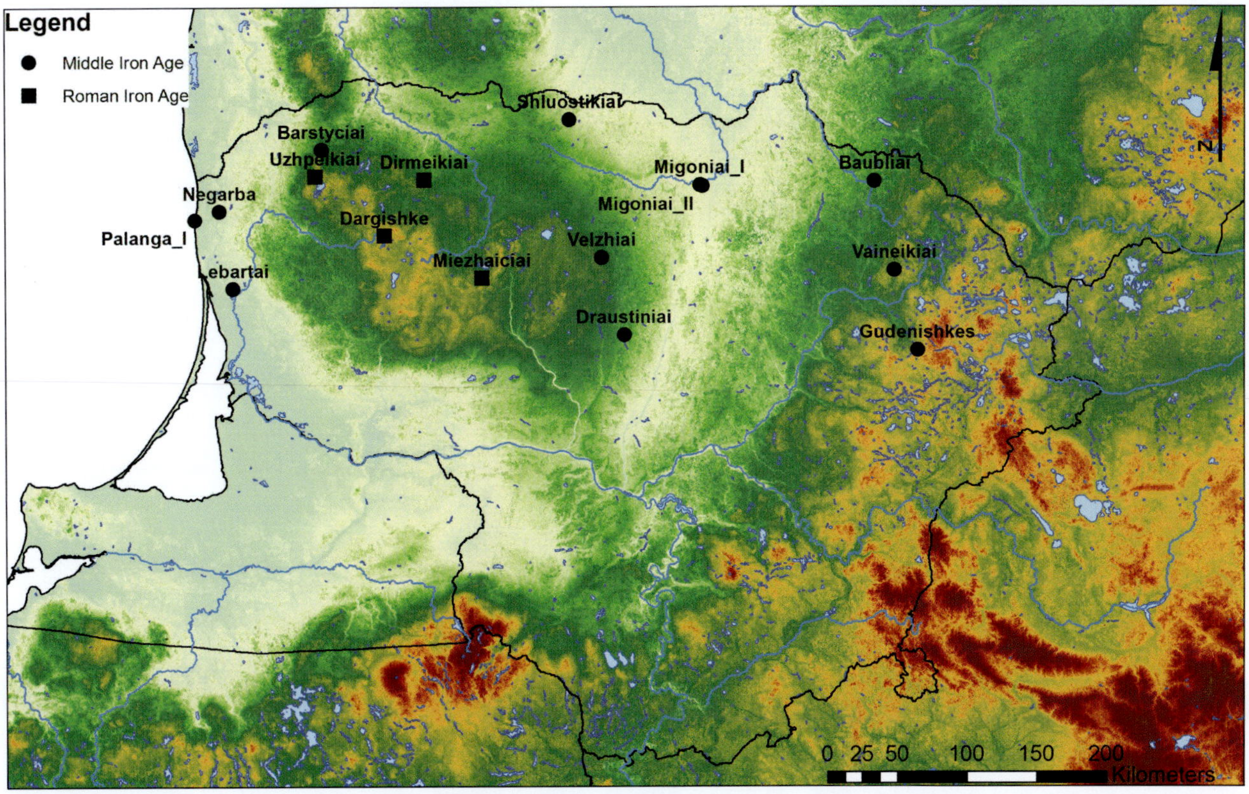


*Fig. 8.1.3.5. Map of Lithuanian wealth deposits.*

The geographical distribution shows clearly that in Lithuania artefact deposits are only found in the northern and central part of the country (Fig. 8.1.3.5.) and there are no finds in the southern half of the country.

## 8.1.4. Selection of artefacts

Intentional selection of artefacts is indicated by the combinations of concealed materials. The most common materials – bronze and silver – are mainly found alone (Fig. 8.1.4.1.). There is only one example of each of them in which silver and bronze respectively are the second major materials. Iron can be found as predominant material only, but it can be in combination with either bronze or stone, never with silver. Iron is never a second major material. The latter indicates that if precious metal or bronzes are deposited then iron is excluded from these assemblages.

The CA analysis of the exact amounts of all materials indicates similar selection principles (Fig. 8.1.4.2.). With the Axis 1 and 2 describing the assemblage with the total inertia of 49.1% and 40% three main clusters emerge: there are silver deposits, bronze deposits, and some finds which contain both materials. The fourth larger group consists of iron deposits in combination with either bronze or stone artefacts.

The picture is the same for the major artefact groups in the deposit. In the crosstab table and bar charts the empty row headings and blue bars indicate artefact groups that are found alone (Fig. 8.1.4.3.). There is a clear tendency towards a single artefact group in Lithuanian deposits. In most cases ornament deposits contain ornaments only and there are only two examples when they are found with coins. Raw materials can be in

| | | Second Material | | | | |
|---|---|---|---|---|---|---|
| | | None | Bronze | Silver | Stone | Total |
| Major Material | Bronze | 7 | 0 | 1 | 0 | 8 |
| | Iron | 1 | 1 | 0 | 1 | 3 |
| | Silver | 4 | 1 | 0 | 0 | 5 |
| **Total** | | **12** | **2** | **1** | **1** | **16** |

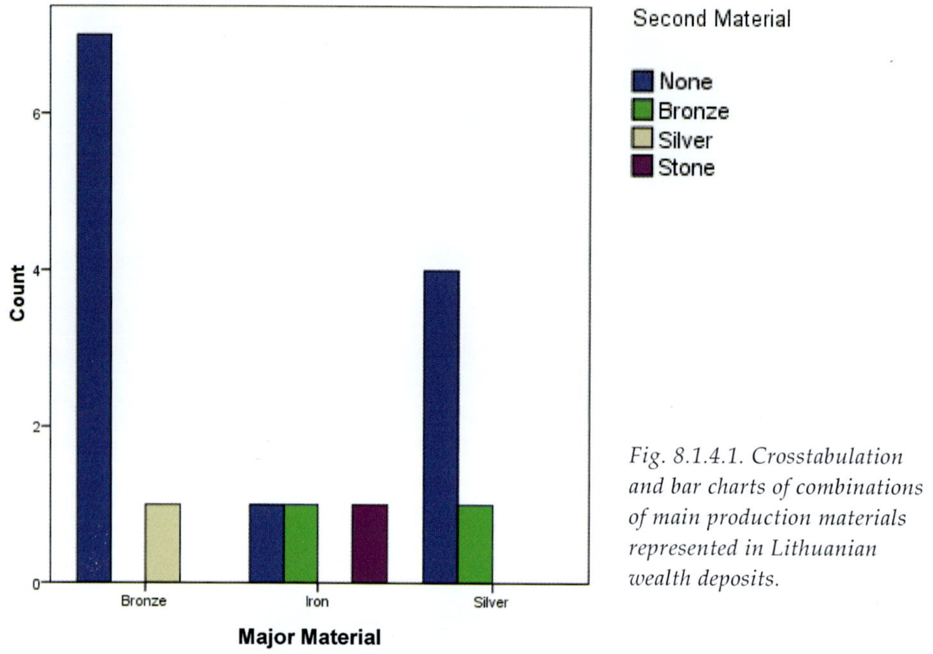


*Fig. 8.1.4.1. Crosstabulation and bar charts of combinations of main production materials represented in Lithuanian wealth deposits.*

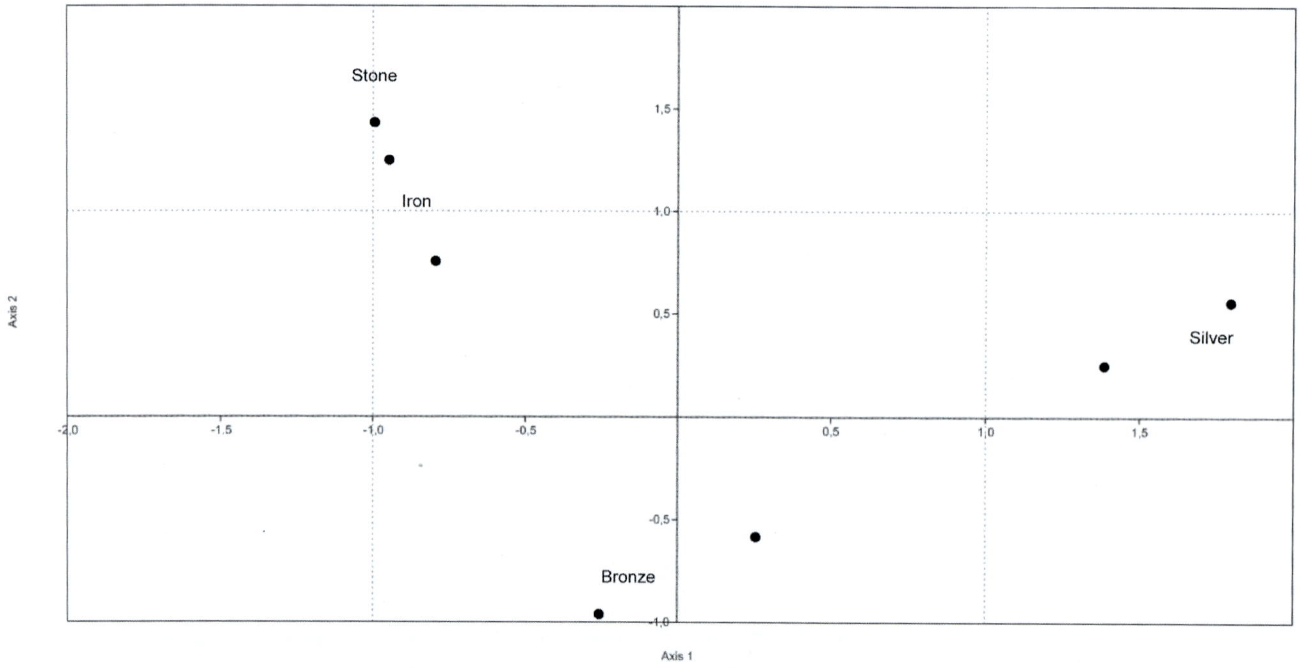


*Fig. 8.1.4.2. Correspondence analysis of combinations of all materials represented in Lithuanian wealth deposits according to the number of represented artefacts.*

| | | Second Artefact Group | | | | |
|---|---|---|---|---|---|---|
| | | – | C | O | T | Total |
| Major Artefact Group | C | 0 | 0 | 1 | 0 | 1 |
| | O | 8 | 1 | 0 | 0 | 9 |
| | Oth | 1 | 0 | 0 | 0 | 1 |
| | R | 1 | 0 | 1 | 0 | 2 |
| | W | 1 | 0 | 1 | 1 | 3 |
| **Total** | | **11** | **1** | **3** | **1** | **16** |

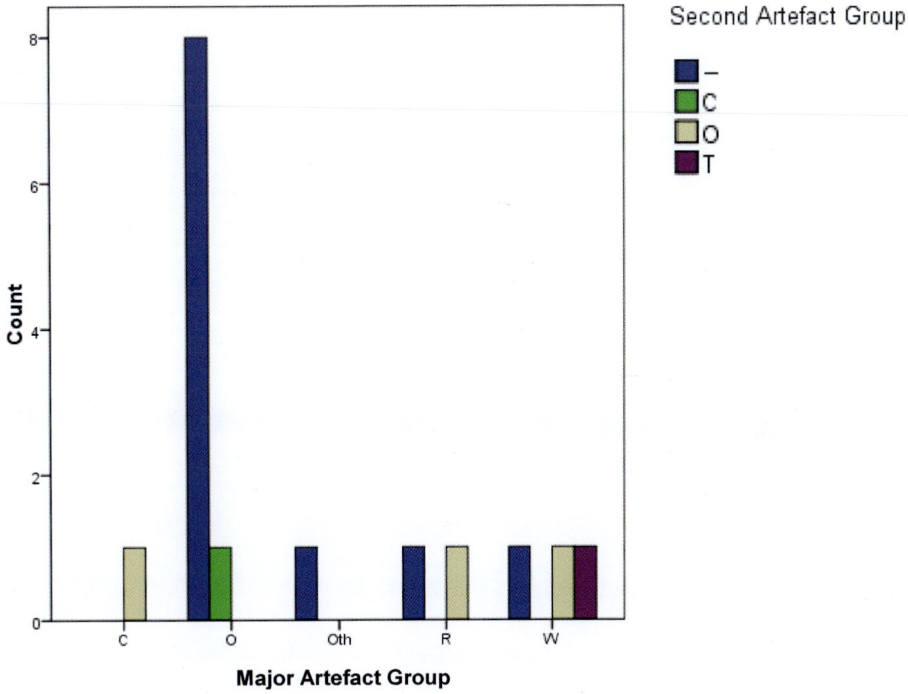


C – Coins, O – Ornaments, Oth – Other, R – Raw Material, W – Weapons, T – Tools.

*Fig. 8.1.4.3. Crosstabulation and bar charts of combinations of main artefact functional groups represented in Lithuanian wealth deposits.*

combination with ornaments, and weapon deposits might include ornaments and tools in them. If ornaments are the most common artefacts in the deposit then they are either the only artefact type or found with coins. However, ornaments can be included as second artefact group in the deposits where coins, raw material and weapons are in the majority.

The CA analysis based on different artefact groups with the total inertia of Axes 1, 2 and 3 are only 38.2%, 31.8% and 17.8% respectively shows some clustering. The results on the scale of Axis 1 and 2 indicate correlation between ornaments and coins (Fig. 8.1.4.4.). Weapon and tool deposits form a separate group. Looking at the distribution between Axis 1 and 3 it becomes clear that the group of raw material is related to both ornaments and coins, but certainly remains separated from weapons and tools. Although problematic due to very small dataset, it can be still concluded that there is a division between ornament finds which are most often found in relation to coins, and weapons-tools deposits.

Looking at the combinations according to artefact types which are found in more than one deposit and taking into account only those deposits which include more than one artefact type the CA (Fig. 8.1.4.5.) with the inertia of Axis 1, 2 and 3 being 29%, 26.2% and 21% respectively, indicates clustering of neck-

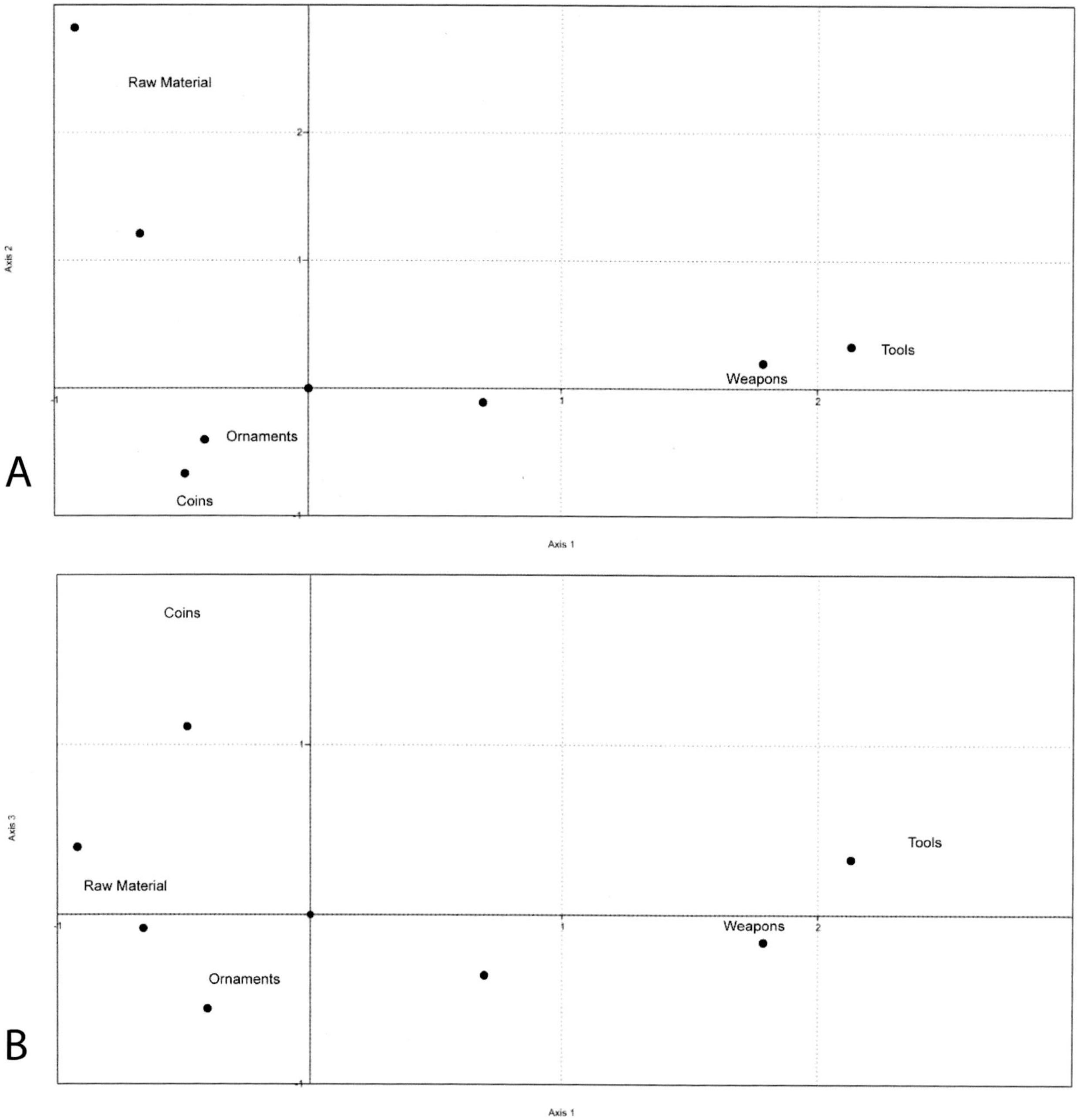


*Fig. 8.1.4.4. Correspondence analysis of combinations of all artefact functional groups represented in Lithuanian wealth deposits. A – Axes 1 and 2; B – Axes 1 and 3.*

rings, then bracelets and coins, and spearheads and axes on the other side of the axis. However, brooches are in between those clearer clusters on both Axis. Raw materials can be related to both of those larger groupings.

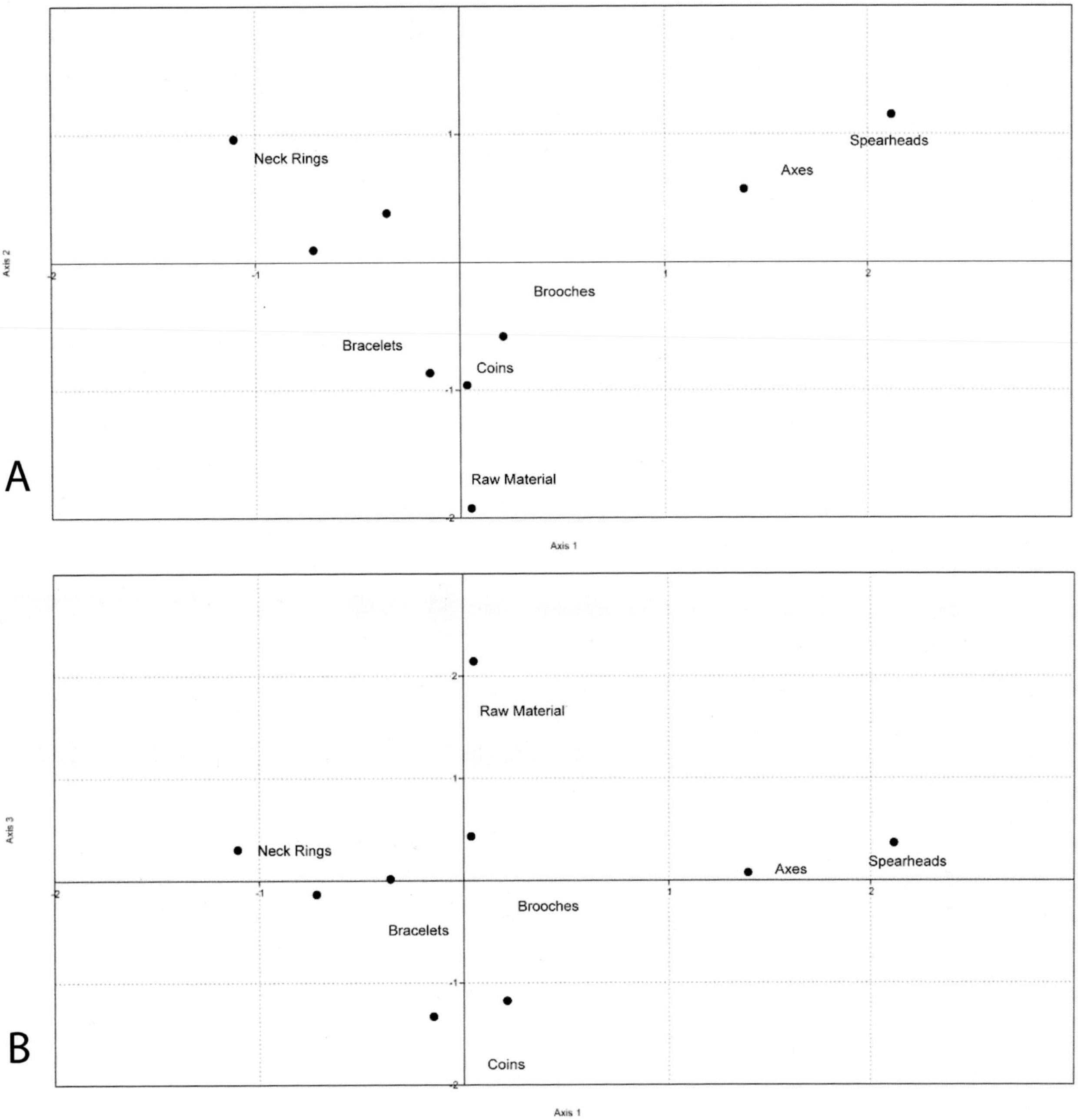


*Fig. 8.1.4.5. Correspondence analysis of combinations of artefact types represented in Lithuanian wealth deposits. A – Axes 1 and 2; B – Axes 1 and 3.*

## 8.1.5. Selection of environment

The crosstab table and bar charts of environments and artefacts (Fig. 8.1.5.1.) show that bog/marsh, being the main environment of concealment, have been used for very different artefact materials. The selection of materials is clearer when looking at the absence rather than presence of particular materials. Iron items are only found in water related conditions such as open water and bog/marsh. At the same time, dry land and archaeological sites contain only deposits where silver or bronze are in majority.

|  |  | Major Material |  |  | Total |
|---|---|---|---|---|---|
|  |  | Bronze | Iron | Silver | Total |
| Environment Subcategory | Archaeological Site | 0 | 0 | 1 | 1 |
|  | Bog/Marsh | 4 | 2 | 3 | 9 |
|  | Open Water | 0 | 1 | 0 | 1 |
|  | Solid Ground | 3 | 0 | 1 | 4 |
|  | Unknown | 1 | 0 | 0 | 1 |
| **Total** |  | **8** | **3** | **5** | **16** |

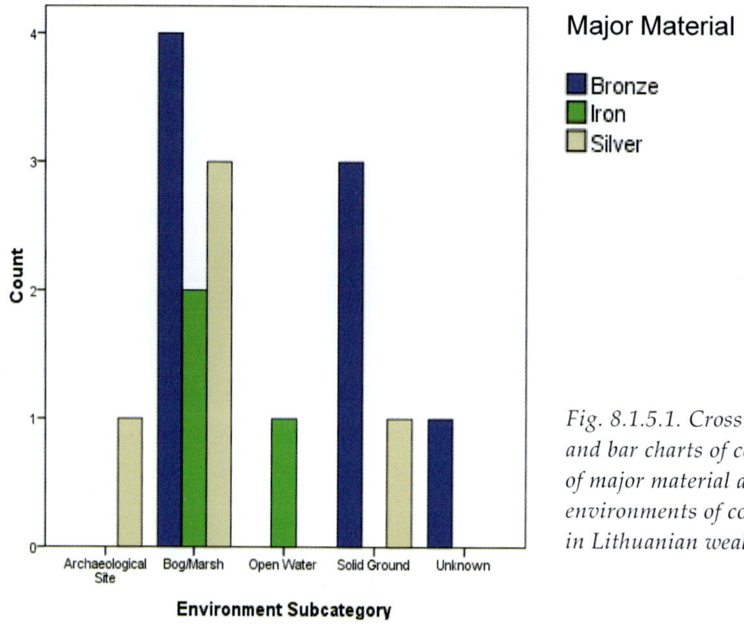


*Fig. 8.1.5.1. Crosstabulation and bar charts of combinations of major material and environments of concealment in Lithuanian wealth deposits.*

| Major Material |  |  | Environment Subcategory |  |  |  |  | Total |
|---|---|---|---|---|---|---|---|---|
|  |  |  | Archaeological Site | Bog/ Marsh | Open Water | Solid Ground | Unknown | Total |
| Bronze | Second Material |  | 0 | 3 | 0 | 3 | 1 | 7 |
|  |  | Silver | 0 | 1 | 0 | 0 | 0 | 1 |
|  | Total |  | 0 | 4 | 0 | 3 | 1 | 8 |
| Iron | Second Material |  | 0 | 1 | 0 | 0 | 0 | 1 |
|  |  | Bronze | 0 | 1 | 0 | 0 | 0 | 1 |
|  |  | Stone | 0 | 0 | 1 | 0 | 0 | 1 |
|  | Total |  | 0 | 2 | 1 | 0 | 0 | 3 |
| Silver | Second Material |  | 1 | 2 | 0 | 1 | 0 | 4 |
|  |  | Bronze | 0 | 1 | 0 | 0 | 0 | 1 |
|  | Total |  | 1 | 3 | 0 | 1 | 0 | 5 |

*Fig. 8.1.5.2. Crosstabulation of combinations of major and second material and environments of concealment in Lithuanian wealth deposits.*

Looking at the combinations when considering the second major material group (Fig. 8.1.5.2.) we see that the patterns remain by and large the same. There are no cases where iron would be the second major material. Thus, it is clear that this material is regarded as suitable for watery conditions only. Combinations of bronze and silver are found in dry land and bog/marsh. However, their combination in those contexts is scarcer and they are most often found alone. Although small in numbers we see some patterning as well as unique outliers on the MCA plot on the basis of main material and environment subcategory (Fig. 8.1.5.3.).

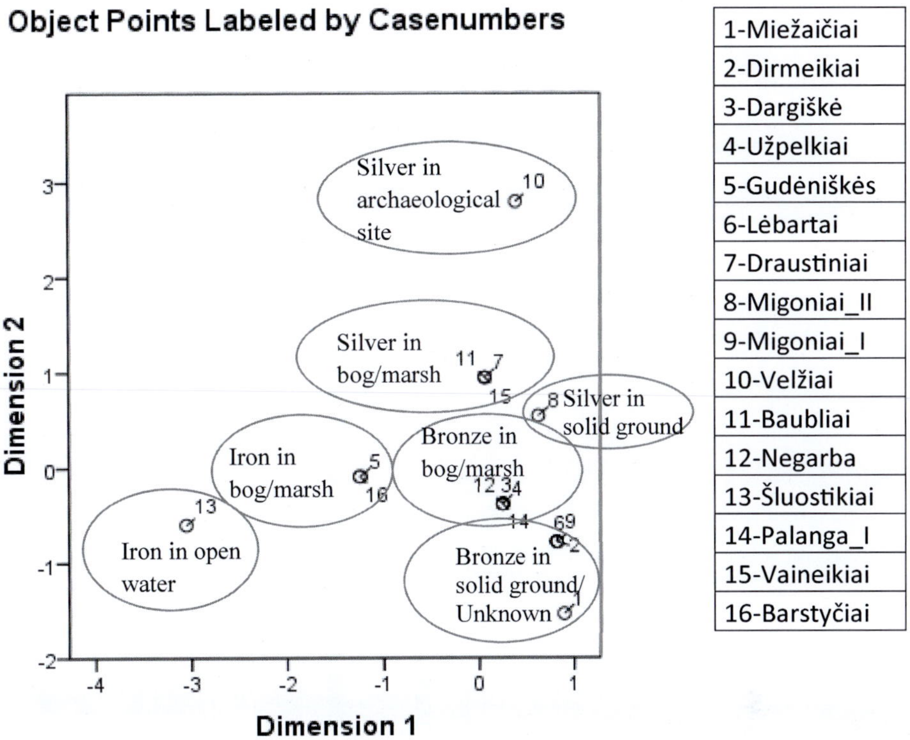


*Fig. 8.1.5.3. MCA plot of combinations of major material and detailed environments of concealment in Lithuanian wealth deposits.*

| | | Major Artefact Group | | | | | Total |
|---|---|---|---|---|---|---|---|
| | | C | O | Oth | R | W | |
| Environment | Solid Ground | 1 | 2 | 1 | 1 | 0 | 5 |
| | Unknown | 0 | 0 | 0 | 1 | 0 | 1 |
| | Watery Condition | 0 | 7 | 0 | 0 | 3 | 10 |
| **Total** | | **1** | **9** | **1** | **2** | **3** | **16** |

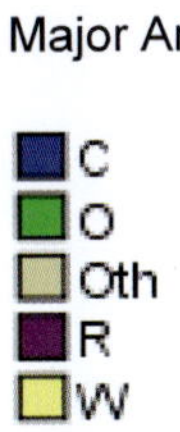


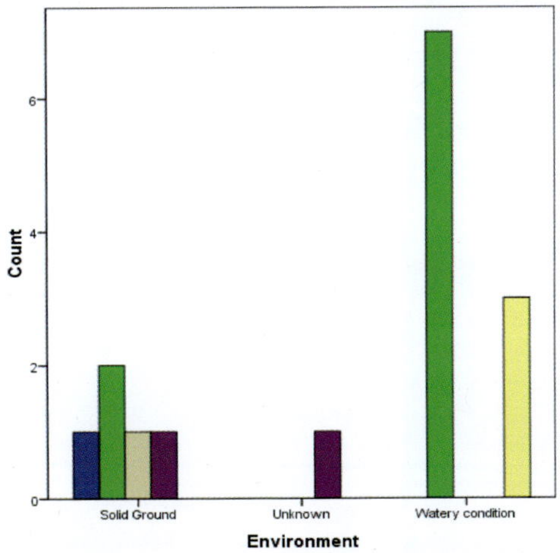


*Fig. 8.1.5.4. Crosstabulation and bar charts of combinations of artefact groups and environments of concealment in Lithuanian wealth deposits.*

C – Coins, O – Ornaments, Oth – Other, R – Raw Material, W – Weapons.

Turning towards artefact groups in different environments there is a broader division based on dry land and watery conditions (Fig. 8.1.5.4.). Most of the ornament deposits and all weapon deposits are found in watery contexts. Dry land, on the other hand contains equal number of different artefact functional

| | | Major Artefact Group | | | | | |
|---|---|---|---|---|---|---|---|
| | | **C** | **O** | **Oth** | **R** | **W** | **Total** |
| Environment Subcategory | Archaeological Site | 0 | 1 | 0 | 0 | 0 | 1 |
| | Bog/Marsh | 0 | 7 | 0 | 0 | 2 | 9 |
| | Open Water | 0 | 0 | 0 | 0 | 1 | 1 |
| | Solid Ground | 1 | 1 | 1 | 1 | 0 | 4 |
| | Unknown | 0 | 0 | 0 | 1 | 0 | 1 |
| **Total** | | **1** | **9** | **1** | **2** | **3** | **16** |

C – Coins, O – Ornaments, Oth – Other, R – Raw Material, W – Weapons.

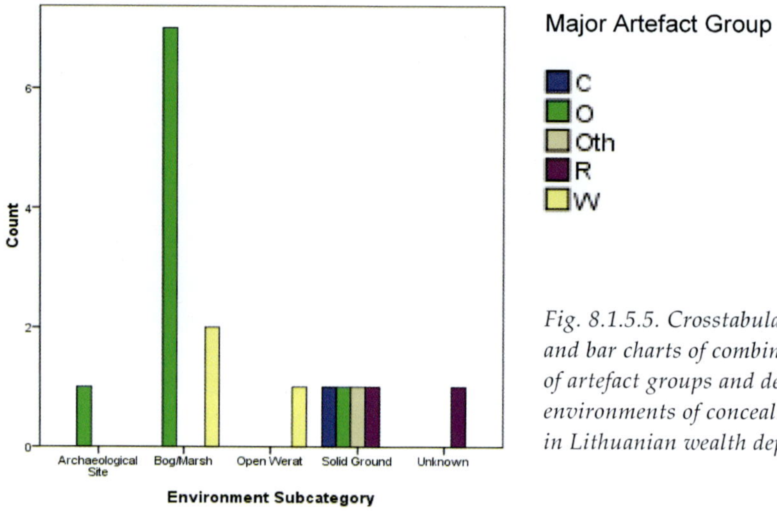


*Fig. 8.1.5.5. Crosstabulation and bar charts of combinations of artefact groups and detailed environments of concealment in Lithuanian wealth deposits.*

| | | Major Artefact Groups | | | | | | | |
|---|---|---|---|---|---|---|---|---|---|
| | | C+O | O | O+C | Oth | R | R+O | W | Total |
| Environment Subcategory | Archaeological Site | 0 | 1 | 0 | 0 | 0 | 0 | 0 | 1 |
| | Bog/Marsh | 0 | 6 | 1 | 0 | 0 | 0 | 2 | 9 |
| | Open Water | 0 | 0 | 0 | 0 | 0 | 0 | 1 | 1 |
| | Solid Ground | 1 | 1 | 0 | 1 | 0 | 1 | 0 | 4 |
| | Unknown | 0 | 0 | 0 | 0 | 1 | 0 | 0 | 1 |
| **Total** | | **1** | **8** | **1** | **1** | **1** | **1** | **3** | **16** |

C – Coins, O – Ornaments, Oth – Other, R – Raw Material, W – Weapons.

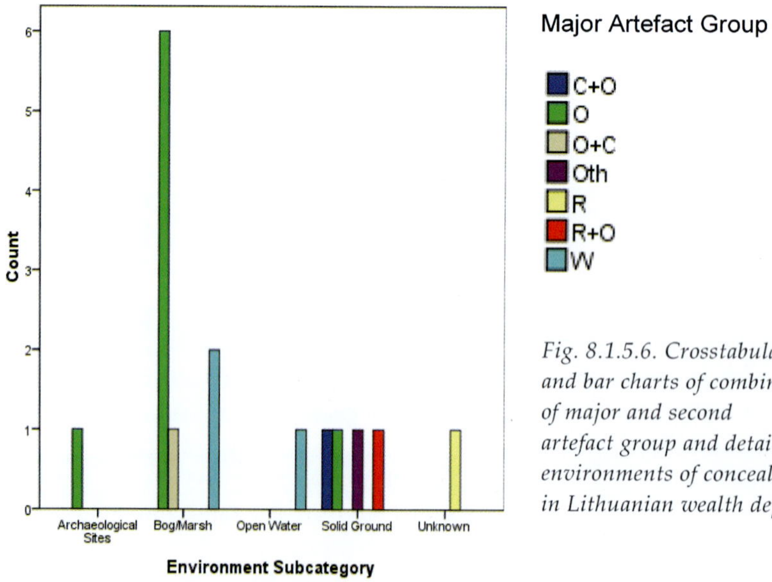


*Fig. 8.1.5.6. Crosstabulation and bar charts of combinations of major and second artefact group and detailed environments of concealment in Lithuanian wealth deposits.*

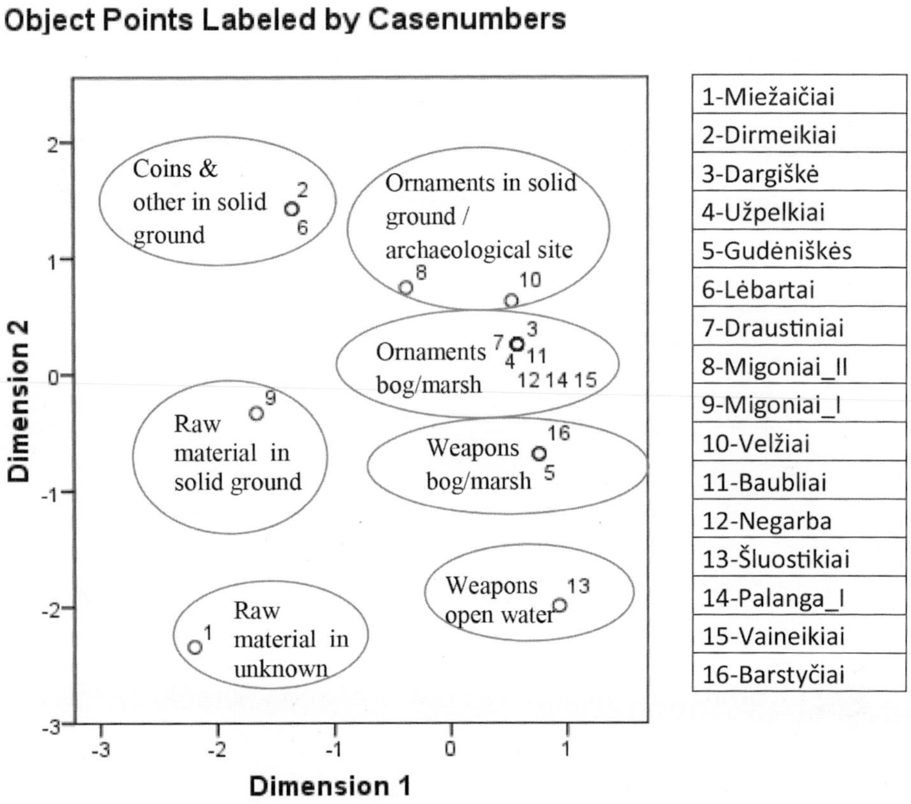


*Fig. 8.1.5.7. MCA plot of combinations of major artefact groups and detailed environments of concealment in Lithuanian wealth deposits.*

groups. When dividing the environments of concealment into more detailed categories similar tendencies with some extra specifications appear (Fig. 8.1.5.5.). Most ornament deposits are found in bog/marsh with only some unique examples from archaeological sites and dry land. Weapon deposits are hidden in watery conditions only, though mostly in bog/marsh with just one example of open water context. Dry land includes the whole variety of artefacts, but weapons are never found in this environment. Similar tendencies are also evident when considering detailed environments of concealment and the two major artefact groups in deposits (Fig. 8.1.5.6.).

MCA according to the environment subcategory and major artefact group shows the main clusters and also the outliers (Fig. 8.1.5.7.). There is one clear pattern: ornaments in bog/marsh and some close examples of weapons in watery conditions. However, in the rest of the cases the examples tend to be outliers than forming clusters.

## 8.1.6. Chronological distribution

It is important to add a temporal background scale for the detailed artefact and environment selections. Starting from the production materials (Fig. 8.1.6.1.) we see that throughout the Roman Iron Age, bronze is the most common material in wealth deposits. However, the numbers of deposited objects remain below ten and there is only one deposit per each century. Only one find in the Roman Iron Age includes silver. This is the Užpelkiai deposit which includes bronze and silver ornaments from the mid-part and from the final centuries of the Roman Iron Age.

A

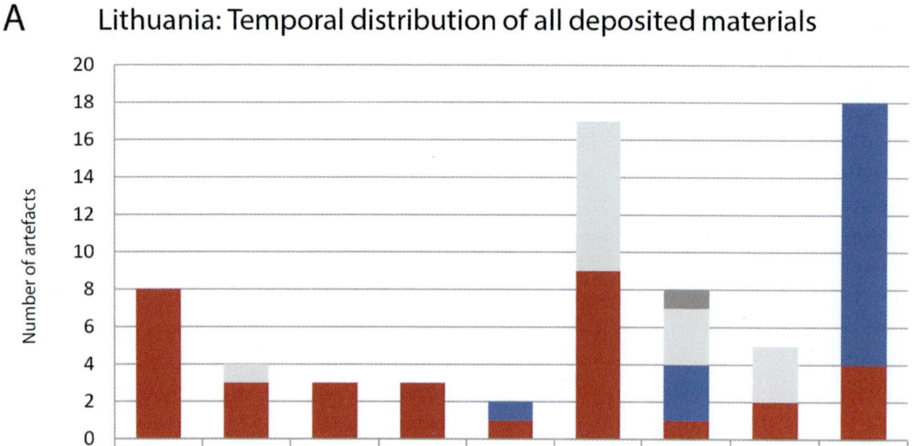


| | 2 | 2-3; 4-5 | 3 | 4 | 6 | 7 | 8 | 9 | 7-8; 10-11 |
|---|---|---|---|---|---|---|---|---|---|
| Stone | 0 | 0 | 0 | 0 | 0 | 0 | 1 | 0 | 0 |
| Silver | 0 | 1 | 0 | 0 | 0 | 8 | 3 | 3 | 0 |
| Iron | 0 | 0 | 0 | 0 | 1 | 0 | 3 | 0 | 14 |
| Bronze | 8 | 3 | 3 | 3 | 1 | 9 | 1 | 2 | 4 |

B

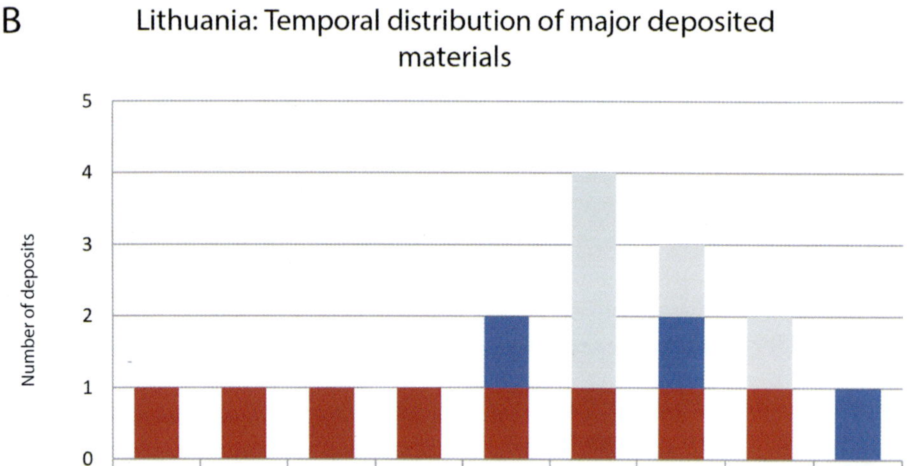


| | 2 | 2-3; 4-5 | 3 | 4 | 6 | 7 | 8 | 9 | 7-8; 10-11 |
|---|---|---|---|---|---|---|---|---|---|
| Silver | 0 | 0 | 0 | 0 | 0 | 3 | 1 | 1 | 0 |
| Iron | 0 | 0 | 0 | 0 | 1 | 0 | 1 | 0 | 1 |
| Bronze | 1 | 1 | 1 | 1 | 1 | 1 | 1 | 1 | 0 |

*Fig. 8.1.6.1. Temporal distribution (centuries AD) of all artefact materials (A) and major materials (B) in Lithuanian wealth deposits.*

Although bronzes continue to be deposited throughout the Middle Iron Age, some considerable changes take place from the 6th century AD onwards. Iron occurs in Lithuanian wealth deposits for the first time. The second change is that silver objects increase in deposits during the second half of the Middle Iron Age peaking in the 7th century. Looking at the distribution according to the main artefact material (Fig. 8.1.6.1. (B)) we see that silver is the main material hidden in the 7th century AD and it is continuously concealed in the following centuries. However, the numbers and proportions of silver items decrease and cede their place to both bronze and iron over time. There is one find-spot – Barstyčiai – which is likely to have been used over a longer period of time having objects from

A Lithuania: Temporal distribution of all artefact groups

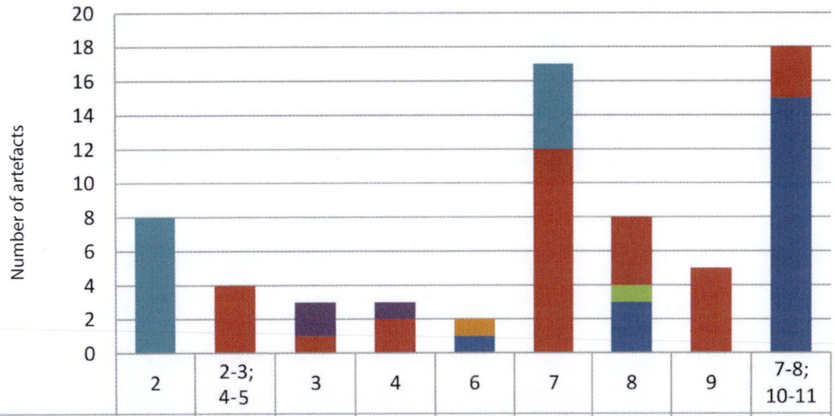


| | 2 | 2-3; 4-5 | 3 | 4 | 6 | 7 | 8 | 9 | 7-8; 10-11 |
|---|---|---|---|---|---|---|---|---|---|
| Other | 0 | 0 | 0 | 0 | 1 | 0 | 0 | 0 | 0 |
| Raw_Material | 8 | 0 | 0 | 0 | 0 | 5 | 0 | 0 | 0 |
| Coins | 0 | 0 | 2 | 1 | 0 | 0 | 0 | 0 | 0 |
| Ornaments | 0 | 4 | 1 | 2 | 0 | 12 | 4 | 5 | 3 |
| Tools | 0 | 0 | 0 | 0 | 0 | 0 | 1 | 0 | 0 |
| Weapons | 0 | 0 | 0 | 0 | 1 | 0 | 3 | 0 | 15 |

B Lithuania: Temporal distribution of major artefact groups

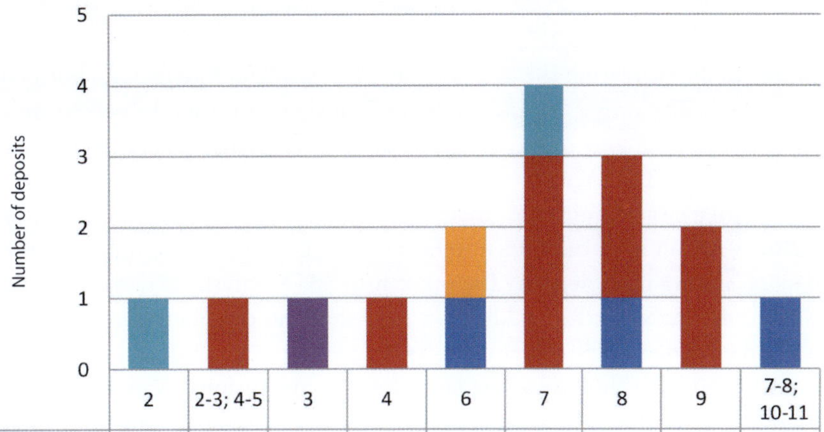


| | 2 | 2-3; 4-5 | 3 | 4 | 6 | 7 | 8 | 9 | 7-8; 10-11 |
|---|---|---|---|---|---|---|---|---|---|
| Other | 0 | 0 | 0 | 0 | 1 | 0 | 0 | 0 | 0 |
| Raw_Material | 1 | 0 | 0 | 0 | 0 | 1 | 0 | 0 | 0 |
| Coins | 0 | 0 | 1 | 0 | 0 | 0 | 0 | 0 | 0 |
| Ornaments | 0 | 1 | 0 | 1 | 0 | 3 | 2 | 2 | 0 |
| Weapons | 0 | 0 | 0 | 0 | 1 | 0 | 1 | 0 | 1 |

*Fig. 8.1.6.2. Temporal distribution (centuries AD) of all artefact groups (A) and major groups (B) in Lithuanian wealth deposits.*

both Middle Iron Age and the following Late Iron Age periods. Iron is the major material in this find, although it also contains some bronzes.

Turning to artefact groups in deposits from a chronological perspective the graphs (Fig. 8.1.6.2. A and B) reveal some extra information. The exact details of artefact groups and types are represented in Figs 8.1.6.3. and 8.1.6.4. The first Roman Iron Age deposit contains raw material only: it is a unique find of eight large bronze bars from Miežaičiai. Bronze remains the main material and a

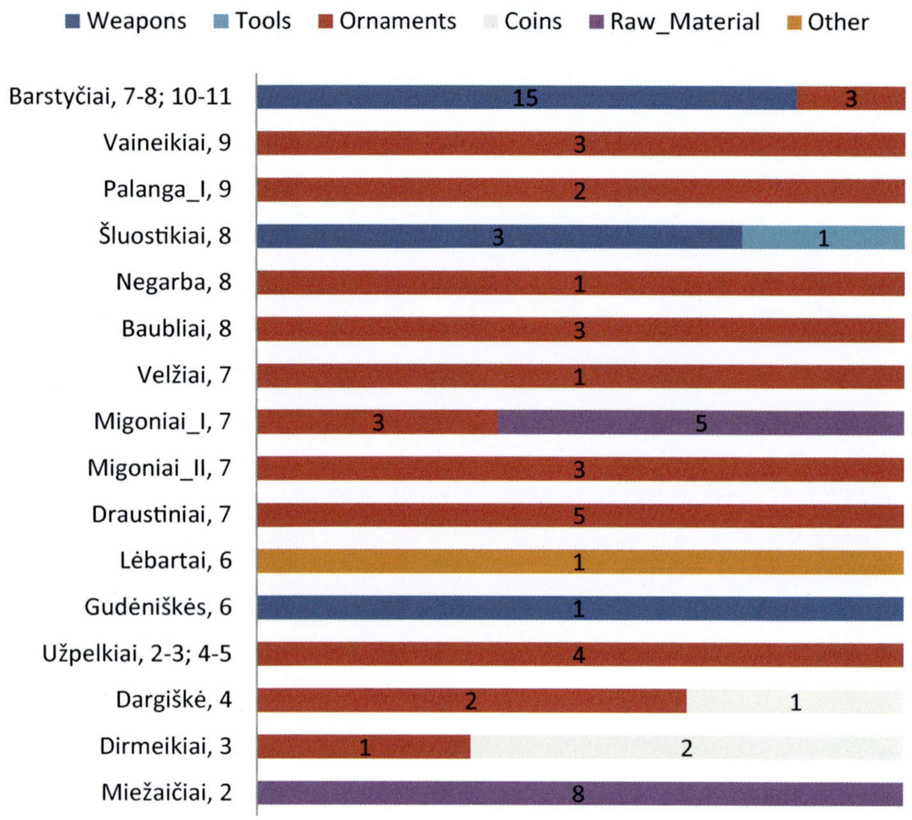


*Fig. 8.1.6.3. Temporal distribution (centuries AD) of artefact groups according to deposits in Lithuanian wealth deposits. The number in deposit name indicates century.*

couple of deposits from the middle of the Roman Iron Age include both coins and ornaments. The only exception is the previously mentioned Užpelkiai find, which consists of ornaments only, though from two different chronological sequences.

The Middle Iron Age introduces weapon deposits for the first time, although they never gain a clear dominance. There are only three deposits in which weapons are in majority and in most cases the numbers remain under five. The only exception is the Barstyčiai long-term deposit. The 6th century AD material is remarkable because it is the only period in the Middle Iron Age where no ornaments are represented and we find only two single object deposits: an axe from Gudėniškės and a bronze comb from Lėbartai. In the case of the latter further conclusions are problematic because there is no reliable information about the exact content of this find. Therefore it is complicated to make further conclusions about artefact groups hidden in this century and it remains an example of a period of unusual deposits. Ornaments are the most common artefact group throughout the second half of the Middle Iron Age. The 7th century raw material addition, which comes from the Migoniai I find, includes at least a couple of bars that are most likely meant to be made into ornaments. As Fig. 8.1.6.4. shows the 7th-9th century deposits include mostly neck-rings stressing the homogeneity of deposits during this time period. The last thing to note is that the numbers of deposited objects, be it ornaments or weapons, remain small compared to Estonian and Latvian material.

Finally the environment of concealment has to be considered (Fig. 8.1.6.5.). The main results are that bog/marsh remains an important environment of concealment throughout the Roman and Middle Iron Age. The first two deposits have been most likely discovered in the dry land, although in the case of Miežaičiai we lack the exact information about its discovery. Dry land environment, including

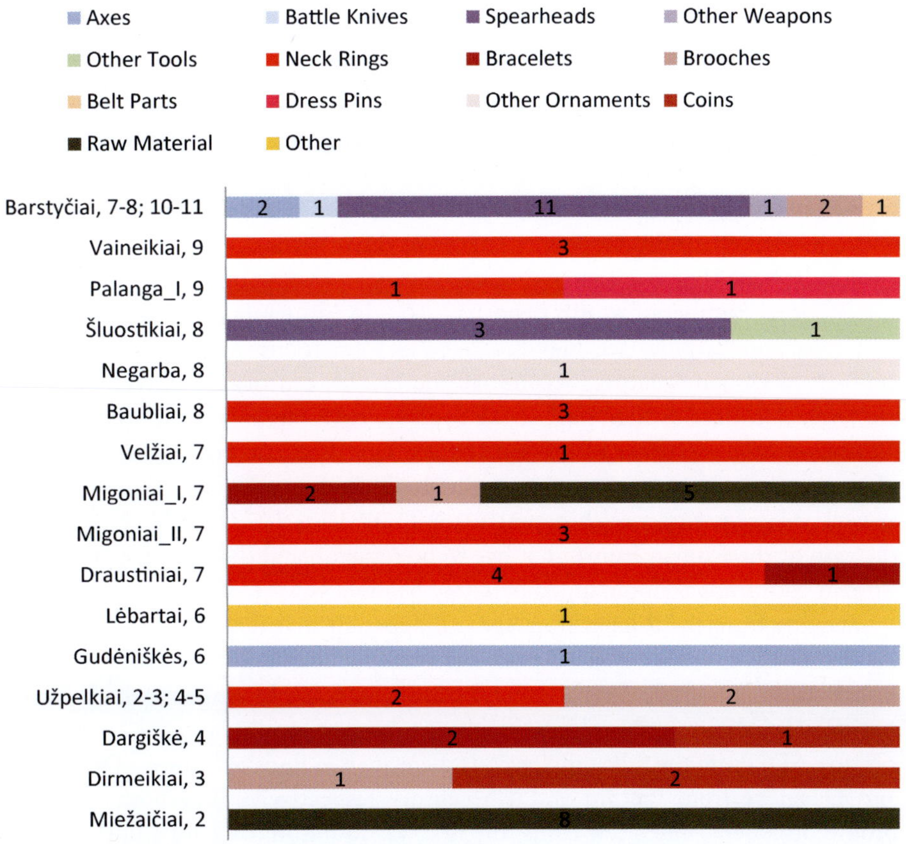


Fig. 8.1.6.4. Temporal distribution (centuries AD) of artefact types according to deposits in Lithuanian wealth deposits. The number in deposit name indicates century.

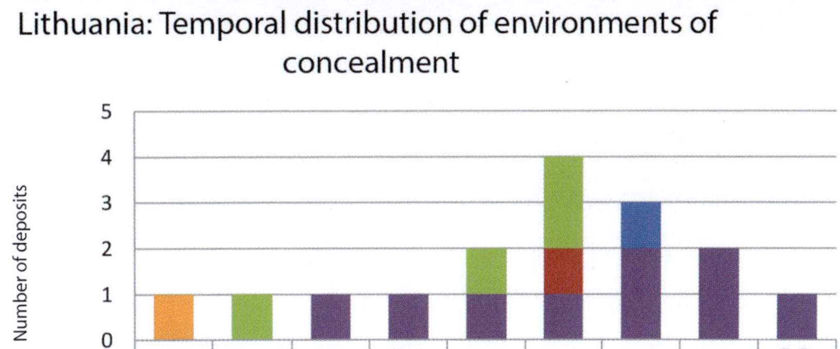


| | 2 | 3 | 4 | 2-3; 4-5 | 6 | 7 | 8 | 9 | 7-8; 10-11 |
|---|---|---|---|---|---|---|---|---|---|
| Unknown | 1 | 0 | 0 | 0 | 0 | 0 | 0 | 0 | 0 |
| Solid ground | 0 | 1 | 0 | 0 | 1 | 2 | 0 | 0 | 0 |
| Open Water | 0 | 0 | 0 | 0 | 0 | 0 | 1 | 0 | 0 |
| Archaeological_Site | 0 | 0 | 0 | 0 | 0 | 1 | 0 | 0 | 0 |
| Bog/Marsh | 0 | 0 | 1 | 1 | 1 | 1 | 2 | 2 | 1 |

Fig. 8.1.6.5. Temporal distribution (centuries AD) of environments of concealment in Lithuanian wealth deposits.

a single example of an archaeological site, is represented only during the first half of the Middle Iron Age. From the 8th century AD onwards, watery conditions, with clear dominance of bog/marsh are preferred.

## 8.2. Practices of wealth depositing in Lithuania: Long-term perspective and the question of change

The following account of wealth deposits in Lithuania is based on the results of analyses presented above, taking into account the detailed description of each wealth deposit as presented in the catalogue. The preliminary MCA combining major artefact groups, material, environment of concealment and century-based dating of deposits indicates some patterns in the different contexts of Lithuanian wealth deposits (Fig. 8.2.1.).

The total number of wealth deposits – 16 – in Lithuania is much smaller than in Latvia and Estonia (see Figs 8.2.2.-8.2.4.) There are never more than four deposits in any one century. Second, all the 1st-9th century AD artefact deposits are located in the northern part of the country, covering only a half of Lithuania. This cannot be the result of limited archaeological research in the southern part of the country, because these areas provide numerous other archaeological sites as well as later period wealth deposits (see Tautavičius 1977; 1978). However, in the case of the Roman Iron Age it has to be remembered that the distribution of Roman coin finds is not mapped here (see below).

Starting from the Roman Iron Age it is apparent that the there is a continuous pattern of approximately one deposit per century. The earliest deposit is an Early Roman Iron Age find of eight large bronze bars from **Miežaičiai** which for the statistical analysis in this thesis has been chronologically situated to the 2nd century AD. From the following periods there are two finds of bronzes: **Dirmeikiai** and **Dargiškė** from the 3rd and 4th century respectively. They both consist of bronze ornaments and a few coins, the first was found in dry land and the second from the boggy/marshy area. A lot more than just a couple of coins and ornaments

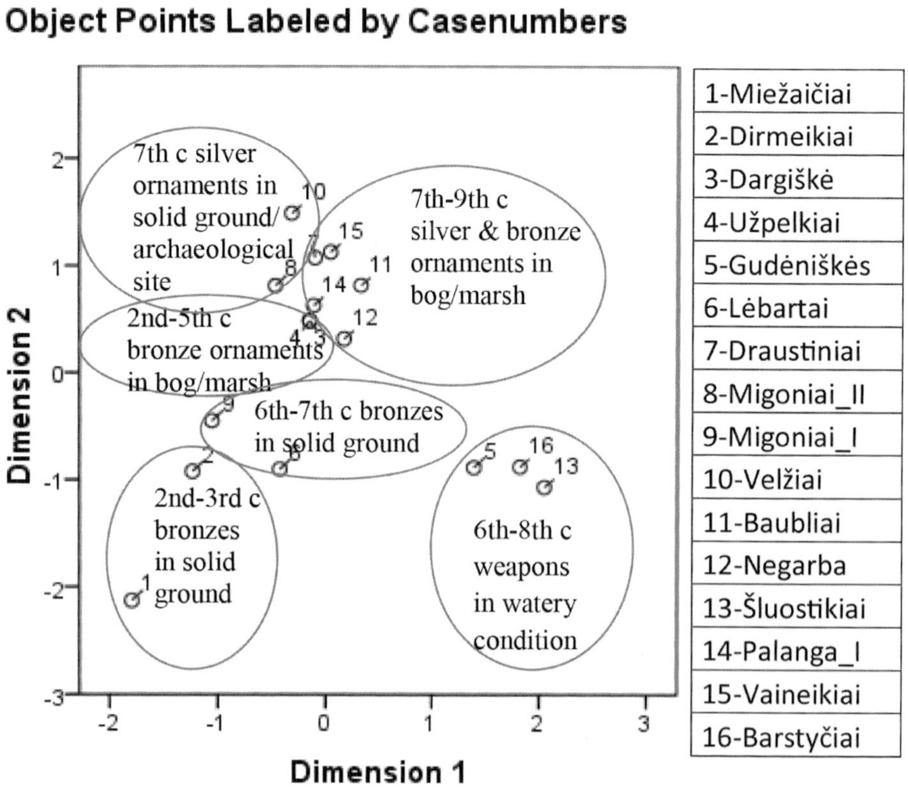


*Fig. 8.2.1. MCA plot of combinations of major artefact groups, materials, detailed environments of concealment and dating of Lithuanian wealth deposits.*

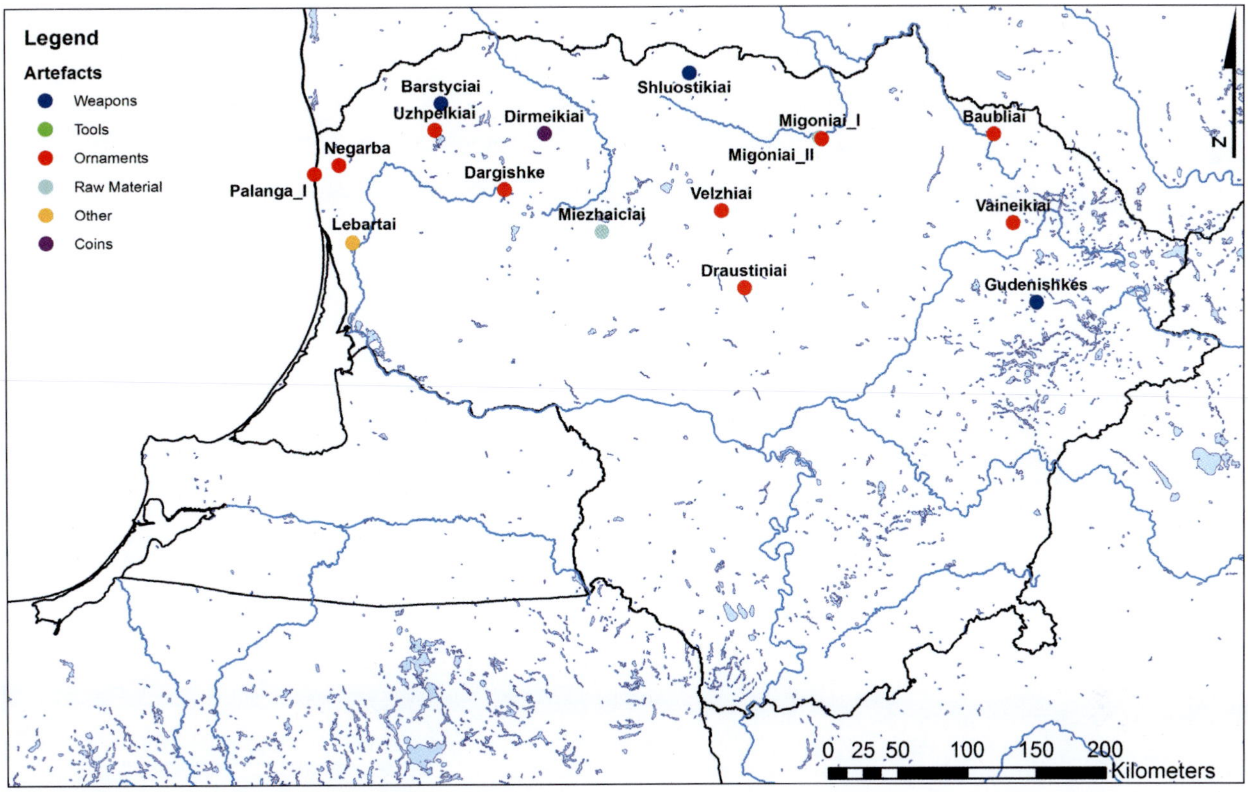


*Fig. 8.2.3. Map of major artefact groups represented in Lithuanian wealth deposits.*

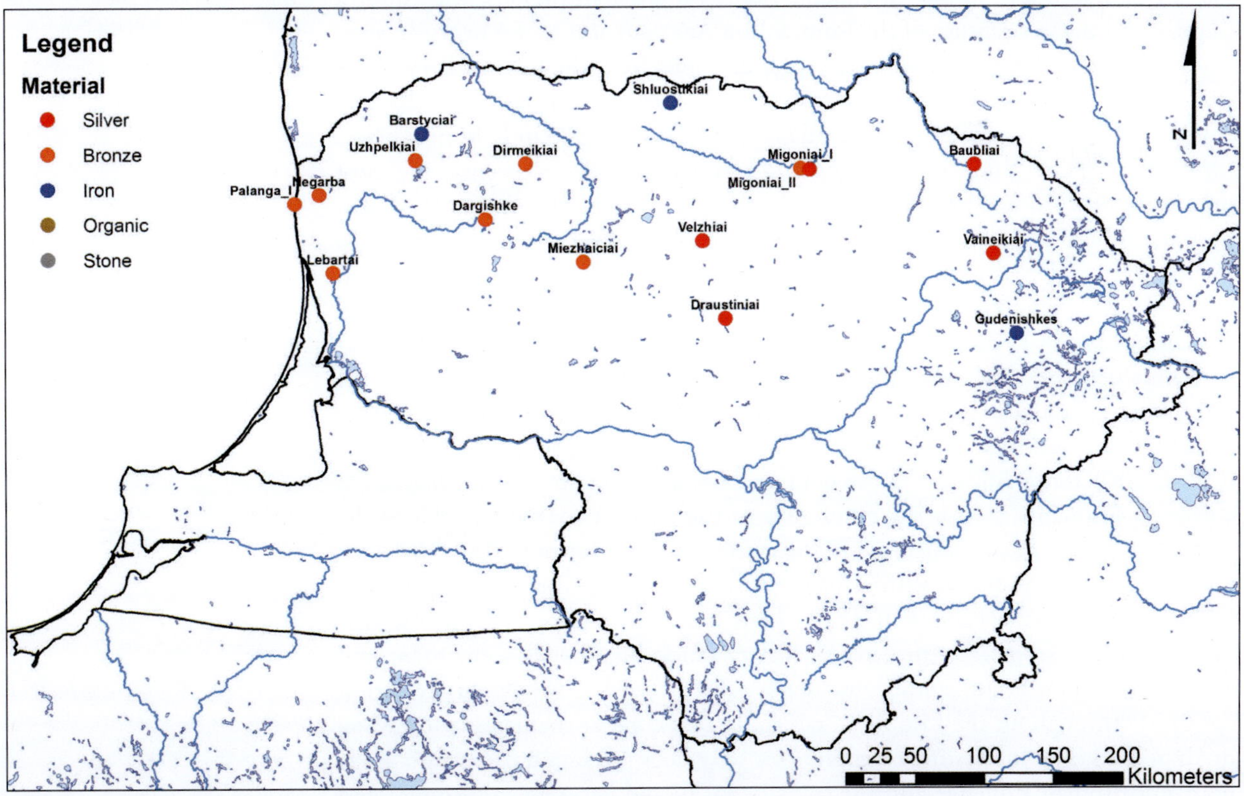


*Fig. 8.2.2. Map of major materials represented in Lithuanian wealth deposits.*

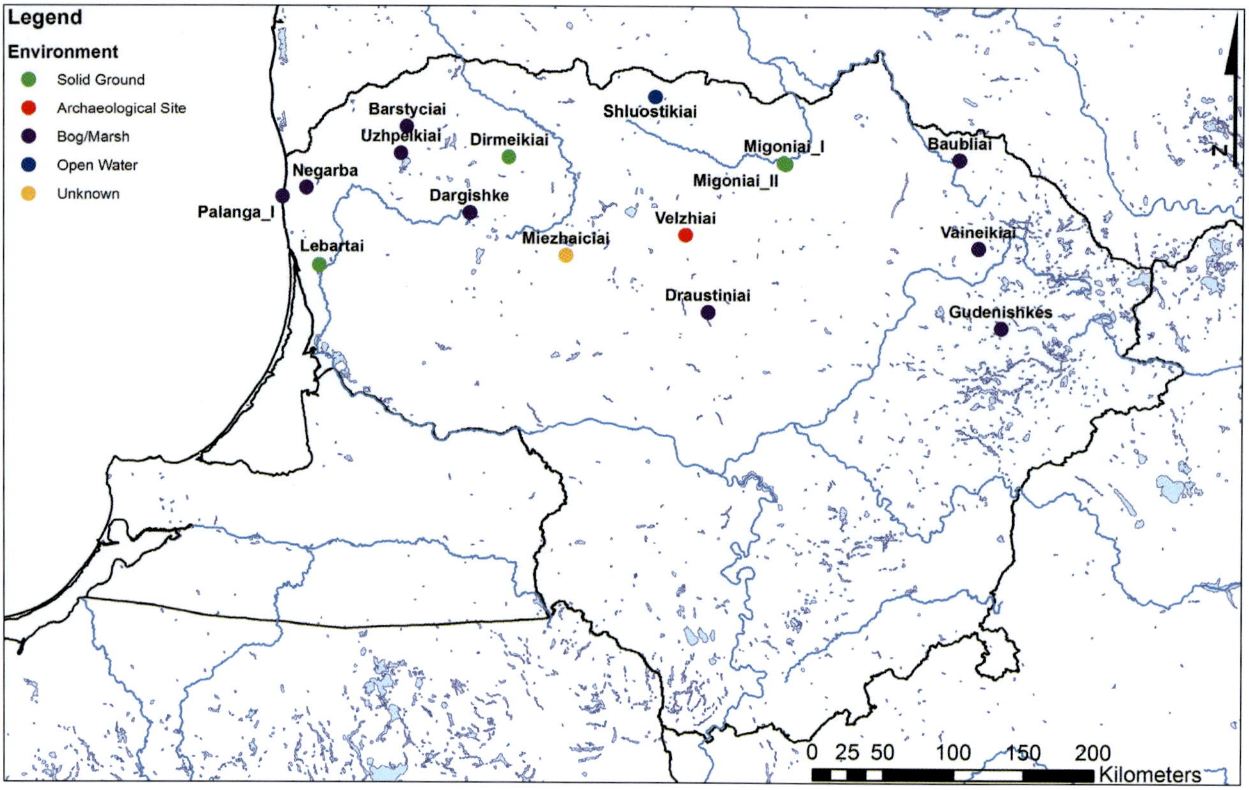


were found (see catalogue), but unfortunately the exact numbers are unknown. The **Užpelkiai** find of bronze ornaments from two different periods (the 2nd-3rd century and the last century of the Roman Iron Age) was also found in bog/marsh.

*Fig. 8.2.4. Map of environments of concealment of Lithuanian wealth deposits.*

One clear common denominator for all the finds from the Roman Iron Age is that they all consist of various forms of bronzes. To these we can also add 11 Roman coin hoards (see Appendix 1.3.). The majority of these contain only bronze pieces (up to 50 coins per find) from the 2nd and 3rd century AD. Bronze was the most important depositional material during the first half of the 1st millennium AD in Lithuania. Additionally, Roman coin hoards expand the area of wealth deposits to the southern regions, although most of them tend to concentrate around the main water routes in the western coast (amber region) and central areas of the country (Michelbertas 2001; Bliujienė 2011, 171-189, fig. 61).

Therefore the first clear cluster of wealth depositional practices in the Lithuanian material is a long-term concept of depositing bronzes which besides Roman coins includes the **Miežaičiai**, **Dirmeikiai**, **Dargiškė**, and **Užpelkiai** deposits. All those finds are located in the small region in the north-western corner of Lithuania, just at the outer edge of the western coastal area where the coin deposits are most numerous (Michelbertas 2001; Bliujienė 2011, 171-189, fig. 61). During the first centuries of the Roman Iron Age the favoured context for depositing has been most likely dry land (not absolutely certain in the case of Miežaičiai). From the 4th century AD onwards bog/marsh seem to prevail as the most appropriate context for depositing. As we see below this tradition continues throughout the Middle Iron Age. In this context the deposit from bog in **Užpelkiai** is an interesting example. Not only does it contain ornaments from both mid-Roman Iron Age and the transitional period between the Roman and

Middle Iron Age, but with its mid-5th century silver brooch it also forms a link to numerous silver deposits in the following period.

In the 6th century AD, for the first time iron as a production material and weapons as artefact group appear in wealth deposits. However, in the 6th century this is only a single axe find from bog, the **Gudėniškės** deposit. As discussed above this find is problematic, because it may also relate to the nearby burial ground. Besides the axe some other artefacts were discovered, but they never reached the museum collections. This single weapon find remains unparalleled and unique until the 8th century AD. There are two other weapon-dominated finds from watery conditions – **Šluostikiai** and **Barstyčiai** –, from the second half of the Middle Iron Age. In the case of the first the chronology is complicated and the time range has been set for 500-900 AD. This might be partly because of the heavily corroded spearheads in the find. However, according to the available archival drawings and in comparison with other similar finds the deposit has been dated to the 8th century AD in the current thesis. The Barstyčiai find is unique in terms of item combinations and chronology. It includes weapons and ornaments from the 7th-8th and 10th-11th AD, indicating a possible long-term use of the same site on different occasions. This fragmentary picture shows that weapon deposits in Lithuania are scarce and contain such a different combination and small number of objects that they do not seem to form a single homogeneous group at all. If the Gudėniškės deposit is in fact a burial assemblage, then weapon deposits appear in Lithuanian deposits only in the last half of the Middle Iron Age. Another important common denominator is that they are all found in watery conditions, be it open water or bog/marsh. The geographical location of the weapon finds is noteworthy: the later two weapon deposits are located near the northern border of the country, but the questionable Gudėniškės deposit is from the eastern part of Lithuania.

In the 6th century AD there are some other unique finds in the Lithuanian material. One of them is the **Lėbartai** deposit, although its outlier status is to some extent a result of poor documentation. It is evident from the graphs and charts that this deposit is unusual. Initially it was a find of bronzes from dry land near the coast of western Lithuania. Unfortunately the fate of those items is unknown and the only available information says that it included several objects from 3rd to 6th century AD, and was hidden most likely in the 6th century AD. From all the artefacts only a bronze comb is known for certain (although its current whereabouts is unknown) and, thus it is assigned to find group 'other' throughout the analysis. Lacking any detailed information about this deposit it is difficult to estimate its relationship to other finds. Its content resembles the above discussed Roman Iron Age deposits of various bronzes.

The other option would be to relate the Lėbartai deposit to another unique discovery from the Middle Iron Age, the **Migoniai I** deposit. This includes bronze bracelets and bars of raw material in various forms discovered in the dry land in the northern-central region of Lithuania. This deposit remains an outlier mainly in comparison with other Middle Iron Age ornament deposits: first, because bronze ornament deposits in the Middle Iron Age are mostly related to watery environment (see below); and second, it is the only find from the Middle Iron Age that has a combination of ornaments and raw material in it. All we can conclude is that, Lėbartai and Migoniai I deposits from the 6th-7th century contain different items from all the other Middle Iron Age deposits and are concealed in dry land.

It might be that they indicate a continuous importance of bronze as a material from the Roman Iron Age onwards. However, without any detailed information it is impossible to make any further conclusions.

The largest group of distinguishable depositional practice is the 7th-9th century AD silver and bronze ornament deposits. A large group of seven finds might be assembled under this category, but there are also some interesting regional nuances. First, there are two 7th century AD finds – the **Migoniai II** and **Velžiai** deposits – which include only silver neck-rings, three and one respectively. They both were discovered in the dry land, Velžiai single neck-ring actually during the excavation of a hill-fort. Thus in comparison with other ornament finds they stand out in terms of the environment of concealment and artefact assemblage.

The group of deposits which include silver and bronze ornaments, hidden in boggy or marshy areas is larger. There are altogether five deposits with such characteristics covering the time period of 7th-9th century AD: **Draustiniai**, **Baubliai**, **Negarba**, **Palanga I** and **Vaineikiai**. With the exception of Negarba they all include, if not contain solely of neck-rings. Draustiniai also has a bronze bracelet besides three neck-rings, Palanga I includes a bronze neck-ring and a dress pin. The Negraba deposit is formed by a large complex bronze pendant and chains which is probably part of the larger ornament set. Looking at the material in more detail it is noticed that **Negarba** and **Palanga I** are the only finds in this group which contain only bronze objects and in which neck-rings do not take a clear dominance. Considering the distribution map we see that they are both located at the coast of western Lithuania. Both finds have contemporary hill-fort and burial grounds in their vicinity. Thus, these two deposits form a separate entity of bronze ornament deposits in bog/marsh from the areas where other contemporary archaeological sites are known.

The **Draustiniai**, **Baubliai** and **Vaineikiai** deposits are different: they contain 3-4 silver neck-rings only. Unfortunately the Vaineikiai ones went to private collections and their current whereabouts remains unknown. In addition to those three, the find of two silver neck-rings from Rokiškis region (see Appendix 1.1.) seems to fit into this pattern. This is also dated to the 7th-8th century AD, but cannot be included in detailed analysis because its exact location and context of discovery is unknown.

All the silver neck-ring finds in Lithuania are located in the north-eastern part of the country. Additionally, the Velžiai and Migoniai II deposits of silver neck-rings fall into the same region and period. Therefore I would argue that we see two different ornament deposit traditions in Lithuania during the second half of the Middle Iron Age. There are western coastal bronze ornaments in watery conditions in the one side of the country, and on the other side, in the north-eastern region, we see a tradition of silver neck-ring deposits both in dry land and bog/marsh.

Several tendencies can be detected about the practices of wealth depositing in 1st-9th century AD Lithuania despite the scarcity of the overall material. First, during the Roman Iron Age the emphasis is put on bronze as a material. It can be found in various artefact forms, but mostly as ornaments and of course coins in the first four/five centuries of the 1st millennium AD. During the first half of the Roman Iron Age the preferred environment of concealment is solid ground, but from the 3rd century onwards bog/marsh are considered most appropriate. Moreover, all the finds from the Roman Iron Age are located in the western part of Lithuania. Bronzes remain represented in the depositional material in the Middle Iron Age. However, with the turn of the period two new materials – iron and silver

– are introduced. Although the first possible weapon deposit in Lithuania might be from the 6th century, more reliable material comes from the second half of the period. Additionally, weapons in general are a very rare find group in Lithuanian deposits. In the Middle Iron Age ornament deposits two distinguishable traditions occur: deposits of bronzes in watery environments in the western coastal area and silver neck-ring deposits in the north-eastern region.

The total quantity of deposits and deposited artefacts is considerably lower in Lithuania than in Latvia and Estonia and they cover a much smaller region. There is only one long-term site in which ornaments and weapon finds are combined. In most cases a clear selection of specific artefact functional groups can be traced. The small number of weapon and almost the total absence of tool finds in Lithuanian material should be also stressed. There is a clear domination of ornament deposits in the Lithuanian material.

*Chapter 9*

# Regional and cross-regional practices of wealth depositing in the eastern Baltic

This chapter provides broader conclusions about the practices of wealth depositing in the eastern Baltic 1st-9th century AD. Country specific and regional as well as cross-border and more widespread practices of wealth depositing are discussed via specific case studies. Only the more widely followed practices are taken into account and the unique outliers discussed under each country (see Chapters 6-8) are not considered here. Comparison of eastern Baltic material and Scandinavian material is discussed in the final subchapter.

The following discussion draws on the theoretical standpoints outlined in Chapter 3, with a special emphasis on answering the 'how' questions by setting the practices of wealth depositing into their contemporary social context. In the first part general cross-regional comparisons of deposits are provided in order to answer how eastern Baltic depositional practices have changed in time and space i.e. how the single events of wealth depositing (micro scale analysis) merge into wider depositional practices. In the second part of the chapter those practices are set into their social context and the macro scale of the analysis is provided. This includes discussing main social developments, stabilities and changes, as expressed by main characteristics of various archaeological features, sites and artefactual data. Resulting overall picture provides a macro scale background – a social structure – in which the depositional practices were situated. In the final parts of these discussion subchapters and presented case studies further conclusions are drawn about the relations between specific wealth depositional practices and their social context. Interpretations provided attempt to answer if and how practices of wealth depositing are influenced by their contemporary social structure and identify relationships between them. This altogether provides a fresh approach in terms of posing, answering and deriving the questions of highly interpretative and meaning-aimed 'why' from the material-based and analytical questions of 'how'.

## 9.1. Geographical and chronological distribution

The chronological distribution of eastern Baltic wealth deposits (Figs 9.1.1.-9.1.2.) shows that there is an increase in the number of deposits throughout the 1st-9th century AD. A clear peak is in the 6th century with 17 deposits. Estonia and Latvia show this peak (eight and seven deposits), but there are only two Lithuanian deposits from the 6th century. This might be related to the problems of artefact chronology, but the total number of deposits from the preceding and following centuries in Lithuania is also small: there are no deposits from the

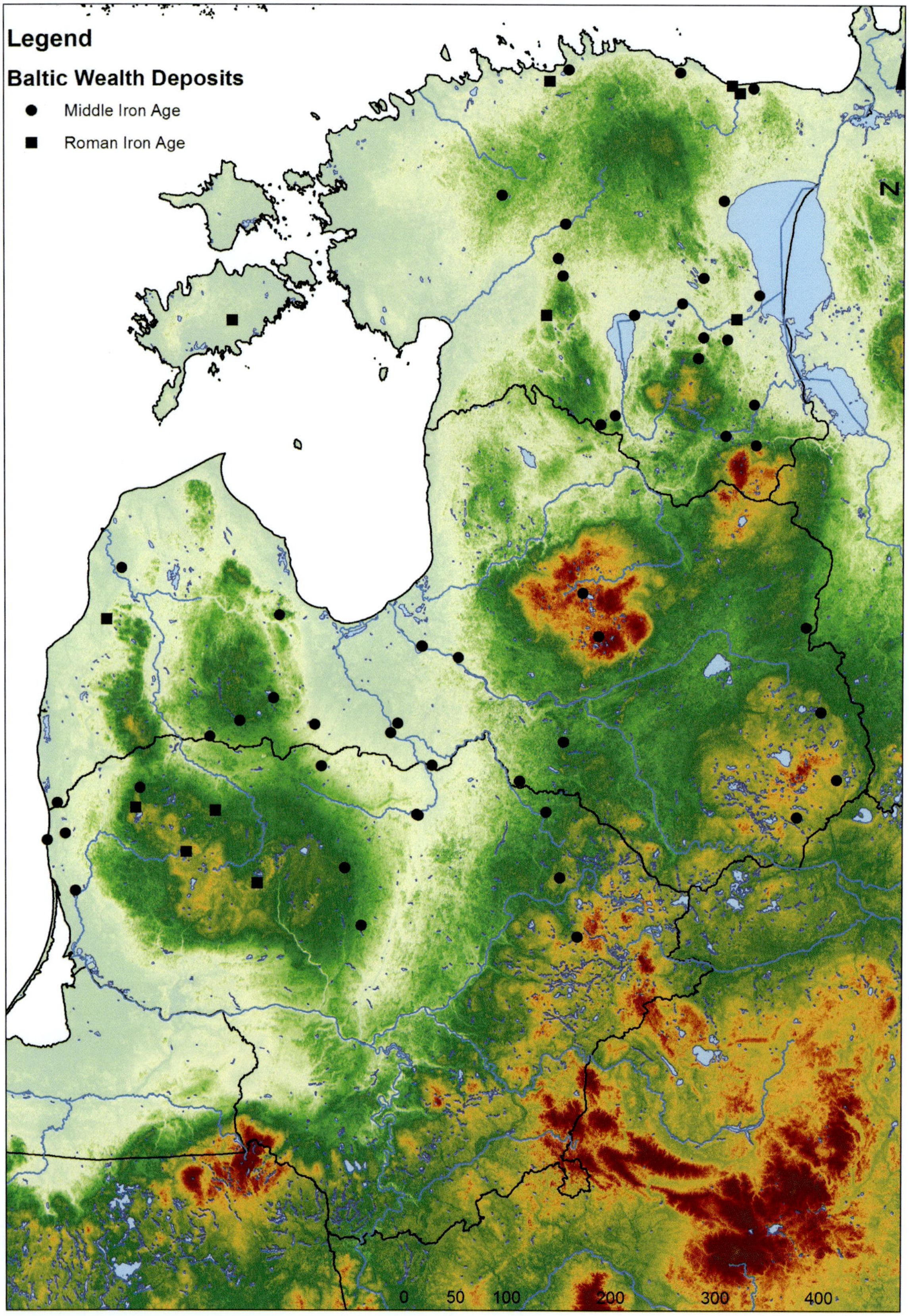


*Fig. 9.1.1. Map of chronological distribution of wealth deposits in the three Baltic countries.*

| | | Country | | | Total |
|---|---|---|---|---|---|
| | | Estonia | Latvia | Lithuania | |
| Dating | 2 | 1 | 0 | 1 | 2 |
| | 2-3; 4-5 | 0 | 0 | 1 | 1 |
| | 3 | 1 | 0 | 1 | 2 |
| | 4 | 3 | 1 | 1 | 5 |
| | 5 | 4 | 4 | 0 | 8 |
| | 6 | 8 | 7 | 2 | 17 |
| | 7 | 2 | 3 | 4 | 9 |
| | 8 | 4 | 5 | 3 | 12 |
| | 9 | 3 | 5 | 2 | 10 |
| | 1-3; 6-7 | 1 | 0 | 0 | 1 |
| | 7-8; 10-11 | 0 | 0 | 1 | 1 |
| | 2-3; 6-7; 12/13 | 1 | 0 | 0 | 1 |
| **Total** | | **28** | **25** | **16** | **69** |

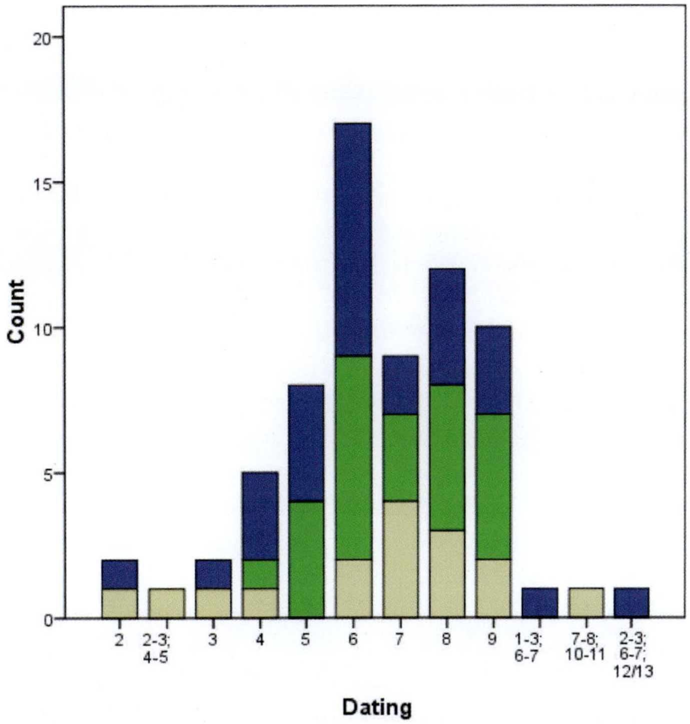


*Fig. 9.1.2. Chronological distribution (centuries AD) of wealth deposits in the eastern Baltic in crosstabulation and bar charts accordingly.*

5th and only four finds from the 7th century, the largest number of finds per century in Lithuania. Therefore it seems that the temporal distribution of wealth depositing in Estonia and Latvia follow the same patterns while Lithuania forms a slightly different entity with fewer deposits in total and a different chronological distribution.

The second general point is the small number of deposits in all three countries in the Roman Iron Age. There are only single deposits per country in the first half of the Roman Iron Age. Estonian material increases in the 4th century, and the single Latvian Roman Iron Age deposit is also from this century. Although this conclusion is biased by the fact that coin hoards are excluded from the analysis most of the Roman coin hoards in Latvia and Lithuania are from the 4th and 5th century. As the majority of Roman Iron Age deposits includes bronzes (mainly ornaments) the chronological distribution seems to relate to the increasing inflow of bronzes from the Roman Empire to the southern regions of the eastern Baltic. There this material could have been recast into other bronze artefacts and distributed more widely, including north towards Estonia. The small number of Roman coin hoards in Estonia supports the idea that the bronzes were acquired from its southern neighbours and not from direct connections to the Roman world. An increase in the number of deposits and items concealed begins only in the 5th century onwards when two new materials – silver and iron – enter the stage of wealth concealment.

Although the three Baltic countries are comparable in regional terms the number of depositions varies considerably country by country (Fig. 9.1.2.). In Estonia the total amount of wealth deposits –28 – is the largest of the three countries. More importantly, they are concentrated in the eastern part of the country and the western areas are almost without deposits. There are also gaps in the main distribution area of deposits which may be explained by natural conditions such as the historically heavily forested and upland areas in the central regions of north-eastern Estonia.

The twenty five deposits from Latvia are distributed throughout the country. However, here too some empty zones can be identified. In Estonia the western regions lack deposits, but in Latvia the densest distribution is in the western half of the country. The region with almost no wealth deposits in Latvia is in the north. In the north-eastern areas during the Middle Iron Age this cannot be the result of no population, because there are at least some archaeological sites in the area (Apals *et al.* 2001, fig. 175). The almost complete lack of archaeological sites in north-western Latvia shows that this area was very sparsely inhabited during the 1st-9th century AD. There is an empty border zone between the deposits in Latvia and Estonia indicating the absence of the tradition of wealth depositing in northern Latvia, but its clear existence in southern Estonia. It seems that there really were different attitudes towards the treatment of valuables in Latvia and Estonia, and the existence of cultural borders is also evident in the Iron Age archaeological material. It is most likely a natural border, Haanja Upland in the south-eastern corner of Estonia, served as a cultural border between Estonia and Latvia. Its highest peak Suur Munamägi Hill (318 m a.s.l.) is the highest point in the Baltic countries.

The picture is more complex in Lithuania. The number of wealth deposits (excluding coin hoards) is smaller – only 16. This is significant because Lithuania is the largest of the three Baltic countries. According to the distribution map there are no wealth deposits in the southern half of the country and all the 1st-9th century wealth deposits are from the northern regions. This reflects the actual archaeological data, because there are archaeological sites and similar finds of artefact deposits in the western, central and south-eastern part of the country which include both Roman coin hoards or other deposits from later periods (see the maps in Tautavičius (ed.) 1975; Tautavičius 1977; 1978; Jākobsons 1999, 91; Michelbertas 2001). The southern border of the distribution of the wealth deposits in the 1st-9th century eastern Baltic seems to run from east to west along the central part of Lithuania and it seems that there were quite different attitudes towards depositing valuables in its northern and southern regions. The second important note is that most of the Lithuanian wealth deposits have close parallels in Latvian material. Very often the distribution of wealth deposits in spatial and temporal terms as well as their content and context are alike in those two countries, especially around their current political borders. The only exception is the chronological distribution which is closer between Estonia and Latvia. However, as the numbers of deposits in Lithuania are small and the chronology slightly problematic, the context and content of the finds seem to be more reliable comparisons. Therefore, it is argued that Latvia and Lithuania form a unitary whole with several cross-regional depositional practices. The latter is also supported by the similarities of other archaeological finds and sites in these regions. This has resulted in the discussion of cross-country ethnozones of the Balts *e.g.* Curonians, Semigallians, Selonians, in Latvian and Lithuanian archaeological scholarship having its roots in the early 20th century and Soviet period research tradition (e.g. Griciuvienė 2005; 2007; 2009; see also Oras 2012a).

### 9.1.1. Content and context

There are several important similarities and differences in the context and content of the eastern Baltic wealth deposits which allow further conclusions about cross-regional and local depositional practices. These become more evident when the data is divided according to the chronology of finds country by country.

The general overview graphs showing the temporal distribution of materials and artefact types in three Baltic countries (Figs 9.1.1.1., 9.1.1.2.) indicate relevant patterns. The Roman Iron Age with its very few finds is dominated by bronze ornaments. Iron, especially weapons, first appears in the 5th century AD and continues in almost the same proportions until the end of the period under discussion. Ornaments made of silver or bronze either remain the most common artefact groups or are found as frequently as weapon deposits throughout this 800-years period.

Dividing the same material according to the country (Figs 9.1.1.1., 9.1.1.2.) demonstrates some important regional tendencies. Weapons appear in Latvian and Lithuanian material a couple of centuries earlier than in Estonia, in the 5th century in Latvia and in the 6th in Lithuania. Additionally, in Latvia they form the majority of all artefact deposits in the 5th and 6th century. At the same time ornament deposits remain in the majority in Estonia. In the 5th century they include deposits of bronzes, in the 6th they consist only of silver ornaments or single vessels. At the time when weapons and tools are concealed in Estonia in the second half of the Middle Iron Age, Latvian and Lithuanian material is dominated by silver and bronze ornament deposits. A combination of general and country based graphs of the main artefacts and materials provides some additional conclusions about the practices of wealth depositing. For instance, we see more variety in the content of bronzes (coins, raw material and coins) in Roman Iron Age Lithuania than in Estonia and Latvia (ornaments only). Silver ornaments emerge first in the 4th-5th century but increase from the 6th century onwards. The majority of silver deposits in terms of main material in a deposit as well as the number of concealed silver artefacts is from Estonia and Latvia (12 and 11 silver dominated deposits with a total of 69 and 34 silver objects respectively). In Lithuania the number of silver deposits is only five with 15 silver objects in total (see Figs 6.1.3.1. for Estonia, 7.1.3.1. for Latvia, 8.1.3.1. for Lithuania). It looks as if there were regional rules about where and how silver was deposited. Long-

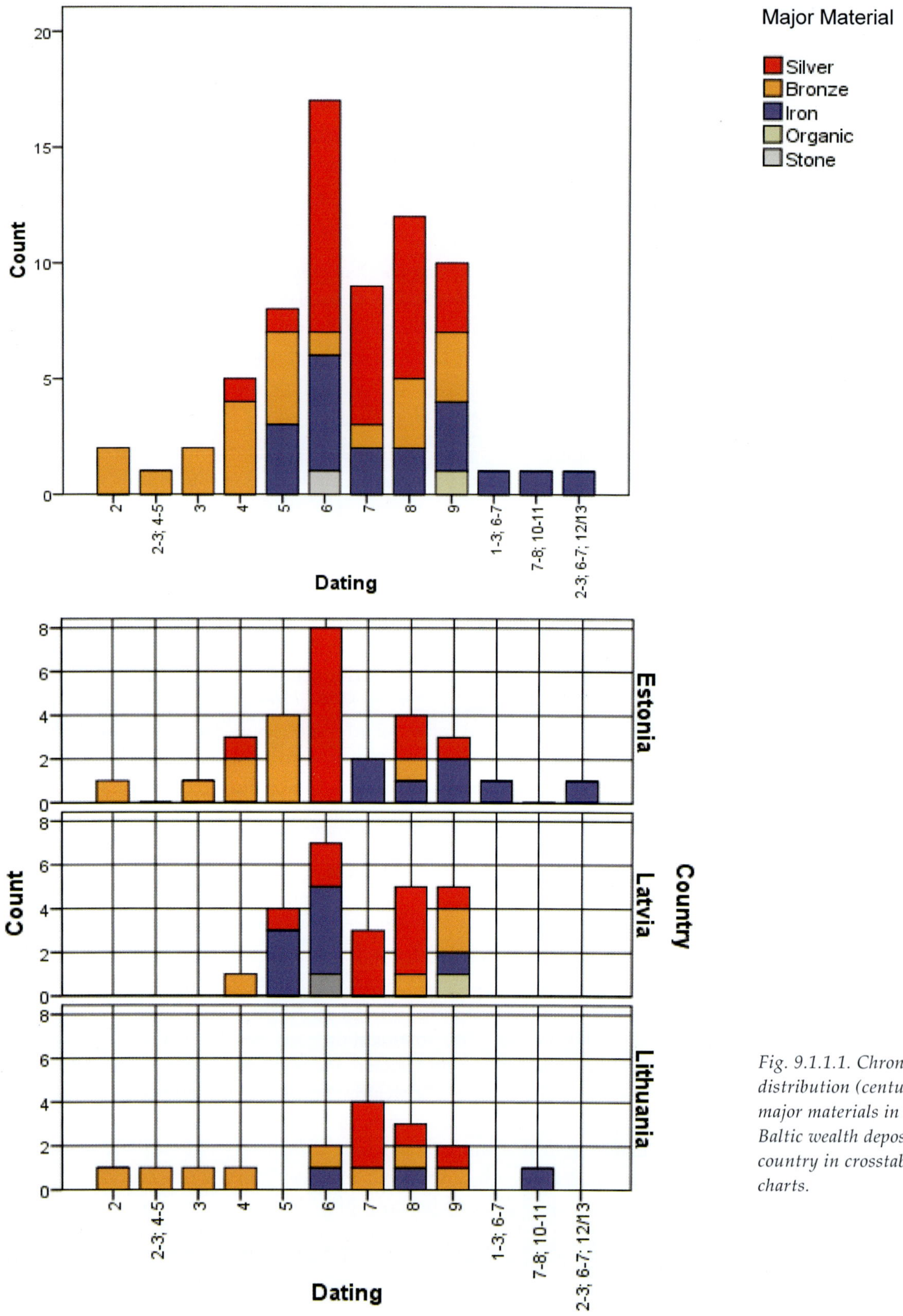


*Fig. 9.1.1.1. Chronological distribution (centuries AD) of major materials in the eastern Baltic wealth deposits and by country in crosstabulation bar charts.*

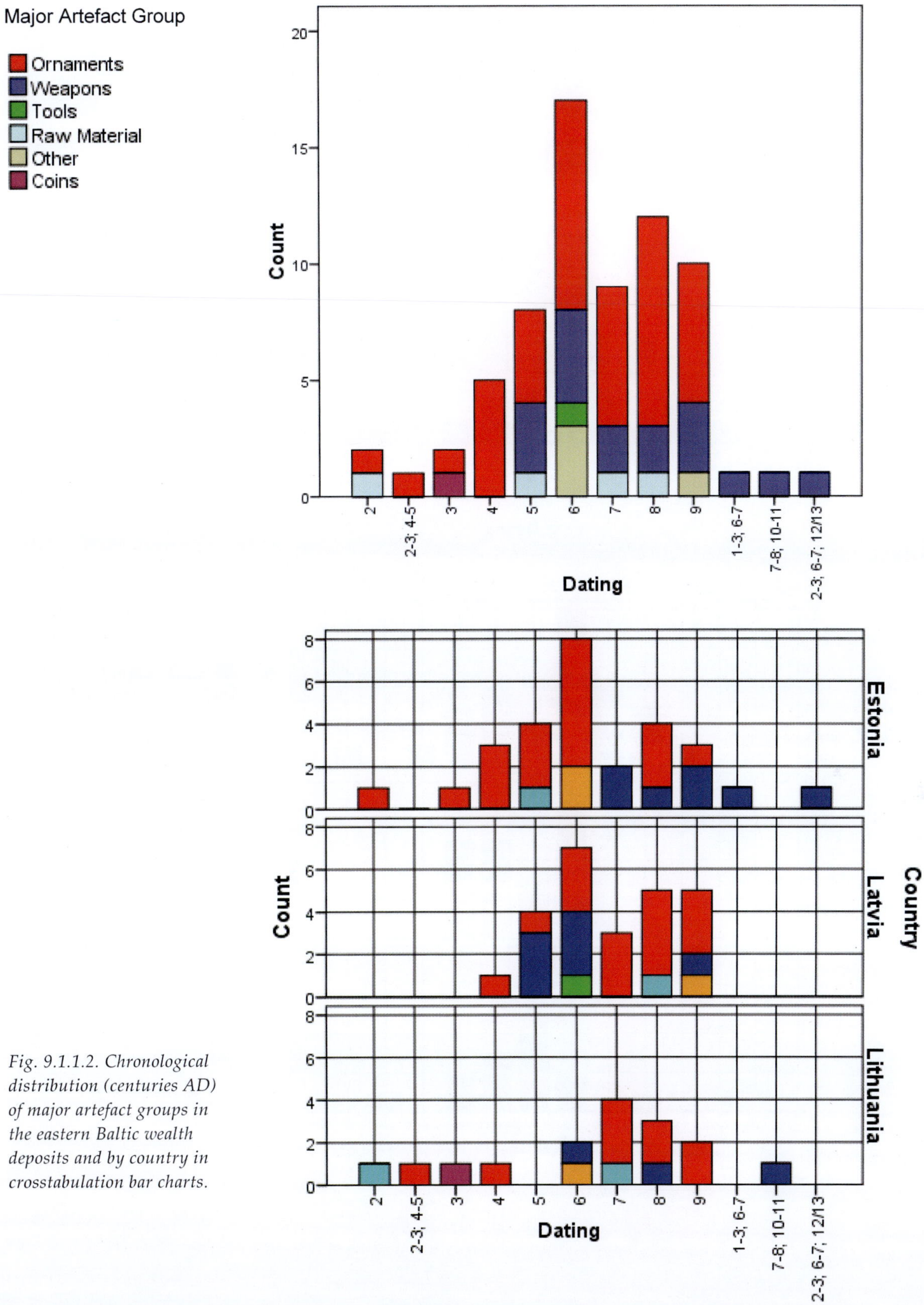


*Fig. 9.1.1.2. Chronological distribution (centuries AD) of major artefact groups in the eastern Baltic wealth deposits and by country in crosstabulation bar charts.*

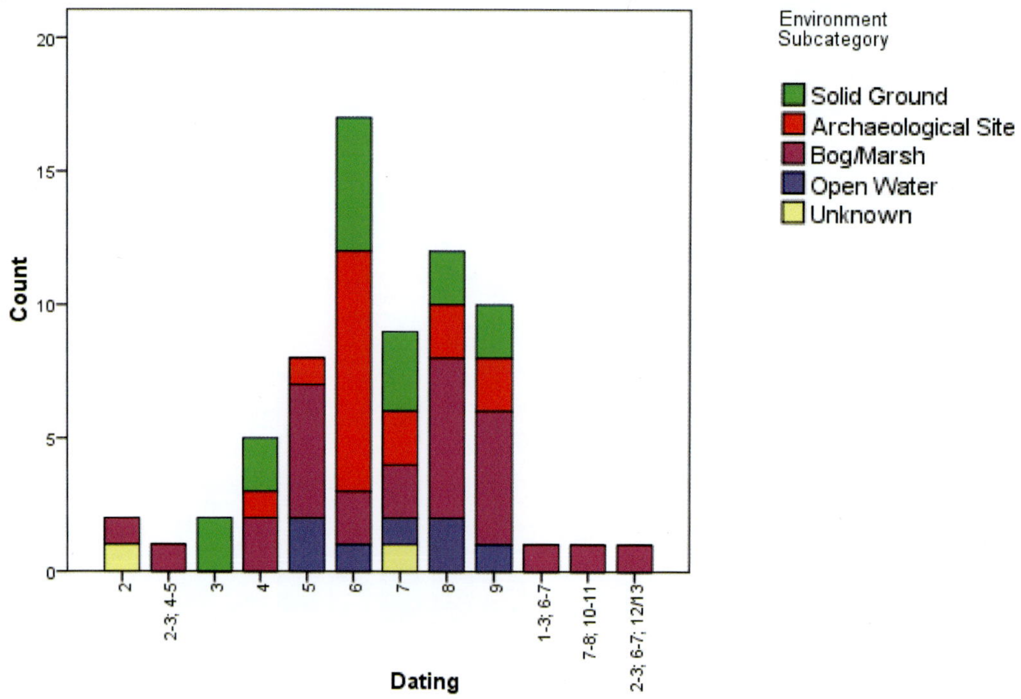


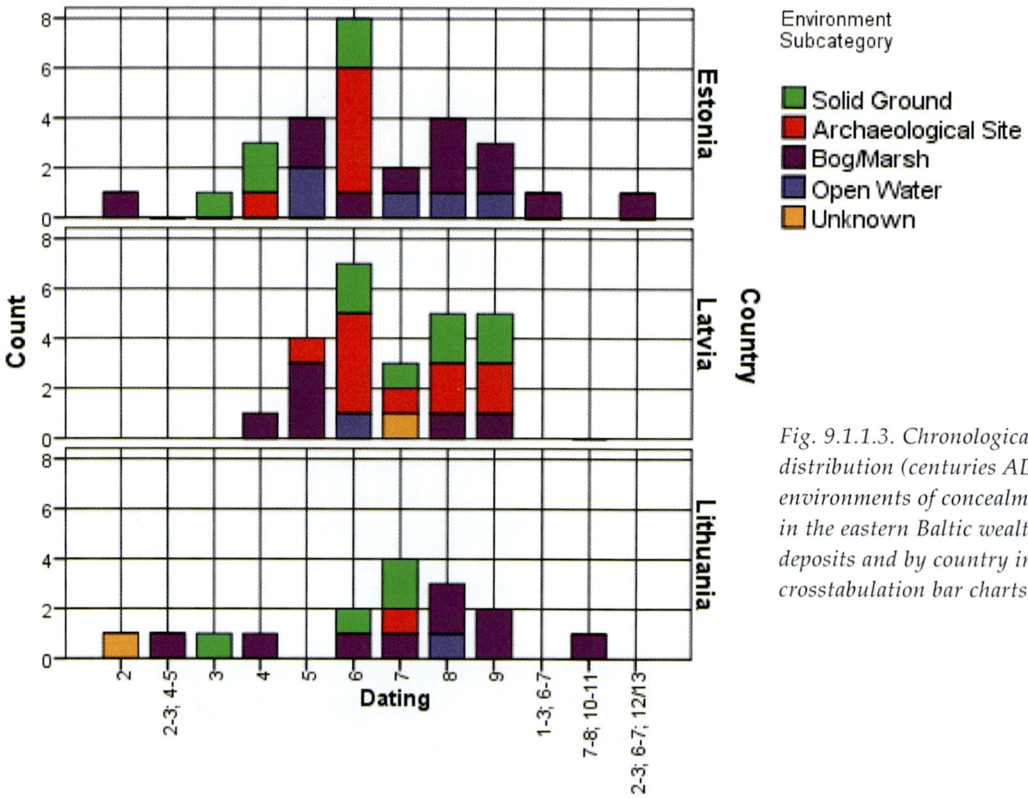


*Fig. 9.1.1.3. Chronological distribution (centuries AD) of environments of concealment in the eastern Baltic wealth deposits and by country in crosstabulation bar charts.*

term depositional sites, a phenomenon that appears in Estonia and Lithuania will be discussed in detail in the following subchapter.

One aspect of artefact content of the deposit can be followed in all the three Baltic countries. There is often a clear dominance of a single material and artefact functional group. However, weapons seem to be more often combined with ornaments in Latvia and Lithuania and in those cases the material of the ornaments is bronze (see Figs 6.1.4.1.-6.1.4.5. for Estonia, 7.1.4.1.-7.1.4.5. for Latvia, and 8.1.4.1.-8.1.4.5. for Lithuania). In Estonia the mixture of weapons-tools with ornaments is unusual. Concealment of bronzes either with or without iron seems to be related to social status or gender based selection of deposited items. Silver is never combined with iron in any of the eastern Baltic deposits. The concept of silver deposits as a separate entity, kept free from any iron items, seems to be a cross-cultural phenomenon, while attitudes towards bronzes are more loose and variable.

The chronological overview (Fig. 9.1.1.3.) shows that the most popular environment of concealment for the eastern Baltic wealth deposits is bog or marsh. This continued as the most common choice throughout the Roman and Middle Iron Age. The only exceptions are the 6th and 7th century when suddenly dry land environments, including in or in the vicinity of archaeological sites, take over. Open water remains marginal and is related to Middle Iron Age deposits only. Country based graphs of the environments of concealment show that most of the open water deposits are found in Estonia. Archaeological sites are most numerous in Estonia and Latvia, but almost absent in Lithuania. In Estonia there is a chronological tendency towards wetter environments of concealment, but in Latvia it is directly the opposite. In Lithuania watery sites remain the most popular environment of concealment throughout the centuries. All the long-term deposits are found in bog and marsh.

Combining the data on materials and artefacts with the environments of concealment in a geographical and temporal scale gives a further insight into regional and cross-regional practices of wealth depositing (see Figs 9.1.1.4 and 9.1.1.5.). In Estonia we see a clear depositional tradition in terms of selecting depositional items to be deposited on archaeological sites. Archaeological sites contain only ornaments or 'other' artefact types (silver vessels in both cases) and these are all predominantly silver deposits. Latvian material from archaeological sites is more varied including nearly all the functional groups and materials. The chronological distribution indicates that in the first half of the Middle Iron Age mostly iron items such as tools and weapons are found in Latvian archaeological sites, but in the last part of the period mainly bronze ornaments can be found there. At the same time silver ornaments seem to be more frequent in dry land environment. However, while most of the Estonian archaeological sites are burial grounds, in Latvia they also include hill-forts and settlements. They are mostly found during large-scale excavations, which demonstrates the variety of materials that might be concealed in hill-fort contexts and revealed only in large-scale excavation projects. Lithuania has only one find from an archaeological site and it is a hill-fort.

Watery environments, including open water and bogs/marshes, contain different functional groups and materials in all three Baltic countries. It looks as if these places have been favourable environments for concealment throughout the 800 years. However, the chronological distribution indicates once again the changes in the most popular types of artefacts that have been deposited in water-

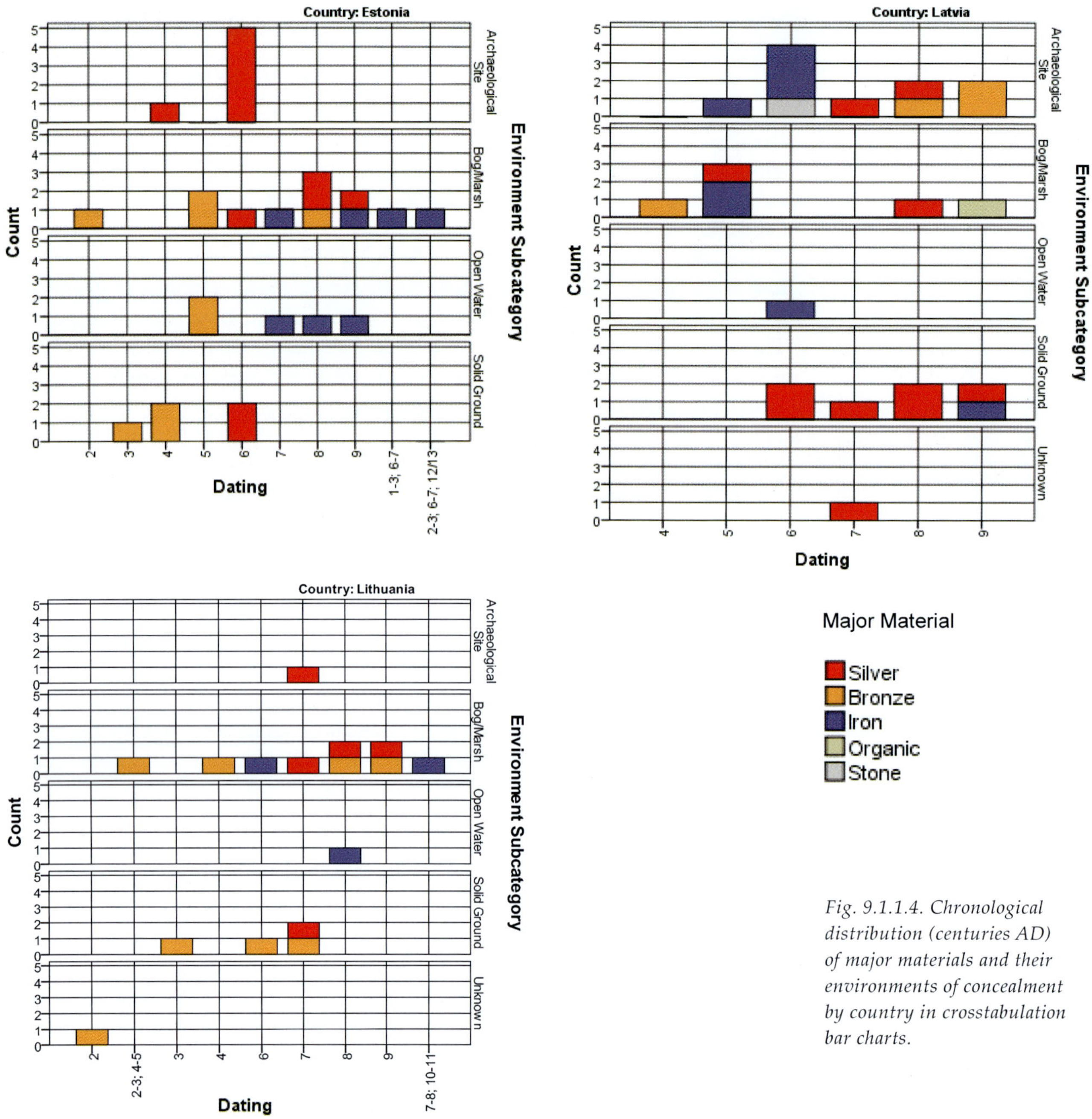


*Fig. 9.1.1.4. Chronological distribution (centuries AD) of major materials and their environments of concealment by country in crosstabulation bar charts.*

related contexts: bronzes in the Roman and early Middle Iron Age, weapons in the Middle Iron Age, silver ornaments (mainly neck-rings, see also below) in the final centuries of the Middle Iron Age. One important aspect is that both in Latvia and Lithuania open water has only iron artefacts (weapons), while in Estonia the same number of deposits of bronzes can be found in this environment, all from the 5th century. In the later centuries similarly to Latvia and Lithuania only iron in the form of weapons is found in open water in Estonia as well.

Dry land has been used for depositing mainly ornaments in Estonia and Latvia, but a more variable selection of items in Lithuania. Only one example of a weapon deposit from Latvia is from a dry land context. Dry land or archaeological

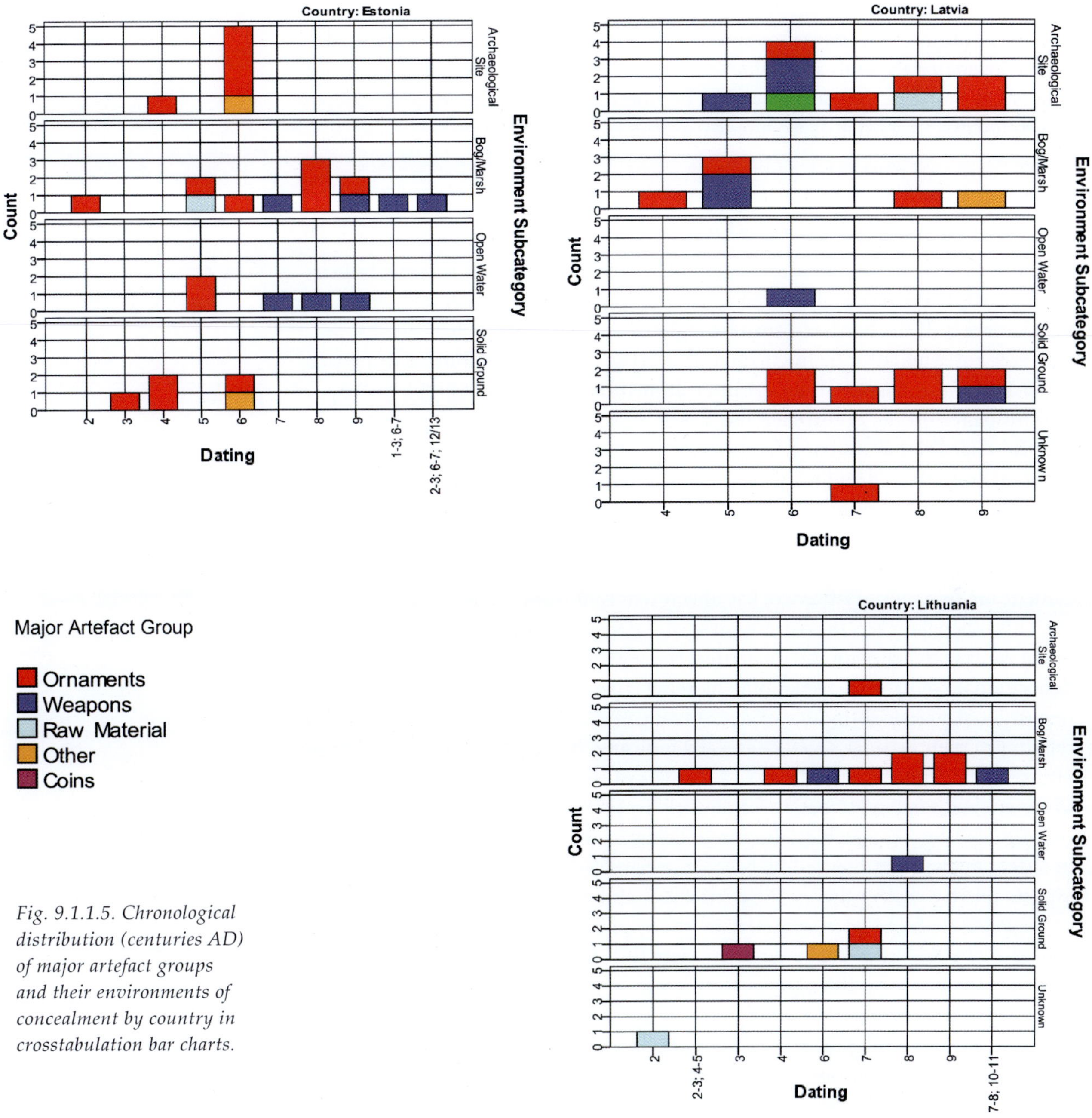


*Fig. 9.1.1.5. Chronological distribution (centuries AD) of major artefact groups and their environments of concealment by country in crosstabulation bar charts.*

sites were a preferable environment of concealment in Estonia up to the 6th century but in the following centuries the Estonian ornament deposits move to water-related conditions. In Lithuania a considerable number of later ornament deposits are also from watery conditions. Differently from those two in Latvia the proportion of Middle Iron Age ornaments in watery conditions compared to dry land environments is small. The majority of silver ornaments, mainly silver neck-rings, in Latvia are from dry land and this particular depositional tradition is traced in Latvian material already in the 6th century AD. Similar ornament deposits in Estonia and Lithuania are from slightly later periods, from the 7th-9th century AD. Thus it seems that the origin of the silver neck-ring deposits is in Latvian territory where they are concealed in dry land conditions. Later when expanding towards south and north this practice became more variable in terms of the environment of concealment and now also watery conditions were used.

As raw materials, tools and 'other' only occur in single instances it is impossible to identify any clear pattern. They can be found at different times and different environments, very often as unique discoveries in only one country.

## 9.2. Regional and cross-regional practices of wealth depositing in social context

To understand regional and cross-regional depositional practices better it is necessary to analyse the results discussed above in comparison with their contemporary social context. If the borders drawn by regional and widespread depositional practices (set out as micro scale in Chapter 3) overlap with the distribution of particular social context (macro scale) it can be argued that social context has an important influence on the occurrence and development of depositional practices. The specific depositional practices are shown on distribution maps which combine different contextual data on a geographical and chronological scale. Figures 9.2.1 and 9.2.2. concentrate on the chronological distribution of materials and major artefact groups. Figures 9.2.3. and 9.2.4. add the environment of concealment. To make the point about cross-country and regional depositional practices more evident modern country borders have been removed from these maps.

This subchapter sets the patterns of wealth depositional practices into a broader social context. It relies on the theoretical framework outlined in Chapter 3: single depositional events with overlapping material characteristics form widely followed depositional practices (inductive micro scale analysis); the latter are analysed in relation to their broader social context as indicated by developments and changes occurring in various materialities and features of the overall archaeological record in given temporal and spatial framework (macro scale analysis). Accordingly, the aim of the case studies discussed below is to consider how depositional practices might be influenced by broader social developments and how these two aspects relate to each other at different times and areas. In doing so an overview of available archaeological material in the vicinity of particular find groups is provided. Information about different sites (hill-forts, settlements, burials) and cultural circumstances (foreign contacts, economy, social hierarchy or heterarchy) are taken into consideration. In most cases the available material is fragmentary and not all archaeological sites and social aspects can be included. Therefore sometimes the comparisons are based on either just a few archaeological remains or very broad generalisations. Some of the site types cannot be considered at all due to the lack of research in particular areas. However, an attempt is made to take into account the closest material both in spatial and temporal terms in order to ensure that the most relevant and direct connections between wealth depositional traditions and broader social context can be drawn.

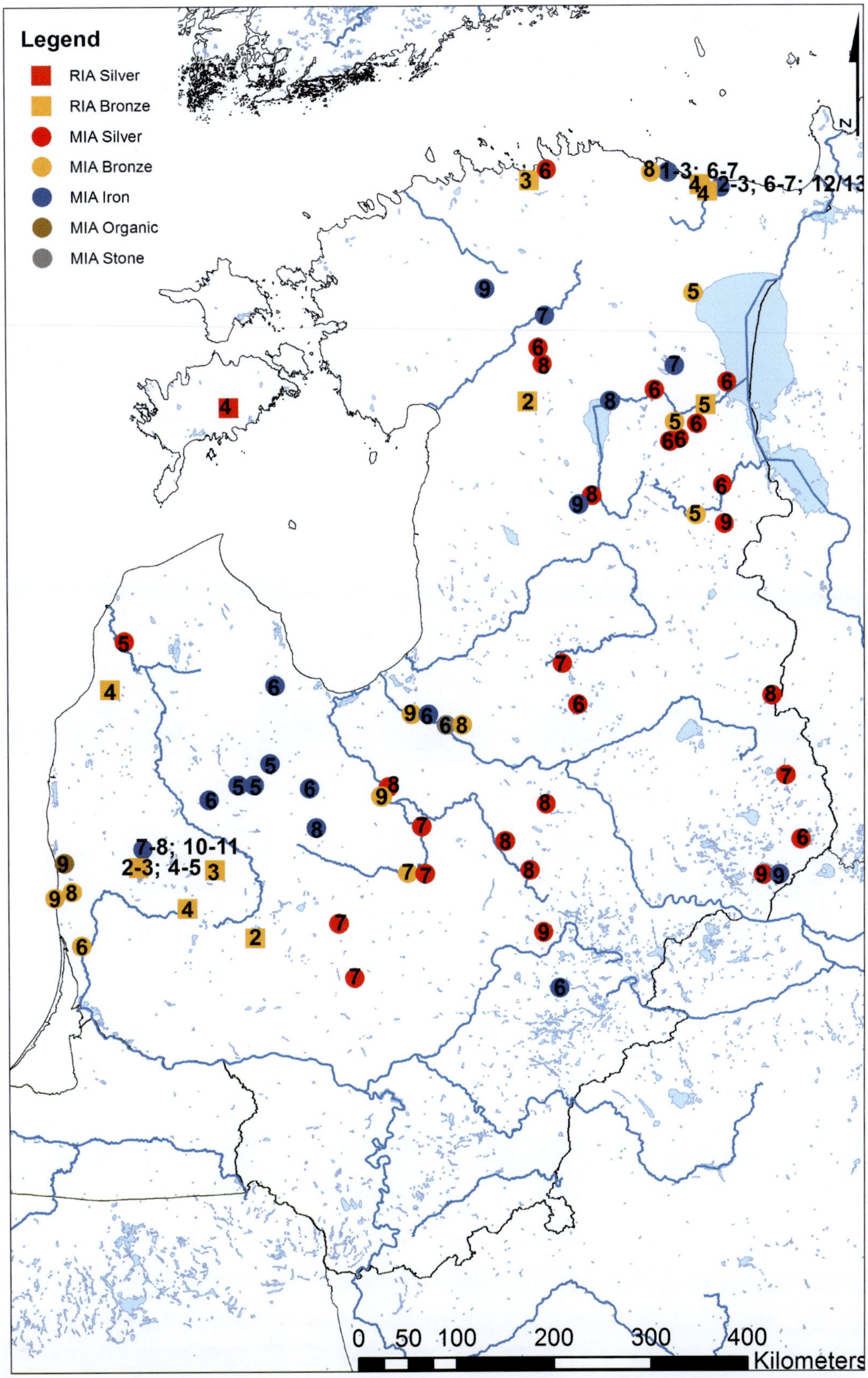


*Fig. 9.2.1. Distribution map of major materials of eastern Baltic wealth deposits and their chronology. Number on the symbol indicates the dating (century AD) of the deposit.*

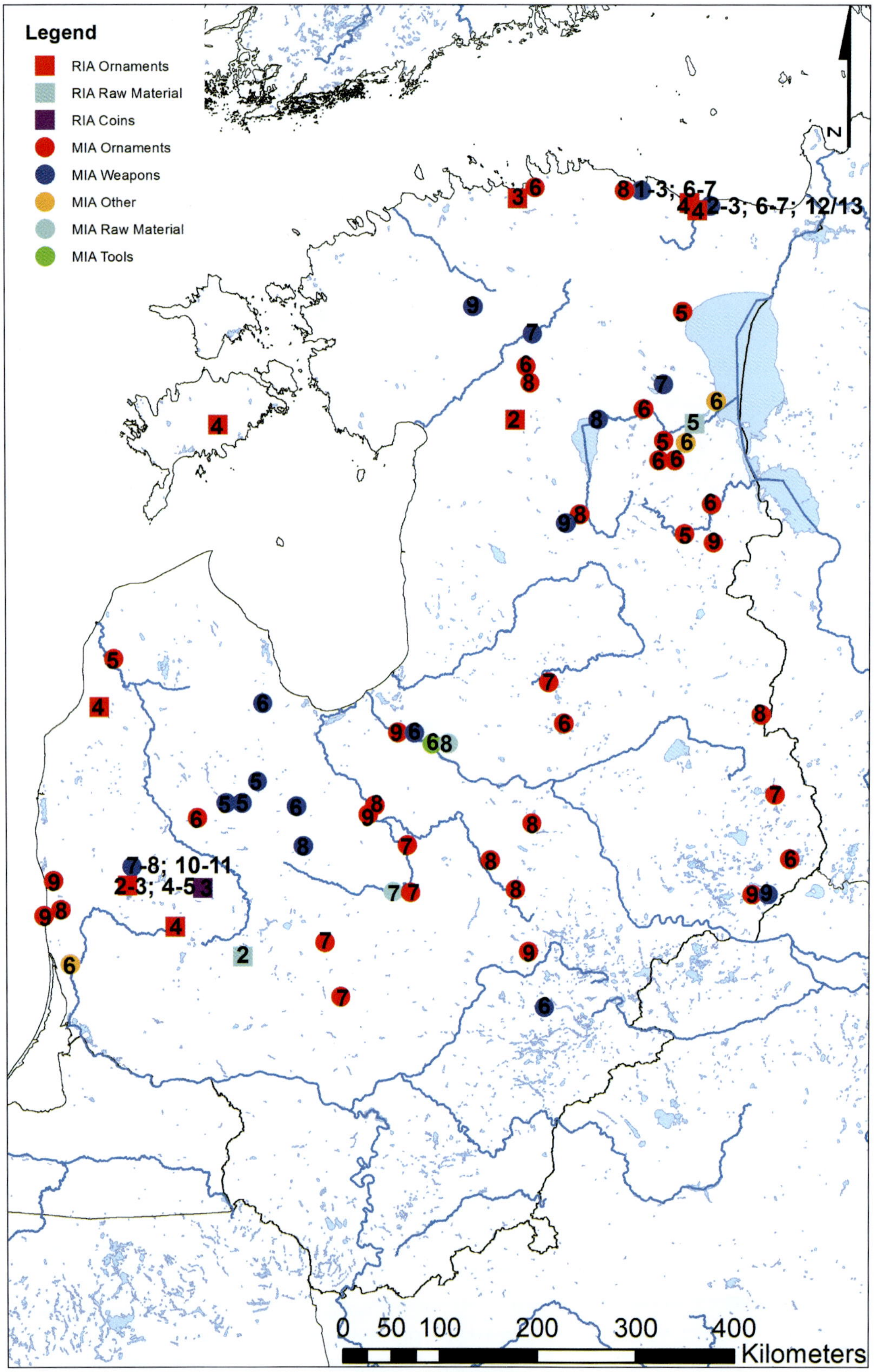


*Fig. 9.2.2. Distribution map of major artefact groups of eastern Baltic wealth deposits and their chronology. Number on the symbol indicates the dating (century AD) of the deposit.*

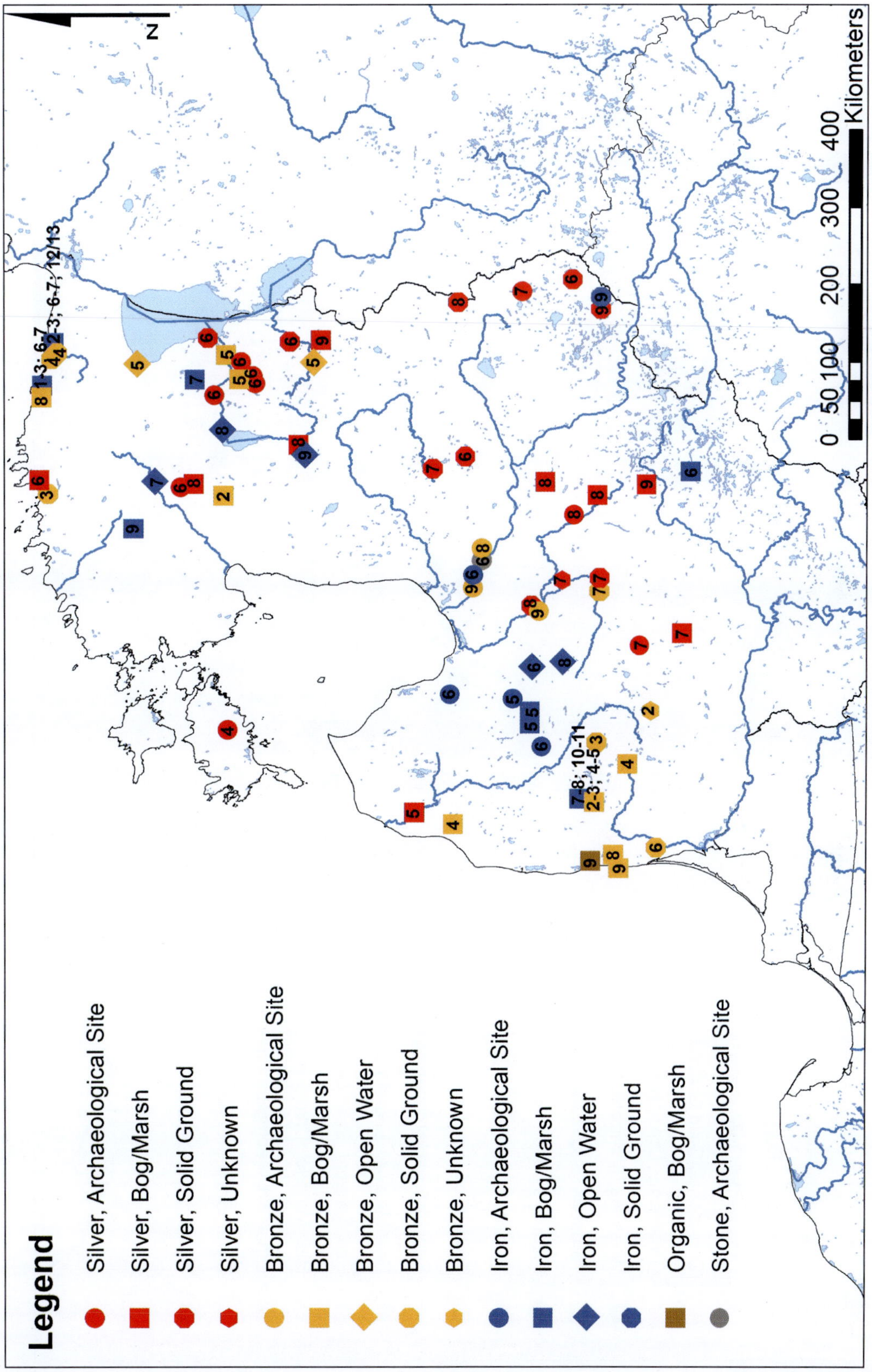


*Fig. 9.2.3. Distribution map of major material, environment of concealment and chronology of eastern Baltic wealth deposits. Number on the symbol indicates the dating (century AD) of the deposit.*

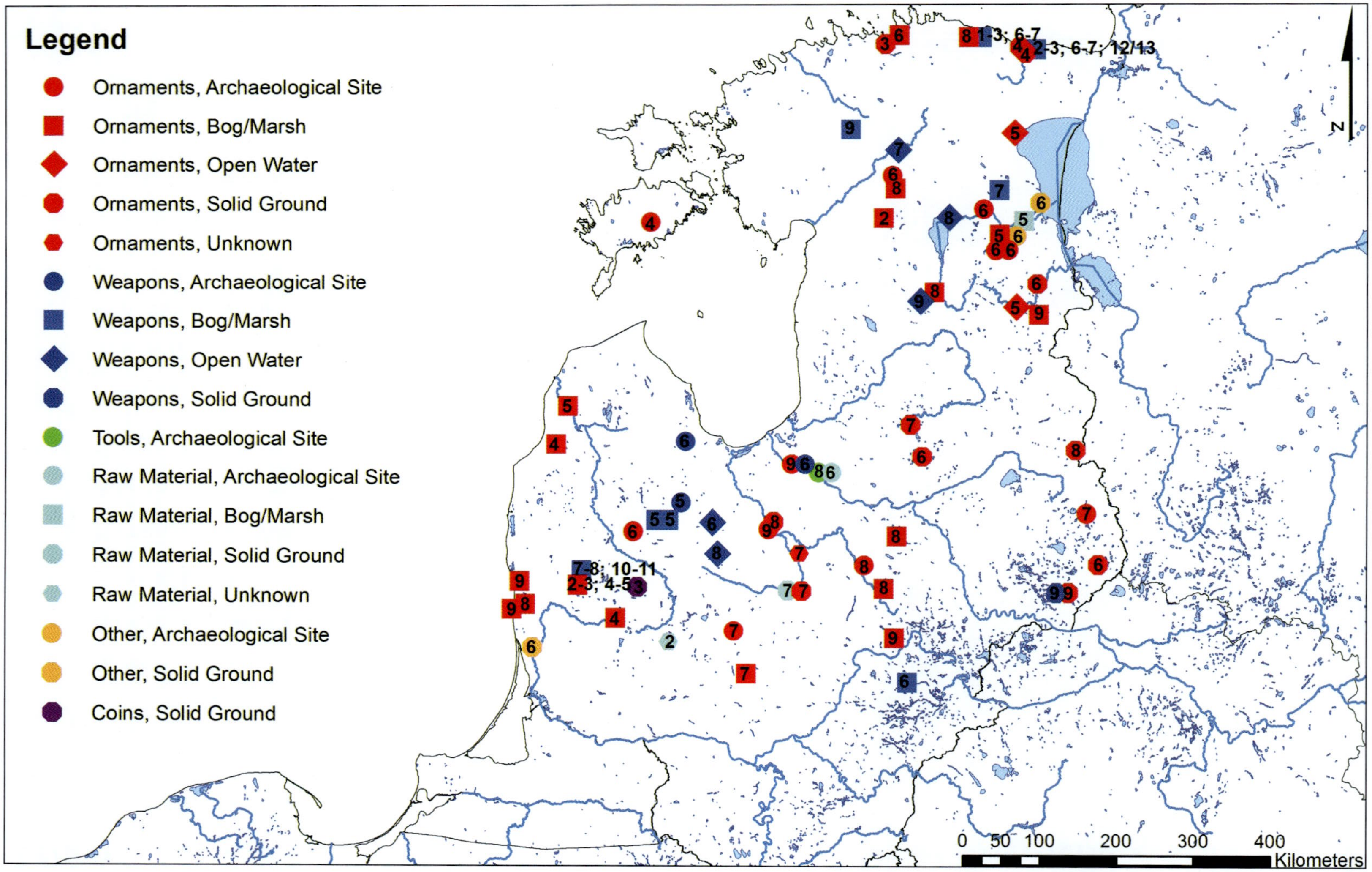


*Fig. 9.2.4. Distribution map of major artefact group, environment of concealment and chronology of eastern Baltic wealth deposits. Number on the symbol indicates the dating (century AD) of the deposit.*

### 9.2.1. Roman Iron Age bronze deposits in the eastern Baltic

One of the earliest examples of a cross-regional depositional practice is the deposits of bronzes in the Roman Iron Age. The number of Roman Iron Age bronze deposits is not large – five in Estonia, only one in Latvia and four in Lithuania. In most cases these are bronze ornaments, but in Estonia and Lithuania there are also examples of raw material (Miežaičiai and Kavastu), or even a bronze lamp (Kavastu), whilst in Latvia only a single bronze ornament (Alsungas) has been discovered. In Lithuania these deposits also include coins. The largest number of Roman coin hoards is from Lithuania (over 10 hoards), followed by Latvia (around 5 hoards) and Estonia (only 2 hoards). Most of the Roman Iron Age bronze deposits are found in relation to main water routes, either in the vicinity of coastal areas or in the region of larger rivers. Their environment of concealment is divided between dry land and bog/marsh. In Latvia and Lithuania the selection of the environment of concealment is related to artefacts: ornaments in bog and marsh, coins and raw material in dry land. In Estonia that division is not evident: some ornament deposits in the north-east coast are found in dry land and bronze bars from Kavastu were discovered in a peat bog. The differences in depositing bronzes in the north and south of the eastern Baltic are reflected in the content and social contexts of these finds.

It seems that the content of Roman Iron Age deposits in the eastern Baltic depends on the abundance of bronzes. Indeed, this is one of the most important social context (macro scale) influence reflected in wealth deposits, but also in very different archaeological features and materialities at the same time. The amount and the intensity of inflow of bronzes was different in the three Baltic countries, as indicated by coin hoards and other Roman import finds. In Lithuania we see a rich variety of Roman objects in different contexts. In Latvia the number of imports is smaller, but nevertheless significant. Estonia remains behind its two southern neighbours and here Roman imports seem to be substituted with bronze ornaments. This suggests that the amount and scale of availability, use and re-use of bronzes in Lithuania was the largest of the three countries. Latvia formed a kind of hinterland, with fewer imports and fewer bronze deposits. Estonia with the same quantity of Roman Iron Age bronzes as Lithuania only includes ornament finds which have probably been produced in and imported from its southern neighbours. The northern Baltic region remained a periphery for the Roman world and thus the forms of items as well as ways of acquiring bronzes were different here. It can be also argued that although similar in many ways the three Baltic countries followed some different depositional traditions during the Roman Iron Age (see case studies below). It is only in the Middle Iron Age that Latvia and Lithuania start to approach each other, whilst Estonia remains separate.

#### 9.2.1.1. Case study 1: 3rd-4th century AD bronze deposits in northern Estonia

One of the earliest Estonian Roman Iron Age wealth deposits consist of ornaments, mainly neck-rings, dating from the 3rd-4th century AD and concealed in a dry land environment. Three of those deposits – **Mustmätta, Liimala** and **Kiiu** – are situated in the coastal region of Estonia. The first two are only a few kilometres from each other in the north-eastern Estonia, Kiiu is further away on the northern coast of Estonia.

Hill-forts are in general rare in Roman Iron Age Estonia. There are some hill-forts in the area where Roman Iron Age wealth deposits are found, but usually they are from the preceding or following periods. If Roman Iron Age activities on them are known they are indicated by single radiocarbon dates or stray finds, and the cultural layer is very thin (Jaanits *et al.* 1982, 220; Tamla 1996; Lang 2007b, chapter 2; Tõnisson 2008, nos 36-40). There is a specific site group of small fortified and/or hilltop settlements (Schmiedehelm 1955, fig. 53; 1956, fig. 29; Lang 2007b, fig. 56, 57-74). Although not numerous, hilltop settlements have a long history going back to the Late Bronze Age and extending to the Middle Iron Age. They are located in the coastal, central and south-eastern regions of Estonia and some of them are situated close to the deposits of bronzes. The material on those sites is very similar to ordinary open settlements. They were inhabited by single households, but their location in the landscape indicates additional protection and/or (symbolic) control purposes. It has been argued that those peculiar settlement sites, that stand out in the overall landscape, are indicators of continuous display of social hierarchy in the Roman Iron Age (Lang 2007b, 74).

The material from Roman Iron Age open settlements is neither thoroughly studied nor abundant. Very few open settlements have been excavated. The area of settlements is usually small with a thin cultural layer (Lang 2007b, 50-51). On the basis of available material it has been argued that north-eastern Estonia was densely inhabited in the Bronze and Early Iron Ages (Lang 2007b, fig. 15). Some long-term settlement analyses have suggested that there is a gradual increase in population, especially along the northern coast of Estonia in the Purtse River region where both the Liimala and Mustmätta deposits are located (Schmiedehelm 1956; Lang 2007b, 83-86). The western part of the northern coast from where the single bronze deposit from Kiiu is known is located in the border area of this densely inhabited region (Lang 1996, 261, 414-416, fig. 122; 2000, 191-195).

The main cemetery type in Estonia during the Roman Iron Age is *tarand*-graves (Lang 2007b, 192-196). These are rectangular stone constructions that are sometimes filled with smaller stone rubble. Burials are usually cremated and scattered within the construction. These are collective burials which mostly belong to single families and include very homogeneous grave goods. *Tarand*-graves are distributed all over Estonia but they are most numerous in the northern coastal (especially north-eastern), central and southern parts of the country (Jaanits *et al.* 1982, plate XII; Lang 2007b, 191-216). Finds in *tarand*-graves in northern Estonia include mainly bronze ornaments such as neck-rings, fibulae, bracelets, finger-rings, and pins. The variety of burial goods becomes particularly abundant in the 3rd-4th century AD including brooches, bracelets, finger-rings, neck-rings, pins, mounts, drinking horn rims, shield parts, and battle knives (Scmiedehelm 1955, fig. 55; 1956, 149-150; Lang 2007b, 193-194). The latter three more unusual find groups are dated already to the turn of the Roman Iron Age to Migration Period. Iron items remain rare all over Estonia and provide only some examples of tools, such as socketed axes, sickles, scythes, knives, and awls (Schmiedehelm 1955). A change in burial customs emerges from the 4th century AD onwards. At first we see some single individual burials among the collective cremations in the north-eastern Estonia. In the 5th-6th century AD also some separate inhumations next to old *tarand*-graves appear with some previously unknown burial goods such as spearheads, single-edged swords, also bracelets and brooches (Schmiedehelm 1955, fig. 55; 1956, 153). This is an indication of social changes happening in the last decades of the Roman Iron Age:

the emergence of single outstanding leaders of the society who have earned a special treatment and place among other collective burials.

In this context of emerging individuality an unparalleled burial custom in the northern coast of Estonia must be discussed. This is located in Valkla, not far from the Kiiu find. The finds from *tarand*-graves around and from the same time as Kiiu deposit are very moderate (Lang 1996, 267, 313-320). At the same time there is a short-term and very small-scale emergence of so-called *bauta*-stone graves that have been connected with similar grave types in Sweden (Vassar 1966; Lang 1996, 324-325; 2007b, 216-217; Jonuks 2009, 222-223). These graves differ from local *tarand*-graves in form and content. *Bauta*-stone graves are cremation burials in pits, marked with a standing stone. Burial goods include mainly small bronze ornaments (finger-rings, pins) and tools (awl, knives). The Kiiu deposit itself has been also argued to be another example of this unique burial tradition (Vassar 1966) but more recent scholarship seems to dismiss this interpretation (Lang 1996, 314, 328; 2007b, 247; Jonuks 2009, 231).

Comparing the artefacts from wealth deposits and other archaeological sites reveals some more interesting conclusions about this local depositional practice. Most of the Roman Iron Age deposits consist of neck-rings and neck-rings are also very popular in grave goods, especially in northern Estonia. Neck-rings with trumpet-shape terminals are one of the earliest types which are known from the 2nd century until the end of 4th century AD. They are thought to come from Latvia, western Lithuania, eastern Prussia (see also Rzeszotarska-Nowakiewicz 2010). The majority of those neck-rings is found in the northern, some also in southern, but none from central Estonia (Moora 1938, 264-267, map IV; Lang 2007b, 211). However, the massive forms are known from wealth deposits only and they are not represented in burial goods (Moora 1938, 36; Schmiedehelm 1955, fig. 11). Such neck-rings are imported items not commonly spread among and worn by every member of the society. It is a type of ornament that was proportionally more common in the wealth deposits than in burial goods.

Turning to other types, the twisted wire neck-rings with loop-shape terminals as found in Liimala and Mustmätta are not very numerous but spread in the same area and contexts where the trumpet-shaped neck-rings are distributed (Moora 1938, 264-299; Lang 2007b, 211-212). Most common are neck-rings with mushroom- or knob-shaped terminals. They are found in both burials and wealth deposits (e.g. Kiiu, Mustmätta) in the northern and central regions of Estonia, while hundreds of those types are known from Latvia and Lithuania (Moora 1938, map VIII; Lang 2007b, 212).

Neck-ring finds in wealth deposits and burials indicate foreign contacts especially with the southern regions of the eastern Baltic. Further contacts, especially with the Roman Empire are rather scarce in Estonia, especially compared to Roman import finds in Latvia, Lithuania and Poland. Roman coin finds are few and have been discovered in the coastal regions or in connection to major water routes in the inland Estonia (Schmiedehelm 1955, fig. 54: 2; Vassar 1956, fig. 43). As described above, there are only two reliable Roman coin hoards from Estonia: from Juminda peninsula in the northern coast of Estonia and Kastna at the western coast of Estonia (Kiudsoo 2013). Other Roman import items include foil beads and some fibulae (Lang 2007b, 257).

The overall picture indicates that during the Roman Iron Age foreign contacts and interests are directed towards south and other eastern Baltic regions. Estonia remains in the role of periphery, if not hinterland, for the Roman world. All Estonian 3rd-4th century AD wealth deposits are located in the coastal region, two of them – Mustmätta and Liimala – in close vicinity to each other. These areas are continuously densely populated. Burial tradition is based on collective burials with homogeneous burial goods. Neck-rings are abundant, but the total numbers indicate that not all the deceased were accompanied by those often imported items. Several neck-rings are discovered in burial goods, but the massive forms of trumpet-shaped terminals are only found in wealth deposits. Thus, in the case of neck-rings in general and especially their massive forms, only a small part of the society is related to those particular objects. It has been suggested that some of the neck-rings are related to women, although in the southern parts of the eastern Baltic they are also found with weapons in male burials (Moora 1938, 273, 298). Thus, the gender-based distinction remains problematic, and it seems that neck-rings indicate some outstanding individuals who can afford to acquire and own such special objects.

This relates to an interpretation proposed by Jonuks (2009, 233) that neck-ring finds that often are a combination of massive (non-functional), and smaller wearable examples are the personal belongings of a particular member of the society. They are signs of social and religious elite. This interpretation is also supported by the previous discussions that we start to see increased individuality in burials in north-eastern and northern Estonia from the 4th century onwards. It is indicated by single inhumations besides scattered cremations and some examples of *bauta*-stone graves. In this sense the Kiiu find in north-west Estonia which is slightly earlier than Liimala and Mustmätta in north-east Estonia suggests the earliest indication of possibly high-status individual related wealth deposit. The concept of individuality might have moved gradually from west to east as shown in Early Iron Age burial customs and wealth deposits in north-east Estonia. However, the Mustmätta deposit of 16 neck-rings might have been put together from items of different periods, gathered in a longer time span (Vassar 1943, 148; Jonuks 2009, 231). Therefore a direct relation to a single person is questionable, but the assemblage might have formed on the basis of possessions of several individuals hidden together at the same time. In comparison with Liimala and Mustmätta neck-ring deposits, the Kiiu deposit still remains different with its mushroom-shape terminal neck-rings also a brooch and a finger-ring. Those objects are abundant in contemporary burial goods. The deposit looks more like a complete set of personal ornaments and might be interpreted as a cenotaph burial. Its close vicinity to Valkla *bauta*-stone graves might support this idea even more.

The overall picture of the Roman Iron Age deposits in Estonia stresses, first, the importance of bronze as a material, and second, the importance of imports, especially neck-rings. The latter seem to indicate higher status of some members of the society, the emergence of local elite, be it social, military or religious, who started to display their status especially in the second half of the period. This is also supported by the changes in burial material which start to indicate individual burials among the communal ones and emerging hierarchy in settlement systems. In this sense the Estonian Roman Iron Age wealth deposits fit well into the general social pattern of the period.

### 9.2.1.2. Case study 2: Roman Iron Age bronze deposits in north-western Lithuania

The earliest Roman Iron Age depositional practice in Lithuania is different from Estonian examples because of the content and social contexts of these finds. All these deposits of bronzes – **Miežaičiai, Dirmeikiai, Dargiškė, Užpelkiai** – are located in the inland regions of north-west Lithuania.

Hill-forts in Lithuania are well known already during the Roman Iron Age (Tautavičius (ed.) 1975; Michelbertas 1986, 261; Lang 2007a, 158). However, similarly to Estonian Roman Iron Age finds there are very few hill-forts in the region where deposits of bronzes are located (Zabiela 2003, fig. 1; although see Bliujienė 2010, 143 for relation of Užpelkiai deposit to hill-fort Pilalė). The material on Roman Iron Age settlements is problematic, because very few settlements have been excavated. Based on the distribution of cemeteries local scholars have discussed possible migrations from west to east in the first half of the Roman Iron Age, which resulted in intensified settlement patterns in the area where bronze deposits are found (Žulkus 2004, fig. 23; Asaris *et al.* 2008, 39; for critical discussion see Lang 2007a, 164-166). However, such an inference arguing the movement of people is largely based on superficial appearance of burial grounds and is therefore problematic without any comparisons with local settlement material and detailed studies of burial sites, especially their chronology. Thus the proposed migrations remain hypothetical propositions.

The main burial tradition in the region is inhumation graves in barrows with stone constructions (Tautavičius 1977, 184-185). Burial goods include ornaments and tools, weapons appear from the 5th century AD onwards (Griciuvienė 2005, 19-22). From the mid-2nd century AD the selection of buried ornaments increases and becomes more variable. In the coastal region the deceased are buried in flat inhumation graves surrounded with circular stone constructions, which are sometimes joined with each other (Tautavičius 1975 (ed.), map 1, 6, 7; Banytė-Rowell 2001). The burial goods are rich. Females have variety of ornaments and tools, male graves include fewer ornaments, but more weapons and tools. Roman coins and miniature vessels, sometimes also parts of horses, are added as specific regional burial goods. Coins found in western Lithuanian burials are often placed in small birch bark boxes, which might also contain typical miniature ceramic vessels, sometimes also bracelets and brooches (Michelbertas 1995, 84). Bracelets, neck-rings and brooches similar to the ones concealed in the 3rd-4th century AD deposits from Dirmeikiai, Dargiškė and Užpelkiai are found in contemporary burials in northern and western Lithuania (Tautavičius 1978, 152-153, maps 9, 25; Michelbertas 1986). The combination of bronze coins and ornaments in burials is also very similar to some of the wealth deposits. In this sense the main objects in the deposits do not seem to differ much from the burial material and indicate a very similar evaluation and combination of artefacts. Change seems to happen in the later quarter of the Roman Iron Age, because Užpelkiai brooches remain somewhat different from the previously discussed items (see below).

Western Lithuania is the richest region for discovery of Roman coins as hoards, stray finds and burial goods. The majority of Roman coins and other imports found in Lithuania are from western and central Lithuania, mainly from burials in the first and in hoards in the latter region (Michelbertas 1995; 2001; Bliujienė 2011). Imports might have arrived in the north-western regions of Lithuania via large inland water routes as well as from the sea (Banytė-Rowell 2004; Bliujienė 2011, 171-189, fig. 61), which was especially important from the mid-3rd century AD onwards. In the 3rd century there is a decrease in foreign contacts and imports, while the majority of import is now beads and coins are far fewer. This correlates with the distribution of coin finds: 75% of Roman coins found in Lithuania are from the 2nd century AD (Michelbertas 1995; 2001). In burials the coins mainly date from the 2nd-3rd century AD, in hoards mainly 4th-5th century AD. Therefore the wealth deposits of Roman coins and ornaments from Dirmeikiai and Dargiškė bridge a gap and witness a change in general wealth concealment: from abundance of coins and imports mainly in burials in the 2nd – early 3rd century AD, to less imports in general and mainly concealed in hoards in the 4th-5th century AD. They also occur in the period when the main import routes change from inland water routes to marine regions. However, both deposits are situated in the inland regions of north-west Lithuania and still have very similar combinations of objects to western region burial traditions.

The same items are found in hoards and graves so there is no clear distinction between those two practices of wealth display and concealment in Lithuania. The main objective seems to be the value and evaluation of one material – bronze – which can be obtained, combined and concealed in different forms like ornaments and coins, burials and wealth deposits. Perhaps we are looking at the deep-rooted and gradual need for bronzes utilized in social displays of everyday- and afterlife. This might have been initiated by a constant inflow of Roman coins and other imports as a result of the amber trade in these regions of the Baltic (Bliujienė 2011). The region benefited from a favourable location as well as growing demand and development from the outside i.e. politics and interests of the Roman Empire. The earliest find – Miežaičiai deposit of large bronze bars form the first centuries of the Roman Iron Age – confirms this development and indicates early availability, evaluation, workmanship and corresponding local demand for bronzes. This deposit is after all a cache of bronze in the form of raw material bars which must have originated from melted bronze objects and was meant for further manufacturing processes.

It is likely that in the case of north-west Lithuania we are looking at the open, active and wealthy bronze-oriented region which could allow larger amounts of this raw material thanks to favourable spatial and temporal conditions. The bronze inflow happened through both inland water-routes as well as via the sea. It is interesting that iron production started to develop at the same time in eastern and southern Lithuania (Salatkienė 2009, 54, 247) and the earliest furnaces in the western part of the country are from the mid-1st millennium AD (Asaris *et al.* 2008, 119). It can be speculated that coastal and western regions did not have a direct need and perhaps also time invest into this 'secondary' raw material, because they had a direct access to the inflow of bronzes. This could have been also the currency for buying iron items from the neighbouring regions. However, it remains an open question, why the wealth deposits containing mainly artefacts concentrate in the inner regions of north-west Lithuania, not in the coastal area which is the richest for its Roman import and coin deposits. Perhaps coins and bronzes were in active daily use in the coastal area due to continuous inflow and trade. The central regions formed a periphery area where the daily use and trade with bronzes was moderate and it was necessary to conceal and store bronzes to keep them safe over longer periods.

The social context changes in the 5th-6th century AD. Previous barrows are replaced by flat ground inhumations (Tautavičius (ed.) 1975, map 1, 6, 7) and there is a decrease in the number of burials. It has been also argued that the burials in Užpelkiai cemetery in the 5th-6th century AD are not really proper burials of ordinary community members but offerings to the ancestors (Bliujienė 1998, 281). The selection of deposited items changes at the same time. The earlier neck-rings deposited in Užpelkiai are ordinary and found in numerous burials, but the later finds are of special character. A cross-bow fibula with a star-shaped foot is a rare type of find in north-western and western Lithuania (Tautavičius 1978, map 28). Cross-bow brooches with ring decorations are more numerous, but only a small part of them are made of silver as we see in the case of Užpelkiai (Tautavičius 1978, 153, map 26). Both of these types are dated to the end of the Roman Iron and beginning of the Middle Iron Age. Thus, the artefact selection of the second deposit(s) in Užpelkiai differs from the previous Roman Iron Age deposits of bronzes that were very similar to burial goods. Depositional traditions start to move towards more unique artefact types and materials. Previous trading contacts feeding the bronze use in western Lithuania come to an end in the 5th century AD. This was also connected with the general political and social developments taking place in Europe at that time. Thus, the developments and changes in social, economic and political scales had a significant effect on the development of depositional practices in Iron Age Lithuania.

### 9.2.1.3. Case study 3: 5th century AD bronze deposits in eastern Estonia

Another clearly regional practice of wealth depositing is deposits of bronzes in eastern Estonia – **Vagula, Reola, Piilsi**, perhaps also **Kavastu** – from the so-called Migration Period (450-550 AD). This looks like a direct further development of northern tradition of bronze ornament deposits. The difference now is that the bronze ornament finds are from watery conditions in eastern Estonia and most of the artefact types can be found in contemporary burials.

The earliest evidence of the Migration Period activities at hill-forts and sometimes settlements at their foot in eastern Estonia are usually only some radiocarbon dates, very thin occupation layers or a few potsherds under the later strata (Laul 2001, 17-26; Lavi 2002; Veldi 2006; Tvauri 2012, fig. 2, 43-45). It is known from earlier find material that south-eastern Estonia was permanently settled at least during the Early Bronze Age and that the tradition of hill-forts arrives first into this area from southern regions during the Late Roman Iron Age (Lang 2007b, 88-89). Very little is known about open settlements and no firm data on those sites has been recorded. Lacking any detailed analysis of settlement and burial chronology, it still has been proposed on the basis of burial forms and distribution that the settlement pattern intensifies in south-eastern Estonia from the 2nd century AD onwards and spreads northwards in the 3rd century AD (Laul 2001, 205-206). This statement is problematic without any detailed material substantiation, but slightly more reliable data on the intensified settlement patterns is related to increased agricultural activities indicated by pollen data.

However, this picture does not seem to apply to the surroundings of the Piilsi wealth deposit. There is a complete lack of any contemporaneous sites in the vicinity of this find. There are only a few finds from the later centuries of the

Middle Iron Age in this region and even these are at a distance from the deposit (Lang 2007b, figs 15, 116; Tvauri 2012, figs 2-4). Landscape surveys carried out in the region as part of this project did not reveal any new relevant sites either (see Oras 2009, map 14.1). Thus, it seems that the Piilsi wealth deposit has been concealed in an uninhabited region. The location of the find at the bank of Piilsi River is noteworthy because this water route leads to Lake Peipus which is one of the largest and most important water routes in north-eastern Europe.

The main burial tradition is *tarand*-graves with collective cremation burials continues up to the first centuries of the Middle Iron Age and covers the whole region. In the 4th century AD no new *tarands* are built but the burials continue in the old constructions or at their vicinity. Typical finds include ornaments such as fibulae, disc-brooches, beads, finger-rings, pins, some neck-rings, dress pins, whilst tools and weapons are rare (Moora 1938; Laul 2001; Lang 2007b, 198-201).

Comparing the burial material with the artefacts in the deposits it becomes evident that the same objects are found in both contexts. This applies very clearly to the simpler forms of objects such as Reola bracelets and brooches which are found in large numbers in several cemeteries (Laul 2001). Unfortunately we do not know the exact content of the Vagula deposit and it has been only noted that besides the elaborate enamel-decorated disc-brooch several rings were found. It is unknown whether the numerous rings mentioned in relation to this find refer to neck-rings, bracelets or both. Although the latter are often found in south-eastern *tarand*-graves, neck-rings are rare. Therefore it is very difficult to estimate whether the content of this find follows the same pattern as burial goods or not. The preserved enamel-decorated disc-brooch from Vagula has a few parallels in Estonia, northern Latvia, eastern and south-western Lithuania and north-western Poland (Moora 1938, map. XIV). The closest parallel to Vagula brooch is located in southern Finland and according to Estonian scholars they are imported from western Lithuania (Laul 2001, 114) or Dnepr region (Tamla & Kiudsoo 2005, 18). The items found in the Vagula wealth deposit resemble contemporary burial goods, but some of them must have had a slightly special character. This is indicated by the likely imported items, elaborately decorated brooch and possible inclusion of less common neck-ring.

The Piilsi deposit shares the same characteristics to contemporary burial material. Similar ornaments have been discovered in several cemeteries (Moora 1938; Schmiedehelm 1955, figs 20, 24, 30, 37). However, there are some items that seem to be imported. For instance a cross-bow brooch with star-shaped foot is mainly found in coastal Poland, western Latvia and Lithuania (Moora 1938, map XII; Bitner-Wroblewska 2001, fig. 11). One difference compared to the Vagula and Reola deposits is the larger number of neck-rings in Piilsi, including a neck-ring with overlapping terminals of Scandinavian origin (Lang 2007b, 212). The Piilsi deposit as the northernmost example of this depositional tradition is a collection of items of very different types and origins which still share some characteristics with the contemporary burial goods.

The Kavastu bronze lamp and bars deposit might also be considered as part of this depositional group. The dating of the fuel residue to the 5th – first half of the 6th century AD makes it possible to place this deposit in the last decades of the Roman Iron Age or early Middle Iron Age. It is located in the same eastern Estonia area with long-term settlement patterns and similar burial traditions. The lamp and bar fragments were found in a peat bog at the bank of Emajõgi River which connects to the Lake Peipus in the east. It is geographically not far from the Reola find and is related to the main water routes in eastern Estonia just like the Piilsi deposit, while the content, location and the environment of concealment distinguish the find from its Roman Iron Age counterparts. The Kavastu deposit indicates the importance of foreign contact and might relate to importing bronze as an important valuable via inland water routes. On the other hand, the environment of concealment makes the economic interpretation problematic except if we were to consider an accident during transportation.

The 5th century AD wealth deposits clearly speak for the importance of bronze as a production material. During the 2nd century AD most of the bronze ornaments in the southern Estonia were imported from the south, but in the 3rd century AD raw material besides the finished objects is brought in and local ornaments are now produced (Laul 2001, 211-212). However, the Reola and Vagula deposits consist of intact items, which seems to dismiss the possibility of pure raw material concealment. In addition, considering the environment of concealment – bog in Reola and lake shore in Vagula –the possibility to retrieve the items is complicated. In the case of Reola it is also known that potsherds, a bone object and a larger wooden construction were found in the same area where the bronzes were discovered. In the description of the finding circumstances of the Kavastu deposit it was also mentioned that some bones were discovered. Although the artefact content of those two finds is different, their geographical closeness and similar concealment contexts resemble Scandinavian Pre-Roman and Roman Iron Age deposits of bronzes, bones and ceramics which have been interpreted as agriculture and fertility related rituals. In the case of Vagula such or indeed any other interpretation remains debateable due to lack of detailed information. Considering the context of intensifying settlement patterns and homogeneous burial material, the interpretation of community rituals looks most likely.

The deposit of Piilsi is different. Its specific content and location in the cultural landscape suggests its unparalleled nature. The items concealed date from the Roman Iron Age up to the 5th century AD and some of them are fragmented or bent. Estonian archaeologists have interpreted the find as economic hoard, possibly collected as scrap-metal during grave robberies with an aim to gather raw material (Tvauri 2012, 222-223). During the documentation of the find some oak planks were recorded at the same depth at which the find was discovered (Moora 1935). It is difficult to estimate whether these wooden remains might refer to a landing site at the river. The assemblage of different object types of different origin and forms indicates the importance of material as opposed to specific selection of special artefact types. A more economic character for this find is also indicated by its location close to the previously mentioned larger water route of Lake Peipus. Perhaps this remote and uninhabited river bank area was a kind of nodal point to which various bronzes (acquired through different means including grave robbery) were collected in order to transport and trade them into other regions of Estonia or even further.

Two slightly different aims and depositional practices of collection of bronzes can be followed in Estonian 5th century material, but the fact that all those deposits are located in the easternmost regions of Estonia gives an additional point of conclusion. Their location and relation to the larger water routes indicates large-scale changes in the main trade and communication routes at the turn of the Roman and Middle Iron Age which moved from the sea to inland. This regional depositional tradition seems to rely on the importance of bronze as a material, which now was coming from the central and south-eastern regions of Europe via inland water routes. However, the contemporary social context in this region shows a stable continuation of Roman Iron Age developments, indicated by a prolonged use of old burial constructions and very little indication of violence or warrior ideology either in terms of hill-forts or burial goods. The idea of evaluating bronze was continued as in previous centuries, but now there was just more of it for both burial goods and wealth deposits.

### 9.2.2. Middle Iron Age weapon and tool deposits in the eastern Baltic

In the 5th and 6th century, different developments in social context as well as depositional practices emerge in the southern regions of the eastern Baltic. For the first time in the 1st millennium AD eastern Baltic weapons occur in wealth deposits. This change towards warrior ideology in social context, reflected in contemporary burials, fortifications and settlements, is another example of macro scale interrelations between the practices of wealth depositing and wider social developments. In Latvia two weapon deposits from Kokmuiža are concealed in the last half of the 5th century close to each other. The Kokmuiža I deposit with its 1280 objects, of which 986 are weapons, is so far the largest weapon deposit in the eastern Baltic. The 5th and 6th centuries provide five more examples of weapon-dominated iron deposits from Latvia raising the total number of such finds in Latvia to the highest level within the whole region of the eastern Baltic in the Middle Iron Age. All these weapon deposits are situated in the western central region of Latvia, in the area of so-called Semigallians. Similar, but smaller, weapon deposits are found in the same cultural region in Lithuania. These are slightly later, starting from the 7th century and found also in the water related environments.

Latvian and Lithuanian weapon deposits differ from those found in Estonia. A small proportion of Estonian weapon and tool deposits have earliest artefacts from the Early Roman Iron Age, but most of them are dated around the 7th century AD and later. There is also a geographical gap between the distribution of Latvian and Estonian weapon deposits. The earliest Estonian iron deposits are in the coastal regions in north-east Estonia, the chronologically following ones are situated in central regions. Although it is possible to relate the development of iron deposits in Estonia to overseas connections, the early date and content of north-eastern Estonian finds (agricultural tools besides weapons) argues against that option. Besides, Latvian and Lithuanian weapon deposits are not a coastal phenomenon, but inland developments. The difference is also evident in the content: in Estonia usually no ornaments are found in weapon deposits, but Latvian and Lithuanian weapon-tool deposits often include some additional functional groups. These are mainly small personal paraphernalia and parts of dress accessories such as bracelets, brooches, rings, dress pins. The overall picture in Latvia and Lithuania is quite similar to Scandinavian Roman Iron Age weapon deposits: iron items, mainly weapons (some of them non-local), and personal belongings concealed in watery conditions, indicating that the assemblage has been created on the basis of warrior equipment.

### 9.2.2.1. Case study 1: 5th-8th century AD weapon deposits in Latvia and Lithuania

The 5th-6th century weapon deposits in Latvia – **Kokmuiža I & II, Kalnamuiža, Vecmokas, Cibēni, Rūsiši** – are located in the southern and central regions of the country. Geographically close are the 7th-8th century Lithuanian weapon deposits from **Šluostikiai** and **Barstyčiai.**

The region which has produced most of the Latvian and Lithuanian weapon and tool deposits in watery conditions was one of the most densely populated areas at that time. Local scholars have suggested both inner colonisation (Apals *et al.* 2001, 447; Jarockis 2004; Zemītis 2004; Radiņš 2006, 83) and changes in economic bases as the reasons for intensified population. An important innovation was the use of iron ploughshares, which first appears in western Latvia. This meant that thicker and tougher clay soils could be ploughed and it was possible to expand to areas that could not be turned into arable lands before (Apals *et al.* 2001, 449-450; Lang 2007a, 215).

New hill-forts are built and old ones re-used (Tautavičius (ed.) 1975, 225; Vasks 1999, 56-58; Apals *et al.* 2001, 445-449; Griciuvienė 2005, 24-25). Many sites become more strongly fortified and a new complex of sites, hill-forts and associated settlements, emerges. There are also several open settlements known from this period. A general tendency was a development from a single farm settlement system to either village-based settlements or hill-fort and settlement complexes.

Burial traditions are also changing. In the 5th and 6th century AD the barrows are no longer built. At first, the deceased are buried in old barrows, then next to the barrows and gradually in brand new flat inhumation cemeteries further away from the old barrows (Tautavičius 1977, maps 2, 4; 8; Apals *et al.* 2001, 446, 453; Griciuvienė 2005). Burial goods include weapons for men and agricultural tools and ornaments for both men and women. The weaponry set is limited consisting mainly of a single edged battle knife, and a couple of spearheads. Axes were also used as typical weapons, while swords, belt-parts and rings are rarer (Tautavičius 1996; Vaškevičiūtė 2000; 2007; Griciuvienė 2005). Sometimes also a drinking horn, tweezers and horse gear were included in male burials. These have been interpreted as indicators of wealth and high status of the deceased. Higher social status might be also expressed by a larger number of spearheads, but also accompanying neck-rings and brooches (sometimes silver plated). A general tendency seems to be an increase of weapons and the emergence of some richer burials with more abundant weapons, sometimes also ornaments and horse gear. Women's ornaments become more variable in time including head-decorations, breast chains with dress pins, bracelets, sometimes also neck-rings. Garment accessories and neck-rings are found in male burials as well, but women wore more and lighter, men single and massive examples.

These social developments have an influence on the interpretation of weapon and tool deposits. It has been argued that a larger quantity of weapons in burials does not always correlate with the increased number of military conflicts (Härke 1990). However, in the current case study the information on hill-forts, including intensified fortification work, and various contacts in the region seem to indicate at times of unease and conflicts. This is also supported by a more detailed analysis of artefact content in the deposits.

Axes are typical weapons in the Middle Iron Age eastern Baltic. However, socketed forms are more common in western areas of southern-central Latvia and shafted ones are mainly found in the eastern regions. To the west only socketed axe types appear, while to the east only shafted axes are in use (Tautavičius 1977, 156-157, maps 62-63; Vaškevičiūtė 2000, 154). Battle knives are the main close combat weapons in this southern-central region of Latvia and swords are rare here. Other types of weapons such as spearheads are more widely distributed.

The Kokmuiža I and II, Vecmokas, Kalnamuiža, Šluostikiai and Barstyčiai deposits mostly contain spearheads which are common throughout Middle Iron Age. The most common axe types in those finds are socketed versions. However, the Kokmuiža I and the Barstyčiai deposits also contain a considerable proportion of shafted axes. In Kokmuiža II and Kalnamuiža finds a number of belt buckles are included. None of the Latvian deposits seem to have any single-edged battle knives in them, but they do contain swords: the first are typical local weapons, but the latter are rare artefact types in this region. Thus, it can be argued that non-local artefacts have been concealed in some of those weapon deposits.

It is likely that Middle Iron Age weapon deposits in Latvia and Lithuania are remains of invading and deceased troops, as has been argued for earlier Scandinavian weapon deposits. The number of deposited weapons in Latvian examples is rather large and they have all been discovered in the vicinity of hill-forts, which supports a military interpretation. Additionally, all the ornaments and personal equipment are characteristic to male burials indicating gender based selection. Southern and central Latvia and northern Lithuania consisted of several autonomous political groups (Radiņš 2006, 90), which were actively involved in the everlasting struggles of local small warrior groups. Emerging and competing regional centres might have caused conflict, especially in times of population growth and expansion onto new arable lands. The Barstyčiai find is also in the position which might be regarded as the border area between the coastal and inland culture regions. Thus, both internal and external conflict might be the triggers for the Middle Iron Age wealth deposits in central-southern Latvia and central-northern Lithuania. However, the quantity of tools (especially in Vecmokas), and blacksmithing items might suggest a non-military background for some of these deposit. Without more detailed chronology one cannot exclude the possibility of different depositional events forming larger finds.

The two wealth deposits in the same region found in contemporary cemeteries, Cibēni and Rūsiši in Latvia, are of different character. The inventory of those deposits is very similar to contemporary burial goods including socketed axes and spearheads, scythes and other tools, but not swords and belt-fittings, with the addition of a battle knife at Rūsiši. Those two reflect single sets of male warrior equipment, probably of high status as indicated by horse gear and a drinking horn. At Cibēni the placement of objects is similar to other burials in the cemetery: surrounded by slabs of stones. These wealth deposits could be interpreted as cenotaphs of lost high-status male individuals (Stepiņš 1939, 46; Kazakevičius & Malonaitis 2006, 75).

The overall archaeological material in the region suggests that the Middle Iron Age is characterised by political and social rivalry, conflicts and warrior ideology in this densely inhabited region. This is indicated by numerous weapons in burials and by active use as well as destruction of hill-forts. Taking into account that in Latvia these deposits are from the earliest 200 years of the Middle Iron Age, but in Lithuania the deposits are from the following centuries, the practices seem to have begun in Latvia. We can trace the spread of weapon deposits, perhaps with migrations and military contacts between invaders and locals towards the south. The Barstyčiai find in Lithuania, which contains chronologically at least two different deposits of weapons, might indicate repeated conflict situations in this area.

However, the total number of weapons deposited in Lithuania (19 weapons) is far smaller than the numbers from Latvia (1179) and Estonia (193). The tradition of weapon deposits in Lithuania is distributed on a very small scale in one specific northern region. It does not mean that weapons were not in circulation in other parts of Lithuania at that time. There are numerous weapons found in Roman and Middle Iron Age burials which in some regions include also horse gear or even a horse itself. The situation rather shows that there were different attitudes to weapons and related depositional practices in Middle Iron Age Lithuania. In most parts of the country they were in active use and buried with the dead warriors, but in northern Lithuania they were also concealed as wealth deposits. These examples still remain moderate for the number of deposits and weapons concealed. Weapon deposits become more abundant in Lithuania only from the Viking Age onwards (Tautavičius 1977, 131-133; Bliujienė 2010).

#### 9.2.2.2. Case study 2: 6th-8th century AD weapon deposits in northern and central Estonia

One of the largest and most widespread practices of wealth depositing in Middle Iron Age Estonia is deposits of iron objects, mainly weapons but also a few tools, in different watery conditions. There are three such deposits in the central-eastern part of Estonia – **Kaabe, Igavere** and **Rikassaare** –and two more from north-eastern Estonia – **Kunda I** and **Alulinn**. Most of those finds are single deposits from the 7th and 8th century AD. The north-eastern deposits are examples of depositional practices where the same place has been used for depositing iron objects for several centuries: 1st-3rd and 6th-7th century AD in the case of Kunda I, and 2nd-3rd, 6th-7th and 12th/13th century AD in the case of Alulinn. However, the majority of objects in the latter two are also from the 6th-7th century AD. The Rikassaare and Kaabe finds are found at riverbanks, all the other finds were discovered in bogs or marshy areas.

The 6th century AD is a period when hill-forts start to emerge in abundance (Jaanits *et al.* 1982, fig. 165; Lavi 2002; Tõnisson 2008; Tvauri 2012, 43-51, figs 3-4). The first large-scale fortifications are related to this and the following century. Sometimes also a settlement is located at the foot of those forts. Quite a number of hill-forts are distributed in the eastern part of the country. The material on open settlements sites in these regions is unfortunately scarce. Although over 50 open settlements are known from the Middle Iron and Viking Age in Estonia, their exact date remains problematic because only a few of them have been excavated. So far the number of pre-Viking Age open settlements remains only around five (Tvauri 2012, fig. 3) and this number cannot reflect the actual distribution of settlement sites during the 6th-7th century AD. The latter is also indicated by a wider distribution of various cemeteries throughout Estonia. The main site types cover the same regions where most of the Estonian Middle Iron Age deposits have been discovered.

In recent years a new debate about the development of settlement patterns and its changes has emerged. Tvauri (2012, 307-312; 2014) has argued that the lack of information on settlement sites might reflect the actual situation: there was a considerable and sudden decrease in inhabited areas during the 6th-7th century AD which he has related to the climatic catastrophe of the so-called 536 AD dust veil event. This climatic catastrophe was first discussed by Baillie (1994) and was later taken further by several archaeologists (Axboe 2001; Gräslund & Price 2012). According to Tvauri population decrease is indicated in the distribution of different archaeological finds and pollen diagrams. However, the problem is that both pollen data and chronology of archaeological sites based on artefacts is dated to a wide period of the 5th-7th century AD. At the same time the pollen diagrams in the western and north-western Estonia as well as in the islands indicate increased human impact instead. Thus the exact pinpointing of the reasons for and extent of this particular change in settlement patterns and land-use is still problematic. Despite these difficulties, the influence of the possible 536 AD climate catastrophe and following settlement decrease in central and north-eastern Estonia has been argued (Tvauri 2012, 307-308; 2014).

However, the general development of settlement systems and subsistence economy indicates quite gradual processes. Permanent field systems spread widely in northern and western Estonia from the Bronze Age onwards. The first strip-fields occur in north-western and north-eastern Estonia around the 7th and 8th century AD (Lang 1996, 496; Lang 2007c; Tvauri 2012, 95-99). That achievement has been related to the emergence of a new settlement system, village based societies instead of single farmsteads (Lang 1996, 371; 2007c, 314). As a result, one can talk about settlement continuity and development into a more controlled and centralised system in coastal regions. This opens the questions of subsistence and land ownership, political leadership and community relations. The same developments are not so clearly followed in the central regions of the country, but a continuous settlement with minor fall-backs, and gradual use of hill-forts and settlements at their foot, are characteristic of these regions. The eastern part of Estonia is also one of the earliest extensive prehistoric iron production areas (Peets 2003a-b). There are several such iron smelting sites in the regions of weapon and tool deposits.

Burial customs in the central and north-eastern regions indicate continuity and conservatism. The main burial tradition here remains cremation or inhumation in stone structures, mainly re-use of old *tarand*-graves, including their border areas (Jonuks 2009, 243-244; Tvauri 2012, 254-256). This is indicated by a few Middle Iron Age artefact finds and later bones scatters in stone constructions. However, the problem is that there are very few dates and the exact use period of these graves remains unanswered. The burial goods in the north-eastern, eastern and central regions are limited throughout the Middle Iron Age. Weapons appear from the 5th-6th century AD onwards but are scarce (Schmiedehelm 1955, fig. 55; Jonuks 2009, 250). They never reach such an abundance as in the rich burials in western and northern Estonia or in Saaremaa Island which include weapons, tools, silver and bronze ornaments and other prestigious items (Ligi 1995, 228). Such examples are Kirimäe cremation pit in western Estonia (Schmiedehelm 1924), Proosa stone cairn field in northern Estonia (Deemant 1978) and the Lepna and Paju mortuary houses (Tamla & Jaanits 1977; Mägi 2006) or the recent discovery of the Salme ship burials in Saaremaa Island (Konsa et al 2009; Peets *et al.* 2011).

The general context indicates gradually developing and more stable social circumstances in the areas of weapon and tool deposits. This is one of the most densely and continuously settled regions of Estonia with permanent field systems developing into strip-fields and settlement units grouping gradually into villages. People keep on using old burial structures. An abundance of iron production sites in eastern Estonia shows available sources (bog ore) and technological achievements in this region. Such conditions support continuous social development into stronger and stable communities. However, an uncertainty and insecurity are indicated by the emergence of hill-forts and the increasing number of weapon finds. These tendencies have made scholars assume that from the 6th century AD onwards a warrior ideology starts to reach the northern regions of the eastern Baltic (Ligi 1995, 233; Jonuks 2009, 263-266).

The deposits of weapons and tools in watery conditions could be considered as indicators of warrior ideology in times of conflict. Times of conflict, questions of power relations and ownership are also indicated in the overall archaeological record drawing direct connections between depositional practices and social developments. However, the exact interpretation of each of these finds is slightly different because the details of their main characteristics diverge. There are only few contemporaneous archaeological sites known in the close vicinity of the Kaabe and Rikassaare deposits. Rikassaare also stands out for its clear selection and placement of items: only spearheads (shafted at the time of deposit) and battle knives in two rows, points facing. The find-spot is in a border area between major historically developed administrative units which might have already existed in prehistory. The find has been interpreted as a symbolic material manifest of a political treaty after a violent conflict between different power units (Mandel & Tamla 1977; Tamla 1995). Although Kaabe does not share all those specific characteristics its location in the most important southern Estonian water route, River Emajõgi, also indicates a possible border area. However, located at the estuary of the river it is also possible that we are dealing with ritual practices marking the importance of this geographical feature and its main functions: crossing the large water route, perhaps also a community border. There are numerous such single weapon and tool finds in Scandinavian Viking Age material at main water routes and bridges which have been interpreted as ritual offerings relating to Viking Age mythology (Lund 2004, 2005, 2006, 2008). Kaabe's later, 8th century AD, date and the fact that only two items were found supports this interpretation.

The situation is different in the case of Igavere, and even more with the Alulinn and Kunda I deposits. Those three finds are surrounded by a variety of contemporary archaeological sites including settlements, hill-forts, burial grounds etc. In the case of Igavere an iron production site is known nearby. They include both weapons and tools and are from boggy-marshy areas as opposed to the previously discussed finds in open-water environment. Igavere seems to be an example of a single deposit, but Kunda and Alulinn have evidence of gradual and long-term use of depositional places and continuous selection of the same materials and types of objects over very long period. Those deposits are located in the centre of inhabited areas and reflect the most topical events in the contemporary society: weapons as possible signs of violent times and increasing importance of warrior ideology; smithy tools in Kunda, and cauldrons in Kunda and Igavere as signs of iron production development; agricultural tools as possible indicators of changing land-use systems and agricultural production in Alulinn and Kunda. The long-term iron deposits support the idea of continuous and stable occupation and its development into more complex and centralised system. Slightly later period finds in vicinity inland regions like Rikassaare and Igavare might have their background in conflicts between these two i.e. coastal and inland areas. The turbulent times in the 7th and 8th century in eastern regions of central Estonia are also indicated by the abundance of hill-forts.

The tradition of weapon deposits in Estonia is a local development: deriving from the long-term iron deposits in north-east Estonia which also include tools, and becoming weapon-dominated in the 7th and 8th century in the central regions of Estonia. The analysis of iron artefact deposits in Estonia strengthens the concept of region-specific depositional traditions. Weapons are an important addition to the overall archaeological material during the Middle Iron Age. However, they are found in rather different and regionally determined contexts: in rich burials accompanied often by imported and precious metal ornaments in western and north-western Estonia, but mainly in wealth deposits in central and north-eastern Estonia. The lack of weapons in the south-eastern regions where ornament deposits seem to prevail instead is particularly remarkable (see below). One possible explanation is that the warrior ideology is not as prevalent in the south-eastern areas as in other regions. In the central and northern areas the population decline, possibly related to 6th century climate catastrophe, was not so rapid and substantial as suggested for southern regions. The settlement growth in there was gradual and the social situation in these regions is described by intensive settlement and land-use systems, increase in communal networks, including of military character, and power centralisation. Estonian iron artefact deposits either surrounded by various contemporary sites or located in emptier border regions seem to reflect exactly those social developments.

### 9.2.3. Middle Iron Age ornament deposits in the eastern Baltic

There are three main traditions of ornaments deposits in the Middle Iron Age eastern Baltic. The earliest silver ornament deposits are the 4th century AD unique silver deposit from Kaali, Saaremaa Island, and the 5th century AD silver neck-ring from Piltene, western Latvia. However, it takes another century before one can see a wider practice of silver ornament deposits, and it emerges in the eastern regions in the eastern Baltic instead. There are two contemporaneous traditions of concealing silver. Imported silver ornament and vessel deposits hidden in burial areas occur in the 6th century AD in the south-eastern and southern regions of central Estonia. The tradition of concealing only silver neck-rings emerges on a much larger geographical and chronological scale. It starts in the 6th century AD in eastern Latvia and spreads to Lithuania and Estonia in the following centuries, lasting up to the 9th century AD. This tradition does not occur in the western parts of Latvia and Lithuania. There the previously discussed weapon deposits from the first half of the Middle Iron Age dominate, followed by a regional tradition of depositing bronze ornaments in watery conditions to the west of these weapon and tool deposits, and bronze ornaments in hill-forts to the east. These separate depositional practices overlap with the variations in regional social context as indicated by specific archaeological remains in these areas. They provide another argument for direct relations between contemporary social developments and practices of wealth depositing which become evident at the level of comparative macro scale analysis as expressed in the theoretical discussion above.

There are several region-specific selections for depositing silver in the Middle Iron Age eastern Baltic. In Latvia and Lithuania the division runs across the north-south axes of these two countries. In the west silver neck-rings are found in elite, usually male, burials and very rarely in wealth deposits. In the east silver neck-rings are unusual in burials, but are found in wealth deposits. In Estonia, silver ornaments are only found in wealth deposits in southern regions, only in burials in western and north-western parts of the country, and in neither in the north-eastern and central Estonia. In the latter region wealth deposits consist of iron objects instead. The exact details of those regional traditions of depositing and evaluating specific object classes are discussed in the case studies and general conclusions below.

Another important regional divergence is the general attitude towards silver ornaments in the three Baltic countries, which is particularly evident when considering neck-rings. The Middle Iron Age silver neck-rings found in Estonia are most likely of Baltic (Latvian, Lithuanian) origin. However, in southern regions of the eastern Baltic these specific ornament types are made of both silver and bronze and deposited in both wealth deposits and burials, although there is a clear geographical division in those depositional practices (see below). The further north, in Estonia, mostly silver examples are found and two separate consistent traditions emerge: in the western and northern regions they are found in only a few rich elite, possibly male burials, but in the central and southern part of the country only in wealth deposits.

### 9.2.3.1. Case study 1: 6th century AD imported silver in burial grounds in southern and central Estonia

A distinct regional depositional practice in Estonia is the tradition of depositing silver objects in the vicinity of burial areas. These 6th century finds of dominantly Baltic-origin silver ornaments, sometimes with a few bronze, iron and gold items, in **Paali I and II**, **Kardla**, **Villevere**; and Byzantine silver vessels in **Kriimani** and **Varnja** form the major part of the highest peak of deposits per century in Estonia. They are all located in the central southern region of Estonia and found in dry land, mostly in the vicinity of or in the stone graves. Their distribution area partly overlaps with the earlier 5th century AD bronze deposits and chronologically they are either contemporaneous with or shortly precede the 6th-8th century AD weapon-tool deposits located in the north-east and central Estonia. No such assemblages – combinations of neck-rings, brooches, bracelets, or imported silver vessels – are found in Latvia and Lithuania. It is a specific small-scale Estonian depositional tradition which has no parallels in the southern regions of the eastern Baltic (see also Oras 2013).

The general developments in terms of hill-forts and settlements discussed under 6th-8th century AD weapon deposits also apply to these regions. There is an expansion of hill-forts and considerable fortification works can be detected at them during these centuries, especially in the eastern part of Estonia. Sometimes open settlements develop at the foot of those hill-forts. Material on settlement sites is scarce and it has been argued that the possible 536 AD climate catastrophe influenced the settlement in the southern Estonia considerably (Tvauri 2012; 2014). Pollen diagrams show a decrease in human influence and settlement patterns seem to become sparser in central and southern regions, but this cannot be dated more precisely than with the first two centuries of the Middle Iron Age. In addition, the occupation of the hilly and forested southern regions of Estonia must have been less dense compared to the coastal region plains. Thus even a small crisis, either environmental or social, might have affected the sparsely populated southern regions more severely.

An important economic change happens in the 6th century AD. This is the emergence of the first permanent field systems in southern Estonia (Laul & Kihno 1999, 12; Konsa 2005, 19-20), based on the appearance of cornflower in the pollen diagrams. Cornflower is a by-product of rye grown in permanent field systems and it almost never appears with the rye grown in slash-and burn fields. Tvauri (2014) has related this development to climate catastrophe, because compared to wheat and barley rye is suitable for colder climates. As we are discussing societies who rely on agriculture, this would have had an impact on day-to-day life. With the emergence of permanent field systems the society has to address the questions of land ownership and division because land use is more constrained and prescribed with a change from extensive land-use to intensive (Lang 2007c, 313). Thus, the 6th century AD in southern Estonia faced several noteworthy economic and social processes.

The burial material from the 6th century AD is diverse (Laul 2001; Jonuks 2009, 242-254; Tvauri 2012, chapter 6). One of the new forms of burials is cremation in stone cairns and other irregular heaps of stones from the 4th century AD onwards. The second tradition is the long-term custom of underground cremation burials in pits (Lillak 2006). The use of old *tarand*-graves continues up to the 6th century AD although no new *tarands* are built from the 4th century onwards. Most of the silver ornament deposits from burial areas seem to be related with those burial grounds and belong chronologically to the final use phase of the old stone graves. A new burial practice – cremations in barrow cemeteries – appears in south-eastern Estonia in the 6th century AD. These barrows are distributed immediately to the east and south of the regions where silver deposits in the vicinity of burial areas are located (Scmiedehelm & Laul 1970, table 1; Aun 1992, fig. 54-55). For some centuries the use of *tarand*-graves and cremation barrow cemeteries existed together and there are examples in south-eastern Estonia where the two burial types are found next to each other. It seems that quite different burial traditions continue, occur and coexist in the southern Estonia whilst some of the old traditions are gradually abandoned in the first centuries of the Middle Iron Age.

There is one common denominator which is characteristic to all those variable burial traditions. Burial goods in all those cemeteries in the southern Estonia are moderate including mainly pottery, some bronze ornaments, to lesser extent also iron items such as tools. Weapons appear in Estonian burials from the Migration Period onwards, but they are found in western and northern Estonia, while in the southern regions weapons are rare throughout the first half of the Middle Iron Age (Jonuks 2009, 250; Tvauri 2012, 181).

The inclusion of weapons is not the only criterion which distinguishes the depositional practices of the inland-southern and coastal north-western areas. There are some distinctive regional tendencies in the distribution of silver ornaments in Estonia. The ornaments concealed in southern Estonian wealth deposits are Baltic origin, but these items are not only a southern Estonian phenomenon. They have been found with the weapons in the same rich Middle Iron Age burials in western and northern Estonia. Thus it seems that there are two different traditions of displaying and concealing wealth: in the south-eastern parts of the country silver is only found in wealth deposits, but in the northern and western regions it is buried with the dead, often with weapons and other imported wealth objects.

The deposits of two silver vessels from Varnja and Kriimani (see Quast *et al.* 2010) share some similarities with the silver ornament deposits. However, these items are of much more remote origin – they are produced in the late 5th century AD in the Byzantine Empire and thus must have travelled a long distance to the north. Their possible deposition time has been estimated to the 6th century AD. The relation to silver ornament deposits is not only their material and import character. The Kriimani bowl was hidden in an earlier *tarand*-grave. Unfortunately there is not sufficient data to decide whether this vessel indicates the final use-phase of a stone grave or if it was abandoned already centuries before the deposit. The Varnja vessel is of the same date and origin, but its environment of concealment is problematic. So far there is no clear evidence of a burial ground in the area of the deposit. It was found under a stone and it is possible that stone grave has been destroyed with later agricultural activities (Oras 2009, no. 18). Both of those finds are imported items of southern origin, made of material and in a form which is not found in local burial goods. In addition, their location is related to important main water routes of southern-central Estonia, Lake Peipus in the case of Varnja and River Emajõgi in Kriimani. They seem to be closely related to contemporary imported silver ornament deposits in the area of burial grounds in terms of content, chronology and geographical location.

The interpretation of those silver deposits is not a simple task. The overall archaeological material in the first half of the Middle Iron Age in southern Estonia seems to indicate several significant changes and developments: emergence of hill-forts, changes in subsistence systems, but possibly also in settlement patterns and climate. There is a variety of different burial grounds: among the old and newly built stone construction graves the tradition of sand barrow cemeteries emerges in the south-eastern corner of Estonia. In all those cemeteries burial goods remain very limited, including mainly ceramics or bronze ornaments. The appearance of non-local precious metal items of Baltic or even Byzantine origin is certainly unusual. Such processes indicate a time of rapid developments and need for adaptation to the changed economic, social and environmental conditions. The 6th century AD is also part of the Migration Period when turbulence was common throughout Europe. This must have had an influence on the depositional practices. Indeed, the 6th century provides the highest number of deposits and silver objects within a single century. As this regional practice of silver deposits has a close connection with old and long-term use of stone graves and it does not spread into the area of sand barrows, it looks like a specific locally developed culturally constrained depositional tradition. The inclusion of Baltic artefacts is then perhaps confusing, but it must be considered that these are some of the earliest silver objects in Estonia. The knowledge of and experience with local silver-smithing must have been in its early phase and reworking this material into local objects was probably not yet carried out. The other explanation is that it was fashionable to own foreign items as indicators of wealth.

One possible explanation for those deposits has been religious or ritual activities: an offering to the supernatural powers in order to cope with and change the unfavourable climate and deteriorating subsistence conditions (Tvauri 2014).

However, looking at the overall archaeological material it still remains unclear whether the primary source for all this was a single climate catastrophic event. Perhaps it is worth considering the results of gradual social development and larger historical processes such as great migrations, or indeed combinations of all these elements. Without more precise and in-depth material analysis I think it would be a mistake to reduce it all to a single mid-6th century AD climatic event which does not seem to have had a similar impact throughout even such a small country as Estonia.

Another possible explanation is that we are seeing a kind of closing ritual or homage paid to old burial areas. As the overall material in the deposits is foreign it remains an open question whether it arrived in Estonia with migrations from the south or through foreign contacts and trade. If there was a sudden climate worsening and drop in settlement density perhaps there was a rapid population decrease which meant that several areas in southern Estonia remained empty or at least sparsely populated. This would have given an opportunity for new groups of people, whether from the south or east. Influence from the south has been argued on the basis of the distribution of hill-forts, while eastern connections have been widely debated in relation to barrow cemeteries (Tvauri 2007). There is a possibility that as part of occupying deserted regions and finding the material remains of previous communities these visible monuments were reused by the new-comers with their fancy imported valuables. However, the deposition by incoming migrants is contradicted by the fact that the same imported items are also found in the western and northern Estonian burials where gradual local population has been presumed. Thus, the import items do not necessarily have to suggest migrants. Finally, one cannot exclude the possibility that those sites were thought to provide necessary landscape marker and perhaps some extra unearthly protection to the important, maybe even communal, valuables which for some reason were never retrieved (Jonuks 2009, 255-256).

The social and possibly environmental changes that we see in the overall archaeological material in southern Estonia possibly triggered a sudden emergence of more unusual depositional activities, be it related to social or religious rituals or purely practical. Rich burial goods indicate rivalling elite, a very small part of the community in the northern and western burials. In the southern and central regions the communality-aspect seems to prevail for a much longer period, as indicated by burial practices and goods. If southern and central areas were less populated compared to northern and western Estonia then for the sparsely located and single farmstead based communities there might have been also less need or indeed possibility for power centralisation. This also explains the lack of displaying valuables of the elite via grand-scale burial events. It is more plausible to talk about communal depositional activities in southern Estonia where the silver deposits in previous burial areas might be symbols of a communal 'bank' or ritual-related activities and assembly places. This community related interpretation in the southern regions is also supported by the logical reasoning that in times of economic, political and subsistence crises cooperation, support and community relations become particularly important. Such comparisons of regional ways of concealing valuables and their relations to local social contexts exemplify the importance of detailed analysis of depositional practices (micro scale) and their social conditions at the macro scale in order to understand the interrelated nature between the two.

### 9.2.3.2. Case study 2: 8th-9th century AD bronze ornaments in the eastern Baltic

Towards the end of the Middle Iron Age, in the 8th-9th century AD, there is another depositional practice that might be seen as cross-regional on a general scale, but very local when considering the exact details of these finds. These are deposits of bronzes, mainly ornaments, in the western coast of Lithuania and Latvia – **Palanga I, Negraba** and **Tīras purvs** – and in the three largest hill-forts in Latvia – **Ķente II, Mūkukalns II, Mežotne**. The common denominator is evidently bronze ornaments. However, detailed regional distribution and the environment of concealment suggest differences in these practices. The coastal finds of Palanga I, Negraba and Tīras purvs indicate some gender-based depositional activities in the bogs and marshes. The deposits from Latvian hill-forts are located inland, around the main water routes. Bronze ornament deposits there seem to reflect social and economic, especially local manufacturing and trading centres.

All the Latvian hill-fort finds are from the southern central part of the country. Therefore the characteristics of archaeological sites discussed under the Latvian and Lithuanian weapon-tool deposits also apply to these finds. The most relevant key aspects are the increase in the number of hill-forts and density of settlement patterns, emergence of new hill-fort and settlement complexes, intensified agricultural activity, warrior ideology expressed by weapon rich burial goods, independent and rivalling regional centres.

An increase in the number of hill-forts and growth of settlements is particularly evident along the Daugava River (Vasks 1999, 58-59). In Ķente and Mūkukalns hill-forts the considerable improvements of fortification structures are seen in the first half of the Middle Iron Age (Stubavs 1976; Graudonis 1978). Ķente is one of the best examples of gradually developing hill-fort and settlement complexes with the evidence of being damaged at least three times during the Middle Iron Age.

Craft specialisation and the local production of weapons, tools and bronze ornaments takes place in these hill-fort and settlement complexes. Some of the earliest iron smelting sites are known in the hill-forts and settlements at the banks of Daugava River. They start in the Roman Iron Age and continue to flourish in the following periods, including at Ķente and Mūkukalns (Daiga 1964; Apals *et al.* 2001, 449-451; Radiņš 2006, 83). Plant remains and agricultural tools discovered during excavation in these sites indicate increased agricultural activities. Hill-forts and settlements across the major water routes are thus political, military and economic centres, controlling movement of people and production of goods.

The earlier deposits in the Latvian Middle Iron Age hill-forts are the 6th century AD Ķente I and Mūkukalns III finds. They contain iron items, weapons and tools, while the latter are in majority. The Ķente I and Mūkukalns III deposits are reflections of not only the military importance of their find-spots, but also evidence of local iron production and agricultural activities. They might have been ordinary tools concealed or left behind accidentally in the context of unexpected attack or alternatively, as argued by Stubavs, religion-related deposits for fertility and fire or Sun cult concealed in the local social and political centres (1976, 142).

As those two earlier deposits contain mundane tools, the change in depositional traditions in hill-fort contexts in the last centuries of the Middle Iron Age becomes even more telling. The three later deposits – Ķente II, Mūkukalns II and Mežotne –

include only bronzes: a neck-ring from Mūkukalns II, brooches and bracelets form Mežotne, and bracelets with some raw material possibly for ornament production from Ķente II. The slightly earlier 7th century AD Migoniai I bronze deposit from Lithuania also contains ornaments and raw materials and thus falls into the same depositional category: it too was found near one of the larger rivers and not far from the contemporary hill-fort. All the bronze items concealed in those deposits are ordinary ornament types that are often discovered in contemporary burials. On a larger scale these deposits seem to suggest changes in the functions of hill-forts and settlement systems in the Middle Iron Age: from iron production for local economic and political needs (practical tools and weapons) to jewellery production of mainly bronze ornaments for local elite or trade.

A detailed analysis of archaeological material from the last phase of the Middle Iron Age provides some additional evidence for this development. During the 8th century AD the inhabitants around Ķente hill-fort moved into the fortified area and the open settlement was no longer so densely populated. In Mežotne additional fortifications were built at the turn of the 8th and 9th century AD (Stubavs 1976; Apals *et al.* 2001, 448). The material culture from these centuries indicates several changes in these regions. The bracelets from Ķente II and the neck-ring from Mūkukalns II are very similar to the objects found in eastern Latvia, indicated by local scholars as Latgallian (Urtāns 1970; Ciglis 2001) and Selonian regions (Ciglis 2006; Griciuvienė 2007, 40-43). Burial customs change at the same time in central Latvia, which local scholars relate to intensified outside contacts, possibly also some small-scale population movements from the east (Apals *et al.* 2001, 448; Radiņš 2006, 83-86). Additional foreign contacts at the Daugava hill-forts are indicated by Scandinavian-origin objects. The general character of the sites in the 8th-9th century AD along the Daugava reflects increased number of foreign contacts with neighbouring and more distant regions and need for better protection of inhabited areas. In this context, the deposits of bronzes as most common valuables and specialised handicraft items might be interpreted as valuables hidden during a time of sudden attack.

Latvian hill-fort deposits and their overall social background indicate a functional change of this site group. Hill-forts started off as local centres of agriculture based subsistence economy where the local elite inhabited the fortified site as a way of symbolising warrior ideology, while most of the population remained at the settlement site at the foot of the hill-fort. Towards the end of the period hill-forts become local production and trading sites. They turn into protected occupation areas for the larger community and the basis of prestige goods production and trading. This is another example how social developments are reflected in the practices of concealing valuables.

The social context for the 8th-9th century AD bronze ornament deposits in western Lithuania and Latvia shares some similar characteristics to Latvian hill-fort finds. During the 7th-8th century AD larger fortification works take place in numerous Lithuanian hill-forts, especially in the western part of the country (Tautavičius (ed.) 1975, 225; Lang 2007a, 189). Northern and north-western parts of Lithuania are densely populated reaching the highest peak of settlement distribution in this region.

Changes happen in the 7th century AD when a sudden mixture of burial customs and a decrease in settlement density has been shown (Bliujienė 2006, 185). The inhumation burials that used to be surrounded by stone circles are now created without stone constructions and this long-term region-specific burial tradition seems to come to an end (Asaris *et al.* 2008, 45-47). From the 8th century AD onwards cremations appear and the coastal region merges with central Lithuania cremation burial tradition (Tautavičius 1977, 189; 1996, 331; Žulkus 2004, 247-250). Scandinavian contacts increase in the coastal area of Latvia and Lithuania in the 7th century AD (Nerman 1958; Žulkus 2004; Asaris *et al.* 2008, 49-56). Thus, in this area we can talk about, first, long-term settlement and gradual population growth, and, second, changes in burial traditions and increased foreign contacts in the second half of the period. The wealth deposits in this region belong to the later period.

Several scholars have argued that important social developments take place in western Lithuania in the second half of the Middle Iron Age. Political elite with military power and professional warrior retinue seems to emerge besides the ordinary peasant groups (Žulkus 2004, 245; Bliujienė 2006; Asaris *et al.* 2008, 57). Palanga region has a special position in this: some of the very few new cemeteries with prestigious items such as silver ornaments and swords are started there (Bliujienė 2006, 185-188; Vaškevičiūtė 2007, 219-220; Asaris *et al.* 2008, 46, 80). Thus the region of late Middle Iron Age bronze deposits stands out for newly created burial grounds and elite warrior and wealth display in them.

Despite these changes and developments in social relations, foreign contacts, archaeological sites and material culture, the items deposited in the 8th-9th century AD in western Lithuania follow the local pattern and are often found in contemporary burials. The objects from the Palanga I deposit are local female ornaments. Cruciform pins become an exclusively female ornament in the second half of the Middle Iron Age and the same can be assumed about twisted bronze neck-rings (Bliujienė 1999, 235, 242-243; Banytė-Rowell 2006, fig. 4; Jērums 2008, 71). The same applies to the complex pendant from Negraba which is typical female accessory often attached with cruciform dress pins. We are dealing with local female ornaments concealed in watery conditions and surrounded by contemporary hill-forts, cemeteries and settlements. The western coastal Latvian 8th-9th century AD Tiras purvs find of male items is conceptually very similar and geographically close to Lithuanian female ornament deposits. One Estonian later find, the Kunda II deposit from the north-eastern coast includes bronze dress pins, a finger-ring and a strike-a-light stone. These two resemble the belongings of a single person and are similar to Latvian and Lithuanian finds. We might be facing a widely spread 8th-9th century AD coastal depositional tradition, possibly relating to gender identities and reflecting the changes in general social life or some unexpected events in the lives of particular persons. However, the small data-set leaves this speculation still open for the debate.

The discussion of 8th-9th century bronze deposits in the eastern Baltic – bronzes in central Latvian hill-forts and gender based deposits in the coastal regions – shows how a detailed insight into the depositional practices and a consideration of regional social contexts reveals variations of what first looks like a very similar depositional tradition. In these examples one can see two different depositional outcomes of similar contemporary social developments.

### 9.2.3.3. Case study 3: Middle Iron Age silver neck-ring deposits in the eastern regions of the eastern Baltic

The final example of the cross-regional practices of wealth depositing is the most intriguing one. So far there have been no widely followed depositional traditions which are found throughout the three Baltic countries in the 1st-9th century AD. The only exception is the deposits of silver neck-rings. The majority of them contain only this specific artefact group although the number of rings varies from one to eleven and types can be quite different. As a general tendency we see a decrease in the number of deposited neck-rings over time. The tradition appears first in the 6th century in central-eastern Latvia and continues throughout the Middle Iron Age occurring later in south, east and north. All the finds are located in the eastern or central eastern regions of the three Baltic countries. Environments of concealment vary by country and century: the earlier, 6th-7th century AD, finds are most often found in dry land, whilst in the later 8th-9th century deposits wet contexts dominate. Despite some differences, it is a very long-term and stable depositional tradition with its own chronological phases: larger numbers of silver neck-rings in dry land in earlier deposits, followed by smaller numbers of neck-rings in watery conditions in later deposits.

The earliest finds in this group are 6th century deposits from **Lejaslepji** and **Miškiņeva** in Latvia (seven and four rings respectively). The **Viira** deposit from Estonia includes 11 rings (four in museum collections) and these are similar types to some of the rings in Latvian counterparts. In the 7th century the number of deposited neck-rings decreases and the forms of rings from **Ķišukalns**, **Lejasļūdi** and **Podži** are different from previous deposits including neck-rings with profoundly faceted or plain, undecorated overlapping terminals. At the same time this depositional tradition appears for the first time in central Lithuania where we find the **Migoniai II**, **Draustiniai** and **Velžiai** deposits which all include faceted terminal neck-rings. The 8th century is the peak of this depositional tradition providing three examples from Estonia – **Navesti**, **Hummuli**, **Loosi** – four from Latvia – **Baltinava**, **Saulītes**, **Dumpji**, **Mūrnieki** –, and one – **Baubliai** – from Lithuania. The types of neck-rings correlate with geographical distribution: profoundly faceted and loop-hooklet terminals in the south, and saddle-shape or slightly faceted overlapping terminals in the north. In the 9th century the tradition starts to decline as the number of deposits goes down to two – **Sauleskalns I** and **Vainekiai** located respectively in the south-east corner of Latvia and north-east corner of Lithuania.

The area of silver neck-ring deposits in Latvia and Lithuania is very rich in hill-forts (Apals *et al.* 2001, fig. 175; Vaitkevičius 2005, 75; Simniškytė 2005; 2006a, 151-153). Some of them are in the close vicinity of those particular wealth deposits. The general hill-fort material seems to indicate that more substantial and large scale fortification works took place during the 7th-8th century AD (Tautavičius (ed.) 1975, 226; Zabiela 2003, fig. 1, table 1) and the number of weapons in the find material increases considerably (Grigalavičienė 1992a-b).

The population becomes denser in the eastern Latvia and Lithuania with several old settlements being reused and expanded (Apals *et al.* 2001, 447; Simniškytė 2006a-b). Settlements also emerge at the foot of the hill-forts and some of them become manufacturing centres producing iron objects, but also jewellery and textiles (Daiga 1964; Grigalavičienė 1992a-b; Atgāzis 2006; Simniškytė 2006a;

Vasks 2006a). However, something happens towards the end of the Middle Iron Age in the north-eastern part of Lithuania, when this area becomes sparsely settled (Tautavičius 1996, 333-334; Simniškytė *et al.* 2003; Simniškytė 2006a) as indicated by some single farmstead sites with thin cultural layer and little human impact in pollen data. The revival of growing population in this region has been suggested from the 7th century AD onwards. Thus, the overall social picture in the eastern Latvia and Lithuania suggests uneasy times, possible violence or population movements, need for extra fortification work, but also interruptions, decreases and changes in settlement chronology and patterns.

Similar social developments are evident in Estonian material. There are numerous settlement sites, hill-forts and also hill-fort and settlement complexes in the regions where silver neck-ring deposits are found (Tõnisson 2008; Tvauri 2012, figs 3-4). Settlement patterns start to intensify in the south-eastern regions of Estonia at the end of the Middle Iron Age and the early centuries of the Viking Age (Tvauri 2012, 311-312). When comparing settlement distribution with the silver neck-ring deposits it becomes evident that these wealth deposits are situated in the border regions of the main settlement clusters in south-east and central-south Estonia. This also applies when considering contemporary Latvian material, because very few sites are known at the border of north-eastern Latvia, especially to the south of the Loosi and Hummuli finds (Apals *et al.* 1974, figs 59, 90).

Although the main settlement units in southern Estonia were still based on single farmsteads there are some local centres – larger hill-fort and settlement complexes – in the core areas of the region where silver neck-rings are found. Such examples include Rõuge in south-eastern corner of Estonia and Tartu by River Emajõgi. Those and other similar complexes have been regarded as important trade and manufacturing centres at which both political power and economic wealth concentrated from the early Viking Age onwards. In south-eastern Estonia much of the wealth and status of those sites was arguably based on the early Viking Age fur trade (perhaps also wax and honey): complexes of hill-forts and settlements acted as nodal points at which these valuables were collected in order to transport them further south and east (Ligi 1995, 234; Leimus & Kiudsoo 2004). This is also supported by the earliest Viking Age coin hoards in south-eastern Estonia.

The main burial custom in the Middle Iron Age eastern Lithuania is barrows with inhumations. There are several round barrows with rich burial goods and horse burials in east (Vaitkevičius 2005) and north-east Lithuania (Simniškytė 2006b). However, in time barrow cemeteries are no longer built and deceased are buried either in old barrows, next to them or into separate areas using new burial type – flat cemeteries with inhumation burials (Tautavičius 1977, maps 2, 4, 8; 1996, 327-333; Apals *et al.* 2001, 446; Balode *et al.* 2005, 34; Simniškytė 2009). Besides this, cremation burials also start to emerge gradually. Typical grave goods for women are bronze head-dresses, chain ornaments and bracelets, sometimes also tools; men have weapons and ornaments. The quantity of weapons increased throughout the Middle Iron Age, but became more homogenised in the last centuries of the period (Simniškytė 2006a-b; Kurila 2009, 191). Some male burials are particularly rich including unique goods such as tweezers, horse gear and silver neck-rings. These indicate clearer social hierarchy and centralised power relations.

The main burial tradition in south-eastern and -western Estonia in the second half of the Middle Iron Age are the previously discussed sand barrows with cremations in the south-eastern corner of Estonia and the more widely distributed reused stone graves or underground cremations pits (Tvauri 2012, chapter 6). All those graves include very few burial goods, precious metal items and weapons are especially rare. Distribution of burial grounds in the region of Estonian silver neck-ring deposits (according to appendices in Oras 2009) shows that all those deposits are located in the areas of stone-graves (either reused old or newly built), but to the east of them is the main distribution area of sand barrows. Loosi is one of the three sites where these two different burial traditions meet (Schmiedehelm & Laul 1970). It seems that the Estonian 8th-9th century AD silver neck-ring deposits are closely related to the groups of stone-grave users and deposited at the settlement border areas of these communities.

Comparing the material from hill-forts, settlements and burials it is evident that silver neck-rings in the eastern regions of the Baltic countries are rare items in any other context than wealth deposits. Neck-rings are normal grave goods, but they are mostly made of bronze (Tautavičius 1978, 151; Griciuvienė 2005; 2007). Sometimes silver neck-rings are found in burials and then they are usually associated with elite males (Vaitkunskienė 1995, 97-99, 102; Apals *et al.* 2001, 452) whereas most of such burials are located in the central and western part of Latvia and Lithuania (compare Bliujienė 2010, fig. 11 and Bliujienė & Curta 2011, fig. 17). Some types of neck-rings seem to have been produced for wealth depositing only. One such types is neck-rings with overlapping and profoundly faceted terminals which are only made of silver and found mostly in hoards and only in rare occasions in rich male burials (Tautavičius 1978, 151; Griciuvienė 2005, 73).

The same applies to Estonian 8th-9th century AD material. The neck-rings in those wealth deposits seem to be imported items and are rarely found in other contexts (Tvauri 2012, 158-159). Similar neck-rings to those from Navesti and Hummuli but made of bronze are known from an inhumation burial at Kivti in eastern Latvia (Šnore 1993, tab. II and III). Rings like the one from Loosi are known from Požerė inhumation cemetery in northern Lithuania (Tautavičius 1984, fig. 8). No such finds as in Hummuli and Navesti are found elsewhere in Estonia. The neck-rings with saddle-shaped terminals as in Loosi are more common, but only silver examples are found, whereas not in burials but only in later Viking Age hoard finds.

The overall social context in the area of silver neck-ring deposits in Latvia and Lithuania gives an impression of competitive and restless times. The numerous and intensely populated hill-forts, but also increase in and standardisation of warrior equipment in burial goods indicate the centralisation of military and regional power. Some hill-forts are burnt down and the material culture indicates military focus. Burial traditions change from barrow cemeteries to flat inhumation burials. In the north-east Lithuania population fluctuations are indicated in pollen diagrams and general archaeological material. The reasons for the settlement gaps might be economic such as bad harvest years, famine or hunger which killed or made people move; or to some extent political such as outside invaders and war activities. This altogether gives a picture of unstable settlement patterns, active foreign contacts (also of military nature), development of local manufacturing, competition for the prestige, control of land ownership and larger groups of people.

Estonian 8th-9th century AD material shows some resemblance to Latvia and Lithuania. Hill-forts are abundant and becoming local trading and manufacturing centres. However, settlement patterns show a gradual spread and intensification without any serious fall-backs. Differently from its southern counterparts burial goods in the area of silver neck-ring deposits are limited and weapons are still quite rare. Estonian neck-ring finds also seem to be related to the old tradition of stone graves, not with the more recent barrow cemeteries. However, it needs to be emphasised that compared to Latvia and Lithuania Estonian deposits emerge later. It might be that this particular tradition of wealth depositing has its roots in southern – Balts – regions and has spread north in later centuries.

Most of the neck-ring deposits in Latvia and Lithuania have been discovered outside cemeteries and settlements, but not too far from them. As we saw above, deposits of iron weapon-tool or later gender related bronze deposits in the western and central Latvia and Lithuania are close to contemporary archaeological sites. It seems that we are facing two sides of the same coin – expression of warrior ideology and social rivalry, but the selection of objects and concealment context divides these countries into two parts. In the west it is expressed by iron weapon-tool or bronze deposits in the vicinity of archaeological sites, and silver neck-rings in rich male burials. In the east the same goals are achieved by depositing silver neck-rings in natural sites while weapons and bronze items remain mostly in the realm of burial goods. This might represent Scandinavian influence in western and central regions and more eastern-related traditions in the other side of these countries. The shared characteristic for both is the masculine character of the deposits which seems to derive from the centralisation and display of power and wealth.

Estonian material does not allow drawing direct connections with the single local elite members or male paraphernalia. However, the clear selection of artefact type and material as well as their distribution and relation to other archaeological sites suggests similarities to eastern Latvian and Lithuanian silver neck-ring finds. Estonian silver neck-ring deposits are also located further away from the main settlement areas. One possible explanation for the Estonian deposits would be that they are evidence of social struggle and possible population growth. This is supported by the distribution and cultural landscape location of those finds and would fit with the general context of increased population and denser settlement patterns from the end of the Middle Iron Age onwards. The abundance of hill-forts and increased foreign contacts also suggest possible economic and military developments. The Loosi find at the border of two different burial traditions might indicate a possible maximum extent of available and arable lands.

Despite some social and chronological differences the tradition of silver neck-ring deposits in the 6th-9th century AD eastern Baltic is a remarkable cross-regional depositional practice. The exact interpretations of these finds might differ regionally and depend on the main characteristics of the contemporary social context. However, purely economic-based explanations of those finds in terms of safe-keeping can be excluded due to the long-term homogeneity of artefact selection. Baltic archaeologists have related silver neck-ring deposits to demonstration of high status of the depositor and to communal symbolic practices (Vasks 1999, 66; Simniškytė 2006a, 157; 2009, 106). These artefacts are rare and special objects in their contemporary context. We are most likely dealing with the social display symbolising changing power relations and ownership questions in the eastern regions of the eastern Baltic throughout the Middle Iron Age.

## 9.3. Eastern Baltic regional comparisons

Case studies discussed above have provided several examples of why it is a fruitful approach to first of all conduct a detailed micro scale analysis of wealth deposits in order to recognise large scale depositional practices, and thereafter set those practices into wider social contexts. Interpretations of wealth deposits gained via applying such a comparative micro and macro scale analysis opens considerably more nuanced and hopefully better argued discussions about the reasons why those deposits were concealed in the first place and their natural embeddedness in contemporary social circumstances. As a result one should not talk about wealth deposits as a self-contained archaeological find group, but as deeply rooted practices founded on their cultural and historical context.

The case studies represented indicate several geographical divisions of the practices of wealth depositing as well as differences in the availability and evaluation of wealth objects in the 1st-9th century AD eastern Baltic. These are particularly evident when considering and comparing more abundant Middle Iron Age material.

In Latvia and Lithuania, weapons and silver are a universal category of valuables. Weapons are found in burials throughout Latvia and Lithuania. However, in the region where silver neck-ring deposits are found weapon-tool deposits are lacking and silver is rare in burials. In the regions where weapon-tool deposits are located silver can be found more often in burials, while silver ornament deposits are not concealed there. The regional division into east-west is thus based on the existence or lack of weapon-tool deposits, and the depositional context of silver, which is concealed either in burials in the west or wealth deposits in the east. Estonia is divided into three regions with: a) only silver in wealth deposits but without any weapons and silver ornaments in burials in the south, b) silver and weapons in burials, but without any wealth deposits in the west and north-west, and 3) weapons in wealth deposits and burials but lack of silver in both burials and wealth deposits in the north-east and central regions.

It suggests that the military display and possible conflict situations evident throughout Latvia and Lithuania had reflections in coastal regions of Estonia, but not in the southern part of the country. This contradicts the distribution of hill-forts in Estonia because the earliest ones seem to be located in the south-eastern part of the country. One explanation would be that the spread of attitudes towards and active use of weapons can be related to sea connections. The earliest weapons occur in burials and wealth deposits in coastal regions, while weapon deposits in central areas are slightly later. The second explanation is that weapons were needed in combat and therefore not removed from the circulation in southern Estonia for practical reasons. The direct relation between weapons in graves and increase in military conflicts has been questioned in the case of the Anglo-Saxon burial material (Härke 1990). This, however, seems to contradict the contemporary state of affairs among the southern neighbours of Estonia, where not only weapons in burials and wealth deposits, but also hill-fort and settlement material suggest conflict situations. The other point to consider is the assigned military nature of hill-forts. Perhaps it is necessary to reconsider all the other possible functions a hill-fort might have. The list includes social and economic nodal points, sites of gathering and dwelling for the whole communities or some outstanding members of the community. Of course, the protective and military aspect cannot be totally excluded, but perhaps this occurrence of hill-forts in the southern regions of Estonia is not so contradictory with the lack of weapons in the region. The abundance of silver wealth deposits in the area might indeed indicate the success of hill-fort based settlement, production and economic system which at first did not necessarily have to include a direct military function, but rather served as an accumulation point of and a protective means to economic wealth.

In Latvia and Lithuania silver neck-rings have a close relation to rich elite male, possibly warrior burials, because they are often found with abundant weaponry and other prestigious male paraphernalia. In the southern countries the connection between the deposits and warrior ideology seems to persist throughout the Middle Iron Age and across the whole countries. However, the total number of weapons in Lithuania is very small and ornament deposits form the majority of Lithuanian finds. This indicates different attitudes and functions of different object groups within the smaller regions of the eastern Baltic. Therefore, the comparison of ornament and weapon-tool deposits in the three countries and their more detailed social contexts is a good example of importance of analysing depositional practices not only on a large- and cross-regional scale, but also in comparison with different regional social contexts. It helps to bring out the differences and similarities of the specific regions and alter our explanations of what might look at first like a very similar depositional practice.

There are more regional small-scale practices of wealth depositing in Estonia, while more widespread, cross-country patterns emerge in Latvia and Lithuania. Specific regional practices in Estonia include Early Middle Iron Age deposits of bronzes which might relate to Roman Iron Age depositional practices. This is followed by the unique tradition of depositing imported silver ornaments and vessels in burial areas in the south-eastern and central areas of Estonia, which chronologically precedes and partly overlaps with the weapon and tool deposits in north-eastern and central regions. Latvia and Lithuania share similar ideas about weapon deposits in the Middle Iron Age but also have similar deposits of bronzes in the last centuries of this period. There are some depositional practices that are characteristic to all the three Baltic countries indicating a much wider spread of ideas and cultural activities. Such examples might be the deposits of bronzes in all three countries in the Roman Iron Age or the tradition of silver neck-ring deposits in the Middle Iron Age. However, as discussed above, even those more widely distributed practices have their own region-specific nuances that at an in-depth analysis might result in quite different final interpretations.

## 9.4. Practices of wealth depositing east and west of the Baltic Sea

The regional and cross-regional practices of wealth depositing in the 1st-9th century AD eastern Baltic are now discussed in the broader Baltic Sea context. Comparisons with Scandinavian, Polish and Finnish materials draw on detailed discussions and examples presented in Chapter 5. Since elaborate references to specific sites, datasets and depositional practices can be found in there, only wider conclusions and more general discussions are cited and discussed in further details in this chapter.

There is considerable regional variability in the Iron Age depositional material in the Baltic Sea area. This bias might be related to the variable development of scholarship and interest in this specific archaeological find group. It is evident that Scandinavian archaeologists have published considerably more in this field. However, the number and content of intentionally concealed artefact deposits shows different regional practices of wealth depositing.

The first difference is the sheer quantity of deposits and their chronological distribution. Southern Scandinavia has the greatest concentration of wealth deposits with over 50 weapon deposits and countless precious metal finds (Hagberg 1984; Hedeager 1992; Jensen 2006; Andersson 2011). The number of separate artefacts deposits in Estonia, Latvia and Lithuania is around 20 per country and only about ten in Finland (coin hoards excluded).

The earliest intentional artefact deposits in Scandinavia which mainly include organic material, pottery and stone artefacts, are traced back to the Mesolithic and carry on until the historical periods (e.g. Becker 1974; Harck 1984; Stjernquist 1997; Carlie 1998). As discussed in Chapter 5 a number of Roman and Germanic Iron Age booty sacrifices (e.g. Ejsbøl, Nydam, Vimose) also contain similar earlier substrate of organic and mineral deposits (Ørsnes 1988; Pauli Jensen 2009; Rau 2010). A few similar Pre-Roman Iron Age deposits of organic and ceramic material are found in Poland (Makiewicz 1988), but in most of the eastern Baltic such early traditions are missing. Although Bronze Age deposits are found in all three Baltic countries, there seems to be a gap in the last half of the 1st millennium BC in the eastern Baltic, especially in comparison with the rich material from Scandinavia. There are some hints of bone and other organic material being deposited in Estonian finds of Reola and Kavastu. However, these have not been preserved nor recorded properly and the chronology or relation to those particular deposits remains unclear.

On a chronological scale, there are numerous Roman Iron Age finds in Scandinavia, but in the eastern Baltic most deposits are dated to the second half of the 1st millennium AD. Scandinavian Iron Age weapon deposits in watery conditions begin already in the Pre-Roman Iron Age (Randborg 1995), though the majority belongs to the Roman Iron Age and often contain hundreds of objects, including horse gear, tools, ornaments, personal belongings, even coins and other precious metal items (Ilkjær 2003). There are also examples of weapon deposits from the following periods, which usually include fewer artefacts (Nørgård Jørgensen 2008a, 104-120). Polish weapon deposits (Makiewicz 1992; Raddatz 1993; Nowakiewicz & Rzeszotarska-Nowakiewicz 2012), although smaller in terms of deposited items and overall number of finds, resemble Scandinavian traditions.

Eastern Baltic weapon deposits differ in many ways. They emerge later, from the 5th century AD onwards, and the combinations of different functional groups are less variable than in Scandinavia. There is usually a clear dominance of one material or artefact group in the eastern Baltic material. The number of deposited items is usually smaller, although the Kokmuiža I find with its 1200 items is quite close to its western counterparts. As the number of artefacts in later Scandinavian deposits decreases, the amounts of objects concealed in east and west Baltic become comparable in the later parts of the Iron Age.

There are also some other similarities. One important shared characteristic is that most of the iron deposits, usually dominated by weapons, are found in water-related conditions along both coasts of the Baltic Sea. Like many Scandinavian weapon deposits, some eastern Baltic items also indicate possible pre-depositional destruction. Many Scandinavian weapon deposit locales like Illerup (Ilkær 2000), Nydam (Rau 2010), Vimose (Pauli Jensen 2009), Porskjær (Nørgård Jørgensen

2008a) and Kragehul (Iversen 2010) have been used on several occasions and some of the earliest deposits in the places where weapon deposits occur date back to the Pre-Roman Iron Age or even earlier. The only examples of really long-term used sites in eastern Baltic are the north-east Estonian Alulinn and Kunda I deposits in which the first items date from the beginning of the 1st millennium and continue throughout the Middle Iron Age. Their coastal location might indicate influences from the Scandinavian depositional traditions. However, differently from Scandinavia, they also include agricultural and smithy tools (sickles, scythes, coal trowels) and their chronology is much wider.

Considering artefactual comparisons with other archaeological sites some additional east-west differences emerge. In Iron Age and early medieval Anglo-Saxon and southern Scandinavian contexts the number of weapons in burials decreases according to the increase of weapons in bog deposits (Hedeager 1992; Hines 1997; Härke 2000), but the same phenomenon cannot be traced in most of the eastern Baltic. When weapons occur in wealth deposits they are also found in burials in Latvia and Lithuania. However, in the north-eastern and central part of Estonia burials do not include the same richness of weapons as evident in contemporary iron deposits.

The border-line between the two traditions of weapon-tool deposits in the eastern and western Baltic seems to run in northern Poland where a few Scandinavian style deposits have been discovered. The difference is in the abundance of deposits, number of artefacts concealed and combination of artefact types: personal equipment, luxury warrior paraphernalia and jewellery are usually excluded in the Baltic countries where merely combinations of iron tools and weapons can be found. The most Scandinavian type deposit in three Baltic countries remains the Kokmuiža I deposit from Latvia, which resembles western Baltic counterparts in terms of environment, number of objects and the set of items concealed. There are very few Roman and Middle Iron Age iron deposits in Finland (Kivikoski 1973; Huurre 1995). Therefore it looks as if the northern border of this depositional tradition runs along the northern coast of Estonia.

Although precious metal is found in the eastern Baltic deposits the main difference between the depositional practices on the two coasts of the Baltic Sea lies in this subgroup of finds. Firstly, the number of gold finds in Scandinavia greatly exceeds its eastern neighbours (Jørgensen & Petersen 1998; Andersson 2011). The Migration Period in Scandinavia is called the 'golden age', but in the three Baltic countries and Finland gold is rare in burials and wealth deposits. There is only one gold find, a neck-ring from Kardla in Estonia, a single gilded neck-ring from Piltene, and an animal-head terminal neck-ring from Nousianen (Hackman 1905, 213-214) in the eastern Baltic wealth deposits. Silver is more common, though not the most abundant material. Most of the ornaments are made of bronze. Even the vast majority of Roman coin finds in the Baltic countries are bronze as opposed to the numerous silver and gold coins found in Scandinavia and Poland (Bursche 2002; Ciołek 2010). There are no gold bracteates or gold-foil figures – artefact groups which are numerous in Scandinavia (Andrén 1991; Lamm 2004; Ratke 2009) – in the eastern Baltic. The hack-silver finds known in Scandinavia prior to the Viking Age (Fabech 1990) are absent in the Baltic countries.

One cross-regional tradition that shows some connections between Scandinavian and Baltic ornament deposits is ring deposits. There seems to be a cross-cultural phenomenon of evaluating rings, be it a neck-ring or bracelet, as a specific depositional object on the both coasts of the Baltic Sea. This is clearly indicated by the eastern Baltic silver neck-ring deposits and numerous gold ring finds in Scandinavian Roman and Migration Period material (Helg 1990; Hedeager 1991; 1992; Rasch 2004). In both regions they are found in watery conditions as well as dry land. Scandinavian scholars have interpreted such exquisite ring finds as symbolic expressions of ritual and political power, rank, leadership and created high-status relationships (Lund Hansen 2001; Hedeager 2011, 165-168, 205). These finds, however, differ in their material in east and west – mainly gold in Scandinavia and silver in the eastern Baltic. They also tend to be slightly earlier in Scandinavia. As the earliest silver ring deposits in the eastern Baltic, the Piltene gilded silver neck-ring and the Kaali set of neck-ring and bracelets are from the western coast areas, they might indicate the western Baltic origin of this tradition and connections between the two regions at that time (Helg 1990). However, the majority of the Middle Iron Age eastern Baltic silver neck-ring deposits concentrate in eastern regions and thus might form a separate and locally developed depositional tradition.

The second major difference is the context in which precious metal is found. Scandinavia is famous for its gold found in settlement contexts, especially central places such as Gudme, Lundeborg, Sorte Muld and Uppåkra (Hårdh & Larsson (eds) 2002; Adamsen *et al.* (eds) 2009; Henriksen 2010). Most of the eastern Baltic silver deposits are found outside settlement contexts. The problem remains that very few eastern Baltic settlement sites have been excavated. However, very little evidence of precious metal is known from more extensively studied hill-forts and silver is also rare in burials. This suggests that most of the Roman and Middle Iron Age precious metal in the eastern Baltic comes from wealth deposits.

In terms of precious metal finds Poland follows along the same lines of Scandinavian material. It has a vast quantity of Roman coins, several gold deposits containing bracteates, rings, military paraphernalia (Godłowski 1980), but also some separate silver finds (Bitner-Wroblewska 2010, 150-151). Resemblance in the content and context of weapon finds in Scandinavia and Poland was discussed above. Thus it seems that the Baltic countries together with Finland, with very little Roman or Middle Iron Age deposits at all, formed a peripheral area where precious metal reached in smaller quantities and less often. This peripheral status resulting in less wealth objects and materials (such as high quality Roman import, coins and gold) can be traced already in the Roman Iron Age.

In conclusion, although eastern Baltic wealth depositional material does share some broad similarities with the Scandinavian contemporary sites, there are several significant differences that argue for locally developed depositional concepts. Scandinavia takes a dominant role in terms of the amount and the content of finds, including higher value materials and well as variability of objects concealed. Poland is a middle-ground between eastern and western Baltic depositional traditions. The main find groups known from the Scandinavian Iron Age material like organic, pottery or stone deposits and weapons in watery conditions, coin hoards, and various precious metal deposits are also represented in Polish Roman and Migration Periods finds, although usually in smaller quantities. Similarities to Scandinavian deposits are visible both in terms of main artefact types and chronology.

Clearer differences between the eastern and western Baltic regions as well as within Scandinavia and Baltic countries seem to relate to the geographical latitude. The number and variability of wealth deposits decreases towards the north. But there are also some interesting deviations in this general picture. One of the best examples is the changing position of Lithuania. Roman coin hoards are more abundant in Lithuania than in Latvia, Estonia and Finland. Lithuania, especially its western and southern part, is quite similar to Polish and Scandinavian material in the Roman Iron Age. However, in later periods and when considering non-numismatic material the number of deposits from 1st-9th century AD Lithuania is small. In fact, Lithuania provides the least examples from the three Baltic countries during this period. All these finds are located in the northern half of the country. Lithuania is an intermediate area between the two depositional traditions – sometimes participating in the southern Baltic and Scandinavian, sometimes in the eastern Baltic wealth system.

Another broader conclusion is that most of the wealth depositing practices in Scandinavia and Poland occur later (if at all) in the eastern Baltic. The character of depositional traditions in the Baltic countries often expresses specific eastern (e.g. silver neck-ring deposits) or very small-scale (e.g. long-term iron weapon-tool deposits in coastal Estonia, silver deposits in burial areas in central-south Estonia) depositional traditions that do not have direct parallels in Scandinavia. These could be considered as expressions of particular eastern Baltic communities of depositional practices. Scandinavia and Poland share the earliest and richest of the main depositional traditions. This most likely derived from and resulted in a more active position in the wider European social and political negotiations. Baltic countries and Finland remained in a peripheral status with their own, possibly quite different social and political connections, networks of trade as well as valuables that are also reflected in the movement, availability and concealment of wealth. Finland with its very few Roman and Middle Iron Age wealth deposits indicates the northern border to this particular wealth concealment tradition in the Baltic Sea area during the first eight centuries of the 1st millennium AD.

The situation changes considerably in the Viking Age. Now, new power lines and economic interests, eastward directed trading routes, as well as different forms and functions of precious metal result in the creation of new peripheries, hinterlands and core areas. For the first time in the 1st millennium AD, the Baltic countries and Finland start to play a role comparable to Scandinavia as a result of developments in broader social context: wider contacts and active engagement in the relations between different European and further eastern regions.

*Chapter 10*

# Conclusions

The aim of this thesis was to show that the acts of concealing valuables are not autonomous phenomena, but form an important part of the past society and the whole archaeological picture. Wealth deposits directly depend on and influence the development of past social contexts. As eastern Baltic 1st-9th century AD material indicates it is possible to identify widely followed cultural practices of wealth depositing which relate to broader social processes and developments. Some are small-scale and regional, others more widely distributed practices. A few extend over modern political borders, even across the Baltic Sea as is evident from the comparison with Scandinavian and Polish material. Therefore the hypothesis presented in the introduction of the thesis – wealth depositing is a cultural practice which relates to and derives from various past cultural phenomena and changes in time and space in accordance with those processes – has been well supported.

From the methodological perspective this study combined several theoretical concepts from social sciences. I began with a point of view that wealth depositing is a cultural practice that both depends on as well as influences the broader social structure behind it. The starting point was to consider each deposit as an example of a widely followed concealment practice. Moving from a single event (one wealth deposit) to widely followed, and therefore culturally prescribed depositional practices was based on comparing different depositional contexts. These contexts include combinations of artefacts and their production materials, environment of concealment and its location in the landscape, but also the chronology of the deposits. For comparing and relating a single wealth deposit (an event) and social structure, the concepts of micro and macro scale were employed. The first is constituted by single events (wealth deposits) and developed further into the level of practice when several deposits cluster due to their overlapping depositional contexts and close spatial and temporal distribution. Macro scale was derived from the broader archaeological dataset from hill-forts to burials, and environmental data to general artefact record, altogether indicating other social developments and changes. Putting those two scales – micro and macro – together, enabled the comparisons of whether and how depositional practices depend on the wider social processes. The identification of depositional practices and their changes, as well as their relation to social structure is best recognised in a long-term perspective. Thus this study also emphasised the importance and fruitfulness of studying longer time periods when doing research on depositional practices and their relations to social context. Similar approaches have been used before, but these are mostly based on a single group of depositional material (e.g. wetland deposits, pit deposits in settlements, deposits of bronzes). Current research combined the complete range of depositional practices from different environments and artefact groups over 800 years in order to exemplify the ways in which one could better understand the practices of wealth depositing and their changes in spatial and temporal terms and in relation to broader social developments.

The main theoretical contribution of this study was a shift from explicit meaning related 'why' questions to the questions of 'how'. The aim was to tackle previous interpretational shortcomings, such as often unsubstantiated oppositional categorisations of deposits into ritual and economic, with a considerably modified essence of questions posed to this material. Instead of asking why those concealments were made and what is the meaning behind them, the perspective was now if and how these depositions change in time and space; whether they are unique separate examples or form more widely followed (communities of) practices; and most importantly how do they relate to and reflect different aspects of contemporary social context and developments. Answering the latter is in many ways still a reply to 'why'-question, providing some interpretative reasoning about how and why these particular depositional practices came to be. However, these answers derive from different, more data substantiated and comparative background. They emphasise the embeddedness of depositional practices in their social context and are arguably less speculative than attempts to give a single meaning and function to a wealth deposit.

Another contribution of this research to the study of wealth deposits was developing and testing different possibilities of data categorisation and specific analyse methods. It was aimed to show how a depositional practice as a social act in essence can be read from numeric or categorical data with the help of statistical methods. This was done by comparing contextual characteristics of each wealth deposit at different levels: artefact assemblage, material assemblage, relations between artefact and material assemblage and the environments of concealment, and all those together in a chronological scale. I employed both quantitative and qualitative methods for identifying the specific depositional practices and their spatial and temporal distribution. In doing so, the biases of specific analytical methods and problems relating to data categorisation and input were emphasised. As the results indicate, all those analyses provide relevant outcome for establishing the practices of wealth depositing and unique outliers in this dataset. However, comparisons of those results exemplify the issues that should be kept in mind when applying those methods and categorisation principles not only for the analysis of wealth deposits but in material culture studies in general. The best and most complete picture can be formed when combining the information gained through different data categories and methods, while keeping in mind the specifics of each dataset and the importance of those characteristics that cannot be expressed numerically or categorically. Therefore, the discussions of data collection, categorisation and analytical methods employed in this research should be of value to anyone interested in the studies of intentional artefact deposits.

There were several premises to be fulfilled in the discussion of different practices of wealth depositing. First, the material needs to be as wide as possible. This means that it is necessary to include all kinds of different contexts and contents of deposits as long as there is a good argument that the items have been intentionally concealed. This is also why the concept of wealth deposit – assemblages of one or more valued object/s that is/are hidden deliberately as an intended separate deposition of selected object(s) into a selected place in a specific, distinguishable manner – was introduced. This umbrella term includes different materials, functional groups and environments of concealment which makes it possible to recognize regionally and temporally developing practices of wealth depositing.

The second premiss is the question of context. Patterns in wealth depositing are established as a result of comparative analysis of different depositional contexts and their combinations. This is based on detailed contextual information about artefacts, their functional groups, environment of concealment, and the exact location and chronology of each deposit. That data enables further analysis of the similarities and differences between different deposits and makes widely followed practices as well as unique examples of wealth depositing recognisable.

The final important prerequisite for distinguishing depositional practices and their development is long-term perspective and geographical scale. Depositional practices, especially their developments and changes, become evident only in a long-term perspective. This is why a broad time-period of 800 years was chosen in the current study. Another relevant aspect is to include the finds from larger geographical areas. This helps to identify small-scale and regional practices, but also to distinguish cross-regional and more widely followed depositional practices. Comparing those with other aspects of social context and changes traced in archaeological sites it is possible to talk about closed or shared cultural regions with local or widespread depositional acts. The current thesis has provided several examples of both (see Chapter 9).

The details of the characteristics of each wealth deposit and their depositional patterns are provided country by country in Chapters 6-8. Chapter 9 contains the analysis of the extent to which interdependence of depositional practices and broader social developments can be identified. Several general tendencies in the eastern Baltic material of wealth depositional practices should be emphasised, because they indicate some regional aspects of the practices of wealth depositing compared to other parts of the Baltic Sea. They also might be used as further points of reference when posing questions about practices of wealth depositing in any other region and time period where such archaeological source material is available. Therefore, the concluding remarks below indicate the tendencies which can be read from wealth deposits and exemplify the importance of a cross-regional and long-term perspective.

Most of the eastern Baltic 1st-9th century AD depositional practices are small-scale and regional supporting the idea of socially impelled communities of practice, although these regions also cross some of the modern political borders. The latter examples include Middle Iron Age weapon deposits or personal item assemblages from watery contexts in Latvia and Lithuania. It is noteworthy that despite the acknowledged problematic nature of drawing ethnic borders based on archaeological material both of those cross-country practices correlate to the traditional historical Semigallian and Curonian ethnozones. Estonia seems to form a separate entity with its own local developments of depositional practices compared to several shared characteristics between Latvia and Lithuania. Explanations might lie in the existence of cultural borders (Finno-Ugrians and Balts) and/or different chronological developments in social contexts. However, there is also an example of a depositional practice which can be found throughout the area under discussion: silver neck-ring deposits in the eastern regions of the eastern Baltic. Although covering several centuries of the Middle Iron Age and having different spatial and temporal concentrations, its consistent content and regional distribution indicates the potential of distinguishing cross-cultural depositional phenomena within larger geographical and longer time frames.

Some generalisations about the chronological distribution of wealth deposits in the eastern Baltic Iron Age can be made. First there is an increase in the quantity of deposits over time: there are far less wealth deposits (Roman coin hoards are excluded) from the Roman Iron Age than from the Middle Iron Age in all three Baltic countries. The peak centuries for the quantity of deposited items and number of deposits per century are in the first half of the Middle Iron Age (5th-7th century AD). After that the number of deposits, and the number of items deposited together decreases. As the same tendency applies to all three countries it indicates similar and widespread cultural attitudes towards valuables of different forms and the practices carried out with them during that period. Explanations for this might be related to disruption related to the Migration Period in Europe or the possible environmental crisis of the so-called 536 AD dust veil event (see Chapter 9.2). However, it is not clear how much direct influence those specific phenomena had in these northern regions. One could perhaps also consider local social developments, like power struggles and changes in ownership relations or social hierarchy, which might have coincided with these large-scale events and triggered the intensified depositional practices.

Another general tendency is that wealth deposits reflect chronological developments in the economy and foreign contacts like trade, availability of different resources, also the use and production of metals. For instance, in the Roman Iron Age when bronze is the most widespread material for ornaments most of the deposits consist of bronzes. The main inflow feeding this system was based on Roman imports, mainly coins, coming in as a result of the amber trade. Most numerous and variable are bronze finds (including Roman coins) in the southern part of the eastern Baltic which was active in this trade system. Further north the deposits become scarcer and homogenised. Around the middle of the 1st millennium AD two new materials – silver and iron – emerge, while the number of deposited bronzes remains the same in Lithuania and starts to fall in Estonia and Latvia. The emergence of iron in wealth deposits, on the other hand, correlates well with the increased iron production in those countries. The amount of silver might be related to increased foreign contacts and interest in a new and rare material. The earliest silver deposits are the 4th and 5th century silver ornament deposits from Kaali and Piltene. As both of them are in the western regions of the eastern Baltic, the origin of the earliest silver in these areas might be related to seafaring. However, in later periods the concentration of silver deposits moves to eastern regions and in combination with the distribution of silver in burial goods very different import routes, contacts and valuation systems can be presumed.

Artefact functional groups and their combinations seem to be most relevant when considering specific practices of wealth depositing in the eastern Baltic Iron Age. Chronologically an important development is the emergence of weapons in wealth deposits in the first half of the Middle Iron Age. This correlates with the increased number of weapons in burials. Although the relationship between warfare and weapons in burial goods is debatable, it can argued that weapon deposits indicate times of turbulence and violence in all the three Baltic countries. Ornaments, on the other hand, seem to be chosen for depositing in very different times. They can be found in Estonian Roman Iron Age and 5th century bronze deposits or 6th century silver ornament deposits. The stability and peaceful nature of those social contexts is arguably indicated by the lack of weapons in contemporary burial goods while hill-forts are not very common either. However, the tradition of silver neck-ring deposits in Latvia and Lithuania is related to the regions and centuries where times of turbulence and warrior ideology are constantly evident in the overall archaeological record. As those artefact types have been mainly related to elite male warriors in the areas where they form part of the burial assemblage we might be dealing with the diverse regional expressions of contemporary social developments in the eastern regions of the eastern Baltic.

One wide-spread phenomenon is the combination of artefact functional groups. It is evident in all three countries that weapons are hardly ever combined with silver ornaments. Mostly there are distinct divisions between iron (weapons and tools) and silver and/or bronze (ornaments) deposits. In Latvian and Lithuanian material there are a few personal bronze ornaments found in larger weapon deposits but in Estonia there are no combinations of ornaments and weapons. Additionally, in the case of the first two these ornaments are mainly parts of male warrior sets. The second cross-temporal phenomenon is the importance of neck-rings in wealth deposits. Neck-rings are the artefact type found most often throughout the 1st-9th century AD in all three countries. They tend to dominate the content of the deposit if they are not the sole type. Such general patterns suggest that there were strict limitations for selecting artefacts to be deposited which again indicates accepted cultural rules for wealth depositing.

The environment of concealment does not seem to be the most important aspect of the specific depositional practices. One of the problems here is the changing nature of the landscape and the difficulties of distinguishing the exact environment of concealment without in-depth geological studies. On a general scale different artefacts can be concealed in different environments. However, some generalisations about the distinct practices can be made even here. Iron is hardly ever found in ordinary dry land, but if found in non-watery conditions then in contemporary burial grounds or hill-forts. Bronze is found in both watery and dry land environments but the deposits of silver items never appear in open water conditions, although they can be often found in bog/marsh. Chronologically the Roman Iron Age seems to be dominated by finds in dry land (including archaeological sites) whereas from the mid-1st millennium AD different water-related contexts start to emerge more often. Although only general conclusions about the environment of concealment can be made, there are several temporal and regional environmental tendencies in combination with artefact assemblages that are described in detail in Chapters 6-9.

Identification of distinct practices derived from clear intentional selection and combination of artefacts and environments of concealment in time and space are one of the most important results of this thesis. The second larger goal was exemplifying the importance of the contemporary social context. This is relevant when trying to provide further interpretations and explanations of the specific depositional practices. The broader social context background for each depositional practice was based on combining all the available material from contemporary and nearby archaeological sites. This approach encounters several difficulties, because the state of research of archaeological sites and environmental material is uneven in different regions. The main problems include uncertainties of site chronologies and the clear over-representation of burial material compared to any other archaeological sites. Despite those problems, it was argued that without considering the developments and changes in other archaeological sites the picture of wealth depositional practices would be incomplete. The relevance of detailed social context is best exemplified in the case studies provided in Chapter 9. As a result of these case studies it can be concluded that it is essential to examine the overall archaeological record in order to understand the development of depositional practices and their relationship to broader social processes. This is the above-discussed new and modified way of answering important 'why' questions via better argued responses to 'how': how depositional practices change in time and space and relate to the developments in a wider social scale respectively.

There are several examples in the current thesis that exemplify this argument. One of them is the discussion of Roman Iron Age deposits of bronzes in different parts of the three Baltic countries: the amount and form of deposited bronzes relates to the areas of influence of the Roman Empire. In the case of the Estonian 4th-5th century AD depositional tradition one might also add the increasing importance of stressing the individuality of some members of the society which is reflected in both wealth deposits and Late Roman Iron Age burial customs. Another example of the relevance of social context is the contextualisation and long-term development of weapon deposits in the eastern Baltic: they all seem to have a close relationship to military activities and times of conflict. However, the emergence of such developments is earlier in Latvia and Lithuania, while in Estonia it does not seem to reach southern regions before the end of the Middle Iron Age or even later. Regional social developments which can be read from the wealth deposits are also indicated in burials, to some extent also hill-forts. The third important instance was the distinct practice of silver neck-ring deposits. In Latvia and Lithuania these deposits most likely correlate with male warrior leaders and political rivalry, but the social context of silver ornament deposits in Estonia does not have a direct correlation with increasing military activities. In Latvia and Lithuania silver neck-rings are found throughout the Middle Iron Age in wealthy male warrior graves in the western regions, but only in wealth deposits in eastern areas, while in Estonia silver neck-rings seem to be a specific artefact type only used for wealth depositing in the later part of the Middle Iron Age. The necessity of such detailed analysis of changes in social context is also exemplified by the cases where very similar material characteristics of wealth deposits are evident, but where the social context suggests nuances that might alter further interpretation of specific regional depositional traditions. The latter include the Late Middle Iron Age bronzes in western Latvia and Lithuania and in Latvian hill-forts: the first indicating gender based individual-related depositional traditions, the others showing developments of power, trade and production centres at hill-fort and settlement complexes.

These are just a few examples to show how conclusions about specific depositional practices can be made only when considering and comparing broader social contexts, larger regions and longer time periods. As indicated by the specific regional case studies and general cross-regional discussion in Chapter 9 the choice of artefacts to be concealed and the location of the deposition depend on broader social contexts. On the other hand, wealth deposits play their own part in creating, maintaining or changing this contemporary social context. There is a constant interplay between wealth deposits and social context. However, those relations are not always straight-forward and universal, but can have their own subtleties, regional preferences and local developments. Therefore it should be emphasised that no depositional tradition with its own local social context should be taken as a model to be applied to other times and regions, but they all have to be considered as an organic whole case by case, region by region, practice by practice.

A more general outcome of the thesis is the demonstration of the main and distinct regional traditions of wealth depositing in the 1st-9th century AD Baltic Sea area. There is a clear divide between north and south in the Baltic Sea area in terms of wealth deposits. The same division also applies to east and west. The material of wealth deposits seems to be accumulated in the south-western regions, southern Scandinavia and Scania, Poland, and is almost lacking in north-eastern areas, especially Finland. The southern border of the eastern Baltic depositional traditions discussed in this thesis runs from east to west across Lithuania. As explained above, the distribution of wealth deposits in Lithuania does seem to be the result of objective data and it is likely that the concept of wealth depositing was not followed in the southern half, especially in the inland regions of the country. Therefore southern and central Lithuania are a border zone between two depositional traditions: there is a different content and number of wealth deposits in the eastern and northern Baltic compared to its western and southern regions. The depositional traditions in Poland, mainly in its coastal regions, correlate by and large with the rich Scandinavian material. Although usually smaller in numbers and content of deposits Polish material provides instances of all the main Scandinavian depositional traditions. Latvia and Lithuania share several cross-regional practices of wealth depositing with closer patterns in spatial terms as well as content of finds. Estonia is a separate entity which is characterised by regional depositional practices, although some of them may be drawn from and influenced by its southern neighbours. The northern border of the active tradition of wealth depositing before the Viking Age overlaps with the Estonian borders. As there are very few 1st-9th century AD wealth deposits in Finland it seems that the Gulf of Finland creates a natural border to the tradition of wealth depositing in the Baltic Sea area before the Viking Age. The northern part of Scandinavia can be characterised as having fewer examples of typical Scandinavian Iron Age intentional artefact deposits. As the information about wealth deposits to the east of the three Baltic countries is scarce and not published as a cohesive study, conclusions about the possible distribution and continuation of wealth concealment there remain an open, but certainly relevant question worth further enquiry.

Finally, some further suggestions can be made about the research development of the current topic. One of the main drawbacks of the current study remains the limited total number of deposits considered. Only 69 deposits for 800 years does not allow very firm conclusions and indeed the results of some of the statistical analysis did not give satisfactory results. In this sense the choice of suitable methods for this specific dataset might be reconsidered. However, most of the results indicated clear depositional traditions and the results are also supported by simpler qualitative analysis.

A solution to some statistical problems emerged in the thesis could be alternative data categorisation principles. Firstly, as the detailed data analysis and case studies showed, there is no direct need to divide the material according to current political borders. There are several coinciding depositional practices in Latvia and Lithuania, some even found in all the three Baltic countries. Representing the material on a country bases does ease the reader to find concentrated information about one specific region, but at the same time weakens the statistical argument due to a small data set. The latter is also the reason why political borders were dismissed in the final analysis in Chapter 9. Second possibility would be to abandon century-based chronological distribution and use arbitrary time units covering two or more centuries *e.g.* Early and Late Roman Iron Age, Migration Period and Pre-Viking Age, or Early and Late Middle Iron Age. This might also solve some of the detailed artefact chronology derived issues discussed at the beginning of core chapters 6-8. Additionally, the resolution of decoding changes in depositional practices would not suffer much either. Finally it would be worthwhile rethinking some alternative ways for categorising artefact functional groups and types. Division of artefacts into single functional groups remains currently slightly problematic, especially in the case of objects that have several use categories: axes, belt parts, knives. One possibility would be to give up function-based categorisation and rely on object types solely. However, a solution based on artefact type is problematic in the case of current dataset because it would scatter the material considerably and allow only a small part of it to be included in several statistical analyses. Functional categorisation allows merging several smaller types into larger function-based entities. This thesis tried to combine both, pointing out pros and cons for each.

Additional consideration relating to the overall picture of the wealth deposits' material is the question of non-metal deposits in the eastern Baltic. There are examples of bone, ceramic, stone and wood deposits in Poland, Scandinavia, also in Finland and many other parts of Europe but no such finds could be included in the current thesis. It is possible that this indicates the lack of this particular practice in the eastern Baltic. However, it is just as likely that this kind of data has not yet been considered and looked for, perhaps not even properly recorded. As the current thesis is largely based on published material it is likely that it lacks some of the material deposited. Therefore archive materials and museum catalogues should be re-examined to see if any such deposits have been found in the eastern Baltic.

The second future research prospect that arises from the detailed contextualisation of each wealth deposit is the significance of object and deposit biography, including detailed study of both artefacts and their find-spots. The relevant questions would include a detailed artefact description and analysis, more precise chronology, and the origin and production methods of artefacts. If possible, excavations of known find-spots and further scientific analysis of the cultural landscape and geographical features would be valuable. This would allow more reliable description of the landscape situation at the time of deposit. Excavation of undisturbed and newly discovered wealth deposits would be extremely useful. The recent discovery of the Kohtla deposit[23] of hundreds of weapons and tools is such a find, which might provide a unique opportunity for studying one Iron Age wealth deposit in full details. For the first time in Estonia it is possible to apply a range of different research methods starting from archaeological excavations and employing all sorts of scientific analysis from environmental to material studies for such a find. The complete set of over 400 artefacts from the first half of the first millennium AD and a detailed documentation of the site provides an opportunity for further analysis and research for years to come. Additionally, the Kohtla find with its content and context – almost exclusively iron items like axes, spearheads

23 As the Kohtla deposit was discovered in August 2013, at the last stage of completing this thesis, unfortunately its full details are yet to be analysed and the find could not be included in the current thesis. For preliminary overview see Oras & Kriiska 2014.

and sickles, hidden in a wetland, not far from the similar Estonian finds of Kunda I and Alulinn deposit – fits very well with the depositional patterns set out in this thesis.

The third approach which partly relates to the object and deposit biography would be an in-depth scientific analysis of deposited artefacts and their environments of concealment. This would include the application of different scientific methods to artefact and environmental studies. Depending on available material and reliability of the location of the deposit in the landscape some approaches might include methods from archaeochemistry and physics: material and production characterisation methods of XRF, SEM-EDS, ICP-MS, dating methods like AMS, SC-AMS, OSL, detailed characterisation of related finds through residue analysis, plant remains and dates, environmental studies with the help of geophysics, geomorphology and pollen studies. The efficiency and relevance of such studies is clearly indicated by the detailed study of the Kavastu bronze lamp in the current study. With this small collaborative project I have only started to investigate what kind of other relevant information might be gained with a detailed science based analysis of wealth deposits.

All these proposed research topics would widen considerably our knowledge and understanding of each deposit and allow further comparative analysis of wealth depositional material. It is likely that they might alter the patterns and interpretations provided in the current study. However, unlike the current thesis, they all presume a considerably smaller scale data selection, a micro-study approach of a single artefact, deposit or group of finds. The first step in such biographical and science-based in-depth studies is thorough knowledge of the overall material and the main problems therein. The latter is an important prerequisite that allows the choice of study material in a more problem-derived way and enables better argued question setting as well as end-results. The current study of the practices of wealth depositing in the 1st-9th century AD eastern Baltic provides excellent foundation for future research on eastern Baltic Iron Age wealth deposits.

# References

## Manuscripts


Allik, H. & Markus, E. 1923. *Pilistvere kihelkonna muinasjäänused.* (Manuscript in TÜ AK, Pilistvere parish.)

Asmer, K. 1930. *kiri: V.A. Eesti rahva Muuseumi Juhatus.* (Manuscript in TÜ AK, Avinurme parish.)

EAA 1384.1.12. Планъ имения Кавастъ. 2nd half of the 19th century. (Map in EAA.) Available at: http://www.ra.ee/kaardid/index.php/et/map/search?place=kavastu&v-mode=grid&q=1. (28.09.2013.)

EAA 854.4.120. План мызных земель принадл. имению Кольк, Ревельскаго уезда и Кусальскаго прихода. 1866. a. (Map in EAA.) Available at: http://www.ra.ee/dgs/_display.php?pth=%2Fkaardid%2Feaa0854%2F004%2F0000120&img=eaa0854_004_0000120_00000_k&tpl=zoomify&fns=EAA.854.4.120&hash=63ed8276072033731ac1896548fa1bfd. (11.04.2009.)

Indreko, R. 1930. *Aruanne Avinurme khl. Piilsi kl. leiust 14. aug. 1930.* (Manuscript in TÜ AK, Avinurme parish.)

Jüriado, A. 1928/1929. *Nõo khk-st ajalooline traditsioon.* (Manuscript in TÜ AK, Nõo parish.)

Kangert, N. 2009. *Metallidetektorid ja arheoloogiapärandi kaitse Eestis: arengud ja hetkeseis.* BA thesis. Tartu: University of Tartu. (Manuscript in TÜ AK.)

Karopun, T. 1922. *Vastseliina muinasjäänuste kirjeldus.* (Manuscript in TÜ AK, Vastseliina parish.)

Laid, E. 1924. *Tori kihelkonna muistised.* (Manuscript in TÜ AK, Tori parish.)

Lieven, O. 1893-1894. *4 kirja [30. mai 1893, 14. juuni 1893, 17. juuni 1893, 17. september 1894]: leiud Kunda tsemendivabriku merglikihist ja Kundast talupoeg Christian Ennu talu maalt [1893–1894].* (Manuscript in TÜ AK, Viru-Nigula parish.)

Liiv, N. 1922. *Lüganuse kihelkond Virumaal.* (Manuscript in TÜ AK, Lüganuse parish.)

Lillak, A. 2006. *Maa-alused põletusmatused Lõuna-Eestis.* Bakalaureusetöö. BA thesis. Tartu: University of Tartu. (Manuscript in TÜ AK.)

Mägi, T. & Haljak, G. 2000. *Muinsuskaitse ametile aruanne.* (Manuscript in TÜ AK, Rapla parish.)

Määr 1922. *Viru-Nigula kihelkonna muinasjäänused.* (Manuscript in TÜ AK, Viru-Nigula parish.)

Note (Juu). 13. VI 1923. *Juuru Palukyla Kunilepa tl leiukoht.* Foto. (Manuscript in TÜ AK, Juuru parish.)

Note (MMg). *Teade: 4 kirvest, odaots, vikat (ERM 14431).* (Manuscript in TÜ AK, Maarja-Magdaleena parish.)

Oras, E. 2009. *Eesti keskmise rauaaja peitvarad.* Magistritöö : MA thesis. Lund-Tartu: Tartu Ülikool: University of Tartu. (Manuscript in TÜ AK.)

Orviku, K. 1930. *Mag. K. Orviku Piilsi leiukohast.* (Käsikiri Manuscript in TÜ AK, Avinurme parish.)

Ots, M. 2006. *Merevaiguleiud Baltimaade kivi- ja pronksiaja muististes.* Magistritöö: MA thesis. Tallinn: Tartu Ülikool: University of Tartu. (Manuscript in TÜ AK.)

Parmas, O. 1925. *Kuusalu kihelkond.* (Manuscript in TÜ AK, Kuusalu parish.)

Püss, V. 1932. *Aruanne muinasleidude registreerimisest V.-Nigula khlk. 1932.a. suvel.* (Manuscript in TÜ AK, Viru-Nigula parish.)

Riisiberg, A. 1921. *Nõo kihelkonna arheoloogiline kirjeldus.* (Manuscript in TÜ AK, Nõo parish.)

Schmiedehelm, M. 1933. *Aruanne kaevamistest Kambja khl. Kambja vl. Paali talu kivikalmel 14.VIII-21.VIII 1933 a.* (Manuscript in TÜ AK, Kambja parish.)

Stepiņš, P. 1940. *Izraukumi Īles Cibēnos - 1940.14.-15.VII.* [LVNM AA no. 279.] (Mansucript in LVNM.)

Suik, A. 1923/1924. *Helme kihelkonna kirjeldus.* (Manuscript in TÜ AK, Helme parish.)

Suurväli, E. 1932. *Lüganuse kihelkond.* (Manuscript in TÜ AK, Lüganuse parish.)

Štšogoleva, J. 2009. *Rooma tooteid Baltikumis.* Bakalaureusetöö. BA thesis. Tartu: University of Tartu. (Manuscript in TÜ AK.)

Tiitsmaa, A. 1921a. *Kodavere [kihelkonnakirjeldus].* (Manuscript in TÜ AK, Kodavere parish.)

Tiitsmaa, A. 1921b. *Maarja-Magdaleena [kihelkonnakirjeldus].* (Manuscript in TÜ AK, Maarja-Magdaleena parish.)

Tiitsmaa, A. 1924. *Kõpu [kihelkonnakirjeldus].* (Manuscript in TÜ AK, Kõpu parish.)

Tõnisson, E. 1957. *Inspektsiooniaruanne Reola rabast Tartu lähedal.* (Manuscript in TÜ AK, Kambja parish.)

Ulst, I. 2012. *The Role of Community Archaeology in Heritage Protection: Responsible Metal Detecting as a Tool for Enhancing the Protection of Archaeological Heritage.* MA thesis. Tartu: Tartu Ülikool: University of Tartu. (Manuscript in TÜ AK) Available at: www.arheo.ut.ee/docs/MA12_Ulst.pdf. (07.11.2013.)

Urgart, O. 1922. *Põlva [kihelkonnakirjeldus].* (Manuscript in TÜ AK, Põlva parish.)

Urgart, O. 1925. *Juuru [kihelkonnakirjeldus].* (Manuscript in TÜ AK, Juuru parish.)

Valk, H. 1988. *Inspektsiooniaruanne Helme kihelkonna kirdeosast, Ala ja Liva küladest 25. okt. 1988. a. ning Elmar Maasiku teateid Helme kihelk. muististe kohta.* (Manuscript in TÜ AK, Helme parish.)

Valk, H. 1993. *Inspektsiooniaruanne Äksi kihelkonna edelaosast 05. juunil 1993. a.* (Manuscript in TÜ AK, Äksi parish.)

Vassar, A. 1943. *Nurmsi kivikalme Eestis ja tarandkalmete areng.* [Doktoritöö]: PhD dissertation. Tartu Ülikool: University of Tartu. (Manuscript in UTL.)

Vedru, G. 2007. *Eksperthinnang. Kahala järve ümbruse tähtsus arheoloogiapärandi seisukohalt.* (Manuscript in TÜ AK, Kuusalu parish.)

## Published sources

Adamsen, C., Hansen, U. L., Nielsen, F. O. & Watt, M. (eds) 2009. *Sorte Muld: Wealth, Power and Religion at an Iron Age Central Settlement on Bornholm*. Denmark: Bornholms Museum.

Ailio, J. 1928. Hattelmalan rautakautinen kätkölöytö. *Suomen Museo* 1928, 51–54.

Aitchison, N.B. 1988. Roman wealth, native ritual: coin hoards within and beyond Roman Britain. *World Archaeology* 20(2), 270–284.

Alseikaitė-Gimbutiene, M. 1946. *Die Bestattung in Litauen in der vorgeschichtlichen Zeit*. Tübingen: H. Laupp.

Ames, K.M. 1991. The archaeology of the longue duree: temporal and spatial scale in the evolution of social complexity on the southern Northwest Coast. *Antiquity* 65(249), 935–945.

Andersson, K. 2011. *Guldålder: Svenska arkeologiska skatter*. Uppsala: Balderson Förlag.

Andrén, A. 1991. Guld och makt – en tolkning av de skandinaviska guldbrakteaternas funktion. Gold and power – the function of the Scandinavian gold bracteates. In: *Samfundsorganisation og regional variation: Norden i romersk jernalder og folkevandringstid: Beretning fra 1. nordiske jernaldersymposium på Sandbjerg Slot, 11–15 april 1989 / edited by C. Fabech & J. Ringtved*. Jutland Archaeological Society publications, 27. Højbjerg: Jysk Arkæologisk Selskab, 245–256.

Apals, J., Atgāzis, M., Daiga, J., Deņisova, R., Graudonis, J., Loze, I., Mugurēvičs, Ē., Stubavs, A., Šnore, E., Zagorskis, F. & Zariņa, A. 1974. *Latvijas PSR arheoloģija*. Rīga: Zinātne.

Apals, J., Mugurēvičs, Ē. & Vasks, A. 2001. *Latvijas senākā vēsture 9.g.t. pr. Kr.–1200.g.* Rīga: Latvijas vēstures institūta apgāds.

Appadurai, A. 1986. Introduction: commodities and the politics of value. In: *The Social Life of Things: Commodities in Cultural Perspective / edited by A. Appadurai*. Cambridge: Cambridge University Press, 3–63.

Appadurai, A. (ed.) 1986. *The Social Life of Things: Commodities in Cultural Perspective*. Cambridge: Cambridge University Press.

Arne, T.J. 1906. Det stora guldfyndet från Sköfde. *Fornvännen* 1906, 92–95.

Arnold, T.M. 1980. Wealth and social structure: A matter of life and death. In: *Anglo-Saxon Cemeteries 1979. The Fourth Anglo-Saxon Symposium at Oxford / edited by P. Rahtz, Tania Dickinson & Lorna Watts*. BAR British series, 82. Oxford: B.A.R., 81–142.

Arrhenius, B. 1995. Women and gold. On the role of women in society at the time of the Great Migrations and their relationship to the production and distribution of ornaments. In: *Produksjon og samfunn om erverv, spesialisering og bosetning i Norden i 1. årtusen e.Kr.: Beretning fra 2. nordiske jernaldersymposium på Granavolden Gjæstgiveri 7.–10. mai 1992 / edited by H.G. Resi*. Oslo: Universitetets Oldsaksamling, 85–96.

Asaris, J., Muižnieks, V., Radiņš, A., Virse, I. & Žeiere, I. 2008. *Kurši senatnē. Couronians in Antiquity*. Rīga: Latvijas Nacionālais Vēstures muzejs.

Atgāzis, M. 2000. Tērvetes senvietas, to pētniecības gaitu sākums un daži senvietu hronoloģijas jautājumi. *Arheoloģija un Etnogrāfija* 20, 18–31.

Atgāzis, M. 2006. Sēlpils Spietiņu apmetne un tās laiks. In: *Pētījumi Sēļu senatnē: Rakstu krājums / edited by I. Melne.* Latvijas nacionālā vēstures muzeja raksti, 11. Arheologija. Rīga: Latvijas nacionālais vēstures muzejs, 11–28.

Aun, M. 1992. = Аун, М. 1992. *Археологические памятники второй половины 1-го тысячелетия н.э. в Юго-Восточной Эстонии.* Tallinn: *Олион.*

Axboe, M. 2001. Amulet pendants and a darkened sun. On the function of the gold bracteates and a possible motivation for the large gold hoards. In: *Roman Gold and the Development of the Early Germanic Kingdoms: Aspects of Technical, Socio-Political, Socio-Economic, Artistic and Intellectual Development, A.D. 1–550 : Symposium in Stockholm, 14–16 November 1997 / edited by B. Magnus.* Konferenser. Kungl. Vitterhets, historie och antikvitets akademien, 51. Stockholm: Almqvist & Wiksell, 119–136.

Bailey, G.N. 1983. Concepts of time in Quaternary prehistory. *Annual Review of Anthropology* 12, 165–192.

Bailey, G.N. 2005. Concepts of time. In: *Archaeology: The Key Concepts / edited by C. Renfrew & P. Bahn.* London: Routledge, 268–273.

Bailey, G. 2007. Time perspectives, palimpsests and the archaeology of time. *Journal of Anthropological Archaeology* 26(2), 198–223.

Baillie, M.G.L. 1994. Dendrochronology raises questions about the nature of the AD 536 dust-veil event. *Holocene* 4(2), 212–217.

Balode, U., Ciglis, J., & Žeiere, I. 2005. *Sēļi un Sēlija.* Rīga: Latvijas Nacionālais vēstures muzejs.

Balodis, F. A. & Tentelis, A. (eds) 1938. *Latviešu vesture.* Riga: Valtera un Rapas.

Banytė-Rowell, R. 2001. Vakarų Lietuvos kapinynų laidosenos ypatumai vėlyvuoju romėniškuoju laikotarpiu. *Archeologia Lituana* 2001(2), 29–47.

Banytė-Rowell, R. 2003. *Zemgaļi senatnē.* Rīga: Latvijas vēstures muzejs.

Banytė-Rowell, R. 2004. The transition of ideas and Northern Lithuania in the Roman Period. In: *Pētījumi Zemgaļu senatnē: Rakstu krājums / edited by R. Ritums.* Latvijas Vēstures Muzeja raksti, 10. Rīga: Latvijas Vēstures Muzejs, 11–24.

Banytė-Rowell, R. 2006. Looking for the watershed between the Middle- and Late Iron Ages in Lithuanian archaeology. In: *Transformatio Mundi: The Transition from the Late Migration Period to the Early Viking Age in the East Baltic / edited by M. Bertasius.* Kaunas: Kaunas University of Technology Department of Philosophy and Cultural Science, 25–39.

Banytė-Rowell, R., Baronas, D., Kazakevičius, V., Vaškevičiūtė, I. & Zabiela, G. 2007. *Lietuvos istorija. II Tomas. Geležies amžius / edited by G. Zabiela.* Vilnius: Baltos Lankos.

Barrett, J.C. 1988. Fields of discourse: reconstituting a social archaeology. *Critique of Anthropology* 7(3), 5–16.

Barrett, J.C. 1994. *Fragments from Antiquity: An Archaeology of Social Life in Britain, 2900–1200 BC.* Social archaeology. Oxford: Blackwell.

Barrett, J.C. 2000. A thesis in agency. In: *Agency in Archaeology / edited by M.-A. Dobres & J.E. Robb.* London: Routledge, 61–68.

Barrett, J.C. 2001. Agency, the duality of structure, and the problem of the archaeological record. In: *Archaeological Theory Today / edited by I. Hodder.* Cambridge: Polity, 141–164.

Baxter, M.J. 1994. *Exploratory Multivariate Analysis in Archaeology.* Edinburgh: Edinburgh University Press.

Baxter, M.J. 2003. *Statistics in Archaeology.* Arnold applications of statistics series. London: Arnold.

Beck, R.A.J., Bolender, D.J., Brown, J.A. & Earle, T.K. 2007. Eventful archaeology: The place of space in structural transformation [with comments]. *Current Anthropology* 48(6), 833–860.

Becker, C.J. 1971. Mosepotter fra Danmarks jernalder: Problemer omkring mosefunde lerkar og deres tolkning. *Arbøger for Nordisk Old Kyndighed og Historie* 1971, 5–60.

Behr, C. 2010. New Bracteate Finds from Early Anglo-Saxon England. *Medieval Archaeology* 54(1), 34–88.

Bemmann, G. & Bemmann, J. 1998. *Der Opferplatz von Nydam: Die Funde aus den älteren Grabungen, Nydam-I und Nydam-II.* Schriften des Archäologischen Landesmuseums, 4. Neumünster: Wachholtz.

Bennike, P. 1999. The Early Neolithic Danish bog finds: A strange group of people! In: *Bog Bodies, Sacred Sites and Wetland Archaeology: Proceedings of a Conference Held by WARP and the National Museum of Denmark, in Conjunction with Silkeborg Museum, Jutland, September 1996 / edited by B. Coles, J. Coles & M. S. Jørgensen.* WARP occasional paper, 12. Exeter: Wetland Archaeology Research Project (WARP), 27–32.

Berggren, Å. 2010. *Med kärret som källa. Om begreppen offer och ritual inom arkeologin.* Vägar till Midgård, 13. Lund: Nordic Academic Press.

Berggren, A. & Stutz, L.N. 2010. From spectator to critic and participant: A new role for archaeology in ritual studies. *Journal of Social Archaeology* 10(2), 171–197.

Bintliff, J.L. 1991. The contribution of an Annaliste / Structural histroy approach to archaeology. In: *The Annales School and Archaeology / edited by J.L. Bintliff.* Leicester: Leicester University Press, 1–33.

Bintliff, J.L. (ed.) 1991. *The Annales School and Archaeology.* Leicester: Leicester University Press.

Bintliff, J. 2004. Time, strucure, and agency: The Annales, emergent complexity, and archaeology. In: *A Companion to Archaeology / edited by J.L. Bintliff.* Blackwell companion to archaeology. Oxford: Blackwell, 174–194.

Bitner-Wroblewska, A. 2001. *From Samland to Rogaland: East-West Connections in the Baltic Basin during the Early Migration Period.* Warszawa: Panstwowe Muzeum Archeologiczne, Stowarzyszenie Naukowe Archeologow Polskich, Oddzial w Warszawe.

Bitner-Wróblewska, A. (ed.) 2007. *Skarby starożytnej Łotwy.* Warszawa: Państwowe Muzeum Archeologiczne. Stowarzyszenie Naukowe Archeologów Polskich, Oddział w Warszawie.

Bitner-Wróblewska, A. 2010. North-eastern Poland in the first centuries AD - A world apart. In: *Worlds apart?: Contacts Across the Baltic Sea in the Iron Age : Network Denmark-Poland, 2005–2008 / edited by U. Lund Hansen & A. Bitner-Wróblewska.* København: Det Kongelige Nordiske Oldkriftselskab, 141–184.

Bliujienė, A. 1998. Investigations at the Užpelkiai cemetery. *Archaeologia Baltica* 3, 277–290.

Bliujienė, A. 1999. *Vikingu epochos kuršiu papuošalu ornamentika.* Vilnius: Diemedžio.

Bliujienė, A. 2006. Role of Cuornians in the eastern Baltic area: The transition process from the Late Migration Period into the Early Viking Age. In: *Transformatio Mundi: The Transition from the Late Migration Period to the Early Viking Age in the East Baltic / edited by M. Bertasius*. Kaunas: Kaunas University of Technology Department of Philosophy and Cultural Science, 183–193.

Bliujienė, A. 2007. *Lietuvos priešistorės gintaras*. Vilnius: Versus Aureus.

Bliujienė, A. 2008. Trade, warfare, looting and hoarding: Attributes of Viking Age contacts across the Baltic Sea. In: *Pētījumi Kuršu senatnē: Rakstu krājums / edited by V.Muižnieks*. Latvijas nacionālā vēstures muzeja raksti. Arheoloģija, 14. Rīga: Latvijas Nacionālais Vēstures muzejs, 167–179.

Bliujienė, A. 2010. The bog offerings of the Balts: 'I give in order to get back'. *Archaeologia Baltica* 14, 136–165.

Bliujienė, A. 2011. *Northern Gold: Amber in Lithuania (c. 100 to c. 1200)*. East Central and Eastern Europe in the Middle Ages, 450–1450, 18. Leiden: Brill.

Bliujienė, A. & Curta, F. 2011. Exotic lands, quixotic friends: Eastern Lithuania and the Carpathian Basin in Late Antiquity and the Early Middle Ages (AD c 380 to c 620). *Medieval Archaeology* 55, 28–64.

Bourdieu, P. 1977. *Outline of a Theory of Practice*. Cambridge: Cambridge University Press.

Bourdieu, P. 1990. *The Logic of Practice*. Cambridge: Polity.

Bradley, R. 1980. Anglo-Saxon cemeteries: Some suggestionsfor research. In: *Anglo-Saxon Cemeteries 1979. The Fourth Anglo-Saxon Symposium at Oxford / edited by P. Rahtz, T. Dickinson & L. Watts*. BAR British series, 82. Oxford: B.A.R., 171–176.

Bradley, R. 1982. The destruction of wealth in later prehistory. *Man* 17(1), 108–122.

Bradley, R. 1987. Stages in the chronological development of hoards and votive deposits. *Proceedings of the Prehistoric Society* 53, 351–362.

Bradley, R. 1988. Hoarding, recycling and the consumption of prehistoric metalwork: Technological change in western Europe. *World Archaeology* 20(2), 249–260.

Bradley, R. 1990. *The Passage of Arms: An Archaeological Analysis of Prehistoric Hoards and Votive Deposits*. Cambridge: Cambridge University Press.

Bradley, R. 1991. Ritual, time and history. *World Archaeology* 23(2), 209–219.

Bradley, R. 1998. *The Significance of Monuments: On the Shaping of Human Experience in Neolithic and Bronze Age Europe*. London: Routledge.

Bradley, R. 2002. *The Past in Prehistoric Societies*. London: Routledge.

Bradley, R. 2003. A life less ordinary: The ritualization of the domestic sphere in later prehistoric Europe. *Cambridge Archaeological Journal*, 13(1), 5–23.

Bradley, R. 2005. *Ritual and Domestic Life in Prehistoric Europe*. London: Routledge.

Braudel, F. 1992. *The Mediterranean and the Mediterranean world in the age of Philip II*. London: HarperCollins.

Brīvkalne, E. 2009. *Mežotnes pilskalna depozīts*. Rīga: Nordic.

Brodie, N., Doole, J. & Renfrew. C. (eds) 2001. *Trade in Illicit Antiquities: The Destruction of the World's Archaeological Heritage*. McDonald Institute monographs. Cambridge: McDonald Institute for Archaeological Research.

Brodie, N. & Tubb, K.W. (ed.) 2002. *Illicit Antiquities: The Theft of Culture and the Extinction of Archaeology*. One world archaeology, 42. London: Routledge.

Brück, J. 1999. Ritual and rationality: Some problems of interpretation in European archaeology. *European Journal of Archaeology* 2(3), 313–344.

Brudenell, M. & Cooper, A.J. 2008. Post-middenism: Depositional histories on later Bronze Age settlements at Broom, Bedfordshire. *Oxford Journal of Archaeology* 27(1), 15–36.

Budd, P. & Taylor, T. 1995. The faerie smith meets the bronze industry: Magic versus science in the interpretation of prehistoric metal-making. *World Archaeology* 27(1), 133–143.

Bulliet, R.W. 1992. Annales and archaeology. In: *Archaeology, Annales, and Ethnohistory / edited by A.B. Knapp*. Cambridge: Cambridge University Press, 131–134.

Burenhult, G. 1991. *Arkeologi i Sverige. 3, Samhällsbyggare och handelsmän*. Höganäs: Wiken.

Bursche, A. 1992. Roman coinage in the Westbalt circle. *Barbaricum* 2, 231–244.

Bursche, A. 2002. Roman coins in Scandinavia. Some remarks from the Continental perspective. In: *Drik - og du vil leve skønt: Festskrift til Ulla Lund Hansen på 60-årsdagen 18. august 2002 / edited by J. Pind, A. Nørgård Jørgensen, L. Jørgensen, B. Storgaard, P.O. Rindel & J. Ilkjær*. Copenhagen: National Museum of Denmark, 69–78.

Campbell, S. & Thomas, S. (eds) 2013. *Internet Archaeology. Special issue: Portable Antiquities: Archaeology, Collecting, Metal Detecting*. York: Internet Archaeology.

Carlie, A. 1998. Käringsjön. A fertility sacrificial site from the Late Roman Iron Age in South-West Sweden. *Current Swedish Archaeology* 6(1998), 17–37.

Carnap-Bornheim, C. von & Ilkjær, J. 1996. *Illerup Ådal. 5. Die Practausrüstungen. Textband*. Jutland Archaeological Society publications, 25: 5. Højbjerg: Jysk arkæologisk selskab.

Carnap-Bornheim, C. von, Hilberg, V., Radiņš, A. & Schopper , F. 2008. *Lettlands viele Völker: Archäologie der Eisenzeit von Christi Geburt bis zum Jahr 1200. Katalog zum Ausstellung im Archäologischen Landesmuseum im Paulikloster, Brandenburg 12. Dezember 2008 bis 19. April 2009, Archäologischen Landesmuseum, Stiftung Schleswig-Holsteinische Landesmuseen Schloss Gottorf, Schleswig 9. Mai 2009 bis 23. August 2009*. 1st ed. Brandenburg: Brandenburgisches Landesamt für Denkmalpflege und Archäologisches Landesmuseum.

Chadwick, A.M. 2012. Routine magic, mundane ritual: Towards a unified notion of depositional practice. *Oxford Journal of Archaeology* 31(3), 283–315.

Chapman, J. 2000. *Fragmentation in Archaeology: People, Places and Broken Objects in the Prehistory of South-Eastern Europe*. London: Routledge.

Christensen, A.E. 2005a. The Roman Iron Age tools from Vimose, Denmark. *Acta Archaeologica* 76(2), 59–86.

Christensen, T. 2005b. En folkekonges død. Et forslag til tolkningen af jernalderens våbenofferfund. *ROMU* 2005, 29–68.

Ciglis, J. 2001. Some notes on the chronology of Latgallian and Selonian artefacts in the Middle Iron Age. *Archaeologia Lituana* 2, 48–64.

Ciglis, J. 2006. Sēlu etnoģenēze austrumbaltijas etnokultūrvēsturisko procesu kontekstā. In: *Pētījumi Sēļu senatnē: Rakstu krājums / edited by I. Melne*. Latvijas nacionālā vēstures muzeja raksti, 11. Arheologija. Rīga: Latvijas nacionālais vēstures muzejs, 29–40.

Ciołek, R. 2010. Goldene Müntzen des 4.-5. Jahrhunderts in den südlichen Ostseegebieten. In: *Worlds apart?: Contacts Across the Baltic Sea in the Iron Age: Network Denmark-Poland, 2005–2008 / edited by U. Lund Hansen & A. Bitner-Wróblewska*. København: Det Kongelige Nordiske Oldkriftselskab, 377–388.

Čivilytė, A. 2004. Pagaminti tam, kad panaudotum? Keletas nežinomos bronzinės liejimo formos (Doviliai, Klaipėdos r.) reikšmių. *Lietuvos archeologija* 25, 221–232.

Čivilytė, A. 2007. Archeologija tarp legendos ir tikrovės – grįžtant prie Šernų statulėlės (Klaipėdos r.) problemos. *Lietuvos Archeologija* 31, 91–108.

Čivilytė, A. 2009. *Wahl der Waffen. Studien zur Deutung der bronzezeitlichen Waffendeponierungen im nördlichen Mitteleuropa*. Universitätsforschungen zur prähistorischen Archäologie, 167. Bonn: R. Habelt.

Clarke, S. 1997. Abandonment, rubbish disposal and 'special' deposits at Newstead. In: *TRAC 96 : proceedings of the Sixth Annual Theoretical Roman Archaeology Conference, Hosted by the Research School of Archaeology and Archaeological Science, The University of Sheffield, March 30th and 31st 1996 / edited by K. Meadows, C. Lemke & J. Heron*. Oxford: Oxbow, 73–81.

Clayton, S.C., Driver, W.D. & Kosakowsky, L.J. 2005. Rubbish or ritual? Contextualizing a Terminal Classic problematical deposit at Blue Creek, Belize: A response to 'Public Architecture, Ritual, and Temporal Dynamics at the Maya Center of Blue Creek, Belize' by Thomas H. Guderjan. *Ancient Mesoamerica* 16(1), 119–130.

Cofta-Broniewska, A. 1993. Miejsca praktyk kultowych ludności grupy kruszańskiej kultury przeworskiej. In: *Wierzenia przedchrześcijańskie na ziemiach polskich / edited by M. Kwapiński & H. Paner*. Gdańsk: Muzeum Archeologiczne w Gdańsku, 77–87.

Conkey, M.W. & Gero, J.M. (eds) 1991. *Engendering Archaeology: Women and Prehistory.* Social archaeology. Oxford: Blackwell.

Cookson, N. 1992. Treasure Trove: dumb enchantment or new law? *Antiquity*, 66(251), 399–405.

Cornell, P. & Fahlander, F. 2002. Microarchaeology, materiality and social practice. *Current Swedish Archaeology* 10, 21–38.

Crumlin-Pedersen, O. & Trakadas, A. (eds) 2003. *Hjortspring: A pre-Roman Iron-Age Warship in Context.* Roskilde: Viking Ship Museum.

Cunliffe, B. 1992. Pits, preconceptions and propitiation in the British Iron Age. *Oxford Journal of Archaeology* 11(1), 69–83.

Daiga, J. 1964. Dzelz ieguves krāsnis Sēlpils Spietiņu apmetnē. *Arheoloģija un Etnogrāfija* 6, 23–37.

Davenport, W.H. 1986. Two kinds of value in the Eastern Solomon Islands. In: *The Social Life of Things: Commodities in Cultural Perspective / edited by A. Appadurai.* Cambridge: Cambridge University Press, 95–109.

Deemant, K. 1978. Über die Ausgrabungen des Steingräberfeldes von Proosa. *Eesti NSV Teaduste Akadeemia toimetised. Ühiskonnateadused* 27(1), 81–83.

DeMarrais, E., Castillo, L.J. & Earle, T.K. 1996. Ideology, materialization, and power strategies. *Current Anthropology* 37(1), 15–31.

DeMarrais, E., Gosden, C. & Renfrew, C. (eds) 2004. *Rethinking Materiality : The Engagement of Mind with the Material World.* McDonald Institute monographs. Cambridge: McDonald Institute for Archaeological Research.

Dobat, A.S. 2008. *Werkzeuge aus kaiserzeitlichen Heeresausrüstungsopfern: Mit besonderer Berücksichtigung der Fundplätze Illerup Ådal und Vimose.* Jernalderen i Nordeuropa, Jysk Arkæologisk Selskabs Skrifter, 61. Moesgård, Aarhus: Jysk Arkæologisk Selskab.

Dobat, A.S. 2013. Between rescue and research: An evaluation after 30 years of liberal metal detecting in archaeological research and heritage practice in Denmark. *European Journal of Archaeology* 16(4), 704–725.

Dobres, M.-A. & Robb, J.E. 2000. Agency in archaeology: paradigm or platitude? In: *Agency in Archaeology / edited by M.-A. Dobres & J.E. Robb.* London: Routledge, 3–17.

Dobres, M.-A. & Robb, J.E. 2005. 'Doing' agency: Introductory remarks on methodology. *Journal of Archaeological Method and Theory* 12(3), 159–166.

Dornan, J.L. 2002. Agency and archaeology: Past, present, and future directions. *Journal of Archaeological Method and Theory* 9(4), 303–329.

Drennan, R.D. 1996. *Statistics for Archaeologists: A Common Sense Approach.* Interdisciplinary contributions to archaeology. New York; London: Plenum.

Ducmane, K. & Ozoliņa, A. 2009. *Latvija Eiropā: Monētu depozīti 1.–20. gadsimtā.* Rīga: Latvijas Nacionālais Vēstures muzejs.

Ebert, M. 1913. Die baltischen Provinzen Kurland, Livland, Estland. *Praehistorische Zeitschrift* V, 498–559.

Engel, C. 1914. *I. Führer durch die vorgeschichtliche Sammlung des Dommuseums.* Riga: Dommmuseum der Gesellschaft für Geschichte und Alterdumskunde der Ostseeprovinzen Russlands.

Engel, C. 1931. *Einführung in die vorgeschichtliche Kultur des Memellandes.* Memel: Verl. Siebert Memeler Dampfboot AG.

Engel, C. 1933. *II. Führer durch die vorgeschichtliche Sammlung des Dommuseums.* Riga: Dommmuseum der Gesellschaft für Geschichte und Alterdumskunde zu Riga.

Engelhardt, C. 1863. *Thorsbjerg mosefund: Beskrivelse af de oldsager som i aarene 1858–61 ere udgravede af Thorsbjerg mose ved Sønder-Brarup i Angel; et samlet fund, henhørende til den aeldre jernalder og bevart i den kongelige samling af nordiske oldsager i Flensborg.* Kjöbenhavn: I commission hos G. E. C. GAD.

Engelhardt, C. 1866. *Denmark in the Early Iron Age: Illustrated by Recent Discoveries in the Peat Mosses of Slesvig.* London: Williams and Norgate.

Engelhardt, C. 1867. *Kragehul mosefund. 1751–1865: Et overgangsfund mellem den ældre jernalder og mellem-jernalderen.* Kjøbenhavn: Pladerne trykte af G. Klingsey, texten i thieles bogtrykkeri, i Commission hos G.E.C. Gad.

Engelhardt, C. 1869. *Vimose fundet.* Kjøbenhavn: Pladerne trykte af G. Klingsey, texten i thieles bogtrykkeri, i Commission hos G.E.C. Gad.

Fabech, C. 1990. Sjörup - an old problem in a new light. *Meddelanden från Lunds Universitets Historiska Museum* 1989-1990, 101–119.

Fabech, C. 1991a. Booty sacrifices in Southern Scandinavia. A reassessment. In: *Sacred and Profane: Proceedings of a Conference on Archaeology, Ritual and Religion: Oxford 1989 / edited by P.Garwood, D. Jennings, R.Skeates & J. Toms.* Monograph, Oxford University Committee for Archaeology, 32. Oxford: Oxford University Committee for Archaeology, 88–99.

Fabech, C. 1991b. Samfundsorganisation, religiøse ceremonier og regional variation. In: *Samfundsorganisation og regional variation: Norden i romersk jernalder og folkevandringstid : beretning fra 1. Nordiske jernaldersymposium på Sandbjerg slot 11–15 april 1989 / edited by C. Fabech & J.Ringtved.* Jutland Archaeological Society publications, 27. Højbjerg: Jysk arkæologisk selskab, 203–212.

Fabech, C. 1994a. Reading society from the cultural landscape: South Scandinavia between sacral and political power. In: *The Archaeology of Gudme and Lundeborg: Papers Presented at a Conference at Svendborg, October 1991 / edited by P.O. Nielsen, K. Randsborg & H. Thrane.* Arkæologiske studier, 10. Copenhagen: Akademisk forlag, Universitetsforlaget i København, 169–183.

Fabech, C. 1994b. Society and landscape. From collective manifestations to ceremonies of the new ruling class. In: *Iconologia sacra : Mythos, Bildkunst und Dichtung in der Religions- und Sozialgeschichte Alteuropas: Festschrift für Karl Hauck zum 75. Geburtstag / edited by H. Keller & N. Staubach.* Arbeiten zur Frühmittelalterforschung, 23. Berlin: de Gruyter, 132–143.

Fabech, C. 1999a. Centrality in sites and landscapes. In: *Settlement and Landscape: Proceedings of a Conference in Århus, Denmark, May 4–7 1998 / edited by C. Fabech & J. Ringtved.* Højbjerg: Jutland Archaeological Society, 455–473.

Fabech, C. 1999b. Organising the Landscape: A matter of production, power and religion. In: *The Making of Kingdoms: Papers from the 47th Sachsensymposium, York, September 1996 / edited by T.Dickinson & D. Griffiths.* Anglo-Saxon studies in archaeology and history, 10. Oxford: Oxford University Committee for Archaeology, 37–47.

Fabech, C. 2001. The spatial distribution of gold hoards in Southern Scandinavia and the geography of power. In: *Roman Gold and the Development of the Early Germanic Kingdoms: Aspects of Technical, Socio-Political, Socio-Economic, Artistic and Intellectual Development, A.D. 1–550 : Symposium in Stockholm, 14–16 November 1997 / edited by B. Magnus.* Konferenser, Kungl. Vitterhets, historie och antikvitets akademien, 51. Stockholm: Almqvist & Wiksell, 189–204.

Fahlander, F. 2003. *The Materiality of Serial Practice: A Microarchaeology of Burial.* Gotarc, 23. Göteborg: Department of Archaeology, Göteborg University.

Ferdinand, J. & Ferdinand, K. 1962. Jernalderofferfund i Valmose ved Rislev. *Kuml: Årbog for Jysk Arkæologisk Selskab* 1961, 47–90.

Fitzpatrick, B.W. 1984. The deposition of La Tène Iron Age metalwork in watery contexts in Southern England. In: *Aspects of the Iron Age in Central Southern Britain / edited by B. Cunliffe & D.Miles.* Monograph, Oxford University Committee for Archaeology, 2. Oxford: Published by the Oxford University Committee for Archaeology, Institute of Archaeology, 178–190.

Flannery, K.V. 1999. Process and agency in early state formation. *Cambridge Archaeological Journal* 9(1), 3–21.

Fletcher, R. 2004. Materiality, space, time, and outcome. In: *A Companion to Archaeology / edited by J.L. Bintliff.* Blackwell companion to archaeology. Oxford: Blackwell, 110–140.

Fontijn, D.R. 2002. *Sacrificial Landscapes: Cultural Biographies of Persons, Objects and Natural Places in the Bronze Age of the Southern Netherlands, c.2300–600 BC 2001.* Analecta Praehistorica Leidensia, 33/34. Leiden: Faculty of Archaeology, University of Leiden.

Fontijn, D.R. 2008. Traders "hoards". Reviewing the relationship between trade and permanent deposition: the case of the Dutch Voorhout hoard. In: *Hoards from the Neolithic to the Metal Ages: Technical and Codified Practices: Session of the XIth Annual Meeting of the European Association of Archaeologists / edited by C. Hamon & B. Quilliec.* BAR international series, 1758. Oxford: Archaeopress, 5–17.

Fuglevik, L.M. 2007. Krigsbytteofringen Illerup A - En alternativ tolkningsramme. *Fornvännen* 102, 225–237.

Gaimster, D. 2004. Measures against the illicit trade in cultural objects: The emerging strategy in Britain. *Antiquity* 78(301), 699–707.

Gaimster, M. 2001. Gold bracteates and necklaces. Political ideas in the sixth century. In: *Roman Gold and the Development of the Early Germanic Kingdoms: Aspects of Technical, Socio-Political, Socio-Economic, Artistic and Intellectual Development, A.D. 1–550 : Symposium in Stockholm, 14–16 November 1997 / edited by B. Magnus.* Konferenser, Kungl. Vitterhets, historie och antikvitets akademien, 51. Stockholm: Almqvist & Wiksell, 143–156.

Gansum, T. 2004. Role the bones – From iron to steel. *Norwegian Archaeological Review* 37(1), 41–57.

Gardner, A. 2002. Social identity and the duality of structure in late Roman-period Britain. *Journal of Social Archaeology* 2(3), 323–351.

Gardner, A. (ed.) 2004. *Agency Uncovered: Archaeological Perspectives on Social Agency, Power, and Being Human.* London: UCL Press.

Garfinkel, Y. 1994. Ritual burial of cultic objects: The earliest evidence. *Cambridge Archaeological Journal* 4(2), 159–188.

Garrow, D. 2012. Odd deposits and average practice. A critical history of the concept of structured deposition. *Archaeological Dialogues*, 19(2), 85–115.

Geary, P. 1986. Sacred commodities: the circulation of medieval relics. In: *The Social Life of Things : Commodities in Cultural Perspective / edited by A. Appadurai.* Cambridge: Cambridge University Press, 169–194.

Gebühr, M. 2000. *Nydam und Thorsberg. Opferplätze der Eisenzeit.* Schleswig: Verein zur Förderung des Archäologischen Landesmuseums.

Geißlinger, H. 1984. Depotfund. Hortfund. In: *Reallexikon der germanischen Altertumskunde / esitor in chief J. Hoops.* Vol. 5. Berlin: de Gruyter, 320–338.

Gell, A. 1998. *Art and Agency: An Anthropological Theory.* Oxford: Clarendon.

Giddens, A. 1979. *Central Problems in Social Theory: Action, Structure and Contradiction in Social Analysis.* London: Macmillan.

Giddens, A. 1999 [1984]. *The Constitution of Society: Outline of the Theory of Structuration.* Cambridge: Polity Press.

Glob, P.V. 1969. *The Bog People: Iron-Age Man Preserved.* London: Faber.

Godłowski, K. 1980. Zur Frage der Völkerwanderungszeitliche Besiedlung in Pommern. In: *Studien zur Sachsenforschung, 2 / edited by H.-J. Hassler.* Hildesheim, 63–102.

Gosden, C. 1994. *Social Being and Time.* Social archaeology. Oxford: Blackwell.

Gosden, C. & Lock, G. 1998. Prehistoric histories. *World Archaeology* 30(1), 2–12.

Gosden, C. & Marshall, Y. 1999. The cultural biography of objects. *World Archaeology* 31(2), 169–178.

Grant, A. 1984. Animal husbandry. In: *Danebury : An Iron Age Hillfort in Hampshire. by Barry Cunliffe with contributions from Lisa Brown [et al.]. Vol 2, The Excavations, 1969–1978: The Finds.* Research report, Council for British Archaeology, 52. London: Council for British Archaeology, 496–548.

Gräslund, B. & Price, N. 2012. Twilight of the gods? The 'dust veil event' of AD 536 in critical perspective. *Antiquity* 86(332), 428–443.

Graudonis, J. 1964. Mūkukalna depozīti. *Arheoloģija un Etnogrāfija* 6, 75–84.

Graudonis, J. 1978. Apdzīvotība un celtniecība Mūkukalna. *Arheoloģija un Etnogrāfija* 12, 24–52.

Grewingk, C. 1887. Archäologische Ausflüge in Liv- und Estland. *Sitzungsberichte der Gelehrten Estnischen Gesellschaft* 1886, 153–171.

Griciuvienė, E. 2005. *Žiemgaliai: Baltų archeologijos paroda : Katalogas = The Semigallians : Baltic Archaeological Exibition: Catalogue.* Vilnius: Lietuvos nacionalinis muziejus.

Griciuvienė, E. 2007. *Sėliai: Baltų archeologijos paroda: Katalogas = The Selonians: Baltic Archaeological Exhibition: Catalogue.* Vilnius: Lietuvos nacionalinis muziejus.

Griciuvienė, E. 2009. *Kuršiai: Genties kultūra laidosenos duomenimis: Baltų archeologijos paroda : Katalogas = The Curonians: Tribe Culture According to the Burial Data: Catalogue.* Vilnius: Lietuvos nacionalinis muziejus.

Grigalavičienė, E. 1980. = *Григалавичене*, E. 1980. *Древнейшие Металлические Изделия В Литве: (II-I Тысячелетия До Н.э.). Вильнюс: Мокслас.*

Grigalavičienė, E. 1992a. Joudonių piliakalnis ir gyvenvietė (Rokiškio raj.). *Lietuvos Archeologija* 9, 41–91.

Grigalavičienė, E. 1992b. Kerelių piliakalnis. *Lietuvos Archeologija* 8, 85–103.

Grinsell, L.V. 1967. Barrow treasure, in fact, tradition, and legislation. *Folklore* 78(1), 1–38.

Gullman, J. 1995. Sveriges största guldskatt i ny belysning - Timboholmsskatten undersökt med modern teknik. *Fornvännen* 90, 213–220.

Hackman, A. 1905. *Die altere Eisenzeit in Finnland. I: Die Funde aus den fünf ersten Jahrhunderten n. Chr.* Helsingfors: F. Tilgmanns Buch- und Steindruckerei.

Hagberg, U.E. 1964. Järnålderns offerfynd ur svenskt perspektiv. *Tor* 10, 222–239.

Hagberg, U.E. 1967. *The Archaeology of Skedemosse [in collaboration with Margareta Beskow; with geological and zoological contributions by Lars-König Königsson and Johannes Lepiksaar]. [Vol.] 1. The Excavation and the Finds of an Öland fen, Sweden. [Vol.] 2. The Votive Deposits in the Skademosse Fen and their Relation To the Iron-age Settlements on Öland, Sweden.* Stockholm: Almqvist & Wiksell.

Hagberg, U.E. 1984. Opferhorte der Kaiser- und Völkerwanderungzeit in Schweden. *Frühmittelalterliche Studien* 18(1984), 73–82.

Hamerow, H. 2006. "Special deposits" in Anglo-Saxon settlements. *Medieval Archaeology* 50, 1–30.

Hammer, Ø., Harper, D.A.T. & Ryan, P.D. 2001. PAST: Paleontological statistics software package for education and data analysis. *Palaeontologia Electronica* 4(1), 9. Available at http://palaeo-electronica.org/2001_1/past/issue1_01.htm (07.11.2013.)

Hammond, G.N. 1982. Treasure trove: Ancient law to preserve archaeological relics. *Antiquity* 56(216), 58–60.

Hamon, C. & Quilliec, B. 2008. Hoards from the Neolithic to the Metal Ages: Technical and codified practices-Introduction. In: *Hoards from the Neolithic to the Metal Ages: Technical and Codified Practices: Session of the XIth Annual Meeting of the European Association of Archaeologists / edited by C. Hamon & B. Quilliec.* BAR international series, 1758. Oxford: Archaeopress, 1–4.

Hansen, J. 2006. Offertradition og religion i ældre jernalder i Sydskandinavien: med særlig henblik på bebyggelsesofringer. *Kuml : Årbog for Jysk Arkæologisk Selskab* 2006, 117–175.

Harck, O. 1984. Gefäßopfer der Eisenzeit im nördlichen Mitteleuropa. *Frühmittelalterliche Studien* 18(1984), 102–121.

Hårdh, B. 1996. *Silver in the Viking Age : A Regional-Economic Study.* Acta archaeologica Lundensia. Series in 8°, 45. Stockholm: Almquist & Wiksell International.

Hårdh, B. (ed.) 2003. *Fler fynd i centrum : materialstudier i och kring Uppåkra.* Acta archaeologica Lundensia. Series in 8°, 45. Uppåkrastudier, 9. Lund: Arkeologiska institutionen.

Hårdh, B. & Larsson, L. (eds) 2002. *Central Places in the Migration and Merovingian Periods: Papers from the 52nd Sachsensymposium, Lund, August 2001.* Uppåkrastudier, 6. Stockholm: Almqvist & Wiksell.

Harding, J. 2005. Rethinking the great divide: Long-term structural history and the temporality of event. *Norwegian Archaeological Review* 38(2), 88–101.

Harding, J. 2006. 'Rethinking the great divide': A reply to Thomas, Olivier and Murray. *Norwegian Archaeological Review* 39(1), 93–96.

Härke, H. 1990. 'Warrior graves'? The background of the Anglo-Saxon weapon burial rite. *Past & Present* 126, 22–43.

Härke, H. 2000. The circulation of weapons in Anglo-Saxon society. In: *Rituals of Power : From Late Antiquity to the Early Middle Ages / edited by F. Theuws & J.L. Nelson.* The transformation of the Roman world, 8. Leiden: Brill, 377–399.

Harris, M. 1976. History and Significance of the EMIC/ETIC Distinction. *Annual Review of Anthropology* 5(1), 329–350.

Haselgrove, C. 1982. Wealth, prestige and power: The dynamics of Late Iron Age political centralisation in south-east England. In: *Ranking, Resource and Exchange: Aspects of the Archaeology of Early European Society / edited by C. Renfrew & S. Shennan.* Cambridge: Cambridge University Press, 79–88.

Haselgrove, C. & Wigg-Wolf, D. 2005. Introduction: Iron Age coinage and ritual practices. In: *Iron Age Coinage and Ritual Practices / edited by C. Haselgrove & D. Wigg-Wolf.* Studien zu Fundmünzen der Antike, 20. Mainz: P. von Zabern, 9–22.

Haselgrove, C. & Wigg-Wolf, D. (eds) 2005. *Iron Age Coinage and Ritual Practices.* Studien zu Fundmünzen der Antike, 20. Mainz: P. von Zabern.

Hauck, K. & Axboe, M. 1985. *Die Goldbrakteaten der Völkerwanderungszeit.* München: Fink.

Hausmann, R. 1905. Eine Bronze-Depotfund mit einer römischen Bronze-Lampe, gefunden zu Kawwast bei Dorpat. *Sitzungsberichten der Gesellschaft für Geschichte und Altertumskunde der Ostseeprovinzen Russland für das Jahr 1905*, 64–74.

Hausmann, R. 1909. *Übersicht über die archäologische Forschung in den Ostseeprovinzen im letzten Jahrzehnt: Vortrag, gehalten auf dem Historikertag zu Riga 1908*. Riga.

Hausmann, R. 1914. Der Depotfund von Dorpat. In: *Baltische Studien zur Archäologie und Geschichte. Arbeiten des Baltischen Vorbereitenden Komitees für den XVI. Archäologischen Kongress in Pleskau 1914. Herausgegeben von der Gesellschaft für Geschichte und Altertumskunde der Ostseeprovinzen Russlands*. Riga: G. Reimer, 97–116.

Hedeager, L. 1991. Gulddepoterne fra ældre germanentid – Forsøg på en tolkning. Migration Period gold hoards – An attempt at interpretation. In: *Samfundsorganisation og regional variation: Norden i romersk jernalder og folkevandringstid: Beretning fra 1. Nordiske jernaldersymposium på Sandbjerg slot 11–15 april 1989 / edited by C.Fabech & J. Ringtved*. Jutland Archaeological Society publications, 27. Højbjerg: Jysk arkæologisk selskab, 203 – 212.

Hedeager, L. 1992. *Iron-Age Societies: From Tribe to State in Northern Europe, 500 BC to AD 700*. Social archaeology. Oxford: Blackwell.

Hedeager, L. 1999. Sacred topography. Depositions of wealth in the cultural landscape. In: *Glyfer och arkeologiska rum: en vänbok till Jarl Nordbladh / edited by A. Gustafsson & H. Karlsson*. Gotarc. Series A, 3. Göteborg: Göteborg University, Department of Archaeology.

Hedeager, L. 2003. Kognitiv topografi: Ædelmetaldepoter i landskabet. In: *Snartemofunnene i nytt lys / edited by P. Rolfsen & F.-A. Stylegar*. Oslo : Universitetet i Oslo, Universitetets kulturhistoriske museer, 147–165.

Hedeager, L. 2011. *Iron Age Myth and Materiality: An Archaeology of Scandinavia, AD 400–1000*. London: Routledge.

Helg, B. 1990. The gold necklet from Kyhl. *Meddelanden från Lunds Universitets Historiska Museum* 1989-1990, 120–128.

Helgesson, B. 2004. Tributes to be spoken of. Sacrifice and warriors at Uppåkra. In: *Continuity for Centuries. A Ceremonial Building and its Context at Uppåkra, Southern Sweden / edited by L. Larsson*. Uppåkrastudier, 10. Acta archaeologica Lundensia. Series in 8°. Lund: Almqvist & Wiksell, 223–239.

Henriksen, M.B. 2010. Gold deposits in the Late Roman and Migration Period landscape – A case study from the island of Funen (Fyn), Denmark. In: *Worlds apart?: Contacts Across the Baltic Sea in the Iron Age: Network Denmark-Poland, 2005–2008 / edited by U. Lund Hansen & A. Bitner-Wróblewska*. København: Det Kongelige Nordiske Oldkriftselskab, 389–432.

Herschend, F. 2009. *The Early Iron Age in South Scandinavia: Social Order in Settlement and Landscape*. Occasional Papers in Archaeology, 46. Uppsala: Department of Archaeology and Ancient History, Uppsala University.

Hicks, D. & Beaudry, M.C. (eds) 2010. *The Oxford Handbook of Material Culture Studies*. Oxford: Oxford University Press.

Hill, J.D. 1995. *Ritual and Rubbish in the Iron Age of Wessex: A Study on the Formation of a Specific Archaeological Record*. BAR British series, 242. Oxford: Tempus Reparatum.

Hines, J. 1989. Ritual hoarding in migration-period Scandinavia: A review of recent interpretations. *Proceedings of the Prehistoric Society* 55, 193–205.

Hines, J. 1997. Religion: the limits of knowledge. In: *The Anglo-Saxons from the Migration Period to the Eighth Century: An Ethnographic Perspective / edited by J, Hines*. Studies in historical archaeoethnology, 2. Woodbridge: Boydell Press, 375–410.

Hingley, R. 2006. The Deposition of iron objects in Britain during the later prehistoric and Roman periods: Contextual analysis and the significance of iron. *Britannia* 37, 213–257.

Hodder, I. 1986. *Reading the Past: Current Approaches to Interpretation in Archaeology.* Cambridge: Cambridge University Press.

Hodder, I. 1999. *The Archaeological Process: An Introduction.* Oxford: Blackwell.

Hollack, E. 1908. *Erläuterungen zur vorgeschichtlichen Übersichtskarte von Ostpreussen im Auftrage des ostpreussischen Provinzial-Verbandes.* Glogau: C. Flemming.

Holman, D. 2005. Iron Age coinage from Worth, Kent and other possible evidence of ritual deposition in Kent. In: *Iron Age Coinage and Ritual Practices / edited by C. Haselgrove & D. Wigg-Wolf.* Studien zu Fundmünzen der Antike, 20. Mainz: P. von Zabern, 265–285.

Holst, M.K. 2013. Krigerne i Alken Enge. In: *Årets gang. Moesgård Museum 2012 / edited by J. Laursen & J.S. Madsen.* Højbjerg: Moesgård Museum, 22–27.

Hoskins, J. 2006. Agency, biography and objects. In: *Handbook of Material Culture / edited by C. Tilley, W. Keane, S. Kühler, M. Rowlands & P. Spyer.* London: SAGE, 74–84.

Huurre, M. 1995. *9000 vuotta Suomen esihistoriaa.* 5. uud. pain. Helsingissä: Otava.

Ilkjær, J. 1984. The weaponfind from Illerup and its implications for the explanation of similar finds from Northern Europe. *Frühmittelalterliche Studien* 18(1984), 83–90.

Ilkjær, J. 2000. *Illerup Ådal: Archaeology as a Magic Mirror.* Højbjerg: Moesgård Museum.

Ilkjær, J. 2003. Danish war booty sacrifices. In: *The Spoils of Victory: The North in the Shadow of the Roman Empire / edited by L. Jørgensen, B. Storgaard and L.G.Thomsen.* Copenhagen: Nationalmuseet, 44–65.

Insoll, T. 2004. *Archaeology, Ritual, Religion.* Themes in archaeology. New York (NY): Routledge.

Iversen, R.B. 2008. Fourth and fifth century war booty from Kragehul. In: *Aktuelle Forschungen zu Kriegsbeuteopfern und Fürstengräbern im Barbaricum: Internationales Kolloquium, unterstützt durch Carlsbergfondet, Schleswig, 15.–18. Juni 2006 / edited by A.Abegg-Wigg & A. Rau.* Schriften des Archäologischen Landesmuseums. Ergänzungsreihe, 4. Neumünster: Wachholtz, 175–192.

Iversen, R.B. 2010. *Kragehul Mose: Ein Kriegsbeuteopfer auf Südwestfünen.* Jysk Arkæologisk Selskabs skrifter, 73. Højbjerg: Jysk Arkæologisk Selskab.

Jaanits, L. Laul, S. Lõugas, V. & Tõnisson, E. 1982. *Eesti esiajalugu.* Tallinn: Eesti raamat.

Jākobsons, F. 1999. *Austrumbaltijas dzelzs laikmeta pētījumi. Rakstu krājums.* Latvijas Vēstures Muzeja raksti, 6. Archeoloģija. Rīga: Latvijas Vēstures Muzejs.

Jarockis, R. 2004. Settlement development in the River Lielupe basin c. 500–1200 AD. In: *Pētījumi zemgaļu senatnē: Rakstu krājums / edited by R. Ritums.* Latvijas Vēstures Muzeja raksti, 10. Rīga: Latvijas Vēstures Muzejs, 59–65.

Jensen, J. 2006a. *Danmarks oldtid. Ældre jernalder, 500 f. Kr.–400 e. Kr.* 2. udg., 1. opl. København: Gyldendal.

Jensen, J. 2006b. *Danmarks oldtid. Yngre jernalder og vikingetid, 400–1050 e. Kr.* 2. udg., 1. opl. København: Gyldendal.

Jērums, N. 2008. Krustadatas Kurzemē. In: *Pētījumi Kuršu senatne: Rakstu krājums / edited by V. Muižnieks.* Latvijas nacionālā vēstures muzeja raksti, 14. Archeoloģija. Rīga: Latvijas nacionālais vēstures muzejs, 57–71.

Johansen, Ø. 1993. *Norske depotfunn fra bronsealderen.* Universitetets oldsaksamlings skrifter, ny rekke, 15. Oslo: Universitetets oldsaksamling.

Johns, C. 1994. Romano-British precious-metal hoards: Some comments on Martin Millett's paper. In: *TRAC 94: Proceedings of the Fourth Annual Theoretical Roman Archaeology Conference, held at the Department of Archaeology, University of Durham, 19th and 20th March, 1994 / edited by S. Cottam [et al.].* Oxford: Oxbow, 107–117.

Johns, C. 1996. The classification and interpretation of Romano-British treasures. *Britannia* 27, 1–16.

Johnsen, H. & Olsen, B. 2000. Hermeneutics and archaeology: On the philosophy of contextual archaeology. In: *Interpretive Archaeology : A Reader / edited by J. Thomas.* London: Leicester University Press, 97–117.

Jonuks, T. 2009. *Eesti muinasusund.* Dissertationes archaeologiae Universitatis Tartuensis, 2. Tartu: Tartu Ülikooli Kirjastus.

Jørgensen, L. 1994. The find material from the settlement of Gudme II: Composition and interpretation. In: *The Archaeology of Gudme and Lundeborg : Papers Presented at a Conference at Svendborg, October 1991 / edited by P.O. Nielsen, K. Randsborg & H. Thrane.* Arkæologiske studier, 10. Copenhagen: Akademisk forlag, Universitetsforlaget i København, 53–63.

Jørgensen, L. 2001. The 'Warriors, soldiers and conscripts' of the anthropology in late Roman and Migration Period archaeology. In: *Military Aspects of the Aristocracy in Barbaricum in the Roman and Early Migration Periods: Papers from an International Research Seminar at the Danish National Museum, Copenhagen, 10–11 December 1999 / edited by B. Storgaard.* Publications from the National Museum. Studies in archaeology and history, 5. Copenhagen: National Museum of Denmark, Danish Collections, 9–19.

Jørgensen, L. & Petersen, P.V. 1998. *Guld, magt og tro: Danske guldskatte fra oldtid og middelalder = Gold, Power, and Belief: Danish Gold Treasures from Prehistory and the Middle Ages.* Copenhagen: Nationalmuseet.

Jørgensen, L., Storgaard, B. & Thomsen, L.G. (eds) 2003. *The Spoils of Victory : The North in the Shadow of the Roman Empire.* Copenhagen: Nationalmuseet.

Joy, J. 2011. Fancy objects in the British Iron Age: Why decorate? *Proceedings of the Prehistoric Society* 77, 205–229.

Joyce, R.A. 2008. Practice in and as deposition. In: *Memory Work: Archaeologies of Material Practices / edited by B.J. Mills & W.H. Walker.* School for Advanced Research advanced seminar series. Santa Fe: School for Advanced Research Press, 25–39.

Joyce, R.A. & Lopiparo, J. 2005. PostScript: Doing agency in archaeology. *Journal of Archaeological Method and Theory* 12(4), 365–374.

Joyce, R. & Pollard, J. 2010. Archaeological assemblages and practices of deposition. In: *The Oxford Handbook of Material Culture Studies / edited by D.Hicks & M.C. Beaudry.* Oxford handbooks. Oxford: Oxford University Press, 291–309.

Jung, J. 1898. *Muinasaja teadus eestlaste maalt.* II, *Kohalised muinasaja kirjeldused Liiwimaalt, Pernu ja Wiljandi maakonnast.* Jurjew: A. Grenzstein.

Kaul, F. 1991. *Gundestrupkedlen: Baggrund og billedverden.* København: Nationalmuseet.

Kaul, F. 1997. Priosløkke and its logistic implications. In: *Military Aspects of Scandinavian Society in a European perspective, AD 1–1300: Papers from an International Research Seminar at the Danish National Museum, Copenhagen, 2–4 May 1996 / edited by A. Nørgård Jorgensen & B.L. Clausen.* Publications from the National Museum. Studies in archaeology & history, 2. Copenhagen: National Museum, 136–145.

Kaul, F. 2003. The Hjortspring find. In: *Hjortspring: A Pre-Roman Iron-Age Warship in Context / edited by O. Crumlin-Pedersen & A. Trakadas.* Ships and boats of the North, 5. Roskilde: Viking Ship Museum.

Kaul, F. 2009. Indflydelser og kontakter i keltisk jernalder. In: *Tollundmandens verden. Kontinentale kontakter i tidlig jernalder / edited by K.M. Boe, T. Capelle & C. Fischer.* Silkeborg: Wormianum, Silkeborg Kulturhistoriske Museum, 9–55.

Kazakevičius, C. & Malonaitis, A. 2006. Sacrifices of weapons in Baltic burials. In: *Transformatio Mundi: The Transition from the Late Migration Period to the Early Viking Age in the East Baltic / edited by M. Bertasius.* Kaunas: Kaunas University of Technology Department of Philosophy and Cultural Science, 73–79.

Keane, W. 2001. Money is no object. Materiality desire, and modernity in an Indonesian Society. In: *The Empire of Things: Regimes of Value and Material Culture / edited by Fred R. Myers.* School of American Research advanced seminar series. Santa Fe: School of American Research Press, 65–90.

Kiudsoo, M. 2005. Eesti kagunurga aardeleiud (Vastseliina-Alūksne keskaegne ühendustee). In: *Uurimusi Setumaa loodusest, ajaloost ja folkloristikast. / edited by M. Aun & Ü. Tamla.* Setumaa kogumik, 3. Tallinn: Ajaloo Instituut, 138–169.

Kiudsoo, M. 2013. New Roman coin find in Estonia. *Archaeological Fieldwork in Estonia* 2012, 289–296.

Kivikoski, E. 1961. *Suomen historia.* Porvoo; Helsinki: WSOY.

Kivikoski, E. 1973. *Die Eisenzeit Finnlands: Bildwerk Und Text.* Neuausgabe. Helsinki: Weilin+Göös.

Kleeman, O. 1935. Die beiden Fibeln von Grobin. In: *Sitzungsberichte der Kurländischen Gesellschaft für Literatur und Kunst* 1934, 1–6.

Knapp, A.B. 1992a. Archaeology and Annales: Time, space, and change. In: *Archaeology, Annales, and Ethnohistory / edited by A.B. Knapp.* Cambridge: Cambridge University Press, 1–21.

Knapp, A.B. 1992b. Independence and imperialism: politico-economic structures in the Bronze Age Levant. In: *Archaeology, Annales, and Ethnohistory / edited by A.B. Knapp.* Cambridge: Cambridge University Press, 83–98.

Knapp, A.B. (ed.) 1992. *Archaeology, Annales, and Ethnohistory.* Cambridge: Cambridge University Press.

Knapp, A.B. & van Dommelen, P. 2008. Past practices: Rethinking individuals and agents in archaeology. *Cambridge Archaeological Journal* 18(01), 15–34.

Knappett, C. 2005. *Thinking Through Material Culture: An Interdisciplinary Perspective.* Archaeology, culture, and society. Philadelphia, PA: University of Pennsylvania Press.

Knappett, C. & Malafouris, L. (eds) 2008. *Material Agency: Towards a Non-Anthropocentric Approach*. New York: Springer.

Koch, E. 1999. Neolithic offerings from the wetlands of eastern Denmark. In: *Bog Bodies, Sacred Sites and Wetland Archaeology: Proceedings of a Conference Held by WARP and the National Museum of Denmark, in Conjunction with Silkeborg Museum, Jutland, September 1996 / edited by B. Coles, J. Coles & M. Schou Jørgensen*. WARP occasional paper, 12. Exeter: Wetland Archaeology Research Project (WARP), 125–131.

Kokowski, A. 1993. W kwestii ofiar i miejsc ofiarnych na ziemiach polskich w młodszym okresie przedrzymskim i okresie rzymskim. In: *Wierzenia przedchrześcijańskie na ziemiach polskich / edited by M. Kwapiński & H. Paner*. Gdańsk: Muzeum Archeologiczne w Gdańsku, 88–97.

Kolendo, J. 1976. Rzekome znalezisko posążków egipskich w Szwekszniach na Litwie. *Rocznik Białostocki* 13, 283–297.

Konsa, M. 2005. Vaade Karula kõrgustikult Lõuna-Eesti muinasajale. *Tartu Ülikooli Lõuna-Eesti keele- ja kultuuriuuringute keskuse aastaraamat* IV, 11–28.

Konsa, M., Allmäe, R., Maldre, L. & Vassiljev, J. 2009. Rescue excavations of a Vendel Era boat-grave in Salme, Saaremaa. *Archaeological Fieldwork in Estonia* 2008, 53–64.

Kopytoff, I. 1986. The cultural biography of things: Commoditization as process. In: *The Social Life of Things : Commodities in Cultural Perspective / edited by A. Appadurai*. Cambridge: Cambridge University Press, 64–91.

Kraszewski, J.I. 1860. *Sztuka U Słowian, Szczególnie W Polsce I Litwie Przedchrześcijańskiéj*. Wilno: A.H. Kirkor.

Kraut, A. 2012. Amendments to the Heritage Conservation Act regarding protection of archaeological monuments in 2011. *Archaeological Fieldwork in Estonia* 2011, 319–332.

Kriiska, A. & Tvauri, A. 2002. *Eesti muinasaeg*. Tallinn: Avita.

Kropotkin, V.V. 1961. = Кропоткин В.В. 1961. *Клады римских монет на территории СССР*. Москва: Издателство Академии наук СССР.

Kulikauskas, P., Volkaitė-Kulikauskienė, R., Tautavičius, A. & Lebedys, J. 1961. *Lietuvos archeologijos bruožai*. Vilnius: Valstybinės ir mokslinės literatūros leidykla.

Kulikauskienė, R. & Rimantienė, R. 1958. *Lietuvių liaudies menas: Senovės lietuvių papuošalai*. Vilnius: Vaga.

Kurila, L. 2009. Socialinis statusas ir lytis: Geležies amžiaus Rytų Lietuvos socialinės organizacijos analizė. *Lietuvos Archeologija* 35, 153–192.

Lamm, J.P. 1997. The Vittene hoard. A gold-treasure from Västergötland in Sweden with continental background. *Peregrinatio Gothica, Supplementum ad Acta Musei Moraviae Scientiae Sociales* 82, 193–200.

Lamm, J.P. 2004. Figural gold foils found in Sweden. A study based on the discoveries from Helgö. In: *Excavations at Helgö XVI. Exotic and Sacral Finds from Helgö / edited by H. Clarke & K. Lamm*. Stockholm: Kungl. Vitterhets historie och antikvitets akademien, 41–142.

Lang, V. 1996. *Muistne Rävala. Muistised, kronoloogia ja maaviljelusliku asustuse kujunemine Loode-Eestis, eriti Pirita jõe alamjooksu piirkonnas. I-II*. Muinasaja teadus, 4. Tallinn: Ajaloo Instituut.

Lang, V. 2000. *Keskusest ääremaaks: Viljelusmajandusliku asustuse kujunemine ja areng Vihasoo-Palmse piirkonnas Virumaal = From Centre to Periphery: Establishment and History of Farming Settlement in Vihasoo and Palmse Area (Virumaa, North Estonia).* Muinasaja teadus, 7. Tallinn: Teaduste Akadeemia Kirjastus.

Lang, V. 2007a. *Baltimaade pronksi- ja rauaaeg.* Tartu: Tartu Ülikooli Kirjastus.

Lang, V. 2007b. *The Bronze and Early Iron Ages in Estonia.* Estonian archaeology, 3. Tartu: Tartu University Press.

Lang, V. 2007c. Muistsed maakasutussüsteemid Eestis. *Ajalooline Ajakiri* 3/4, 291–320.

Larsson, L. (ed.) 2004. *Continuity for Centuries: A Ceremonial Building and Its Context at Uppåkra.* Uppåkrastudier, 10. Lund, Sweden: Almqvist & Wiksell.

Larsson, T.B. 1986. *The Bronze Age Metalwork in Southern Sweden: Aspects of Social and Spatial Organization 1800-500 B.C.* Archaeology and environment, 6. Umeå: Deptartment of Archaeology.

Latour, B. 2005. *Reassembling the Social: An Introduction to Actor-Network-Theory.* Oxford: Oxford University Press.

Laul, S. 2001. *Rauaaja kultuuri kujunemine Eesti kaguosas: (500 e.Kr. – 500 p.Kr).* Muinasaja teadus, 9. Õpetatud Eesti Seltsi kirjad, 7. Tallinn: Ajaloo Instituut.

Laul, S. & Kihno, K. 1999. Viljelusmajandulsiku asustuse kujunemisjooni Haanja kõrgustiku kaguveerul. *Eesti Arheoloogia Ajakiri* 3(1), 3–18.

Laul, S. & Tõnisson, E. 1991. Muistsete sirpide ja vikatite kujunemisloost Eestis. In: *Arheoloogiline kogumik / edited by L. Jaanits & V. Lang.* Muinasaja teadus, 1. Tallinn: Agu, 75–91.

Lavi, A. 2002. Kesk-Eesti idaosa linnamägedest. In: *Keskus, tagamaa, ääreala: Uurimusi asustushierarhia ja võimukeskuste kujunemisest Eestis = Centre, Hinterland, Margin: Studies in the Formation of Settlement Hierarchy and Power Centres in Estonia / edited by V. Lang.* Muinasaja teadus, 11. Tallinn-Tartu: Tartu Ülikool, 233–272.

Leeuw, S.E. van der & McGlade, J. (eds) 1997. *Time, Process, and Structured Transformation in Archaeology.* One world archaeology, 26. London: Routledge.

Leimus, I. & Kiudsoo, M. 2004. Koprad ja hõbe. *Tuna* 4(2004), 31–47.

Lesure, R. 1999. On the genesis of value in early hierarchical societies. In: *Material Symbols : Culture and Economy in Prehistory / edited by J.E. Robb.* Occasional paper, Southern Illinois University at Carbondale. Center for Archaeological Investigations, 26. Carbondale: Center for Archaeological Investigations, Southern Illinois University, 23–55.

Levy, J.E. 1982. *Social and Religious Organization in Bronze Age Denmark: An Analysis of Ritual Hoard Finds.* BAR international series, 124. Oxford: B.A.R.

Lightfoot, K.G. 2001. Traditions as cultural production: Implications for contemporary archaeological research. In: *The Archaeology of Traditions : Agency and History Before and After Columbus / edited by T.R. Pauketat.* Ripley P. Bullen series. Gainesville : University Press of Florida, 237–252.

Ligi, P. 1995. Ühiskondlikest oludest Eesti alal hilispronksi ja rauaajal. In: *Eesti arheoloogia historiograafilisi, teoreetilisi ja kultuuriajaloolisi aspekte / edited by V. Lang.* Muinasaja teadus, 3; Töid arheoloogia alalt, 3. Tallinn: Teaduste Akadeemia Kirjastus, 182–270.

Lillios, K.T. 1999. Objects of memory: The ethnography and archaeology of heirlooms. *Journal of Archaeological Method and Theory* 6(3), 235–262.

Lindeberg, M. 1997. Gold, gods and women. *Current Swedish Archaeology* 5, 99–110.

Lønstrup, J. 1984. Older and newer theories. The find from Thorsberg in the light of new discoveries. *Frühmittelalterliche Studien* 18(1984), 91–101.

Lõugas, V. 1996. *Kaali kraatriväljal Phaethonit otsimas*. Tallinn: Eesti Entsüklopeediakirjastus.

Lõugas, V. & Selirand, J. 1977. *Arheoloogiga Eestimaa teedel*. Tallinn; Valgus.

Lucas, G. 2008. Time and archaeological event. *Cambridge Archaeological Journal* 18(01), 59–65.

Lucero, L.J. 2008. Memorializing place among classic Maya commoners. In: *Memory Work: Archaeologies of Material Practices / edited by B.J. Mills & W.H. Walker*. School for Advanced Research advanced seminar series. Santa Fe: School for Advanced Research Press, 187-205.

Lund Hansen, U. 2001. Gold rings – symbols of sex and rank. Necklaces and bracelets in Scandinavia and Continental Europe from the Late Roman and Migration periods. In: *Roman Gold and the Development of the Early Germanic Kingdoms : Aspects of Technical, Socio-Political, Socio-Economic, Artistic and Intellectual Development, A.D. 1–550 : Symposium in Stockholm, 14–16 November 1997 / edited by B. Magnus*. Konferenser (Kungl. Vitterhets, historie och antikvitets akademien), 51. Stockholm: Almqvist & Wiksell, 157–188.

Lund Hansen, U. & Vennersdorf, M. 2009. Votive finds? In: *Sorte Muld: Wealth, Power and Religion at an Iron Age Central Settlement on Bornholm / edited by C. Adamsen, U. Lund Hansen, F.O. Nielsen & M. Watt*. Denmark: Bornholms Museum, 29–33.

Lund, J. 2004. Våben i vand: Om deponeringer i vikingetiden. *Kuml: Årbog for Jysk Arkæologisk Selskab* 2004, 197–221.

Lund, J. 2005. Thresholds and passages: The meanings of bridges and crossings in the Viking Age and Early Middle Ages. In: *Viking and Medieval Scandinavia / edited by J. Quinn, S. Brink & J.Hines*. Viking and Medieval Scandinavia, 1. Turnhout: Brepols, 109–135.

Lund, J. 2006. Vikingetidens værktøjskister i landskab og mytologi. *Fornvännen* 5, 323–341.

Lund, J. 2008. Banks, borders and bodies of water in a Viking Age mentality. *Journal of Wetland Archaeology* 8, 51–70.

Lund, J. 2009. *Asted og vadested. Deponeringer, genstandsbiografier og rumlig strukturering som kilde til vikingatidens kognitive landskaber*. Acta Humaniora. Oslo: Universitet i Oslo.

Lund, J. & Melheim, A.L. 2011. Heads and tails - minds and bodies: Reconsidering the Late Bronze Age Vestby hoard in light of symbolist and body perspectives. *European Journal of Archaeology* 14(2), 441–464.

Luoto, J. 2010. Suomen esihistoriallisista uhrilöydöistä. In: *Hirviveneestä hullukaaliin – Muinaisuskomukset arkeologisen aineiston tulkinnassa / edited by H. Poutiainen*. Päijät-Hämeen tutkimusseuran vuosikirja. 2008-2009. Hämeenlinna: Päijät-Hämeen tutkimusseura, 12–33.

Madsen, T. (ed.) 1988. *Multivariate Archaeology: Numerical Approaches in Scandinavian Archaeology*. Jutland Archaeological Society publications, 21. Højbjerg: Jutland Archaeological Society.

Mägi, M. 2000. Weapons find and an ancient harbour site at Viltina Käo-Matsi. *Archaeological Filedwork in Estonia* 1999, 92–99.

Mägi, M. 2006. Changing connections, changing society: Burial rites on Iron Age Saaremaa. In: *Transformatio Mundi: The Transition from the Late Migration Period to the Early Viking Age in the East Baltic / edited by M. Bertasius.* Kaunas: Kaunas University of Technology Department of Philosophy and Cultural Science, 51–64.

Magnus, B. 1999. Das große Tier im Moor. In: *Völker an Nord- und Ostsee und die Franken: Akten des 48. Sachsensymposiums in Mannheim vom 7. bis 11. September 1997 / edited by U.von Freeden, U. Koch & A. Wieczorek.* Kolloquien zur Vor- und Frühgeschichte, 3. Bonn: Habelt, 75–82.

Magnus, B. (ed.) 2001. *Roman Gold and the Development of the Early Germanic Kingdoms: Aspects of Technical, Socio-Political, Socio-Economic, Artistic and Intellectual Development, A.D. 1–550 : Symposium in Stockholm, 14–16 November 1997.* Stockholm: Almqvist & Wiksell.

Makiewicz, T. 1988. Opfer und Opferplätze der vorrömischen Eisenzeit in Polen. *Prähistorische Zeitschrift* 63, 81–112.

Makiewicz, T. 1992. Broń jako element rytuałów ofiarnych w okresie przedrzymskim i rzymskim na ziemiach Polski. In: *Arma et ollae: Studia dedykowane Profesorowi Andrzejowi Nadolskiemu w 70 rocznicę urodzin i 45 rocznicę pracy naukowej : sesja naukowa, Łódź, 7–8 maja 1992 r. / edited by M. Głosek, M. Mielczarek, W.Świętosławsk & K. Walenta.* Łódź: Stowarzyszenie Nauk. Archeologów Polskich, Oddz. w Łodzi, 109–128.

Makiewicz, T. 1993. Z badań nad ofiarami i miejscami ofiarnymi na terenie Polski w okresie przedrzymskim i rzymskim. In: *Wierzenia przedchrześcijańskie na ziemiach polskich / edited by M. Kwapiński & H. Paner.* Gdańsk: Muzeum Archeologiczne w Gdańsku, 65–76.

Mandel, M. 1985. = Мандель, М. 1985. Меч в вооружении эстонских племен до 7 века. — Новое в археологии Прибалтики и соседних территорий: сборник статей. Новое в археологии Прибалтики и соседних территорий = Neues in der Archäologie des Ostbaltikums und der Nachbarterritorien = Uut Baltimaade ja naaberalade arheoloogias: сборник статей / Ред. Ю. Селиранд. Таллин: Академия наук Эстонской ССР, Институт истории, 78–85.

Mandel, M. 2003. *Läänemaa 5.–13. sajandi kalmed.* Töid ajaloo alalt, 5. Tallinn: Eesti Ajaloomuuseum.

Mandel, M. & Tamla, T. 1977. Rikassaare relvaleid. *Eesti NSV Teaduste Akadeemia toimetised. Ühiskonnateadused* 26(2), 158–164.

Martin, A. 2005. Agents in inter-action: Bruno Latour and agency. *Journal of Archaeological Method and Theory* 12(4), 283–311.

Mauss, M. 2002. *The Gift : The Form and Reason for Exchange in Archaic Societies.* London: Routledge.

McCall, J.C. 1999. Structure, agency, and the locus of the social: Why poststructural theory is good for archaeology. In: *Material Symbols : Culture and Economy in Prehistory / edited by J.E. Robb.* Occasional paper (Southern Illinois University at Carbondale. Center for Archaeological Investigations), 26. Carbondale: Center for Archaeological Investigations, Southern Illinois University, 16–20.

McGlade, J. & Leeuw, S.E. van der 1997. Introduction: Archaeology and non-linear dynamics – New approaches to long-term change. In: *Time, Process, and Structured Transformation in Archaeology / edited by S. van der Leeuw & J. McGlade*. One world archaeology, 26. London: Routledge, 1–31.

McNiven, I.J. 2012. Ritualized middening practices. *Journal of Archaeological Method and Theory* 19(1), DOI: 10.1007/s10816–012–9130–y. (08.11.2013.)

Meinander, C.F. 1950. *Etelä-Pohjanmaan historia. 1, Esihistoria*. Helsinki: Etelä-Pohjanmaan historiatoimikunta.

Meinander, C.F.V. 1954. *Die Bronzezeit in Finnland*. Suomen Muinaismuistoyhdistyksen aikakauskirja, 54. Helsinki: Suomen Muinaismuistoyhdistys.

Merkevičius, A. 1973. Seniausių Lietuvos metalo dirbinių cheminė sudėtis. *Lietuvos TSR Mokslų akademijos darbai, A serija* 2(43), 87–102.

Merkevičius, A. 2011. *Ankstyvieji Metaliniai Dirbiniai Lietuvoje*. Vilnius: Versus aureus.

Michelbertas, M. 1972. Prekybiniai ryšiai su Romos imperija. In: *Lietuvos Gyventojų Prekybiniai Ryšiai I–XIII a. / edited by M. Michelbertas*. Vilnius: Lietuvos TSR Mokslų akademijos Istorijos instituta, 5–125.

Michelbertas, M. 1986. *Senasis geležies amžius Lietuvoje, I-IV amžius*. Vilnius: Mokslas.

Michelbertas, M. 1995. Römische Münzen in den Gräberfeldern Litauens. *Archaeologia Baltica* 1, 81–87.

Michelbertas, M. 2001. *Corpus der Römischen Funde Im Europäischen Barbaricum: Litauen*. Vilnius: Universität Vilnius Lehrstuhl für Archäologie.

Michelbertas, M. 2007. Archeologiniai lobiai. In: *Lietuvos lobiai*. Kaunas: Šviesa, 8–17.

Miller, D. 2001. Alienable gifts and inalienable commodities. In: *The Empire of Things: Regimes of Value and Material Culture / edited by F.R. Myers*. School of American Research advanced seminar series. Santa Fe: School of American Research Press 91–115.

Miller, D. 2005. Materiality: An introduction. In: *Materiality / edited by D. Miller*. Durham, NC: Duke University Press, 1–50.

Millett, M. 1994. Treasure: Interpreting Roman hoards. *TRAC 94: Proceedings of the Fourth Annual Theoretical Roman Archaeology Conference, Held at the Department of Archaeology, University of Durham, 19th and 20th March, 1994 / edited by S. Cottam [et al.]*. Oxford: Oxbow, 99–106.

Mills, B.J. 2004. The establishment and defeat of hierarchy: Inalienable possessions and the history of collective prestige structures in the pueblo southwest. *American Anthropologist*, 106(2), 238–251.

Mills, B.J. 2008. Remembering while forgetting: Depositional prcatices and social memory at Chaco. In: *Memory Work: Archaeologies of Material Practices / edited by B.J. Mills & W.H. Walker*. School for Advanced Research advanced seminar series. Santa Fe: School for Advanced Research Press, 81–108.

Mills, B.J. & Walker, W.H. 2008. Introduction: Memory, materiality, and depositional practice. In: *Memory Work: Archaeologies of Material Practices / edited by B.J. Mills & W.H. Walker*. School for Advanced Research advanced seminar series. Santa Fe: School for Advanced Research Press, 3–23.

Molvõgin, A. 1976. = Молвыгин А. 1976. Нумизматические находки. *Eesti NSV Teaduste Akadeemia toimetised. Ühiskonnateadused* 1, 77–78.

Moora, H. 1925. Hõbeaare Pilistverest. *Eesti Rahva Muuseumi Aastaraamat* 1, 110–117.

Moora, H. 1929. *Die Eisenzeit in Lettland bis etwa 500 N. Chr.* Verhandlung der Gelehrten Estnischen Gesellschaft, 25. Tartu-Dorpat.

Moora, H. 1935. Der Verwahrfund von Piilsi, Kirchspiel Avinurme. *Õpetatud Eesti Seltsi Aastaraamat* 1933, 283–303.

Moora, H. 1938. *Die Eisenzeit in Lettland bis etwa 500 N. Chr. II. Teil. Analyse.* Verhandlungen der Gelehrten Eestnischen Gesellschaft, 29. Tartu.

Moora, H. 1962. = Моора Х. 1962. Клад V века , найденный в Реола близ гор. Тарту. *Swiatowit* 26 (1962), 343–351.

Moora, H., Laid, E., Mägiste, J. & Kruus, H. 1936. *Eesti ajalugu I: Esiajalugu ja muistne vabadusvõitlus.* Tartu: Eesti Kirjanduse Selts.

Moore, H.L. 1982. The interpretation of spatial patterning in settlement residues. In: *Symbolic and Structural Archaeology / edited by I. Hodder.* Cambridge: Cambridge University Press, 74–79.

Moreland, J.F. 1992. Restoring the dielactic: Settlement patterns and documents in medieval central Italy. In: *Archaeology, Annales, and Ethnohistory / edited by A.B. Knapp.* Cambridge: Cambridge University Press, 112–129.

Munksgaard, E. 1987. Spätantikes Silber. *Frühmittelalterliche Studien* 21(1987), 82–84.

Munn, N.D. 1986. *The Fame of Gawa: A Symbolic Study of Value Transformation in a Massim (Papua New Guinea) Society.* The Lewis Henry Morgan lectures, 1976. Cambridge: Cambridge University Press.

Murray, T. 2006. Comments on Jan Harding (2005): Rethinking the great divide: Long-term structural history and the temporality of the event. Norwegian Archaeological Review 38, 88–101. Structure and event - again. *Norwegian Archaeological Review* 39(1), 82–89.

Myers, F.R. 2001. Introduction: The empire of things. In: *The Empire of Things: Regimes of Value and Material Culture / edited by F.R. Myers.* School of American Research advanced seminar series. Santa Fe: School of American Research Press, 3–61.

Nagevičius, V. 1935. *Mūsų pajūrio medžiaginė kultūra: VIII-XIII amž.: Pryšmančių ir kitų vietų kasinėjimai.* Kaunas: 'Spindulio' sp.

Nakaitė, L. 1959. Senovės lietuvių sidabriniai papuošalai. *Iš lietuvių kultūros istorijos* II, 54–71.

Needham, S.P. 1988. Selective deposition in the British Early Bronze Age. *World Archaeology* 20(2), 229–248.

Nerman, B. 1958. *Grobin-Seeburg: Ausgrabungen Und Funde.* Stockholm: Almqvist & Wiksell.

Nicklasson, P. 1997. *Svärdet ljuger inte: Vapenfynd från äldre järnålder på Sveriges fastland.* Acta archaeologica Lundensia. Series in 4°, 22. Stockholm: Almqvist & Wiksell International.

Nielsen, P.O., Randsborg, K. & Thrane, H. (eds) 1994. *The Archaeology of Gudme and Lundeborg: Papers Presented at a Conference at Svendborg, October 1991.* Copenhagen: Akademisk forlag, Universitetsforlaget i København.

Nielsen, S., Andersen, J.H, Baker, J.A., Christensen, C., Glastrup, J., Grootes, P.M., Hüls, M., Jouttijärvi, A., Larsen, E.B., Madsen, H.B., Müller, K., Nadeau, M.-J., Röhrs, S., Stege, H., Stos, Z.A. & Waight, T.E. 2005. The Gundestrup cauldron: New scientific and technical investigations. *Acta Archaeologica* 76(2), 1–58.

Niskanen, M. 2006. Stature of the Merovingian-period inhabitants from Levänluhta, Finland. *Fennoscandia Archaeologica* 23, 24–36.

Nordqvist, B. 2006. *Offerplatsen Finnestorp. Grävningsredogörelse över de arkeologiska undersökningarna utförda under åren 2000-2004. Arkeologisk undersökning av den fasta fornlämningen RAÄ nr 121, inom fastigheten Finnestorp 2:1, Larvs sn, Vara kommun, lanskapet Västergötland, Västra Götlands län.* Gotarc Series, D Arch. Rep., 63. Göteborg.

Nordqvist, B. 2007. Der Kriegsbeuteopferplatz von Finnestorp in Schweden. *Offa* 61/62(2004/2005), 221–238.

Nørgård Jørgensen, A. 2008a. *Porskjær Mosefund.* Jysk Arkaeologisk Selskab, 59. Århus: Jysk Arkaeologisk Selskab.

Nørgård Jørgensen, A. 2008b. The Porskjær weapon sacrifice - Introduction and preliminary results. In: *Aktuelle Forschungen zu Kriegsbeuteopfern und Fürstengräbern im Barbaricum: internationales Kolloquium, unterstützt durch Carlsbergfondet, Schleswig, 15.–18. Juni 2006 / edited by A. Abegg-Wigg & A. Rau.* Schriften des Archäologischen Landesmuseums. Ergänzungsreihe, 4. Neumünster: Wachholtz, 193–207.

Nowakiewicz, T. & Rzeszotarska-Nowakiewicz, A. 2012. *Jezioro Nidajno koło Czaszkowa na Mazurach: niezwykłe miejsce kultu z okresu późnej starożytności = Lake Nidajno near Czaszkowo in Masuria: A Unique Sacrificial Site from Late Antiquity.* Warszawa: Komitet Nauk Pra- i Protohistorycznych Polskiej Akademii Nauk; Instytut Archeologii Uniwersytetu Warszawskiego; Instytut Archeologii i Etnologii Polskiej Akademii Nauk.

Nowakowski, W. 1988. Metallglocken aus der römischen Kaiserzeit im europäischen Barbaricum. *Archaeologia Polona* 27, 69–146.

Nowakowski, W. 1994. Tintinnabula auf den Ostseeinseln. Die römischen. Bronzeglocken auf den Inseln Gotland und Bornholm. *Fornvännen* 89, 133–143.

Nylén, E., Lund Hansen, U. & Manneke, P. 2005. *The Havor Hoard : The Gold - The Bronzes - The Fort.* Stockholm: Kungl. Kungl. Vitterhets, historie och antikvitets akademiens handlingar. Antikvariska serien 46. Vitterhets, Historie och Antikvitets Akademien.

Olivier, L. 2006. Comments on Jan Harding (2005): Rethinking the great divide: Long-term structural history and the temporality of the event. Norwegian Archaeological Review 38, 88–101. The greatest harmony is born of differences. *Norwegian Archaeological Review* 39(1), 89–93.

Oras, E. 2008. Leiukontekstist tõlgenduseni Eesti noorema rauaaja aarete näitel. *Õpetatud Eesti Seltsi Aastaraamat* 2007, 127–148.

Oras, E. 2010. Ritual wealth deposits in Estonian Middle Iron Age material. *Estonian Journal of Archaeology* 14(2), 123–142.

Oras, E. 2012a. Contemporary polities and archaeology of ethnicity in the Baltic countries: Paradigms of history writing, state politics and personalities in the tradition of archaeological research. *Archaeological Review from Cambridge* 27(2), 111–137.

Oras, E. 2012b. Importance of terms: What is a wealth deposit? *Papers from the Institute of Archaeology* 22(2012), 61–82.

Oras, E. 2013. Eastern Baltic Middle Iron Age Wealth deposits in burial areas: An example of regional cultural practice. *Archaeologia Baltica* 19, 44–62.

Oars, E. & Kriiska, A. 2014. The Kohtla weapon deposit: Preliminary results. *Archaeological Fieldwork in Estonia* 2013, 55–66.

Ørsnes, M. 1963. The weapon find in Ejsbøl mose at Haderslev: Preliminary report. *Acta Archaeologica* 34(1963), 232–247.

Ørsnes, M. 1988. *Ejsbøl I : Waffenopferfunde des 4.-5. Jahrh. nach Chr.* Nordiske fortidsminder. Serie B, 11. København: Det Kongelige Nordiske oldskriftselskab.

Ørsnes, M. & Ilkjær, J. 1993. Votive deposits. In: *Digging Into the Past: 25 Years of Archaeology in Denmark / edited by S. Hvass & B. Storgaard.* Copenhagen: Royal Society of Northern Antiquarie, 215–222.

Ortner, S.B. 1984. Theory in anthropology since the sixties. *Comparative Studies in Society and History* 26(1), 126–166.

Osborne, R. 2004. Hoards, votives, offerings: The archaeology of the dedicated object. *World Archaeology* 36(1), 1–10.

Panagos, P., Van Liedekerke, M., Jones, A. & Montanarella, L. 2012. European Soil Data Centre: Response to European policy support and public data requirements. *Land Use Policy* 29(2), 329–338. DOI:10.1016/j.landusepol.2011.07.003. (08.11.2013.)

Parker Pearson, M. 1999. *The Archaeology of Death and Burial.* Stroud: Sutton.

Pauketat, T.R. 2000. The tragedy of commoners. In: *Agency in Archaeology / edited by M.-A. Dobres & J.E. Robb.* London: Routledge, 113–129.

Pauketat, T.R. 2001a. A new tradition in archaeology. In: *The Archaeology of Traditions : Agency and History Before and After Columbus / edited by T.R. Pauketat.* Ripley P. Bullen series. Gainesville: University Press of Florida, 1–16.

Pauketat, T.R. 2001b. Practice and history in archaeology: An emerging paradigm. *Anthropological Theory* 1(1), 73–98.

Pauketat, T.R. & Alt, S.M. 2004. The making and meaning of a Mississippian axe-head cache. *Antiquity* 78(302), 779–797.

Pauketat, T.R. & Alt, S.M. 2005. Agency in a postmold? Physicality and the archaeology of culture-making. *Journal of Archaeological Method and Theory* 12(3), 213–236.

Pauli Jensen, X. 2008. Vimose revisited - Perspectives and preliminary results. In: *Aktuelle Forschungen zu Kriegsbeuteopfern und Fürstengräbern im Barbaricum : internationales Kolloquium, unterstützt durch Carlsbergfondet, Schleswig, 15.–18. Juni 2006 / edited by A. Abegg-Wigg & A. Rau.* Schriften des Archäologischen Landesmuseums. Ergänzungsreihe, 4. Neumünster: Wachholtz, 137–149.

Pauli Jensen, X. 2009. From fertility rituals to weapon sacrifices. The case of the south Scandinavian bog finds. In: *Glaube, Kult und Herrschaft : Phänomene des Religiösen im 1. Jahrtausend n. Chr. in Mittel- und Nordeuropa ; Akten des 59. Internationalen Sachsensymposions und der Grundprobleme der frühgeschichtlichen Entwicklung im Mitteldonauraum.* Bonn: R. Habelt, 53–64.

Pauli, L. 1985. Einige Anmerkungen zum Problem der Hortfunde. *Archäologisches Korrespondenzblatt* 15(1985), 195–206.

Peets, J. 2003a. Koos rauaga läbi aastatuhandete. In: *Arheoloogiga Läänemeremaades. Uurimusi Jüri Seliranna auks / edited by V. Lang & Ü. Tamla.* Muinasaja teadus, 13. Tallinn-Tartu: Eesti Teaduste Akadeemia Kirjastus, 209–226.

Peets, J. 2003b. *The Power of Iron: Iron Production and Blacksmithy in Estonia and Neighbouring Areas in Prehistoric Period and the Middle Ages = Raua vägi: Raua tootmine ja sepatöö Eestis ja naaberpiirkondades muinas- ja keskajal.* Muinasaja teadus, 12. Tallinn: Teaduste Akadeemia Kirjastus.

Peets, J., Allmäe, R. & Maldre, L. 2011. Archaeological investigations of Pre-Viking Age burial boat in Salme village at Saaremaa. *Archaeological Fieldwork in Estonia* 2010, 29–48.

Pollard, J. 1995. Inscribing space: Formal deposition at the later Neolithic monument of Woodhenge, Wiltshire. *Proceedings of the Prehistoric Society* 61, 137–156.

Pollard, J. 2001. The aesthetics of depositional practice. *World Archaeology* 33(2), 315–333.

Pollard, J. 2008. Introduction: Memory, materiality, and depositional practice. In: *Memory Work: Archaeologies of Material Practices / edited by B.J. Mills & W.H. Walker.* School for Advanced Research advanced seminar series. Santa Fe: School for Advanced Research Press, 41–59.

Pugh, T.W. 2009. Contagion and Alterity: Kowoj Maya appropriations of European objects. *American Anthropologist* 111(3), 373–386.

Puzinas, J. 1935. Biržų apskrities priešistoriniai laikai. *Lietuvškoji enciklopedija* III, 1231–1235.

Puzinas, J. 1938. *Naujausių proistorinių tyrinėjimų duomenys (1918–1938 metų Lietuvos proistorinių tyrinėjimų apžvalga).* Senovės, IV. Kaunas.

Quast, D., Tamla, Ü. with contribution by Felten, S. 2010. Two fifth century AD Byzantine silver bowls from Estonia. *Estonian Journal of Archaeology* 14(2), 99–122.

Raddatz, K. 1987. *Der Thorsberger Moorfund: Katalog: Teile von Waffen und Pferdegeschirr, sonstige Fundstücke aus Metall und Glas, Ton- und Holzgefässe, Steingeräte.* Offa-Bücher, 65. Neumünster: Wachholtz.

Raddatz, K. 1993. Der Wolka-See, ein Opferplatz der Römischen Kaiserzeit in Ostpreußen. *Offa* 49/50(1992/1993), 127–187.

Radiņš, C. 2006. Lower Daugava area in the 1st–11th century. In: *Transformatio Mundi: The Transition from the Late Migration Period to the Early Viking Age in the East Baltic / edited by M. Bertasius.* Kaunas: Kaunas University of Technology Department of Philosophy and Cultural Science, 81–92.

Randsborg, K. 1973. Wealth and social structure as refelcted in the Bronze Age burials - A quantitative approach. In: *The Explanation of Culture Change: Models in Prehistory; Proceedings of a Meeting of the Research Seminar in Archaeology and Related Subjects Held at the University of Sheffield / edited by C. Renfrew.* London: Duckworth, 565–570.

Randsborg, K. 1990. Beyond the Roman Empire: Archaeological discoveries in Gudme on Funen, Denmark. *Oxford Journal of Archaeology* 9(3), 355–366.

Randsborg, K. 1995. *Hjortspring: Warfare and Sacrifice in Early Europe.* Aarhus: Aarhus University Press.

Randsborg, K. 2002. Wetland hoards. *Oxford Journal of Archaeology* 21(4), 415–418.

Rasch, M. 2004. The gold-treasure from Vittene in southwest Sweden = El tesoro áureo de Vittene, suroeste de Suecia. In: *Tecnología del oro antiguo: Europa y América = Ancient Gold Technology : America and Europe / edited by A. Perea, I. Montero & O. García-*

*Vuelta*. Anejos de Archivo Español de Arqueología, 32. Madrid: Consejo Superior de Investigaciones Científicas, Instituto de Historia, Departamento de Historia Antigua y Arqueología, 289–299.

Ratke, S. 2009. Guldgubber – a glimpse into the Vendel period. *Lund Archaeological Review* 15(2009), 149–159.

Ratke, S. & Simek, R. 2006. Guldgubber: Relics of Pre-Christian law rituals? In: *Old Norse Religion in Long-Term Perspectives: Origins, Changes, and Interactions: An International Conference In Lund, Sweden, June 3–7, 2004 / edited by A. Andrén, K. Jennbert & C. Raudvere*. Vägar till Midgård, 8. Lund: Nordic Academic, 303 – 307.

Rau, A. 2010. *Nydam Mose: Die personengebundenen Gegenstande, Grabungen 1989–1999*. Aarhus: Aarhus University Press.

Read, D.W. 2007. *Artifact Classification: A Conceptual and Methodological Approach*. Walnut Creek, CA: Left Coast Press.

Reece, R. 1988. Interpreting Roman hoards. *World Archaeology* 20(2), 261–269.

Renfrew, C. 1986. Varna and the emergence of wealth in prehistoric Europe. In: *The Social Life of Things: Commodities in Cultural Perspective / edited by A. Appadurai*. Cambridge: Cambridge University Press, 141–168.

Resi, H.G. 1995. The Norwegian iron bar deposits: Have they most to tell about production, distribution or consumption? In: *Produksjon og samfunn om erverv, spesialisering og bosetning i Norden i 1. årtusen e.Kr. : beretning fra 2. nordiske jernaldersymposium på Granavolden Gjæstgiveri 7.–10. mai 1992 / edited by H.G. Resi*. Oslo: Universitetets Oldsaksamling, 131–146.

Resi, H.G. 2011. Tre skjeletter og en halsring fra førromersk jernalder deponert i vann og våtmark i Stange, Hedmark. *Viking* 74(2011), 45–66.

Richards, C. & Thomas, J. 1984. Ritual activity and structured deposition in later NeolithicWessex. In: *Neolithic Studies: A Review of Some Current Research / edited by R. Bradley & J. Gardiner*. BAR British series, 133. Oxford: B.A.R. 189–218.

Rieck, F. & Jørgensen, E. 1997. Non-military equipment from Nydam. In: *Military aspects of Scandinavian society in a European perspective, AD 1–1300: Papers from an International Research Seminar at the Danish National Museum, Copenhagen, 2–4 May 1996 / edited by A. Nørgård Jorgensen & B.L. Clausen*. Publications from the National Museum. Studies in archaeology & history, 2. Copenhagen: National Museum, 220–225.

Riekstiņš, H. 1931. Der zweite depotfund von Kokumuiža. In: *Congressus secundus archaeologorum balticorum, Rigae, 19.-23. VIII. 1930*. Acta Universitatis Latviensis. Philologorum et Philosophorum ordinis series. Rigae: Valstspapiru spiestuve, 473–478.

Riekstiņš, H. 1936. 1935. g. ieguvumi numismatikā (pielikumā depozitu un savrupatradumu saraksts ar 2 kartēm). *Senate un Māksla* 1936(1), 85–98.

Robb, J.E. 1999. Secret agents: Culture, economy, and social reproduction. In: *Material Symbols: Culture and Economy in Prehistory / edited by J.E. Robb*. Occasional paper, Southern Illinois University at Carbondale. Center for Archaeological Investigations, 26. Carbondale: Center for Archaeological Investigations, Southern Illinois University, 3–15.

Robb, J.E. 2004. The extended artifact and the monumental economy: A methodology for material agency. In: *Rethinking Materiality: The Engagement of Mind with the Material World / edited by E. DeMarrais, C. Gosden & C. Renfrew.* McDonald Institute monographs. Cambridge: McDonald Institute for Archaeological Research, 131–139.

Robb, J. 2010. Beyond agency. *World Archaeology* 42(4), 493–520.

Robb, J. & Pauketat, T.R. (eds) 2013. *Big Histories, Human Lives: Tackling Problems of Scale in Archaeology.* Santa Fe, N.M.: School for Advanced Research Press.

Robson, E., Treadwell, L. & Gosden, C. (eds) 2006. Who Owns Objects?: The Ethics and Politics of Collecting Cultural Artefacts. Oxford: Oxbow Books.

Rossenberg, van E. 2003. Embedding material culture in perceptions of landscape. A contextual analysis of the deposition of bronzes in Northern Italy. In: *SOMA 2002. Symposium On Mediterranean Archaeology. Proceedings of the Sixth Annual Meeting of Postgraduate Researchers. University of Glasgow, Department of Archaeology, 15–17 February, 2002, Glasgow / edited by A. Brysbaert, N. de Bruijn, E. Gibson, A. Michael & M. Monaghan.* BAR international series, 1142. Oxford: Archaeopress, 157–164.

Rowlands, M.J. 1971. The Archaeological Interpretation of Prehistoric Metalworking. *World Archaeology* 3(2), 210–224.

Rzeszotarska-Nowakiewicz, A. 2010. Neckrings with trumpet-shaped terminals (mit Trompetenden) – Some remarks on traces of contacts in the Baltic basin during the Early Roman Period. In: *Worlds apart?: Contacts Across the Baltic Sea in the Iron Age: Network Denmark-Poland, 2005–2008 / edited by U. Lund Hansen & A. Bitner-Wróblewska.* København: Det Kongelige Nordiske Oldkriftselskab, 315–336.

Sajauskas, S. 2007. Monetų lobiai. In: *Lietuvos lobiai / edited by M. Michelbertas.* Kaunas: Šviesa, 18–45.

Salatkienė, B.K. 2009. *Geležies metalurgija Lietuvoje: Archeologijos duomenys.* Šiauliai: Šiaulių universiteto leidykla.

Salo, U. 1968. *Die Frührömische Zeit in Finnland.* Suomen muinaismuistoyhdistyksen aikakauskirja, 67. Helsinki: Suomen muinaismuistoyhdistys.

Salo, U. 1984. Pronssikausi ja rautakauden alku. In: *Suomen historia I / edited by E. Laaksonen, E. Pärssinen & K. J. Sillanpää.* Espoo: Weilin Göös, 99–256.

Sanden, W.A.B. van der. 1996. *Through Nature to Eternity: The Bog Bodies of Northwest Europe.* Amsterdam: Batavian Lion International.

Schmiedehelm, M. 1924. Der Fund von Kirimäe in Estland. *Suomen Muinaismuistoyhdistyksen Aikakauskirja* 35(1), 3–36.

Schmiedehelm, M. 1934. Keskmise rauaaja aardeleide Kambjast. *Eesti Rahva Muuseumi Aastaraamat* 9-10, 210–224.

Schmiedehelm, M. 1955. = Шмидехельм, М. 1955. *Археологические Памятники Периода Разложения Родового Строя На Северо-Востоке Эстонии (V Век До Н.э. - V Век Н.э.). Таллинн: Эстонское государственное издательство.*

Schmiedehelm, M. 1956. Kirde-Eesti hõimudest I aastatuhande viimasel poolel e.m.a. ja meie ajaarvutuse I aastatuhande algupoolel. In: *Eesti rahva etnilisest ajaloost: Artiklite kogumik / edited by H. Moora.* Tallinn: Eesti Riiklik Kirjastus, 147–159.

Schmiedehelm, M. & Laul, S. 1970. Asustusest ja etnilistest oludest Kagu-Eestis I aastatuhandel. In: *Studia Archaeologica in Memoriam Harri Moora / edited by M. Schmiedehelm, L. Jaanits & J. Selirand.* Tallinn: Valgus, 154–165.

Schovsbo, P.O. 2007. *Tranbær Mosefund 1875-96*. Moesgård, Aarhus: Jysk Arkaeologisk Selskab.

Scott, E. 1991. Animal and infant burials in Romano-British villas: A revitlaization movement. In: *Sacred and Profane: Proceedings of a Conference on Archaeology, Ritual and Religion: Oxford 1989 / edited by P. Garwood, D. Jennings, R. Skeates & J. Toms*. Monograph, Oxford University Committee for Archaeology, 32. Oxford: Oxford University Committee for Archaeology, 115–121.

Seger, T. 1982. The plague of Justinian and other scourges. An anallyses of the anomalies in the development of the Iron Age population in Finland. *Fornvännen* 1982, 184–197.

Selirand, J. & Tõnisson, E. 1963. *Läbi aastatuhandete*. Tallinn: Valgus.

Sewell, W.H. 1992. A theory of structure: Duality, agency, and transformation. *The American Journal of Sociology* 98(1), 1–29.

Shennan, S. 1993. After social evolution: A new archaeological agenda? In: *Archaeological Theory : Who Sets the Agenda? / edited by N. Yoffee & A. Sherratt*. Cambridge: Cambridge University Press, 53–59.

Shennan, S. 1997. *Quantifying Archaeology*. 2nd ed. Edinburgh: Edinburgh University Press.

Shennan, S. 2004. Analythical archaeology. In: *A Companion to Archaeology / edited by J.L. Bintliff*. Blackwell companion to archaeology. Oxford: Blackwell, 3–20.

Sherratt, A. 1992. What can archaeologists learnd from Annalsites? In: *Archaeology, Annales, and Ethnohistory / edited by A.B. Knapp*. Cambridge: Cambridge University Press, 135–142.

Sidrys, R.V. & Luchtanas, A. 1999. Shining axes, spiral pins. Early metal consumption in the East Baltic. *Acta Archaeologica* 70, 165–184.

Siljander, E. & Poutiainen, H. 2010. Päijät-Hämeen rautakautiset aarre- ja korukätkölöidöt. In: *Hirviveneestä hullukaaliin – Muinaisuskomukset arkeologisen aineiston tulkinnassa / edited by H.Poutiainen*. Päijät-Hämeen tutkimusseuran vuosikirja, 2008-2009. Hämeenlinna: Päijät-Hämeen tutkimusseura, 82–101.

Simniškytė, A. 2005. Sėlos kraštas VI-VII-XIII/XIV a.: Teritorinė struktūra ir hierarchija. *Lietuvos Archeologija* 27, 27–48.

Simniškytė, A. 2006a. Sociocultural dynamics in Selonian region (450–700 AD). In: *Transformatio Mundi: The Transition from the Late Migration Period to the Early Viking Age in the East Baltic / edited by M. Bertasius*. Kaunas: Kaunas University of Technology Department of Philosophy and Cultural Science, 151–159.

Simniškytė, A. 2006b. Weapon burial rite in the 2nd half of the 1st millennium. In: *Pētījumi Sēļu senatnē: Rakstu krājums / edited by I. Melne*. Latvijas nacionālā vēstures muzeja raksti, 11. Arheologija. Rīga: Latvijas nacionālais vēstures muzejs, 65–76.

Simniškytė, A. 2009. Memory and Identity: Genuine of fake? Once more on the question of the 'Selonian' culture. In: *Memory, Society, and Material Culture: Papers from the Third Theoretical Seminar of the Baltic Archaeologists (BASE) Held at the University of Latvia, October 5–6, 2007 / edited by A. Šnē & A. Vasks*. Interarchaeologia, 3. Rīga: Latgales Druka, 99–110.

Simniškytė, A., Stančikaitė, M. & Kisielienė, D. 2003. Continuity and discontinuity in the Juodonys archaeological comlex. In: *Arheoloogiga Läänemeremaades. Uurimusi Jüri Seliranna auks / edited by V. Lang & Ü. Tamla*. Muinasaja teadus, 13. Tallinn-Tartu: Eesti Teaduste Akadeemia Kirjastus, 267–286.

Šnore, E. 1993. *Agrā dzelzs laikmeta uzkalniņi Latvijas austrumu daļa*. Riga: Zinatne.

Šnore, E. 1962. = Шноре, Э. 1962. Шпоры городища Асоте и их место в классификации шпор. *Swiatowit*, 24, 557–585.

Šnore, R. 1936. *Latvijas aizvēstures kartes*. Congressus secundus archaeologorum balticorum, Rigae, 19.–23. VIII. 1930. Acta Universitatis Latviensis. Philologorum et Philosophorum ordinis series, T. 1., suppl. 2. Rigae: Latvijas Universitate.

Spangen, M. 2009. Silver hoards in Sámi areas. In: *Recent Perspectives on Sámi Archaeology in Fennoscandia and North-West Russia. Proceedings of the First International Conference on Sámi archaeology, Rovaniemi, 19–22 October 2006 / edited by P. Halinen, M. Lavento & M. Suhonen*. ISKOS, 17. Helsinki: Finnish Antiquarian Society.

Sparrow, C. 1982. Treasure trove: A lawyer's view. *Antiquity* 56(218), 199–202.

Sperling, U. 2013. Der Bronzebruchhort von Tehumardi in Estland – Verstecktes Altmetall oder ritueller Weihefund? Ein Deutungsversuch am Erscheinungsbild der Bronzen. In: *Man, His Time, Artefacts, and Places: Collection of Articles Dedicated to Richard Indreko = Inimene, tema aeg, esemed ja paigad: Richard Indrekole pühendatud artiklite kogumik / edited by K. Johanson & M. Tõrv*. Muinasaja teadus, 19. Tartu: Tartu Ülikool, 261–316.

Stanton, T.W., Brown, M.K. & Pagliaro, J.P. 2008. Garbage of the Gods? Squatters, refuse disposal, and termination rituals among the ancient Maya. *Latin American Antiquity* 19(3), 227–247.

Stenbak, M.K. 1994. Illemose. *Fynske Minder* 1994, 149–180.

Stenberger, M.K.H. 1977. *Vorgeschichte Schwedens*. Neumünster: K. Wachholtz.

Stepiņš, P. 1939. Senkapi 'Liepu kalnā' Rubas. pag. Rūsīšos - Debešos, Jelgavas apr. *Senatne un Māksla* 1939(1), 45–63.

Stjernquist, B. 1997. *The Röekillorna Spring. Spring-Cults in Scandinavian Prehistory*. Stockholm : Almqvist & Wiksell International.

Stubavs, A. 1976. *Ķentes Pilskalns un Apmetne*. Rīga: Zinātne.

Taavitsainen, J.-P. 1990. *Ancient Hillforts of Finland : Problems of Analysis, Chronology and Interpretation with Special Reference to the Hillfort of Kuhmoinen*. Suomen Muinaismuistoyhdistyksen aikakauskirja, 94. Helsinki: Suomen Muinaismuistodistys.

Tallgren, A.M. 1924. Ein wichtiger eisenzeitlicher Fund aus Kunilepa Ksp. Juuru (Jörden). *Sitzungsberichte der Gelehrten Estnischen Gesellschaft* 1923, 50–56.

Tallgren, A.M. 1925. *Zur Archäologie Eestis. 2., Von 500 bis etwa 1250 n. Chr.* Acta et Commentationes Universitatis Dorpatensis, III, 6. Dorpat.

Tallgrens, A.M., Šturms, E., Moora, H. & Baloža, F. 1926. *Latvijas archaioloģija*. Riga: AS Valters un Rapa.

Talvio, T. 2002. *Coins and Coin Finds in Finland, AD 800-1200*. ISKOS, 12. Helsinki: Suomen muinaismuistoyhdistys.

Tamla, T. 1977. Eesti soo- ja rabaleidudest. Tartu Riikliku Ülikooli ÜTÜ ajalooringi kogumik. Ajalooalaseid töid 6, 151–175.

Tamla, T. 1985. Kultuslikud allikad Eestis. In: Rahvasuust kirjapanekuni. Uurimusi rahvaluule proosaloomingust ja kogumisloost / edited by Ü. Tedre. Eesti NSV Teaduste Akadeemia Emakeele Seltsi Toimetised, 17. Tallinn: Eesti NSV Teaduste Akadeemia, 122–146.

Tamla, T. 1995. Einige estnische Moorfunde aus dem ersten Jahrtausend. In: *Archaeology East and West of the Baltic: Papers from the Second Estonian-Swedish Archaeological Symposium, Sigtuna, May 1991 / edited by I. Jansson*. Theses and papers in archaeology. New series A, 7. Stockholm: Department of Archaeology, University of Stockholm, 103–110.

Tamla, T. 1996. Virumaa muinasaeg. In: *Virumaa: Koguteos / edited by K. Saaber*. Tallinn: Lääne-Viru Maavalitsus : Ida-Viru Maavalitsus, 206–244.

Tamla, T. & Jaanits, L. 1977. Das Gräberfeld und das Spätneolithische Siedlungsplatz von Paju. *Eesti NSV Teaduste Akadeemia toimetised. Ühiskonnateadused* 26(1), 64–71.

Tamla, Ü. & Kiudsoo, M. 2005. *Eesti muistsed aarded: [Näituse kataloog: 19.05.2005–05.06.2006 Tallinnas*. Tallinn: Arheoloogiakeskus.

Tautavičius, A. 1977. *Lietuvos TSR archeologijos atlasas. T III. I–XIII a. pilkapynai ir senkapiai*. Vilnius: LTSR Mokslų akademijos Istorijos institutas.

Tautavičius, A. 1978. *Lietuvos TSR archeologijos atlasas. T IV. I–XIII a. radiniai*. Vilnius: LTSR Mokslų akademijos Istorijos institutas.

Tautavičius, A. 1981. Taurapilio 'kunigaikscio' kapas. *Lietuvos Archeologija* 2, 18–43.

Tautavičius, A. 1984. Požerės plokštinis kapinynas. *Lietuvos Archeologija* 3, 93–118.

Tautavičius, A. 1996. *Vidurinis geležies amžius Lietuvoje (V–IX a.)*. Vilnius: Pilių tyrimų centras 'Lietuvos pilys'.

Tautavičius, A. (ed.) 1975. *Lietuvos TSR archeologijos atlasas. T II. Piliakalniai*. Vilnius: LTSR Mokslų akademijos Istorijos institutas.

Thomas, J. 1996. *Time, Culture, and Identity: An Interpretative Archaeology*. London: Routledge.

Thomas, J. 2000. Introduction: The polarities of post-processual archaeology. In: *Interpretive Archaeology : A Reader / edited by J. Thomas*. London: Leicester University Press, 1–18.

Thomas, J., Murray, T., & Olivier, L. 2006. Comments on Jan Harding (2005): Rethinking the great divide: long-term structural history and the temporality of the event. Norwegian Archaeological Review 38, 88–101. *Norwegian Archaeological Review* 39(1), 80–97.

Thomas, N. 1991. *Entangled Objects: Exchange, Material Culture, and Colonialism in the Pacific*. Cambridge, Mass. : Harvard University Press.

Thomas, S. & Stone, P.G. 2009. *Metal Detecting and Archaeology*. The 'heritage matters' series, 2. Woodbridge: Boydell Press.

Tilley, C.Y., Keane, W., Küchler, S, Rowlands, M. & Spyer, P. (eds) 2006. *Handbook of Material Culture*. London: SAGE.

Tõnisson, E. 1962. Eesti aardeleiud 9.–13. sajandist. In: *Muistsed kalmed ja aarded / edited by H. Moora*. Arheoloogiline kogumik, 2. Tallinn: Ajaloo Instituut, Eesti NSV Teaduste Akadeemia, 182–274.

Tõnisson, E. 2008. *Eesti muinaslinnad / compiled and edited by H. Valk & A. Mäesalu, with special contributions from various authors*. Muinasaja teadus, 20. Tartu: Tartu Ülikool.

Torbrügge, W. 1972. Vor- und Frühgeschichtliche Flüssfunde. *Bericht der romischgermanischen Kommission* 51-52(1970-1971), 1–146.

Tvauri, A. 2006. Investigation of the Middle Iron Age. In: *Archaeological Research in Estonia, 1865–2005 / edited by V. Lang & M.Laneman*. Estonian archaeology, 1. Tartu: Tartu University Press, 105–126.

Tvauri, A. 2007. Migrants or natives? The research history of long larrows in Russia and Estonia in the 5th–10th centuries. In: *Slavica Helsingiensia. Special issue: Topics on the Ethnic, Linguistic and Cultural Making of the Russian North / edited by J. Nuorluoto*. Slavica Helsingiensia, 32. Helsinki: Department of Modern Languages at Helsinki University, 247–285.

Tvauri, A. 2012. *The Migration Period, Pre-Viking Age, and Viking Age in Estonia*. Estonian Archaeology, 4. Tartu: Tartu Ülikooli Kirjastus.

Tvauri, A. 2014. The impact of the climate catastrophe of 536–537 AD in Estonia and neighbouring areas. *Estonian Journal of Archaeology* 18(1), 30–56.

Ulst, I. 2010. The problems of 'black archaeology' in Estonia. *Estonian Journal of Archaeology* 14(2), 153.

Undset, I. & Mestorf, J. 1882. *Das erste Auftreten des Eisens in Nord-Europa eine Studie in der vergleichenden vorhistorischen Archäologie*. Hamburg: O. Meissner.

Urtāns, J. 2004. The sacral waters in Zemgale (Semigallia). In: *Pētījumi Zemgaļu senatnē: Rakstu krājums / edited by R. Ritums*. Latvijas Vēstures Muzeja raksti, 10. Rīga: Latvijas Vēstures Muzejs, 89–100.

Urtāns, J. 2008. *Ancient Cult Sites of Semigallia = Zemgales senas kulta vietas*. CCC Papers, 11. Riga: Nordik.

Urtāns, V. 1962. Tīras purva depozīts. *Latvijas PSR Vēstures muzeja raksti: Arheoloģija* 1962, 83–94.

Urtāns, V. 1964. Latvijas 5.–9. gs. depozīti. *Arheoloģija un Etnogrāfija* 6, 39–74.

Urtāns, V. 1970. Etniskās atšķirības apbedīšanas tradīcijās un kapu inventārā Latvijā 5.–9. gs. *Arheoloģija un Etnogrāfija* 9, 61–85.

Urtāns, V. 1977. *Senākie depozīti Latvijā līdz 1200. g.* Riga: Zinatne.

Vaitkevičius, V. 2004. *Studies into the Balts' Sacred Places*. BAR International Series, 1228. Oxford: John and Erica Hedges, Ltd.

Vaitkevičius, V. 2005. Interpreting the east Lithuanian barrow culture. In: *Culture and Material Culture: Papers from the First Theoretical Seminar of the Baltic Archaeologists (BASE) Held at the University of Tartu, Estonia, October 17h–19th, 2003 / edited by V. Lang*. Interarchaeologia, 1. Tartu: University of Tartu, 71–86.

Vaitkevičius, V. 2006. *Senosios Lietuvos šventvietės: Aukštaitija*. Vilnius: Diemedžio leidykla.

Vaitkunskienė, L. 1981. *Sidabras Senovės Lietuvoje*. Vilnius: Mokslas.

Vaitkunskienė, L. 1995. The formation of a warrior elite during the Middle Iron Age in Lithuania. *Archaeologia Baltica* 1, 94–106.

Valatka, V. 1966. Dargėliškės lobis. *Kraštotyra* 25, 165–169.

Vang Petersen, P. 1994. Excavations at sites of treasure trove finds at Gudme. In: *The Archaeology of Gudme and Lundeborg: Papers Presented at a Conference at Svendborg, October 1991 / edited by P. O. Nielsen, K. Randsborg & H. Thrane*. Arkæologiske studier, 10. Copenhagen: Akademisk forlag, Universitetsforlaget i København, 30–40.

Vankina, L., Vasks, A. & Urtāns, V. 1981. *Latvijas senatne ceļvedis pa Latvijas PSR vēstures muzeja ekspozīciju (9. gt. p. m. ē. b. – m. ē. 13 gs)*. Riga: Avots.

Vasiliauskas, E. 2009. Senovės gyvenvietės ir kaimavietės Joniškio rajone. *Archeologiniai tyrinėjimai Lietuvoje 2008 metais*, 250–259.

Vaškevičiūtė, I. 2000. Etnokultūrinė žiemgalių sritis. *Lietuvos Archeologija* 20, 141–157.

Vaškevičiūtė, I. 2007. Semigallian warrior weaponry and its reflection in burial rites in the fifth to the 12th Century AD. *Archaeologia Baltica* 8, 214–222.

Vasks, A. 1999. Latvian archaeology: research and conclusions. In: *Inside Latvian Archaeology / edited by O.W. Jensen, H. Karlsson & A. Vijups*. Gotarc Series A, 2. Göteborg: Göteborg University, Department of Archaeology, 3–87.

Vasks, A. 2006a. Dignājas pilskalna apmetne 1989. un 1990. gada izraukumu gaisimā. In: *Pētījumi Sēļu senatnē: Rakstu krājums / edited by I. Melne*. Latvijas nacionālā vēstures muzeja raksti, 11. Arheologija. Rīga: Latvijas nacionālais vēstures muzejs, 105–120.

Vasks, A. 2006b. Stone grave cemeteries in western Latvia. In: *Etnos ja kultuur: Uurimusi Silvia Laulu auks / edited by H. Valk*. Muinasaja teadus, 18. Tartu; Tallinn: Tartu Ülikool, arheoloogia õppetool, 99–111.

Vasks, A. & Vijups, A. 2004. *Staldzenes Bronzas Laikmeta Depozīts = Staldzene Bronze Age Hoard*. Rīga: SIA Fobo Prints.

Vassar, A. 1956. Lisandeid Eesti hõimude uurimisele Lääne- ja Edela-Eestis I–IV sajandil. In: *Eesti rahva etnilisest ajaloost: Artiklite kogumik / edited by H. Moora*. Tallinn: Eesti Riiklik Kirjastus, 160–190.

Vassar, A. 1966. Sammaskalmetest Eestis. In: *Pronksiajast varase feodalismini. Uurimusi Baltimaade ja naaberalade arhoeloogiast / edited by H. Moora & J. Selirand*. Tallinn: Eesti NSV Teadsuste Akadeemia Ajaloo Instituut, 207–215.

Veldi, M. 2006. Keskusest a kommunikatsionist Kagu- ja Ida-Eestis rauaaja esimesel poolel. In: *Etnos ja Kultuur: Uurimusi Silvia Laulu Auks / edited by H. Valk*. Muinasaja teadus, 18. Tartu-Tallinn: Tartu Ülikool, arheoloogia õppetool, 79–97.

Verlaeckt, K. 2000. Hoarding and the circulation of metalwork in Late Bronze Age Denmark: Quantification and beyond. In: *Metals Make the World Go Round: The Supply and Circulation of Metals in Bronze Age Europe: Proceedings of a Conference Held at the University of Birmingham in June 1997 / edited by C.F. E. Pare*. Oxford: Oxbow Books, 194–208.

*Vogt, J., Soille, P., de Jager, A., Rimaviciute, E., Mehl, S., Foisneau, S., Bódis, K., Dusart, J., Paracchini, M.L., Haastrup, P. & Bamps. C. 2007. A pan-European River and Catchment Database. European Commission. JRC: Luxembourg, (EUR 22920 EN).*

Volkaitė-Kulikauskienė, R. 1943. Stačiūnų kapinyno antkaklės. *Gimtasai kraštas* 31, 80–95.

Volkaitė-Kulikauskienė, R. 1958. *Lietuvos archeologiniai paminklai ir jų tyrinėjimai*. Vilnius: Valstybinės ir mokslinės literatūros leidykla.

Voss, O. 1954. The Høstentorp silver hoard and its period. A study of a Danish find of scrap silver from about 500 A.D. *Acta Archaeologica* 25(1954), 171–219.

Walker, W.H. 1995. Ceremonial trash? In: *Expanding Archaeology / edited by J.M. Skibo, W.H. Walker & A.E. Nielsen*. Salt Lake City: University of Utah Press, 67–79.

Watt, M. 2004. The Gold-Figure Foils ('Guldgubbar') from Uppåkra. In: *Continuity for Centuries. A Ceremonial Building and its Context at Uppåkra, Southern Sweden / edited by L. Larsson*. Uppåkrastudier, 10. Acta archaeologica Lundensia. Series in 8°. Lund: Almqvist & Wiksell, 167–221.

Webley, L. 2008. *Iron Age Households: Structure and Practice in Western Denmark, 500BC–AD200*. Jutland Archaeological Society Publications, 62. Moesgård, Aarhus: Jutland Archaeological Society.

Weiner, A.B. 1985. Inalienable Wealth. *American Ethnologist* 12(2), 210–227.

Weiner, A.B. 1992. *Inalienable Possessions: The Paradox of Keeping-While-Giving*. Berkeley: University of California Press.

Weiner, A.B. 1994. Cultural difference and the density of objects. *American Ethnologist* 21(2), 391–403.

Wenger, E. 1998. *Communities of Practice: Learning, Meaning, and Identity*. Cambridge: University Press.

Wentink, K. & Van Gijn, A. 2008. Neolithic depositions in the northern Netherlands. In: *Hoards from the Neolithic to the Metal Ages: Technical and Codified Practices: Session of the XIth Annual Meeting of the European Association of Archaeologists / edited by C.Hamon & B. Quilliec*. BAR international series, 1758. Oxford: Archaeopress, 29–34.

Wessman, A. 2009. Levänluhta – A place of punishment, sacrifice or just a common cemetery? *Fennoscandia Archaeologica* 26, 81–105.

Wiell, S. 2003. Denmark's bog find pioneer: The archaeologist Conrad Engelhardt and his work. In: *The Spoils of Victory: The North in the Shadow of the Roman Empire / edited by L. Jørgensen, B.Storgaard & L. Gebauer Thomsen*. Copenhagen: Nationalmuseet, 66–83.

Wiker, G. 1999. Gullbrakteatene og deres funnsteder. *Nicolay* 77(1999), 12–20.

Wolf, E.R. 1990. Distinguished lecture: Facing power – Old insights, new questions. *American Anthropologist* 92(3), 586–596.

Yates, D. & Bradley, R. 2010. Still water, hidden depths: The deposition of Bronze Age metalwork in the English Fenland. *Antiquity* 84(324), 405–415.

Zabiela, G. 2003. Lietuvos piliakalniai: Tyrinėjimų aspektas. *Lietuvos Archeologija* 24, 33–56.

Zachrisson, I. 1984. *De samiska metalldepåerna år 1000–1350: I ljuset av fyndet från Mörtträsket, Lappland = The Saami Metal Deposits A.D. 1000–1350: In the Light of the Find from Mörtträsket, Lapland*. Archaeology and environment, 3. Umeå: University of Umeå.

Zapolska, A. 2012. Roman coins from the western part of the west Balt territory. In: *Proceedings of the XIVth International Numismatic Congress, Glasgow 2009 / edited by N. Holmes*. London: Spink of London, 1115–1125.

Žeiere, I. 2008. Par Tīras purva depozīta tekstilmateriāliem. In: *Pētījumi Kuršu senatnē: Rakstu krājums / edited by V. Muižnieks*. Latvijas nacionālā vēstures muzeja raksti. Arheoloģija, 14. Rīga: Latvijas Nacionālais Vēstures muzejs, 129–138.

Zemītis, G. 2004. Gaideļu-Vidaču kapulauka vieta Jaunsvirlaukas un Salgales (Sidrabrenes) pagasta arheoloģisko kontekstā. In: *Pētījumi Zemgaļu senatnē: Rakstu krājums / edited by R. Ritums*. Latvijas Vēstures Muzeja raksti, 10. Rīga: Latvijas Vēstures Muzejs, 181–194.

Žulkus, V. 2004. *Kuršiai Baltijos jūros erdvėje: Monografija*. Vilnius: Versus Aureus.

## Internet sources


CCM River and Catchment Database. http://ccm.jrc.ec.europa.eu/. (11.11.2011.)

Department of Cultural Heritage [Lithuania], Map server, © G.Jucys: Kultūros Paveldo Departamentas. http://www.heritage.lt/km/. (12.11.2013.)

Estonian Land Board Geoportal: Maa-ameti Geoportaal. http://geoportaal.maaamet.ee/est/Kaardiserver-p2.html. (12.11.2013.)

Global Administrative Areas. http://www.gadm.org/. (11.11.2011.)

Illerup Ådal. Et arkæologisk tryllespejl. http://www.illerup.dk/. (25.06.2012.)

KurTuEsi [Maps]. http://www.kurtuesi.lv/maps#. (12.11.2013.)

Latvian Geospatial Information Agency: Latvijas Ģeotelpiskās informācijas aģentūra. http://kartes.lgia.gov.lv/kartes.html. (12.11.2013.)

Mägi, M. 2003. Kaali ja kultuurmaastik. http://www.tlu.ee/UserFiles/Ajaloo%20Instituut/Arheoloogia%20osakond/Kaali%20ja%20kultuurmaastik.pdf. (23.09.2013.)

NGA GEOnet Names Server. http://earth-info.nga.mil/gns/html/. (11.11.2011.)

Oxford English Dictionary. http://www.oed.com/. (04.04.2011.)

PAST. Past 3.x - the Past of the Future. http://folk.uio.no/ohammer/past/. (12.11.2013.)

Portable Antiquities Scheme. http://finds.org.uk/. (04.11.2013.)

Register of Cultural Heritage [Lithuania]: Kultūros vertybių registras. http://kvr.kpd.lt/heritage/. (12.11.2013.)

Register of the maps in the National Archives of Estonia: Rahvusarhiivi kaartide infosüsteem. http://www.ra.ee/kaardid/index.php/et. (12.11.2013.)

Roskilde Museum. Mannerupskatten - sølvskatten fra germansk jernalder. http://www.roskildemuseum.dk/Default.aspx?ID=651. (10.11.2012.)

Skandeborg Museum. Alken Enge - The mass grave at Lake Mossø. http://www.skanderborgmuseum.dk/Alken_Enge-English_version-1070.aspx. (10.07.2013.)

State register of cultural heritage, State Inspection for Heritage Protection [Republic of Latvia]: Valsts aizsargājamo nekustamo kultūras pieminekļu saraksts, Valsts kultūras pieminekļu aizsardzības inspekcija. http://www.mantojums.lv/?cat=742&lang=lv. (12.11.2013.)

The Treasure (Designation) Order 2002. http://www.legislation.gov.uk/uksi/2002/2666/contents/made. (19.04.2011.)

Treasure Act 1996. http://www.legislation.gov.uk/ukpga/1996/24/contents. (19.04.2011.)

X-GIS. Estonian Land Board: X-GIS. Maa-amet. http://xgis.maaamet.ee/xGIS/XGis. (12.11.2013.)

# Abbreviations

## Institutions

AI – Institute of History, Tallinn University (Ajaloo Instituut, Tallinna Ülikool).

AM – Estonian History Museum (Eesti Ajaloomuuseum).

BKM – Sėla Museum, Biržai (Biržų kraštotyros muziejus „Sėla“).

DaM – Daugavpils Museum (Daugavpils Muzejs).

DM – Riga Dome Cathedral Museum (Doma muzeja, Rīgā).

EAA – Estonian Historical Archives (Eesti Ajalooarhiiv).

ERM – Estonian National Museum, Tartu (Eesti Rahva Muuseum).

Helsinki KaM – The National Museum of Finland, Helsinki (Suomen Kansallismuseo).

Jelgavā KPM – Jelgavā History and Art Museum (Jelgavas vēstures un mākslas muzejs, Jelgavā muzejs, prev. Kurzemes provinces muzeja).

KM – Kretinga Museum (Kretingos muziejus).

LMAB – Archives of the Wroblewski Library of the Lithuanian Academy of Sciences (Lietuvos mokslų akademijos Vrublevskių biblioteka).

LNM AR – Lithuanian National Museum, Vilnius (Lietuvos nacionalinis muziejus).

LVNM (LVNM (CVVM)) – Latvian National Historical Museum, Rīga (Latvijas Nacionālais Vēstures muzejs).

OxA – Oxford Radiocarbon Accelerator Unit, Research Laboratory for Archaeology and the History of Art.

PM – Prussian Musem (Prūsijos muzieijus).

RKM – Rokiškis Land Museum (Rokiškio Krasto muziejus).

ŠAM – Aušra Museum, Šiauliai (Šiaulių muziejus „Aušros“).

TÜ – University of Tartu, Archaeology collections (Tartu Ülikool, arheoloogiakogud).

TÜ AK – Archives of the *Kabinet* of Archaeology, University of Tartu (Arheoloogia Kabineti arhiiv, Tartu Ülikool).

UKM – Utena Museum (Utenos kraštotyros muziejus).

UTL – University of Tartu Library (Tartu Ülikooli Raamatukogu).

VDKM – Vytautas the Great War Museum, Kaunas (Vytauto Didžiojo karo muziejus).

ŽMA – Alka Samogitian Museum, Telšiai (Žemaičių muziejus „Alka“).

## Publications

KPM II 1897 – Katalog des Prussia-Museums im Nordflügel des Königlichen Schlosses. Teil II: Die Funde aus der Zeit der heidnischen Gräberfelder (von Christi Geburt bis zur Einführung des Christentums). Königsberg.

MPAR – Materialō po arheologii Rossii. Материалы по археологии России, издаваемые Императорской археологической комиссией. Санкт-Петербург (St Petersburg), 1866-1918.

Otšet – Otšet Imperatorskoi Arheologitšeskoi Komissii. *Отчет* Императорской *Археологической Комиссии*). Санкт-Петербург (St Petersburg), 1882-1888.

Pieminekļu izstāde 1936 – 1936. gadā izrakto pieminekļu izstāde. Rīga.

RK 1896 – Katalog der Ausstellung zum X. archäologischen Kongress in Riga 1896. Riga.

RK 1930 – Katalog der Ausstellung zur Konferenz Baltischer Archäologen in Riga 1930. Riga.

Sammlung – Die vorgeschichtliche Sammlung des Kurzemer (Kurländischen) Provinzialmuseums zu Jelgava (Mitau), 1818-1938. Rīga, 1939.

Sb. GEG – Sitzungsberichte der Gelehrten Estnischen Gesellschaft, 1861-1923; Õpetatud Eesti Seltsi Aastaraamat, 1924-1938; 1988-. Dorpat (Tartu), 1861-1940; 1995-.

Sb. Kurl. – Sitzungsberichte der Kurländischen Gesellschaft für Literatur und Kunst aus den Jahren 1850-1935/1936. Mitau. Rīga, 1850-1937.

Sb. Prussia H – Sitzungsberichte der Alterdumsgesellschaft Prussia. Königsberg, 1875-1924.

Sb. Rig. – Sitzungsberichte der Gesellschaft für Geschichte und Alterthumskunde der Ostseeprovinzen Russlands aus den Jahren 1873-1934. Riga, 1874-1936.

SM – Senate un Māksla. Rīga, 1936-1940.

# Appendices

| Name | Country | Collection | Dating | Artefacts | Find-spot | Environment | Comments | References |
|---|---|---|---|---|---|---|---|---|
| Aesoo I | Estonia | Lost | Middle Iron Age (?) | 4 swords, 1 axe | | Dry land, under big aspen tree, in the vicinity of River Navesti | | Laid 1924, 139 |
| Aesoo II | Estonia | Lost | Middle Iron Age (?) | 1(+) sword, 1(+) spearhead, 1(+) sickles/scythes, 1(+) other iron artefacts | | Unknown | Perhaps belongs together with Aesoo I find | Laid 1924, 139 |
| Põhja-Eesti (North-Estonia) | Estonia | AI 2643: 265-343; Narva Museum | 100-600 | 51 sickles/scythes, 21 spearheads, 5 battle knives, 3 axes | Unknown, North-Estonia, Selja village(?) | Bog | | Grewingk 1887, 165–166; Laul & Tõnisson 1991, 81; Sb. GEG 1886, 165; Tamla 1977, no. 51, 156; Tamla 1995, 103 |
| Grobiņa | Latvia | LVNM 58214, 64387 | 675-700 | 2 brooches (1 silver, 1 gilded bronze) | Somewhere in the Grobiņa area | Unknown | | Kleeman 1935, 1–6, figs 1.a–c, 2.a–b; LV 1938, 127; RK 1896, 23 (no. 328), tab. 6: 7, 9; Sammlung 1939, 16, tab. 17; Tallgrens et al. 1926, 58, fig. 29: 10; Urtāns 1964, 49, no. 13, figs 15–16; Urtāns 1977, 155–156, fig. 63 |
| Ikšķile | Latvia | St. Petersburg State Hermitage Museum 987/1-3 | 600-700 | 3 silver neck-rings | Somewhere in the Ikšķiles area | Unknown | | Urtāns 1964, 52–53, no. 19, fig. 22; Urtāns 1977, 155, fig. 62 |
| Rokiškis | Lithuania | VDKM 1404: 1-2 | 600-800 | 2 silver neck-rings | Somewhere in the Rokiškis area | Unknown | | Kulikauskas et al. 1961, fig. 222; Nakaitė 1959, 57, 59, fig. 1; Tautavičius 1977, 133; Vaitkunskienė 1981, 29; Volkaitė-Kulikauskienė 1943, 92 |

*Appendix 1.1. List of wealth deposits with insufficient contextual information. Only the deposits of artefacts with relevant chronology (within 1st–9th century AD) have been included.*

| Wealth Deposit | TPQ | Coins | Material 1 | Material 2 | Coin details |
|---|---|---|---|---|---|
| Kazzemnieki | 161 | 2 | Silver | Bronze | 1-Hadrianus (117-138); 1-Antonius Pius (138-161) |
| Daugavpils | 337 | 34 | Bronze | | 2-Marcus Vipsanius Agrippa (45-12 BC); 2-Augustus Octavianus (27 BC-14 AD); 2-Claudius I (41-54); 3-Vespasian (69-79); 4-Domitian (81-96); 6-Hadrianus (117-138); 1-Antonius Pius (138-161); 1-Lucius Verus (161-169); 3-Marcus Aurelius (161-180); 3- Faustina II († 175); 1-Lucilla (150-182); 1- Severus Alexander (222-235); 1-Philip the Arab (244-249); 1-Volusianus (251-253); 1-Diocletian (284-305); 1-Constantine the Great (306-337); 1-Not identifyable |
| Priedkalni | 361 | 17 | Bronze | | 3-Not identifyable; 6-Not identifyable; 1-Marcus Vipsanius Agrippa (45-12 BC); 2-Augustus Octavianus (27 BC-14 AD); 1-Germanic (?); 1-Claudius I (41-54); 1- Faustina II († 175)?; 1-Constantine the Great (306-337); 1-Constantius II (337-361) |
| Jelgava | 361 | 13 | Bronze | | 1-Diocletian (284-305); 1-Maximian (285- ca. 310); 1-Maximinus (305-313); 7- Constantine the Great (306-337); 1-Constantius II (337-361); 2-Imitation of a Roman coin |
| **Total: 4** | | **66** | | | |

*Appendix 1.2. Roman coin hoards from Latvia.*

| Wealth Deposit | TPQ | Ornaments | Coins | Material 1 | Material 2 | Coin details |
|---|---|---|---|---|---|---|
| Dirmeikiai | 161 | 1 | 2 | Bronze | | 1-Antoninus Pius (138-161); 1-Hadrianus (117-138) |
| Klaipėda | 161 | | 3 | Bronze | | 1-Augustus Octavianus (27 BC-14 AD); 1-Trajanus (98-117); 1-Antoninus Pius (138-161) |
| Lileikėniai | 161 | | 6 | Bronze | Silver | 5-Roman; 1-Antoninus Pius (138-161) |
| Noreišiai | 161 | | 5 | Bronze | | 1-Hadrianus (117-138); 1-Antoninus Pius (138-161); 1-Faustina I (coined after the death); 2-Unidentifyable |
| Veršvai | 180 | | 7 | Bronze | | 2-Trajanus (98-117); 1-Sabina († 136); 2-Faustina I († 141); 2-Marcus Aurelius (161-180) |
| Algimantai | 192 | | 8 | Bronze | | 1-Antoninus Pius (138-161); 1-Faustina I († 141); 1-Faustina II († 175); 1-Marcus Aurelius (161-180); 1-Lucilla (†183); 1-Crispina (†183); 2-Commodus (180-192) |
| Vilkyčiai | 192 | | 11 | Bronze | | 1-Hadrianus (117-138); 1-Antoninus Pius (138-161); 1-Marcus Aurelius (161-180); 1-Lucius Verus (161-169); 1-Sabina († 136); 1-Faustina I († 141); 1-Faustina II († 175); 1-Commodus (180-192); 1-Crispina († 183); 1-Maximianus (Maiminus?); 1- Unidentifyable (numerous other coins) |
| Saulažoliai | 212 | | 51 | Bronze | | 4-Trajanus (98-117); 5-Hadrianus (117-138); 1-Sabina († 136); 9-Antoninus Pius (138-161); 2-Faustina I († 141); 1-From period 138-161; 9-Marcus Aurelius (161-180); 5-Faustina II († 175); 1-Bronze medalion Geta (209-212), Coined in Tarsus (Kilykien); 1-Commodus (180-192); 1-From period 138-192; 12-Unidentifyable |
| Raseiniai | 235 | | 43 | Bronze | | 3-Consular coins; 1-Domitianus (81-96); 1-Nerva (96-98); 5-Trajanus (98-117); 1-Elius Verus (133-138); 8-Antoninus Pius (138-161); 1-Faustina († 141); 8-Marcus Aurelius (161-180); 1-Faustina II († 175); 3-Caracalla (211-217); 1-Julia Domna († 217); 2-Severus Alexander (222-235); 8-Unidentifyable |
| Dargiškė | 244 | 2 | 1 | Bronze | | 1-A bullion Antoninian of Gordian III (238–244) minted in Nikea (Asia Minor) |
| Janapolė | 244 | | 14 | Bronze | | 2-Severus Alexander (222-235), Coined in Nikaea (Bithynien); 1-Julia Mamaea (†235), Coined in Nikaea (Bithynien); 1-Maximinius I (235-238), Coined in Nikaea (Bithynien); 3-Maximus (235-238), Coined in Nikaea (Bithynien); 7-Gordianus III (238-244), Coined in Nikaea (Bithynien) |
| Kaunas | 423 | | 13 | Bronze | | 1-Victorinus (ca. 265-270); 1-Tetricus I (268-273); 1-Tetricus Sohn ??? (269-273); 1-Probus (276-282); 1-Numerianus (283-284); 1-Carinus (283-285); 1-Alcetus (293-296), Coined in London (Londinum); 2-Galerius (293-311); 1-Crispus (317-326), Coined in Trier (Augusta Trevirorum); 1-Constans I (337-350); 2-Honorius (295-423), Coined in Nicomedia (Bithynien) |
| Palanga_II | | | 30 | Bronze | | 30-Unidentifyable coins |
| **Total: 13** | | **3** | **194** | | | |

*Appendix 1.3. Roman coin hoards from Lithuania*

# CATALOGUE

| Wealth Deposit | ALSUNGAS |
|---|---|
| Collection number | LVNM 64910<br>(prev. DM T XCII 4) |
| Country | Latvia |
| County | Alsunga |
| Municipality | Alsunga |
| Village | Alsungas (Almāle) (Alšvangas) |
| Date Of Discovery | 1885/1886 summer |
| Comments On Discovery | Found during peat cutting at prev. Almāle manour land |
| Dating Of Deposit (century) | 4 |
| Earliest Dating Of Artefacts (AD) | 300 |
| Latest Dating Of Artefacts (AD) | 425 |
| References | Bliujienė 2010, no. 1<br>Moora 1938, 310<br>Sb. Rig. 1887, 6–7<br>Urtāns 1964, 48, no.12, fig. 14 |
| Comments | Donated to the Dome Cathedral Museum by baron T. Fuks on the 11th of February 1887 |

| | |
|---|---|
| Environment | Watery condition |
| Environment Subtype | Bog |

*Alsungas wealth deposit. (Photo: Ester Oras).*

| Artefact Type | Subtype | Amount | Material | Comments On Appearance | Futher Description |
|---|---|---|---|---|---|
| Neck-Ring | Wire wound and small loop terminals | 1 | Bronze | Fragment of a neck-ring, bent in the form of a ring | Diameter 8.5 x 12 cm |

| Wealth Deposit | ALULINN |
|---|---|
| Collection number | AI 1103: 1–24; 1156: 1–12; 1983: 1–35;<br>2794: 6–22; AM 98: 1–18 |
| Country | Estonia |
| County | Ida-Viru |
| Municipality | Lüganuse |
| Village | Aa |
| Date Of Discovery | 1869 |
| Comments On Discovery | Found during digging drainage ditches |
| Dating Of Deposit (century) | 2-3; 6-7; 12/13 |
| Earliest Dating Of Artefacts (AD) | 100 |
| Latest Dating Of Artefacts (AD) | 1200 |
| Manuscripts | Liiv 1922, 19<br>Suurväli 1932, 50 |
| References | Grewingk 1887, 163 ff<br>Jaanits et al. 1982, 283–284<br>Kriiska & Tvauri 2002, 158<br>Lang 2007a, 163<br>Laul & Tõnisson 1991, 81<br>Lõugas & Selirand 1977, 203<br>Mandel & Tamla 1977<br>RK 1896, 20-21 (nos 313–316), tab. 22: 3, 11, tab. 23: 17<br>Sb. GEG 1872, 35<br>Sb. GEG 1873, 32<br>Sb. GEG 1874, 131–132<br>Sb. GEG 1886, 162<br>Tamla 1977, no. 14–15, 158 ff<br>Tamla 1995<br>Tamla 1996, 226<br>Tamla & Kiudsoo 2005, 10–11<br>Tvauri 2012, 292<br>Undset & Mestorf 1882, 171 |
| Comments | In Tamla 1977 confusion about the number of separate deposits: according to him two separate deposits (one 60 m the other 300 m from the enclosure) were discovered and later mixed. According to the earliest sources there still seems to be a single deposit. |

| | |
|---|---|
| Environment | Watery condition |
| Environment Subtype | Bog |
| Depth (cm) | 30-40 |
| Artefact Placement | Found in an area of 1.8–2.4 $m^2$. Some axes and spearheads consist traces of wood i.e. deposited with shafts. |
| Archaeological Site | Hill-fort / enclosure |
| Comments On Find-spot | A boggy area close to the Alulinn hill-fort/enclosure and settlement site. |

| Artefact Type | Subtype | Amount | Material | Comments On Appearance | Futher Description |
|---|---|---|---|---|---|
| Sword | | 3 | Iron | 10 fragments of 3 swords | Dated to the 2nd–3rd century |
| Axe | Socketed | 9 | Iron | 1 fragmented | Some consist traces of wood i.e. deposited with shafts |
| Axe | Shafted | 4 | Iron | | |
| Spearhead | Socketed | 51 | Iron | 19 fragmented | One from the Late Iron Age (9th–13th century); some consist traces of wood i.e. deposited with shafts |
| Other Tool | Harpoon | 1 | Iron | | |
| Sickle/Scythe | Sickle, 1 possible scythe | 27 | Iron | 11 fragmented | |
| Other Iron Object | Fragments of iron artefacts | 3 | Iron | 3 fragmented | |

*Selection of artefacts from Alulinn wealth deposit. (Photo: Ester Oras).*

| Wealth Deposit | BALTINAVA |
|---|---|
| Collection number | LVNM 58124-58127; DaM III 68 (Lost) |
| Country | Latvia |
| County | Baltinava |
| Municipality | Baltinava |
| Village | Baltinava (Baltenau: part of the bigger village Bolwa) |
| Date Of Discovery | 1897 |
| Comments On Discovery | Found in the Baltinava (Baltenau) manor field |
| Dating Of Deposit (century) | 8 |
| Earliest Dating Of Artefacts (AD) | 600 |
| Latest Dating Of Artefacts (AD) | 800 |
| Manuscripts | LVNM archives, Abrenej apr., Baltinavai pag., 1 |
| References | Apals et al. 1974, 151<br>Balodis & Tentelis (eds) 1938, 126<br>Bitner-Wróblewska (ed.) 2007, 490. no. 872<br>Carnap-Bornheim et al. 2008, 26<br>Engel 1933, 74, fig. 15<br>Urtāns 1964, 41–42, no. 1, fig. 1<br>Urtāns 1977, 160, fig. 67<br>Sb. Rig. 1898, 44 |
| Comments | 1 neck-ring (DaM III 68) lost from Daugavpils Museum during German occupation (1941–1944). Total weight of the deposit 1142 g. |

| | |
|---|---|
| Environment | Dry land |

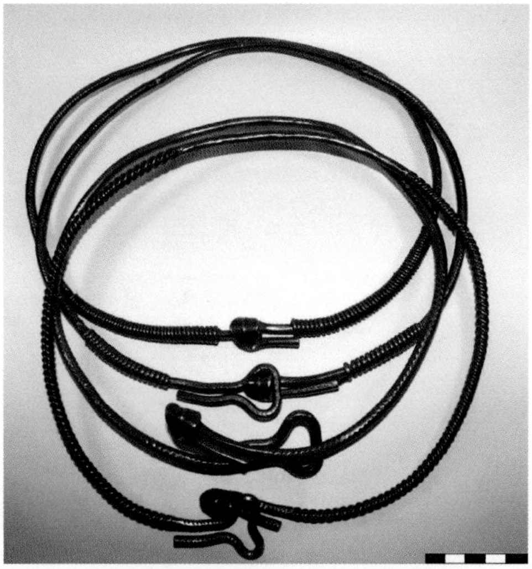

*Baltinava wealth deposit. (Photo: Ester Oras).*

| Artefact Type | Subtype | Amount | Material | Comments On Appearance | Futher Description |
|---|---|---|---|---|---|
| Neck-Ring | Saddle and hooklet terminals | 1 | Silver | | Diameter 23.4 cm, weight 223.97 g |
| Neck-Ring | Saddle and hooklet terminals, wrapped with wire | 1 | Silver | | Diameter 23 cm, weight 215.67 g |
| Neck-Ring | Saddle and hooklet terminals, wrapped with wire | 1 | Silver | | Diameter 24.6 cm, weight 213.48 g |
| Neck-Ring | Saddle and hooklet terminals | 1 | Silver | | Diameter 22 cm, weight 238.95 g |
| Neck-Ring | Saddle and hooklet terminals | 1 | Silver | | Diameter 24.6 cm, weight 250 g |

| Wealth Deposit | BARSTYČIAI |
|---|---|
| Collection number | ŠAM I-A 1520-1539 |
| Country | Lithuania |
| County | Klaipėda |
| Municipality | Skuodas |
| Village | Barstyčiai |
| Date Of Discovery | Unknown |
| Comments On Discovery | Exact circumstances of discovery unknown |
| Dating Of Deposit (century) | 7-8; 10-11 |
| Earliest Dating Of Artefacts (AD) | 600 |
| Latest Dating Of Artefacts (AD) | 1100 |
| References | Bliujienė 2010, 140 ff, no. 2 |
| Comments | Dating range: 600–800; 900–1100 AD |

| | |
|---|---|
| Environment | Watery condition |
| Environment Subtype | Bog |
| Geographical Landscape | Bog or lake |
| Comments On Find-spot | Found possibly in a bog at Barstyčiai forest. |

| Artefact Type | Subtype | Amount | Material | Comments On Appearance | Futher Description |
|---|---|---|---|---|---|
| Spearhead | Socketed | 6 | Iron | | |
| Spearhead | Shafted | 5 | Iron | | |
| Axe | | 2 | Iron | 1 blunt end fragmented | |
| Battle Knife | | 1 | Iron | Fragmented, either blade of a battle knife or a single-edged sword | |
| Other Weapon | Scabbard mounting | 1 | Bronze | | |
| Belt Part | Belt buckle, quadrangular, with mounting | 1 | Bronze | | Quadrangular belt buckle with mounting |
| Brooch | Pennannular brooch | 2 | Bronze | | From later period (10th–11th century) |

*Barstyčiai wealth deposit. (Photo: Gediminas Petrauskas).*

| Wealth Deposit | BAUBLIAI |
|---|---|
| Collection number | VDKM 1090: 1–2;<br>RKM 170 |
| Country | Lithuania |
| County | Panevėžys |
| Municipality | Rokiškis |
| Village | Baubliai (Indriūnai) |
| Date Of Discovery | 1935 |
| Comments On Discovery | Found during field ploughing in a marshy area |
| Dating Of Deposit (century) | 8 |
| Earliest Dating Of Artefacts (AD) | 600 |
| Latest Dating Of Artefacts (AD) | 800 |
| References | Bliujienė 2010, no. 3<br>Griciuvienė 2007, 231–233, 259<br>Michelbertas 2007, 13<br>Tautavičius 1977, 131<br>Volkaitė-Kulikauskienė 1943, 92<br>Vaitkunskienė 1981, 28 |
| Comments | Total weight of the deposit 650 g |

| | |
|---|---|
| Environment | Watery condition |
| Environment Subtype | Marsh |
| Depth (cm) | 30-40 |
| Comments On Find-spot | Boggy and marshy area |

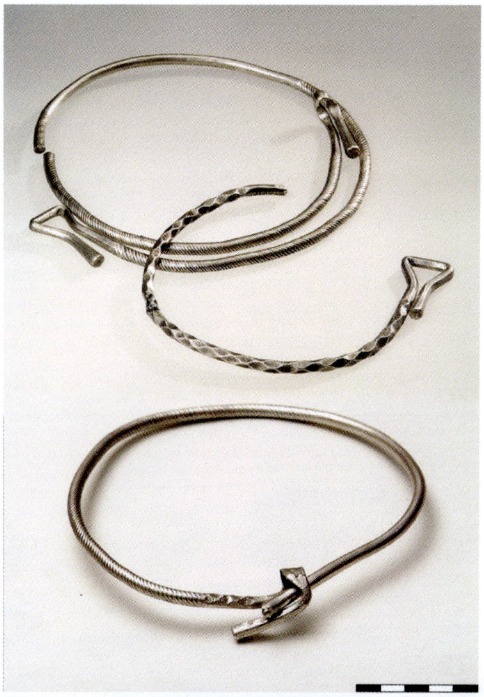

*Baubliai wealth deposit. (Photo: Griciuvienė 2007, 232).*

| Artefact Type | Subtype | Amount | Material | Comments On Appearance | Futher Description |
|---|---|---|---|---|---|
| Neck-Ring | Crutch-shape terminals, faceted | 1 | Silver | 1 fragmented: a half of the neck-ring | Diameter 14.7, thicness 0.7 cm; weight 126.5 g |
| Neck-Ring | Crutch- and saddle-shape terminals, torque imitation | 1 | Silver | | Diameter 19 cm, thickness 0.7 cm; weight 313.7 g |
| Neck-Ring | Saddle-shaped terminals, torque imitation | 1 | Silver | 1 fragmented | |

| Wealth Deposit | CIBĒNI |
|---|---|
| Collection number | LVNM A 10404: 1–9 |
| Country | Latvia |
| County | Dobele |
| Municipality | Annenieki |
| Village | Cibēni |
| Date Of Discovery | 14.–15. 07.1940 |
| Comments On Discovery | Found during excavations at the NW shore of Lake Cibēnu (Kapeņu) burial ground |
| Dating Of Deposit (century) | 5 |
| Earliest Dating Of Artefacts (AD) | 400 |
| Latest Dating Of Artefacts (AD) | 450 |
| Manuscripts | Stepiņš 1940 |

| | |
|---|---|
| Environment | Dry land |
| Environment Subtype | Archaeological site |
| Depth (cm) | 12–25 |
| Markers | Stones? |
| Archaeological Site | Cibēni (Kapeņu) burial ground |
| Comments On Find-spot | Ca. 60–70 cm N from the 1st burial, area surrounded by slabs of stones, interpreted as a cenotaph |

| Artefact Type | Subtype | Amount | Material | Comments On Appearance | Futher Description |
|---|---|---|---|---|---|
| Axe | Socketed | 1 | Iron | | |
| Arrowhead | Socketed | 2 | Iron | One socket broken, but during the excavations | |
| Knife | Knife? | 1 | Iron | Heavily corroded, possibly a knife | |
| Horse Gear | Bridles? | 1 | Iron | Heavily corroded, possibly bridles | |
| Sickle/Scythe | Scythe? | 1 | Iron | Heavily corroded, possibly a scythe | |
| Other Tool | Strike-a-light stone | 1 | Stone | Quadrangular shape, clear signs of wear (groovs on the surface) | |
| Other Tool | Whetstone | 1 | Stone | | |
| Vessel | Drinking horn | 1 | Bronze | Carved ornaments on horn | Horn almost decayed, bronze corroded. Signs of sun-like ornament on the parts of the horn. Attatched with 2 rings. |
| Ring | | 1 | Bronze | | |

*Cibēni wealth deposit. (Photo: Ester Oras).*

| Wealth Deposit | DARGIŠKĖ |
|---|---|
| Collection number | ŽMA 518, 519 |
| Country | Lithuania |
| County | Telšiai |
| Municipality | Telšiai |
| Village | Dargiškė (now Pluotinė?) |
| Date Of Discovery | 1934 |
| Comments On Discovery | Found by a local villager Juozas Bružinskis during working in a field at the foot of small hill |
| Dating Of Deposit (century) | 4 |
| Earliest Dating Of Artefacts (AD) | 244 |
| Latest Dating Of Artefacts (AD) | 350 |
| References | Bliujienė 2010, no. 8<br>Michelbertas 1972, 112, no. 8<br>Michelbertas 2001, no. VIII-03-1/1.1<br>Michelbertas 2007, 12<br>Sajauskas 2007, 20<br>Tautavičius 1977, 131<br>Valatka 1966, 165–169 |
| Comments | Number of ornaments: 2+?; number of coins: 1+? (total of 2 kg but most of them lost over time). Bracelets given to the museum in 1935, coin in 1956. Later on some other coins added to the collection but the relation to this particualr find not entirely certain. |

| | |
|---|---|
| Environment | Watery condition |
| Environment Subtype | Marsh |
| Type Of Container | Ceramic vessel |
| Comments On Find-spot | At the foot of small hill |

| Artefact Type | Subtype | Amount | Material | Comments On Appearance | Futher Description |
|---|---|---|---|---|---|
| Bracelet | Simple ribbon-like bracelet | 2 | Bronze | 1 broken, 1 slightly deformed | |
| Coin | Roman | 1+? | Bronze | | A bullion Antoninian of Gordian III (238–244) minted in Nikea (Asia Minor) |

*Dargiškė wealth deposit with added Roman coins. (Photo: Ester Oras).*

| Wealth Deposit | DIRMEIKIAI |
|---|---|
| Collection number | ŠAM |
| Country | Lithuania |
| County | Telšiai |
| Municipality | Telšiai |
| Village | Dirmeikiai |
| Date Of Discovery | 1955 |
| Comments On Discovery | Found during field ploughing |
| Dating Of Deposit (century) | 3 |
| Earliest Dating Of Artefacts (AD) | 161 |
| Latest Dating Of Artefacts (AD) | 250 |
| References | Kropotkin 1961, 99, no. 1409<br>Michelbertas 1972, 112–113, no. 9<br>Michelbertas 2001, VI-06-2/1.1<br>Tautavičius 1977, 131 |
| Comments | Number of ornaments: 1+?; number of coins: 10+?. More than tens of coins and numerous ornaments found but lost over time. Brooch unidentifiable in the collections. |

| | |
|---|---|
| Environment | Dry land |
| Type Of Container | Ceramic vessel |

| Artefact Type | Subtype | Amount | Material | Comments On Appearance | Futher Description |
|---|---|---|---|---|---|
| Coin | Roman | 1 | Bronze | | Antoninus Pius (138-161) |
| Coin | Roman | 1 | Bronze | | Hadrianus (117-138) |
| Brooch | Cross-ribbed | 1 | Bronze | | |

| Wealth Deposit | DRAUSTINIAI |
|---|---|
| Collection number | VDKM 721: 1–3, 5–6 |
| Country | Lithuania |
| County | Kėdainiai |
| Municipality | Kėdainiai |
| Village | Draustiniai |
| Date Of Discovery | Spring 1935 |
| Comments On Discovery | Found during peat digging or peat ploughing |
| Dating Of Deposit (century) | 7 |
| Earliest Dating Of Artefacts (AD) | 500 |
| Latest Dating Of Artefacts (AD) | 700 |
| References | Alseikaitė-Gimbutienė 1946, 187<br>Bliujienė 2010, no. 10<br>Kulikauskienė & Rimantienė 1958, fig. 284<br>Michelbertas 2007, 13<br>Nakaitė 1959, 55, 59<br>Puzinas 1938, fig. 60:2<br>Tautavičius 1977, 131<br>Vaitkunskienė 1981, 29<br>Volkaitė-Kulikauskienė 1943, 92 |
| Comments | Several artefacts found. Number of ornaments: 5+?. Museum received also a 14th–15th century key (VDKM 721: 4 ) which is not part of this deposit. According to Alseikaitė-Gimbutienė (1946, 187) deposit found in an inhumantion burial. Total weight of the deposit 838.7 g. |

| | |
|---|---|
| Environment | Watery condition |
| Environment Subtype | Bog |

| Artefact Type | Subtype | Amount | Material | Comments On Appearance | Futher Description |
|---|---|---|---|---|---|
| Neck-Ring | Profoundly faceted terminals | 3 | Silver | 1 broken into two pieces, 1 in two terminal fragments | |
| Neck-Ring | Loop and hooklet terminals | 1 | Silver | | |
| Bracelet | Thickened terminals | 1 | Bronze | | |

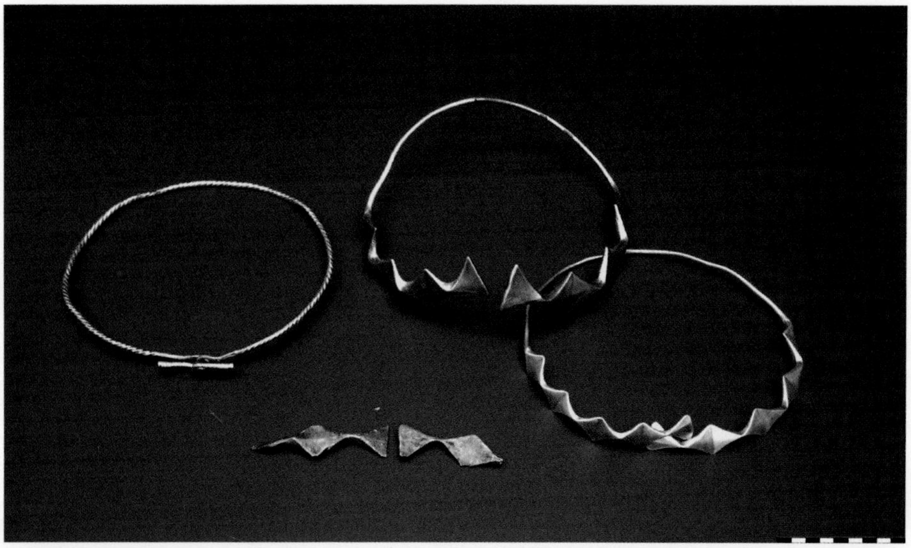

*Artefacts from Draustiniai wealth deposit. (Photo: Arturas Uzgalis).*

| Wealth Deposit | DUMPJI |
|---|---|
| Collection number | LVNM 58121–58123, (prev. DM III 74-76) |
| Country | Latvia |
| County | Bauska |
| Municipality | Mežotne |
| Village | Dumpji (Strēlnieki) |
| Date Of Discovery | Spring 1897 |
| Comments On Discovery | Found during field ploughing. Exact circumsatnces of discovery unclear. |
| Dating Of Deposit (century) | 8 |
| Earliest Dating Of Artefacts (AD) | 675 |
| Latest Dating Of Artefacts (AD) | 725 |
| Manuscripts | LVNM archives |
| References | Balodis & Tentelis (eds) 1938, 126<br>Engel 1933, 65, fig. 6b: 2–4<br>Griciuvienė 2005, 170, 230<br>RK 1930, 109, tab. 25: 2, 26: 3<br>Sb. Rig. 1898, 40–41, 118<br>Urtāns 1964, 42–43, no. 2, fig. 2<br>Urtāns 1977, 157, fig. 64<br>Vankina et al. 1981, 58 |
| Comments | Finds received by the museum in 1898. According to a decsription of a discovery the Didulos family found some prehistoric artefacts. Locals were interviewed on the 11th of July 1928 by V. Ģinters, but the owners of the Dumpji farm did not know anything about the 19th century discovery. Total weight of the deposit 563.3 g. |

| | |
|---|---|
| Environment | Dry land |
| Comments On Find-spot | A Semigallian burial ground located nearby |

| Artefact Type | Subtype | Amount | Material | Comments On Appearance | Futher Description |
|---|---|---|---|---|---|
| Neck-Ring | Flat overlapping terminals with faceted decoration in a middle part | 1 | Silver | One terminal bent but not broken | Diameter 16.8 x 18.6 cm; weight 91.75 g |
| Neck-Ring | Hooklet and conical mushroom-shape terminals, twisted | 1 | Silver | | Diameter 18.8 cm; weight 428.55 g |
| Brooch | Crossbow brooch | 1 | Silver | Fragmented, in 3 pieces | Height of bow 3.6 cm, length 8.2 cm; Weight 44.7 g |

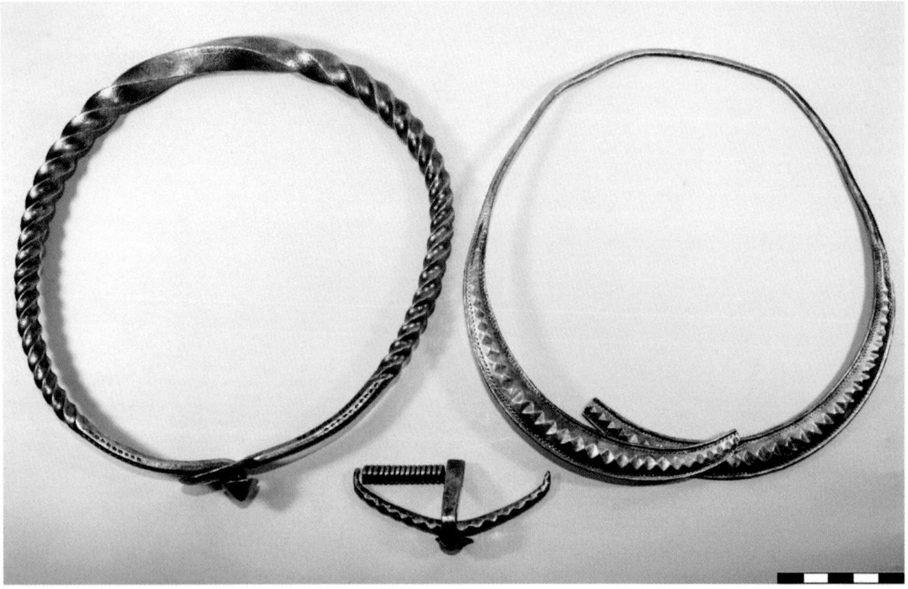

*Dumpji wealth deposit. (Photo: Ester Oras).*

| Wealth Deposit | GUDĖNIŠKĖS |
|---|---|
| Collection number | UKM |
| Country | Lithuania |
| County | Utena |
| Municipality | Utena |
| Village | Gudėniškės |
| Date Of Discovery | 1977 |
| Comments On Discovery | Found during digging drainage ditches and an installation of a water collector |
| Dating Of Deposit (century) | 6 |
| Earliest Dating Of Artefacts (AD) | 400 |
| Latest Dating Of Artefacts (AD) | 600 |
| References | Bliujienė 2010, no. 12<br>Vaitkevičius 2006, 402, fig. 672 |
| Comments | Finds were discovered from time to time at the southern end of the quagmire. Finds may belong to the Gudėniškiai barrows. |

| | |
|---|---|
| Environment | Watery condition |
| Environment Subtype | Bog |

*Gudėniškės wealth deposit. (Photo: Dalius Ribokas).*

| Artefact Type | Subtype | Amount | Material | Comments On Appearance | Futher Description |
|---|---|---|---|---|---|
| Axe | Shafted, narrow blade | 1 | Iron | Fragmented, blade broken off | |

| Wealth Deposit | HUMMULI |
|---|---|
| Collection number | AI 2019 |
| Country | Estonia |
| County | Valga |
| Municipality | Hummuli |
| Village | Puide (Hummuli) |
| Date Of Discovery | May 1896 |
| Comments On Discovery | Found during field ploughing |
| Dating Of Deposit (century) | 8 |
| Earliest Dating Of Artefacts (AD) | 700 |
| Latest Dating Of Artefacts (AD) | 725 |
| Manuscripts | Suik 1923/1924, 91–92 |
| References | Jaanits et al. 1982, 287<br>Jung 1898, 156<br>RK 1896 (no. 673), 107<br>Sb. GEG 1896, 127–128<br>Tvauri 2012, 296 |

| | |
|---|---|
| Environment | Watery condition |
| Environment Subtype | Marsh |
| Depth (cm) | 30-40 |
| Comments On Find-spot | The find-spot located in the small creek valley with a marshy area surrounding |

| Artefact Type | Subtype | Amount | Material | Comments On Appearance | Futher Description |
|---|---|---|---|---|---|
| Neck-Ring | Flat faceted overlapping terminals | 3 | Silver | | |

*Hummuli wealth deposit. (Photo: Ester Oras).*

| Wealth Deposit | IGAVERE |
|---|---|
| Collection number | AI 2712: 45-49; some lost over time |
| Country | Estonia |
| County | Tartu |
| Municipality | Tartu |
| Village | Igavere |
| Date Of Discovery | 1913 |
| Comments On Discovery | Found during field ploughing |
| Dating Of Deposit (century) | 7 |
| Earliest Dating Of Artefacts (AD) | 500 |
| Latest Dating Of Artefacts (AD) | 700 |
| Manuscripts | Note (MMg)<br>Tiitsmaa 1921b, 43, 49 |
| References | Jaanits et al. 1982, 284<br>Lang 2007a, 163<br>Lõugas & Selirand 1977, 160<br>Tamla 1977, no. 6, 161 ff<br>Tamla 1995<br>Tvauri 2012, 292 |
| Comments | Exact numbers of artefacts unknown |

| | |
|---|---|
| Environment | Watery condition |
| Environment Subtype | Marsh |
| Depth (cm) | 15–20 |
| Comments On Find-spot | A marshy, peat-rich area |

*Selection of artefacts from Igavere wealth deposit. (Photo: Ester Oras).*

| Artefact Type | Subtype | Amount | Material | Comments On Appearance | Futher Description |
|---|---|---|---|---|---|
| Sword | | 1 | Iron | | Numerous swords mentioned, all lost over time |
| Axe | Shafted | 4 | Iron | 3 fragmented, blades broken | 1 lost |
| Axe | Socketed | 1 | Iron | | |
| Spearhead | | 1 | Iron | | Numerous spearheads mentioned, all lost over time |
| Other Weapon | Shield boss | 1 | Iron | | Lost |
| Horse Gear | Horse shoe | 1 | Iron | | Lost |
| Sickle/Scythe | Scythe | 1 | Iron | Fragmented | Lost |
| Other Iron Object | Iron plates, couldron(?) | 7 | Iron | Fragmented | Lost |

| Wealth Deposit | KAABE |
|---|---|
| Collection number | AI 3563: 1–2 |
| Country | Estonia |
| County | Tartu |
| Municipality | Rannu |
| Village | Kaabe |
| Date Of Discovery | 1933 |
| Comments On Discovery | Found during river bed deepening works at Emajõgi River ca. 3 km down the stream |
| Dating Of Deposit (century) | 8 |
| Earliest Dating Of Artefacts (AD) | 400 |
| Latest Dating Of Artefacts (AD) | 800 |
| References | Mandel 1985, 80<br>Tamla 1977, no. 33 |
| Comments | According to Mandel (1985, 80) the sword dated to the 2nd–3rd century AD.<br>Currently presumed dating range: 400–800 AD, more likely ca. 700–800 AD or later (pers. comm. Jüri Peets and Andres Tvauri). |

| | |
|---|---|
| Environment | Watery condition |
| Environment Subtype | River |
| Depth (cm) | 150 |

| Artefact Type | Subtype | Amount | Material | Comments On Appearance | Futher Description |
|---|---|---|---|---|---|
| Sword | One-bladed | 1 | Iron | | |
| Axe | Socketed | 1 | Iron | | |

*Kaabe wealth deposit. (Photo: Ester Oras).*

| Wealth Deposit | KAALI |
|---|---|
| Collection number | AI 4915 |
| Country | Estonia |
| County | Saare |
| Municipality | Pihtla |
| Village | Kaali |
| Date Of Discovery | 1976 |
| Comments On Discovery | Found during archaeological excavations |
| Dating Of Deposit (century) | 4 |
| Earliest Dating Of Artefacts (AD) | 200 |
| Latest Dating Of Artefacts (AD) | 450 |
| References | Jonuks 2009, 187, 231<br>Lang 2007a, 47, 162<br>Lang 2007b, 76–77, 246–247<br>Lõugas 1996, 59–62<br>Mägi 2003, 5<br>Tamla & Kiudsoo 2005, 16–17 |
| Comments | According to Mägi (2003, 5) dated to the Pre-Roman Iron Age. Current dating according to the earilest silver items in the eastern Baltic. |

| | |
|---|---|
| Environment | Dry land |
| Environment Subtype | Archaeological site |
| Archaeological Site | Fortified settlement / enclosure / sacrificial site |
| Geographical Landscape | Bank of the Kaali meteor lake |
| Comments On Find-spot | The upper starata of the the Kaali fortified settlement site /enclosure at the NE bank of the Kaali meteor crater and lake |

| Artefact Type | Subtype | Amount | Material | Comments On Appearance | Futher Description |
|---|---|---|---|---|---|
| Neck-Ring | Simple band-like open terminals | 1 | Silver | | Edges with zig-zag ornament |
| Bracelet | Spiral | 2 | Silver | 2 fragmented | Thin, flat silver band, engarved decorative stripes on one terminal |

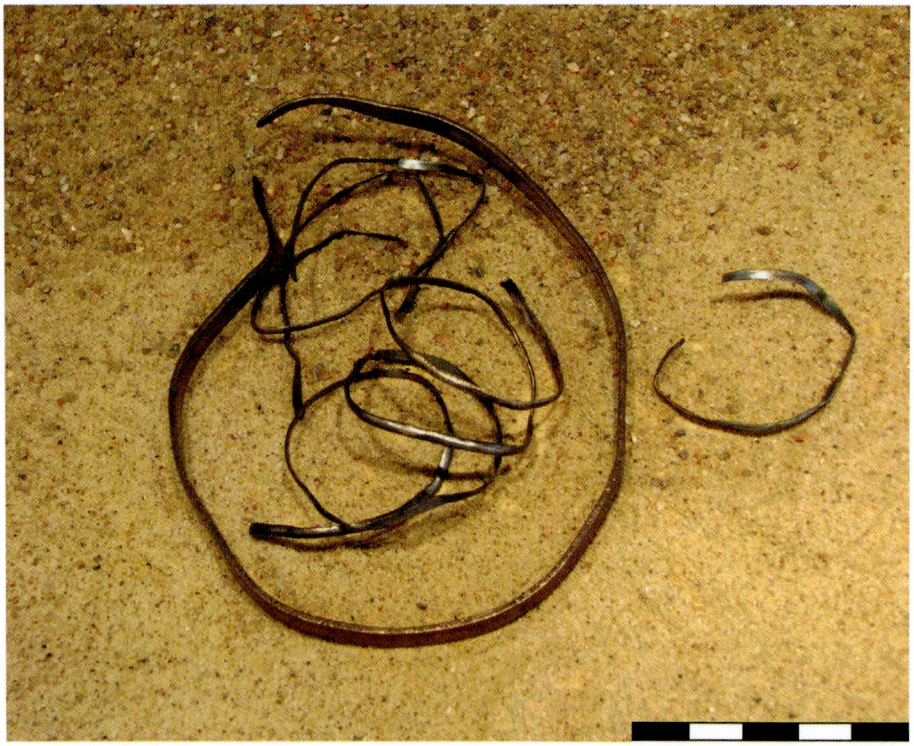

*Kaali wealth deposit. (Photo: Ester Oras).*

| Wealth Deposit | KALNAMUIŽA |
|---|---|
| Collection number | Lost, used to be in the private collections of Kalanamuiža manor owner L. Pālen (Count L. Pahlen) |
| Country | Latvia |
| County | Tērvete |
| Municipality | Tērvete |
| Village | Kalnamuiža Manor, now Tērvete |
| Date Of Discovery | 1888, 8th of August 1892 |
| Comments On Discovery | Found during farm works at Kalnamuiža manor field |
| Dating Of Deposit (century) | 6 |
| Earliest Dating Of Artefacts (AD) | 400 |
| Latest Dating Of Artefacts (AD) | 600 |
| References | Atgāzis 2000, 28<br>Balodis & Tentelis (eds) 1938, 116, 127<br>Bliujienė 2010, 149–150, no. 15<br>Moora 1929, 57, no. 52<br>Riekstiņš 1931, 477<br>RK 1896 (no. 312), 20, tab. 12: 4–5<br>Urtāns 1964, 45, no. 7, fig. 8<br>Urtāns 1977, 149, fig. 54<br>Sb. Kurl. 1892, 25<br>SM 1937, 4, 93–94, fig. 3<br>Tallgrens et al. 1926, 68 |
| Comments | Site excavated after the discovery in 1888 by R. Hausmann and by A. Bīlenštein in 1892. Only two shield bosses have been documented and photographed. |

| | |
|---|---|
| Environment | Watery condition |
| Environment Subtype | River |
| Depth (cm) | 30–40 |
| Markers | Big granite stone |
| Archaeological Site | Close to hill-fort |
| Geographical Landscape | Tērvete Rivulet bank |
| Comments On Find-spot | In a depression in the field, under a large granite boulder, at the Tērvete Rivulet bank. Area had lots of bigger granite stones, the natural soil layer begun under them at the depth of 30 cm. |

| Artefact Type | Subtype | Amount | Material | Comments On Appearance | Futher Description |
|---|---|---|---|---|---|
| Sword | Blade | 1 | Iron | Fragmented | Lost |
| Spearhead | Socketed | 54 | Iron | | Lost, some with barbs, some rhomb-shaped |
| Arrowhead | Socketed | 8 | Iron | | Lost |
| Knife | | 4 | Iron | | Lost |
| Belt Part | Buckle | 9 | Iron | | Lost |
| Horse Gear | Stirrup | 1 | Iron | | Lost, dated to a later period |
| Other Weapon | Shield bosses | 6 | Iron | Fragmented | Lost |
| Other Weapon | Shield bosses | 4 | Iron | | Lost, altogether at least 10 shiled bosses, 2 photographed; one round other conical form |

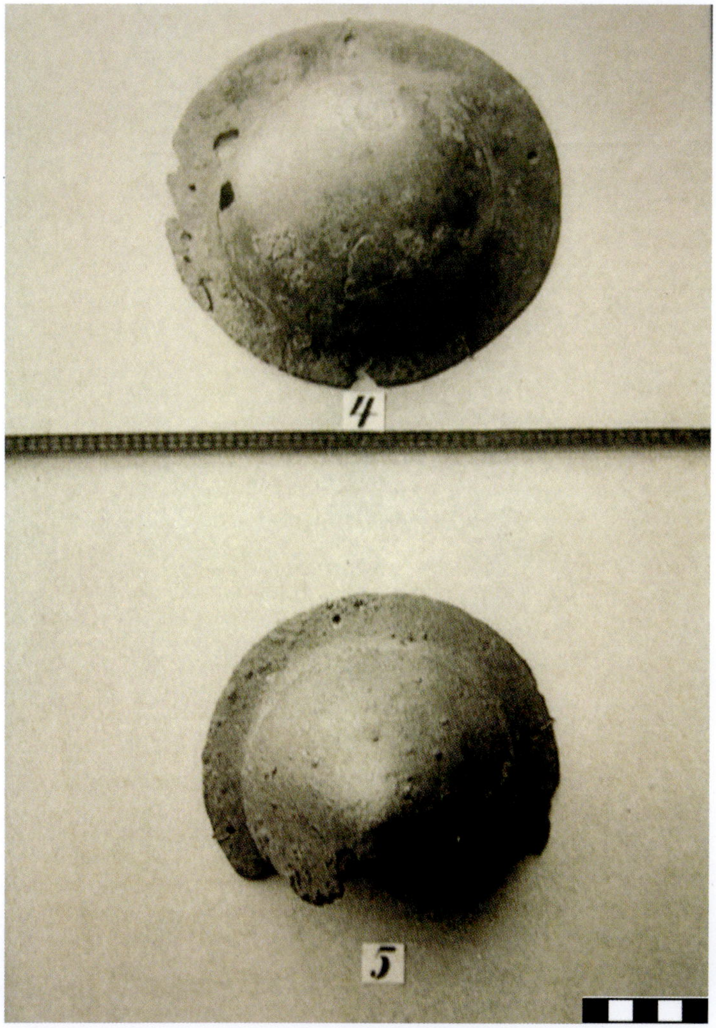


*Shield bosses from Kalnamuiža wealth deposit. (Photo: RK 1896, tab. 12: 4–5).*

| Wealth Deposit | KARDLA |
|---|---|
| Collection number | AI 2415: 1–25 |
| Country | Estonia |
| County | Tartu |
| Municipality | Tähtvere |
| Village | Kardla |
| Date Of Discovery | 1911 |
| Comments On Discovery | Found during farm works, clearing field from stones |
| Dating Of Deposit (century) | 6 |
| Earliest Dating Of Artefacts (AD) | 500 |
| Latest Dating Of Artefacts (AD) | 550 |
| Manuscripts | Jüriado 1928/1929, 7<br>Riisberg 1921, 21<br>Valk 1993 |
| References | Aun 1992, 138 ff<br>Hausmann 1914<br>Jaanits et al. 1982, 286<br>Sb. GEG 1912, 7<br>Selirand & Tõnisson 1963, 127<br>Tamla & Kiudsoo 2005, 20<br>Tvauri 2006, 106, 110<br>Tvauri 2012, 294–295 |

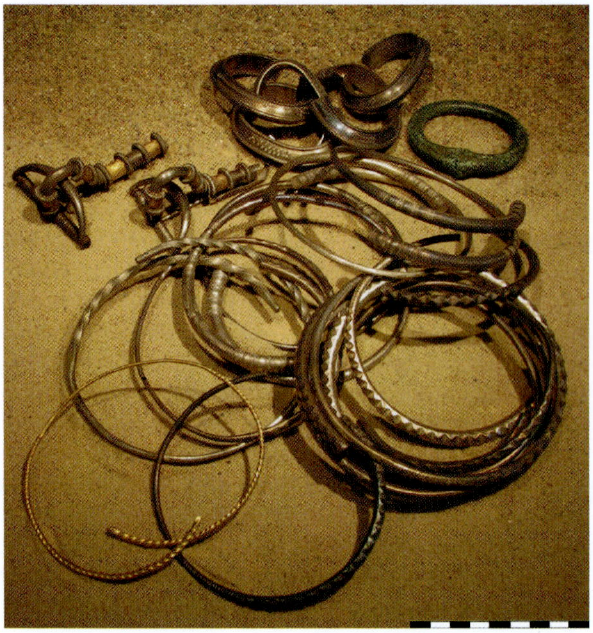

*Kardla wealth deposit. (Photo: Ester Oras).*

| | |
|---|---|
| Environment | Dry land |
| Environment Subtype | Archaeological site |
| Depth (cm) | 45 |
| Markers | Big stone |
| Archaeological Site | Burial area |
| Comments On Find-spot | In a destroyed stone grave, next to a bigger stone. In folk tradition the site is known as an offering site. |

| Artefact Type | Subtype | Amount | Material | Comments On Appearance | Futher Description |
|---|---|---|---|---|---|
| Neck-Ring | Overlapping faceted terminals | 6 | Silver | | |
| Neck-Ring | Overlapping round decorated terminals | 4 | Silver | | |
| Neck-Ring | Overlapping twisted terminals | 1 | Silver | | |
| Neck-Ring | Overlapping twisted terminals | 1 | Gold | | |
| Bracelet | Cast, flaring terminals and a bulky midrib | 5 | Silver | | |
| Bracelet | Massive, cast, thickening terminals | 1 | Bronze | | |
| Brooch | Crossbow brooch | 4 | Silver | 2 fragmented | Golden plate decoration |
| Ring | | 2 | Silver | | |
| Other | Ring-shape rod | 1 | Iron | | Iron rod on which 2 small silver rings |

| Wealth Deposit | KAVASTU |
|---|---|
| Collection number | LVNM 65080 (prev. DM I 324: 1-e) |
| Country | Estonia |
| County | Tartu |
| Municipality | Luunja |
| Village | Kavastu |
| Date Of Discovery | 1902 |
| Comments On Discovery | Found during earth works and drainage at Kavastu Bog |
| Dating Of Deposit (century) | 5 |
| Earliest Dating Of Artefacts (AD) | 427 |
| Latest Dating Of Artefacts (AD) | 557± |
| Manuscripts | EAA 1384.1.12. Планъ имения Кавастъ<br>OxA-27781 & OxA-V-2515-13 (AMS dates of the lamp fuel residue)<br>Štšogoleva 2009, 6–8 |
| References | Ebert 1913, 530, fig. 27<br>Engel 1914, 25–26, fig. 19<br>Hausmann 1905<br>Jaanits et al. 1982, 232, fig. 159<br>Lang 2007b, 257–258, fig. 154<br>Moora et al. 1936, 93–94, fig. 51 |
| Comments | Exact find-spot uncertain. Peat bog marked on the map of EAA 1384.1.12. and location of the deposit estimated according to this. The chronology of the lamp in the Roman Empire Mediterranean context ca. 1st century AD, current chronology according to the AMS dates (1561 ±25 BP, cal. 427-557 AD, 95.4% probability) of the fueld residue in the lamp. |

| | |
|---|---|
| Environment | Watery condition |
| Environment Subtype | Bog |
| Depth (cm) | 120 |
| Comments On Find-spot | Kavastu Bog is at the bank of River Emajõgi. In the area of a discovery some animal bones were noticed but not collected. |

| Artefact Type | Subtype | Amount | Material | Comments On Appearance | Futher Description |
|---|---|---|---|---|---|
| Other | Roman bronze lamp | 1 | Bronze | 2 voluted nozzles, weight 1245 g | Roman (area of Italy, 1st–2nd century) origin, not a province production |
| Raw Material | Bronze bars | 2 | Bronze | | |
| Raw Material | Bronze bars, fragments of an artefact | 2 | Bronze | Fragments of a certain artefact, possibly lamp-stand, 1 with cut-marks | |

*Kavastu wealth deposit. (Photo: Ester Oras).*

| Wealth Deposit | ĶENTE I |
|---|---|
| Collection number | LVNM VI 31: 1441-1444 |
| Country | Latvia |
| County | Ogre |
| Municipality | Ogre town |
| Village | Ķenteskalns in Ogre town |
| Date Of Discovery | 14th of July 1958 |
| Comments On Discovery | Found during the archaeological excavations by A. Stubavs at the Ķente hill-fort |
| Dating Of Deposit (century) | 6 |
| Earliest Dating Of Artefacts (AD) | 475 |
| Latest Dating Of Artefacts (AD) | 525 |
| Manuscripts | LVNM VI archives |
| References | Apals et al. 1974, 152, fig. 80<br>Stubavs 1976, 35–36, fig. 31, tab. XII: 19<br>Urtāns 1964, 54–55, no. 24, fig. 24<br>Urtāns 1977, 145, fig. 50 |

| | |
|---|---|
| Environment | Dry land |
| Environment Subtype | Archaeological site |
| Depth (cm) | 38 |
| Archaeological Site | Ķente hill-fort |
| Comments On Find-spot | The first layer of the second S rampart at the E slope of the fort |

| Artefact Type | Subtype | Amount | Material | Comments On Appearance | Futher Description |
|---|---|---|---|---|---|
| Sickle/Scythe | Sickle | 1 | Iron | Fragmented | Measures 20.85 x 2.25 x 0.32 cm |
| Other Tool | Awl | 1 | Iron | Fragmented | Measures 3.61 x 0.25 cm |
| Other Tool | Strike-a-light stone | 1 | Stone | | Oval; measures 8.12 x 6 x 3.8 cm |
| Other Tool | Stike-a-light stone | 1 | Stone | | Quadrangular; measures 10.6 x 4.5 x 3.05 cm |

*Ķente I wealth deposit. (Photo: Ester Oras).*

| Wealth Deposit | ĶENTE II |
| --- | --- |
| Collection number | LVNM VI 31: 163-167 |
| Country | Latvia |
| County | Ogre |
| Municipality | Ogre town |
| Village | Ķenteskalns in Ogre town |
| Date Of Discovery | 21st of July 1958 |
| Comments On Discovery | Found during the excavations by A. Stubavs at the Ķente southern settlement |
| Dating Of Deposit (century) | 8 |
| Earliest Dating Of Artefacts (AD) | 700 |
| Latest Dating Of Artefacts (AD) | 800 |
| Manuscripts | LVNM archives |
| References | Apals et al. 1974, 151<br>Stubavs 1976, 74–75, fig. 71, tab. III: 5–6<br>Urtāns 1964, 54, no. 23, fig. 23<br>Urtāns 1977, 160, fig. 68 |

| | |
| --- | --- |
| Environment | Dry land |
| Environment Subtype | Archaeological site |
| Depth (cm) | 7–14 |
| Type Of Container | Wooden box (15 x 10–12 x 10 cm) |
| Artefact Placement | 2 bracelets inside each other, raw material rods close to them |
| Archaeological Site | Ķente southern settlement |
| Comments On Find-spot | Ķente S settlement from the first layer of square 9a. Around the deposit was organic-rich dark soil (probably from wooden box) and burnt house remains |

| Artefact Type | Subtype | Amount | Material | Comments On Appearance | Futher Description |
| --- | --- | --- | --- | --- | --- |
| Bracelet | Cuff-shaped sheet bronze, High central welt ornament | 2 | Bronze | Very small, diameter only 4.1. and 3.3 cm | Diameters 5.1 x 3.32 cm and 4.1. x 3.3 cm |
| Raw Material | Plate rods | 3 | Bronze | Two fragmented | Measures 8.7 x 1.1 x 0.35 cm |

*Ķente II wealth deposit. (Photo: Ester Oras).*

| Wealth Deposit | KIIU |
|---|---|
| Collection number | AM 71: 1–5 |
| Country | Estonia |
| County | Harju |
| Municipality | Kuusalu |
| Village | Kiiu |
| Date Of Discovery | 1903 |
| Comments On Discovery | Found during farm works under a stone |
| Dating Of Deposit (century) | 3 |
| Earliest Dating Of Artefacts (AD) | 200 |
| Latest Dating Of Artefacts (AD) | 300 |
| Manuscripts | Parmas 1925, 69 |
| References | Ebert 1913, 528<br>Jonuks 2009, 231–232<br>Lang 1996, 314, 328<br>Lang 2007a, 134, 162<br>Lang 2007b, 211, 217, 247<br>Vassar 1966, 211 |
| Comments | Debatable whether a deposit (Lang 1996, 314, 328) or a burial/cenotaph (Vassar 1966). |

| | |
|---|---|
| Environment | Dry land |
| Markers | Big stone |
| Comments On Find-spot | Under a big stone, which might indicate a burial context. However, contemporary burial sites located over 1 km distance from the find-spot. |

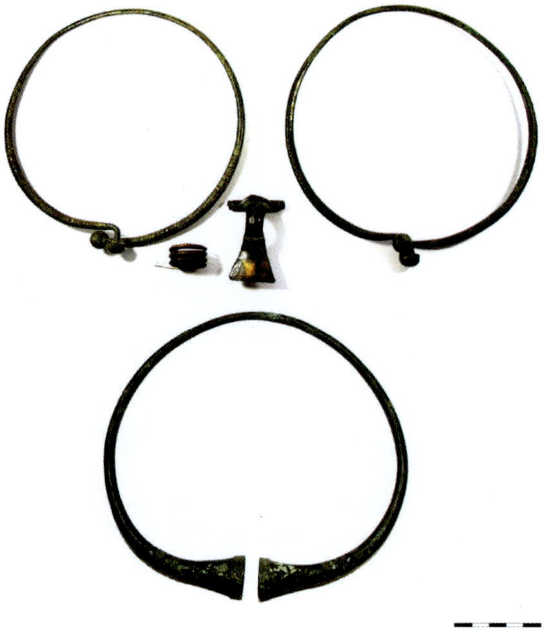

*Kiiu wealth deposit. (Photo: Ester Oras, Krista Sarv).*

| Artefact Type | Subtype | Amount | Material | Comments On Appearance | Futher Description |
|---|---|---|---|---|---|
| Neck-Ring | Trompet-shaped terminals | 1 | Bronze | | |
| Neck-Ring | Mushroom shaped terminals | 2 | Bronze | | |
| Brooch | Head-shield brooch | 1 | Bronze | | |
| Finger-Ring | Spiral ring | 1 | Bronze | | |

| Wealth Deposit | ĶIŠUKALNS |
|---|---|
| Collection number | LVNM 58265 |
| Country | Latvia |
| County | Cibla |
| Municipality | Zvirgzdene |
| Village | Šalupinki |
| Date Of Discovery | Ca. 1939 |
| Comments On Discovery | Found by locals in the settlement site at the foot of the Ķišukalns hill-fort |
| Dating Of Deposit (century) | 7 |
| Earliest Dating Of Artefacts (AD) | 500 |
| Latest Dating Of Artefacts (AD) | 700 |
| Manuscripts | LVNM archives, Ludzas apr., Ciblas pag., 8 |
| References | Urtāns 1964, 51, no.16, fig. 19<br>Urtāns 1977, 153, fig. 59 |
| Comments | Museum bought the items on the 5th of January 1940. Other artefacts handed over to the museum include a bronze penannular brooch and fragments of a bracelet, fragments of bronze cross pendants and spiral bracelets, fragments of an axe. All these artefacts are from later periods (Viking Age and Late Iron Age). |

| | |
|---|---|
| Environment | Dry land |
| Environment Subtype | Archaeological site |
| Archaeological Site | Settlement at the foot of the Ķišukalns hill-fort |
| Comments On Find-spot | Some bones were also noticed in the area, but probably these belong to the settlement activities. No burial-related finds are known in the area. |

| Artefact Type | Subtype | Amount | Material | Comments On Appearance | Futher Description |
|---|---|---|---|---|---|
| Neck-Ring | Overlapping round terminals | 1 | Silver | After finding broken into 3 parts, but later amalgamated together | After finding broken into 3 parts, but later amalgamated together.<br>Diameter 14.4 cm; weight 173.2 g |

*Ķišukalns wealth deposit. (Photo: Ester Oras).*

| Wealth Deposit | KOKMUIŽA I |
|---|---|
| Collection number | LVNM (CVVM) 64376: 1–469;<br>Jelgavā KPM II 1280: 1–111, 1281: 1–28, 1282: 1–4; 1283: 1–2, 1284: 1–155; 3536, 3537: 1–8, 3538: 1–2, 3539, 3919: 1–6, 4096-4097; Helsinki KaM 2021: 64–71;<br>AI 1097;<br>Copenhagen National Museum (4 iron fragments);<br>Moscow National Museum (1 artefact, lost) |
| Country | Latvia |
| County | Auces |
| Municipality | Vītiņi |
| Village | Kokmuiža (Kokumuiža), now Līgotņu |
| Date Of Discovery | 1869 |
| Comments On Discovery | Found during digging drainage ditch in manor field at the foot of the hill in the boggy bed of the River Avīkne |
| Dating Of Deposit (century) | 5 |
| Earliest Dating Of Artefacts (AD) | 450 |
| Latest Dating Of Artefacts (AD) | 525 |
| Manuscripts | LVNM archives |
| References | Apals et al. 1974, 151<br>Balodis & Tentelis (eds) 1938, 116<br>Banytė-Rowell 2003, 72–73<br>Bitner-Wróblewska (ed.) 2007, 250–251<br>Bliujienė 2010, 141 ff, no. 16<br>Carnap-Bornheim et al. 2008, 37<br>Moora 1929, 71–78, 176–179, tab. VIII: 5, tab. IX: 2, 4–6, tab. XI: 5, tab. XXVII: 5–6, tab. XXX: 7–8, XXXI: 8–11<br>Riekstiņš 1931, 477<br>RK 1896, 16, 19, 20 (nos 250, 309–311), tab. 2: 38–39, tab. 3: 10–12, tab. 5: 3–5, tab. 22: 7–9<br>Sb. Kurl. 1869, 367–369<br>Sb. Kurl. 1870, 395–397<br>Sb. Rig. 1901, 126, 138<br>Undset & Mestorf 1882, 167–171<br>Urtāns 1964, 55–56, no. 25, figs 25–27<br>Urtāns 1977, 138–142, figs 45–47<br>Urtāns 2004, 95<br>Urtāns 2008, 84, fig. 18<br>Tallgrens et al. 1926, 68<br>Vankina et al. 1981, 57 |
| Comments | Area excavated by A. Bīlenštein (pastor Bilenstein) in 1869. Altogether information on more than 1260 artefacts weighing 120 kg: some lost, some fragmented, some burnt, some reidentified over time. Thus, estimations of artefact functional groups, exact numbers and artefact types may vary. |

| | |
|---|---|
| Environment | Watery condition |
| Environment Subtype | Marsh |
| Depth (cm) | 45 |
| Type Of Container | Some artefacts possibly in a ceramic vessel |
| Artefact Placement | Artefacts found in the area of ca. 120 $cm^2$. Iron artefacts lower, stone artefacts on top, bronze and silvers items partly in a possible pot and partly between other items. |
| Archaeological Site | Hill-fort |
| Comments On Find-spot | In the boggy bed of River Avīkne |

| Artefact Type | Subtype | Amount | Material | Comments On Appearance | Futher Description |
|---|---|---|---|---|---|
| Sword | Two-bladed | 6 | Iron | Fragments of blades from 6 swords | Amounts vary: 6, 3 |
| Sword | Sword handle | 3 | Iron | Fragmented | |
| Spearhead | Spear- or arrowhead fragments | 472 | Iron | Fragmented | Amounts vary: 472, 17 |
| Spearhead | Socketed | 186 | Iron | Fragmented, broken sockets | Amounts vary: 186, 14, 3 |
| Spearhead | Socketed spearheads or sockets of axes | 134 | Iron | Fragmented | Amounts vary: 134, 18<br>Some of them spearheads, other socketed axes; 67 rusty fragments |
| Axe | Socketed | 131 | Iron | | Amounts vary: 131, 48 |
| Axe | Shafted, narrow blades | 40 | Iron | | Amouns vary: 40, 25.<br>Narrow blades. |
| Axe | Socketed and shafted axes or hoes | 14 | Iron | | Different axes and hoes |
| Knife | | 3 | Iron | | |
| Sickle/Scythe | Sickle | 1 | Iron | | |
| Other Tool | Anvil | 1 | Iron | | Amounts vary: 3, 2, 1 |
| Other Tool | Hammer | 2 | Iron | | Amounts vary: 2, some |
| Other Tool | Mattock /Pick | 1 | Iron | | Amounts vary: 1, some |
| Other Tool | File | 1 | Iron | | Amount estiamted: "some" |
| Other Tool | Hoe | 13 | Iron | | Amounts vary: 13, 6 |
| Other Tool | Oval strike-a-light | 40 | Stone | | Amounts vary: ca. 60, 47, 40, 26 |
| Other Tool | Strike-a-light fragments | 9 | Stone | Fragmented | Amounts vary: 11, 9, 7 |
| Other Tool | Whetstone | 2 | Stone | | Amounts vary: some, 15, 12, 2 |
| Other Tool | Coal trowel | 1 | Iron | | Weight: 124 g |
| Other Tool | Iron sharp-ended tools | 1 | Iron | | Amounts vary: 1, 2, 8 |
| Other Iron Object | Different sharp artefacts | 47 | Iron | Fragmented and deformed | |
| Other Iron Object | Unidentified rusty iron objects | 90 | Iron | | |
| Other Iron Object | Different sharp artefacts | 28 | Iron | Fragmented | Amounts vary: 28, 35 |
| Other Iron Object | Iron fragments | 4 | Iron | | |
| Neck-Ring | | 1 | Bronze | | |
| Bracelet | Including also massive, cast, thickening terminals | 14 | Bronze, Iron | | Amounts vary: 12, 13, 14 |
| Bracelet | | 1 | Silver | | |
| Brooch | Crossbow brooch | 9 | Bronze | | Amounts vary: 7, 9 |
| Finger-Ring | Spiral | 2 | Bronze | | Amounts vary: 2, 3, some |
| Ring | Spiral | 2 | Bronze | | |
| Other Ornament | Chain with pendants | 1 | Bronze | | Chain with pendants |
| Vessel | Drinking horn mounting | 4 | Bronze | | Amounts vary: 6, 4 |
| Raw Material | Thin bronze bands | 1 | Bronze | | Length 4 inches (ca. 8.8 cm) |
| Raw Material | Rod fragments | 5 | Bronze | Fragmented | Amounts vary: 1, 5 |
| Raw Material | Rod | 1 | Silver | | |
| Raw Material | Thin plates of bronze and iron | 6 | Bronze | Rolled-up, fragmented | |
| Raw Material | Raw iron | 3 | Iron | Fragmented | Amounts vary: 3, 5 |

*Selection of artefacts from Kokmuiža I wealth deposit at the exhibition at the Latvian National History Museum. (Photo: Ester Oras).*

*Selection of artefacts from Kokmuiža I wealth deposit. (Photo: Ester Oras).*

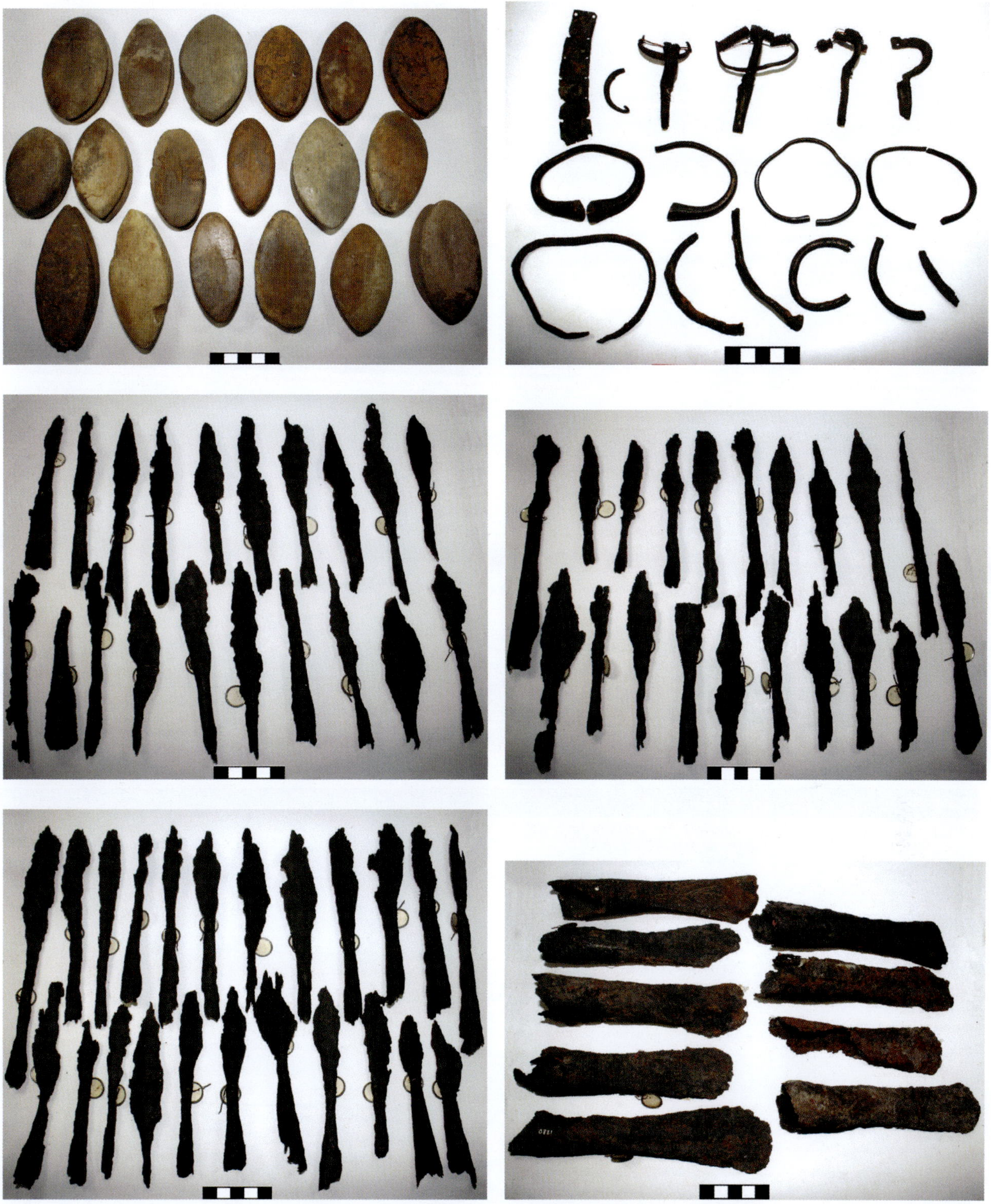

*Selection of artefacts from Kokmuiža I wealth deposit. (Photo: Ester Oras).*

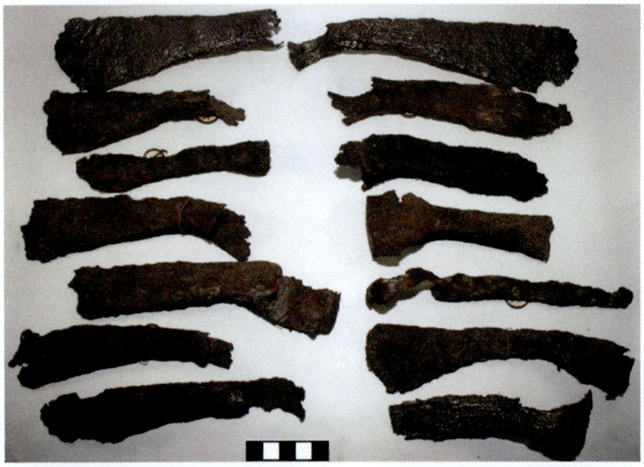

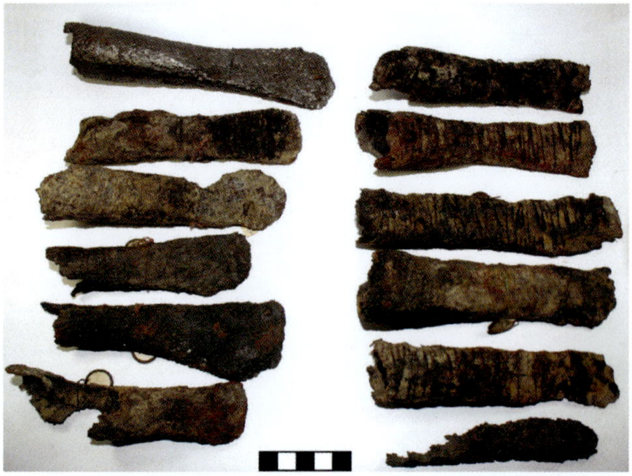

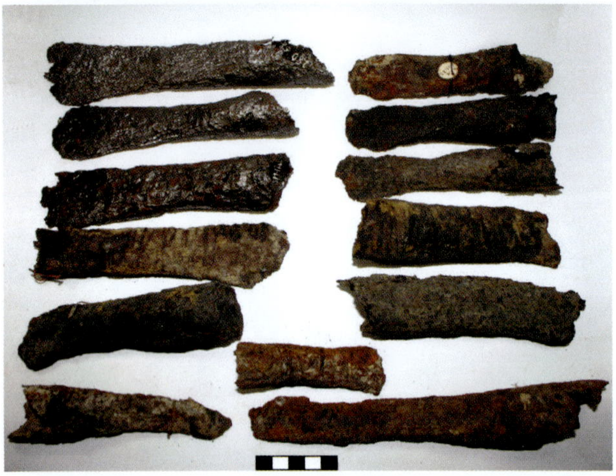

*Selection of artefacts from Kokmuiža I wealth deposit. (Photo: Ester Oras).*

| Wealth Deposit | KOKMUIŽA II |
|---|---|
| Collection number | LVNM 60210 / LVNM A 7027: 1–138 |
| Country | Latvia |
| County | Auces |
| Municipality | Vītiņu |
| Village | Kokmuiža (Kokumuiža), now Līgotņu |
| Date Of Discovery | Beginning of August, 1929 |
| Comments On Discovery | Found during digging ditch in the boggy bed of the River Avīkne |
| Dating Of Deposit (century) | 5 |
| Earliest Dating Of Artefacts (AD) | 450 |
| Latest Dating Of Artefacts (AD) | 525 |
| Manuscripts | LVNM archives 4635–4770b |
| References | Apals et al. 1974, 151<br>Balodis & Tentelis (eds) 1938, 127<br>Bliujienė 2010, 141 ff, no. 17<br>Moora 1938, 312–313, 671, 690, no. 17<br>Riekstiņš 1931<br>Urtāns 1964, 55–59,no. 26, figs 28–29<br>Urtāns 1977, 142–145, figs 48–49<br>Urtāns 2004, 95<br>Urtāns 2008, 84, fig. 18 |
| Comments | Site excavated in 1930 and 1931 by H. Riekstiņš. Mainly fragments and burnt objects were found: ca. 138 artefacts, weighing altogether 16 kg. Some artefacts burnt or fragmented prior the deposition. |

| | |
|---|---|
| Environment | Watery condition |
| Environment Subtype | Marsh |
| Depth (cm) | 45-60 |
| Artefact Placement | The total area of finds ca. 1.5 x 1 m. Stone artefacts on top, iron objects under them. |
| Archaeological Site | Hill-fort |
| Comments On Find-spot | In the boggy bed of the River Avīkne. In the peat at the edges of the trench some charcoal and calcinated bones were noted. At the depth of 45 cm, a 80 x 26 cm timber block was found with charcoal, ashes around it. |

| Artefact Type | Subtype | Amount | Material | Comments On Appearance | Futher Description |
|---|---|---|---|---|---|
| Spearhead | Socketed | 41 | Iron | 30 fragmented | Some include timber in the sockets |
| Axe | Socketed | 1 | Iron | | Contains tumber in the socket |
| Knife | | 9 | Iron | Fragmented | |
| Other Tool | Nail | 4 | Iron | Fragmented | |
| Other Tool | Strike-a-light | 1 | Iron | Fragmented | |
| Other Tool | Oval strike-a-light | 9 | Stone | 2 fragmented | |
| Other Tool | Whetstone | 9 | Stone | 8 fragmented | |
| Other Tool | Spindle whorl | 1 | Stone | | |
| Other Iron Object | Unidentified fragments | 3 | Iron | Fragmented | |
| Other Iron Object | Iron chain fragments | 1 | Iron | Fragmented | Consists of 5 rings |
| Other Iron Object | Unidentified fragment | 1 | Iron | Fragmented | |
| Other Iron Object | Large piece of shlag | 1 | Iron | | |
| Belt Part | Buckles | 2 | Bronze | Fragmented | |
| Belt Part | Buckles | 26 | Iron | Fragmented | |
| Ring | | 2 | Iron | ??? | |
| Neck-Ring | Box-shaped clasp termianls (?), terminals wrapped with wire | 1 | Silver | Burnt and fragmented | |
| Bracelet | Open thickened terminals | 1 | Bronze | Very small, fragmented | Max. outer diameter 3 cm |
| Bead | | 4 | Bone | Burnt | |
| Vessel | Drinking horn mounting | 1 | Bronze | Burnt and fragmented | |
| Other | Comb | 4 | Bone | Burnt and fragmented | |
| Other | Plate / disk | 1 | Bone | Burnt | |
| Other | Unidentified fragments | 14 | Bone | Burnt and fragmented | |

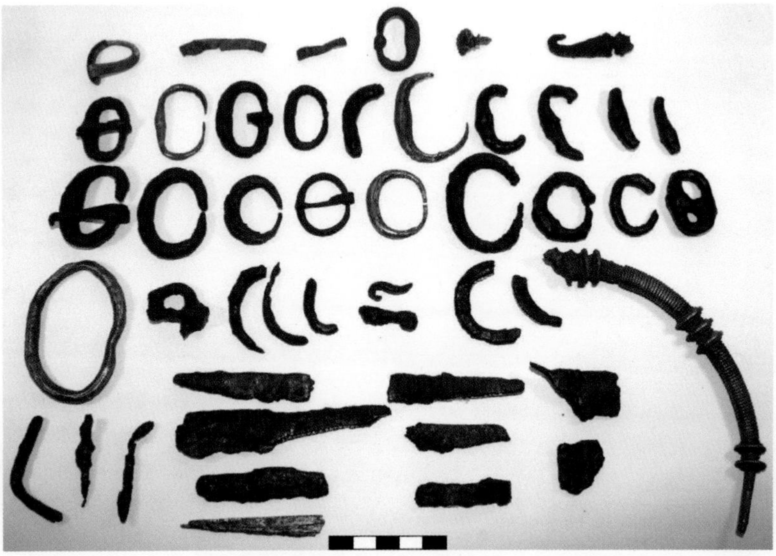

*Selection of artefacts from Kokmuiža II wealth deposit. (Photo: Ester Oras).*

*Selection of artefacts from Kokmuiža II wealth deposit. (Photo: Ester Oras).*

| Wealth Deposit | KOORKÜLA VALGJÄRV |
|---|---|
| Collection number | AI 1569–1571; 2712:11; several artefact lost |
| Country | Estonia |
| County | Valga |
| Municipality | Hummuli |
| Village | Jeti |
| Date Of Discovery | 19th century |
| Dating Of Deposit (century) | 9 |
| Earliest Dating Of Artefacts (AD) | 700 |
| Latest Dating Of Artefacts (AD) | 900 |
| Manuscripts | ERM museum catalogue no. 3224<br>Suik 1923/1924, 94<br>Valk 1988 |
| References | Jung 1898, 154–155<br>Tamla 1977,165<br>Tamla 1985, 139<br>Tvauri 2012, 291 ff |
| Comments | The exact finding circumstances and assemblage uncertain. Some artefacts may belong to later (historical) periods. Find deposited in Valga County Museum. 7 spearheads in the ERM lost and written off from the collections in 1952. |

| | |
|---|---|
| Environment | Watery condition |
| Environment Subtype | Spring |
| Artefact Placement | Spearheads thrust into the spring |

| Artefact Type | Subtype | Amount | Material | Comments On Appearance | Futher Description |
|---|---|---|---|---|---|
| Spearhead | Tanged | 3 | Iron | | 1 lost |
| Axe | Shafted, narrow blade | 1 | Iron | | Numerous, others lost |
| Other Tool | Shear | 1 | Iron | | Lost |
| Other Iron Object | Iron artefacts, parts of iron armour(?) | 1 | Iron | | Lost |
| Coin | Unknown | 1 | Bronze | | Lost, dating and exact numbers unknown |

*Selection of artefacts from Koorküla Valgjärv wealth deposit. (Photo: Ester Oras).*

| Wealth Deposit | KRIIMANI |
|---|---|
| Collection number | AI 1270 |
| Country | Estonia |
| County | Tartu |
| Municipality | Haaslava |
| Village | Kriimani |
| Date Of Discovery | 19th century (before 1877) |
| Comments On Discovery | Found during farm working in a heap of stones |
| Dating Of Deposit (century) | 6 |
| Earliest Dating Of Artefacts (AD) | 475 |
| Latest Dating Of Artefacts (AD) | 600 |
| References | Aun 1992, 142–143<br>Ebert 1913, 545<br>Jaanits et al. 1982, 287<br>Quast et al. 2010<br>Sb. GEG 1877, 103<br>Tallgren 1925, 14<br>Tvauri 2012, 87 |
| Comments | Previously dated to 7th century, produced in late-5th – early-6th century, deposited probably in the 6th century. Dating range: 475–525/600. |
| Environment | Dry land |
| Environment Subtype | Archaeological site |
| Depth (cm) | 10–30 |
| Markers | Heap of stones |
| Archaeological Site | Possible stone (tarand) grave |
| Comments On Find-spot | Under a heap of stones: a porbable destroyed stone (*tarand-*)grave, because some of the stones were placed in a row. |
| Comments On Artefacts | Vessel |

| Artefact Type | Subtype | Amount | Material | Comments On Appearance | Futher Description |
|---|---|---|---|---|---|
| Vessel | | 1 | Silver | Post-depositional fragmentation, Reconstructed in 2010. | Produced in late-5th – early-6th century, deposited probably in the 6th century. Reconstructed in 2010 (see Quast & Tamla with contribution by Felten 2010). |

*Kriimani wealth deposit. (Photo: Volker Iserhardt, Römisch-Germanisches Zentralmuseum in Quast et al. 2010, fig. 3).*

| Wealth Deposit | KUNDA I |
|---|---|
| Collection number | AI 1858: 1–16, 1884–1890 |
| Country | Estonia |
| County | Lääne-Viru |
| Municipality | Viru-Nigula |
| Village | Kunda |
| Date Of Discovery | 1893-1894 |
| Comments On Discovery | Found in Kunda bog during marl digging |
| Dating Of Deposit (century) | 1–3; 6–7 |
| Earliest Dating Of Artefacts (AD) | 1 |
| Latest Dating Of Artefacts (AD) | 700 |
| Manuscripts | Lieven 1893-1894<br>Määr 1922, 9<br>Püss 1932 |
| References | Jaanits et al. 1982, 284<br>Lang 2007a, 163<br>Mandel & Tamla 1977, 161–162<br>RK 1896, 21 (no. 317–318), tab. 22: 12–13, tab. 28: 20–21<br>Sb. GEG 1893 [1894], 126<br>Tallgren 1925, 24<br>Tamla 1977, no. 30, 157 ff<br>Tamla 1995<br>Tamla 1996<br>Tvauri 2012, 292–293 |
| Comments | Copper coins and 3 more axes found in closeby area in 1885–1887.<br>Dating range: 1–200; 500–700. |

| | |
|---|---|
| Environment | Watery condition |
| Environment Subtype | Bog |

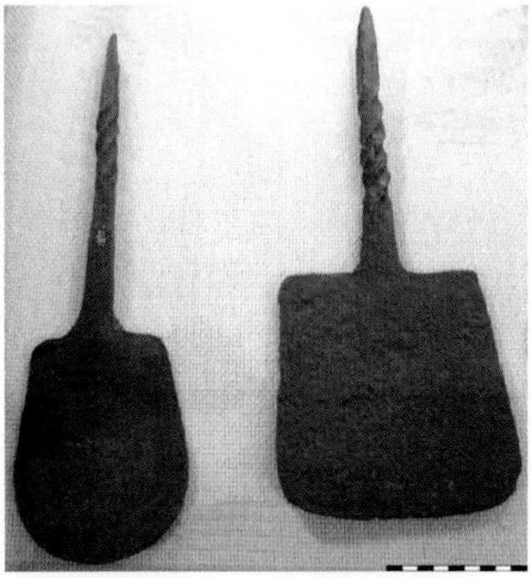

*Selection of artefacts from Kunda I wealth deposit. (Photo: Ester Oras).*

| Artefact Type | Subtype | Amount | Material | Comments On Appearance | Futher Description |
|---|---|---|---|---|---|
| Sword | | 1 | Iron | Fragmented | |
| Spearhead | | 5 | Iron | | |
| Axe | Shafted, 1 with a thin blade (dated to the 1st–2nd century) | 8 | Iron | Fragmented | 1 thin bladed, 1st–2nd century |
| Axe | Shafted | 1 | Iron | | |
| Other Tool | Coal trovel | 2 | Iron | | |
| Other Iron Object | Iron plates | 2 | Iron | Fragmented | Possibly cauldon parts? |
| Other Iron Object | Fragments of iron artefacts | 4 | Iron | Fragmented, inlcuding 1 possible sword fragment | |

*Selection of artefacts from Kunda I wealth deposit. (Photo: Ester Oras).*

| Wealth Deposit | KUNDA II |
|---|---|
| Collection number | AM 88: 112–115; some artefacts lost |
| Country | Estonia |
| County | Lääne-Viru |
| Municipality | Viru-Nigula |
| Village | Kunda |
| Date Of Discovery | End of the 19th century (1893?) |
| Comments On Discovery | Found in Kunda bog during marl digging |
| Dating Of Deposit (century) | 8 |
| Earliest Dating Of Artefacts (AD) | 600 |
| Latest Dating Of Artefacts (AD) | 800 |
| Manuscripts | Määr 1922, 1, 9<br>Püss 1932, 14, 25 |
| References | Jaanits et al. 1982, 283<br>Sb. GEG 1893, 126<br>Tvauri 2012, 291, 296 |

| | |
|---|---|
| Environment | Watery condition |
| Environment Subtype | Bog |

| Artefact Type | Subtype | Amount | Material | Comments On Appearance | Futher Description |
|---|---|---|---|---|---|
| Finger-Ring | | 1 | Bronze | | Lost |
| Dress Pin | Ring-shape terminal | 2 | Bronze | Fragmented | |
| Other Tool | Oval strike-a-light stone | 1 | Stone | | Lost |

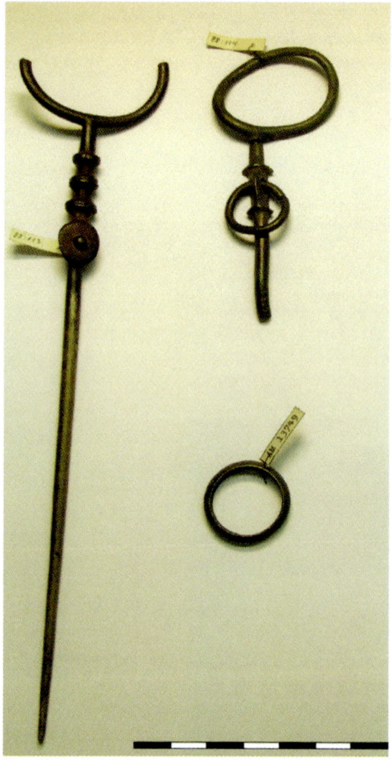

*Selection of artefacts from Kunda II wealth deposit. (Photo: Ester Oras).*

| Wealth Deposit | LĖBARTAI |
|---|---|
| Collection number | PM 6522 (until 1945); current location unknown |
| Country | Lithuania |
| County | Klaipėda |
| Municipality | Klaipėda |
| Village | Lėbartai |
| Date Of Discovery | End of the 19th century |
| Comments On Discovery | Found during farm work under the stump of an elm tree |
| Dating Of Deposit (century) | 6 |
| Earliest Dating Of Artefacts (AD) | 500 |
| Latest Dating Of Artefacts (AD) | 600 |
| References | Engel 1931, 84<br>Hollack 1908, 92<br>KPM II 1897, 34, no. 165<br>Michelbertas 2007, 13<br>Sb. Prussia H. 19, 1895, 252<br>Tautavičius 1977, 132 |
| Comments | Artefacts found, but an exact find-spot and artefact content unknown.<br>Donated to Prussia Museum by Mr Rittergutsbesitzer Scheu (Heydekrug region).<br>According to the descriptions artefacts dating from the 3rd–6th century. |

| | |
|---|---|
| Environment | Dry land |
| Depth (cm) | 40–50 |
| Comments On Find-spot | Under the stump of an elm tree. Some burial grounds are known closeby. |

| Artefact Type | Subtype | Amount | Material | Comments On Appearance | Futher Description |
|---|---|---|---|---|---|
| Other | Comb | 1 | Bronze | A bronze comb with long haft | Lost? |

| Wealth Deposit | LEJASLEPJI |
|---|---|
| Collection number | LVNM A 8300: 1-6, A 9050 |
| Country | Latvia |
| County | Madona |
| Municipality | Vestiena |
| Village | Vestiena |
| Date Of Discovery | 1905 |
| Comments On Discovery | Found in local farm land |
| Dating Of Deposit (century) | 6 |
| Earliest Dating Of Artefacts (AD) | 400 |
| Latest Dating Of Artefacts (AD) | 600 |
| Manuscripts | LVNM archives, Madonas apr., Vestienas pag., 16 |
| References | Apals et al. 1974, 151<br>Balodis & Tentelis (eds) 1938, 114, 126<br>Griciuvienė 2005, 169, 232–233<br>Moora 1938, 319, 346–347, 691–692<br>Urtāns 1964, 51–52, no. 18, fig. 21<br>Urtāns 1977, 149–150, fig. 55<br>Vankina et al. 1981, 58, fig. 27: 1 |
| Comments | Museum received 6 rings on the 21st of January 1937, another one on the 28th of January 1937. Area excavated in June 1934. Total weight of the deposit 1092.61 g. |

| | |
|---|---|
| Environment | Dry land |

| Artefact Type | Subtype | Amount | Material | Comments On Appearance | Futher Description |
|---|---|---|---|---|---|
| Neck-Ring | Overlapping faceted terminals | 3 | Silver | 1 fragmented | Diameter 19.2 cm; weight 175.3 g;<br>Diameter 18.5 cm; weight 183.82 g;<br>Diameter 19.5 cm; weight 164.6 g |
| Neck-Ring | Hooklet terminals, slightly faceted | 1 | Silver | 1 fragmented (1 terminal missing) | Diameter 22.1 cm; weight 215.42 g |
| Neck-Ring | Overlapping faceted terminals | 1 | Silver | Fragmented, half of the ring | Diameter 14.8 cm; weight 140.1 g |
| Neck-Ring | Overlapping twisted terminals | 1 | Silver | | Diameter 19.8 cm; weight 92.22 g |
| Neck-Ring | Thin, faceted terminals | 1 | Silver | | Diameter 18.7 cm; weight 77.25 g |

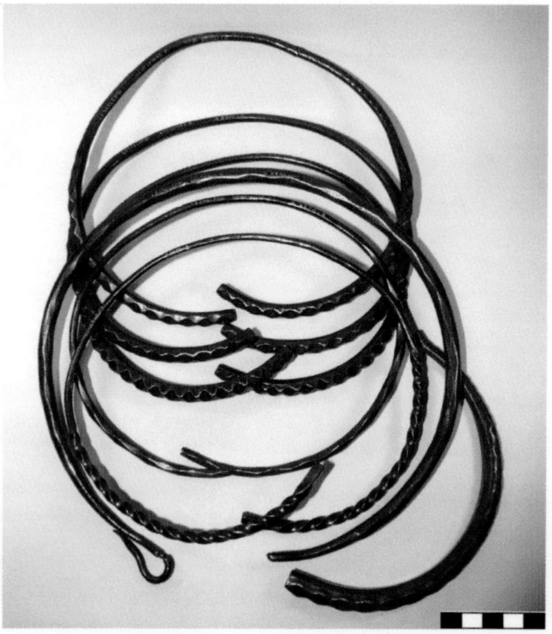

*Lejaslepji wealth deposit. (Photo: Ester Oras).*

| Wealth Deposit | LEJASĻŪDI |
|---|---|
| Collection number | LVNM 58060 |
| Country | Latvia |
| County | Vecpiebalga |
| Municipality | Taurene |
| Village | Ļūdi |
| Date Of Discovery | 1924 or 1925 |
| Comments On Discovery | Found by a local peasant during digging ground at the meadows |
| Dating Of Deposit (century) | 7 |
| Earliest Dating Of Artefacts (AD) | 600 |
| Latest Dating Of Artefacts (AD) | 650 |
| Manuscripts | LVNM archives, Cēsu apr., Taurenes pag., 13 |
| References | Šnore 1936, 48, no. 145<br>Urtāns 1964, 45, no. 6, fig. 7<br>Urtāns 1977, 155, fig. 61 |
| Comments | Received by the museum in 1933, donated by J. Rungula. |

| | |
|---|---|
| Environment | Dry land |

| Artefact Type | Subtype | Amount | Material | Comments On Appearance | Futher Description |
|---|---|---|---|---|---|
| Neck-Ring | Profoundly faceted terminals | 1 | Silver | | Diameter 26.4 cm; weight 252.5 g |

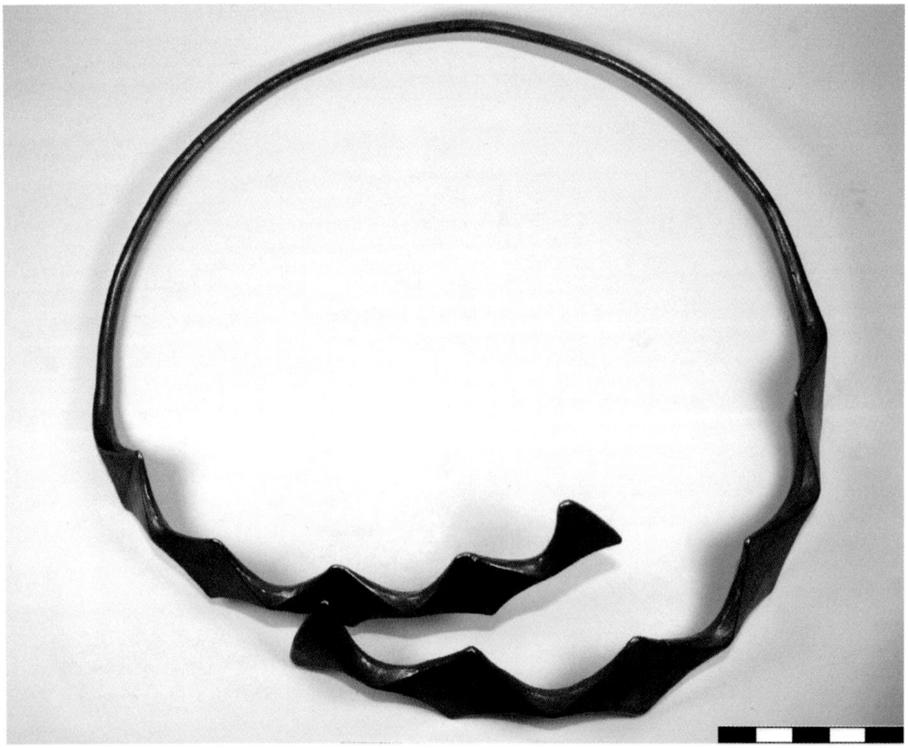

*Lejasļūdi wealth deposit. (Photo: Ester Oras).*

| Wealth Deposit | LIIMALA |
|---|---|
| Collection number | AI 3774: 1 - 2 |
| Country | Estonia |
| County | Ida-Viru |
| Municipality | Lüganuse |
| Village | Liimala |
| Date Of Discovery | 1938 |
| Comments On Discovery | Found during farm works |
| Dating Of Deposit (century) | 4 |
| Earliest Dating Of Artefacts (AD) | 275 |
| Latest Dating Of Artefacts (AD) | 325 |
| References | Jaanits et al. 1982, 220–221, 231, fig. 147<br>Jonuks 2009, 230–233, 242<br>Lang 2007a, 162<br>Lang 2007b, 211, 246–247, fig. 149<br>Rzeszotarska-Nowakiewicz 2010, 320–324, plate V: 9<br>Schmiedehelm 1955, fig. 46 |

| | |
|---|---|
| Environment | Dry land |
| Markers | Stones? |
| Archaeological Site | Burial area? |
| Geographical Landscape | Limestone cliff |
| Comments On Find-spot | In a field situated at the limestone cliff in the area of the field where stones in a row were noticed (probable stone grave e.g. *tarand*-grave?) |

| Artefact Type | Subtype | Amount | Material | Comments On Appearance | Futher Description |
|---|---|---|---|---|---|
| Neck-Ring | Massive, trumpet-shaped terminals | 1 | Bronze | | |
| Neck-Ring | Loop-shaped terminals, twisted bronze wire | 1 | Bronze | | |

*A massive neck-ring from Liimala wealth deposit. (Photo: Ester Oras).*

| Wealth Deposit | LOOSI |
|---|---|
| Collection number | AI 721: 1-3 |
| Country | Estonia |
| County | Võru |
| Municipality | Vastseliina |
| Village | Loosi (Hindi) |
| Date Of Discovery | II half of the 19th century (before 1866) |
| Comments On Discovery | Found during digging a drainage ditch in the small marshy field area |
| Dating Of Deposit (century) | 9 |
| Earliest Dating Of Artefacts (AD) | 750 |
| Latest Dating Of Artefacts (AD) | 900 |
| Manuscripts | Karopun 1922, 45–46 |
| References | Aun 1992, 138 ff<br>Jaanits et al. 1982, 287<br>Kiudsoo 2005, 142<br>Sb. GEG 1866, 29–30<br>Tamla 1977, no. 48, 163<br>Tõnisson 1962, no. 96, 200<br>Tvauri 2012, 296 |

| | |
|---|---|
| Environment | Watery condition |
| Environment Subtype | Marsh |
| Comments On Find-spot | A possible wooden construction was noticed in the closeby area |

| Artefact Type | Subtype | Amount | Material | Comments On Appearance | Futher Description |
|---|---|---|---|---|---|
| Neck-Ring | Saddle and hooklet terminals | 3 | Silver | 2 fragmented | |

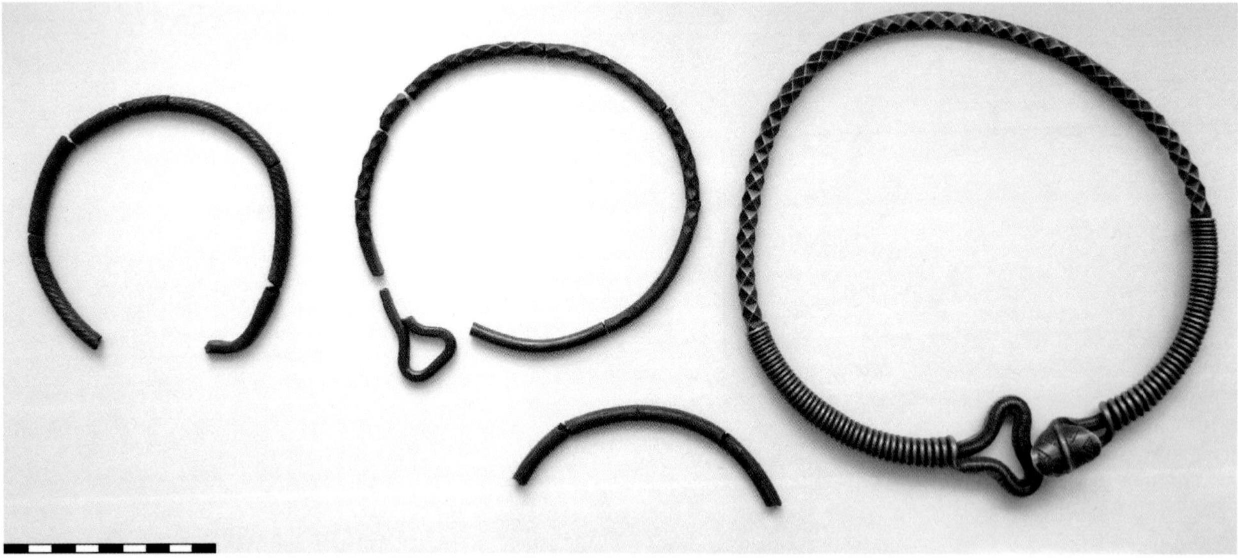

*Loosi wealth deposit. (Photo: Ester Oras).*

| Wealth Deposit | MEŽOTNE |
|---|---|
| Collection number | LVNM 64609: 2–3, 6–7<br>LVNM 64609: 1, 4, 5 (Lost during German occupation (1941–1944)) |
| Country | Latvia |
| County | Bauska |
| Municipality | Mežotne |
| Village | Rundāles |
| Date Of Discovery | 6th of September 1939 |
| Comments On Discovery | Found during excavations at Mežotne hill-fort by V. Ģinters. |
| Dating Of Deposit (century) | 9 |
| Earliest Dating Of Artefacts (AD) | 800 |
| Latest Dating Of Artefacts (AD) | 825 |
| Manuscripts | LVNM archives |
| References | Apals et al. 1974, 151<br>Brīvkalne 2009<br>SM 1939, 4, 36-38, figs 21–22<br>Urtāns 1964, 43–44, no. 3, figs 3–4<br>Urtāns 1977, 163, fig. 70 |

| | |
|---|---|
| Environment | Dry land |
| Environment Subtype | Archaeological site |
| Type Of Container | Textile |
| Markers | Hill-fort rampart |
| Archaeological Site | Mežotne hill-fort |
| Comments On Find-spot | In the 10th layer of the hill-fort rampart in the W-part of the plateau close to the debris of burnt fortification wall. Burnt bone fragments and weapons were found closeby (interpreted as remains and belongings of defenders who remained under the collapsed fortification wall). |

| Artefact Type | Subtype | Amount | Material | Comments On Appearance | Futher Description |
|---|---|---|---|---|---|
| Bracelet | Spiral | 2 | Bronze | Fragmented, 1 bracelet deformed | Ornamented plate |
| Brooch | Crossbow brooch, animal head-like terminals | 1 | Bronze | | Nail made of iron, dated earlier: 7th–8th century, lost |
| Brooch | Crossbow brooch with crossplates | 1 | Bronze | Fragmented | Nail and central part made of iron, some parts lost |
| Brooch | Penannaular brooch with rolled-up terminals | 1 | Bronze | Fragmented | |
| Brooch | Penannular brooch with faceted terminals | 2 | Bronze | | Lost |

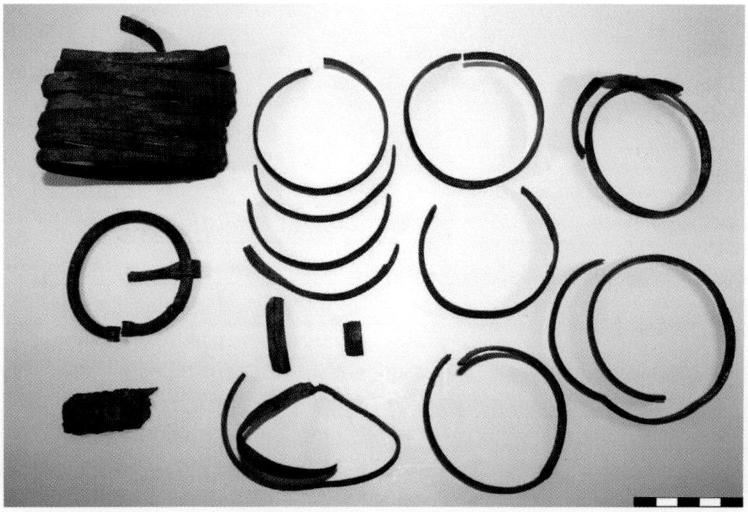

*Selection of artefacts from Mežotne wealth deposit. (Photo: Ester Oras).*

*Selection of artefacts from Mežotne wealth deposit. (Photo: LVNM Archeology Department Archives, AA 529).*

| Wealth Deposit | METSKÜLA |
|---|---|
| Collection number | AI 2513: 88; one neck-ring lost |
| Country | Estonia |
| County | Viljandi |
| Municipality | Suure-Jaani |
| Village | Metsküla / Kõpu |
| Date Of Discovery | In 1880s |
| Comments On Discovery | Found during digging a drainage ditch |
| Dating Of Deposit (century) | 2 |
| Earliest Dating Of Artefacts (AD) | 1 |
| Latest Dating Of Artefacts (AD) | 200 |
| Manuscripts | Tiitsmaa 1924, 13 |
| References | Ebert 1913, 527–528<br>Hausmann 1909, 45–47<br>Jaanits et al. 1982, 221, 231, fig. 148<br>Jonuks 2009, 231–234, 242<br>Lang 2007a, 162<br>Lang 2007b, 247, fig. 150<br>Rzeszotarska-Nowakiewicz 2010, 324, 329–330, plate IX: 14<br>Schmiedehelm 1955, 163<br>Vassar 1956, 185 |
| Comments | Artefacts dated to the Late Pre-Roman Iron Age (ca. 250 BC – 100 AD); deposition according to the similar finds of Mustmätta and Liimala dated to the Roman Iron Age (50–450 AD). Accoridng to Rzeszotarska-Nowakiewicz 2010 finds date from the Late Pre-Roman Iron Age, with parallels from Prussia and western-Baltic. Thus latest possible dating for the deposit around 2nd century AD. |

| | |
|---|---|
| Environment | Watery condition |
| Environment Subtype | Marsh |
| Depth (cm) | 120 |
| Geographical Landscape | Small drumlins |
| Comments On Find-spot | Marshy area between small drumlins |

| Artefact Type | Subtype | Amount | Material | Collection No | Futher Description |
|---|---|---|---|---|---|
| Neck-Ring | Massive upwards bent trompet shaped termianls | 1 | Bronze | AI 2513: 88 | Repaired before in prehistoric times (Ebert 1913, 527; Hausmann 1914, 45–47) |
| Neck-Ring | Thin, simple | 1 | Bronze | Lost | Compared to the massive one, thinner and simpler one, lost |

*A massive neck-ring from Metsküla wealth deposit. (Photo: Ester Oras).*

| Wealth Deposit | MIEŽAIČIAI |
|---|---|
| Collection number | ŠAM I-A 247–250; VDKM 1911: 1–4 |
| Country | Lithuania |
| County | Šiauliai |
| Municipality | Kelmė |
| Village | Miežaičiai; Mažaičiai |
| Date Of Discovery | 1931 |
| Dating Of Deposit (century) | 2 |
| Earliest Dating Of Artefacts (AD) | 1 |
| Latest Dating Of Artefacts (AD) | 200 |
| References | Kulikauskas et al. 1961, 107, fig. 68<br>Merkevičius 1973, 94<br>Michelbertas 1986, 212<br>Michelbertas 2007, 12<br>Nagevičius 1935, 90<br>Tautavičius 1977, 132<br>Volkaitė-Kulikauskienė 1958, 115, fig. 84 |
| Comments | Dated to the beginning of the 1st millennium AD on the basis of chemical analysis (higher i.e. 26% Zn inclusion) of the 4 bars. According to Michelbertas (2007, 12) deposit most probably from the Early Iron Age. Exact circumstances of discovery unknown. |

| | |
|---|---|
| Environment | Unknown |

| Artefact Type | Subtype | Amount | Material | Comments On Appearance | Futher Description |
|---|---|---|---|---|---|
| Raw Material | Rod (bar) | 8 | Bronze | Triangular cross-section; length 37–47 cm | Dated to the I millennium AD on the bases of chemical analysis (higher i.e. 26% Zn inclusion) of 4 rods, although first thought to be from the Bronze Age |

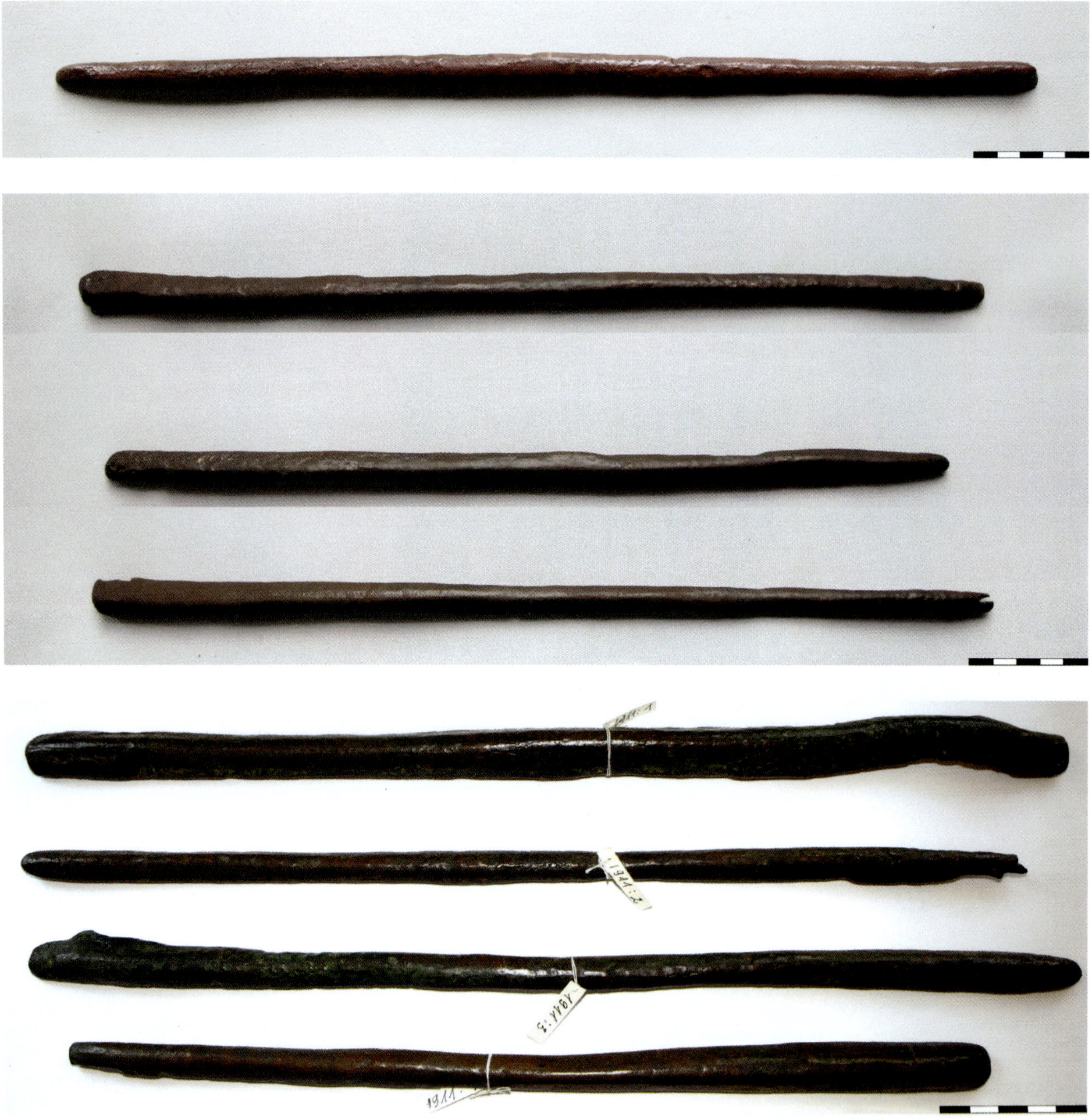

*Miežaičiai wealth deposit. (Photo: Ester Oras, Audronė Šapaitė, Arturas Uzgalis).*

| Wealth Deposit | MIGONIAI I |
|---|---|
| Collection number | BKM |
| Country | Lithuania |
| County | Panevėžys |
| Municipality | Pasvalys |
| Village | Migoniai |
| Date Of Discovery | 1931 |
| Comments On Discovery | Found during field ploughing |
| Dating Of Deposit (century) | 7 |
| Earliest Dating Of Artefacts (AD) | 600 |
| Latest Dating Of Artefacts (AD) | 700 |
| References | Michelbertas 2007, 13–14<br>Puzinas 1935, 1235<br>Tautavičius 1977, 132<br>Volkaitė-Kulikauskienė 1958, 115–116 |
| Comments | Unfinished artefacts, interpreteted as jeweller's hoard |

| | |
|---|---|
| Environment | Dry land |
| Depth (cm) | 30–40 |
| Comments On Find-spot | Depth derived from finding circumstances (ploughing) |

| Artefact Type | Subtype | Amount | Material | Comments On Appearance | Futher Description |
|---|---|---|---|---|---|
| Bracelet | | 2 | Bronze | Unfinished | |
| Brooch | Crossbow brooch | 1 | Bronze | Unfinished | |
| Raw Material | Rod / bar | 1 | Bronze | Traingular cross section | Length 18.5 cm, width 2.3 cm; thickness 1.7 cm |
| Raw Material | Rod / bar | 1 | Bronze | Fragmented, cut terminals, triangular cross section | Similar to longer one, length 11.2 cm |
| Raw Material | Raw material for ornament production | 1 | Bronze | | Long and narrow bar, possibly raw material for ornament production |
| Raw Material | | 2 | Bronze | Bent | Unfinished bracelets or other ornaments, triangular edges |

*Migoniai I wealth deposit. (Photo: Ester Oras).*

| Wealth Deposit | MIGONIAI II |
|---|---|
| Collection number | BKM |
| Country | Lithuania |
| County | Panevėžys |
| Municipality | Pasvalys |
| Village | Migoniai |
| Date Of Discovery | 1940s |
| Comments On Discovery | Found in the fields of Migoniai village |
| Dating Of Deposit (century) | 7 |
| Earliest Dating Of Artefacts (AD) | 500 |
| Latest Dating Of Artefacts (AD) | 700 |
| References | Michelbertas 2007, 13–14<br>Tautavičius 1977, 132<br>Vaitkunskienė 1981, 29<br>Volkaitė-Kulikauskienė 1943, 92<br>Volkaitė-Kulikauskienė 1958, 116, fig. 85 |

| | |
|---|---|
| Environment | Dry land |

| Artefact Type | Subtype | Amount | Material | Comments On Appearance | Futher Description |
|---|---|---|---|---|---|
| Neck-Ring | Loop and hooklet terminals | 2 | Silver | 1 fragmented, loop part missing | |
| Neck-Ring | Profoundly faceted terminals | 1 | Silver | Facets ornamented | |

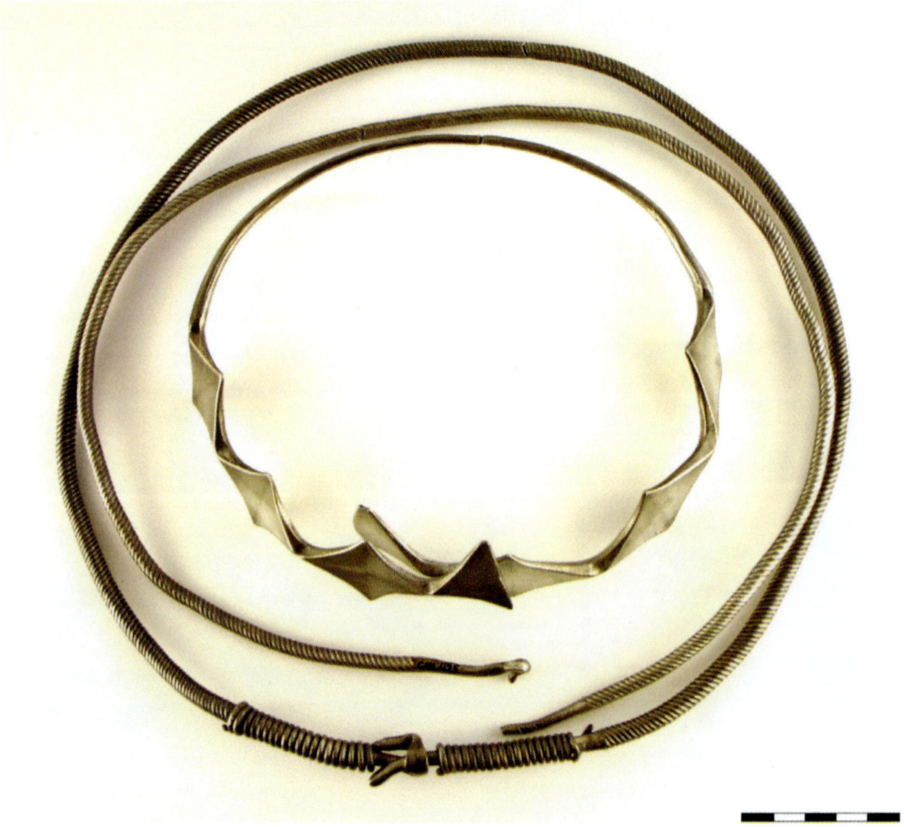

*Migoniai II wealth deposit. (Photo: Ester Oras).*

| Wealth Deposit | MIŠKIŅEVA |
|---|---|
| Collection number | St Petersburg State Hermitage Museum 966/1–4 |
| Country | Latvia |
| County | Ludza |
| Municipality | Istra |
| Village | Miškiņeva (Istras) |
| Date Of Discovery | September 1878 |
| Comments On Discovery | Found during sand digging |
| Dating Of Deposit (century) | 6 |
| Earliest Dating Of Artefacts (AD) | 400 |
| Latest Dating Of Artefacts (AD) | 600 |
| Manuscripts | St Petersburg State Hermitage Museum catalogue |
| References | Apals et al. 1974, 151<br>Balodis & Tentelis (eds) 1938, 126<br>MPAR 1890, 50, tab. VIII: 1,3, 10–11<br>Moora 1929, 83, no. 83<br>Moora 1938, 315–319, fig. 39<br>Urtāns 1964, 51, no. 17, fig. 20<br>Urtāns 1977, 148–149, fig. 53<br>Vaitkunskienė 1981, 32 |
| Comments | Total weight of the deposit 1445.9 g |

| | |
|---|---|
| Environment | Dry land |
| Geographical Landscape | Sand plain |
| Comments On Find-spot | Sandy field |

| Artefact Type | Subtype | Amount | Material | Comments On Appearance | Futher Description |
|---|---|---|---|---|---|
| Neck-Ring | Hooklet and loop shape terminals | 2 | Silver | Terminals wrapped with wire | |
| Neck-Ring | Spoon (shell) shaped terminals with silver hook | 2 | Silver | Terminals wrapped with wire | 1 neck-ring has been repaired during its inital use period |

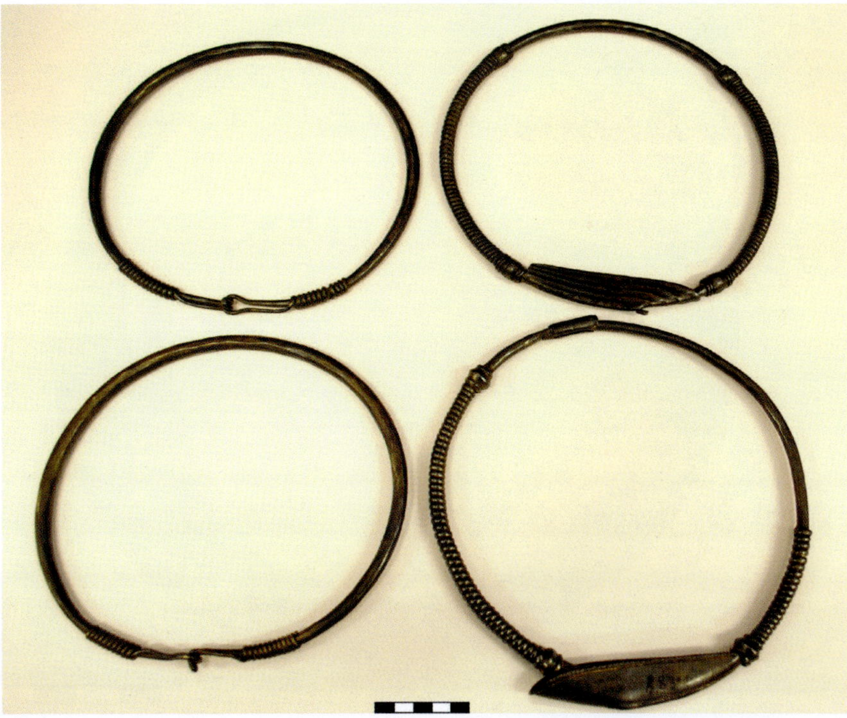

*Miškiņeva wealth deposit. (Photo: Ester Oras).*

| Wealth Deposit | MŪKUKALNS II |
|---|---|
| Collection number | LVNM A 11848: 748 |
| Country | Latvia |
| County | Salaspils |
| Municipality | Salaspils |
| Village | Spolītes |
| Date Of Discovery | 24th of July 1961 |
| Comments On Discovery | Found during excavations at the Mūkukalns hill-fort |
| Dating Of Deposit (century) | 9 |
| Earliest Dating Of Artefacts (AD) | 775 |
| Latest Dating Of Artefacts (AD) | 825 |
| Manuscripts | LVNM archives, no. 401 |
| References | Graudonis 1964, figs 1, 4<br>Urtāns 1964, 53, no. 21<br>Urtāns 1977, 160–161, fig. 69 |

| | |
|---|---|
| Environment | Dry land |
| Environment Subtype | Archaeological site |
| Depth (cm) | 68 |
| Markers | Large granite stone slate |
| Archaeological Site | Mūkukalns hill-fort |
| Comments On Find-spot | In sooty soil under a large stone slate of the rampart's stone pavement in the SW part of the hill-fort (during cleaning the second layer/beginning of the third layer in square XVII). |

| Artefact Type | Subtype | Amount | Material | Comments On Appearance | Futher Description |
|---|---|---|---|---|---|
| Neck-Ring | Overlapping terminals with facet-like decoration | 1 | Bronze | | Diameter 17.5 x 18.7 cm |

*Mūkukalns II wealth deposit. (Photo: Ester Oras).*

| Wealth Deposit | MŪKUKALNS III |
|---|---|
| Collection number | LVNM 163184:1000–1013 |
| Country | Latvia |
| County | Salaspils |
| Municipality | Salaspils |
| Village | Spolītes |
| Date Of Discovery | 23rd of August 1962 |
| Comments On Discovery | Found during excavations at the Mūkukalns hill-fort. |
| Dating Of Deposit (century) | 6 |
| Earliest Dating Of Artefacts (AD) | 475 |
| Latest Dating Of Artefacts (AD) | 525 |
| Manuscripts | LVNM archives AA 402 |
| References | Graudonis 1964, figs 1, 5–9<br>Urtāns 1964, 53–54, no. 22<br>Urtāns 1977, 145–146, fig. 51 |

| | |
|---|---|
| Environment | Dry land |
| Environment Subtype | Archaeological site |
| Depth (cm) | 52-70 |
| Type Of Container | Ceramic vessel? |
| Artefact Placement | Most of the spearheads' directed towards S, two to N. Axes facing opposite direction from each other |
| Markers | Stone pile |
| Archaeological Site | Mūkukalns hill-fort |
| Comments On Find-spot | N slope of the Mūkukalns hill-fort (square XXVI) in the middle of a small oval stone pile. On and near the deposit 2 potsherds (bottom shard with a diametre of ca. 10 cm, and a fragment of a body part of the vessel) were found, but the relation with the deposit is unclear. |

| Artefact Type | Subtype | Amount | Material | Comments On Appearance | Futher Description |
|---|---|---|---|---|---|
| Spearhead | Socketed | 5 | Iron | | |
| Axe | Shafted | 2 | Iron | | |
| Knife | | 2 | Iron | | |
| Sickle/Scythe | Sickle | 5 | Iron | | |

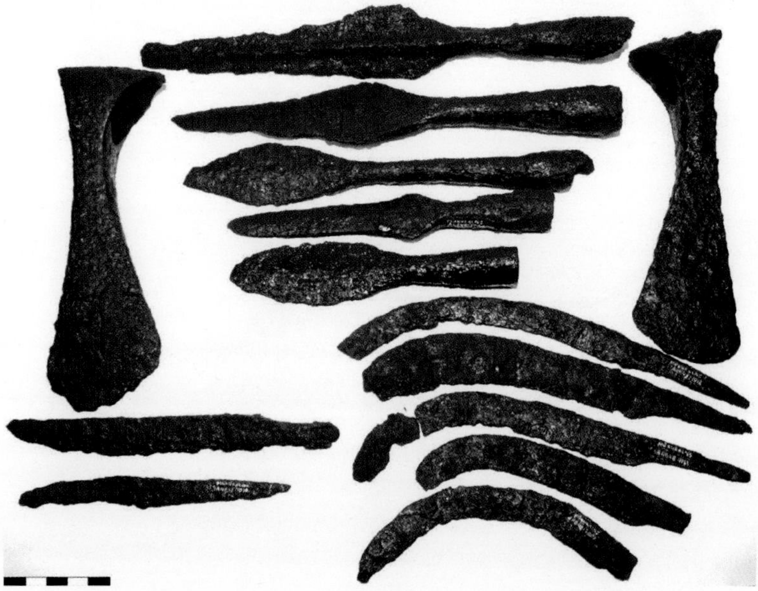

*Mūkukalns III wealth deposit. (Photo: Ester Oras).*

| Wealth Deposit | MŪRNIEKI |
|---|---|
| Collection number | LVNM 163258: 1–2 |
| Country | Latvia |
| County | Nereta |
| Municipality | Nereta |
| Village | Mūrnieki |
| Date Of Discovery | 1937 |
| Comments On Discovery | Found by A. Lapiņš. |
| Dating Of Deposit (century) | 8 |
| Earliest Dating Of Artefacts (AD) | 675 |
| Latest Dating Of Artefacts (AD) | 725 |
| Manuscripts | LVNM VI archives |
| References | Urtāns 1964, 45–46, no. 8, fig. 9<br>Urtāns 1977, 157–158, fig. 65<br>Vankina et al. 1981, fig. 28 |
| Comments | The finds were received by the Museum on the 12th of August 1960. Total weight of the deposit 554 g. |

| | |
|---|---|
| Environment | Dry land |
| Environment Subtype | Archaeological site |
| Archaeological Site | Mūrnieki settlement site |
| Comments On Find-spot | Mūrnieki settlement site located in the close vicinity of the deposit |

| Artefact Type | Subtype | Amount | Material | Comments On Appearance | Futher Description |
|---|---|---|---|---|---|
| Neck-Ring | Loop and hooklet terminals | 1 | Silver | | Diameter 24.5 cm; weight 245.7 g |
| Neck-Ring | Profoundly faceted terminals | 1 | Silver | | Diameter 24 x 25 cm; weight 308.2 g |

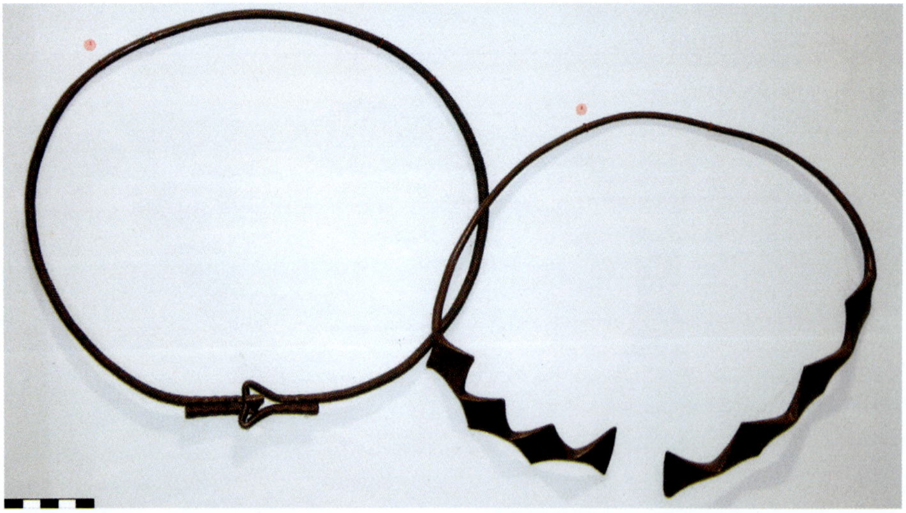

*Mūrnieki wealth deposit. (Photo: Ester Oras).*

| Wealth Deposit | MUSTMÄTTA |
|---|---|
| Collection number | AI 3890: 1–16 |
| Country | Estonia |
| County | Ida-Viru |
| Municipality | Lüganuse |
| Village | Mustmätta |
| Date Of Discovery | 28.05.1940 |
| Comments On Discovery | Found during field ploughing / harrowing |
| Dating Of Deposit (century) | 4 |
| Earliest Dating Of Artefacts (AD) | 275 |
| Latest Dating Of Artefacts (AD) | 325 |
| Manuscripts | Vassar 1943, 148 |
| References | Jaanits et al. 1982, 220–221, 231, fig. 147<br>Jonuks 2009, 231–234, 242<br>Lang 2007a, 162<br>Lang 2007b, 211, 247, fig. 132<br>Rzeszotarska-Nowakiewicz 2010, 320–324, plate V: 8<br>Schmiedehelm 1955, fig. 45<br>Tamla & Kiudsoo 2005, 12–13 |
| Comments | According to Vassar (1943, 148) artefacts can be dated in the time span of 200 years |

| | |
|---|---|
| Environment | Dry land |
| Depth (cm) | 20–30 |

| Artefact Type | Subtype | Amount | Material | Comments On Appearance | Futher Description |
|---|---|---|---|---|---|
| Neck-Ring | Trumpet-shaped terminals | 8 | Bronze | 1 fragmented | 2 very massive examples |
| Neck-Ring | Mushroom-shaped terminals | 5 | Bronze | 1 fragmented | |
| Neck-Ring | Conical terminals | 2 | Bronze | 1 neck-ring fragmented into 4 pieces | |
| Neck-Ring | Twisted bronze wire with loop-shape terminals | 1 | Bronze | | |

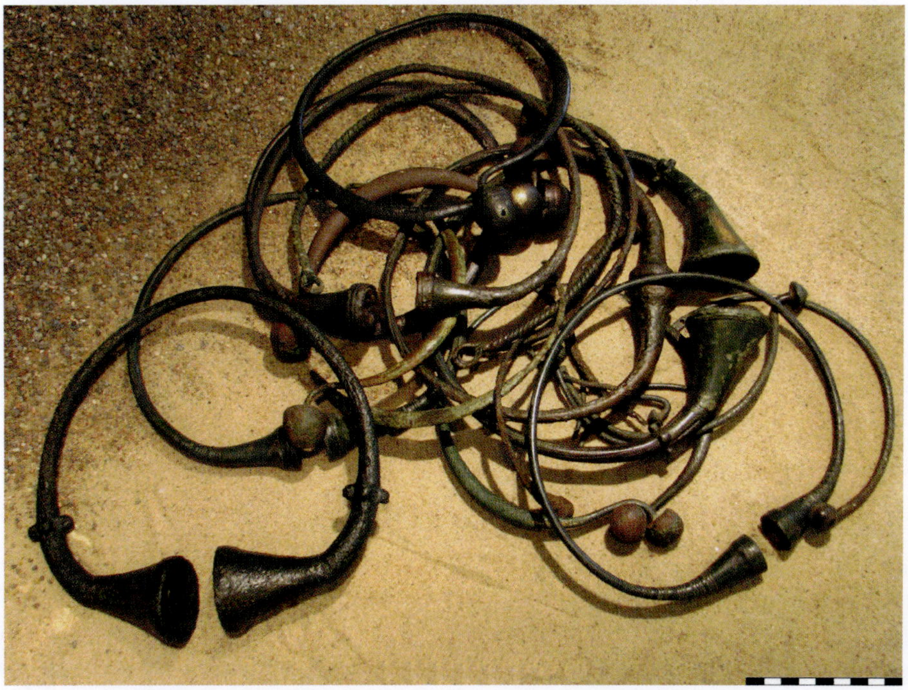

*Mustmätta wealth deposit.*
*(Photo: Ester Oras).*

| Wealth Deposit | NAVESTI |
|---|---|
| Collection number | AI 3842 |
| Country | Estonia |
| County | Viljandi |
| Municipality | Suure-Jaani |
| Village | Navesti |
| Date Of Discovery | October 1938 |
| Comments On Discovery | Found during field ploughing |
| Dating Of Deposit (century) | 8 |
| Earliest Dating Of Artefacts (AD) | 700 |
| Latest Dating Of Artefacts (AD) | 725 |
| Manuscripts | AI museum catalogue no. 3842 |
| References | Tamla 1977, no. 42, 162–163<br>Tvauri 2012, 296 |

| | |
|---|---|
| Environment | Watery condition |
| Environment Subtype | Marsh |
| Depth (cm) | 20 |
| Comments On Find-spot | Peat rich marshy area, on top of the natural watersand layer |

| Artefact Type | Subtype | Amount | Material | Comments On Appearance | Futher Description |
|---|---|---|---|---|---|
| Neck-Ring | Flat faceted overlapping terminals | 1 | Silver | | Broken during discovery |

*Navesti wealth deposit. (Photo: Ester Oras).*

| Wealth Deposit | NEGARBA |
|---|---|
| Collection number | KM GEK 4097 |
| Country | Lithuania |
| County | Klaipėda |
| Municipality | Kretinga |
| Village | Senkai |
| Dating Of Deposit (century) | 8 |
| Earliest Dating Of Artefacts (AD) | 650 |
| Latest Dating Of Artefacts (AD) | 800 |
| Manuscripts | Pers. comm. Audronė Bliujienė |
| References | Tautavičius 1978, 80<br>Bliujienė 2013, 239, fig. 150 |
| Comments | According to Tautavičius (1978, 80) dating 8th–9th century |

| | |
|---|---|
| Environment | Watery condition |
| Environment Subtype | Bog |
| Archaeological Site | Hill-fort |
| Comments On Find-spot | Peat bog |

| Artefact Type | Subtype | Amount | Material | Comments On Appearance | Futher Description |
|---|---|---|---|---|---|
| Other Ornament | Complex bronze-pendant with chains | 1 | Bronze | | Possibly part of a cruciform dress pin |

*Negarba wealth deposit. (Photo: Donatas Butkus).*

| Wealth Deposit | PAALI I |
|---|---|
| Collection number | AI 3235: 90–92 |
| Country | Estonia |
| County | Tartu |
| Municipality | Kambja |
| Village | Paali |
| Date Of Discovery | 1932 |
| Comments On Discovery | Found during archaeological excavations at the Paali *tarand*-grave by M. Schmiedehelm |
| Dating Of Deposit (century) | 6 |
| Earliest Dating Of Artefacts (AD) | 500 |
| Latest Dating Of Artefacts (AD) | 550 |
| Manuscripts | Schmiedehelm 1933 |
| References | Aun 1992, 138<br>Jaanits et al. 1982, 286<br>Schmiedehelm 1934<br>Selirand & Tõnisson 1963, 125–126<br>Tvauri 2006, 110<br>Tvauri 2012, 295 |

| | |
|---|---|
| Environment | Dry land |
| Environment Subtype | Archaeological site |
| Depth (cm) | 20-40 |
| Artefact Placement | Neck-rings on top of each other, brooch in the middle of neck-rings |
| Markers | Stone |
| Archaeological Site | Tarand-grave |
| Comments On Find-spot | 0.75 m S from the Paali tarand-grave, under a big stone |

| Artefact Type | Subtype | Amount | Material | Comments On Appearance | Futher Description |
|---|---|---|---|---|---|
| Neck-Ring | Overlapping twisted terminals | 1 | Silver | | |
| Neck-Ring | Overlapping round decorated terminals | 1 | Silver | | 1 faceted terminals |
| Brooch | Crossbow brooch | 1 | Silver | | |

*Selection of artefacts from Paali I wealth deposit. (Photo: Ester Oras).*

| Wealth Deposit | PAALI II |
|---|---|
| Collection number | AI 3235: 235–244 |
| Country | Estonia |
| County | Tartu |
| Municipality | Kambja |
| Village | Paali |
| Date Of Discovery | 1932 |
| Comments On Discovery | Found during road construction works close to the Paali *tarand*-grave |
| Dating Of Deposit (century) | 6 |
| Earliest Dating Of Artefacts (AD) | 500 |
| Latest Dating Of Artefacts (AD) | 550 |
| Manuscripts | Schmiedehelm 1933 |
| References | Aun 1992, 138<br>Jaanits et al. 1982, 286<br>Schmiedehelm 1934<br>Selirand & Tõnisson 1963, 125–126<br>Tvauri 2006, 110<br>Tvauri 2012, 295 |

| | |
|---|---|
| Environment | Dry land |
| Environment Subtype | Archaeological site |
| Depth (cm) | 100 |
| Type Of Container | Birch bark vessel |
| Archaeological Site | Tarand-grave |
| Comments On Find-spot | 2.75 m N from the Paali tarand-grave tarand wall |

| Artefact Type | Subtype | Amount | Material | Comments On Appearance | Futher Description |
|---|---|---|---|---|---|
| Neck-Ring | Overlapping round decorated terminals | 2 | Silver | | |
| Bracelet | Cast, flaring terminals and a bulky midrib | 1 | Silver | | |
| Bracelet | Massive, cast, thickening terminals | 1 | Bronze | | |
| Brooch | Crossbow brooch | 2 | Silver | | Axis made of iron, cocered with gold foil |
| Brooch | Crossbow brooch with a triangular foot | 1 | Silver | | |
| Finger-Ring | Spiral ring | 1 | Bronze | Fragmented | |
| Belt Part | Buckle | 1 | Bronze | | Similar to Gotlandic examples |
| Belt Part | Mount with a hoop | 2 | Bronze | | |
| Other Ornament | Small bronze spirals | 4 | Bronze | | |

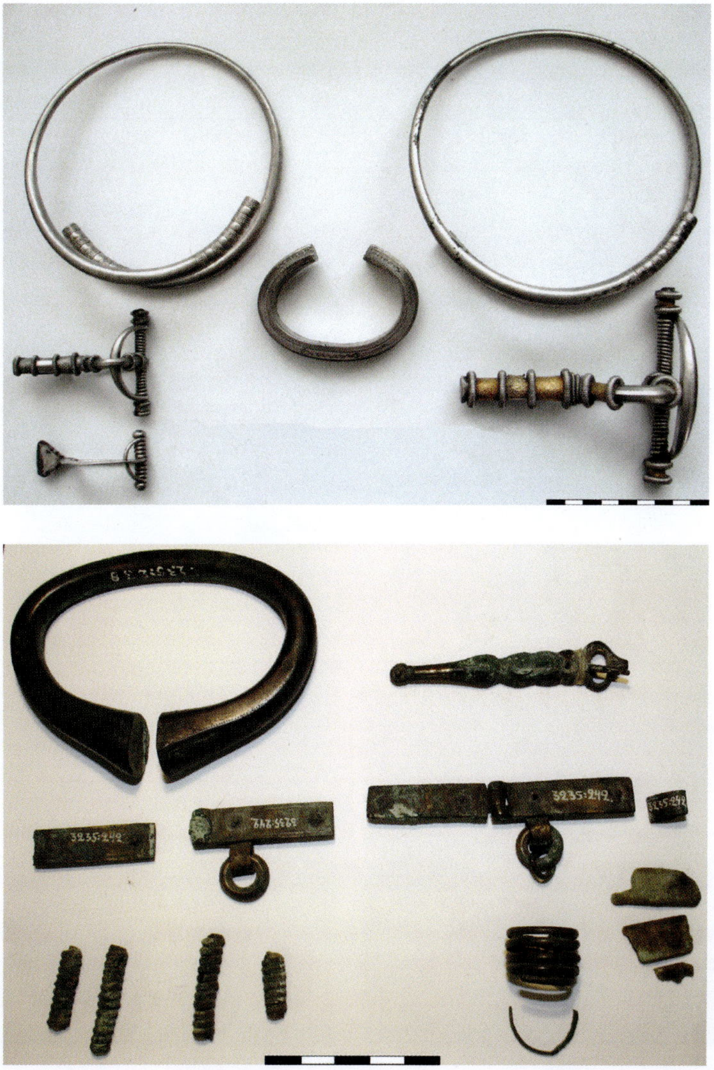

*Paali II wealth deposit. (Photo: Ester Oras).*

| Wealth Deposit | PALANGA I |
|---|---|
| Collection number | VDKM 784: 1–2 |
| Country | Lithuania |
| County | Klaipėda |
| Municipality | Palanga town |
| Village | Palanga (town) |
| Date Of Discovery | 1936 |
| Comments On Discovery | Found during digging drainage ditches in the marshy area E of the town |
| Dating Of Deposit (century) | 9 |
| Earliest Dating Of Artefacts (AD) | 700 |
| Latest Dating Of Artefacts (AD) | 900 |
| References | Bliujienė 2010, 143, no. 19<br>Tautavičius 1977, 132 |
| Comments | Number of ornaments: 2+?. Probably more artefacts found but only some received by the Museum |

| | |
|---|---|
| Environment | Watery condition |
| Environment Subtype | Marsh |
| Comments On Find-spot | Marshy-boggy area, probably in the region of 2 nearly bogged-up lakes, close to burial ground |

| Artefact Type | Subtype | Amount | Material | Comments On Appearance | Futher Description |
|---|---|---|---|---|---|
| Neck-Ring | Tongued bow, loop and hooklet terminals | 1 | Bronze | Fragmented | |
| Dress Pin | Cruciform head | 1 | Bronze | | |

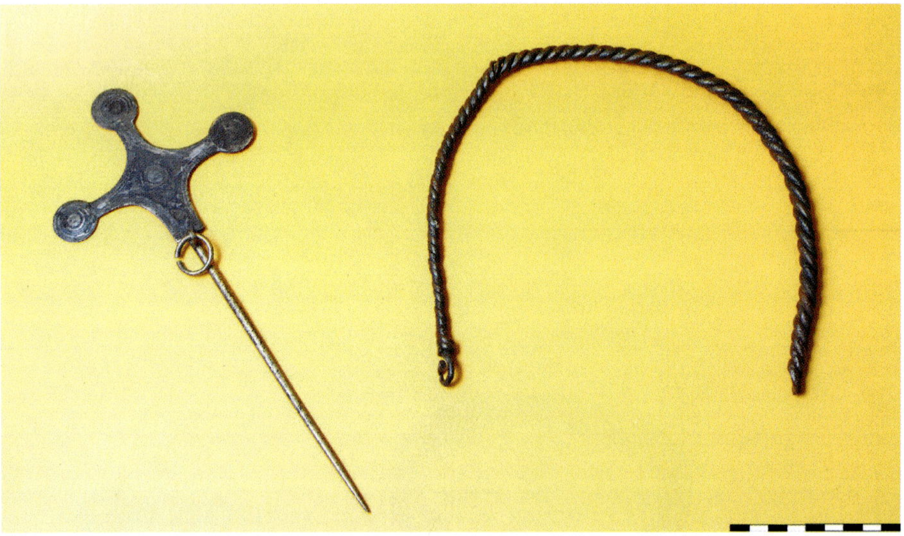

*Palanga I wealth deposit. (Photo: Arturas Uzgalis).*

| Wealth Deposit | PALUKÜLA | |
|---|---|---|
| Collection number | AI 2483: 1–61; 2499: 1–9, 6512 | |
| Country | Estonia | |
| County | Rapla | |
| Municipality | Kehtna | |
| Village | Paluküla | |
| Date Of Discovery | 1921 | |
| Comments On Discovery | Found during field ploughing | |
| Dating Of Deposit (century) | 9 | |
| Earliest Dating Of Artefacts (AD) | 750 | |
| Latest Dating Of Artefacts (AD) | 900 | |
| Manuscripts | Mägi & Haljak 2000<br>Note (Juu)<br>Urgart 1925, 6 | |
| References | Jaanits et al. 1982, 356–357<br>Kriiska & Tvauri 2002, 179<br>Mandel 2003, 148<br>Selirand & Tõnisson 1963, 124 | Tallgren 1924<br>Tallgren 1925, 10 ff<br>Tvauri 2006, 107<br>Tvauri 2012, 223 |
| Comments | In 2000, the area was controlled with a metal detector and a single bracelet was found. Some objects are fragments of wood: possibly shafts of spearheads. | |

| | |
|---|---|
| Environment | Watery condition |
| Environment Subtype | Marsh |
| Depth (cm) | 30–40 |
| Artefact Placement | Artefacts placed between the 3 bent swords |
| Markers | Stone |
| Comments On Find-spot | Marshy area, artefacts placed next to a big stone |

| Artefact Type | Subtype | Amount | Material | Comments On Appearance | Futher Description |
|---|---|---|---|---|---|
| Sword | Two-edged | 5 | Iron | 3 bent, 1 represented by a pommel and cross guards, all burnt | |
| Spearhead | Socketed | 23 | Iron | 2 fragmented, all burnt | |
| Knife | | 5 | Iron | 1 fragmented, 2 burnt | |
| Horse Gear | Spur | 1 | Bronze | Fragmented and burnt | |
| Other Tool | Wedge-shaped strike-a-light with an openwork central section | 1 | Iron | Burnt | Central part with a bronze ornament |
| Neck-Ring | Broadening, ribbed, overlapping terminals with round cross-section | 2 | Bronze | Fragmented and burnt | |
| Bracelet | Massive, cast, thickening terminals | 1 | Bronze | | |
| Bracelet | Massive, spiral, triangular cross-section | 4 | Bronze | 3 fragmented, 1 bent | |
| Brooch | Owl brooch | 1 | Bronze | Fragmented and burnt | Possibly covered with silver gilding |
| Brooch | Crossbow brooch | 5 | Bronze | 4 fragmented and burnt | 2 flat crossbow brooches with poppy-head terminals |
| Brooch | Penannular brooches with rolled and facated, including rare examples in Estonian context | 14 | Bronze | 5 fragmented, without nails/pins | |
| Brooch | Penannular brooch | 3 | Iron | 2 fragmented | |
| Dress Pin | Ring-headed | 2 | Bronze | 1 fragmented, 2 burnt | 1 covered with silver gilding |
| Other | Timber fragments | 2 | Organic | Sharpened and coverd with rust - possibly shafts of spearheads | |
| Other Iron Object | Function unknown | 1 | Iron | Burnt | |

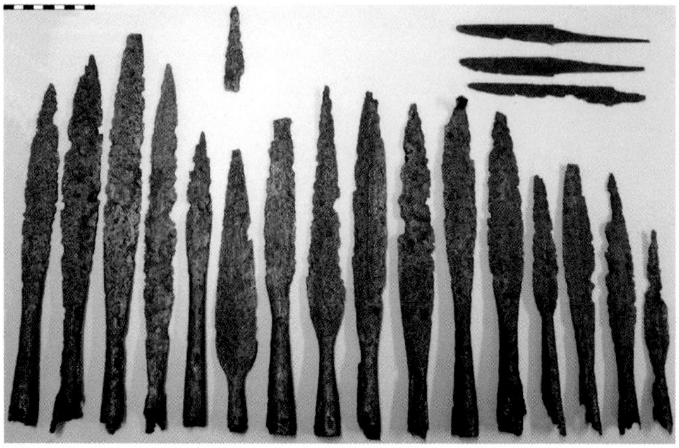

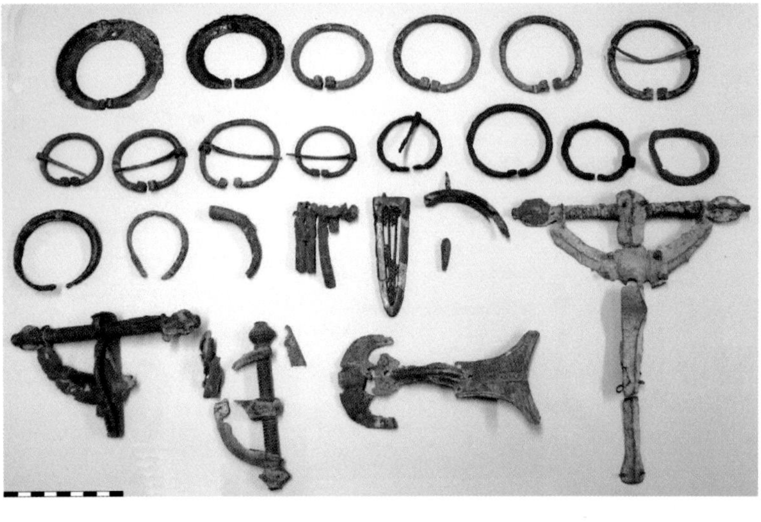

*Selection of artefacts from Paluküla wealth deposit. (Photo: Ester Oras).*

| Wealth Deposit | PIILSI |
|---|---|
| Collection number | AI 2719: 1–41 |
| Country | Estonia |
| County | Ida-Viru |
| Municipality | Lohusuu |
| Village | Piilsi |
| Date Of Discovery | 1930 |
| Comments On Discovery | Found during earth works in the Piilsi River area |
| Dating Of Deposit (century) | 5 |
| Earliest Dating Of Artefacts (AD) | 450 |
| Latest Dating Of Artefacts (AD) | 500 |
| Manuscripts | Asmer 1930<br>Indreko 1930<br>Orviku 1930 |
| References | Jaanits et al. 1982, 281<br>Moora 1935<br>Tamla 1977, no. 18, 162<br>Tvauri 2006, 110<br>Tvauri 2012, 221–222, 231 |
| Comments | The finder Karl Amser handed in some Late Iron Age (1050-1200 AD) bronze bracelets a year later. Their covering patina layer is green and different from the deposit's brown patina and thus most likely the artefacts were found in different places. |

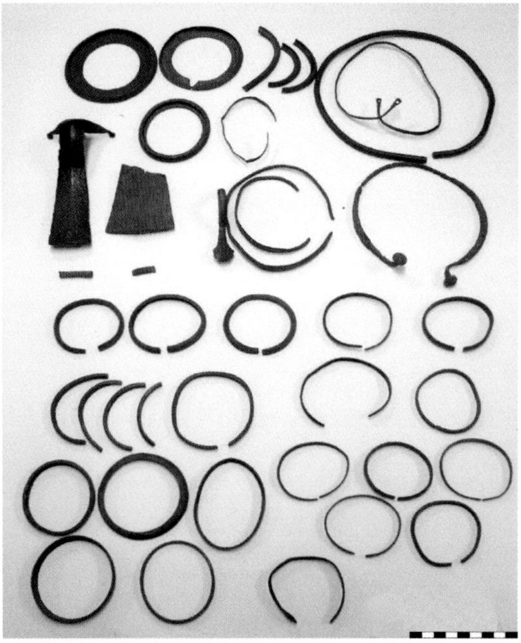

*Piilsi wealth deposit. (Photo: Ester Oras).*

| | |
|---|---|
| Environment | Watery condition |
| Environment Subtype | River |
| Depth (cm) | 80–90 |
| Markers | At the same depth some oak tree planks were found hinting at a possible wooden construction |
| Comments On Find-spot | Old river bed. The upper layer is clayish sod, at the depth of the deposit the soil is darker (organic rich?) and consists some fragments of wood. |

| Artefact Type | Subtype | Amount | Material | Comments On Appearance | Futher Description |
|---|---|---|---|---|---|
| Neck-Ring | Ridged end-plates | 3 | Bronze | Fragmented | Scandinavian parallels |
| Neck-Ring | Plate terminals with punched holes | 1 | Bronze | Deformed | |
| Neck-Ring | Thickening terminals | 1 | Bronze | | |
| Neck-Ring | Mushroom shaped terminals | 1 | Bronze | | |
| Bracelet | Simple, band-like | 17 | Bronze | | |
| Brooch | Penannular brooch with enamel decoration | 1 | Bronze | | Enamel decoration |
| Brooch | Crossbow brooch with star-shape terminal | 1 | Bronze | Fragmented | |
| Brooch | Eye brooch | 2 | Bronze | Fragmented | |
| Ring | 2 flat, made of bronze sheet plates | 11 | Bronze | 4 fragmented | Possibly froms a stacking bracelet |
| Other Ornament | Small cilynders | 2 | Iron | | |
| Other Ornament | Bronze spiral | 1 | Bronze | | Part of the eye brooch? |

| Wealth Deposit | PILTENE |
|---|---|
| Collection number | LVNM 58201 |
| Country | Latvia |
| County | Ventspils |
| Municipality | Piltene |
| Village | Piltene |
| Date Of Discovery | April 1870 |
| Comments On Discovery | Found during digging a ditch in the Piltene forrest |
| Dating Of Deposit (century) | 5 |
| Earliest Dating Of Artefacts (AD) | 400 |
| Latest Dating Of Artefacts (AD) | 500 |
| Manuscripts | LVNM archives, Ventspils apr., Piltenes pag., RD 40 |
| References | Balodis & Tentelis (eds) 1938, 126<br>Bliujienė 2010, no. 23<br>Engel 1914, 28–29, fig. 46<br>Engel 1933, 65, fig. 6b: 1<br>Moora 1929, 90, no. 94<br>Moora 1938, 338, 341, fig. 40: 1<br>RK 1896, 23 (no. 329), tab. 3: 9<br>Sb. Rig. 1880, 137<br>Tallgrens et al. 1926, 62, fig. 32: 2<br>Urtāns 1964, 59, no. 28, fig. 31<br>Urtāns 1977, 137-138, fig. 44 |

| | |
|---|---|
| Environment | Watery condition |
| Environment Subtype | Marsh |
| Depth (cm) | 120 |

| Artefact Type | Subtype | Amount | Material | Comments On Appearance | Futher Description |
|---|---|---|---|---|---|
| Neck-Ring | Overlapping round decorated terminals with gilded bands | 1 | Silver | Worn and fragmented (repaired) | Diameter 17.6 x 16.9 cm; weight 593.64 g Repaired in the middle |

*Piltene wealth deposit. (Photo: Ester Oras).*

| Wealth Deposit | PODŽI |
|---|---|
| Collection number | LVNM 58062 |
| Country | Latvia |
| County | Bauska |
| Municipality | Brunava |
| Village | Podži |
| Date Of Discovery | 1920s |
| Comments On Discovery | Found at the bank of Ceraukstes River. Exact circumstances of discovery unclear. |
| Dating Of Deposit (century) | 7 |
| Earliest Dating Of Artefacts (AD) | 500 |
| Latest Dating Of Artefacts (AD) | 700 |
| Manuscripts | LVNM archives, Bauskas apr., Panemunes pag., 9 |
| References | Apals et al. 1974, 151<br>Moora 1938, 341, 700<br>Šnore 1936, 51, no. 200<br>Urtāns 1964, 44, no. 4, fig. 5<br>Urtāns 1977, 153, fig. 60 |
| Comments | The museum received the finds on the 1st of February 1931 (bought from Jāņa Dručkas). |

| | |
|---|---|
| Environment | Unknown |
| Geographical Landscape | Ceraukses River |

| Artefact Type | Subtype | Amount | Material | Comments On Appearance | Futher Description |
|---|---|---|---|---|---|
| Neck-Ring | Overlapping round decorated terminals | 1 | Silver | Fragmented | Weight 322.77 g, diameter 16.3 cm |

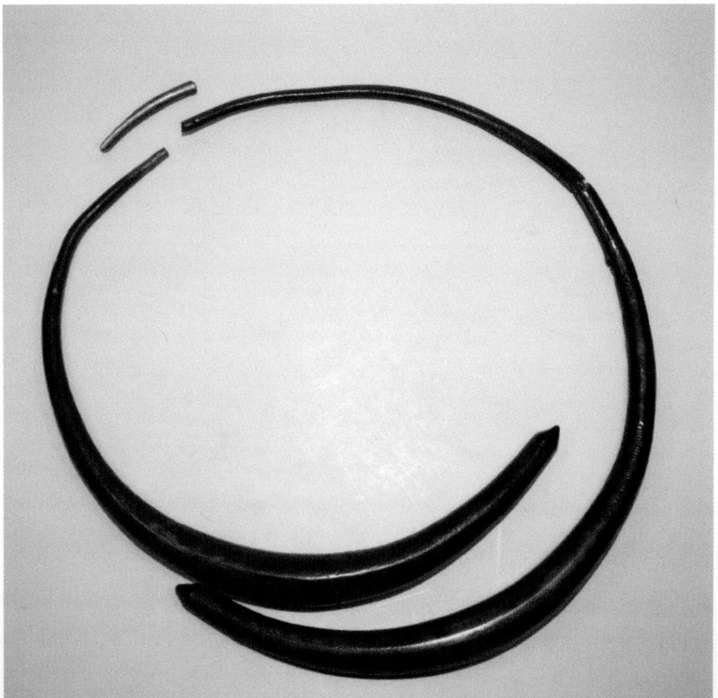

*Podži wealth deposit. (Photo: Ester Oras).*

| Wealth Deposit | REOLA |
|---|---|
| Collection number | AI 4102: 1–11 |
| Country | Estonia |
| County | Tartu |
| Municipality | Ülenurme |
| Village | Reola |
| Date Of Discovery | 1954 |
| Comments On Discovery | Found during peat cutting in the Reola bog |
| Dating Of Deposit (century) | 5 |
| Earliest Dating Of Artefacts (AD) | 450 |
| Latest Dating Of Artefacts (AD) | 500 |
| Manuscripts | Tõnisson 1957 |
| References | Aun 1992, 138 ff<br>Jaanits et al. 1982, 281<br>Moora 1962<br>Tamla 1977, no. 34, 162<br>Tamla 1985, 140 |
| Comments | In addition to bronze artefacts a bone item was found, but has been lost over time. |

| | |
|---|---|
| Environment | Watery condition |
| Environment Subtype | Bog |
| Depth (cm) | 100 |
| Artefact Placement | Some close together, others slightly further away |
| Comments On Find-spot | Probably in a hag. In the closeby area finds of animal bones and ceramics, ca. 200 m to the W of the deposit a wooden construction was noticed. Unfortunately no other finds are stored in museums. |

| Artefact Type | Subtype | Amount | Material | Comments On Appearance | Futher Description |
|---|---|---|---|---|---|
| Bracelet | Simple, band-like, one with traingular cross-section | 8 | Bronze | 2 bent | |
| Brooch | Cross-ribbed | 3 | Bronze | | |
| Other | Bone artefact | 1 | Bone | | Lost |

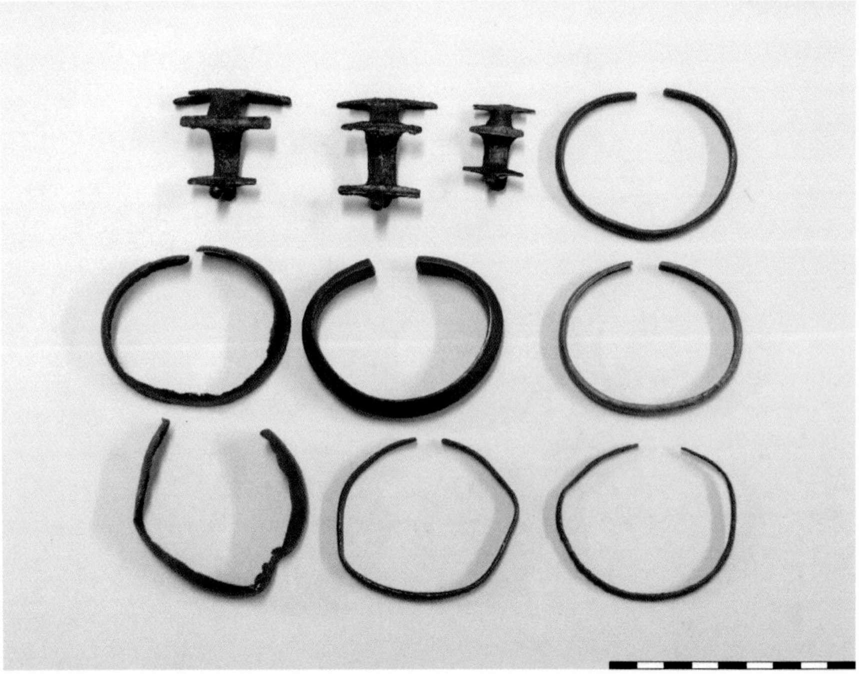

*Reola wealth deposit. (Photo: Ester Oras).*

| Wealth Deposit | RIKASSAARE |
|---|---|
| Collection number | AI 4484: 1–16 |
| Country | Estonia |
| County | Järva |
| Municipality | Türi |
| Village | Rikassaare |
| Date Of Discovery | 1969 |
| Comments On Discovery | Found during digging drainge ditches at the bank of the Prandi River |
| Dating Of Deposit (century) | 7 |
| Earliest Dating Of Artefacts (AD) | 550 |
| Latest Dating Of Artefacts (AD) | 650 |
| References | Jaanits et al. 1982, 283<br>Kriiska & Tvauri 2002, 158<br>Mandel & Tamla 1977<br>Tamla 1977, no. 21, 156 ff<br>Tamla 1995<br>Tvauri 2006, 113<br>Tvauri 2012, 292 |

| | |
|---|---|
| Environment | Watery condition |
| Environment Subtype | River |
| Depth (cm) | 20-40 |
| Artefact Placement | Tips of spearheads together, probably thrust in the ground with shafts |
| Comments On Find-spot | Peat-rich field area at the bank of the Prandi River |

| Artefact Type | Subtype | Amount | Material | Comments On Appearance | Futher Description |
|---|---|---|---|---|---|
| Spearhead | Socketed | 54 | Iron | | Some consist wood fragemnts in the socket |
| Battle Knife | | 7 | Iron | | |

*Selection of artefacts from Rikassaare wealth deposit. (Photo: Ester Oras).*

*Selection of artefacts from Rikassaare wealth deposit. (Photo: Ester Oras).*

| Wealth Deposit | RŪSIŠI |
|---|---|
| Collection number | LVNM A 9510: 1–33 (CVVM 62644) |
| Country | Latvia |
| County | Saldus |
| Municipality | Ruba |
| Village | Debeši |
| Date Of Discovery | March 1938 |
| Comments On Discovery | Found at the Semigallian burial area |
| Dating Of Deposit (century) | 6 |
| Earliest Dating Of Artefacts (AD) | 475 |
| Latest Dating Of Artefacts (AD) | 525 |
| Manuscripts | LVNM archives |
| References | Šnore 1962, 577–578<br>Stepiņš 1939, 45–46<br>Urtāns 1977, 147–148, fig. 52 |
| Comments | Excavated after the discovery the deposit in 1938 and 1940 by P. Stepiņš |

| | |
|---|---|
| Environment | Dry land |
| Environment Subtype | Archaeological site |
| Artefact Placement | Spearhead includes timber in the socket |
| Markers | Stones? |
| Archaeological Site | Burial ground |
| Geographical Landscape | Hill |
| Comments On Find-spot | In the Semigallian burial ground under the pile of burnt stones and sooty soil (a probable hearth?) |

| Artefact Type | Subtype | Amount | Material | Comments On Appearance | Futher Description |
|---|---|---|---|---|---|
| Spearhead | Socketed | 1 | Iron | | Includes timber in the socket |
| Battle Knife | | 1 | Iron | | |
| Knife | | 4 | Iron | | |
| Horse Gear | Spur | 4 | Iron | | |
| Horse Gear | Bit | 1 | Iron | | |
| Sickle/Scythe | Scythe | 2 | Iron | | |
| Other Tool | Awl | 2 | Iron | | |
| Other Tool | Hoe | 1 | Iron | | |
| Other Iron Object | Hook | 1 | Iron | | |
| Bracelet | Ornamented | 5 | Bronze | 2 fragmented | Middle raised area |
| Brooch | Crossbow brooch | 1 | Bronze | | |
| Dress Pin | | 1 | Iron | | |
| Other Ornament | Spirals | 3 | Bronze | 2 ragmented | |
| Ring | | 2 | Iron | | |
| Vessel | Drinking horn mounting | 2 | Bronze | 1 fragmented | |
| Other | Iron slag | 1 | Iron | | Probably more than 1 |

*Rūsiši wealth deposit. (Photo: Ester Oras).*

| Wealth Deposit | SAULESKALNS I |
|---|---|
| Collection number | LVNM A 8889: 2–4; LVNM<br>Riga A 8889: 1 (silver neck-rings lost) |
| Country | Latvia |
| County | Krāslava |
| Municipality | Kombuļi |
| Village | Lielie-Unguri |
| Date Of Discovery | 4th of May 1936 |
| Comments On Discovery | Found during earth works |
| Dating Of Deposit (century) | 9 |
| Earliest Dating Of Artefacts (AD) | 800 |
| Latest Dating Of Artefacts (AD) | 900 |
| Manuscripts | LVNM Archives, Daugavpils apr., Krāslavas pag, Sauleskalns - kulta vieta, 7 (533)<br>LVNM Archives, Daugavpils apr., Krāslavas pag, Sauleskalns - kulta vieta, 8 (488) |
| References | Pieminekļu izstāde 1936, 14<br>Urtāns 1964, 46–47, no. 10, figs 11–12<br>Urtāns 1977, 164, fig. 72 |
| Comments | 1 silver neck-ring lost. Area examined by P. Stepiņš in 1937. |

| | |
|---|---|
| Environment | Dry land |
| Depth (cm) | 30 |
| Markers | Close by a 5 x 2 m stone clustering of 20 cm-diameter stones |
| Archaeological Site | Sauleskalns known as later period ritual site |
| Comments On Find-spot | In dark sooty soil, stones under the deposit (probable hearth?) |

| Artefact Type | Subtype | Amount | Material | Comments On Appearance | Futher Description |
|---|---|---|---|---|---|
| Neck-Ring | Twisted wire, tetrahedric terminals | 1 | Silver | | Lost, diameter 20.7 cm |
| Neck-Ring | Saddle and hooklet terminals, two separate attached parts | 1 | Silver | Fragmented | Diameter 19.2 x 17.6 cm |
| Neck-Ring | Overlapping rhombic cross-section terminals | 1 | Silver | Twisted together | Diameter 10.2 cm |
| Brooch | Owl brooch | 1 | Bronze | Fragmented | Covered with silver foil |

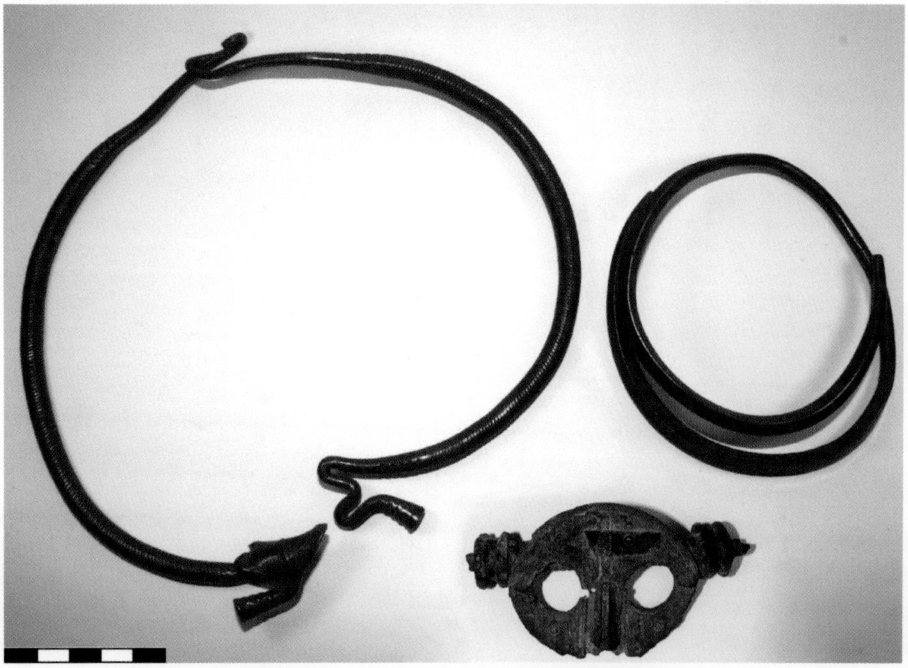

*Selection of artefacts from Sauleskalns I wealth deposit. (Photo: Ester Oras).*

| Wealth Deposit | SAULESKALNS II |
|---|---|
| Collection number | LVNM A 9407: 1–20 (Lost from Daugavpils Museum during German occupation (1941-1944)) |
| Country | Latvia |
| County | Krāslava |
| Municipality | Kombuļi |
| Village | Lielie-Unguri |
| Date Of Discovery | 18th of August 1937 |
| Comments On Discovery | Found during earthworks |
| Dating Of Deposit (century) | 9 |
| Earliest Dating Of Artefacts (AD) | 800 |
| Latest Dating Of Artefacts (AD) | 900 |
| Manuscripts | LVNM Archives, Daugavpils apr., Krāslavas pag, Sauleskalns - kulta vieta, 9 (1059) |
| References | Urtāns 1964, 47–48, no. 11, figs 12–13<br>Urtāns 1977, 164, fig. 73 |
| Comments | Lost from Daugavpils Museum during German occupation (1941-1944). |

| | |
|---|---|
| Environment | Dry land |
| Depth (cm) | 30 |
| Artefact Placement | All arrowheads together and placed in the same direction. Possibly deposited with the shafts. |
| Archaeological Site | Sauleskalns known as later period ritual site |
| Comments On Find-spot | Wood remains of shafts visible in the ground i.e. possibly thrust into ground or placed there with shafts. Not far from the find-spot (close to a sightseeing tower) an iron axe was found. |

| Artefact Type | Subtype | Amount | Material | Comments On Appearance | Futher Description |
|---|---|---|---|---|---|
| Arrowhead | Shafted | 19 | Iron | | Lost, lengths 6.6-10.9 cm: width 0.7-2.7 cm |
| Arrowhead | Socketed | 1 | Iron | | Lost, length 5.9 cm; width 1.6 cm |

*Sauleskalns II wealth deposit. (Photo: Urtāns 1977, fig. 73).*

| Wealth Deposit | SAULĪTES |
|---|---|
| Collection number | LVNM 58211-58213 |
| Country | Latvia |
| County | Viesīte |
| Municipality | Viesīte |
| Village | Saulītes (Germ. Wahrenbrock) (Saulìht-Gesinde beim Wahrenbrock) |
| Date Of Discovery | 21st of May 1882 |
| Comments On Discovery | Found during digging linen soaking ditch |
| Dating Of Deposit (century) | 8 |
| Earliest Dating Of Artefacts (AD) | 675 |
| Latest Dating Of Artefacts (AD) | 725 |
| Manuscripts | LVNM archives, Jēkabpilj apr., Vārnavas pag., 2 |
| References | Balodis & Tentelis (eds) 1938, 126<br>RK 1896, 60–61 (no. 485), tab. 16: 8<br>Sammlung 1939, 16, tab. 15<br>Sb. Kurl. 1882, 17, 23–24, tab. I<br>Urtāns 1964, 46, no.9, fig. 10<br>Urtāns 1977, 157–158, fig. 66<br>Vankina et al. 1981, 58 |
| Comments | Silver neck-rings and a leather belt were found. Relation between the neck-rings and belt uncertain. Total weight of neck-rings 1438.8 g. |

| | |
|---|---|
| Environment | Watery condition |
| Environment Subtype | Marsh |
| Depth (cm) | 45 |
| Artefact Placement | Neck-rings on top of each other |
| Comments On Find-spot | Marshy-boggy area in sandy ground |

| Artefact Type | Subtype | Amount | Material | Comments On Appearance | Futher Description |
|---|---|---|---|---|---|
| Neck-Ring | Profoundly faceted terminals | 2 | Silver | | Diameter 23.7 x 29.6 and 23.8 x 32.7 cm; weight 702.65 and 430.2 g |
| Neck-Ring | Loop and hooklet terminals | 1 | Silver | | Diameter 24.3 x 27.2 cm; weight 305.95 g |
| Other | Belt | 1 | Organic (leather) | | Lost, lenght ca. 18.75 cm |

*Saulītes wealth deposit. (Photo: Roberts Kaninš).*

| Wealth Deposit | ŠLUOSTIKIAI |
|---|---|
| Collection number | ŽMA 6578; 7859–7861 (spearheads written off from the collections due to bad state of preservation) |
| Country | Lithuania |
| County | Šiualiai |
| Municipality | Joniškios |
| Village | Šluostikiai |
| Date Of Discovery | 1956, 1958 |
| Comments On Discovery | Found during ditch deepening works at the Vešėtinis Rivulet |
| Dating Of Deposit (century) | 8 |
| Earliest Dating Of Artefacts (AD) | 500 |
| Latest Dating Of Artefacts (AD) | 900 |
| References | Bliujienė 2010, 143, no. 30<br>Vasiliauskas 2009, 255–256 |

| | |
|---|---|
| Environment | Watery condition |
| Environment Subtype | River |
| Markers | Flat boulder rock |

| Artefact Type | Subtype | Amount | Material | Comments On Appearance | Futher Description |
|---|---|---|---|---|---|
| Spearhead | Socketed | 3 | Iron | Heavily corroded | 1 with long socket and rhomb-shape blade. Dated in catalogue to 9th–13th century; written off from the museum collections |
| Other Tool | Spindle whorl | 1 | Stone | | Small, cylinder shape |

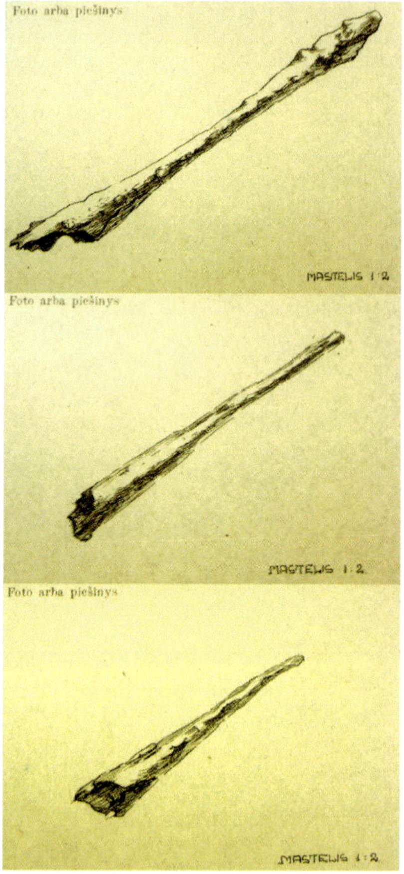

*Šluostikiai wealth deposit. (Photo: Ester Oras, ŽMA Archives).*

| Wealth Deposit | TĪRAS PURVS |
|---|---|
| Collection number | LVNM A 9170: 1–28 |
| Country | Latvia |
| County | Rucava |
| Municipality | Rucava |
| Village | Tīras |
| Date Of Discovery | 26th of May – June 1936 |
| Comments On Discovery | Found during peat cutting by J. Barbānu in a centre of the bog |
| Dating Of Deposit (century) | 9 |
| Earliest Dating Of Artefacts (AD) | 800 |
| Latest Dating Of Artefacts (AD) | 850 |
| Manuscripts | LVNM archives, AA 166 |
| References | Apals et al. 1974, 151–152, fig. 79<br>Bliujienė 2010, 150, 156, no. 31<br>Pieminekļu izstāde 1936, 12–14<br>Urtāns 1962, 83–94, figs 1-8, tab. I–II<br>Urtāns 1964, 49–51, no. 15, figs 17–18<br>Urtāns 1977, 163, fig. 71<br>SM 1937, 4, 94–97<br>Žeiere 2008<br>Vankina et al. 1981, 57 |
| Comments | Area studied later by P. Stepiņš. |

| | |
|---|---|
| Environment | Watery condition |
| Environment Subtype | Bog |
| Depth (cm) | 110-150 |
| Type Of Container | Wrapped in textile, pushed down with a pole |
| Artefact Placement | Surrounded with pine stakes, over the find a horizontal bar was placed, a shield placed under artefacts, lower another shield and some textiles were found, artefacts covered with large woollen cloth. |
| Markers | Stakes? |
| Comments On Find-spot | Between upper light brown 110 cm thick and lower 45 cm thick, black peat layers. Under the peat a white sand layer. |

| Artefact Type | Subtype | Amount | Material | Comments On Appearance | Futher Description |
|---|---|---|---|---|---|
| Other Weapon | Shield boss | 1 | Iron | Fragmented | Diameter 85.5 cm, shiled boss 13.1 x 10.5 cm |
| Other Weapon | Shield | 2 | Organic (fur tree) | | Measures 68 x 11.8 x 1.4 cm; 31.5 x 5.7 x 1.2 cm |
| Other Tool | Awl | 1 | Bronze (bronze and wood) | | Awl with a wooden handle |
| Bracelet | Ornamented, massive | 1 | Bronze | | Diameter 9.1 cm |
| Brooch | Penannular brooch with cylindrikal terminals | 1 | Bronze | | |
| Other Ornament | Spiral | 2 | Bronze | Fragmented | |
| Ring | Spiral | 2 | Bronze | | |
| Ring | | 1 | Iron | | Diameter 3.1 cm |
| Belt Part | Belt mountings | 2 | Bronze | | Ornamented, length 3.1-3.2 cm |
| Belt Part | Belt buckle | 1 | Bronze | | |
| Vessel | Drinking horn mounting | 1 | Organic (horn) | | |
| Other | Bag | 1 | Organic (leather) | | |
| Other | Bands | 3 | Organic (leather) | | Part of the bag (?) |
| Other | Textile, woollen band | 2 | Organic (wool) | | |
| Other | Tablet woven and other woollen textile fragments | 25 | Organic (wool) | | |
| Other | Textile, ball of woollen yarn | 1 | Organic (wool) | | |

| Artefact Type | Subtype | Amount | Material | Comments On Appearance | Futher Description |
|---|---|---|---|---|---|
| Other | Timber fragments | 1 | Organic (wood) | | Exact number unknown |
| Other | Footware | 1 | Organic (wool) | | |
| Other | Small sticks | 31 | Organic (deciduous tree) | | Length 4.4–83 cm |
| Other | Toggle / Buckle | 10 | Organic (wood) | | Conical or round terminals; lenght 7.3–8.9 cm |
| Other | Stake | 9 | Organic (pine wood) | Burnt | Stakes' ends burnt to sharpen |

*Selection of artefacts from Tīras purvs wealth deposit at the exhibition at the Latvian National History Museum. (Photo: Ester Oras).*

| Wealth Deposit | UŽPELKIAI |
|---|---|
| Collection number | VDKM 662: 1–4 |
| Country | Lithuania |
| County | Telšiai |
| Municipality | Plungė |
| Village | Užpelkiai |
| Date Of Discovery | 1909-1910 |
| Comments On Discovery | Found during peat digging in Tyreliai bog |
| Dating Of Deposit (century) | 2–3; 4–5<br>(150–300 AD & 350–450 AD) |
| Earliest Dating Of Artefacts (AD) | 150 |
| Latest Dating Of Artefacts (AD) | 450 |
| References | Bliujienė 2010, 140 ff, no. 32<br>Kulikauskas et al. 1961, fig. 230<br>Michelbertas 2007, 14<br>Moora 1938, 140, footnote 3<br>Puzinas 1938, fig. 64: 1<br>Tautavičius 1977, 133<br>Vaitkevičius 2004, 41<br>Vaitkunskienė 1981, 29, fig. XV |
| Comments | Artefacs previously thought to be from burial.<br>Received from the finder by J. Mickevičius in 1931 and handed over to the museum. |

| | |
|---|---|
| Environment | Watery condition |
| Environment Subtype | Bog |
| Depth (cm) | 150 |
| Archaeological Site | Hill-fort |
| Comments On Find-spot | Found in Tyreliai peat bog |

| Artefact Type | Subtype | Amount | Material | Comments On Appearance | Futher Description |
|---|---|---|---|---|---|
| Neck-Ring | Box-shape clasp terminal | 2 | Bronze | Fragmented and burnt(?) | |
| Brooch | Crossbow brooch | 1 | Silver | | Notched ring decoration, clearences between ringlets decorated with gold (?) plates |
| Brooch | Star-shape foot | 1 | Bronze | Fargemented | Without a spiral part and a bow, covered with silver foil |

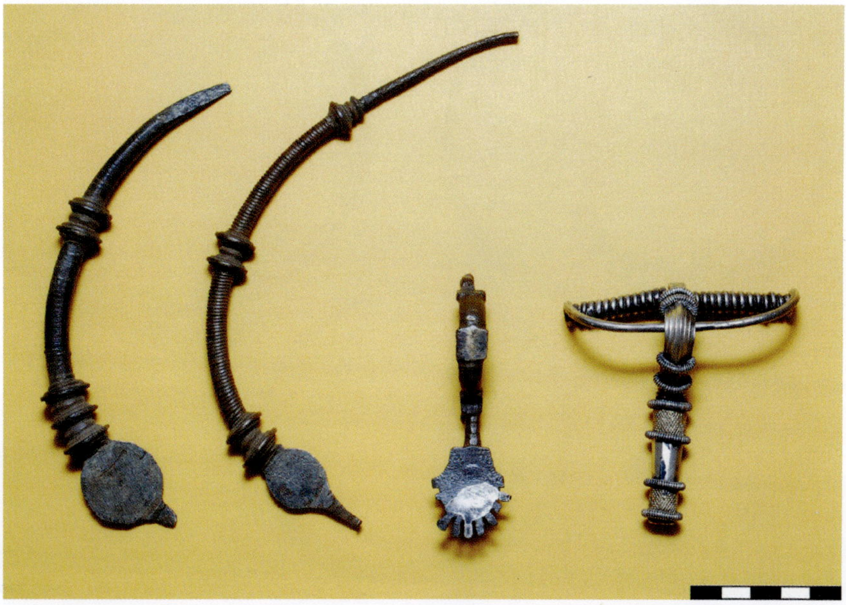

*Užpelkiai wealth deposit. (Photo: Arturas Uzgalis).*

| Wealth Deposit | UURI |
|---|---|
| Collection number | AM A 287: 1–5 |
| Country | Estonia |
| County | Harju |
| Municipality | Kuusalu |
| Village | Uuri |
| Date Of Discovery | 1921 / 1922 |
| Comments On Discovery | Found during field ploughing at the bank of Pudisoo Bond |
| Dating Of Deposit (century) | 6 |
| Earliest Dating Of Artefacts (AD) | 500 |
| Latest Dating Of Artefacts (AD) | 550 |
| Manuscripts | EAA 854.4.120.<br>Vedru 2007, 12 |
| References | Jaanits et al. 1982, 287<br>Lang 1996, 328–329<br>Tvauri 2012, 296 |

| | |
|---|---|
| Environment | Watery condition |
| Environment Subtype | Marsh |
| Depth (cm) | 30 |

| Artefact Type | Subtype | Amount | Material | Comments On Appearance | Futher Description |
|---|---|---|---|---|---|
| Neck-Ring | Overlapping faceted terminals | 2 | Silver | | |
| Neck-Ring | Overlapping round decorated terminals | 1 | Silver | | |
| Bracelet | Massive, cast, thickening terminals | 1 | Bronze | Fragmented | |
| Brooch | Crossbow brooch | 1 | Silver | Fragmented | |

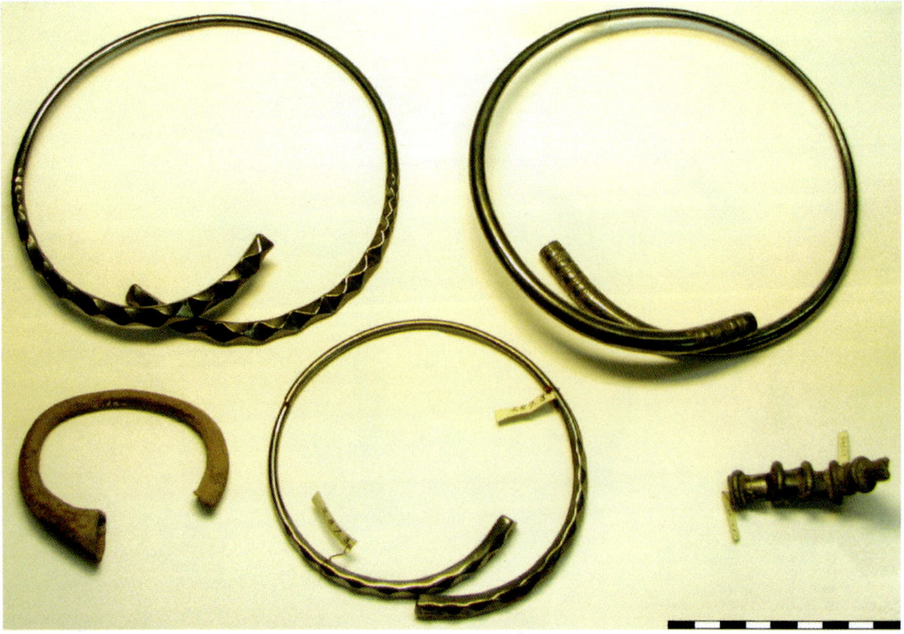

*Uuri wealth deposit. (Photo: Ester Oras).*

| Wealth Deposit | VAGULA |
|---|---|
| Collection number | AI 2616 |
| Country | Estonia |
| County | Võru |
| Municipality | Võru |
| Village | Vagula |
| Date Of Discovery | Beginning of the 20th century |
| Comments On Discovery | Found during farm works at the coast of the Vagula Lake |
| Dating Of Deposit (century) | 5 |
| Earliest Dating Of Artefacts (AD) | 450 |
| Latest Dating Of Artefacts (AD) | 525 |
| References | Jaanits et al. 1982, 281, 283, plate IX<br>Jonuks 2009, 229, 231, 256<br>Kriiska & Tvauri 2002, 158–159<br>Lang 2007a, 210<br>Tamla & Kiudsoo 2005, 18–19 |
| Comments | Different rings and brooches mentioned (altogether 8 kg), most lost, data based on memories of the finder 30 years later. |

| | |
|---|---|
| Environment | Watery condition |
| Environment Subtype | Lake |

| Artefact Type | Subtype | Amount | Material | Comments On Appearance | Futher Description |
|---|---|---|---|---|---|
| Brooch | Disk-shaped brooch with enamel decoration | 1 | Bronze | | Decorated with glass enamel, imported (probably from Dnepr River area) |

*A brooch from Vagula wealth deposit. (Photo: Ester Oras).*

| Wealth Deposit | VAINEIKIAI |
| --- | --- |
| Collection number | Unknown, private collections(?) |
| Country | Lithuania |
| County | Panevėžys |
| Municipality | Rokiškis |
| Village | Vaineikiai |
| Date Of Discovery | 1943 |
| Comments On Discovery | Found during ploughing a drained peat bog |
| Dating Of Deposit (century) | 9 |
| Earliest Dating Of Artefacts (AD) | 700 |
| Latest Dating Of Artefacts (AD) | 1200 |
| References | Bliujienė 2010, no. 33<br>Tautavičius 1977, 133 |
| Comments | Finds were taken into a private collection, current location unknown. |

| | |
| --- | --- |
| Environment | Watery condition |
| Environment Subtype | Bog |
| Artefact Placement | Neck-rings on top of each other, bound together |

| Artefact Type | Subtype | Amount | Material | Comments On Appearance | Futher Description |
| --- | --- | --- | --- | --- | --- |
| Neck-Ring | Corded | 3 | Silver | | Private collection, current location unknown |

| Wealth Deposit | VARNJA |
| --- | --- |
| Collection number | LVNM DM I 1365 |
| Country | Estonia |
| County | Tartu |
| Municipality | Peipsiääre |
| Village | Varnja |
| Date Of Discovery | 1895 |
| Comments On Discovery | Found during farm works |
| Dating Of Deposit (century) | 6 |
| Earliest Dating Of Artefacts (AD) | 491 |
| Latest Dating Of Artefacts (AD) | 600 |
| Manuscripts | Tiitsmaa 1921a, 14–15 |
| References | Aun 1992, 142<br>Ebert 1913, 545<br>Engel 1914, 29, fig. 45<br>Hausmann 1909, 41<br>Jaanits et al. 1982, 287<br>Quast et al. 2010<br>Sb. GEG 1885, 213–214<br>Tallgren 1925, 14<br>Tvauri 2012, 87 |
| Comments | Vessel produced during the reign of Emperor Anastasius I (491–518 AD), deposed probably in the 6th century.<br>Dating range: 491–518/600. |

| | |
| --- | --- |
| Environment | Dry land |
| Markers | Stone |
| Comments On Find-spot | Found in the field under a stone (possible detsroyed stone grave?) |

| Artefact Type | Subtype | Amount | Material | Comments On Appearance | Futher Description |
|---|---|---|---|---|---|
| Vessel | Byzantine silver vessel | 1 | Silver | Fragmented | Stamped in the bottom with manufacturer and production stamps of Emperor Anastasius I (491–518 AD) |

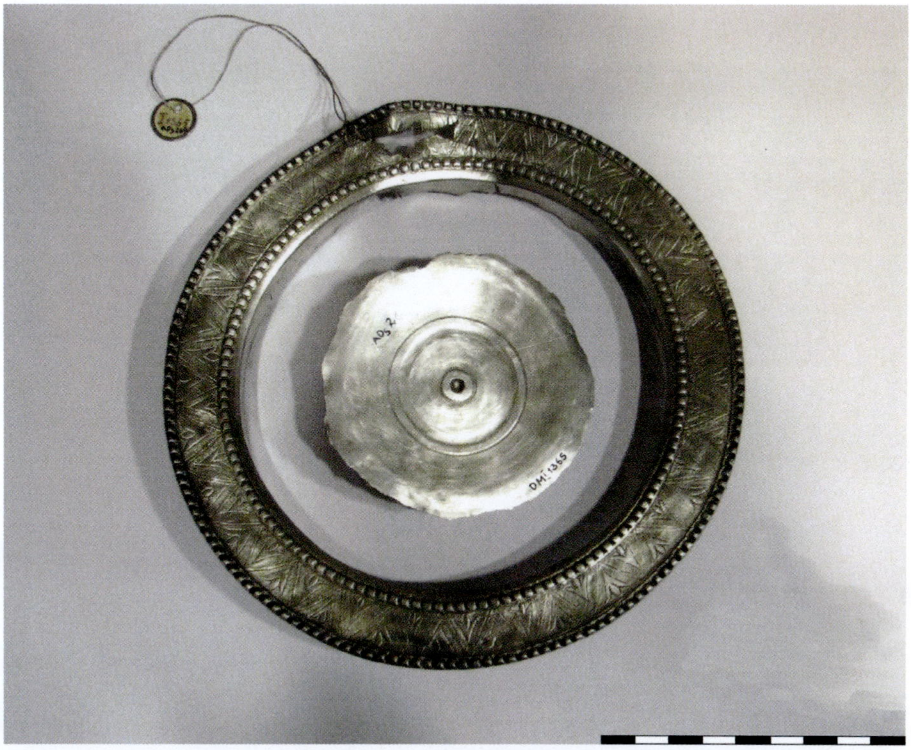

*Varnja wealth deposit. (Photo: Ester Oras).*

| Wealth Deposit | VECMOKAS |
|---|---|
| Collection number | Jelgavā KPM 2056: 1–21, 2057: 1–24, 2058: 1–11; several artefacts lost over time |
| Country | Latvia |
| County | Tukums |
| Municipality | Tume |
| Village | Vecmokas |
| Date Of Discovery | 1908 |
| Comments On Discovery | Found at the foot of hill-fort |
| Dating Of Deposit (century) | 6 |
| Earliest Dating Of Artefacts (AD) | 500 |
| Latest Dating Of Artefacts (AD) | 600 |
| References | Balodis & Tentelis (eds) 1938, 127<br>Moora 1929, 179, no. 84<br>Moora 1938, 572<br>Otšet 1908, 172, fig. 235<br>Riekstiņš 1931, 477<br>Sammlung 1939, 16, tab. 12: 1–2, 12–13, tab. 13: 6–7<br>Tallgrens et al. 1926, 68<br>Urtāns 1964, 59–60, no. 29, figs 32–34<br>Urtāns 1977, 150–153, figs 56–58 |
| Comments | Donated to Kurzeme province Jelgavā Museum by baron Elsene. Most of the items currently lost, some in Jelgavā Museum. Some artefacts fragemneted, some burnt. |

| | |
|---|---|
| Environment | Dry land? |
| Environment Subtype | Archaeological site |
| Archaeological Site | Skamaņu hill-fort |
| Comments On Find-spot | At the foot of the hill-fort. Detailed finding circumstances unknown. The foot of the fort currently surrounded by boggy and marshy area. |

| Artefact Type | Subtype | Amount | Material | Comments On Appearance | Futher Description |
|---|---|---|---|---|---|
| Spearhead | Socketed | 24 | Iron | Some burnt | Measures 16.4–33.6 x 2–3.9 cm, socket diameter 1.5–2.6 cm, lost(?) |
| Axe | Socketed | 12 | Iron | | Measures 14–21 x 3.2–5.3 cm, socket diameter 2.8–4.4 cm, lost(?) |
| Sickle/Scythe | Scythe | 11 | Iron | 7 fragmented | Mostly lost(?) |
| Other Tool | Oval strike-a-light stone | 1 | Stone | Fragmented | Measures 5.1 x 3.6 cm, lost(?) |
| Other Tool | Whetstone, oblong | 1 | Stone | | Length 19.7 cm, lost(?) |
| Neck-Ring | | 1 | Bronze | Fragmented | Length 10.1 cm, diameter 0.6 cm |
| Dress Pin | Different forms incl. Double mushroom-head, triangular head | 6 | Bronze | 3 fragmented | Some with rings and spiral attached; Measures 11.8–17.7 cm, some lost(?) |

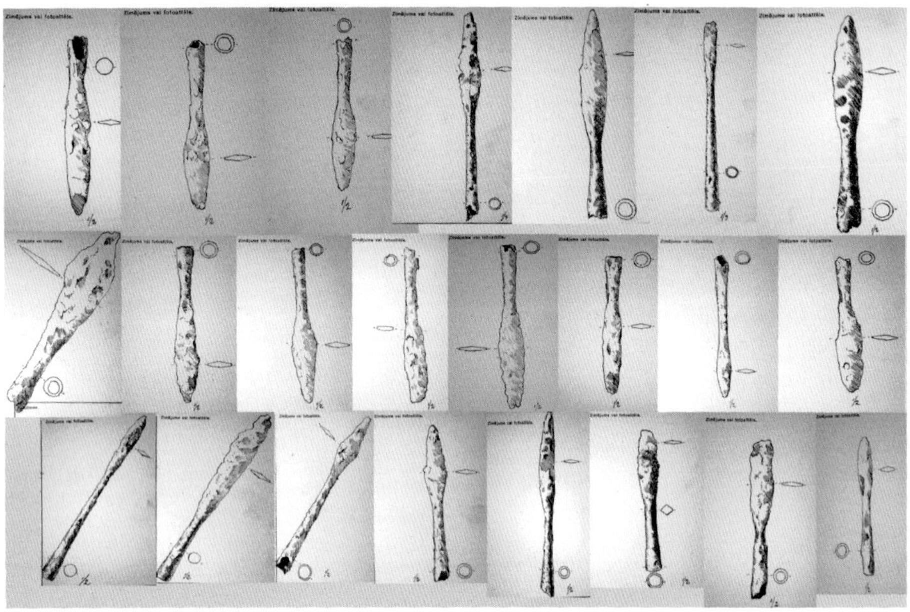

*Selection of artefacts from Vecmokas wealth deposit. (Photo: Ester Oras, Jelgavā KPM Archives).*

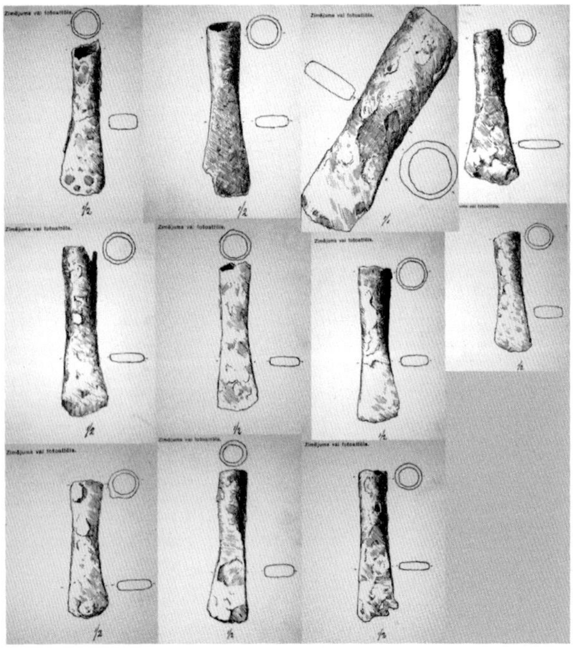

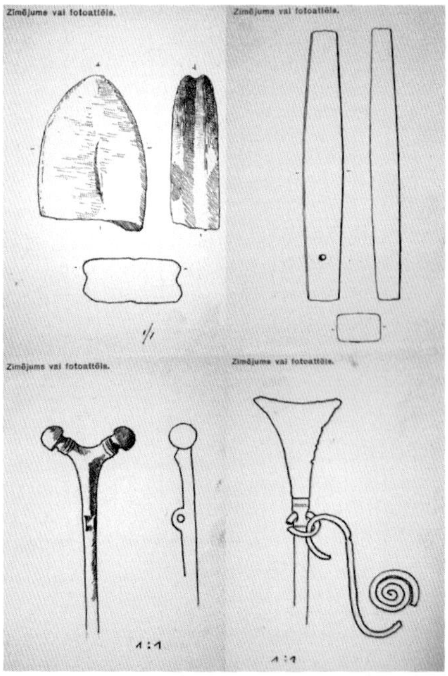

*Selection of artefacts from Vecmokas wealth deposit. (Photo: Ester Oras).*

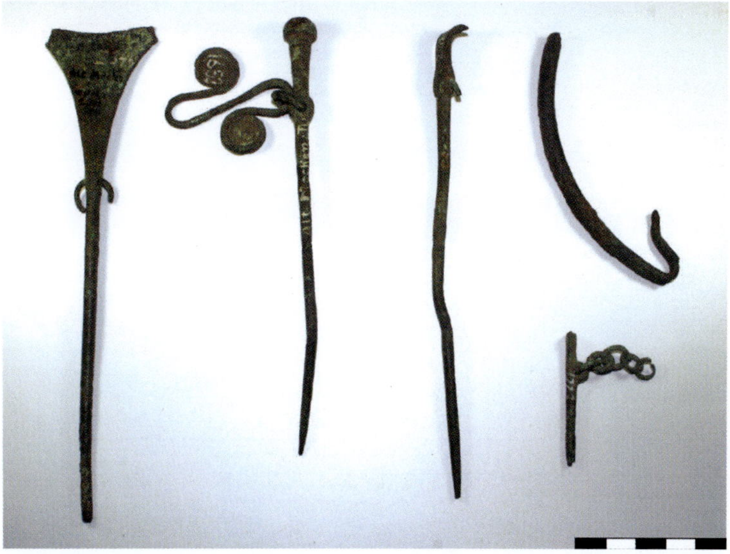

| Wealth Deposit | VELŽIAI |
|---|---|
| Collection number | ŠAM I-A 108 |
| Country | Lithuania |
| County | Šiauliai |
| Municipality | Radviliškis |
| Village | Velžiai |
| Date Of Discovery | 1969 |
| Comments On Discovery | Found during excavations on the Velžiai hill-fort |
| Dating Of Deposit (century) | 7 |
| Earliest Dating Of Artefacts (AD) | 600 |
| Latest Dating Of Artefacts (AD) | 700 |
| References | Tautavičius 1977, 133<br>Vaitkunskienė 1981, 29 |

| | |
|---|---|
| Environment | Dry land |
| Environment Subtype | Archaeological site |
| Archaeological Site | Hill-fort |

| Artefact Type | Subtype | Amount | Material | Comments On Appearance | Futher Description |
|---|---|---|---|---|---|
| Neck-Ring | Profoundly faceted terminals | 1 | Silver | | |

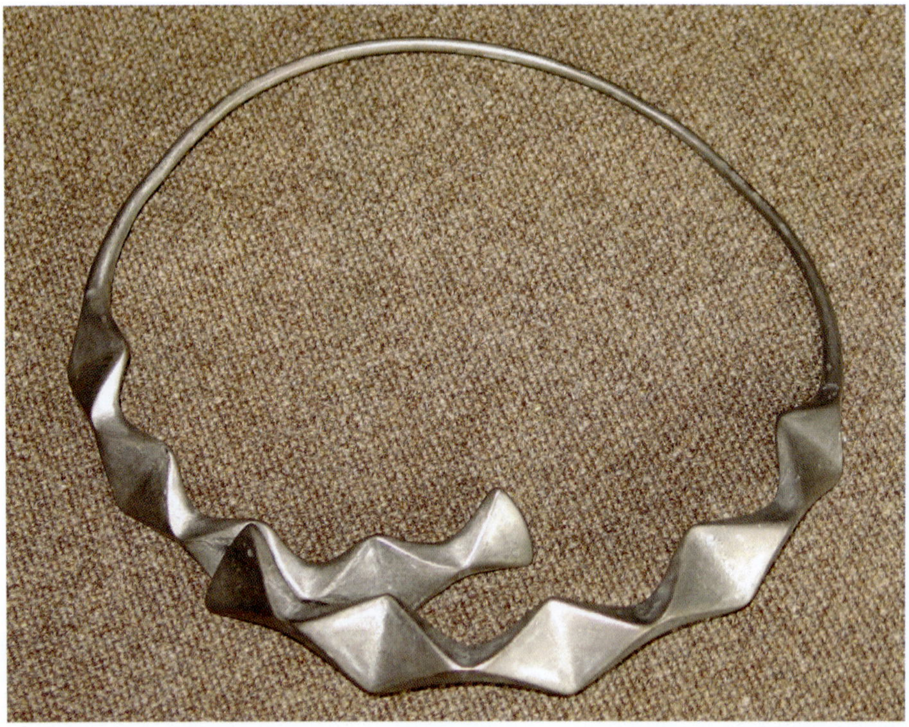

*Velžiai wealth deposit. (Photo: Audronė Šapaitė).*

| Wealth Deposit | VIIRA |
|---|---|
| Collection number | AI 1529: 1–4; some lost |
| Country | Estonia |
| County | Põlva |
| Municipality | Veriora |
| Village | Viira |
| Date Of Discovery | 1882 |
| Comments On Discovery | Found during field working at the potato field of the Viira manor |
| Dating Of Deposit (century) | 6 |
| Earliest Dating Of Artefacts (AD) | 450 |
| Latest Dating Of Artefacts (AD) | 550 |
| Manuscripts | Urgart 1922, 8 |
| References | Aun 1992, 138 ff<br>Jaanits et al. 1982, 287<br>RK 1896 (no. 677), 107<br>Sb. GEG 1883, 30–31<br>Tamla & Kiudsoo 2005, 22<br>Tvauri 2012, 295 |
| Comments | 7 neck-rings lost. |

| | |
|---|---|
| Environment | Dry land |
| Depth (cm) | 120 |
| Geographical Landscape | Closeby is a steep sandstone denudation at the bank of the Võhandu River |

*Selection of artefacts from Viira wealth deposit (Photo: Ester Oras).*

| Artefact Type | Subtype | Amount | Material | Comments On Appearance | Futher Description |
|---|---|---|---|---|---|
| Neck-Ring | Hooklet and loop shape terminals | 11 | Silver | | 7 lost over time; silver content ca. 60% |

| Wealth Deposit | VILLEVERE |
|---|---|
| Collection number | AI 2489: 1-12 |
| Country | Estonia |
| County | Järva |
| Municipality | Türi |
| Village | Villevere |
| Date Of Discovery | 1920 |
| Comments On Discovery | Found during field ploughing |
| Dating Of Deposit (century) | 6 |
| Earliest Dating Of Artefacts (AD) | 450 |
| Latest Dating Of Artefacts (AD) | 550 |
| Manuscripts | Allik & Markus 1923, 7–8 |
| References | Jaanits et al. 1982, 287<br>Moora 1925<br>Selirand & Tõnisson 1963, 127<br>Tamla & Kiudsoo 2005, 24–25<br>Tvauri 2006 107, 110<br>Tvauri 2012, 294 |
| Comments | From the lands of the same farm also 5 other bronze artefacts were discovered, but lost over time. |

| | |
|---|---|
| Environment | Dry land |
| Environment Subtype | Archaeological site |
| Depth (cm) | 30–40 |
| Type Of Container | Textile |
| Archaeological Site | Burial area |
| Comments On Find-spot | In a vicinity of a stone-graves area |

| Artefact Type | Subtype | Amount | Material | Comments On Appearance | Futher Description |
|---|---|---|---|---|---|
| Neck-Ring | Hooklet and loop shape terminals | 5 | Silver | 4 fragmented, including 2 in small fragments | |
| Neck-Ring | Overlapping faceted terminals | 3 | Silver | 1 fragemnted and bent | |
| Bracelet | Cast, flaring terminals and a bulky midrib | 1 | Bronze | | |
| Brooch | Crossbow brooch | 1 | Silver | | |
| Ring | Spiral ring | 1 | Silver | Fragmented | |
| Ring | | 1 | Silver | Fragmented | |

*Villevere wealth deposit. (Photo: Ester Oras).*